EUROPE'S JUSTICE DEFICIT?

The gradual legal and political evolution of the European Union has not, thus far, been accompanied by the articulation or embrace of any substantive ideal of justice going beyond the founders' intent or the economic objectives of the market integration project. This absence arguably compromises the foundations of the EU legal and political system since the relationship between law and justice—a crucial question within any constitutional system—remains largely unaddressed. This edited volume brings together a number of concise contributions by leading academics and young scholars whose work addresses both legal and philosophical aspects of justice in the European context. The aim of the volume is to appraise the existence and nature of this deficit, its implications for Europe's future, and to begin a critical discussion about how it might be addressed. There have been many accounts of the EU as a story of constitutional evolution and a system of transnational governance, but few which pay sustained attention to the implications for justice.

The EU today has moved beyond its initial and primary emphasis on the establishment of an Internal Market, as the growing importance of EU citizenship and social rights suggests. Yet, most legal analyses of the EU Treaties and of EU case-law remain premised broadly on the assumption that EU law still largely serves the purpose of perfecting what is fundamentally a system of economic integration. The place to be occupied by the underlying substantive ideal of justice remains significantly underspecified or even vacant, creating a tension between the market-oriented foundation of the Union and the contemporary essence of its constitutional system. The relationship of law to justice is a core dimension of constitutional systems around the world, and the EU is arguably no different in this respect.

The critical assessment of justice in the EU provided by the contributions to this book will help to create a fuller picture of the justice deficit in the EU, and at the same time open up an important new avenue of legal research of immediate importance.

Europe's Justice Deficit?

Edited by
Dimitry Kochenov
Gráinne de Búrca
and
Andrew Williams

·HART·
PUBLISHING
OXFORD AND PORTLAND, OREGON
2015

Published in the United Kingdom by Hart Publishing Ltd
16C Worcester Place, Oxford, OX1 2JW
Telephone: +44 (0)1865 517530
Fax: +44 (0)1865 510710
E-mail: mail@hartpub.co.uk
Website: http://www.hartpub.co.uk

Published in North America (US and Canada) by
Hart Publishing
c/o International Specialized Book Services
920 NE 58th Avenue, Suite 300
Portland, OR 97213-3786
USA
Tel: +1 503 287 3093 or toll-free: (1) 800 944 6190
Fax: +1 503 280 8832
E-mail: orders@isbs.com
Website: http://www.isbs.com

© The editors and contributors severally, 2015

The editors and contributors have asserted their right under the Copyright, Designs and Patents Act 1988, to be identified as the authors of this work.

Hart Publishing is an imprint of Bloomsbury Publishing plc.

All rights reserved. No part of this publication may be reproduced, stored in a retrieval system, or transmitted, in any form or by any means, without the prior permission of Hart Publishing, or as expressly permitted by law or under the terms agreed with the appropriate reprographic rights organisation. Enquiries concerning reproduction which may not be covered by the above should be addressed to Hart Publishing Ltd at the address above.

British Library Cataloguing in Publication Data
Data Available

ISBN: 978-1-84946-527-4

Typeset by Compuscript Ltd, Shannon
Printed and bound in Great Britain by
CPI Group (UK) Ltd, Croydon CR0 4YY

Preface

The relationship of law to justice is a core dimension of constitutional systems around the world and the EU cannot be different in that respect. The European Union today has certainly moved beyond the initial emphasis purely on the establishment of an Internal Market, as the growing importance of, inter alia, EU citizenship and social rights suggests. Yet, most legal doctrine and academic analyses of the EU treaties and case-law is premised broadly on the assumption—which is fundamentally incorrect, we submit—that EU law still largely serves the purpose of perfecting what is essentially a system of economic integration. The place to be occupied by the underlying ideal of justice in the European legal context—a crucial issue for any legal or political system—thus remains significantly underspecified or even *vacant*, creating a tension between the market-oriented foundation of the Union and the contemporary essence of its constitutional system.

Indeed, the gradual constitutional evolution of the European Union has not been accompanied by the articulation or embrace of any ideal of justice going beyond the founders' intent or beyond the economic objectives of the market integration project. Even worse: the word 'justice' came, in contemporary euro-speak, to signify nothing more than the formalistically correct functioning of the numerous European organs and institutions—a tiny fraction of what this concept actually stands for. The justice vacuum emerging in Europe where the market is divorced from constitutionalism compromises the essential foundation of the EU legal system since the relationship between law and justice remains largely unaddressed.

The book you are holding in your hands brings together 30 contributions by leading scholars whose work addresses both legal and philosophical aspects of justice to make an attempt to start remedying this situation. Justice is more than a formalistic component of 'the Area of Freedom, Security, and Justice'. The very fact that the need arose to re-emphasise this obvious reality demonstrates the extent of the problem Europe is facing. Besides restating the problem, the aim of this collection is to appraise the existence and nature of the justice deficit, its implications for Europe's future, and to begin a critical discussion about how it might be addressed.

The initial ideas underlying the majority of the chapters included in this collection were discussed at an authors' colloquium in London, in September 2012, kindly hosted by the LSE European Institute. The editors are grateful to Damian Chalmers of LSE and to their schools for making the colloquium possible. The transcript of the debates is available as EUI Working Paper (LAW 2013/11) entitled *Debating Europe's Justice Deficit: The EU, Swabian Housewives, Rawls, and Ryanair* and is a natural companion of this volume. The scholars who only participated in the *Housewives* deserve a special word of thanks: the London debate definitely helped enrich and contextualise the approach to justice embraced by the authors of this collection. We are grateful to the editorial assistants in Groningen and New York, who helped with this endeavour. Justin Lindeboom, Adam McCann, Daniël HK

Overgaauw, Suryapratim Roy (who also contributed a chapter) and Jonathan Silberstein Loeb: thank you. Last but not least, we are thankful to Grisha Kochenov, who painted the uneasy Europe for the cover.

With academic literature largely preoccupied with analysis and appraisal of the objectives stated in the Treaties, the justice dimension of Europe's development has received remarkably little attention. We hope that a critical assessment of justice in Europe based on the premise that economic integration cannot anymore, in all academic honesty, be presented as a suitable framework to analyse the European legal space, will help to shape an exciting multi-faceted picture of the justice deficit in the EU, thus opening up an important new avenue of legal research of immediate importance. There have been too many accounts of the EU as a story of constitutional evolution and a system of transnational governance with little or no attention to the implications for justice. Ignoring justice is not sustainable.

The editors, May 2014

Short Table of Contents

Preface v
Short Table of Contents vii
Full Table of Contents xi
List of Contributors xix
List of Abbreviations xxi
List of Figures xxiii
Table of Cases xxv
Table of Treaties and Legislation xxxi

1. Europe's Justice Deficit Introduced 1
   Dimitry Kochenov and Andrew Williams

Part One

2. The Ought of Justice 21
   Dimitry Kochenov

3. The Problem(s) of Justice in the European Union 33
   Andrew Williams

4. Justice, Injustice and the Rule of Law in the EU 51
   Sionaidh Douglas-Scott

5. The Question of Standards for the EU: From 'Democratic Deficit'
   to 'Justice Deficit?' 67
   Oliver Gerstenberg

6. Justice as Europe's Signifier 79
   Suryapratim Roy

7. 'Constitutional Justice' and Judicial Review of EU Legislative Acts 97
   Dorota Leczykiewicz

Part Two

8. Politicising Europe's Justice Deficit: Some Preliminaries 111
   Michael A Wilkinson

9. Whose Justice? Which Europe? 137
   Agustín José Menéndez

10. We the People: EU Justice as Politics 153
    Daniel Augenstein

11. Swabian Housewives, Suffering Southerners: The Contestability
    of Justice as Exemplified by the Eurozone Crisis 165
    Danny Nicol

viii *Short Table of Contents*

12. Is Transnational Citizenship (Still) Enough? 177
    Justine Lacroix

Part Three

13. The Evolving Idea of Political Justice in the EU:
    From Substantive Deficits to the Systemic Contingency
    of European Society 193
    Jiří Přibáň

14. Justice and the Right to Justification: Conceptual Reflections 211
    Jürgen Neyer

15. Justice, Democracy and the Right to Justification:
    Reflections on Jürgen Neyer's Normative Theory of the
    European Union 227
    Rainer Forst

16. Disproportionate Individualism 235
    Stavros Tsakyrakis

17. Justice in and of the European Union 247
    Neil Walker

18. Social Legitimacy and Purposive Power: The End,
    the Means and the Consent of the People 259
    Gareth Davies

Part Four

19. Social Justice in the European Union: The Puzzles of
    Solidarity, Reciprocity and Choice 277
    Juri Viehoff and Kalypso Nikolaïdis

20. The Preoccupation with Rights and the Embrace of
    Inclusion: A Critique 295
    Alexander Somek

21. A Reply to Somek 311
    Andrew Williams

22. Taking Change Seriously: The Rhetoric of Justice and the
    Reproduction of the Status Quo 319
    Damjan Kukovec

23. Victimhood and Vulnerability as Sources of Justice 337
    András Sajó

24. Conceptions of Justice From Below: Distributive Justice
    as a Means to Address Local Conflicts in European Law
    and Policy 349
    Fernanda G Nicola

25. *Qu'ils mangent des contrats*: Rethinking Justice in
    EU Contract Law 367
    Daniela Caruso

Part Five

26. Just Fatherlands? The Shoah in the Jurisprudence of Strasbourg 381
    Carole Lyons

27. An Idea of Ecological Justice in the EU 401
    Jane Holder

28. Freedom of Expression and Spatial (Imaginations of) Justice 417
    Antonia Layard

29. The Just World 435
    Dimitry Kochenov

30. Conclusion 459
    Gráinne de Búrca

Index 465

Full Table of Contents

Preface v
Short Table of Contents vii
Full Table of Contents xi
List of Contributors xix
List of Abbreviations xxi
List of Figures xxiii
Table of Cases xxv
Table of Treaties and Legislation xxxi

1. Europe's Justice Deficit Introduced...1
   Dimitry Kochenov and Andrew Williams
       I. 2
       II. 6
       III. 8
       IV. 12
       V. 17
       VI. 18

Part One

2. The Ought of Justice 21
   Dimitry Kochenov
     I.   Justice as the Foundational Assumption..22
     II. The Normative Starting Point: The EU is a Suitable
          Agent of Justice..25
     III. The Empirical Starting Point: Inadequate Treatment
          of Justice in the EU 26
     IV. The First Approach: Presumed Justice..27
     V. The Second Approach: Rhetorical Justice 28
     VI. The Third Approach: Silence About Justice 29
     VII. A Reminder..30

3. The Problem(s) of Justice in the European Union 33
   Andrew Williams
     I.   Introduction..33
     II. Substantive Justice and the EU..35
     III. Elements of Justice for the EU 38
         A.   Distributive Justice..39
         B.   Political Justice 42
         C.   Inter-generational Justice 43
         D. Criminal Justice 47
     IV. Addressing the Justice Deficit..48

xii *Full Table of Contents*

4. Justice, Injustice and the Rule of Law in the EU 51
   Sionaidh Douglas-Scott
   I. Introduction 51
   II. Injustice in the EU 52
   III. The Perplexities of Justice in the EU 57
   IV. The Rule of Law and Critical Legal Justice 58
   V. Injustice Explored 61
   VI. Conclusion 65

5. The Question of Standards for the EU: From 'Democratic
   Deficit' to 'Justice Deficit?' 67
   Oliver Gerstenberg
   I. The Question of Standards 67
   II. The EU as an Experimentalist Arrangement 68
   III. The ECJ as an Experimentalist Court 73
        A. The Right to Healthcare: The Need to Take
           Individual Circumstances of Pain and Suffering
           More Fully into Account 73
        B. Adjudicating Consumer Contracts: Attentiveness to
           an Implicit Human Rights Dimension 75
   IV. Coda 77

6. Justice as Europe's Signifier 79
   Suryapratim Roy
   I. Introduction 79
   II. The Signifying Capacity of Justice 80
   III. Foreclosing Justice by Institutional Self-legitimation 82
   IV. Foreclosing Justice Through Privileged Referents 85
        A. 'Justified Structures of Justification' as Referent 85
        B. Democracy as Referent 88
   V. Institutional Violence and the Individual 90
        A. The Market as Europe's Signifier 90
        B. The Inverted Monism of Institutional Violence 92
        C. Tethering Justice 94
   VI. Conclusion 95

7. 'Constitutional Justice' and Judicial Review of EU Legislative Acts 97
   Dorota Leczykiewicz
   I. 'Justice', EU Constitutionalism and Judicial Review 97
   II. Standards of Constitutional Justice Applicable to
       the European Court of Justice 99
   III. The Charter of Fundamental Rights as a Vehicle
        of Constitutional Justice 103
   IV. Judicial Review—The Question of Legitimacy or Justice? 107

Part Two

8. Politicising Europe's Justice Deficit: Some Preliminaries 111
   Michael A Wilkinson
   I. Introduction 111
   II. Conceptualising a Justice Deficit 113
   III. Historicising a Justice Deficit: The Role of the State 115
   IV. Historicising a Justice Deficit: The Role of Ideology 118
   V. Framing the EU's Social Justice Deficit............................... 122
   VI. Politicising Justice Deficits 128
   VII. Democratising the Justice Deficit? 132

9. Whose Justice? Which Europe? 137
   Agustín José Menéndez
   I. Introduction 137
   II. Justice or Democratic Politics? 138
   III. European Constitutional Law as a Democratic Straitjacket:
        How it Came to be and how to Start Liberating Ourselves 146
   IV. Conclusion 150

10. We the People: EU Justice as Politics 153
    Daniel Augenstein
    I. Austerity 153
    II. Piecemeal Justice 155
    III. Political Unity 158
    IV. Fundamental Rights in the European Market Polity 160
    V. To Each his Own? 162
    VI. Conclusion 164

11. Swabian Housewives, Suffering Southerners: The Contestability
    of Justice as Exemplified by the Eurozone Crisis 165
    Danny Nicol
    I. Introduction 165
    II. Contestable Justice: Pre-eurozone Crisis Examples 167
    III. Eurozone Crisis and Justice 168
    IV. The Role of the Scholar 171
    V. The Depoliticisation of Justice 173
    VI. Conclusion 175

12. Is Transnational Citizenship (Still) Enough? 177
    Justine Lacroix
    I. Introduction: Transnational Citizenship as a Normative
       and Realistic Concept 177
    II. *Demoicracy* in Crisis 180
    III. Some Doubts About the 'Third Way' 183
    IV. A Universal Field of Rights? 185
    V. Conclusion 189

xiv *Full Table of Contents*

Part Three

13. The Evolving Idea of Political Justice in the EU: From Substantive Deficits to the Systemic Contingency of European Society 193
    Jiří Přibáň
    I. Introduction 193
    II. The Legal and Political Concept of Justice: Preliminary Theoretical Distinctions 194
    III. Political Justice as the Categorical Imperative of Law and the State 196
    IV. Political Justice, the State and the EU 198
    V. From Theoretical Contexts to the Legal Text: The Lisbon Treaty and Democratic Legitimacy 200
        A. The EU As the Balance Between Efficiency and Democratic Legitimacy 200
        B. The Principle of Representative Democracy and Its Adoption by the European Union 202
        C. The Union's Deficit of Representative Democracy and Its Constitutional Strengthening at the Member State Level 203
        D. Legislating for the EU's Participatory and Direct Democracy, Constructing the EU's Civil Society? 204
    VI. The Lisbon Treaty and the Juridification of Political Justice 205
    VII. Legitimacy Without Justice? On the EU's Politicisation and Depoliticisation 206
    VIII. Political Justice and European Polity as Outcomes of Functional Differentiation of European Society 207
    IX. Concluding Remarks: On Functional Differentiation of European Society, Politics and Justice 208

14. Justice and the Right to Justification: Conceptual Reflections 211
    Jürgen Neyer
    I. Why not Democracy? 211
    II. The Better Alternative 212
        A. What is Justice? 212
        B. What is a Justification? 215
        C. Substantial and Procedural Preconditions of Justifications 217
        D. Limits to the Right to Justification 221
        E. Justified Structures of Justification 222
    III. The EU's Justice Deficit 223

15. Justice, Democracy and the Right for Justification: Reflections on Jürgen Neyer's Normative Theory of the European Union 227
    Rainer Forst
    I. Introduction 227
    II. Why not Democracy? 228

	III.	Alternatives...229
	IV.	European Democracy...233

16. Disproportionate Individualism..235
    Stavros Tsakyrakis
    I.   A Tale of Two Societies 235
    II. A Prima Facie Right to Everything?..237
    III. The Liberty of Human Rights..241
    IV. Human Rights and the Courts...244
    V.   Conclusion...245

17. Justice in and of the European Union..247
    Neil Walker
    I.   Introduction: In the Name of European Justice 247
    II. The Agility of Justice 247
    III. The Elusive Legitimacy of the EU..250
    IV. Four Approaches to Polity Legitimacy...251
    V.   Justifying Justification..256

18. Social Legitimacy and Purposive Power: The End, the Means
    and the Consent of the People...259
    Gareth Davies
    I.   Introduction...259
    II. Legitimacy: Substance, Process and Emotion.................................261
    III. The Expressive Role of Law 263
    IV. Conferral, Functional Powers and the EU's
         Instrumental Orientation 265
         A.   The Way Law is Made 266
         B.   Technical Regulation 268
         C.   Adjudication...269
         D.   Framing the Law: The Denial of Choice 271
    V.   The Political Context of Instrumentality..272
    VI. Conclusion...273

Part Four

19. Social Justice in the European Union: The Puzzles of
    Solidarity, Reciprocity and Choice 277
    Juri Viehoff and Kalypso Nicolaïdis
    I.   Introduction...277
    II. Domestic Social Justice: Content and Grounds..............................279
         A.   Benchmark of Equality...280
         B.   Fair Equality of Opportunity..281
    III. Is social Justice Unavailable in the EU? Solidarity
         As a Prerequisite 282
         A.   The Meaning of Solidarity..282
         B.   The Solidarity Compass: Interest, Community,
              Altruism and Obligation 283

            (i) Self-interest versus Community 284
            (ii) Altruism versus Political Obligation 285
    IV. Is Social Justice Fundamentally Different in the EU?
        Reciprocity as the Common Core 287
    V. How Is Social Justice Different in the EU?
        Constrained Choice as an EU Marker 290
    VI. Conclusion 292

20. The Preoccupation with Rights and the Embrace
    of Inclusion: A Critique 295
    Alexander Somek
    I. The New Kid on the Block 295
    II. The A and Ω 297
    III. The Category Mistake 300
    IV. A Right that Really Isn't One 302
    V. An Implied Self-critique 303
    VI. The Merit of Being Part of the Whole 305
    VII. Rawls 306
    VIII. Inclusion 307
    IX. Conclusion 309

21. A Reply to Somek 311
    Andrew Williams
    I. A General Response: A Romantic Notion 311
    II. A Specific Response 314
    III. A Contradictory Conclusion 317

22. Taking Change Seriously: The Rhetoric of Justice
    and the Reproduction of the Status Quo 319
    Damjan Kukovec
    I. Introduction 319
    II. Reproduction of Hierarchies and the Periphery 320
    III. Justice and Social Transformation 323
    IV. Social Europe and Conceptualism of Contemporary
        Legal Thought 324
    V. Justice as Inclusion of the Other and Constitutionalisation 330
    VI. Projecting Visions that Expand the Range of Social Options 334
    VII. Conclusion 336

23. Victimhood and Vulnerability as Sources of Justice 337
    András Sajó
    I. Introduction 337
    II. Generating Justice Claims on the Basis of 'Status' 338
        A. Victimhood 338
        B. Vulnerability 343
    III. Consequences of Status Claims on Restorative
        and Redistributive Policies 347
    IV. Conclusion 347

24. Conceptions of Justice from Below: Distributive Justice as a
    Means to Address Local Conflicts in European Law and Policy 349
    Fernanda G Nicola
    I. Introduction 349
    II. Displacing the Neutrality of the Federal Judiciary
        and its Federalism Doctrines 352
    III. Distributive Justice in Adjudication 356
    IV. In Search of Distributive Justice in Cohesion Policy 359
    V. The *Idea of Justice* as a Comparative Development
        Framework 361
    VI. Three Children, a Flute and the ECJ Jurisprudence 362
    VII. Conclusion 365

25. *Qu'ils mangent des contrats*: Rethinking Justice in
    EU Contract Law 367
    Daniela Caruso
    I. Introduction 367
    II. Internal Critique and Suggestions from Within 369
        A. Perils of Deliberation 369
        B. Focusing on Vulnerable Consumers 372
        C. Producing Better Knowledge 372
        D. Making Up for Asymmetries 375
        E. Contracts and Competence Creep 375
    III. The External Critique: Beyond Contract Law 376
        A. Whither Contracts? 376
        B. Property, Family and Association 377
    VI. Conclusions 378

Part Five

26. Just Fatherlands? The Shoah in the Jurisprudence
    of Strasbourg 381
    Carole Lyons
    I. Introduction 381
    II. The Legend of the Just Men 389
    III. The Court of Grief 390
    IV. *Nomen est Numen* 392
        A. *Stolperstein* 1—X (The Auschwitz Survivor) 393
    V. The Wrong Kind of Justice? 394
        B. *Stolperstein* 2—X (The SS Officer) 395
        C. *Stolperstein* 3—Heinz Jentzsch (SS Guard) 395
    VI. No Shoah? 396
    VII. 'The Holocaust on Your Plate' 397
        D. *Stolperstein* 4—PETA 397
    VIII. The Origin is the Goal 398
    IX. Ending 399

xviii *Full Table of Contents*

27. An Idea of Ecological Justice in the EU 401
    Jane Holder
    I. Introducing Ecological Justice 401
    II. Seeking Ecological Justice in Natura 2000 403
    III. Moving Towards Ecological Justice 405
        A. Spatial Justice and Territorial Cohesion 407
        B. Environmental Justice 408
        C. Ecological Justice 410
        D. Relation- and Context-Based Ecological
           Review Principles 413
           (i) Integrity 414
           (ii) Resilience 414
           (iii) Coherence 415
    IV. Conclusions 415

28. Freedom of Expression and Spatial (Imaginations of) Justice 417
    Antonia Layard
    I. Introduction 417
    II. *Raël v Switzerland* 419
    III. Towards a Spatial Understanding of *Raël* 422
        A. Splices 423
        B. Legal–Spatial Imaginaries 425
        C. Spatial Imaginations of a European Public Sphere 429
    IV. Conclusion 433

29. The Just World 435
    Dimitry Kochenov
    I. Introduction 435
    II. Introducing Key Elements of the Argument 437
    III. The Case for Taking Reality into Account 441
    IV. The Just World and the Law 446
    V. The Scope of Justice and the Law 448
    VI. Broader Implications 450
        A. For Democracy 451
        B. For the Myth of Justice in Law 451
        C. For Legitimacy 452
        D. For the Procedural–Substantive Justice Divide 453
        E. For Equality 453
        F. For the EU's Federal Structure 454
        G. For EU Citizenship 455
    VII. Conclusion 456

30. Conclusion 459
    Gráinne de Búrca

Index 465

List of Contributors

Daniel Augenstein — Assistant Professor, Department of European and International Public Law, Tilburg University

Gráinne de Búrca — Florence Ellinwood Allen Professor of Law, Faculty Director, Hauser Global Law School, Director, Jean Monnet Center for International and Regional Economic Law and Justice, New York University School of Law

Daniela Caruso — Professor of Law, Boston University School of Law

Gareth Davies — Professor of European Law, Department of Transnational Legal Studies, VU University Amsterdam

Sionaidh Douglas-Scott — Professor of European and Human Rights Law, Faculty of Law, University of Oxford

Rainer Forst — Professor of Political Theory and Philosophy, Goethe-University Frankfurt am Main, Permanent Fellow at the Institute of Advanced Study in Bad Homburg

Oliver Gerstenberg — Reader in Law and Director of the Centre for International Governance, University of Leeds School of Law

Jane Holder — Professor in Environmental Law, Faculty of Law, University College London

Dimitry Kochenov — Chair in EU Constitutional Law, Faculty of Law, University of Groningen

Damjan Kukovec — SJD Candidate, Harvard Law School

Justine Lacroix — Professor, Department of Political Science, Université Libre de Bruxelles

Antonia Layard — Professor of Law, University of Bristol Law School

Dorota Leczykiewicz — Marie Curie Fellow, European University Institute, Florence, and Research Fellow, Oxford Institute of European and Comparative Law

Carole Lyons — Lecturer in Law, Robert Gordon University Aberdeen

List of Contributors

Agustín José Menéndez — Professor, ARENA Centre for European Studies, University of Oslo and University of León

Jürgen Neyer — Professor of European Politics, Faculty of Social and Cultural Sciences, European University Viadrina Frankfurt (Oder)

Danny Nicol — Professor of Public Law, Department of Advanced Legal Studies, University of Westminster

Fernanda G Nicola — Professor of Law, American University Washington College of Law

Kalypso Nicolaïdis — Professor of International Relations, Director of the Centre for International Studies and Faculty Fellow, St Antony's College, University of Oxford

Jiří Přibáň — Professor, Cardiff University Law School

Suryapratim Roy — PhD Candidate, Faculty of Law, University of Groningen

András Sajó — Judge, European Court of Human Rights, University Professor and Founding Dean of the Department of Legal Studies, Central European University, Budapest

Alexander Somek — Charles E Floete Chair in Law, University of Iowa College of Law

Stavros Tsakyrakis — Professor of Constitutional Law, University of Athens

Juri Viehoff — Research Fellow, Centre for Ethics, University of Zurich

Neil Walker — Regius Professor of Public Law and the Law of Nature and Nations, University of Edinburgh Law School

Michael A Wilkinson — Associate Professor of Law, London School of Economics and Political Science

Andrew Williams — Professor of Law, University of Warwick School of Law

List of Abbreviations

AFSJ — Area of Freedom, Security and Justice
AG — Advocate General
BvE — *Verfassungsstreitigkeiten zwischen Bundesorganen*
BVerfG — *Bundesverfassungsgericht*
BVerfGE — *Entscheidungen des Bundesverfassungsgerichts*
BvR — *Verfassungsbeschwerden*
CA2 — United States Court of Appeals 2nd Circuit
Cal App — California Appellate Court
CAP — Common Agricultural Policy
CBDR — Common But Differentiated Responsibility
CCT — Constitutional Court of South Africa
CEE — Central and Eastern Europe
CESL — Common European Sales Law
CFR — Charter of Fundamental Rights of the European Union
DCFR — Draft Common Frame of Reference
DR — Decisions and Reports of the European Commission on Human Rights
EAW — European Arrest Warrant
EC — European Community
ECB — European Central Bank
ECCG — European Consumer Consultative Group
ECR — European Court Reports
EEC — European Economic Community
ECHR — European Convention on Human Rights
ECtHR — European Court of Human Rights
ECJ — European Court of Justice, Court of Justice of the EU
ECommHR — European Commission on Human Rights
EG — Estates Gazette
EHRR — European Human Rights Reports
EMU — Economic and Monetary Union
ERDF — European Regional Development Fund
ESM — European Stability Mechanism
ETS — Emissions Trading Scheme
EU — European Union
EUI — European University Institute
EWCA — Court of Appeal of England and Wales
EWHC — High Court of England and Wales
FCA — Federal Court of Australia
GC — Grand Chamber
GCt — General Court
GDP — Gross Domestic Product
GMO — Genetically Modified Organism
HCA — High Court of Australia
HMSO — Her Majesty's Stationery Office

IBA — Important Bird Area
IMF — International Monetary Fund
ILM — International Legal Materials
IROPI — Imperative Reasons of Overriding Public Interest
LA — Supreme Court of Louisiana
LEQS — LSE 'Europe in Question' Series
NGO — Non-Governmental Organisation
NHS — National Health Service
NZHC — High Court of New Zealand
OECD — Organisation for Economic Co-operation and Development
OJ — Official Journal of the European Union
OMC — Open Method of Coordination
OMT — Outright Monetary Transactions
PL — Plenary Session
RSCAS — Robert Schuman Centre for Advanced Studies, EUI, Florence
SAC — Special Area of Conservation
SCR — Supreme Court Reports of Canada
SME — Small and Medium Enterprises
SPA — Special Protection Area
TEU — Treaty on European Union
TFEU — Treaty on the Functioning of the European Union
TWAIL — Third World Approaches to International Law
TWC — Trials of War Criminals Before the Nuremberg Military Tribunal
UNECE — United Nations Economic Commission for Europe
UNTS — United Nations Treaty Series
US — Supreme Court of the United States
ÚS — *Ústavní soud*, Constitutional Court of the Czech Republic
VAT — Value Added Tax
WTO — World Trade Organisation
ZACAC — South African Competition Appeal Court

List of Figures

Figure 4.1: Darmstadt, Residenzschloss, Fassade zum Marktplatz Justitia 61
Figure 4.2: Copenhagen, Jens Galschiøt, 'Survival of the Fattest' 62
Figure 19.1: The Conceptual Space of Solidarity 284
Figure 28.1: Swiss Raëlian Movement Poster Campaign 420

Table of Cases

European Court of Justice

Case C-370/12 *Thomas Pringle v Government of Ireland, Ireland and the Attorney General* (ECJ, 27 November 2012) 6, 126, 154, 155, 162

Joined Cases C-293/12 and C-594/12 *Digital Rights Ireland v The Minister of Communications, Marine and Natural Resource* (ECJ, 8 April 2014) 104, 105

Case C-86/12 *Adzo Domenyo Alokpa and Others v Ministre du Travail, de l'Emploi et de l'Immigration* (ECJ, 10 October 2013) 91

Case C-583/11 P *Inuit Tapiriit Kanatami and Others v European Parliament and Council* (3 October 2013) 101

Case C-426/11 *Mark Alemo-Herron v Parkwood Leisure Ltd* (ECJ, 18 July 2013) 106

Case C-415/11 *Mohamed Aziz v Caixa d'Estalvis de Catalunya, Tarragona i Manresa (Catalunyacaixa)* (ECJ, 14 March 2013) 4, 75, 76

Case C-399/11 *Stefano Melloni v Ministerio Fiscal* (ECJ, 26 February 2013) 52, 99, 106

Case C-283/11 *Sky Österreich GmbH v Österreichischer Rundfunk* (ECJ, 22 January 2013) 105

Case C-256/11 *Murat Dereci and Others v Bundesministerium für Inneres* [2011] ECR I-1131 91

Case C-618/10 *Banco Español de Crédito SA (Banesto) v Joaquín Calderón Camino* (ECJ, 14 June 2012) 76

Joined Cases C-584/10 P, C-593/10 P and C-595/10 P *European Commission v Yassin Abdullah Kadi* (ECJ, 18 July 2013) 101

Case C-366/10 *Air Transport Association of America and Others v Secretary of State for Energy and Climate Change* [2011] ECR I-13755 93

Case C-360/10 *Belgische Vereniging van Auteurs, Componisten en Uitgevers CVBA (SABAM) v Netlog NV* (16 February 2012) 106

Case C-70/10 *Scarlet Extended SA v Société belge des auteurs, compositeurs et éditeurs SCRL (SABAM)* [2011] ECR I-11959 106

Case C-434/09 *Shirley McCarthy v Secretary of State for the Home Department* [2011] ECR I-3375 .... 91, 455

Case C-348/09 *PI v Oberbürgermeisterin der Stadt Remscheid* [2012] ECR 1-6355 86

Case C-236/09 *Association belge des Consommateurs Test-Achats ASBL and Others v Conseil des ministers* [2011] ECR I-773 106

Joined Cases C-92/09 and C-93/09 *Volker und Markus Schecke GbR and Hartmut Eifert v Land Hessen* [2010] ECR I-11063 104

Case C-34/09 *Gerardo Ruiz Zambrano v Office national de l'emploi (ONEm)* [2011] ECR I-1177 .... 90, 270, 455

Case C-515/08 *Criminal proceedings against Vítor Manuel dos Santos Palhota, Mário de Moura Gonçalves, Fernando Luis das Neves Palhota, Termiso Limitada* [2010] ECR I-9133 162

Case C-407/08 P *Knauf Gips v European Commission* [2010] ECR I-6375 104

Case C-271/08 *European Commission v Federal Republic of Germany* [2010] ECR I-7087 162

Case C-2/08 *Amministrazione dell'Economia e delle Finanze and Agenzia delle entrate v Fallimento Olimpiclub Srl* [2009] ECR I 7501 82
Case C-405/07 P *Kingdom of the Netherlands v Commission of the European Communities* [2008] ECR I-8301 266
Case C-346/06 *Dirk Rüffert v Land Niedersachsen* [2008] ECR I-1989 .... 363, 364
Case C-345/06 *Gottfried Heinrich* [2009] ECR I-1659 60
Case C-212/06 *Government of the French Community and Walloon Government v Flemish Government (Belgian care insurance scheme)* [2008] ECR I-1683 357
Case C-15/06 *Regione Siciliana v Commission of the European Communities* [2007] ECR I-2591 350
Case C-438/05 *International Transport Workers' Federation and Finnish Seamen's Union v Viking Line ABP and OÜ Viking Line Eesti* [2007] ECR I-10779 .... 3, 4, 56, 73, 88, 167, 301, 323, 357
Joined Cases C-402/05 P and C-415/05 P *Yassin Abdullah Kadi and Al Barakaat International Foundation v Council and Commission* [2008] ECR I-6351 .... 101, 102
Case C-341/05 *Laval un Partneri Ltd v Svenska Byggnadsarbetareförbundet and Others* [2007] ECR I-11767 .... 3, 4, 56, 73, 88, 167, 271, 301, 329, 333, 357
Case C-417/04 *Regione Siciliana v Commission of the European Communities* [2006] ECR I-3881 350
Case C-372/04 *R, on the application of Yvonne Watts v Bedford Primary Care Trust and Secretary of State for Health* [2006] ECR I-4325 .... 4, 73, 74
Case C-234/04 *Rosmarie Kapferer v Schlank & Schick GmbH* [2006] ECR I 2585 82
Joined Cases C-154/04 and C-155/04 *R, on the application of Alliance for Natural Health v Secretary of State for Health* [2005] ECR I-6451 107
Case C-27/04 *Commission of the European Communities v Council of the European Union* [2004] ECR I-6649 126
Joined Cases C-453/03, C-11/04, C-12/04 and C-194/04 *R, on the application of ABNA Ltd v Secretary of State for Health and Food Standards Agency* [2005] ECR I-10423 103
Case C-403/03 *Egon Schempp v Finanzamt München V* [2005] ECR I-6421 .... 30, 455
Case C-210/03 *R, on the application of: Swedish Match AB and Swedish Match UK Ltd v Secretary of State for Health* [2004] ECR I-11893 107
Case C-176/03 *Commission of the European Communities v Council of the European Union* [2005] ECR I-7879 83
Case C-147/03 *Commission of the European Communities v Republic of Austria* [2005] ECR I-5969 270
Case C-200/02 *Kunqian Catherine Zhu and Man Lavette Chen v Secretary of State for the Home Department* [2004] ECR I-9925 .... 270, 455
Case C-148/02 *Carlos Garcia Avello v Belgian State* [2003] ECR I-11613 270
Case C-36/02 *Omega Spielhallen- und Automatenaufstellungs-GmbH v Oberbürgermeisterin der Bundesstadt Bonn* [2004] ECR I-9609 161
Case C-491/01 *R v Secretary of State for Health, ex parte British American Tobacco (Investments) Ltd and Imperial Tobacco Ltd* [2002] ECR I-11453 .... 103, 107
Case C-224/01 *Gerhard Köbler v Republik Österreich* [2003] ECR I 10239 82
Case C-183/00 *María Victoria González Sánchez v Medicina Asturiana SA* [2002] ECR I-3901 357

Case C-50/00 P Unión de Pequeños Agricultores v Council of the
European Union [2002] ECR I-6677 83
Case C-413/99 Baumbast and R v Secretary of State for the Home
Department [2002] ECR I-7091 270
Case C-184/99 Rudy Grzelczyk v Centre public d'aide sociale
d'Ottignies-Louvain-la-Neuve [2001] ECR I-6193 .... 270, 271
Case C-376/98 Federal Republic of Germany v European Parliament
and Council of the European Union [2000] ECR I-841 .... 266, 267
Case C-256/98 Commission of the European Communities v French
Republic [2000] ECR I-2487 403
Case C-292/97 Kjell Karlsson and Others [2000] ECR I-2737 102
Case C-180/97 Regione Toscana v Commission of the European
Communities [1997] ECR I-5245 350
Case C-95/97 Région Wallonne v Commission of the European
Communities [1997] ECR I-1787 350
Case C-158/96 Raymond Kohll v Union des caisses de maladie [1998]
ECR I-1931 353
Case C-85/96 María Martínez Sala v Freistaat Bayern [1998] ECR I-2691 270
Case C-3/96 Commission of the European Communities v Kingdom
of the Netherlands [1998] ECR I-3031 403
Case C-44/95 R v Secretary of State for the Environment, ex parte:
Royal Society for the Protection of Birds [1996] ECR I-3805 406
Case C-233/94 Federal Republic of Germany v European Parliament
and Council of the European Union [1997] ECR I-240 107
Case 5/88 Hubert Wachauf v Bundesamt für Ernährung und Forstwirtschaft
[1989] ECR 2609 102
Case 186/87 Ian William Cowan v Trésor public [1989] ECR 195 270
Case 302/86 Commission of the European Communities v Kingdom
of Denmark [1988] ECR 4607 406
Case 294/83 Parti écologiste 'Les Verts' v European Parliament [1986]
ECR 1339 .... 100, 159
Case 240/83 Procureur de la République v Association de défense des
brûleurs d'huiles usages (ADBHU) [1985] ECR 531 406
Case 44/79 Liselotte Hauer v Land Rheinland-Pfalz [1979] ECR 3727 161
Case 8/74 Procureur du Roi v Benoît and Gustave Dassonville [1974] ECR 837 77
Case 4/73 J Nold, Kohlen- und Baustoffgroßhandlung v Commission
of the European Communities [1974] ECR 491 102
Case 11/70 Internationale Handelsgesellschaft mbH v Einfuhr- und
Vorratsstelle für Getreide und Futtermittel [1970] ECR 1125 .... 99, 102, 160
Case 6/64 Flaminio Costa v ENEL [1964] ECR 585 .... 121, 159, 389
Case 26/62 NV Algemene Transport- en Expeditie Onderneming
van Gend en Loos v Nederlandse Administratie
der Belastingen [1963] ECR (English Special Edition) 1 .... 23, 159, 389

General Court

Case T-187/11 Mohamed Trabelsi and Others v Council of
the European Union (GCt, 28 May 2013) 104
Case T-18/10 Inuit Tapiriit Kanatami and Others v European
Parliament and Council of the European Union [2011] ECR II-5599 101
Case T-16/04 Arcelor v European Parliament and Council of the
European Union [2004] ECR II-211 93

xxviii *Table of Cases*

Case T-81/97 *Regione Toscana v Commission of the European
  Communities* [1998] ECR II-2889 350
Case T-585/93 *Stichting Greenpeace Council (Greenpeace International)
  and others v Commission of the European Communities*
  [1998] ECR I-1651 406

European Court and Commission of Human Rights

Al Nashiri v Poland App No 28761/11 60
Janowiec and Others v Russia App Nos 55508/07 and 29520/09
  [2014] 58 EHRR 30 (ECtHR (GC), 21 October 2013) 383, 384, 387
Horváth and Kiss v Hungary App No 11146/11 (ECtHR,
  29 January 2013) 345
PETA Deutschland v Germany App No 43481/09 [2012]
  ECHR 1888 (ECtHR, 8 November 2012) 386, 388, 390, 397, 398
Mouvement Raëlien Suisse v Switzerland App No 16354/06
  [2012] ECHR 1598 (ECtHR (GC), 13 July 2012) 417, 418, 419, 423,
                                                                                    424, 427, 428, 430
Janowiec and Others v Russia App Nos 55508/07 and
  29520/09 (ECtHR, 16 April 2012) 383, 384, 387
LZ v Slovakia App No 27753/06 (ECtHR, 27 September 2011) 386
MSS v Belgium and Greece App No 30696/09 [2011] 53
  EHRR 2 (ECtHR (GC), 21 January 2011) 15, 346
Hoffer and Annen v Germany App Nos 397/07 and 2322/07
  [2011] ECHR 46 (ECtHR, 13 January 2011) 397
Alajos Kiss v Hungary App No 38832/06 (ECtHR, 20 May 2010) 346
Kononov v Latvia App No 36376/04 (ECtHR (GC) 17 May 2010) 384
Oršuš and Others v Croatia App No 15766/03 (ECtHR, 16 March 2010) 346
Women On Waves and Others v Portugal App No 31276/05
  (ECtHR, 3 February 2009) 428
Kononov v Latvia App No 36376/04 (ECtHR, 24 July 2008) 384
EB v France App No 43546/02 (ECtHR (GC), 22 January 2008) 346
DH and Others v Czech Republic App No 57325/00 [2008] 47
  EHRR 59 (ECtHR (GC), 13 November 2007) 346
Poznanski and Others v Germany App No 25101/05 (ECtHR, 3 July 2007) 386
Mamidakis v Greece App No 35533/04 (ECtHR, 11 January 2007) 245
Garaudy v France App 65831/01 [2003] ECHR IX
  (ECtHR, Admissibility Decision, 7 July 2003) 397
Appleby and Others v the United Kingdom App No 44306/98 [2003]
  ECHR 222 [2003] 37 EHRR 783 (ECtHR, 6 May 2003) 424, 432
Anthony Sawoniuk v United Kingdom App No 63716/00
  (ECtHR, Admissibility Decision, 29 May 2001) 394
Witzsch v Germany App No 41448/98 (ECtHR, Admissibility Decision,
  20 April 1999) 397
Lehideux and Isorni v France App No 24662/94 [1998] ECHR 90 [2000]
  30 EHRR 665 (ECtHR (GC), 23 September 1998) 397
Slowik v Poland App No 30641/96 (ECommHR Decision, 16 April 1998) 386
Marais v France App No 31159/96 86 DR 184 (ECommHR Decision,
  24 June 1996) 397
Honsik v Austria App No 25062/94 83 DR 77 (ECommHR Decision,
  18 October 1995) 397

Abdulaziz, Cabales and Balkandali v United Kingdom App Nos 9214/80, 9473/81 and 9474/81 Series A No 94 [1985] 7 EHRR 471 (ECtHR (PL), 28 May 1985)... 346
Sporrong and Lönnroth v Sweden App Nos 7151/75 and 7152/75 Series A No 52 (ECtHR (PL), 23 September 1982)... 236
Ilse Hess v United Kingdom App No 6231/73 2 DR 72 (ECommHR Decision, 28 May 1975) 394
Heinz Jentzsch v Germany App No 2604/65 (ECommHR Decision, 6 October 1970) 394, 395, 396
De Becker v Belgium App 214/56 Series A No 4 (ECtHR, 27 March 1962)... 389
Ilse Koch v Germany App No 1270/61 (ECommHR Decision, 8 March 1962) 394
X v Germany App No 920/60 (ECommHR Decision, 19 December 1961) 394, 395
X v Germany App No 627/59 (ECommHR Decision, 14 December 1961) 387, 389, 392, 394, 395

Australia

Minister for Home Affairs of the Commonwealth v Zentai [2012] HCA 28 (15 August 2012) 382, 392
Australian Competition and Consumer Commission v GM Holden Ltd [2008] FCA 1428 (18 September 2008).. 93

Austria

Judgment No 6 Ob 321/04f (Austrian Supreme Court of Justice, 12 October 2006)........ 390

Belgium

Judgment No 11/2009 (Constitutional Court of Belgium, 21 January 2009).................... 358

Canada

Law v Canada (Minister of Employment and Immigration) [1999] 1 SCR 497 (25 March 1999) 339
Egan v Canada (AG) [1995] 2 SCR 513 (25 May 1995).. 339

Czech Republic

Judgment No 19/08 Pl ÚS (Constitutional Court of the Czech Republic, 26 November 2008) 203

Germany

BVerfG 2 BvR 1390/12 (12 September 2012)... 6, 154
BVerfG 1 BvR 699/06 (22 February 2011)... 432
BVerfG 2 BvE 2/08 (30 June 2009) 203
BVerfGE 90, 241, 1 BvR 23/94 (13 April 1994)... 338
BVerfGE 89, 155, 2 BvR 2134/92 and 2159/92 (12 October 1993) 139, 396
BVerfGE 54, 143, 2 BvR 854/79 (23 May 1980).. 239

The Netherlands

Stichting Mothers of Srebrenica v The Netherlands and the United Nations
  ECLI:NL:RBDHA:2014:8748 (District Court, The Hague, 16 July 2014) 25

New Zealand

New Zealand Climate Science Education Trust v National Institute of
  Water and Atmospheric Research Limited [2012] NZHC 2297 (7 September 2012) 93

South Africa

Minister of Economic Development and Others v Competition Tribunal and
  Others, South African Commercial, Catering and Allied Workers Union
  (SACCAWU) v Wal-Mart Stores Inc 110/CAC/Jul11 and 111/CAC/Jun11
  [2012] ZACAC 6 (9 October 2012) 326
City Council of Pretoria v Walker [1998] CCT 8/97 (17 February 1998) 339
President of the Republic of South Africa and Another v Hugo [1997]
  CCT 11/96 (18 April 1997) 339

United Kingdom

City of London v Samede and Others [2012] EWCA Civ 160 (22 February 2012) 432
School of Oriental and African Studies v Persons Unknown [2010] 49 EG 78
  (EWHC, 25 November 2010) 432

United States

Association of Irritated Residents v California Air Resources Board
  No A132165 (Cal App, 1st Dist, 19 June 2012) 93
Massachusetts v Environment Protection Agency 549 US 497 (2 April 2007) 93
Gratz v Bollinger 539 US 244 (23 June 2003) 342
New Orleans Campaign for a Living Wage v City of New Orleans
  825 So.2d 1098 (LA, 4 September 2002) 364
City of Cleburne Tex v Cleburne Living Center 473 US 432 (23 April 1985) 343
Lawrence County v Lead-Deadwood School District 469 US 256 (9 January 1985) 355
Regents of University of California v Bakke 438 US 265 (28 June 1978) 342
Norwalk Core v Norwalk Redevelopment Agency 395 F2d 920 (CA2, 7 June 1968) 342
Heart of Atlanta Motel, Inc v US 379 US 241 (14 December 1964) 343
Parker v Brown 317 US 341 (4 January 1943) 354
United States v Carolene Products Co 304 US 144 (25 April 1938) 347
Lochner v New York 198 US 45 (17 April 1905) 235

Other Courts and Tribunals

US v Otto Ohlendorf et al (Einsatzgruppen) United States Military
  Tribunals at Nuremberg (1948) Case No 9, TWC Vol IV 1 391
Case No 9, The Zyklon B Case, The Trial of Bruno Tesch and Two Others
  Law Reports of Trials of War Criminals, United Nations War
  Crimes Commission, Vol 1, London, HMSO (1947) 385

Table of Treaties and Legislation

EU Treaties and the Charter of Fundamental Rights

Charter of Fundamental Rights of the European
   Union 2000 .... 42, 49, 55, 103–7, 161–62
   Art 7 105
   Art 16 106
   Art 47 .... 101, 104, 106, 162
   Art 48(2) 106
   Art 51(1) 162
   Art 52(1) 104–6
      (3) 104
      (4) 104
Fiscal Compact *see* Treaty on Stability, Coordination and Governance
   in the Economic and Monetary Union 2012
Single European Act 1986 406
Treaty of Amsterdam 1999 .... 52, 203, 378
Treaty establishing the European Coal and Steel Community 1951 251
Treaty establishing the European Economic Community 1957 .... 163–65, 251, 378
   Art 2 163
Treaty establishing the European Community (Nice consolidated version)
   Art 60 102
   Art 130(a) 359
      (b) 359
      (c) 359
      (d) 359
   Art 301 101
   Art 308 101
Treaty establishing the European Stability Mechanism 2011 .... 124, 126, 154–55, 162
Treaty on European Union (Maastricht) 1992 .... 177, 203, 249, 296
Treaty on European Union (Lisbon consolidated version) 2007 .... 166, 285
   Preamble 200
   Art 2 .... 23–25, 30, 55, 59, 98, 181–82, 203
   Art 3 .... 24, 27, 55, 167, 408
      (1) 24, 298–99
      (2) 55
      (3) 54
      (3)(2) 24
   Art 5(3) 100
      (4) 100
   Art 6(3) 98, 104
   Art 7 .... 24, 45, 60
   Art 10 .... 200, 203
   Art 11 200
      (4) 204

xxxii *Table of Treaties and Legislation*

Art 19 99
  (3) 99
Art 24 99
Treaty on the Functioning of the European Union 2007 (consolidated version) 166
  Art 4(2) 100
  Art 9 55
  Art 18 453
  Art 24 204
  Art 26 267
  Art 56 363
  Art 81 378
  Art 106 167
  Art 113 266
  Art 114 .... 265–67, 377
  Art 125 .... 126, 144, 155
    (1) 155
  Art 135 83
  Art 174(2) 359
  Art 192 266
  Art 227 204
  Art 256 99
  Art 258 .... 24, 99
  Art 259 .... 24, 99
  Art 260 24
  Art 263 .... 99, 103
  Arts 263–265 99
  Arts 267–276 99
  Art 275 103
  Art 280(4) 83
  Art 289(3) 101
  Art 345 378
  Art 352 266
  Protocol No 3 on the Statute of the Court of Justice of the
    European Union 99
Treaty of Lisbon 2007 .... 47, 60, 103–4, 106, 200, 203–5, 207, 359, 376
Treaty of Nice 2001 203
Treaty of Paris *see* Treaty establishing the European Coal and Steel Community 1951
Treaty of Rome *see* Treaty establishing the European Economic Community 1957
Treaty on Stability, Coordination and Governance in the Economic
  and Monetary Union 2012 .... 124, 126, 296
  Art 3(1)(a) 140
    (b) 140
    (d) 140
    (e) 140
  Art 7 54–55

EU Secondary Legislation

Regulations
Reg 1466/97 on the strengthening of the surveillance of budgetary positions and the
  surveillance and coordination of economic polices [1997] OJ L209/1 126

Table of Treaties and Legislation xxxiii

Art 2(a) 140
Art 5(1) 140
Art 6(3) 140
Reg 1467/97 on speeding up and clarifying the implementation of the
excessive deficit procedure [1997] OJ L209/6 126
Art 2(1)(a) 140
Reg 1173/2011 on the effective enforcement of budgetary surveillance
in the euro area [2011] OJ L306/1 .... 54–55, 142, 296
Reg 1174/2011 on enforcement measures to correct excessive
macroeconomic imbalances in the euro area [2011] OJ L306/8 .... 54–55, 142, 296
Reg 1175/2011 amending Reg 1466/97 [2011] OJ L306/12 .... 54–55, 142, 296
Reg 1176/2011 on the prevention and correction of macroeconomic
imbalances [2011] OJ L306/25 .... 54–55, 142, 296
Reg 1177/2011 amending Reg 1467/97 [2011] OJ L306/33 .... 54–55, 142, 296
Reg 1215/2012 on jurisdiction and the recognition and enforcement
of judgments in civil and commercial matters [2012] OJ L351/1 369
Reg 472/2013 on the strengthening of economic and budgetary
surveillance of Member States in the euro area experiencing or
threatened with serious difficulties with respect to their financial
stability [2013] OJ L140/1 .... 142, 296
Reg 473/2013 on common provisions for monitoring and assessing
draft budgetary plans and ensuring the correction of excessive deficit
of the Member States in the euro area [2013] OJ L140/11 .... 142, 296

Directives
Dir 79/409 on the conservation of wild birds [1979] OJ L103/1 .... 403, 411
Art 4 411
Dir 85/337 on the assessment of the effects of certain public and
private projects on the environment [1985] OJ L175/40 404
Dir 85/577 to protect the consumer in respect of contracts negotiated
away from business premises [1985] OJ L372/31 368
Dir 89/552 on the coordination of certain provisions laid down by law,
regulation or administrative action in Member States concerning the
pursuit of television broadcasting activities [1989] OJ L298/23 105
Dir 92/43 on the conservation of natural habitats and of
wild fauna and flora [1992] OJ L206/7 .... 401–5, 410, 412, 414–16
Preamble 402
    recital 4 404
    recital 6 403
Art 1(i) 415
Art 4 403
Art 5 403
Art 6(3) 404, 414
    (4) 402, 404–5, 410, 415
Art 10 403
Annex I 404
Annex II 404
Annex III 403
Dir 93/13 on unfair terms in consumer contracts [1993] OJ L95/29 .... 75–76, 368, 370
Dir 96/61 concerning integrated pollution prevention and control
[1996] OJ L257/6 404

Dir 96/71 concerning the posting of workers in the framework of the
  provision of services [1997] OJ L18/1 363–64
    Art 3(8) 364
Dir 97/7 on the protection of consumers in respect of distance
  contracts [1997] OJ L144/19 368
Dir 1999/44 on certain aspects of the sale of consumer goods and
  associated guarantees [1999] OJ L171/12 368
Dir 2000/43 implementing the principle of equal treatment between
  persons irrespective of racial or ethnic origin [2000] OJ L180/22 409
Dir 2000/60 establishing a framework for Community action in the
  field of water policy [2000] OJ L327/1 401
Dir 2001/37 on the approximation of laws, regulations and administrative
  provisions concerning the manufacture, presentation and sale of tobacco
  products [2001] OJ L194/26 103
    Art 5 103
Dir 2003/109 concerning the status of third-country nationals who are
  long-term residents [2003] OJ L16/44 185
Dir 2004/113 implementing the principle of equal treatment between
  men and women in the access to and supply of goods and services
  [2004] OJ L373/37 106
Dir 2005/29 concerning unfair business-to-consumer commercial
  practices in the internal market [2005] OJ L149/22 369
Dir 2006/24 on the retention of data generated or processed in connection
  with the provision of publicly available electronic communications services
  or of public communications networks [2006] OJ L105/54
    Art 6 105
Dir 2011/85 on requirements for budgetary frameworks of the Member
  States [2011] OJ L306/41 .... 54–55, 142, 296

Decisions
Dec 70/243 on the replacement of financial contributions from Member
  States by the Communities' own resources [1970] OJ L94/19 148
Framework Dec 2002/584 on the European arrest warrant and surrender
  procedures between Member States [2002] OJ L190/1 106
Dec 2011/199 amending Art 136 of the TFEU with regard to a stability
  mechanism for Member States whose currency is the euro [2011] OJ L91/1 153

International Conventions, Treaties

Aarhus Convention on Access to Information, Public Participation in
  Decision-Making and Access to Justice in Environmental Matters 1998 .... 46, 404
European Convention on Human Rights
  1950 .... 102, 104, 119, 236, 331, 382–88, 392–99,
                              417–22, 424, 430, 460
    Art 5 395
      (3) 396
    Art 7(2) 396
    Art 8 76
    Art 9 419
    Art 10 .... 386, 396–98, 417, 419
      (2) 419

Art 17	397
Art 34	387
Protocol No 1, Art 1	236

National

France
Declaration of the Rights of Man and of the Citizen 1789
Art 17	236

Germany
Basic Law	220
Art 103(2)	396

United States
Civil Rights Act 1964	343
Constitution, First Amendment	237

1
Europe's Justice Deficit Introduced

DIMITRY KOCHENOV AND ANDREW WILLIAMS

THE AMBITION OF this volume is to explore the notion of justice and its relationship with law in the context of the European Union. It seeks to appraise the existence and nature of any perceived justice deficit in Europe, its implications for Europe's future, and to begin a critical discussion about how this deficit might be addressed should it be identified as a problem. The time to do this is ripe. The EU has moved beyond its initial and primary emphasis on the establishment of an Internal Market. Politically, socially and economically, the EU is engaged in a vast array of concerns that impact on people's lives. Yet, most academic analyses of the European legal reality remains premised broadly on the assumption that EU law still largely serves the purpose of perfecting what is fundamentally a system of economic integration. This view and this system have outlived themselves. Both are in need of fundamental reform.[1] Whatever shape such reform will take, it is bound to touch upon the sensitive issues of justice and injustice. This being said, the place to be occupied by any substantive ideal of justice in the European legal context remains significantly underspecified, even vacant, creating a tension between the market-oriented foundation of the Union and the contemporary essence of its constitutional system.[2] A market, however successful, cannot supply the constitutional core of the Union.[3]

Underlying this volume are two key appreciations: first, normative, that it *is* appropriate to talk about justice in terms of the EU; and second, empirical, that justice in this context has, despite exceptions, been inadequately theorised and examined academically and institutionally.[4] Overall this volume hopes to remedy the latter by providing the opportunity for the former, thereby moving the study of European law and integration forward. The time has come to establish the essential

---

[1] See, eg, AJ Menéndez, 'Editorial: A European Union in Constitutional Mutation?' (2014) 20 *European Law Journal* 127; AJ Menéndez, 'The Existential Crisis of the European Union' (2013) 14 *German Law Journal* 453; D Kochenov, 'The Citizenship Paradigm' (2013) 15 *Cambridge Yearbook of European Legal Studies* 196; A Williams, 'Taking Values Seriously: Towards a Philosophy of EU Law' (2009) 29 *Oxford Journal of Legal Studies* 549.
[2] Eg Williams, 'Taking Values Seriously', n 1 above; A Williams, *The Ethos of Europe* (Cambridge, Cambridge University Press, 2009); D Kochenov and R Plender, 'EU Citizenship: From an Incipient Form to an Incipient Substance? The Discovery of the Treaty Text' (2012) 37 *European Law Review* 369.
[3] See also N Nic Shuibhne, 'The Resilience of EU Market Citizenship' (2010) 47 *Common Market Law Review* 1597.
[4] See D Kochenov 'The Ought of Justice' in this volume, 21.

links between the numerous issues and perspectives on justice, providing an overarching agenda for the scholarly engagement with this area in the near- to mid-term future. That is the aim of this book.

The volume aims to address several inter-related dimensions of justice in the context of the European legal landscape, focusing predominantly, but not exclusively, on the European Union, while also taking the wider Council of Europe context into account. The main claim of this book is confirmed by all the chapters and restated in the conclusion. Simply put it is that a mature legal system as the EU now is, cannot remain justice-blind. The EU cannot avoid dealing with innumerable justice claims, which already—in an atmosphere of justice deficit—create numerous problems.

By bringing together a large number of contributors, all invited to share their concerns about justice in this context and, in many cases, to engage in debate amongst themselves in the process, we hope to make the notion of justice more visible for the EU. Taking justice seriously is the underlying rationale for this collection.

I

The book is arranged as a flow of ideas. It opens with Dimitry Kochenov's explanation of the starting point of thinking behind the deficit: justice is to be expected of Europe, but has not so far received sufficient attention[5] and Andrew Williams' restatement of a key normative starting point: the EU *already* is an actor of justice (and injustice) and should be approached as such. Moreover, crucially, justice should necessarily possess a substantive meaning, rather than be relegated to the procedural[6] corners of the fabric of EU's legal–political essence. Four key aspects of justice in the EU are analysed: distributive, inter-generational, political, and criminal. Williams ponders, in particular, on the question of the standards of justice against which each of the aspects of justice he outlines is to be measured in the context of European integration. Posing questions rather than providing answers, his chapter advocates a proactive rather than a passive stance in dealing with the justice issues in the EU, stating which justice areas the EU should be taking seriously and why. A key sub-theme emerging from the chapter—akin to the point made by Alexander Somek later in this volume—consists in restating the problematic nature of trying to approach justice issues as human rights problems,[7] thereby attempting to interpret away the key ethical choices which the EU is constantly facing.[8] Rather, justice should be viewed as a key value underlying the construction of the European legal–political space that should not be approached in the light of legitimacy alone. In fact, the issues of justice on the one side and of legitimising the EU on the other, should better be treated separately, as 'sophisticated arguments

---

[5] ibid.
[6] 'Superficial', in Williams' categorisation: A Williams, 'The Problem(s) of Justice in the European Union' in this volume, 33, at 34.
[7] See also, in similar vein, A Sajó, 'Victimhood and Vulnerability as Sources of Justice' in this volume, 337.
[8] On the natural multiplicity of such choices remember, for instance, Rawls' example of the children and a flute: J Rawls, *A Theory of Justice* (Cambridge, MA, Harvard University Press, 1971).

about legitimacy might divert attention from the declaration of *should* but would not displace it'.[9]

Sionaidh Douglas-Scott's chapter develops this analysis. She first emphasises the EU's ability to do *injustice* focusing on concrete examples.[10] These include the EU's Area of Freedom, Security and Justice (AFSJ), the EU's handling of the financial crisis—a recurrent theme in this volume[11]—and social justice, where she focuses on the decisions in *Viking*[12] and *Laval*.[13] While the cases given in the chapter may not be viewed as examples of injustice by all the scholars engaged in justice analysis,[14] it is reasonable to state that the way in which we conceive of the EU may affect how we understand its capacity to do justice.[15] Yet, our pre-set vision of the EU cannot deny the '*should*-question', as Kochenov and Williams framed it: however the EU is understood, justice and injustice already play a role. Recognising this fully, Douglas-Scott presents a Rule of Law-centred concept of 'Critical Legal Justice' to supply the cornerstone of our assessment of the EU.

Should more attention be paid to justice in the EU—and especially once a normative decision has been taken that this should indeed be the case—the key question arising relates to standards. Who is to fashion the standards of justice? Oliver Gerstenberg considers that any easy answers are unlikely, given the complexity of both the notion of justice and the EU's own organisation: the hierarchical and constantly contested interplay between the individual levels in the multi-layered structure of the EU is very sophisticated—much more so than is usually claimed. Key in this respect is to ensure that the system of justice is adequately equipped to fully accommodate Europe's multiple pluralisms.

Gerstenberg thus cautions against pretending that the EU can have a unitary concept of justice. If correct, then the relevance of democratic procedure destined to enable the elaboration and fine-tuning of the possible competing conceptions becomes crucial. It is thus, as Agustín Menéndez, too, argues,[16] not 'justice replacing democracy', but the development of the two hand-in-hand that is required. Gerstenberg's starting idea of a justice conception includes, first, 'equal respect for the diversity of conceptions of good life' and, secondly, 'equal concern for the interest of all members of the society'.[17]

Although the resulting idea of justice—as with Douglas-Scott—is quite thin, it is also dynamic and malleable, enabling its possible real-life application. At the core of

---

[9] Williams, 'The Problem(s) of Justice', 37.

[10] See also J Shklar, *The Faces of Injustice* (New Haven, CT, Yale University Press, 1992).

[11] See, inter alia, also the contributions by AJ Menéndez, 'Whose Justice? Which Europe?' in this volume, 137, and D Nicol, 'Swabian Housewives, Suffering Southerners: The Contestability of Justice as Exemplified by the Eurozone Crisis' in this volume, 165.

[12] Case C-438/05 *International Transport Workers' Federation and Finnish Seamen's Union v Viking Line ABP and OÜ Viking Line Eesti* [2007] ECR I-10779.

[13] Case C-341/05 *Laval un Partneri Ltd v Svenska Byggnadsarbetareförbundet and Others* [2007] ECR I-11767.

[14] See D Kukovec, 'Taking Change Seriously: The Rhetoric of Justice and the Reproduction of the Status Quo' in this volume, 319.

[15] S Douglas-Scott, 'Justice, Injustice and the Rule of Law in the EU' in this volume, 51.

[16] Menéndez, 'Whose Justice? Which Europe?' in this volume, 137.

[17] O Gerstenberg, 'The Question of Standards for the EU: From "Democratic Deficit" to "Justice Deficit?"' in this volume, 67.

the chapter is the legal–philosophical engagement with the 'sovereignist objection' as formulated, inter alia, by Nagel, which consists of the impossibility of positive obligations of justice beyond the state.[18] While Nagel can be dismissed morally and ethically,[19] Gerstenberg takes the objective limits of Member State sovereignty in today's EU as his starting point. Doing nothing because of how sovereignty is understood is not sustainable in the face of current justice claims. Moreover, the discontinuity of the political conception in the contemporary EU can legitimately be exposed as an exaggeration: the EU offers a political continuum along the EU–Member State lines. In particular, the presumed separation between the economic and the social in the EU—one being largely supranational, the other largely national—simply does not stand in practice.

Thus, according to Gerstenberg, the EU emerges as a continuous discursive space of pluralist engagement. The Court of Justice of the European Union (ECJ) plays the key role in this context: the dualities economic/social and national/supranational are now blurred and emerge in a far more complex light than initially imagined. It is an 'experimentalist Court'[20] and should be regarded as such. Gerstenberg employs several examples to demonstrate how the Court's case-law, viewed from a strictly national sovereignty perspective as harmful supranational mingling with Member State competences, actually, when viewed in the context of the complex pluralist space of justice emerging in Europe, is furthering justice ideals. *Yvonne Watts* is one such example.[21] *Aziz* is another.[22] One cannot help but place *Viking* and *Laval* into the same context.[23] The ECJ, looking at EU citizens and their concerns demands a nuanced and justified approach to justice issues, bypassing the long-established national status quo unless it can be properly justified.[24] Ironically, in such a context the ECJ seemingly emerges as a true justice actor—sensitive and non-authoritarian—in contrast to Douglas-Scott's observation in her contribution.

It takes liberation from the blinding ideology of absolute sovereignty to see the just nature of *Watts*, *Viking* and *Laval*, as Gerstenberg reminds us: 'it is the *European sphere* that opens up a forum for principled moral considerations of personhood,

---

[18] T Nagel, 'The Problem of Global Justice' in T Nagel, *Secular Philosophy and the Religious Temperament: Essays 2002–2008* (Oxford, Oxford University Press, 2010). In the context of the EU, this position has been strongly advocated by Richard Bellamy. See, eg, R Bellamy, 'Political Justice for an Ever Closer Union of People' in G de Búrca, D Kochenov and A Williams (eds), *Debating Europe's Justice Deficit* (2013) EUI Working Papers LAW 2013/11.

[19] A Williams, 'The EU, Interim Global Justice and the International Legal Order' in D Kochenov and F Amtenbrink (eds), *The European Union's Shaping of the International Legal Order* (Cambridge, Cambridge University Press, 2013) 38.

[20] Gerstenberg, 'The Question of Standards for the EU' in this volume, 67, at 73.

[21] Case C-372/04 R, *on the application of Yvonne Watts v Bedford Primary Care Trust and Secretary of State for Health* [2006] ECR I-4325.

[22] Case C-415/11 *Mohamed Aziz v Caixa d'Estalvis de Catalunya, Tarragona i Manresa (Catalunyacaixa)* (ECJ, 14 March 2013).

[23] Case C-438/05 *Viking Line* [2007] ECR I-10779 and Case C-341/05 *Laval un Partneri* [2007] ECR I-11767.

[24] See also G Davies, 'The Humiliation of the State As a Constitutional Tactic' in F Amtenbrink and PAJ van den Bergh (eds), *The Constitutional Integrity of the European Union* (The Hague, TMC Asser Press, 2010).

need, and circumstance'.[25] His recommendation for the future of justice in the EU underlines the need to sustain the precious complex discursive field emerging across the layers of government in Europe and fostered by the EU.

Drawing on the fact that justice is never explained in European legal discourse, a need arises to trace its current function in the European legal context: the key research point of Suryapratim Roy's chapter in this collection, which argues that justice is used as a rhetorical tool to provide legitimacy for other principles and institutional decisions. An analogous process is at work in scholarly critique of institutional justice, where justice appears subservient to scholarly preferences for other principles. Justice is therefore subjugated to particular ways of understanding and advocating the importance of democracy and fairness: 'as far as the EU is concerned, justice appears to be an empty signifier tethered to the self-justifying referent of institutional stability'.[26]

Building on this insight, Roy's chapter assumes that justice too can and should acquire a voice of its own. Roy argues that it is necessary to identify and work against such instrumentalist 'inverse monism' where institutional speech-acts shape the discourse of social organisation and individual contestation.[27] Indeed, 'it is necessary to shape the law to support justice, rather than perpetuate institutional preferences'.[28] The inevitability of defining justice according to institutional preferences tempts the conclusion that justice cannot possibly have a voice of its own within the institutional constraints of the European legal order. This may be true if the aim is to give space to all the meanings that justice can possibly have, but the chapter recognises the necessity for institutional restraint of infinite meanings to maintain social order.

Roy ultimately advocates the construction of a legal space that facilitates the assessment and contestation of such restraint, termed as 'institutional violence'.[29] Such a legal space may require institutional change as well as interpretive ingenuity, but fits well within the idea of a narrative of the complex experimental discursive field, which is Europe, as advocated by Gerstenberg.

To collect even more systematic evidence on the actual role of justice in the reasoning practices of the ECJ, Dorota Leczykiewicz focuses in her contribution on the specific area of validity challenges involving EU acts. Leczykiewicz argues that 'the language of "justice" will bring about a beneficial change only if it is used to perform new tasks, currently not carried out by concepts such as political or social legitimacy'.[30] This position is tested by focusing on constitutional (rather than administrative) review of EU acts. Among the key problems outlined in this regard is the low threshold of standards adopted by the ECJ in the course of judicial review, undermining the aspirations of justice: a '"justice-as-justification" deficit'[31] in the words of the author.

---

[25] Gerstenberg, 'The Question of Standards for the EU' in this volume, 67, at 75.
[26] S Roy, 'Justice As Europe's Signifier: Towards a More Inclusive Hermeneutics of the European Legal Order' in this volume, 79, at 83.
[27] ibid, 92.
[28] ibid, 95.
[29] ibid, 90.
[30] D Leczykiewicz, '"Constitutional Justice" and Judicial Review of EU Legislative Acts' in this volume, 97.
[31] ibid, 99.

II

A separate sub-set of questions emerges when the inter-relationship between the justice deficit and the political is considered. Should justice be an apolitical force or should the deficit be politicised? Strong arguments in favour of the latter are contained in the chapters by Michael Wilkinson and Agustín José Menéndez, while Daniel Augenstein comes to the same conclusion with an emphasis on the role of fundamental rights in the European construct. Arguments for politicisation are particularly acute in the specific context of the EU, given that the 'apolitical' reality of integration—our contemporary Union—has largely failed justice. The 'apolitical' construct emphasises the Internal Market, depoliticising the economic sphere. Moreover, fundamental rights have been turned into the key aids for economic integration, losing their broader justice-related functions.[32]

This is the core warning and insight provided by Menéndez and also Wilkinson: politicisation—via democratic politics—should be the prerequisite of dealing with justice, since the alternative is a constant reconfirmation of the problematic idea that supranational economic integration is beyond the reach of justice.

Crucial in this discussion is the distinction between legitimation and politicisation: the latter does *not* have legitimacy as the only goal. Agustín Menéndez takes the reader through a number of convincing examples from the history of ideas since antiquity, which illustrate different (still) available ways to deploy justice to kill politics. He focuses on three such strategies in particular—justice as an alternative to politics; apolitical justice as a way to preserve the political community; depoliticisation of justice through the emphasis on the impartiality—associating them with three political philosophers: Plato, Hobbes, and Godwin. Menéndez's conclusion resulting from the application of the triumvirate of approaches to the EU is that— come the crisis—the EU's approach to economic and monetary policy has been effectively purged of politics in the most Platonic fashion,[33] posing a threat to the harmonious development of the Union.

Wilkinson turns to the roots of European integration to represent them as a recalibration of Wolfgang Streek's dilemma[34] regarding the relationship between market and social justice. This has been done, famously, through constraining *both* democracy and capitalism.[35] Such an approach to building the Union in Europe brought about dangerous consequences: the Internal Market, as interpreted and implemented by the EU institutions, came to be presented in naturalistic terms, excluding interventions informed by justice and politics: 'the source of authority [now lies] apparently "beyond the sphere of power"'.[36]

---

[32] See D Augenstein, 'We the People: EU Justice As Politics' in this volume, 153.
[33] Menéndez, 'Whose Justice? Which Europe?' in this volume, 137, at 139: 'It is not hard to see Platonic streaks in the contemporary debates on the European crises'.
[34] See, for key literature citations, n 8 and the accompanying text in MA Wilkinson, 'Politicising Europe's Justice Deficit: Some Preliminaries' in this volume, 111, at 112.
[35] ibid, 113ff.
[36] ibid, 130. Augenstein's reliance on Case C-370/12 *Thomas Pringle v Government of Ireland, Ireland and the Attorney General* (ECJ, 27 November 2012) and the BVerfG's *ESM* judgment (BVerfG 2 BvR 1390/12 (12 September 2012)) allows him to make this point with particular clarity: Augenstein, 'We the People' in this volume, 153, at 154ff.

Europe's Justice Deficit Introduced 7

It seems to be clear that 're-politicisation' will most likely require a virtually complete reinvention of the European unification project. Moreover, it does not imply the repatriation of powers to the national level: more ingenious approaches have to be found for it to be effective. Menéndez, while strongly opposed to the idea of 'justice deficit', seeing it as a way to entrench depoliticisation of the EU even further, offers one such approach, branding it as 'democratic tactics' (as opposed to bringing about constitutional moments) and an attempt to expose the cleavages and deeply divided class structures now not infrequently hidden behind the façades of the states, mistakenly presented as the natural units of justice.

For Augenstein, whose chapter proceeds along similar lines, but adopts the Weilerian fundamental rights/fundamental boundaries distinction[37] as a starting consideration, it is the function of fundamental rights that has to be the focus of potential reform to bring about a just Union in Europe: fundamental rights should be reconceptualised in such a way that their current dependence (frequently downplayed in euro-speak but decipherable in the case-law and policy) on the Internal Market-thinking should give way to a non-market conception. He states that 'as long as fundamental rights are reduced to a function of economic integration, and delimited by virtue of the expediencies of financial reform, they will not muster the political strength to break the EU's vicious circle between output legitimacy and economic self-interest'.[38]

Danny Nicol's chapter enriches the politicisation of the justice deficit perspective by moving beyond the political. His central argument is that justice, rather than being simply political, is *party political*.[39] This is so since justice, as presented by Nicol, is 'something we argue about'[40] and party politics structures this process. His argument is in harmony with Menéndez's: justice should not be deployed to annihilate valid concerns related to the state and the indispensability of democracy for the EU. Unlike Menéndez, however, Nicol comes to this conclusion by illustrating the multiplicity of perfectly valid readings of what is just and what is not, tapping into the context of addressing the Eurozone crisis as well as ECJ's case-law[41] and EU law in general. The chapter contrasts the views of Laski and von Hayek to restate its point at the doctrinal plane: plentiful mutually contradictory reasonable approaches to justice are possible.[42] Arguing for justice as justification—like Neyer and Forst do[43]—when approached in this vein seems to imply a refusal to see that 'it is precisely the EU's existing system of justification which has consistently privileged the interests of

---

[37] JHH Weiler, 'Fundamental Rights and Fundamental Boundaries: On the Conflict of Standards and Values in the Protection of Human Rights in the European Legal Space' in JHH Weiler, *The Constitution of Europe: 'Do the New Clothes Have an Emperor?' and Other Essays on European Integration* (Cambridge, Cambridge University Press, 1999).

[38] Augenstein, 'We the People' in this volume, 153, at 164.

[39] Nicol, 'Swabian Housewives, Suffering Southerners' in this volume, 165, at 170.

[40] ibid, 165.

[41] For more on the innate partiality of the ECJ see, Fernanda Nicola's chapter in this volume, 349. See also, eg, G Davies 'Abstractness and Concreteness in the Preliminary Reference Procedure: Implications for the Division of Powers and Effective Market Regulation' in N Nic Shuibhne (ed), *Regulating the Internal Market* (Cheltenham, Edward Elgar, 2006).

[42] Nicol, 'Swabian Housewives, Suffering Southerners' in this volume, 165, at 171.

[43] See the chapters by R Forst, 'Justice, Democracy and the Right for Justification: Reflections on Jürgen Neyer's Normative Theory of the European Union' in this volume, 227, and J Neyer, 'Justice and the Right to Justification: Conceptual Reflections' in this volume, 221.

8   *Dimitry Kochenov and Andrew Williams*

private enterprise, setting in train the pro-corporation bias which has arguably led to the Eurozone crisis'.[44] The divergent legitimate conceptions of justice are informed, argues Nicol, by party politics: scholars are recommended to disclose their political affiliation before embarking on any justice-related analytical journeys. The obvious problem with such reasoning, it seems, is that it entirely ignores the deeper meaning of justice—the universal common denominator, on which all reasonable people, no matter what their political colours are—can unquestionably agree. Such common denominator can be the boundary of humanity, inherent in all, left or right.[45]

Justine Lacroix turns to the citizen in her analysis. Approaching citizenship as an open-ended process, rather than merely self-governance, she connects the concepts of justice, legitimacy and rights by linking all three to the idea of citizenship. Leaning in the direction of Daniel Augentein's contribution, Lacroix awards full preference to fundamental rights, making them part of the very definition of what justice is to mean in the complex context of the EU. Justice in this reading is 'a determined quest to construct a universal field of rights'.[46] To make this possible, one needs to realise the actual place of diversity and pluralism in our ranking of values. In this sense saying that justice is contested and could mean anything (or that it is party-political) can legitimately be contested by pointing out in Jan-Werner Müller's terms (as Justine Lacroix does), that 'Diversity and pluralism are not values in the same sense as liberty and democracy ... It is liberty and democracy that European intellectuals need to defend'.[47] Since citizenship is an important legal status, reducing it to a form of political action is wrong,[48] with far-reaching implications for the politicisation of justice as the key approach to solving the justice deficit.

Alexander Somek, inspired by Aristotle's *Nicomachean Echics* provides a convincing end to the justice versus politics discussion:

> Justice is about giving persons their due. Due is what is lawful. Lawful is what comports with law. What is law in a certain type of society depends on what that society is. A society is, from a distributive perspective, what its members deem to be meritorious. Merit stands for what society believes should be rewarded with goods, influence and, most importantly, political power.[49]

III

The intricate connection between legitimacy and political justice is at the heart of Jiří Přibáň's contribution. Moving from Hans Kelsen[50] to Niklas Luhmann,[51] he

---

[44]   Nicol, 'Swabian Housewives, Suffering Southerners' in this volume, 165, at 175.
[45]   See D Kochenov, 'The Just World' in this volume, 435.
[46]   J Lacroix, 'Is Transnational Citizenship (Still) Enough?' in this volume, 177, at 180.
[47]   J-W Müller, 'The Failure of European Intellectuals?' *Eurozine* (11 April 2012) www.eurozine.com/articles/2012-04-11-muller-en.html.
[48]   Lacroix, 'Is Transnational Citizenship (Still) Enough?' in this volume, 177, at 183.
[49]   A Somek, 'The Preoccupation with Rights and the Embrace of Inclusion: A Critique' in this volume, 295, at 305 (footnotes omitted).
[50]   H Kelsen, *The Pure Theory of Law* (Berkeley, CA, University of California Press, 1960).
[51]   N Luhmann, *Paradigm Lost: Die ethische Reflexion der Moral* (Frankfurt, Suhrkamp, 1990); N Luhmann, *Law As a Social System* (Oxford, Oxford University Press, 2004); N Luhmann, *Ausdifferenzierung des Rechts: Beiträge zur Rechtssoziologie und Rechtstheorie* (Frankfurt, Suhrkamp, 1981); and N Luhmann, *Legitimation durch Verfahren* (Frankfurt, Surhkamp, 1969/1983).

outlines the inherent tension between law and justice for the positivists: political justice has a clearly distillable dangerous potential: 'it semantically unifies what needs to be functionally differentiated in a modern society; namely politics and law'.[52] Given that political justice is legitimately viewed as an avenue of legitimising law and politics alike, the idea of legitimation through justice comes to the fore and has to be scrutinised. In this sense, distinguishing between what Přibáň terms as 'normative' and 'operative' concepts of legitimacy is vital.[53]

Operative legitimacy, embraced in the EU since its creation, welcomes Europeans into a fairytale post-conflictual world where political institutions do not enjoy coercive power.[54] It will not be a surprise for anyone that such a world in fact does not exist: hard political decisions remain the assumption behind technocratic exercises; a post-conflictual world then largely amounts to removing any possibility of contesting the fundamentals. In the EU, as we have seen above, this is the Internal Market ideology. In this context Přibáň asks whether the EU 'needs to constitute legally its "categorical imperative" of political justice and determine its content'.[55] The key finding underlying it is, of course, that the EU, although possessing an autonomous legal system, 'operates *without* the foundationalist legitimising principle of political justice' (emphasis added).[56] The EU, in its current form then emerges as 'post-conflict' and, crucially, '*value free*'.

In contrast, Jürgen Neyer expresses a belief that justice should be a *substitute* for democracy in European integration.[57] He views justice as a largely procedural exercise removed from politics. The main function of such procedural justice according to Neyer, is to appease the ruled, who enjoy 'a right to justification'[58]—whose voice is presumably heard in the course of the generation of, and the statement of reasons for, the policies adopted. Striving for legitimacy without democracy thus emerges as Neyer's main goal.

The key question, as he formulates it, is 'under which theoretical premises the EU can be justified convincingly'?[59] The EU is presumed to be non-democratic by choice,[60] from which follows that its legitimation should not be sought in anything akin to democracy. Justice is then offered as a notion to replace democracy in the context of EU's justification. While providing a tentative answer to several wrongs from which European integration is believed to be suffering—especially the democratic deficit, which it interprets away—Neyer's account is blind to the 'ought' of justice, as it does not concern itself either with just outcomes (replaced by procedurally sound justifications) or with the ultimate standards against which such

---

[52] J Přibáň, 'The Evolving Idea of Political Justice in the EU: From Substantive Deficits to the Systemic Contingency of European Society' in this volume, 193, at 198.
[53] ibid, 199.
[54] Compare with A Badiou, *Ethics: An Essay on the Understanding of Evil* (London, Verso, 2001); and S Žižek, 'Against Human Rights' (2005) 34 *New Left Review* 10.
[55] Přibáň, 'The Evolving Idea of Political Justice' in this volume, 193, at 199.
[56] ibid, 206.
[57] Neyer, 'Justice and the Right to Justification' in this volume, 211. See also the monograph on which the chapter builds: J Neyer, *The Justification of Europe: A Political Theory of Supranational Integration* (Oxford, Oxford University Press, 2012).
[58] Neyer, 'Justice and the Right to Justification' in this volume, 211, at 213.
[59] ibid, 212.
[60] ibid, 211.

justification occurs (which should emerge as 'working agreements'[61] in the context of justificatory discourse).

While the added value of stating reasons is undisputed,[62] one could argue that justice reduced to stating reasons does not emerge as justice at all.[63] If the Internal Market is the EU's grand narrative then should justification of any policy take place against the market? If only the discourse plays a role, this ignores the potential legitimacy of expecting substantively just outcomes, which could be problematic. Once democracy and justice are viewed as mutually replaceable elements of societal organisation, the rightful instrumental importance of both in improving our lives is undermined. Moreover, psychological research demonstrates that the value of procedures as opposed to what are believed to be just outcomes is somewhat overrated by lawyers and political scientists.[64] Reducing justice to justification, although probably appealing to some as a rhetorical device, is thus potentially nothing more than a *reduccio ad absurdum*, or, in Rainer Forst's words, an '*Ersatz* or placebo discourse'.[65]

Beside all the scholars whose views have been described above, who argue that justice should not rhetorically substitute democracy *à la* Neyer, as this will amount to a denial of both, Rainer Frost takes a different view and is particularly vocal in his contribution in distancing himself—as an academic who launched the justice as justification idea—from Neyer's interpretation of his theories.[66] Forst's key objection rests in his understanding that the democracy–legitimacy link is vital to making justification work, as 'a just political order is a democratic normative order'.[67] Without democracy, a right to justification necessarily becomes something different from a right to becoming an *agent* of justification. Agency is of key importance here; Frost's justification is the justification by free citizens whereas Neyer's justification might be interpreted as only a justification for the passive recipients of procedural justice. In Forst's view, Neyer is oblivious to the fact that, inter alia, 'the rule-making authority must be constituted by those subjected to its norms'.[68]

---

[61] EO Eriksen, *The Unfinished Democratization of Europe* (Oxford, Oxford University Press, 2009) 51; J Habermas, 'Wahrheitstheorien' in H Fahrenbach (ed), *Wirklichkeit und Reflexion. Walter Schulz zum 60. Geburtstag* (Pfullingen, Neske, 1973) 218.

[62] M Kumm, 'Institutionalising Socratic Contestation: The Rationalist Human Rights Paradigm, Legitimate Authority and the Point of Judicial Review' (2007) 1(2) *European Journal of Legal Studies* 142.

[63] Justice then threatens to become merely an act of balancing, allowing all the substance to be interpreted away, if need be. See, eg, S Tsakyrakis, 'Disproportionate Individualism' in this volume, 235. See also S Tsakyrakis, 'Proportionality: An Assault on Human Rights?' (2009) 7 *International Journal of Constitutional Law* 468.

[64] For the psychological insights on this see, eg, L Heuer et al, 'The Role of Resource and Relational Concerns for Procedural Justice' (2002) 28 *Personality and Social Psychology Bulletin* 1468; K van den Bos, EA Lind and HAM Wilke, 'The Psychology of Procedural and Distributive Justice Viewed from the Perspective of Fairness Heuristic Theory' in R Cropanzano (ed), *Justice in the Workplace: From Theory to Practice*, vol 2 (Mahwah, NJ, Erlbaum, 2001) 49.

[65] Forst, 'Justice, Democracy and the Right for Justification' in this volume, 227, at 234.

[66] R Forst, *Das Recht auf Rechtfertigung. Elemente einer konstruktivistischen Theorie der Gerechtigkeit* (Frankfurt, Suhrkamp, 2007); R Forst, *The Right to Justification. Elements of a Constructivist Theory of Justice* (New York, NY, Columbia University Press, 2012), R Forst, *Justification and Critique. Towards a Critical Theory of Politics* (Cambridge, Polity Press, 2013).

[67] Forst, 'Justice, Democracy and the Right for Justification' in this volume, 227, at 234.

[68] ibid, 229.

Ultimately, however, it might matter little whether the justification discourse is politicised or not, since calling 'justification' a 'right' could be a categorical mistake, as Alexander Somek argues later in the volume. If justification, rather than being split from a right is taken as any right's inherent part, the justice that both Forst and Neyer argue for is nothing more than an argument for the protection of human rights.[69]

Unlike Forst, Stavros Tsakyrakis, in his contribution, is troubled by the essence of justification as such. He suggests—in departure from both Forst's and Neyer's thinking—that justification, as well as the related idea of balancing, is dangerous and unjust, viewing the starting point of the balancing ideology as 'a prima facie right to everything'.[70] Focusing on human rights adjudication in Europe in particular, Tsakyrakis' worry is that 'from the state of nature, proportionality lets Hobbes into the city'.[71] Putting aside unrestrained individualism promoted by the institutions and the law, the consequences of this are twofold. First, we are witnessing a constant glorification of a minimal authority, which is unable to become a serious actor of justice. Indeed, non-intervention—that is, the inability to do substantive justice—is as such not infrequently presented as just. Secondly, we are necessarily witnessing the erosion of the substance of any rights whatsoever—even those the minimal intervention attempting to further justice has managed to bring about: a prima facie right to everything amounts, in fact, to a right to 'nothing in particular'.[72]

Bringing about legitimacy through procedural justice is thus potentially very problematic on a number of accounts. This is not to dismiss the crucial justice–legitimacy connection, but to warn against particularly narrow placebo approaches to justice which create more problems than they solve.

Neil Walker's contribution restates the justice–legitimacy connection through a complex global assessment, without attempting to interpret away the key disagreements and main difficulties. It outlines six key-types of justice (personal, interpersonal, sectoral, institutional, polity-holistic, and global) only to find that while there is place for all of them *in* the EU context—which Walker explains by one of the key attributes of justice, its agility—the picture changes once these approaches are used to measure the justice *of* the Union. Walker's concern is the EU's nature as a self-standing polity and the problem of measuring the 'legitimacy of its contribution to the world'.[73] When justice is used to legitimise what the EU does—the 'in the EU' in Walker's terms—its potential is radically different compared with legitimising what the EU is—the 'of the EU' perspective.

Can it be though, that the EU's own essential design features not directly related to democracy and the division of powers between the Union and the Member States, undermine its ability to generate legitimacy? Gareth Davies makes precisely such a claim, focusing on the goal-oriented nature of the Union's powers. His chapter contains a serious counter-argument to the claims of those who view the politicisation of the EU as a panacea.

---

[69] Somek, 'The Preoccupation with Rights' in this volume, 295, at 303.
[70] Tsakyrakis, 'Disproportionate Individualism' in this volume, 235, at 237.
[71] ibid, 236.
[72] ibid, 239.
[73] N Walker, 'Justice in and of the European Union' in this volume, 247, at 250.

Davies reminds us that in a purposeful system like that of the EU, the contestation of the main goals pre-programmed in the founding documents is simply impossible, expectedly reducing the appeal of politicisation. Politicisation does not fly when the starting position is the denial of choice. Moreover, goal-oriented systems dangerously understate the importance of the irrational in the context of political life—and seemingly irrational concerns can have important expressive value going to the core of identity. If many political debates cannot boast any grain of rationality, as they address deeply held frustrations, biases and fears of the people, the goal-oriented nature of a legal–political system can indeed be regarded as an additional serious obstacle on the way to politicisation.

Politics, when condemned by the EU to instrumentality,[74] is hardly politics at all, undermining legitimacy. The EU by design is incapable of addressing subjective human harms. Worse still, it seems to be contaminating the Member States through a spill-over of this structural incapacity: 'national politics', in the words of Davies, 'ceases to be an effectively meaningful debate about society, but becomes a mere adjunct to expertise—at worst an irrelevance, at most a supervisory role'.[75] As a result, social legitimacy—already structurally decapitated at the supranational level—is undermined in the Member States as well. With the irrational ruled out as deficient or irrelevant, identities can be harmed, as people—profoundly interested in and attached to seemingly purely irrational concerns—feel deceived by the political system, which emerges as failing to recognise them for who they are. Davies' starting point lies in taking emotions seriously when conducting legal analysis.[76] From Davies' perspective, the EU is blind to the expressive role of the law, undermining politics.

IV

The contribution co-authored by Juri Viehoff and Kalypso Nicolaïdis turns to the mechanics of social justice, engaging with a number of theories to supply common ground for social justice theorizing in the EU context. The chapter first focuses on dismissing the worries expressed by a handful of scholars contributing to the volume, Menéndez in particular, that the rising profile of justice in the EU can undermine its legitimacy by making democracy concerns less relevant. Although justice and politics are intimately connected, the democratic deficit does not prevent thinking about justice in the EU either. Viehoff and Nicolaïdis submit that the EU naturally 'provides a fertile testing ground for hybrid theories of justice',[77] differing as it does both from the contemporary states and from the global sphere.

Building on this insight, the chapter then critically engages with three claims: that social solidarity in the EU is impossible since substantive solidarity among EU citizens is lacking; that social justice in the EU is different since goods to be

---

[74] G Davies, 'Social Legitimacy and Purposive Power: The End, the Means, and the Consent of the People' in this volume, 259.

[75] ibid, 272.

[76] See also A Sajó, *Constitutional Sentiments* (New Haven, CT, Yale University Press, 2011).

[77] J Viehoff and K Nicolaïdis, 'Social Justice in the European Union: The Puzzles of Solidarity, Reciprocity and Choice' in this volume, 277, at 279.

distributed on the basis of reciprocity at the national and supranational levels are different; and that as a voluntary association of states—such as the EU—does not need to be concerned with social justice. These are dismissed as simplistic, as the reasons behind endorsing socio-economic justice in the EU, which is so different from the Member States collectively composing it, can be radically different from the state-level reasons, making criticisms inspired by the latter obsolete: Joseph Weiler's 'oranges and apples' argument applied to justice.

As the EU emerges as a de facto and also de jure actor of justice, the question of distributions comes to the fore once we move beyond the political aspects of justice. Alexander Somek's contribution is a forceful reminder of this state of affairs. It is centred on a critique of the offer of human rights protection as a way to solve EU's justice problems, which some of the scholars—most notably Andrew Williams in his *Ethos of Europe*—have suggested. As Williams' 'Reply to Somek' makes clear, however, remedying the justice deficit through rights was merely one claim out of many: a suggestion of what could be possibly done—moving beyond maximalist idealistic and highly unrealistic accounts—once the *Ethos* diagnosed the flaws from which the Union is suffering.

The indictment of the human rights ideology as a possible tool of justice—as sounded by Somek—is based on the realisation that the legal essence of justice and rights is simply different—the first one is about establishing and honouring what is owed to whom, while the second is about the protection of what has already been determined. Justice is *not* about human rights. In particular, this concerns social justice, as those concerned with rights 'remain largely oblivious of how the burdens and benefits of social cooperation ought to be allocated'.[78] This perspective provides an additional criticism of Neyer's and Forst's views: if justice is a right to justification, than we are not speaking about justice at all: as rights constantly collide, justification why a right can be used or not is 'already part and parcel of the right itself',[79] as Somek remarks. If this is the case, the idea of justice through justification is 'nothing else, and not more than, the protection of rights'.[80] Justification thus has nothing to do with justice, should justice be viewed as something different from the protection of rights.

Somek moves his analysis one step further—a distinction is made in his piece between 'equality' and 'inclusion'. The first can only be claimed in a political context where justice considerations play a crucial role. The second is the operation of equality considerations in an apolitical environment. That there is no real equality in the EU—either in practice, or as a legal principle functioning independently of the structural considerations of the Internal Market has been long established: the EU has been accused of being 'only selectively relevant in certain specific areas of [EU] law ... and ... does not have a single coherent role in [Union] law'.[81]

---

[78] Somek, 'The Preoccupation with Rights' in this volume, 295, at 297.
[79] ibid, 303.
[80] ibid.
[81] G de Búrca, 'The Role of Equality in European Community Law' in A Dashwood and S O'Leary (eds), *The Principle of Equal Treatment in EC Law* (London, Sweet and Maxwell, 1997) 15. See also JHH Weiler, 'Europa: "Nous coalisons des Etats nous n'unissons pas des hommes"' in M Cartabia and A Simoncini (eds), *La sostenibilità della democrazia nel XXI secolo* (Bologna, Il Mulino, 2009) 54.

Somek's 'inclusion' applies precisely in those 'certain specific areas' of EU law and does not connect with justice directly, as the Union has never offered any ethical—let alone rational explanations—for some of the key assumptions underlying the principle,[82] which is also insulated from democracy.[83] It is certain that in the context of the citizens' Europe mere moving around cannot be accepted as such a rational explanation: negative bias vis-à-vis those who make a rational decision *not* to cross the invisible borders within the Internal Market cannot provide an ethical foundation for the law.[84]

That apolitical systems cannot produce equality as opposed to inclusion is supported by a reading of the whole body of ECJ case law to date, as well as the practical day-to-day operation of the law, which, while operating under the banner of rights, necessarily ignores key interests which do not enjoy a privileged access to the Internal Market. These interests are as diverse as those of a mother of a sick child,[85] a region,[86] or, indeed, a Member State on the periphery of the Union.[87] The law reinforces pre-established hierarchies making deviations from them impossible.

This aspect of production of injustice in the EU is the main concern of Damjan Kukovec's contribution to this collection, which demonstrates that the whole internal logic of operation of the Union reinforces the status quo of power relationships in the context of the Internal Market: the interests of the centre are always privileged in the EU compared with those of the periphery, and the law—legal scholarship included[88]—reinforces the gap that divides the Europe of the centre from the Europe of the periphery. Usually, EU law does not quite work for the peripheral claims. The trouble with justice then, following Kukovec, is that 'the rhetoric of justice could also entrench existing legal thinking, which reproduces the current hierarchies in the European Union and the world in general today'.[89]

In particular, this happens through the reproduction of the existing hierarchies through the built-in understandings of the weaker party entrenched in the legal system and usually not open to contestation. Among the examples are crucial

---

[82] See, for a critical analysis, D Kochenov, 'Citizenship Without Respect: The EU's Troubled Equality Ideal' (2010) *Jean Monnet Working Papers* (NYU Law School) No 08/10.

[83] In this context, the implications of inclusion for our understanding of the essence of EU's democracy are far reaching: 'That the Union appears to be consistent with inclusion, and not with democratic justice, reveals how deeply it is at odds with democracy': Somek, 'The Preoccupation with Rights' in this volume, 295, at 309.

[84] The first voices emerge in the literature aiming at counterbalancing the logic of EU law activation based on movement with a right distilled based on the Treaties. See, eg, S Iglesias Sánchez, 'A Citizenship Right to Stay? The Right Not to Move in a Union Based on Free Movement' in D Kochenov (ed), *EU Citizenship and Federalism: The Role of Rights* (Cambridge, Cambridge University Press, 2015) (forthcoming).

[85] N Nic Shuibhne, '(Some of) the Kids are All Right' (2012) 49 *Common Market Law Review* 349.

[86] FG Nicola, 'Conceptions of Justice from Below: Distributive Justice As a Means to Address Local Conflicts in European Law and Policy' in this volume, 349; D Kochenov, 'Regional Citizenships in the EU' (2010) 35 *European Law Review* 307.

[87] Kukovec, 'Taking Change Seriously' in this volume, 319.

[88] Rallying for the perceived interests of the trade unions of the centre against the basic interests of the periphery in the vein of Douglas-Scott's analysis of *Viking* and *Laval* in this volume (among many others) is a wonderful illustration of the point Kukovec is making. See also U Belavusau, 'The Case of *Laval* in the Context of the Post-Enlargement EC Law Development' (2008) 9 *German Law Journal* 2279.

[89] Kukovec, 'Taking Change Seriously' in this volume, 319.

aspects of the day-to-day functioning of the EU, including far-reaching presumptions, which are often in practice unjust, as they are blind to the social reality: 'that free movement/autonomy claims are always neoliberal, that the weakest claims will always be the social ones, that justice comes from the realisation of the social claim, that the poor and the marginalised will automatically benefit from them',[90] and many others. It is thus vital to ensure that justice is not used as a pretext to obstruct development through making the contestation of the established compromises impossible. Kukovec's vision of justice is to make 'a quest for change and social transformation' (emphasis omitted).[91]

One of the established hierarchies which is problematic from the perspective presented by Kukovec is critiqued by Judge Sajó in his chapter, where the focus is on the role played by victimhood and vulnerability in the context of distributive justice claims. The history of the development of entitlements related to vulnerability in several jurisdictions is presented to provide a stepping stone for the analysis of the current approaches in the context of the Council of Europe law, which have direct implications for EU law. Sajó, in his contribution, looks specifically at perceived vulnerability as a source of distributive justice claims: the rising 'social respectability' of victimhood. Vulnerability has traditionally been an important vehicle for the generation of the expectations of justice, particularly concerning certain identifiable minority groups persecuted through history. Some recent moves in legislation and the case-law of the highest courts in Europe seem to indicate, however, that the scope of vulnerability as a potential activator of justice claims seems to be growing, as refugees, to take one example, seem now to be regarded as a 'vulnerable group'.[92] *En gros* group vulnerability seems to be becoming 'a source of new legitimacy'[93] and even extends as far as simple socio-economic conditions of the new vulnerable. The question that András Sajó asks in his contribution is, in a nutshell, how far vulnerability arguments can be stretched and where the legitimate border-line lies for the reasonable connection between vulnerability and justice: 'what are the legal implications of victimhood/vulnerability for legislation and for the courts, and in particular, do they trigger obligations of restorative or redistributive "state action"?'[94] The chapter is a call for caution in the deployment of vulnerability and victimhood as a foundation of distributive justice claims: 'humanitarian concerns are distinct from human rights',[95] in the words of Judge Sajó.

Fernanda Nicola focuses in her contribution on 'justice from below', contrasting the national and supranational visions of justice with the local and regional ones, exposing conflicting visions. The conflicts about justice, her chapter claims, are often resolved with no regard to local concerns and understandings, which poses a problem for the successful development of justice in Europe. This problem will not disappear by itself, and is likely to remain acute in the medium to long term.

---

[90] ibid, 327.
[91] ibid, 319.
[92] *MSS v Belgium and Greece* App No 30696/09 [2011] 53 EHRR 2 (ECtHR (GC), 21 January 2011).
[93] Sajó, 'Victimhood and Vulnerability' in this volume, 337, at 338.
[94] ibid, 337.
[95] ibid, 348.

One of Nicola's main insights is that 'EU law destabilises traditional and internal distribution of powers by creating unstable multilevel governance alliances with conflicting political goals and different conceptions of justice'.[96] The natural question that arises is whether such destabilisations should necessarily be presented in a negative light. The EU's function at the national (just as at the local level) can also legitimately be viewed as challenging the established status quo. Already this is potentially valuable from the point of view of justice, as it allows for rethinking of established understandings, which are accepted without any critical engagement.[97] The main problem with such questioning though is that, as Nicola points out, local viewpoints and visions of justice are usually 'collapsed into [those] of their Member States',[98] depriving the local level of a voice. The chapter thus sounds a very legitimate alarm looking at the internationalisation of local and regional justice claims in the EU's context of multilevel governance. Nicola's analysis builds on two theoretical insights: American legal realism, which questions the neutrality of the supranational level[99] and Amartya Sen's reading of justice, revealing the multiplicity of logics behind the legitimate formation of preferences, thus complicating a traditional Rawls' presentation. Deployed in the context of seeking justice at the local level in the EU, the combination of the two produces a strong argument in favour of taking local concerns more seriously.

Although the majority of the scholars contributing to this volume come from the camp of public law, Daniela Caruso makes it abundantly clear in her chapter that private law is also prone to suffer from the deficit this volume aims to appraise. Caruso analyses the Social Justice Manifesto,[100] which made an attempt to push the Commission in the direction of 'a socially conscious law of private exchange'.[101] While the Manifesto was consequential, Caruso argues, a much broader deployment of private law as an instrument of social justice is possible, potentially affecting other fields of law, rather than contracts. In this respect, while more can be expected of private law, Kukovec's analysis is instrumental for the contextualisation of the possible limitations of the Manifesto approach. Caruso's perspective can be regarded as potentially threatening to the establishment of new strict hierarchies, rather than ensuring their easy contestability.[102] What is unquestionable, however, is that in order to take the justice deficit seriously, it is crucial to move beyond the realm of public law alone, as private law, too, has vital potential for justice and injustice generation.

---

[96] Nicola, 'Conceptions of Justice from Below' in this volume, 349, at 350.
[97] Kumm, 'Institutionalising Socratic Contestation', n 62 above; Davies 'The Humiliation of the State', n 24 above.
[98] Nicola, 'Conceptions of Justice from Below' in this volume, 349, at 350.
[99] In the vein of Davies, 'Abstractness and Concreteness in the Preliminary Reference Procedure', n 41 above.
[100] Study Group on Social Justice in European Private Law, 'Social Justice in European Contract Law: A Manifesto' (2004) 10 *European Law Journal* 653, 663–64.
[101] D Caruso, '*Qu'ils mangent des contrats*: Rethinking Justice in EU Contract Law' in this volume, 367.
[102] Kukovec, 'Taking Change Seriously' in this volume, 319.

V

Delving into the legal history of how Europe has dealt with the dark areas of its past, Carole Lyons' contribution offers a general overview of the way European courts have confronted the Holocaust, focusing on the European Court of Human Rights (ECtHR), but also noting the silence of the ECJ. Lyons' contribution in this collection stands as a meticulous reminder of the ultimate injustice. The parallel story of *Costa v ENEL* and Holocaust survivors' cases is very telling: the perspective the chapter adopts may not be familiar to the majority of students of European law, who are used to approaching their subject in an ahistorical fashion, treating it in complete detachment from the mass murder that preceded the case-law they study by less than 20 years. Looking at the treatment of the Holocaust by the ECtHR—a parallel story to the maturation of the Internal Market—Lyons comes up with a periodisation of the Holocaust cases, moving from Amnesia (1950–80) through Negationism (1990s) to Particularity (2010s). The evolution of the case-law demonstrates that the Strasbourg human rights protection *acquis* is now trying to confront the silence of the past, thereby emerging significantly enriched.

Jane Holder continues along the generational justice line by looking at the ecological aspects of justice. In her chapter ecological justice is defended as an emerging category formulated in opposition to the environmental, as the former rejects the 'human-centred foundation' of justice, which the environmentalists take for granted. The chapter analyses the relevant EU law *acquis* in seeking the elements of ecological justice in Natura 2000,[103] adopting the 'non-anthropocentric paradigm of justice'[104] as its starting normative position. Whether one embraces this starting point or not (and here some moral convictions are required, turning this into an issue of moral choice) it demonstrates the richness of the possible visions of justice.

Another illustration of how innumerable the approaches to justice can be is supplied by the appeals to legal geography forming the core of Antonia Layard's analysis. Layard extends the idea of justice deficit to come up with a formulation of the 'spacial deficit' in Europe, arguing—with the use of the freedom of expression—that not enough attention is paid to the special (re)production of justice in Europe. The starting insight of the chapter is that space does not exist in itself, as it is legally produced. The resulting social product does not represent a neutral reality, making justice considerations particularly relevant. In other words, part of the justice deficit is necessarily spacial.[105] The spacial justice approach prompts the use of methodological techniques utilised by law and society scholars, and attuned to exploring multiplicities through scaling, place and space. Using such techniques the chapter explores what we mean when we refer to a European legal space, whether there might be multiple views on what constitutes justice depending on their relation to legal consciousness, and how we can understand the different objects and subjects of EU justice.

---

[103] Council Directive 92/43/EEC of 21 May 1992 on the conservation of natural habitats and of wild fauna and flora ('Habitats Directive') [1992] OJ L206/7.
[104] J Holder, 'An Idea of Ecological Justice in the EU' in this volume, 401, at 411.
[105] A Layard, 'Freedom of Expression and Spatial (Imaginations of) Justice' in this volume, 417.

The last in the collection of chapters is Dimitry Kochenov's contribution, pushing the limits of the notion of justice beyond the legal realm in an attempt to enrich it through a broad interdisciplinary vision. Based on an overview of the most recent literature from psychology, evolutionary biology, social anthropology and a number of other fields, the chapter reminds the readers that justice is infinitely richer and bigger than law, as its socio-biological roots extend beyond human societies. The broader approach to justice is capable of informing an understanding and construction of the law, boasting far-reaching implications also in the context of the Union in Europe, as the chapter demonstrates. The core of the analysis revolves around two concepts. The first one, drawing on Melvin Lerner's scholarship,[106] is the Just World—a sub-conscious implicit belief that the world is fair and that everyone eventually gets what he or she deserves, which is at the core of human psychology. The second one, drawing on Susan Opotow's scholarship,[107] is the scope of justice. In a nutshell, the scope of justice is the field where the Just World functions. All that falls outside the scope of justice is simply ignored, again subconsciously, no matter what: even if the most inequitable and outrageously unfair things happen, the Just World cannot be compromised by anything, which is outside the scope of justice. These insights allow us to approach the concept of justice in law in a new light and can have far-reaching effects on the understanding of the key concepts besides justice, including, inter alia, legitimacy, democracy and equality.

VI

The conclusion of the book by Gráinne de Búrca underlines the importance of giving full consideration to justice in the context of the future development of European law and European studies. Crucially, taking justice seriously does not imply diminished attention to democracy and human rights in the European legal context. Rather, it provides an additional important component, contributing to the improvement of our understanding of European integration and also to designing a better Union for the future. Outlining key issues of importance emerging from the contributions included in this volume, de Búrca is faithful to the main task of this collection: 'to begin to grapple with the complex issues posed by asking questions about the justice of EU policies and the justice of the EU policy'.[108] She is the author of the question mark in the title of this book.

---

[106] See MJ Lerner and S Clayton, *Justice and Self-Interest* (Cambridge, Cambridge University Press, 2011) (and the literature cited therein).
[107] See S Opotow, 'Is Justice Finite?' in L Montada and MJ Lerner (eds), *Social Justice in Human Relations: Current Societal Concerns About Justice*, vol 3 (New York, NY, Plenum, 1996).
[108] G de Búrca, 'Conclusion' in this volume, 459, at 463.

Part One

2

The Ought of Justice

DIMITRY KOCHENOV[*]

DISCUSSING JUSTICE IN Europe can potentially be distorted—if not undermined—by taking an unhelpfully dogmatic view of the sui generis specificity of the European integration project,[1] which some scholars are ready to embrace as a legitimate ground for what one could present as a pretext for a relative *diminution* of justice-related concerns in Europe.[2] It is suggested that a strong normative position in favour of justice as a founding consideration behind EU law is indispensable in this context, to dismiss the 'justice impossible' and 'justice irrelevant' lines of thought outright as unhelpful, misleading, and, ultimately out of touch with reality.

The argument of this brief chapter is thus twofold and very simple. First, dismissing justice as a non-issue in the European context means being guilty of knowingly building a justice-blind (read: unjust) legal system, which cannot possibly be a legitimate aspiration and should thus be avoided at any cost. Secondly, the students of integration seem to be guilty of overlooking or downplaying justice concerns citing merely rhetorical, often sui generis-inspired arguments and displaying statist views of justice ignoring the EU's obvious far-reaching potential as an actor of justice and injustice shaping our lives—a view which is bound to change as the EU legal system matures.

The chapter restates the normative importance of justice and makes an attempt to find its reflection in the mainstream literature on EU law, only to uncover three deficient approaches to justice: presumed justice, rhetorical justice and silence about justice. All three fall short of reflecting the EU's nature as a justice actor. Building on these normative and empirical observations it is possible to add one more element

---

[*] I am overwhelmingly grateful to Andrew Williams and Gráinne de Búrca for their input, as well as to the participants of the London workshop on the justice deficit for inspiration. This text draws in part on the paper prepared by all the editors for the launch of the London workshop on the justice deficit. For an overview of the workshop, see G de Búrca, D Kochenov and A Williams (eds), *Debating Europe's Justice Deficit: The EU, Swabian Housewives, Rawls and Ryanair* (2013) *EUI Working Papers* LAW 2013/11.

[1] Such specificity, although clearly decipherable, should not be overstated. See, for a brilliant dismissal of the sui generis mythology, R Schütze, 'On "Federal" Ground: The European Union as an (Inter)National Phenomenon' (2009) 46 *Common Market Law Review* 1046; R Schütze, *From Dual to Cooperative Federalism: The Changing Structure of European Law* (Oxford, Oxford University Press, 2009).

[2] See, for a strong criticism of this view, A Williams, 'Promoting Justice After Lisbon: Groundwork for a New Philosophy of EU Law' (2010) 30 *Oxford Journal of Legal Studies* 1. See also A Williams, 'The EU, Interim Global Justice and the International Legal Order' in D Kochenov and F Amtenbrink (eds), *The European Union's Shaping of the International Legal Order* (Cambridge, Cambridge University Press, 2013).

to the list of the deficits the EU suffers from, as outlined by Joseph Weiler in a masterful analysis of the EU's DNA, which included democratic deficit and political deficit.[3] The third element is the justice deficit, which this volume will analyse.

I. JUSTICE AS THE FOUNDATIONAL ASSUMPTION

Justice is the essential basis on which any legal–political system builds its structures. Indeed, the main function of such systems could be termed as the articulation and backing of justice claims. This is particularly true of the constitutional systems,[4] as opposed to purely administrative/managerial constellations of rules[5]—even though these, too, normally implicitly incorporate a certain ideology of justice as an essential element next to other considerations, be it internal coherence, expediency, efficiency or profit. Constitutional law is legitimately expected to wrap itself in the garbs of a justice ideal and to liaise with democracy for this ideal's fine-tuning and re-articulation to ensure the legal system's continuous success and legitimacy.

Crucially, justice is necessary not only for the law to be effective. Rather, it is indispensable for the law to be worthy of the glorifying term. In this sense, justice considerations are quite different from those of democracy and legitimacy and should thus not be confused with either of the two, which require serious treatment on their own.

Approaching the EU in this light, it is necessary to realise that presenting legitimacy as the main issue of relevance, if not the main junction of justice, undermines a more fundamental question—what *should* be done?[6]—a question which is not necessarily about social acceptability and which might imply hard choices, if not the taming of majoritarian interests and concerns. Likewise—and for the same reason—justice cannot be collapsed into democracy or legitimately presented as a replacement thereof.[7] Crucially, however, while distinct from democracy and legitimacy, justice is seemingly at least as important in the context of each legal system's development and day-to-day operation.

Approached from the vantage point of justice, the EU and its law produces a most curious impression, as while it is now undisputed that it is a dynamic constitutional

---

[3] JHH Weiler, 'Deciphering the Political and Legal DNA of European Integration: An Exploratory Essay' in J Dickson and P Eleftheriadis (eds), *Philosophical Foundations of European Union Law* (Oxford, Oxford University Press, 2013).

[4] For an overview, see, M Tushnet, *Advanced Introduction to Comparative Constitutional Law* (Cheltenham, Edward Elgar, 2014). For a classical presentation of the EU as a constitutional system see JHH Weiler, *The Constitution of Europe: 'Do the New Clothes Have an Emperor?' and Other Essays on European Integration* (Cambridge, Cambridge University Press, 1999). See also G de Búrca and JHH Weiler (eds), *The Worlds of European Constitutionalism* (Cambridge, Cambridge University Press, 2012).

[5] On 'global administrative law' see B Kingsbury, N Krisch and RB Stewart, 'The Emergence of Global Administrative Law' (2005) 68 *Law and Contemporary Problems* 15; in the EU context, see P Lindseth, *Power and Legitimacy: Reconciling Europe and the Nation-State* (Oxford, Oxford University Press, 2010). For a compelling presentation of EU administrative law, see P Craig, *EU Administrative Law* (Oxford, Oxford University Press, 2012).

[6] A Williams, 'The Problem(s) of Justice in the European Union' in this volume, 33, at 36.

[7] See, for an analysis, D Nicol, 'Can Justice Dethrone Democracy in the European Union? A Reply to Jürgen Neyer' (2012) 50 *Journal of Common Market Studies* 508.

system[8] of an ever-growing complexity and importance, both at the level of the individuals[9] and, crucially, at the level of the *Herren der Verträge*[10]—as the Member States are ever dependent on Brussels' ability to regulate a fast-growing array of issues—'justice' is definitely not the term illuminating EU law and legal theory. Even worse, when invoked—for instance in the context of the Area of Freedom Security and Justice (AFSJ)—its meaning is reduced to an unfamiliar narrow reading of judicial efficiency and definitely fails to capture justice's deep potential.[11] In this sense all the EU's documents about justice appear either to have nothing to do with or to severely understate the potential and the core meaning of this notion,[12] turning justice into a mere rhetorical device to help uphold any institutional choice.[13] The case-law of the European Court of Justice (ECJ) is not an exception in this regard.[14]

Although most likely a value on which the Union is founded,[15] it is questionable whether the Treaty reference to the operation of EU values 'in a society in

---

[8] For a most reliable textbook, see R Schütze, *European Constitutional Law* (Cambridge, Cambridge University Press, 2012). In fact, the literature even moved beyond that, emphasising the republican nature of the Union: A von Bogdandy, 'The Prospect of a European Republic: What European Citizens are Voting on' (2005) 42 *Common Market Law Review* 913.

[9] The essential idea of serving the citizen goes directly back to the foundational case-law of the 1960s: eg Case 26/62 *NV Algemene Transport- en Expeditie Onderneming van Gend en Loos v Nederlandse Administratie der Belastingen* [1963] ECR (English Special Edition) 1. A Vauchez, 'The Transnational Politics of Judicialization. Van Gend en Loos and the Making of EU Polity' (2010) 16 *European Law Journal* 1; D Kochenov, 'The Citizenship Paradigm' (2013) 15 *Cambridge Yearbook of European Legal Studies* 196.

[10] On the nature of the complex structure of EU law see, eg, G Letsas, 'Harmonic Law' in J Dickson and P Eleftheriadis (eds), *Philosophical Foundations of European Union Law* (Oxford, Oxford University Press, 2012); Schütze, *From Dual to Cooperative Federalism*, n 1 above; Schütze, 'On "Federal" Ground', n 1 above; K Lenaerts and K Gutman, '"Federal Common Law" in the European Union: A Comparative Perspective From the United States' (2006) 54 *American Journal of Comparative Law* 1; J-C Piris, 'L'Union européenne: vers une nouvelle forme de fédéralisme?' (2004) 41 *Revue trimestrielle de droit européenne* 23; D Sidjanski, 'Actualité et dynamique du fédéralisme européen' (1990) 341 *Revue du marché commun* 655.

[11] See, eg, S Douglas-Scott, 'Justice, Injustice, and the Rule of Law in the EU', in this volume, 51, at 52, where she argues that 'within the EU's AFSJ, freedom and justice have been sacrificed to the needs of security'. For the general presentation of the AFSJ, see, eg, CC Murphy and D Acosta Arcarazo (eds), *EU Security and Justice Law after Lisbon and Stockholm* (Oxford: Hart Publishing, 2014). You will find nothing on justice in the sense adopted in this volume either in Murphy and Acosta Arcarazo, or in any other leading work on the AFSJ.

[12] This can be illustrated by the discussion documents prepared by the Commission for the *Assises de la Justice* conference in Brussels, in autumn 2013, which was the flagship event sponsored by Directorate-General Justice aimed at 'Shaping Justice Policies in Europe for the Years to Come', www.ec.europa.eu/justice/events/assises-justice-2013/index_en.htm. In the debate, as framed by the Commission, justice only received an extremely narrow procedural meaning within the context of particular activities aimed at judicial cooperation and the combating of crime. The same could be said about the scholarly works too numerous to be cited, turning justice in the context of the EU into a curious sub-category of efficiency.

[13] See, for an analysis, S Roy, 'Justice As Europe's Signifier: Towards a More Inclusive Hermeneutics of the European Legal Order' in this volume, 79.

[14] See, eg, the analysis by Suryapratim Roy (ibid) and Dorota Leczykiewicz ('"Constitutional Justice" and Judicial Review of EU Legislative Acts' in this volume, 97).

[15] Art 2 of the Consolidated version of the Treaty on European Union [2012] OJ C326/13 (TEU). The provision does not list justice among the values of the Union *sensu stricto*, deploying it as an attribute of the societies of the Member States. This gave rise to scholarly claims that justice is, in the words of Sionaigh Douglas-Scott, 'not presented as one of the EU's founding values'—a position, which is probably too categorical not to be questioned, especially given that Art 2 TEU eventually uses the word 'justice', which is seemingly deployed as an assumption underlying all the values listed in that provision. See S Douglas-Scott, 'The Problem of Justice in the European Union' in J Dickson and P Eleftheriadis (eds), *Philosophical Foundations of European Union Law* (Oxford, Oxford University Press, 2013) 414.

which ... justice ... prevail[s]'[16] is a sufficient indication that justice became one of the *goals* of European integration in the sense of the Treaties,[17] to convey the sense that European integration should be instrumental in the achievement of justice. To agree with Sionaidh Douglas-Scott, read together, Articles 2 and 3 of the Treaty on European Union (TEU) 'present themselves as a rather incoherent jumble':[18] the clear picture of the role to be played by justice fails to emerge from the text. This poses a serious problem in the context of the goal-oriented methodology of interpretation of the provisions of EU law.[19] Although the *telos* of integration seems to be inspired by and require the formation of a particular type of constitutionalism,[20] corresponding to the culture of justification, rather than authority,[21] the actual implantation of such constitutionalism in all the Member States is a claim open to contestation.[22] Moreover, equating proportionality and giving reasons with a substantive ideal of justice to underpin and inform all the integration exercise is obviously problematic.[23]

Mere values—although they are binding on the EU, which has to promote them,[24] as well as being, to some extent at least, even enforceable as law[25]—cannot boast an ability to provide strict guidance in the context of the development of the EU externally[26]

---

[16] Art 2 TEU.

[17] Equally see Art 3(3)(2) TEU, mentioning 'social justice'—this is as well as the 'area of freedom, security and justice' of Art 3(1) TEU, which the Union 'shall offer its citizens'.

[18] Douglas-Scott, 'The Problem of Justice', n 15 above, 413.

[19] Eg A von Bogdandy and J Bast, 'The European Union's Vertical Order of Competences: The Current Law and Proposals for Reform' (2002) 39 *Common Market Law Review* 227.

[20] V Perju, 'Proportionality and Freedom—An Essay on Method in Constitutional Law' (2012) 1 *Global Constitutionalism* 334.

[21] M Cohen-Eliya and I Porat, *Proportionality and Constitutional Culture* (Cambridge, Cambridge University Press, 2013).

[22] J-W Müller, 'Eastern Europe Goes South: Disappearing Democracy in the EU's Newest Members' (2014) 93(2) *Foreign Affairs* 14; B Bugarič, 'Protecting Democracy and the Rule of Law in the European Union: The Hungarian Challenge' (2014) *LEQS Papers* No 79/2014; D Kochenov, V Poleshchuk and A Dimitrovs, 'Do Professional Linguistic Requirements Discriminate?—A Legal Analysis: Estonia and Latvia in the Spotlight' (2013) 10 *European Yearbook of Minority Issues* 137; M Bánkuti, G Halmai and KL Scheppele, 'Hungary's Illiberal Turn: Disabling the Constitution' (2012) 23 *The Journal of Democracy* 138.

[23] S Tsakyrakis, 'Proportionality: An Assault on Human Rights?' (2009) 7 *International Journal of Constitutional Law* 468; S Tsakyrakis, 'Disproportionate Individualism' in this volume, 235; A Somek, 'The Preoccupation with Rights and the Embrace of Inclusion: A Critique' in this volume, 295.

[24] Art 3(1) TEU is unequivocal about this aim of the Union: 'The Union's aim is to promote peace, its values and the well-being of its peoples'.

[25] Art 7 TEU is nothing but a clear mechanism to enforce Art 2 TEU. It is quite obvious that the inclusion of Art 2 TEU in the Treaties does not exclude the possibility of deploying other enforcement mechanisms available in the Treaties, including Arts 258, 259 and 260 of the Consolidated version of the Treaty on the Functioning of the European Union [2012] OJ C326/47 (TFEU) and others: C Closa, D Kochenov and JHH Weiler, 'Reinforcing Rule of Law Oversight in the European Union'(2014) *EUI Working Papers* RSCAS No 2014/25. On Art 7 TEU, see W Sadurski, 'Adding Bite to a Bark: The Story of Article 7, EU Enlargement, and Jörg Haider' (2010) 16 *Columbia Journal of European Law* 385.

[26] M Cremona, 'Values in EU Foreign Policy' in M Evans and P Koutrakos (eds), *Beyond the Established Legal Orders: Policy Interconnections Between the EU and the Rest of the World* (Oxford, Hart Publishing, 2011); P Leino and R Petrov, 'Between "Common Values" and Competing Universals' (2009) 15 *European Law Journal* 654; D Kochenov, 'The Issue of Values' in R Petrov and P Van Elsuwege (eds), *The Application of EU Law in the Eastern Neighbourhood of the European Union* (London, Routledge, 2014).

and also internally,[27] which would ensure their definitive ability to inform the law. While there are numerous good reasons for this—from the potential vagueness and the contested nature of values, to the natural disagreements about their content and the degree to which they are to be reached among the Member States[28]—the lacunae in the law resulting from the current state of affairs are as numerous as they are clear. Formal incorporation in Article 2 TEU notwithstanding, justice thus never left the field of amorphous desiderata of EU values (on an optimistic reading of Article 2) remaining merely confined to most questionable effects in law.

In this context it becomes apparent that the place to be played by justice in the European legal context remains highly underspecified at a number of levels—from scholarship and institutional practice, to the treaty text. The EU's approach to justice is evidently deficient, to the detriment of the Union's appeal, effectiveness and overall success, one can suggest.[29] It is crucial that justice concerns be introduced into the fabric of the European legal system: something that has not been done—as noted in the introduction to this volume—on at least two crucial levels: normative (as an indispensable starting point of our thinking about the European legal context—the EU and the Council of Europe included), and theoretical (as the way in which scholars have been approaching the issues of justice in Europe until now).

II. THE NORMATIVE STARTING POINT: THE EU IS A SUITABLE AGENT OF JUSTICE

The scope of justice potentially applicable to the EU should be considered broadly rather than narrowly.[30] Some commentators have disagreed that the EU can be

---

[27] J-W Müller, 'The EU As a Militant Democracy or: Are there Limits to Constitutional Mutations Within the Member States' (2014) 165 *Revista de Estudios Políticos*; A von Bogdandy and M Ioannidis, 'Systemic Deficiency in the Rule of Law: What it is, What has been Done, What can be Done' (2014) 51 *Common Market Law Review* 59; D Kochenov, 'Europe's Crisis of Values' (2014) 48 *Revista catalana de dret públic* 106; J-W Müller, 'Safeguarding Democracy Inside the EU. Brussels and the Future of the Liberal Order' (2013) *Transatlantic Academy Paper Series 2012–2013* No 3; M Dawson and E Muir, 'Enforcing Fundamental Values: EU Law and Governance in Hungary and Romania' (2012) 19 *Maastricht Journal of European and Comparative Law* 469.

[28] For some valid reasons see, eg, Douglas-Scott, 'The Problem of Justice', n 15 above.

[29] See, for a profound analysis, A Williams, 'Taking Values Seriously: Towards a Philosophy of EU Law' (2009) 29 *Oxford Journal of Legal Studies* 549. The current problematic situation does not prevent the Union form promoting its values—whether connected with justice or not—in the third countries: Petrov and Van Elsuwege, *The Application of EU Law*, n 26 above. The success of this exercise, in essence, is highly questionable, examples of its problematic nature ranging from ensuring the basic adherence to values internally, to such adherence at EU's borders, like in Srebrenica, where, in the words of Joseph Weiler, 'all these immobile soldiers were, like all of us, firm believers in human rights, solidarity, and all the other values we profess ... but evidently, they lacked the virtues necessary to enact them' (Weiler, 'Deciphering the Political and Legal DNA of European Integration', n 3 above, 143). See also *Stichting Mothers of Srebrenica v The Netherlands and the United Nations* ECLI:NL:RBDHA:2014:8748 (District Court, The Hague, 16 July 2014); A Williams, *The Ethos of Europe* (Cambridge, Cambridge University Press, 2010) ch 2. As to ensuring that the values are complied with by the Member States joining the Union, this is at least as problematic, as the values are, strictly speaking, not a part of the *acquis*, so the standard of values to check and promote in the course of the pre-accession process simply does not exist: eg, D Kochenov, 'Overestimating Conditionality' in I Govaere et al (eds), *The European Union and the World: Essays in Honour of Marc Maresceau* (Leiden, Martinus Nijhoff, 2014).

[30] See also A Williams 'The Problem(s) of Justice in the European Union' in this volume, 33.

plausibly identified as a site for (distributive) justice on the basis that it is not a state. However, the starting assumption is that associating justice only with the state is not tenable as a convincing moral or practical argument. Not only do justice considerations possess relevance for the individual, the family and sub-state structures, as well as profoundly affected societies before states entered the stage of history. The sensitivity to justice is also one of the fundamental socio-biological features of all human beings,[31] constituting an essential part of our moral landscape.[32]

In this context it becomes clear that cooperation between states, whether regionally or otherwise, which has constructed institutions to manage transnational ventures should not constrain the standards of justice which should be applied.[33] Rather, standards applied to particular institutions should reflect the nature of the goals of cooperation and the impact their decisions have on the lives of their constituents or those outside their borders.

The EU and its institutions have undeniably assumed considerable power and influence within and beyond the Member States, affecting the interests of individuals, corporations and states. It possesses significant capabilities to generate (as well as to address) injustices internally and externally. It is thus untenable to proceed on the assumption that justice is not what one should legitimately expect of the European Union. The starting normative assumption that justice is of relevance for the EU is thus fully justified and has to be adopted, as it would be untenable not to reaffirm the *ought* of justice. To agree with Damjan Kukovec, 'lawyers fundamentally construct social reality, and the burden to reconstruct it importantly lies in their hands'.[34] The EU is undoubtedly bound to be approached as a justice actor.

III. THE EMPIRICAL STARTING POINT: INADEQUATE TREATMENT OF JUSTICE IN THE EU

The whole body of doctrinal thinking about the Union in Europe supports the second consideration mentioned above: justice as a founding value of the Union underlying the text of the treaties and superseding the *acquis* as such has been constantly neglected by the institutions, including the Court of Justice, and by scholars alike.[35] This regrettable reality ensures that the rare instances of a search for justice in the EU context stand in a particularly stark contrast with the discipline's mainstream.[36]

---

[31] For an overview, see, MJ Lerner and S Clayton, *Justice and Self-Interest* (Cambridge, Cambridge University Press, 2011). For an analysis, see D Kochenov, 'The Just World' in this volume, 435.

[32] W Sadurski, 'Social Justice and Legal Justice' (1984) 3 *Law and Philosophy* 329.

[33] A Williams, 'The EU, Interim Global Justice', n 2 above. As nicely put by Daniel Augenstein in his contribution 'We the People: EU Justice As Politics' in this volume, 153, at 157: 'it is simply too late to tame the European beast with a new functional discipline, or to seek political refuge in the international order of states'.

[34] D Kukovec, 'Taking Change Seriously: The Rhetoric of Justice and the Reproduction of the Status Quo' in this volume, 319, at 336. See, for a global restatement of this point, P Allott, *Eunomia* (Oxford, Oxford University Press, 1990); P Allott, *The Health of Nations: Society and Law Beyond the State* (Cambridge, Cambridge University Press, 2002).

[35] For a masterful and convincing diagnosis see Williams, *The Ethos of Europe*, n 29 above.

[36] See, most importantly, ibid; Douglas-Scott, 'The Problem of Justice', n 15 above; M Poiares Maduro, 'A New Governance for the European Union and the Euro: Democracy and Justice' (2012) *EUI Working Papers* RSCAS No 2012/11.

The extent of the problem is so vast that no detailed perusal of the literature is required: the deviations from the main trend of not awarding justice any importance whatsoever are so rare that one can legitimately conclude that justice considerations barely play any role at all in the literature.

While a number of trends in the literature may be outlined, three key approaches to classifying these trends may be tentatively sketched, none of which give justice in the EU legal context the serious treatment it deserves. In the context of numerous explanations as to why justice is not the altar of the European cathedral and how EU law, instead of being rooted in the idea of justice to underpin its development and to justify its existence,[37] is downgraded—substantively and procedurally—to constant restatements of the treaty text,[38] one thing is clear: 'the market now stands alone, without a mantle of ideals', as aptly put by JHH Weiler.[39] The grand promise of European integration ended up being hijacked, if not consumed by the Internal Market which was designed to serve as the main tool to bring about this promise's fulfilment.[40] In this sense Sionaidh Douglas-Scott's question 'what possible meaning can be given to "social justice" as an aspiration in Article 3 TEU, for an EU which has for so long focused on a market-driven ideology?'[41] seems particularly acute.

The idea of justice is not the centerpiece of the European project. The key approaches to justice focus on the assumption that the EU is and has been just from its very inception, never mind its day-to-day operation, failures and successes; that justice is an instrumental tool to deal with democracy and legitimacy problems; and that justice considerations do not deserve too much attention, requiring scholars to focus on more down-to-earth issues. The three approaches thus come down to presumed justice, rhetorical justice and silence about justice. However different their treatment of justice is, all three approaches described below are unanimous in dismissing justice as an important factor to be taken into account seriously at the current stage of integration. It is either outright irrelevant, instrumental in interpreting away Europe's ills, or a nod in the direction of the noble presumptions concerning Europe's past. Consequently, the place to be occupied by the idea of justice in the context of the European integration exercise remains, to this day, largely vacant.

IV. THE FIRST APPROACH: PRESUMED JUSTICE

The first approach (and the most atypical of the three) views justice as a fundamental underlying value informing the Union and its law from its very inception: the overarching response to the disillusionment and loss of the Second World War and preceding totalitarianisms plaguing the majority of European states[42] and a

---

[37] G Morgan, 'European Political Integration and the Need for Justification' (2007) 14 *Constellations* 332.
[38] Williams, 'Taking Values Seriously', n 29 above.
[39] JHH Weiler, 'Bread and Circus: The State of the European Union' (1998) 4 *Columbia Journal of European Law* 223, 231.
[40] D Kochenov, 'The Citizenship Paradigm' (2013) 15 *Cambridge Yearbook of European Law and Policy* 196.
[41] Douglas-Scott, 'The Problem of Justice', n 15 above, 416.
[42] See Tony Judt's *Postwar* (London, Penguin, 2006) for a global story of Europe's (re)building.

definitive desire for a fundamental change embodied in the radical impulse behind the framing of supranational integration in Europe.[43] On this reading, Europe's very raison d'être reflects this approach, aspiring to demonstrate in deed that a radical rethinking of international relations—even if within the framework of only one continent[44]—is possible.[45] This would imply limitations on democracy[46] and the freedom of markets alike,[47] forcing stronger ties of necessity between European states, bound by a messianic programme.[48] Although this is probably the most plausible story behind the very idea of the revolutionary Pescatorean *droit de l'intégration*,[49] it is difficult to argue that the Union managed to preserve an intimate connection with the founders' promise of justice. As Andrew Williams has compellingly argued, at the current stage of integration justice is definitely not a part of Europe's ethos.[50] Once the EU is approached from this vantage point, Danny Nicol's vision of it may be correct: the time indeed appears to be ripe to dismiss the 'quasi-religious belief' with which 'generations of EC/EU scholars grew up' that 'the Treaty of Rome basically met the demands of justice'.[51] This naïveté about the innate justness and perpetual glorification of the elusive golden age in the past is most unhelpful in the current circumstances:[52] a critical appraisal is required. Such an appraisal is long overdue.

V. THE SECOND APPROACH: RHETORICAL JUSTICE

The second approach to justice in the European legal context views this ideal, when bundled with justification, as a natural way to bring about strengthened legitimacy for the supranational legal structures. In essence, it thus aims at concluding the democratic deficit debate[53] with appeals to justice, according to the latter a largely

---

[43] Weiler, 'Deciphering the Political and Legal DNA of European Integration', n 3 above, 146–49.
[44] This, notwithstanding the fact that the presumption of continued colonisation of Africa was at the essence of the European integration project: D Custos, 'Implications of the European Integration for the Overseas' in D Kochenov (ed), *EU Law of the Overseas* (The Hague, Kluwer Law International, 2011).
[45] G de Búrca, 'Europe's *raison d'être*' in D Kochenov and F Amtenbrink (eds), *The European Union's Shaping of the International Legal Order* (Cambridge, Cambridge University Press, 2013); P Allott, 'The European Community Is Not the True European Community' (1991) 100 *Yale Law Journal* 2485.
[46] J-W Müller, *Contesting Democracy: Political Ideas in Twentieth Century Europe* (New Haven, CT, Yale University Press, 2011).
[47] See MA Wilkinson, 'Politicising Europe's Justice Deficit: Some Preliminaries' in this volume, 111.
[48] Weiler, 'Deciphering the Political and Legal DNA of European Integration', n 3 above, 146–49.
[49] P Pescatore, *Le droit de l'intégration* (Leyde, Sijthoff, 1972).
[50] Williams, *The Ethos of Europe*, n 29 above.
[51] D Nicol, 'Swabian Housewives, Suffering Southerners' in this volume, 165.
[52] In the context of dealing with the financial crisis the EU is turning into a powerful actor of injustice in the eyes of many. See, eg, the analysis in the chapters by AJ Menéndez, 'Whose Justice? Which Europe?' in this volume, 137; Nicol, 'Swabian Housewives, Suffering Southerners' in this volume, 165; and Wilkinson, 'Politicising Europe's Justice Deficit' in this volume, 111.
[53] A Føllesdal and S Hix, 'Why There is a Democratic Deficit in the EU: A Response to Majone and Moravcsik' (2006) 44 *Journal of Common Market Studies* 533; A Moravcsik, 'In Defence of the Democratic Deficit: Reassessing Legitimacy in the European Union' (2002) 40 *Journal of Common Market Studies* 603.

procedural, albeit a very important role.[54] Awarding justice such a role is potentially dangerous, as it narrows down the meaning of justice to a very limited understanding, which cannot be fine-tuned through democratic procedures, deploying the notion as a vehicle of all-out depoliticisation of the European integration exercise. This seems to be yet another take on a potentially questionable strategy of appealing to justice going back to Plato's antiquity, no more, no less.[55] Justice is thus offered as a potentially powerful tool to depoliticise the debate about the EU's current troubles, interpreting away the democratic deficit popular among scholars.[56] Assuming that justice is (much) more than a rhetorical tool to get rid of some occasional perceived discomforts of democracy (however imperfect), this approach could emerge as boasting only a minimal added value, helping little both in the understanding of justice *and*, crucially, in building a better Union in Europe.

VI. THE THIRD APPROACH: SILENCE ABOUT JUSTICE

The third approach to justice in the EU (which also enjoys the most popularity) is infinitely less ambitious in essence, than the two mentioned above, as it sees—mistakenly, as this collection aims to demonstrate—no problem with the current state of affairs, rehearsing twists and turns of ECJ case-law uniquely and exclusively with the context of market integration in mind—the time has come to spell it out explicitly—with no fundamental idea underlying the essence of the integration exercise that would go beyond the Internal Market[57] and the presumed economic prosperity that it is supposed to bring, however ironical such a take seems in the context of dealing with the economic crisis in the EU's South.[58]

Regrettably, this approach is observable in the great majority of EU legal writing and also case-law, driving—blindly—past the issues of justice and injustice. As

---

[54] J Neyer, *The Justification of Europe. A Political Theory of Supranational Integration* (Oxford, Oxford University Press, 2012); J Neyer, 'Justice, Not Democracy: Legitimacy in the European Union' (2010) 48 *Journal of Common Market Studies* 903. Such a vision of the role (to be) played by justice in the European legal context has sparked controversy and sound criticism: D Nicol, 'Can Justice Dethrone Democracy in the European Union' (2012) 50 *Journal of Common Market Studies* 508; See also the chapters by Nicol, 'Swabian Housewives, Suffering Southerners' in this volume, 165; R Forst, 'Justice, Democracy and the Right for Justification: Reflections on Jürgen Neyer's Normative Theory of the European Union' in this volume, 227; and Somek, 'The Preoccupation with Rights' in this volume, 295.

[55] Menéndez, 'Whose Justice? Which Europe?' in this volume, 137, at 138ff and Forst, 'Justice, Democracy and the Right for Justification' in this volume, 227.

[56] For an account of the desirable future for the EU which is diametrically opposed to Neyer's see, eg, Miguel Poiares Maduro's proposal on the politicisation of the Union: Poiares Maduro, 'A New Governance', n 36 above.

[57] For important attempts to do away with such a narrow view of the EU's legal essence see, eg, J Dickson and P Eleftheriadis (eds), *Philosophical Foundations of European Union Law* (Oxford, Oxford University Press, 2012); Williams, *The Ethos of Europe*, n 29 above; JHH Weiler, 'On the Distinction Between Values and Virtues in the Process of European Integration' (2010) Institute for International Law and Justice, International Legal Theory Colloquium Spring 2010 (unpublished).

[58] AJ Menéndez, 'Editorial: A European Union in Constitutional Mutation?' (2014) 20 *European Law Journal* 127; AJ Menéndez, 'The Existential Crisis of the European Union' (2013) 14 *German Law Journal* 453; Nicol, 'Swabian Housewives, Suffering Southerners' in this volume, 165.

might be expected, such blindness fails to summon the appeal of justice in response to the questions posed by the burning issues of EU's future. It ignores the Union's values,[59] undermines coherence of the vertical division of powers in the EU,[60] and is blind to the non-economically active and to the non-cross-border individual (all the relevant terms being very loosely defined).[61] It is prone to generate citizenship without respect,[62] while turning men and women into silent recipients of the Internal Market's at times punishing wisdom,[63] taking no considerations of justice into account.[64] Silence about justice would be sustainable, one can argue, in the Garden of Eden, where joy reigns and no injustice is done. It is flawed, however, to be silent about justice while the EU is emerging—in theory, but in reality too—as a potentially powerful actor of injustice.

As all three approaches demonstrate, the gradual legal and political evolution of the Union in Europe has not, thus far, been accompanied by the articulation or embracing of any substantive ideal of justice going beyond the founders' intent or the economic objectives of the market integration project.[65] This is how the possible justice deficit—bound up, necessarily, with an indictment of the mainstream EU legal scholarship that has consistently failed to ask the justice question—comes to light:[66] in the context of the European Union the crucial bond between law and justice remains, to this day, largely unaddressed.

VII. A REMINDER

All three approaches are thus inadequate in essence: all fail to flesh out the justice-inspired logic which is bound to underpin the essence of the EU and its functioning.

---

[59] Since the values enumerated in Art 2 TEU are not directly related to the Internal Market *acquis*, the EU does not even have the tools to ensure they are complied with. For an overview, see, eg, Closa, Kochenov and Weiler, 'Reinforcing Rule of Law Oversight', n 25 above.

[60] For a global assessment, see D Kochenov (ed), *EU Citizenship and Federalism: The Role of Rights* (Cambridge, Cambridge University Press, 2015) (forthcoming).

[61] N Nic Shuibhne, '(Some of) the Kids are Alright: Comment on *McCarthy* and *Dereci*' (2012) 49 *Common Market Law Review* 349; A Tryfonidou, *Reverse Discrimination in EC Law* (The Hague, Kluwer Law International, 2009); M Poiares Maduro, 'The Scope of European Remedies: The Case of Purely Internal Situations and Reverse Discrimination' in C Kilpatrick, T Novitz and P Skidmore (eds), *The Future of Remedies in Europe* (Oxford, Hart Publishing, 2000).

[62] D Kochenov, 'Citizenship Without Respect' (2010) *Jean Monnet Working Papers* (NYU Law School) No 08/10.

[63] Weiler, 'Bread and Circus', n 39 above; JHH Weiler, 'Europa: "Nous coalisons des Etats nous n'unissons pas des homes"' in M Cartabia and A Simoncini (eds), *La sostenibilità della democrazia nel XXI secolo* (Bologna, Il Mulino, 2009); N Nic Shuibhne, 'The Resilience of EU Market Citizenship' (2010) 47 *Common Market Law Review* 1597, 1608; Somek, 'The Preoccupation with Rights' in this volume, 295.

[64] Unless 'justice' relates to tidying-up the application of the Internal Market rules, however absurd the consequences. The case of *Schempp* is most frequently cited as an illustration: it is not absurd, the ECJ tells us, that whether the principle of non-discrimination is applicable essentially depends on the nationality of one's former wife: Case C-403/03 *Egon Schempp v Finanzamt München V* [2005] ECR I-6421. For an inspiring analysis, see E Spaventa 'Seeing the Wood Despite the Trees? On the Scope of Union Citizenship and its Constitutional Effects' (2008) 45 *Common Market Law Review* 13, 36–39.

[65] Williams, 'Taking Values Seriously', n 29 above.

[66] See also Somek's 'The Preoccupation with Rights' in this volume, 295, arguing that EU law scholarship has been the servant of the project, failing to address the fundamentals.

A change in the scholarly vision of the EU as well as in its self-positioning vis-à-vis the issues of justice and injustice is thus indispensable for the integration project's success, which is the main line of thinking behind this edited volume. This change requires the embracing of a normative position: the EU should emerge as an actor of justice not only silently, de facto, but also de jure and at the theoretical plane.

Any audit of justice must be based on an understanding of the range of justice that might be assessed. Building on this central proposition—and inspired by Andrew Williams' thinking—two questions follow: an empirical and an ethical one. These are the following: What forms of justice (and injustice) *are* encountered in the EU? What forms *should* be pursued? The book, as it proceeds, touches upon both. These questions only make sense, however, once the *ought* of justice in the EU legal context is asserted normatively: a reminder, which is the modest aim of this brief contribution.

3

The Problem(s) of Justice in the European Union

ANDREW WILLIAMS

I. INTRODUCTION

OF COURSE, JUSTICE should always be a conundrum for any institution, a 'first virtue' and perhaps a first problem too. It is a problem that can never be wholly resolved either. There will always be a need for re-evaluations of its meaning, scope and application. This might suggest charting the 'problems' of justice in the EU is futile. If the territory is so unstable, so fluid, what value might there be in undertaking such a review? Wouldn't it be out of date as soon as it was crafted? Wouldn't any calculated 'deficit' be nothing more than a passing political opinion?

My intention in this chapter is not to affix justice conclusively to a particular set of problems or to resolve those problems. Neither is it to be constrained by the EU's own apparent sense of what 'justice' means. Too frequently the Union's institutions produce literature which seems only to recognise justice in highly limited terms.[1] Even the recently launched European e-justice portal, 'conceived as a future electronic one-stop-shop in the area of justice', is concerned with only very limited justice themes.[2] Rather, this contribution provides a sense of those problems of justice which I believe the EU must take much more seriously, to the point where they become the focus of its future direction and constitution. Their current under-development or even absence is where I see the greatest and systemic deficit of justice in the EU. They are not counterweighted by adherence to the itemised values now constitutionally enshrined: democracy, the rule of law, freedom, equality, respect for human rights. In particular, heavy reliance on respect for human rights to resolve substantive justice issues (fundamentally concerned with the fair distribution of benefits and burdens) is an erroneous approach. Although I have argued elsewhere that looking to human rights might be a *means* towards deeper

---

[1] See, eg, European Commission, 'Proposal for a Regulation of the European Parliament and of the Council establishing for the period 2014 to 2020 the Justice Programme' COM (2011) 759 which refers to justice simply as 'promoting judicial cooperation in civil and criminal matters'.
[2] See www.e-justice.europa.eu/home.do?action=home&plang =en.

substantive justice, I do not hold they are the solution.[3] They certainly do not fulfil that role at present.

Although these problems of substantive justice are neither ahistorical nor unique to the Union, they are affected by the novel environment created by the intersection of varying European supranational 'institutions', social, political, economic, legal, bureaucratic. For some, this makes for a complicated setting where justice ceases to have much of a role at all. I do not hold with that view. For me, we may be faced with acute complexity here but that should encourage us to recognise justice in unfamiliar places and forms, not to dismiss it as irrelevant.

I should say in passing that in the process of charting what I take to be the most salient problems of justice, I do not intend to promote any *theory* of justice for the EU (although my very choice of justice issues might be interpreted in this way). Instead, I will talk about the parameters of justice which I argue *should* apply to the Union. It is only when we consider the potential scope of applicable justice that we can begin to think whether justice is being or should be or can be fulfilled here.

To explore the problems of justice in the EU, I have split the chapter into two parts. First, I argue generally that a more sophisticated understanding and language of justice *should* have a role in the Union. This serves not only to illustrate the fallacy in avoiding the subject (as the EU has largely done in all but name) but also to gain a better sense of justice in the Union's likely future. Much depends on whether ideas of *substantive* as opposed to superficial justice are capable of application in the EU as things stand. By superficial I mean those obligations which merely require some basic commitment not to breach certain minimal standards of behaviour associated with any particular obligation or responsibility. And by substantive I mean, as I have said, issues focused on the fairness of distribution of benefits and burdens within a community.

There are, of course, some who will disagree that this is even possible, that the EU cannot equate to a society at any meaningful level, without necessarily disagreeing that the EU should be subject to some lesser standards of superficial justice. But often, those limited standards will only be negative in character; the EU being assessed for its impact on the lives of people and condemned or praised on balance accordingly. However, I argue that this is an unnecessarily restrictive approach. There is no good reason why the EU cannot be treated as offering a form of 'society' or community, that this was always its purpose and has been in some form its reality, and that positive justice obligations should also be contemplated if the substantive issue of distribution as I have described is to be addressed.

Second, I outline the four most salient dimensions of justice which I believe the EU should and could embrace following my argument in the first part. In brief they are: redistributive, political, inter-generational, and criminal. The first three of these are perhaps capable of being read as tripartite aspects of a similar theme. However, I think that there is value at this moment in time in treating them separately. The fourth is currently treated as procedural. However, the notion of

---

[3] A Williams, *The Ethos of Europe: Values, Law and Justice in the EU* (Cambridge, Cambridge University Press, 2010).

criminal responsibility across borders suggests to me a much deeper commitment that inhabits substantive justice concerns.

II. SUBSTANTIVE JUSTICE AND THE EU

It is a predictable argument that the EU should have no role to play in pursuing justice beyond a very limited and procedural conception. Some would no doubt say that justice requires a shared community when it comes to any substantive claims resulting in a redistribution of wealth (economistic justice). The state is said to remain the only valid entity where this form of justice might be imposed. It is only here, so runs the claim, where the bonds between people are sufficiently strong and the interests sufficiently shared and the power sufficiently coordinated, to enable (involuntary) redistribution to take place (primarily through some form of central taxation). Any attempt at replicating these assumed responsibilities *beyond* state boundaries is likely to stretch the bonds of shared benefit and burden to breaking point. Thus, on this reasoning, inter-state cooperative ventures cannot fulfil substantive justice goals. It is only in the closed community of shared citizenship that justice can be enforced legitimately.

Much of this argument is based on two inter-related ideas. First, that it is only at the state level that sufficient power can be exercised to enforce mutual obligations. Second, the coercive institutions needed to undertake this enforcement have to be considered legitimate by those affected: otherwise the institutions are unlikely to sustain their authority over any protracted time. Democratic institutions are considered a necessary and desirable prerequisite to attain that legitimacy.

If such reasoning is followed, the EU can easily be condemned as an unsuitable location for substantive justice. It is patently not a state (lacking the monopoly of means for exercising violence in the classic definition) and what institutions it possesses are afflicted by an enduring democratic deficit. Even if this is debatable (and indeed it has been much debated) we can accept the premise of comparative deficiency at least for now.

However, this reasoning should not be taken for granted as making irrelevant deeper considerations of justice for the EU. Admittedly, talking about justice becomes difficult when we look at those areas where obligations require intervention in the affairs of states *and* a basic proposition is adopted that such intervention can only be undertaken by 'legitimate' institutions. In other words, if the EU is deemed illegitimate (because it is undemocratic, corrupt, inefficient, unrepresentative, etc) then substantive notions of justice cannot have any real place here. How can it oversee any fair distribution of benefits and burdens across and within borders if it is deemed a debased institution? Who would accept the sacrifice this might entail? Even if the institution might compare favourably with any particular state government, the idea of an illegitimate institution without any direct societal connection seems to be a complete disqualification for substantive justice.[4] The only

---

[4] See, eg, T Nagel, 'The Problem of Global Justice' (2005) 33 *Philosophy and Public Affairs* 113.

question then becomes: how *un*just is the EU? And the result of such an evaluation will either be that the EU should be abolished or it should be restricted to a very narrow range of operations, none of which would involve interference directly or indirectly in the internal affairs of sovereign states.

This is both a political and philosophical position. I disagree on both counts. I do not hold with the political position if only because my intuition tells me the *idea* of a European Union is essentially a good thing. Of course, if the EU is formed and operates predominantly as a conduit for *in* justice and the systemic violation of the rights of people (which it might well be), then this intuition may give way to negative judgement.[5] The contributions of Agustín Menéndez and Sionaidh Douglas-Scott in their chapters might indeed provoke caution on my part. Nonetheless, although I accept the desirability of the *existence* of the EU based on an appreciation of a perceived goodness of cooperation and integration between states and their peoples, this does not mean that I accept that its current constitutional foundations vis-á-vis justice are satisfactory or properly reflect this ideal of union.

Even if my intuitive political position is accepted, the philosophical objection to justice through the EU also needs to be countered. In my view, it would be valuable to separate the problem in this context into two fundamental questions: *should* the EU become involved in justice (the ethical element); and *does* it have the capacity and capabilities to become involved (the empirical element)? The first is intimately connected with political sensibilities, as I have already suggested. The second can at least be founded on experience, on evidence accrued of past behaviour as well as a plausible appreciation of future potential.

Taking these two matters in turn, the ethical is perhaps superficially the easier to deal with. It would have to be based on an appreciation that substantive justice entailing some redistribution is fundamental for the realisation of any other interstate obligations of justice (other than the most minor commitments). Without some sharing of wealth, no substantial justice claims could be met. In this, care must be taken to distinguish justice as a value. Much has been made of the EU's new appreciation of constitutionalised values, but in my view distributive justice lies beneath them all. It may not be recognised as such but in theory its absence would disable any fulfilment of human rights, freedom, equality, democracy or the rule of law. Determining a fair distribution of benefits and burdens is the essential question of purpose for all these values.

With this in mind, the ethical question could be resolved by a sequence of statements of belief which are vaguely cosmopolitan in character: (1) we believe that our moral obligations to others should *not* be constrained by historically constructed state borders; (2) if we are to iron out inequalities amongst people wherever they live (which may change from time to time) then those who are rich should give resources to those who are poor regardless of their location; (3) to have a chance of succeeding in this distribution we have to work together; (4) to help us achieve this efficiently, institutions to coordinate activity are necessary; (5) if the distribution is to cross borders in line with our obligations then cross-border institutions would

---

[5] There are a number of authors in this book who may make this evaluation.

make sense; (6) there is good reason to ensure that standards of operative justice (based on principles of good administration) are applied to these institutions. Of course, we could add another statement of quality: that these cross-border institutions would be more legitimate if managed by representatives who were democratically elected from all locations affected. However, the basic six-part sequence is more concerned with efficient realisation and administration of the founding justice obligation rather than providing some deeper legitimacy.

If accepted, this position would not preclude the EU, for all its democratic failings, from satisfying the scheme envisaged above. Once the political determination was made that it *should* realise justice-based obligations across borders then its role (at least in part) could be to fulfil that aim. Principles of good administration founded on the thinner end of the value of the rule of law would police its operations in that respect.[6]

From this point on, the sophisticated arguments about legitimacy might divert attention from the declaration of *should* but it would not displace it. Rather, a counter-position would be needed to say the original sequence was less desirable than another that did *not* seek to extend obligations beyond national borders. It seems to me fruitless to go in that direction. We either decide one way or another as a matter of constitutional principle. If there is any ambiguity in this respect (for instance, the obligation is acknowledged only rhetorically but there is permanent quibbling about the extent to which it should be realised) then the political decision has in effect been made *against* adopting the obligation. We are, instead, in the realm of 'charity' where there is always a choice whether to fulfil some justice aim or not, a choice that is often not exercised.

Once a decision *is* made to embrace substantive justice obligations the second, empirical element, must still be addressed. Does the EU have the capacity to fulfil the ethical aim? Has it demonstrated the ability to coordinate the determination of its members (states and individuals) for the benefit of substantive justice? Has it acquired access to the necessary resources, both administrative and financial? Has it created an enabling legal and constitutional structure?

I have written before on this subject and suffice to say here that the evidence is equivocal.[7] On balance, however, there is some cause to say (in particular through development and humanitarian policy, regional policy, the promotion of social and economic rights) the EU institutions have revealed some qualities one might expect of an agent capable of fulfilling substantive justice aims. Despite a relatively limited budget, the EU still manages significant amounts of funds some of which are distributed in one form or another. It also is involved in the macro to the micro level

---

[6] Joseph Raz considers the rule of law in terms of its thin and thick interpretations. The former is more concerned with fairness of procedure, etc, the latter has been equated with a whole theory of social justice. J Raz, 'The Rule of Law and Its Virtue' in RL Cunningham (ed), *Liberty and the Rule of Law* (College Station, TX, Texas A&M University Press, 1979).

[7] See A Williams, 'The EU, Interim Global Justice and the International Legal Order' in D Kochenov and F Amtenbrink (eds), *The European Union's Shaping of the International Legal Order* (Cambridge, Cambridge University Press, 2013).

in what might reasonably be considered as justice related issues.[8] That is not to say that it operates in accordance with any defined principle of justice in mind. But it is to say that it displays some of the characteristics necessary to fulfil the empirical justice requirement. Even Menéndez in his critique of the EU's current form of distribution being focused on the national or regional in effect acknowledges this.[9] Though he sees this as undesirable and profiting the elite not the individual poor, and probably therefore being an empty distribution, the capacity for the EU to be engaged in substantive justice is acknowledged. Of course whether it is enabled to do so and if so which path it takes in practice is another matter.

It is also arguable that the EU has developed sophisticated operational virtues which ensure that good administration again is plausible in the operation of substantive justice realisation. Of course, we can draw on Bernard Connolly's exposure of corrupt practices and we can point to many instances where resources have been wasted appallingly, but the standards of operational justice assumed through the good administration discourse *are* at least recognised and recognisable in the EU.[10]

All of this, admittedly scanty, evidence, suggests that the EU *is* practicably capable of responding to constitutionally adopted substantive justice principles. If we also accept the ethical position that the EU *should* be committed to substantive justice and that this should be a political imperative, then where does that leave us? Which elements of substantive justice should the EU embrace seriously? Clearly there is a spectrum of possibility here but to my mind there are four that stand out. They stand out because they have particular resonance in a cross-border venture such as the EU and, I suggest, are feasible in David Miller's words (but not his philosophical context) as containing 'principles that members of [a given society which I take to include one encompassed by the EU borders] could be brought to accept by reasoned discussion, which means that the principles cannot have implications that those citizens would find abhorrent'.[11] These elements of justice are considered below.

III. ELEMENTS OF JUSTICE FOR THE EU

The four substantive justice themes which I argue should be taken more seriously by and within the EU are (A) distributive, (B) inter-generational, (C) political, and (D) criminal. These seem to me to be the most salient given the nature of the EU as an inter-state cooperative venture. They also seem to me to be worthy of greater attention in EU studies and politics. Of course, they are all the creatures of politics and it is difficult to see any political movement which seeks seriously to develop all of these justice issues through the EU. Nonetheless, I argue that there are obscure

---

[8] Again development and humanitarian policies together with the commitment to respect and now promote human rights could indicate this.
[9] See AJ Menéndez, 'Whose Justice? Which Europe?' in this volume, 137ff.
[10] B Connolly, *The Rotten Heart of Europe: The Dirty Wars for Europe's Money* (London, Faber & Faber, 1995).
[11] D Miller, *Justice for Earthlings: Essays in Political Philosophy* (Cambridge, Cambridge University Press, 2013) 37.

indications, buried within the EU's history and practices, which suggest that such development is not implausible.

A. Distributive Justice

There is no politically or constitutionally enshrined obligation for the EU to oversee any process of redistribution of wealth and resources either within or outside its borders. The language of solidarity and economic cohesion and social justice appears occasionally but is hardly central. The same could be said for most states, no doubt. Nonetheless, it is this form of justice that I suggest underpins all disputes about the nature of the EU as an inter-state venture. Although few would deny that self-interest has governed the Union as a realised project, few also would deny that its genesis has been rooted in more altruistic ideas. It is when these two facets seem to conflict (self-interest versus altruism) that many conceptual tensions about the EU's direction appear. This has occurred not only in terms of relations between states but also between states and other collectivities: ethnic groups, economic classes, regions. When state perceptions of interest have collided with concern over the welfare of people who are not defined by geography alone (the Roma, the poor, the deprived elderly, the vulnerable) then the EU has been faced with an ethical choice which at least countenances some redistributive process.

Similarly, it is at least possible to connect the whole philosophy of the Internal Market with an intention that the benefits and burdens of the society of Europe should be more fairly distributed. Removing national economic boundaries under the rhetoric of 'freedom' might provoke some to argue that the EU is facilitating this fairer distribution, if only in part. But I think it would be stretching the imagination, and certainly the language *and* history of the Union in this respect, to support this position. Who really benefits? Menéndez in his contribution doubts that the individual is really the subject of the EU project in any justice terms. Rather, it is the elite or corporate class who gains the fruits of any distribution. Nonetheless, it is possible to point to the rather mythical identities of the 'consumer' or 'worker' or 'dependent' or 'rights bearer' and make a connection of benefit arising because of the EU's intervention through the guise of the free market.[12]

But how extensive is this beneficial element for the individual? If there is no constitutional commitment to redistribution, does that mean there are no redistributive tendencies lurking within the EU's structure? Not necessarily. The practice of specific policies may reflect a contrary indication. They may reveal the scale and depth of any redistributive inclinations (if any) which might lie beneath the constitutional surface.

Internally, there are a number of areas where some form of redistribution may be the effect if not the avowed intention. Cohesion policy or regional development policy, although limited, and other means of assisting least developed Member States have seen funds move across borders over the EU's history. Providing funds for underdeveloped areas of the EU suggests a willingness to transfer some monies.

---

[12] Menéndez, 'Whose Justice? Which Europe?' in this volume, 137ff.

40 *Andrew Williams*

But how real this transfer is, is almost impossible to tell. There are few if any studies that lay bare with any clarity the net value of distribution through EU initiatives. No one seems able to say authoritatively who the beneficiaries of membership are. We are left with conjecture as to the effective movement of wealth from the rich countries to the poor areas of Europe. Thus, when the EU announces EUR 6–8 billion for boosting youth employment in June 2013 it is treated with cynicism by political leaders and public alike.[13] Who really gets the money?

Some evidence appears in relation to those states that have joined the Union over the years that seem to have experienced considerable benefit from membership. The support of infrastructure projects, movement of industry to these regions and the net receipt of funds through the annual EU budget have given the impression of some redistribution. Ireland was typically held up as a success story of membership for many years. But with austerity now a feature of the European economy, this net benefit appears considerably less concrete. Greece, Portugal, Cyprus, Hungary, Spain and Ireland all seem to have shed the attractive fiction that EU membership somehow transferred long-term wealth into these economies from the more prosperous states. If that was once true for the many, it seems now only true for the very few.

The various Eurozone bail-outs and banking support packages made available to some of these countries support this negative conclusion. These are (relatively) short-term loan arrangements with strong (some say detrimental to the poorest) budgetary conditions attached that give no indication of any distribution whatsoever. Substantive equality is not a driver of the rhetoric, the policy or the detailed provisions. Of course, at some point in the future it may be possible to argue that a distribution of sorts has taken place through these bail-out schemes. The same argument can be made for the existence of the Internal Market as a whole, the theory basically reliant on a trickle-down type analysis: the people at the bottom benefitting after the people at the top pass it on in some form. Similarly, there is an undercurrent discourse which presumes that helping poor states by imposing conditions restricting wasteful expenditure is for the people's own good: in other words, there is a sort of enforced fairness by preventing waste and corruption.

None of this is accompanied, though, with general guiding principles of distribution. The likelihood then is that any resources acquired by the recipient countries will have propped up the wealthiest rather than improved the condition of the poorest. The whole scandal of the global banking crisis has seen rich institutions receive the benefit of massive investment. Can it really be said that those least well-off have somehow benefitted too? All the indicators of disparity between rich and poor suggest not, or at best suggest the benefit for the poorest is simply negligible.[14]

But if macro-finance analysis cannot tell us whether there is any meaningful distribution happening in practice, can any other fields produce a more informative idea?

---

[13] See Debating Europe at www.debatingeurope.eu/2013/07/04/is-europe-doing-enough-to-tackle-youth-unemployment/.

[14] See in particular the warning and data issued by the Organisation for Economic Co-operation and Development (OECD) in its report *Growing Unequal? Income Distribution and Poverty in OECD Countries* (Paris, OECD Publishing, 2008), and its more recent report *Divided We Stand: Why Inequality Keeps Rising* (Paris, OECD Publishing, 2011).

If we see the development of equality as a matter of distributive justice then the history of the EU in this area is perhaps a little more definitive. There is common agreement that EU regulation and case-law has overseen great changes in employment practices to the advantage of women. Whether the same can be said for ethnic minorities or the disabled or the aged is another matter. But the equal pay commitment and anti-discrimination initiative has altered the terrain of inequality considerably over the last 50 years. Given what I have said already about the capability of the EU to operate as an institution for distributive justice, this is an important although perhaps not massively significant contribution for half a century's work. A clear economic link, in theory, could be made between such measures and a redistribution of wealth across the social spectrum.

Similarly, it could be said that the freedom of movement principles have enabled many to escape from poor life conditions. Social justice language, too, pervades many initiatives on delivering social and economic rights. And no doubt figures could be obtained to show that the general standard of living within the EU has risen over the half century and more of its existence. It is dubious though that we could call this a fair distribution. The EU still records the high, if not increasing, level of those in or at risk of poverty. In 2011, Eurostat recorded that 24.2 per cent of the EU's population were in this category. In 2010 it was 23.6 per cent. And this increasing figure is only an average across the Union. In Romania, Bulgaria and Latvia the figure is more than 40 per cent in 2011 compared with 15 per cent in the Netherlands. Unemployment in Greece ran at 26.8 per cent in March 2013 whilst only 5.3 per cent in Germany.[15]

None of these statistics do anything to suggest that any distribution is either planned or delivered through the auspices of the EU. And if it were planned or intended or hoped then there has been a massive failure of delivery.

Turning to external affairs, the record of allocating resources for the developing world looks superficially impressive. The EU is lauded as the single biggest donor in the world and has been for some time. But it still fails to meet the collective target of 0.7 per cent of gross national product (GNP) set by the United Nations. And this of course takes no account of the exploitation of resources and the net benefits of trade which may well see any such transfer of monies reduced or turned negative.

Such a scanty review of both internal and external distribution cannot of course do justice to this theme. But there is sufficient evidence to suggest that the distribution of wealth does not figure within the EU's DNA as a matter of justice. It is simply not possible to impute any such motivation. Ulrich Beck and Edgar Grande's claim that the EU can be seen as a flawed cosmopolitan venture in essence has not been proven.[16] That does not mean that one *should* not be introduced. Indeed, I would argue that the EU nonetheless rests in a state of advantage vis-á-vis distributive justice. Like any wealthy person, it has the means. And in its case has developed the infancy of some distributive tendencies. Will it ever go any further than that? Probably not so long as the market is the cohering theme of European union.

---

[15] For latest data see Eurostat, 'People at Risk of Poverty or Social Exclusion', www.epp.eurostat.ec.europa.eu/statistics_explained/index.php/People_at_risk_of_poverty_or_social_exclusion.

[16] U Beck and E Grande, *Cosmopolitan Europe* (Cambridge, Polity Press, 2007).

But having a directed discussion on this is of primary importance. The whole enterprise seems closed to such debate at present. And that gives vent to those who criticise and condemn the EU as a vehicle for capital and the elite. In the absence of greater regard for distributive justice beyond technical legal measures of equality or freedom of movement, the critique will only gain political ground.

B. Political Justice

I do not accept that when it comes to justice there should be an either/or approach: distributive or political justice. The two are compatible. Thus, if distributive (and arguably any other form of) justice is to be tenable in the EU, requiring evaluative decisions about how benefits and burdens are to be spread both within and beyond its borders, then some form of just 'government' is desirable.[17]

We could call this 'procedural' justice in the sense that decisions must accord with some agreed standards. Liberal theory has often seen the contents of the rule of law as a reasonable source in this respect, valuing non-arbitrary decision making amongst other qualities. But I take 'political justice' as a better descriptor.

Essentially the problem of justice in this respect is: how should decisions be made and who should make those decisions? Most contemporary political accounts require a democratic system of some kind to underpin the process, even though it is not inconceivable to be just without democracy. Nonetheless, a lack of respect for democratic decision making continues to trouble those who see the exercise of power by an institution, which is not directly elected, to be a threat to national sovereignty and each state's democratic superstructure. It is plausible therefore to see the nature of democracy within the EU as fundamental to its political justice. That being so, is political justice really a problem here?

If we look at its record, the EU displays quite a remarkable evolution in terms of inter-state democracy. The European Parliament is an extraordinary institution, although perhaps for the wrong reasons. On its positive side, it represents the most developed attempt to construct an international democratic system. It may lack powers comparable with national parliaments but it nonetheless exercises a degree of control and influence which is unparalleled in international affairs. What authority it does have (through co-decision procedures, veto powers and powers of inquiry) is not insubstantial. We should also recognise the role of the Ombudsman, the right of petition, and the identification of political rights in the EU Charter of Fundamental Rights. There may still be a significant practical distance between representatives and people, induced by the sheer size of constituency, one which stretches to breaking point any sense of accountability, but the mechanisms are there to develop.

That potential for further evolution should not be ignored from a political justice perspective. It suggests that the empirical question (can the EU be a vehicle for political justice?), should be answered positively.

---

[17] Undoubtedly, some believe this is not necessary and that the technocrat or expert is better placed to make these decisions. Menéndez in his contribution to this book nicely points to the Plato inspired idea of an enlightened elite being trusted to make distributive or other decisions for the populace in EU thinking, 137, at 138–39.

Of course, such an optimistic interpretation must not ignore the dangers of the system. Lack of political engagement by the electorate with turnout in the 2009 elections averaging 43 per cent (lowest Slovakia 19 per cent; highest Belgium 91 per cent, which in law demands participation by its electorate, and the United Kingdom 34 per cent) suggests a widespread public disaffection. Whether that is a general product of a disillusioned age or a failure of the EU to engage with the public (or a combination of these and other factors) is difficult to tell. But it is something which has to be addressed if the democratic line is to be pursued further.

None of this answers the ethical question though: should the EU be (more) democratic and if so what form should this take? If it operated purely as an administrative vehicle to fulfil the politically agreed policies of government representatives, then an argument could be made that greater popular involvement would only be a distraction. But if the EU continues to hold wide ranging competences affecting the daily lives of its citizenry (as well as others beyond its borders) then a robust system of representation and accountability seems to me a prerequisite. No doubt that is a reason for some to argue that those competencies should be withdrawn or scaled down until that system exists. But as things stand, there is a strong reason for greater representative *and* participatory democratic control, accompanied in the meantime by a more intensive accountability. Perhaps that is best organised around different policies and competences rather than trying to acquire some kind of democratic universal model. The sophistication of representation should match the complexity of the institution and the dimensions of justice such complexity requires, as well as the depth to which it is involved in those policies.

That may be the underlying problem for the EU and political justice. Thinking and critique has invariably focused on providing *a* solution. But perhaps this is neither feasible nor desirable. Instead, the multiplicity of the Union and its concerns suggests we need a far more flexible model operating under a parliament of scrutiny rather than parliament of dubious decision-making power. Thus we might expect more representation/participation when it comes to matters with the greatest impact on the lives of individuals but a more distant or delegated representation in more arcane issues (competition regulation for instance). Then the debate about political justice would not become so easily discarded as being too complicated to resolve.

For some time, though, the institutional appetite has been for obscurity. There may be a discourse of transparency and participation but the EU remains a creature of corridors and lobby rooms and private discussions. Perhaps that is inevitable given its current form of political justice, which is rooted in a realist perspective where the need to address the so called 'national interest' remains paramount. Breaking that monopoly of political control seems to me to be a precondition for developing political justice so that other forms of justice are not prejudiced too. Indeed, other forms of justice might be enhanced.

C. Inter-generational Justice

The call for a more publicly recognisable form of political justice may be particularly relevant for my next salient problem of justice: the righting of inter-generational wrongs. In other words, to what extent should the EU take responsibility for resolving the 'wrongs' committed by its constituents in the past (and how far back should that go) as well as in the present that are predicted to have some detrimental impact in the future?

Philosophical notions of responsibility hardly provide much guidance here, particularly in a legal order which overlaps with national law on the one hand and international law on the other. Although it is commonplace to ascribe some sense of responsibility for wrongs committed by a state for past unjust actions,[18] or indeed hold states and other entities responsible for damages that are likely to result from current actions, this does not easily become transposed to the EU. Of course, if we accept the EU as practically a 'primary agent of justice', a polity responsible for the acts of its institutions as a separable entity from its constituents, then we can make inter-generational justice claims just as we might for states. But this would still most likely require the EU to 'inherit' as it were the wrongs of its constituent states.

Probably few would argue for such transference. Those states without a history of colonialism may bridle at the prospect of contributing to any redress claimed from the obvious perpetrator. That would be correct except where perhaps the EU and all its constituent states continued to benefit from the wrong of colonialism. There are those who see that as exactly the case here. The trade relations imposed, the reliance on migrant workers from the ex-colonial South (whatever the purported attempts to keep some out), the continuing exploitation of their resources (now increasingly their workforce as well as their oil and other raw materials) through supported corporate enterprises, all point to a benefit enjoyed by all. That might make one think that if responsibility for colonialism is just then the EU should be involved in its realisation.

Any responsibility would flow more readily if it was determined that the EU (rather than its members) had exercised power in its own right which led to wrongs committed in the past or impacts wrongly on the future. So, if the EU passes legislation which, say, requires states to adopt environmental or economic or social policies that are (predictably?) harmful to people, then a justice claim could be envisaged. But of course the EU only infrequently has this direct power. That does not mean responsibility is dismissed merely because of sporadic interventions. In principle obligations of justice should remain in the field of collective responsibility which we are often happy to impose on nations.[19] Nonetheless, if the EU adopts a 'secondary agent of justice' role (a creature of its Member States) then the prospects for recognising direct obligations of justice are much reduced. Much depends, therefore, on our reading of what the EU has evolved into. Again this is as much about policy application as constitutional framework, which provides little in the way of responsibility allocation to the EU for past or future wrongs.

Indeed, the EU's recognition of justice which spans past, present and future generations is not impressive. Certainly the EU has drawn a very distinct line between its

---

[18] See for instance K-C Tan, 'Colonialism, Reparations and Global Justice' in J Miller and R Kumar (eds), *Reparations: Interdisciplinary Inquiries* (Oxford, Oxford University Press, 2007).
[19] See particularly D Miller, *National Responsibility and Global Justice* (Oxford, Oxford University Press, 2007).

Member States' colonial past and its own development and external affairs policies. Although originally, international development policy was focused on the overseas territories still retained by France in the 1960s, the colonial heritage was never accepted explicitly. Neither has there developed an appreciation of the exploitation and damage done by the colonial enterprise of many of its Member States.

Should this be a matter of justice for the EU? The arguments against are no doubt forceful. Why should a cooperative international venture take on the sins of its members? If we restricted our thinking to purely the present, we might find it difficult to believe that the EU as an institution should take on any responsibility for the conduct of its Member States either internally or externally. Would it be acceptable to say that the foreign wars entered into by the United Kingdom and France over the past 10 years, for instance, should be a subject for redress by the EU as a whole? It would be hard to see many sign up to such a constituting policy, if only because those states which were not involved in any past or current sin would deny any responsibility as naturally accruing. Whether one could make an argument of omission would probably depend on determining that the EU had the power to intervene. Given the highly restrictive wording of Article 7 of the Treaty on European Union (TEU)[20] it is doubtful any intervention would have been plausible in the case of the Iraq War for instance.[21]

And yet, the EU often promotes its collective nature to the point that disaggregating 'sins' in such a way sounds disingenuous. The Union may have been founded on a sense of projection into a better future, turning a collective back on a vicious past, but this should not mean it has no role to play in matters of justice emanating from its members previous wrongs. Indeed, the EU signed the Terezin Declaration on Holocaust Era Assets[22] in 2009 which acknowledged the moral responsibility to secure some form of restitution for Nazi looted property. A very small step but there is at least some recognition that the EU should help facilitate these justice issues within and beyond its borders.

How much further could and should it go for past wrongs? The prospects are thin at best. If the Member States do not themselves admit any ongoing responsibility then the likelihood of the EU intervening in some meaningful fashion must be small. Will it engage at all with the long standing claims about reparations emanating from the Nazi era? The matter is a live one as recent stories attest but it is difficult to see EU intervention as likely.[23]

And if the past is a foreign country for the EU, how strange is the future? The focus of attention is on the environmental matters which accompany economic development. Here we perhaps stumble across a greater sense of obligation and duty arising from a justice issue. Over the past 40 years or so, the EU has accepted that it should be concerned with the degradation of the habitat within and beyond its Member States. The relative strength of the continental green movement in

---

[20] Consolidated version of the Treaty on European Union [2012] OJ C326/13 (TEU).
[21] For a review of this impotent power here, see A Williams, 'The Indifferent Gesture: Article 7 TEU, the Fundamental Rights Agency and the UK's Invasion of Iraq' (2006) 1 *European Law Review* 3.
[22] The text is available at www.holocausteraassets.eu/program/conference-proceedings/declarations/.
[23] See S Daley, 'As Germans Push Austerity, Greeks Press Nazi-Era Claims' *The New York Times* (New York, 5 October 2013).

Germany and other countries has helped place the topic on the policy map. Of course, the pre-eminent justice issue is situated in the present (concerned as it is has been with matters of pollution and climate change considered to be affecting citizens already) but there are many programmes premised on the need to protect the interests of future generations. Again the debate has to be how far this responsibility to do something just should go.

At the forefront of these initiatives has been the 1998 Aarhus Convention.[24] Access to justice in the environment sphere was the point of this instrument. Its objective was 'to contribute to the protection of the right of every person of present and future generations to live in an environment adequate to his or her health and well-being' (Article 1) but it did so through encouraging obligations of providing access to information, participation *and* review (what it termed access to justice). The main thrust since could be said to be enforcement of environmental standards for the benefit of citizens or concerned organisations. Superficially, this might suggest the EU is wholly engaged with this justice issue. But it is arguable that the Aarhus Convention has shifted focus to procedure rather than substance. By concerning itself primarily with how parties can find out information about environmentally affected projects, can participate in reviews of projects, and can access courts in the latter, the EU has sidestepped any calls for radical action for the benefit of future generations (a recent consultation seems to reinforce this emphasis).[25] Justice is conceived as *access* to justice, which in turn is largely conceived as access to affordable informal or formal review of decisions. Whether this really encourages action on behalf of or by those most likely to suffer the impact of environmental degradation is doubtful. It is the poorest who tend to bear the brunt and they tend not to be well represented whatever the regulations offer.

All in all, then, is there evidence that inter-generational justice is accepted as an ethical demand on the EU? From the environmental perspective it is at least arguable that the EU is seen as a plausible agent for engagement in environmental matters. Further than this would be difficult to contend with any conviction. There is no appetite to assume responsibility for (or even recognition of) past injustices. Colonialism externally, nationalism and extremism internally, hardly register if at all. Perhaps this is a just position to adopt: many would argue that it would be wrong to penalise current generations for such matters. But the EU has turned its back on the past other than with limited and tangential expressions of concern. We might hear strong noises about the need for states such as Serbia and Bosnia to prosecute war criminals before they could possibly join the Union but they have hardly been replicated in internal approaches to crimes committed in earlier eras by original Member States.[26] That suggests an historical hypocrisy when it comes to inter-generational justice that looks unlikely to be altered any time soon.

---

[24] United Nations Economic Commission for Europe (UNECE) Aarhus Convention on Access to Information, Public Participation in Decision-Making and Access to Justice in Environmental Matters (25 June 1998) 38 ILM 515 (1999), 2161 UNTS 447.

[25] European Commission, 'Consultation on Access to justice in environmental matters—options for improving access to justice at Member State level', www.ec.europa.eu/environment/consultations/access_justice_en.htm.

[26] The lukewarm approach by key Member States since the 1950s to prosecuting war crimes associated with the Holocaust remains an enduring stain.

D. Criminal Justice

If justice has attained any significant rhetorical presence in the EU's lexicon, it is in the field of criminal justice. 'What should the EU owe its constituents in responding to criminal wrongs whether committed cross-border or within a nation state?' has developed into a searching ethical question. One could be forgiven, however, for dismissing this particular item from the general justice discussion above. The approach of the EU has been fairly anodyne and proceduralistic in this field. There has been little investigation into understanding what might be considered sufficiently 'wrong' to warrant Euro-wide responses other than vague challenges of economy and more specific challenges to some individual rights. Instead, the matter has been largely focused on pragmatic issues: how the EU can help facilitate more efficient policing and avoid criminal behaviour taking advantage of open borders but closed jurisdictions. Only recently has there also developed some thought to standardise fair trial rights.

In more detail, at the formal level, there are three areas of current activity here. First, 'prevention' has seen the development of the European Crime Prevention Network as an organisation constructed to support activity at national level. But its role is largely confined to information sharing. Second, 'prosecution' has now assumed some importance as a potential area for Union involvement. Ever since the prospect of a European prosecutor was introduced in the Lisbon Treaty, many EU critics have suggested this is one more unacceptable move towards federalisation. Nonetheless, by focusing for now on trans-border type crimes: drug and human trafficking, internet child abuse, cybercrime, victims' rights and of course terrorism, the EU has sketched a fairly broad albeit bordered remit for itself. Some of these initiatives undoubtedly make sense particularly in those areas where individual Member States have unimpressive records. And few can argue cogently against some of the attendant beneficial economies and efficiencies of inter-state cooperation. Some might no doubt go so far as to see human rights enhanced in certain countries when the EU turns to constructing minimum standards, for instance in setting rights for the accused in pre-trial procedures.

But of course with benefits come burdens. This is where the negative justice issues really bite. What are the dangers of a European prosecutor with the power to bring proceedings against the citizens of Member States? How threatening is the European Arrest Warrant system for nationally observed rights? What are the hazards of a European police force operating outside national systems of scrutiny and accountability?

It is not impossible to conceive of satisfactory answers in theory to these questions. Whether they would be reflected in practice is quite another matter. But the starting point should not perhaps be pessimistic. If European wide corrective justice was deemed a sensible thing then any problems associated with its delivery should, as in any system, be the subject of continuing assessment. Certainly the argument that the EU by definition and necessity *will* be unjust if it operates in the criminal justice realm seems intuitively absurd.

Perhaps the most powerful intellectual argument rests more on philosophy than practice. Most criminal justice systems in liberal democratic societies are predicated on the conceit that they are the product of popular consent if not design. In other words, there is a political philosophic tradition which aligns corrective justice with democracy: the former acquiring legitimacy through the conscious assent of the people. Thus when reform is needed (as it invariably does to respond to contemporary social ills) there is a basic trust that change will be the result of reasonable deliberation and consensus.[27]

This is a myth in most societies. Perhaps not an unhealthy myth, but still it is quite an article of faith to expect governments to reform criminal justice systems in such an ideal way. Often this is plainly not the case. Witness the restrictions on liberties following national responses to the perceived threat of terrorism. Most of the time the public are, at best, tangentially involved in these changes.

The question then is whether at European level this myth would be further challenged. Would the disjuncture between decision makers and public be even more stretched than at the national level? So far the experience of public engagement in any measures agreed through the EU is not promising. The faith placed in national political systems may be waning but it is hardly greater in the EU.

All this suggests that the criminal justice sphere does and will continue to raise significant questions of practical justice for the EU. And in my view that is right. It makes sense for cross-border responses to crime and wrongdoing to reflect cross-border criminality. Although it is not without its dangers, something inherent in any development of justice, this is an area that appears justifiably an EU matter. Perhaps we have to look at a more radical development if criminal justice is to be substantive as opposed to merely procedural. For instance, should an EU public prosecutor examine the behaviour of states when it comes to their practices of exclusion of minorities rather than reserve such matters to inadequate and toothless administrative action? Should a prosecutor not examine the interweaving connections between banks in their laundering of drug money and prosecute those who facilitate it? Should he or she not consider the criminal responsibility for those complicit in gross breaches of human rights who are citizens of the EU (whether or not they are officials of Member States) rather than leaving this to the International Criminal Court? These are challenges that no doubt will be ignored but nonetheless should at least be pondered if the implications of criminal justice at an EU level are to be truly considered.

IV. ADDRESSING THE JUSTICE DEFICIT

There can be no doubt that there are significant other justice aspects which I have not considered. Nothing I have said suggests that these other dimensions are unworthy of attention. I have merely focused on what I see as the most pressing. In each case it seems to me that questions of justice are relevant and to date have failed to find expression in such deeper terms. Often the vocabulary of rights is used to plug

---

[27] See generally, A Duff et al (eds), *The Trial on Trial*, vols 1–3 (Oxford, Hart Publishing, 2004) which explores the development of criminal process through a comparative perspective and raises the prospect of a normative theory of the criminal trial which has purchase in this context.

this gap.[28] However at the moment, there is no coherence in this respect. Rights are used as a deflection from justice questions.[29] The tendency seems to be to use the language of rights to avoid grasping the justice nettle rather than, as I have argued, using rights as a *means* of introduction to justice supranationally.[30]

Until salient elements of justice are taken seriously in the EU, until the discourse of justice is reflected in political debate and action, we are confined to critical scrutiny and advocacy. In other words, it should always be an essential task vis-á-vis any regime exercising powers of governance, to measure that regime in terms of standards of justice. Assessing levels of *injustice* tends to be the result—which Sionaidh Douglas-Scott makes clear in this volume. But the question remains: what standards should such assessments be measured against?

This is where identifying and defining the aspects of justice (which I have done only partially above) is necessary. These justice issues deserve recognition as *applicable* to the EU. That is a necessary first step. We should as a matter of course be calculating the EU's role in each case. And in each case we should be determining what kind of obligations should be owed to both its citizens and all those with whom it comes into contact. What we should not be doing is dismiss their relevance, which has been the general tendency (with some exceptions) to date.

It seems to me that this requires, as a minimum, clear obligations of justice; clear standards attached to those obligations; clear means of assessing performance in relation to those standards (accountability); and clear means of enforcement.

At present we have little clarity in any of these, which is hardly surprising when justice is unrecognised as an adequately articulated concept. However, in the absence of that the EU may nonetheless have provided an unwitting answer. We have one source of both law and political consensus: respect for human rights. The trouble is: which human rights? The EU Charter of Fundamental Rights provides some basis to begin. Whether it is capable of addressing redistributive or global justice demands (which I believe should be accepted by the EU on the basis that it has accepted some limited cosmopolitan obligations in this respect) is another matter.

But at least we can find popular support and political acceptance of human rights. That must be a beginning in my view of any inter-state cooperative venture that seeks to develop a sense of community rather than pursue wealth for its members (states, corporations or individuals). It does not mean human rights replace justice. Rather it is an avenue towards making substantive justice a deep commitment for the EU.

---

[28] I address this particular alternative to substantive justice in A Williams, 'A Reply to Somek' in this volume, 311.
[29] See A Somek, 'The Preoccupation with Rights and the Embrace of Inclusion: A Critique' in this volume, 295; and my reply, ibid.
[30] See Williams, *The Ethos of Europe*, n 3 above.

4

Justice, Injustice and the Rule of Law in the EU

SIONAIDH DOUGLAS-SCOTT

I. INTRODUCTION

Justice is as much an issue for the EU as it is for any state or social institution. According to John Rawls:

> Justice is the first virtue of social institutions, as truth is to thought. A theory however elegant and economical must be rejected or revised if it is untrue; likewise laws and institutions no matter how efficient and well-arranged must be reformed or abolished if they are unjust.[1]

While I do not argue for the application of Rawls' actual theory of justice to EU law, I do argue that justice, or perhaps rather injustice, raises especially salient issues for the contemporary EU. In some recent actions dealing with particularly pressing issues, the EU has not added value but caused injustice. This chapter will give some particular examples. Unfortunately, however, the resolution of these injustices is not readily apparent. In particular it may be that some of these states of affairs are specifically attributable to the sui generis nature of the EU—to its complex actuality as neither purely sovereign state, creature of international law, nor federal or confederal body. The inchoate status of the EU presents singular challenges for justice.

The earlier sections of this chapter are mainly descriptive in nature, and set out some examples of injustices caused by EU actions. In these sections, I do not argue for an understanding of justice in any particular sense but rather proceed on the basis that justice is a value whose importance is immediately recognisable in some sort of 'thin' or Dworkinian 'pre-interpretive' sense,[2] and should surely be acknowledged by an EU that wishes to proclaim its values. Later in the chapter, however, I consider the concept of justice in greater detail. In that context, I argue that some limited solution to the problem of justice may be found in the specific relation of justice to law, in a concept I name Critical Legal Justice. However, I also argue that justice should not be conceived only as legal justice. In the concluding parts of the

---

[1] J Rawls, *A Theory of Justice* (Cambridge, MA, Harvard University Press, 1971) 3.
[2] See R Dworkin, *Law's Empire* (Cambridge, MA, Harvard University Press, 1986).

chapter I argue that, while, on broader reflection the concept of justice may appear to be so elusive as to be an ideal or utopian, that it is the diagnosis of *injustice* that is itself crucial. Indeed, justice is more likely to move people in its absence, in its antithesis of injustice, rather than as an academic, abstract exercise that ultimately fails to convince. I analyse the notion of injustice in some detail, drawing on philosophical literature, arguing that it is injustice that motivates and propels action, and the highlighting of injustice does its own work. Such an approach is of relevance to the EU and its present predicaments.

II. INJUSTICE IN THE EU

This section engages with some notably salient instances of justice, or injustice, in the EU: operation of its 'Area of Freedom, Security and Justice' (AFSJ); responses to the financial crisis; and approaches to the idea of 'social justice'.

The AFSJ proclaims the term 'Justice' in its very title, and so naturally invites an assessment of its capacity to deliver justice. The AFSJ came into being in 1997, instigated by the Treaty of Amsterdam,[3] and was supposed to make the EU citizen feel closer to the EU and more included by it. Regrettably, however, it has become almost a commonplace to state that, within the EU's AFSJ, freedom and justice have been sacrificed to the needs of security.

Within the scope of the AFSJ, the EU is able to adopt all sorts of measures that have not been traditionally associated with EU action, including measures on terrorism, asylum, privacy and security, the fight against organised crime, and criminal justice. The AFSJ takes up a large part of the EU legislator's time, with no sign that the pace is slowing. Crucially, within the scope of the AFSJ are areas that have been considered core state powers, at the heart of constitutional law, such as the provision of security, the development of public values and the relation between the individual and public authorities.

A specific example of actual injustice perpetrated by the AFSJ attaches to the European Arrest Warrant (EAW). There has been repeated criticism of the manner in which the EAW has functioned in concrete cases.[4] Human rights organisations have raised concerns about the disproportionate arrests, violations of procedural rights and the impossibility in some countries for an innocent person to appeal against a decision to be surrendered. These problems have escalated with the increase in the number of EAWs, the overwhelming majority of which relate to minor crimes. The human rights safeguards in EAW procedures need to be increased. The EU's Stockholm programme suggests review of the EAW, and, where appropriate, 'to increase efficiency and legal protection for individuals in the process of surrender'.[5]

---

[3] Treaty of Amsterdam amending the TEU, the Treaties Establishing the European Communities and Certain Related Acts [1997] OJ C340/1.

[4] As well as the challenges brought in national constitutional courts and in the ECJ. In particular, Case C-399/11 *Stefano Melloni v Ministerio Fiscal* (ECJ, 26 February 2013) raises concerns.

[5] Council of the European Union, 'The Stockholm Programme—An open and secure Europe serving and protecting the citizens' (2 December 2009) No 17024/09, 3.

This review is urgently needed, although efficiency should not be at the expense of rights.

For the AFSJ to be balanced, without security dominant, there needs to be satisfactory common protection of rights throughout the EU, and reciprocal trust between Member States' criminal justice systems in order for mutual recognition systems, such as the EAW, to work. But such trust cannot be built overnight and EU states do not offer equivalent protection of human rights, nor deliver uniform standards of justice. Part of the problem is a failure of supranationalism. What is it about freedom, security and justice that requires their realisation at EU level? And in any case, is there sufficient consensus at EU level as to how they should be understood? There has been too little reflection about this. Consequently, as illustrated by the EAW, problems emerge, and a dominant emphasis on security (ie automatic surrender) is at the expense of justice and the protection of rights. Integration appears one-sided, an Internal Market in security enjoying greater realisation than progress in human rights, freedom or justice.

This relates to the understanding given to 'justice' in the specific context of the AFSJ. Overwhelmingly the focus has been on the administration of justice. Such an interpretation is clearly articulated by the vocabulary of some language versions of the EU treaties. In Dutch and German, for example, *Recht* generally does not have the same associations as 'Justice' in English or in French, but usually connotes a narrower concern for law and order.[6] The EU's 1998 Vienna Action Plan[7] asserted the need of 'bringing to Justice those who threaten the freedom and security of individuals and society' and therefore a need for crime control, for justice to be administered, for judicial cooperation. Justice is perceived as a means of dealing with those who threaten society, rather than being understood in any richer, substantive sense.

* * *

However, it is the handling of the recent financial crisis within the Eurozone that presents perhaps the most immediate example of injustice in the EU. The EU's treatment of this crisis has not been masterly. Since its onset, EU Member States and institutions have proceeded in an ad hoc, event driven way, instigating a seemingly incessant series of obscure and highly complex measures with drastic consequences for the peoples of Europe. What has often been overlooked in the widespread commentary on the euro's troubles is that this crisis is as much one of governance as of economics and finance. The EU has not provided adequate institutional mechanisms and structures for monetary union. Indeed, the common currency has proved to be a major fault line of European integration.

If we examine the details of EU action in the context of the Eurozone crisis, we can see that the scope and impact of these measures has often been formidable, as for example, those imposed by the 'conditionality' clauses in bail-out agreements.

---

[6] Although the Dutch and German *Recht* may also mean 'right' as well as 'law'.
[7] Action plan of the Council and the Commission on how best to implement the provisions of the Treaty of Amsterdam on an area of freedom, security and justice—Text adopted by the Justice and Home Affairs Council of 3 December 1998 [1999] OJ C19/1.

Beyond specific bail-out packages, hugely wide-ranging general legislative measures have also been introduced. For instance, the 2011 reinforcement of economic governance colloquially known as the 'Six-Pack'[8] implemented the most comprehensive reinforcement of economic governance in the EU and the Eurozone since the launch of the Economic and Monetary Union (EMU). Under this, the European Court of Justice (ECJ) and European Commission have the power to scrutinise national budgets prior even to scrutiny by national parliaments (a huge challenge to democracy in itself). If Member States fail to reduce their debts or refuse budgetary suggestions from Brussels, they can be subject to enforcement measures, which can lead to fines of up to 0.05 per cent of Gross Domestic Product (GDP). Further, Member States will only avoid fines or other sanctions if a qualified majority in the Council votes against them, a procedure which might be seen as amounting to 'semi-automatic' sanctions.[9] All of these measures were adopted with little debate and a minimum of public awareness. Most Europeans have little idea that these changes, involving such inroads into their governments' economic sovereignty, have taken place.

We can also be a little more specific about the ways in which these measures wreak injustice. First, many of them have brought the EU into conflict with human rights treaties generally, as well as its own treaties and proclaimed values. Article 3(3) of the Treaty on European Union (TEU)[10] sets the objective of 'a highly competitive social market economy'. It would be hard to argue that measures and reforms such

---

[8] The EU 'Six Pack' sets out provisions for fiscal surveillance, strengthening the earlier Stability and Growth Pact (under which general government deficits must not exceed 3% of GDP and public debt must not exceed 60% of GDP). The 'Six-Pack' consists of five Regulations and one Directive, applicable to all 27 EU Member States, but with some specific rules for Euro-area Member States, especially regarding financial sanctions. Regulation (EU) No 1173/2011 of the European Parliament and of the Council of 16 November 2011 on the effective enforcement of budgetary surveillance in the euro area [2011] OJ L306/1; Regulation (EU) No 1174/2011 of the European Parliament and of the Council of 16 November 2011 on enforcement measures to correct excessive macroeconomic imbalances in the euro area [2011] OJ L306/8; Regulation (EU) No 1175/2011 of the European Parliament and of the Council of 16 November 2011 amending Council Regulation (EC) No 1466/97 on the strengthening of the surveillance of budgetary positions and the surveillance and coordination of economic policies [2011] OJ L306/12; Regulation (EU) No 1176/2011 of the European Parliament and of the Council of 16 November 2011 on the prevention and correction of macroeconomic imbalances [2011] OJ L306/25; Council Regulation (EU) No 1177/2011 of 8 November 2011 amending Regulation (EC) No 1467/97 on speeding up and clarifying the implementation of the excessive deficit procedure [2011] OJ L306/33; Council Directive 2011/85/EU of 8 November 2011 on requirements for budgetary frameworks of the Member States [2011] OJ L306/41. See also now: European Commission, 'Communication from the Commission. A blueprint for deep and genuine economic and monetary union: Launching a European debate' COM (2012) 777 final/2.

[9] Reverse Qualified Majority Voting was introduced for Eurozone measures by Regulation (EU) No 1173/2011 on the effective enforcement of budgetary surveillance in the Euro area, which forms part of the 'Six Pack' measures. It is also applied more generally in the context of Eurozone measures by Art 7 of the Treaty on Stability, Coordination and Governance in the Economic and Monetary Union ('Fiscal Compact') (2 March 2012) text available at www.european-council.europa.eu/media/639235/st00tscg26_en12.pdf.

[10] Consolidated version of the Treaty on European Union [2012] OJ C326/13 (TEU).

as those of the 'Six Pack', or conditions for the bail-outs, are compatible with a social market economy, or with the provisions of Article 9 of the Treaty on the Functioning of the European Union (TFEU)[11] which states that

> In defining and implementing its policies and activities, the Union shall take into account requirements linked to the promotion of a high level of employment, the guarantee of adequate social protection, the fight against social exclusion, and a high level of education, training and protection of human health.

Nor do measures, such as those in bail-out provisions which impose unilateral cuts on wages, pensions, public spending, and restrict collective bargaining, enhance the objective of social justice set out in Article 3 TEU. A further criticism is that Article 7 of the Fiscal Compact Treaty, which deals with the excessive deficit procedure, requires the Member States in the Council to support the Commission in its decision to take disciplinary proceedings against another Member State, and to base their voting decisions exclusively on matters of fiscal probity,[12] and thus to have no regard to other matters which might also be relevant, such as key constitutional principles, and human rights matters. Such a requirement does not comply with other provisions in the EU treaties, particularly those that set out the importance of a plurality of values for the EU, such as human rights, solidarity and equality in Article 2 TEU.

To summarise the injustices of the Eurozone crisis: certain of these measures appear to contradict the EU's avowal of social justice in Article 3 TEU, as well as infringing some human rights, for example, those of collective bargaining and freedom of association in the EU Charter of Fundamental Rights. Further, notably, the crisis of the Euro is also a crisis of governance, of failed supranationalism, of a failure to perceive the dangers of integration at one level (monetary union) without integrating in other areas (namely economic, or fiscal union).

The solution to this crisis is not obvious. Few Member States desire the deeper union and central control of a fiscal union. So action continues to be ad hoc and fragmented, and it seems that much of the resultant injustice is attributable to the very fact of unsatisfactory, unbalanced integration.[13]

**

The capacity of the EU to cause injustice is equally acute if we turn to social justice issues. Article 3 TEU states that the EU 'shall promote social justice'.[14] However, it seems that the EU may have an institutional inability to deliver social justice. This is

---

[11] Consolidated version of the Treaty on the Functioning of the European Union [2012] OJ C326/47 (TFEU).

[12] Art 7 Fiscal Compact reads: 'the Contracting Parties whose currency is the euro commit to support the proposals or recommendations submitted by the European Commission where it considers that a Member State of the European Union whose currency is the euro is in breach of the deficit criterion in the framework of an excessive deficit procedure'.

[13] Ie EMU assumes a level playing field. But states are not equal in this union. Conditions that work for Germany do not work for Greece or Ireland.

[14] Art 3(2) TEU reads: 'It shall combat social exclusion and discrimination, and shall promote social justice and protection, equality between women and men, solidarity between generations and protection of the rights of the child'.

because such a policy remains highly unlikely[15] as a harmonised common policy for the EU when its Member States are so divided as to whether social welfare should be market driven or redistributionist (although the Eurozone crisis now seems to have imposed austerity throughout the EU). There is no consensus as to the desirability of a redistributive EU social policy. EU action is restricted to low minimum standards acceptable to all states, or the very limited redistributive functions in the fields of regional development policy and the varying budgetary contributions of its Member States. Given these circumstances, as Fritz Scharpf has asserted,

> European integration has created a constitutional asymmetry between policies promoting market efficiencies and policies promoting social protection and equality. National welfare states are legally and economically constrained by European rules of economic integration, liberalization, and competition law, whereas efforts to adopt European social policies are politically impeded by the diversity of national welfare states, differing not only in levels of economic development and hence in their ability to pay for social transfers and services but, even more significantly, in their normative aspirations and institutional structures.[16]

Notably and notoriously, the ECJ has asserted the equivalence of fundamental market freedoms and fundamental rights. In both *Viking Line*[17] and *Laval*[18] it was claimed that market freedoms of the applicant undertakings had been restricted by trade union collective action. Although the Court recognised the right to take collective action as a 'fundamental right', in both cases it was interpreted as a 'restriction' on a market freedom, to be exercised proportionately. However, such reasoning is highly contestable and destructive of fundamental rights. As has so often been the case in the EU, the Internal Market lies at the centre of things, and proportionality functions to ensure that market integration is not too greatly diminished. In these circumstances, social justice is very likely to be compromised. Yet we should not forget that 'social justice' is a complex, malleable notion, amenable to protectionism of labour privileges of wealthier EU states at the expense of newer EU states anxious to access new labour markets. In such circumstances, how to understand 'social justice' in the EU?

The preceding paragraphs have given brief sketches of how EU actions may wreak injustice. Notably, the EU's role as a transnational actor has been identified as one of the exacerbating features. If this is so, then arguably, a possible resolution might be the repatriation of the EU's powers, an end to the project of EU integration, dissolution of the euro, dismantling of the AFSJ—a eurosceptic's dream. Yet such a solution is hardly realistic. In the first case, EU Member States themselves are scarcely exemplars of justice and democracy. Further, the EU's transnational integration exemplifies a necessary and unavoidable drive, at a time in which global forces, global financial markets, environmental and security threats, render states incapable of acting alone, however greatly they might wish to. The state, inadequate

---

[15] See, however, for a powerful argument in favour of distributive social justice in the EU, P Van Parijs, *Just Democracy: The Rawls–Machiavelli Programme* (Colchester, ECPR Press, 2011).
[16] FW Scharpf, 'The European Social Model: Coping with the Challenges of Diversity' (2002) *MPIfG Working Papers* 02/8, www.mpi-fg-koeln.mpg.de/pu/workpap/wp02-8/wp02-8.html.
[17] Case C-438/05 *International Transport Workers' Federation and Finnish Seamen's Union v Viking Line ABP and OÜ Viking Line Eesti* [2007] ECR I-10779.
[18] Case C-341/05 *Laval un Partneri Ltd v Svenska Byggnadsarbetareförbundet and Others* [2007] ECR I-11767.

and powerless in the face of global forces, must seek transnational solutions. Yet these very transnational solutions themselves further injustice and insecurity.

III. THE PERPLEXITIES OF JUSTICE IN THE EU

How then, should we understand the concept of justice within the EU? The previous section was not premised on any specific interpretation. The obvious predicament is that achieving justice in a supranational community such as the EU raises particularly complicated issues, given the EU's convoluted, intricate, pluralist legal space. In this context, the question of how to achieve justice becomes highly salient but also Herculean.

Further, interrogating the nature of justice in the EU presents the concept of justice in its diversified forms—namely, substantive and procedural, distributive and corrective. For example, the problems of the AFSJ often turn on issues of corrective justice, whereas the question of securing social justice in the EU raises very thorny issues of distributive justice. Therefore, across the wide range of EU affairs, many aspects and instances of justice are at issue.

The incomplete, inchoate nature of the EU polity also creates further problems. For the way in which we conceive the EU may affect how we understand its capacity to do justice. So, for example, if we see it as becoming more state-like in nature, then it may appear more capable of generating the affective bonds necessary for a richer, deeper concept of justice. Furthermore, as already argued, some examples of the EU's present injustices appear to have been generated by its very existence as a supranational project. Unless the EU becomes a superstate (a form undesired by most) it will always have competences in some areas and very limited powers in others. Yet urgent crises—9/11, Eurozone—require swift solutions, which, however, the EU will be perceived as lacking the full legitimacy to dispense. So there is a sense in which injustice (and not just inefficiency) is built into the very nature of the EU. An end to, or reversal of, integration provides no obvious solution. A vicious circle exists. The imperatives of globalisation render cooperation necessary, yet they exacerbate the injustices rendered by the failures and imbalances of integration.

There is also a further complication. The problems and complexities of justice in the EU are exacerbated by the complexities and possible pluralism of the concept of justice itself. Justice has an all-embracing aspect—no community or institution, however large or small, ought to escape its remit. Yet justice often appears so elusive as to be a utopian ideal. There is no conclusive way of interrogating it. It may be understood in a rich, substantive sense, or as a complex of fair procedures. It may be deemed to be closely tied to particular circumstances, or proclaimed as a universal good, for all times. It clearly has a close relationship with law, but also functions as an external standard with which to evaluate law. Perhaps unsurprisingly, then, Jacques Derrida interprets justice as a complex of *aporia*—demanding immediate action, yet infinite time, knowledge and wisdom in order to do 'justice'.[19] Indeed,

---

[19] J Derrida, 'Force of Law: "The Mystical Foundation of Authority"' in D Cornell and M Rosenfeld (eds), *Deconstruction and the Possibility of Justice* (New York, NY, Routledge, 1992).

Douzinas and Geary suggest that justice is somewhat of a philosophical failure, given that no society or ideology has yet developed an accepted theory of justice, and it is probably fair to assume that no such theory can be developed.[20] One might even inquire, perhaps with a postmodern twist, how it is possible to do justice to justice? More concretely, what position should a viable legal and political theory of the EU take if it is, on the one hand, anxious to avoid an impossibly uniform account of justice, yet also cautious of those postmodern theories which decry grand narratives and embrace a plurality of justices, but also seem unworkable both in their fixity with the ideal and in their pessimism about the actual legal world?

Given this predicament, it is unrealistic (at least at present) to expect the EU to offer and apply an overarching, substantive theory of justice. The circumstances of the EU (for example, a lack of solidarity or consensus among its Member States as to the desirability of EU redistributive social welfare policies)[21] render agreement on substantive justice unlikely. This is a regrettable state of affairs. I am not denying the desirability of social justice. It remains a crucial aspiration. But, in the context of the EU, a quest for the possibility of a richer, more substantive justice, has utopian elements. The better way, I argue, is to focus on *injustice* as motivational, and a call to action. *Injustice as a call to action* will be my second way of framing justice, and I will return to it later in this chapter.

On the other hand, I do argue that a sufficient consensus exists for the realisation of *another* notion of justice in the EU. In short, this argument takes the form that, in addition to prioritising the fulfilment of human rights, the EU should seek to achieve *legal* justice through robust adherence to the Rule of Law. For it is this very manifestation of justice which has been notably absent in many EU activities.

IV. THE RULE OF LAW AND CRITICAL LEGAL JUSTICE

Law and justice have a very close relationship, a special affinity. Justice is seen as a peculiarly legal virtue. People go to law because they feel some sense of injustice, which they hope law will address. Law presents itself as a form of governance that is distinct from power and from personal rule, and it holds out the prospect of justice.

Yet, law and justice may be linked without the positing of an intrinsic connection. Justice may also be seen as external to law, as a measure by which law may be assessed, as a standard, an ideal, to which law should aspire. So to raise the crucial connection between law and justice is also to allude to its ambiguity—is justice essential and intrinsic to law, or an external measure by which we assess law? Or

---

[20] C Douzinas and A Geary, *Critical Jurisprudence* (Oxford, Hart Publishing, 2005) ch 4.

[21] There is also a lack of consensus among political philosophers as to the possibility of justice at the international or transnational level. See eg J Rawls, *The Law of Peoples* (Cambridge, MA, Harvard University Press, 2001); also T Nagel, 'The Problem of Global Justice' (2005) 33 *Philosophy and Public Affairs* 115. Others disagree—eg T Pogge (ed), *Global Justice* (Oxford, Blackwell, 2001); D Held, *Democracy and the Global Order: From the Modern State to Cosmopolitan Governance* (Stanford, CA, Stanford University Press, 1996). See especially, J Habermas, 'Democracy, Solidarity and the European Crisis' lecture delivered in Leuven (26 April 2013), www.kuleuven.be/communicatie/evenementen/evenementen/jurgen-habermas/democracy-solidarity-and-the-european-crisis, in which Habermas argues for greater solidarity between EU Member States.

perhaps it can be both, depending on how we understand justice? Philip Selznick expresses the complexity of the situation in this way:

> It is important to preserve the distinction between Law as an operative system and Justice as a moral ideal. But clear distinctions are compatible with—indeed they are important preconditions of—theories that trace connections and reveal dynamics. Law is not necessarily just, but it does promise Justice.[22]

This, I argue, is the best way to conceptualise the relationship between law and justice—that law is not necessarily just but it does promise justice.

The Rule of Law is what is very often understood by the concept of 'legal justice', importantly acknowledging it as form of justice. There exists a strong intuition that power, position and status should not corrupt justice, and the Rule of Law functions to constrain the abuse of power. The Rule of Law has traditionally been seen to require laws to rest on legal norms that are general in character, relatively clear, certain, public, prospective, and stable, as well as recognising the equality of subjects before the law.[23] Some would add to this the protection of fundamental rights,[24] and this broader interpretation will be adopted here. Its benefits can be stated simply. Observance of the Rule of Law enhances certainty, predictability and security both among individuals, and between citizens and government, as well as restricting governmental discretion. It restricts the abuse of power. Thus it has both private and public law functions—an attraction in the world of growing legal pluralism.

Elsewhere I have argued that the Rule of Law be recast as Critical Legal Justice, which adheres strongly to the *values* that the Rule of Law protects.[25] A belief in the Rule of Law does not commit one to a consequent belief in law as rules, nor in law as a strongly bounded, autonomous discipline. It does not commit one to the legal theory of legal positivism—nor to any other legal theory for that matter. That is why I prefer to recast this concept as Critical Legal Justice, in order to distinguish it from discredited understandings of the Rule of Law.[26] I also wish to identify it more clearly with *justice*, rather than with, for example, the bland identification of the Rule of Law as a value in Article 2 TEU, whose content is empty and undefined.[27]

Critical Legal Justice does not require that actual, substantive laws form rule-like systems, but rather that certain structural components be applied to shore up laws, or even eject them, where necessary. The application of Critical Legal Justice involves, at its best, a remorseless and pervasive holding to account, and attention to the detail of law making and transparency. This is not to argue that the rule of law exhausts justice, but rather that it is an essential element of it.

---

[22] P Selznick, *The Moral Commonwealth: Social Theory and the Promise of Community* (Berkeley, CA, University of California Press, 1992) 443–44.
[23] See, eg, J Raz, 'The Rule of Law and Its Virtue' (1977) 93 *Law Quarterly Review* 195, 196.
[24] See, eg T Bingham, *The Rule of Law* (London, Allen Lane, 2010).
[25] See eg S Douglas-Scott, *Law After Modernity* (Oxford, Hart Publishing, 2013).
[26] Namely, those understandings of the Rule of Law which have been perceived as overly formalist and blind to difference.
[27] Notably the Rule of Law is nowhere defined in the EU treaties and different Member States have different understandings of it—ie *Etat de Droit* in France, *Rechtsstaat* in Germany, and so on. See also L Pech, '"A Union Founded on the Rule of Law": Meaning and Reality of the Rule of Law As a Constitutional Principle of EU Law' (2010) 6 *European Constitutional Law Review* 359.

It is also particularly needed in the EU. The *lack* of the Rule of Law has been glaring and damaging in areas of EU affairs. Cases such as *Viking Line* and *Laval*, for all that they may be vaunted as examples of a strenuous 'integration through law', are not examples of the application of the Rule of Law but instead present an unpredictable, slanted application of a principle (ie free movement of goods). What will constitute a 'restriction' on trade, what restrictions will be proportionate, becomes ever more uncertain. The classification of a fundamental right merely as a restriction on trade is surely a wrong turning in EU law's cohabitation with capitalism rather than the predictable application of clear law?

Further examples are to be found in the lack of access to courts in the criminal law pillar of the EU (at least until the Lisbon Treaty);[28] or in the lack of institutional balance which has granted too much power to unelected, unaccountable agencies such as Eurojust and Europol, or to Member State executives in the Council; in less than transparent, almost secretive law making[29]—this suggests a *dearth* rather than the presence of the Rule of Law. This is also evident in the Eurozone, of whose measures Steve Peers recently commented: that '(they) fail the test of transparency, because of their near-total complexity and unreadability, scattered across a dozen primary, secondary and soft-law sources, with more to come'.[30] Further, the experience of actions taken in the course of the 'war on terror', such as the willingness of some EU states to accept landing of US flights in the course of 'extraordinary rendition',[31] and the unwillingness of the EU to take any action against those states under Article 7 TEU, also suggests that the Rule of Law, along with human rights, has been lost in a search for 'expedient' measures.

Therefore, I identify the Rule of Law, recast as Critical Legal Justice, understood in what I term a 'Thin+' sense (ie incorporating legally enforceable human rights) as a form of 'legal justice' that can enforce law's promise to do justice. However, I do not argue for it as an example of a transcendental, idealist theory, but rather, to use a prosaic term, as elements in the legal toolbox. Critical Legal Justice and human rights provide a background theory of justice (itself the product of a practical consensus around a variety of different accounts) within which law can operate. Understood in a non-perfectionist, non-ideal sense, they offer a meaningful mechanism by which legal institutions may avoid causing injustice—and thereby a contribution to a better world. There exists a sufficient consensus for us to embrace their use.

---

[28] Treaty of Lisbon amending the Treaty on European Union and the Treaty Establishing the European Community [2007] OJ C306/1.

[29] See, eg, Case C-345/06 *Gottfried Heinrich* [2009] ECR I-1659. The Convention of Prüm, dealing with justice and security matters, also provides a fine example of opaque law making: Convention between the Kingdom of Belgium, the Federal Republic of Germany, the Kingdom of Spain, the French Republic, the Grand Duchy of Luxembourg, the Kingdom of the Netherlands and the Republic of Austria on the stepping up of cross-border cooperation, particularly in combating terrorism, cross-border crime and illegal migration ('Prüm Convention') (27 May 2005), www.auswaertiges-amt.de/cae/servlet/contentblob/607278/publicationFile/158731/VertragstextBGBl.pdf.

[30] S Peers, 'Analysis: Draft Agreement on Reinforced Economic Union (REU Treaty)' *Statewatch* (21 December 2011), www.statewatch.org/analyses/no-164-reu-treaty.pdf.

[31] For which now see the application lodged against Poland at the European Court of Human Rights (ECtHR) on 6 May 2011, *Al Nashiri v Poland* App No 28761/11, in which it is alleged that Poland hosted a secret CIA prison at a military intelligence training base in Stare Kiejkuty where the applicant was held incommunicado and tortured.

V. INJUSTICE EXPLORED

Finally, I return to the notion of justice outside of the law. The Rule of Law, however recast, cannot overcome the feeling of lack we experience at injustice, the desire for something more.

An awareness of visual images of justice aids our understanding of this point. The usual image of justice with the scales, often to be found at law courts, such as that displayed in Figure 4.1, and readily associated with the Rule of Law, appears bland and is less emotive or captivating than the following image which represents injustice.

The second image (Figure 4.2) presents the work of the Danish sculptor Jens Galschiøt. This piece is entitled 'Survival of the Fattest', and it was displayed in Copenhagen harbour in December 2009 at the time of the G15 climate change summit.

Figure 4.1: Darmstadt, Residenzschloss, Fassade zum Marktplatz Justitia

Figure 4.2: Copenhagen, Jens Galschiøt, 'Survival of the Fattest'

It depicts an obese European *Justitia*, dangling the scales of justice in her right hand, supported by an emaciated African man. Galschiøt has stated that the sculpture represents the 'self-righteousness of the rich world', which sits on the backs of the poor while 'pretending to exert justice'.[32] Galschiøt deliberately placed 'Survival of the Fattest' next to 'The Little Mermaid' in Copenhagen harbour, in a bid to ensure coverage and attention. In doing this, Galschiøt contrasts the statue from Hans Christian Anderson's fairy tale with the shocking but undeniable realism of his own work, as if to compare the objectives of the climate change conference with fantasies and fables. It is a striking work, beautiful in its way, but borne out of a compulsion to change things, to shock people into doing justice. The chimneys at the other side of the harbour, billowing out smoke, also add to the irony, conveying an image of a duplicitous west, profiting off the backs of the poor, and polluting the environment at the same time, while appearing to work hard to prevent global warming. This work also conveys its message far more effectively and memorably than so many speeches of politicians, or musings of philosophers.

This second image supports my final point. It is extremely difficult to agree upon a theory of justice in the abstract, or even on an overarching theory that may apply in concrete circumstances, such as those of the EU. This contrasts with the immediacy of emotion that injustice provokes. The world that we inhabit, let alone the EU, is violently unjust. Douzinas and Gearey refer to the 'great paradox' in which

[32] See 'Jens Galschiøt: Portrait of a Sculptor' available at www.aidoh.dk.

'we know injustice when we come across it … but when we discuss qualities of justice both certainty and emotion recede…. Justice and its opposite are not symmetrical'.[33] As they also note, justice is far more likely to move people in its breach, than as an academic exercise or 'piece of rhetoric that fails to convince or enthuse'. It is injustice that motivates and propels action. Hence Figure 4.2 seems far more compelling than Figure 4.1.

An awareness of injustice avoids an over-focus on ideals and takes account of the contextual inspiration for our sense of justice, the fact that we derive it from our experiences and responses to varieties of situations. It is a sense of injury that comes first, which is then followed by a demand for justice, a factor which explains the difficulty we experience in trying to explain in positive terms what justice is.

Judith Shklar argues that we miss much if we focus only on justice, and reduce injustice to the rejection and breakdown of justice, treating injustice as the anomaly. For Shklar, scepticism gives injustice its due, recognising that our judgements are often made in the dark, and that we should have doubts as to their validity.[34] This parallels Bernard Williams' view that we have no reason to believe that the world is fully intelligible to us, nor that it is receptive to our moral interests and purposes.[35] To believe otherwise is to engage in wishful thinking. Morality relies on sentiments, both positive and negative. Justice is a set of practices and procedures developed from our responses to injury and wrongdoing, a notion born of experience—of sympathy, compassion, pain, suffering and outrage.

In the 2000s, there has been a turn toward non-ideal theorising about justice. A notable exponent of this type of theorising is the Nobel laureate, Amartya Sen, who has been critical of accounts such as those of Rawls, for being overly focussed on an ideal, 'transcendental' theory of justice and, as a consequence, unable to offer practical guidance for remedying injustice in an increasingly borderless world. Sen argues that, 'a theory of Justice that can serve as the basis of practical reason must include ways of judging how to reduce injustice and advance justice, rather than aiming only at the characterization of perfectly just societies …'.[36]

We have no reason to expect that a perfectly just society will be achievable in the near future, or indeed, ever. Given the inescapable diversity of human practices and capabilities, and the plurality and pluralism of values, there exists no common standard, no single unit of measurement for justice. What is needed is a theory of justice for an imperfect world, which will enable us to move from a situation of 'more unjust' to 'less unjust'. This is a comparative exercise, which cannot be assisted by transcendental theory. Instead, Sen's 'realisation focussed comparison' focuses on a shared sense of *injustice* which people possess, enabling them to agree that a given situation is unjust, even if they cannot agree on one single reason why they believe this is so. Therefore, although the existence of diversity makes it difficult to advocate a single standard of social or distributive justice, in Sen's case this does not lead

---

[33] C Douzinas and A Geary, *Critical Jurisprudence: The Political Philosophy of Justice* (Oxford, Hart Publishing, 2005) 28.
[34] J Shklar, 'Giving Injustice its Due' (1989) 98 *Yale Law Journal* 1135.
[35] As expressed, eg, in B Williams, *Ethics and the Limits of Philosophy* (London, Fontana, 1985).
[36] A Sen, *The Idea of Justice* (London, Allen Lane, 2009) ix.

to the conclusion that the idea of global justice is a myth. Indeed, Sen believes that the most pressing instances of injustice occur at international level, that they need to be addressed, and that it is just the very attachment to a demanding ideal of a perfect justice which *disables* us from finding the means to tackle global injustice. Ideal theories of justice require, at the very least, extremely sophisticated, developed institutions, such as those of the modern state, to implement them. Yet such an approach is disabling when it comes to the global arena, where organisational structures are weak, and there is little prospect of sufficiently realised powerful institutions. As a result, theorists such as John Rawls or Thomas Nagel deem global redistributive justice unlikely or impossible.

Instead, Sen believes that we should focus on the plurality of reasons that may lead us to believe a situation to be unjust. For example, we may not agree on the reasons why we believe the war in Iraq to be unjust but we may nonetheless agree that it is unjust. Our starting point should be the reflection that our determination of what justice requires in a particular situation is initially motivated by *feelings of injustice*. However, this emotional reaction must, for Sen, be coupled with the exercise of reason. Although our emotions should not be ignored, it is necessary to deploy critical scrutiny to determine what lies beneath them.[37] Further, our decisions must be able to withstand public scrutiny, and so *public reason* is necessary to combat injustice.[38]

However, while fairness might seem to demand impartiality, this need not lead to a singular, unique conception of a just society, for there exist diverse ways in which people may be impartial. Rawls' mode of impartiality rests on the contractual basis of his thought experiment, which assumes a clearly defined, closed, self-contained society. Instead of an 'Original Position', Sen prefers the approach to fairness adopted by Adam Smith, whose *Theory of Moral Sentiments*[39] employs the notion of an 'Impartial Spectator'. For Smith, the impartial spectator is a creature produced by the moral power of the imagination, 'the man within the breast' who shapes the moral sensibility of an ethically sensitive person. It is not 'the eternal voice of conscience or of the deity; but in reality ... that of the world to which we belong'.[40] However, Smith's spectator does not just represent an ideal, for he requires one to look at issues 'with the eyes of other people', and from the viewpoint of 'real spectators'. Thus the plurality of impartial reasoning is ensured.

It might be thought that to derive moral principles from a basis in human sentiment risks relativism—namely, the derivation of moral value from subjective emotional reactions to particular circumstances or events. However, for David Hume, this danger is avoided by his argument that *common* emotional reactions are experienced when human beings react to similar circumstances: 'the great resemblance among all human creatures' that 'must very much contribute to make us enter into

---

[37] ibid, 39.

[38] ibid, 122.

[39] A Smith, *The Theory of Moral Sentiments* (Oxford, Clarendon Press, 1976) 125. In making reference to Smith's *A Theory of Moral Sentiments*, Sen is part of a broader rehabilitation of Smith from the clutches of libertarian, free-market capitalism, to which the more superficial, but dominant reading of Smith's other major work, *The Wealth of Nations*, has given rise.

[40] Per N Phillipson, *Adam Smith: An Enlightened Life* (London, Allen Lane, 2010) 157.

the sentiments of others'.[41] For Hume, therefore, morality is founded on universal sentiments. To be sure, Hume distinguished two kinds of emotion—first, those self-interested emotions, of the sort that Hobbes stressed in his theory of social contract as the origin of society, but also, on the other hand, those universal sentiments drawn from 'principles of humanity', which he believed formed the basis of moral judgements, thus refuting any claim that the emotions may only form the basis of negative, self-interested judgements, by stressing the role also played by sympathy and benevolence. However, it should be noted that, in Hume's theory, reason also has its part to play, functioning as a calculator, or instrument of analysis, aiding humans in understanding their emotions. Reason and emotion are therefore compounded and inseparable, and work together in the formation of moral judgements, providing a motivation for moral action in a way that reason alone (in the cool and disengaged form it finds in rational philosophy) is unable to do.

These thinkers of the Scottish Enlightenment stressed the importance of emotion to our moral imagination, emotions which allow us to place ourselves in the circumstances of others, and to feel sympathy and compassion. Furthermore, and crucially, recent work in neuroscience and psychology strengthens the arguments of Smith and Hume, confirming that certain aspects of emotion and feeling are crucial for rationality.[42]

The key point here is that an account of justice which acknowledges the role played by the emotions in identifying injustice, and the contribution of our emotions to our reasoned ethical judgements, not only more accurately represents the nature of our ethical thought, but is better placed to *motivate* citizens. We place unrealistic demands on citizens if we start with justice as an ideal, pre-existing, neutral, and self-produced by a rational conception, such as in the work of Kant, who requires us to act, 'not from inclination, but duty ... the necessity to act out of reverence for the law'.[43] But this is uninspiring for most people—it represents a distant icon, or even a delusion. It is injustice, and its emotional sources, which inspire most people. Philosophy and social psychology, therefore, are *both* crucial components of our moral reasoning.

VI. CONCLUSION

Where does this leave justice? If justice is acknowledged as somewhat of a philosophical failure, and yet still a powerful intuition, and injustice provokes strong emotion, then perhaps justice is best envisaged as a discourse of absence, something which does not belong to the order of being, is always desired, to come, unachieved.

---

[41] D Hume, *A Treatise of Human Nature*, ed LA Selby-Bigge, 2nd ed rev PH Nidditch (Oxford, Clarendon Press, 1978) 318.

[42] Eg, Jorge Moll et al have used neuroimaging techniques to identify the areas of the brain regions activated by basic and moral emotions, and found that emotional experience is linked to moral appraisal (J Moll et al, 'The Neural Correlates of Moral Sensitivity: A Functional Magnetic Resonance Imaging Investigation of Basic and Moral Emotions' (2002) 22 *Journal of Neuroscience* 2730).

[43] I Kant, 'Perpetual Peace: A Philosophical Sketch' in H Reiss (ed), *Kant's Political Writings* (Cambridge, Cambridge University Press, 1970).

As an object of our fantasies, the content of justice is always subjective and indeterminate. We are left with a sense of *injustice* as a motivator, a call to resistance, instilling us with a sense of responsibility to some sort of action, in Amartya Sen's words, 'a matter of actualities, of preventing manifest injustice in the world, of changes, large or small, to people's lives—the abolition of slavery, improvement of conditions in the workplace—realization of an improvement in the lives of actual peoples'.[44]

This, I think should be the response to the injustice of the EU—one of resistance and action: of scepticism, scrutiny, protest and critique—to look closely at each measure adopted by the EU and to resist greater infringements of our liberty in the name of security, to demand transparency and resist measures taken under EMU which violate human rights and 'values' proclaimed at the forefront of the EU's treaties—rather than agonising over a finely tuned theory of justice.

---

[44] Sen, *The Idea of Justice*, n 33 above, ch 1.

5

The Question of Standards for the EU: From 'Democratic Deficit' to 'Justice Deficit?'

OLIVER GERSTENBERG*

> Justice is the first virtue of social institutions ...[1]

I. THE QUESTION OF STANDARDS

THERE IS TODAY a longstanding, continuing debate about the EU's 'democratic deficit'.[2] But should that debate about the EU's 'democratic deficit' now be replaced by a—new—debate about the EU's 'justice deficit?' Is it, in other words, advisable to shift the focus away from (or beyond) democracy to a (search for a) more comprehensive—EU-wide and perhaps genuinely EU-specific—'substantive ideal of justice' (as the editors of this volume invite us to ask and may even be suggesting)?

In what follows, I wish to strike a cautionary note as regards this shift of paradigm and will argue that the focus on *democratic procedure* remains appropriate. That is so, because, as I will argue, the hope for an overlapping consensus on a shared *conception of socio-economic justice* may appear as both surprising and unrealistic in today's ideologically deeply divided EU. In the past, theorists of justice often focused on two combined elements which an inter-subjectively shared conception of justice must meet, namely, first, an equal respect for the diversity of conceptions of the good life that characterises pluralist, western societies, and, second, an equal concern for the interest of all members of the society concerned.[3] Yet not only are shortfalls from justice inevitable, but Europeans fail to share a common conception of justice at all and, equally importantly, are likely to persistently and sharply (yet often reasonably) disagree about what counts as a shortfall from justice in the

---

* For comments and discussion, I would like to thank Gráinne de Búrca, Dimitry Kochenov and Richard Bellamy.
[1] J Rawls, *A Theory of Justice* (Cambridge, MA, Harvard University Press, 1971) 3.
[2] *Cf* JHH Weiler, 'The Political and Legal Culture of European Integration: An Exploratory Essay' (2011) 9 *International Journal of Constitutional Law* 678.
[3] For a representative statement, *cf* P Van Parijs, 'Justice for All and the European Union', www.philosophersforchange.org/2012/01/18/justice-for-all-and-the-european-union/.

context of law application. The lack of consensus, then, is driven just as much by disagreements about questions of socio-economic justice (socio-economic rights, for example) as by disagreements over matters of conceptions of the good life and basic cultural values; and there are bound to be deep disagreements among libertarians, liberals and others about economic justice, independent of disagreements about religious and cultural values.

Against this background of reasonable, justice-related disagreement, the focus on *democratic procedures* here can be seen to have a decisive advantage by allowing citizens to address the role of the EU multilevel system of law in making the process of policy formulation and implementation—at both the domestic and the EU level— more pluralistic, discursive and participatory. And I also want to suggest that, from the specific and important perspective of EU law and its application, that advantage is of importance when it comes to disarming a longstanding standard worry of lawyers as regards the incorporation of socio-economic rights in constitutional law and as regards the separation of powers principle: the concern with European judges seizing on ambiguous (but ambitious) constitutional provisions to issue broad rulings that usurp the legitimate prerogatives of democratically responsible domestic legislatures. Call this the *democratic–sovereigntist* concern or objection.

In what follows, I will therefore address the question of how the background concern with justice—'the first virtue of all institutions'—can be translated into a research programme which is focused on enhancing the democracy-sustaining, experimentalist dimension and potential of the EU Rule of Law.

II. THE EU AS AN EXPERIMENTALIST ARRANGEMENT

The specific advantage of a morally demanding democracy-reinforcing and experimentalist account of the role of the EU and its legal system, then, lies in disarming the sovereigntist objection and in its capacity of accommodating Europe's multiple pluralisms: its institutional, ideological, cultural diversity.

Consider the sovereigntist objection in more detail. To those who raise this objection, the EU appears to be an unlikely candidate for the possibility of an extension of both justice and democratic legitimacy beyond the nation state. Consider, for instance, Thomas Nagel's striking claim that the cause for any resistance against such an extension is not merely the absence of a *demos* and of a European civil society but also the concern that a more deeply integrated EU

> would be subject to claims of legitimacy and justice that are more than the several European populations are willing to submit themselves to, [a concern, which] reflects in part their conviction that they are not morally obliged to expand their moral vulnerabilities in this way.[4]

Underlying Nagel's concern is the important premise that political authority must— because of its coercive imposition—meet particularly exacting normative standards:

---

[4] T Nagel, 'The Problem of Global Justice' in T Nagel, *Secular Philosophy and the Religious Temperament: Essays 2002–2008* (Oxford, Oxford University Press, 2010) 88.

the standards associated with egalitarian justice. But, then, because the EU is not a *nation state*, the normative standards outside or beyond the state are correspondingly less demanding.[5] Outside the state there is no justice: no moral obligation of the European peoples 'to expand their vulnerabilities in this way'.

Nagel's concern draws on the familiar distinction between *defensive, negative* and *positive* fundamental and human rights. Whereas the former merely 'set universal and pre-political limits to the legitimate use of power, independent of special forms of association', the latter, by contrast, for their identification and realisation depend on associative–political obligations between and among the citizens within the nation state, as the proper locus of socio-economic justice. Nagel's conception of socio-economic justice is a *political* one: Socio-economic justice, he argues, 'depends on positive rights that we do not have against all other persons or groups, rights that arise only because we are joined together with certain others in a political society under strong centralised control'[6] exerted by a sovereign. Whereas the most basic *negative, defensive rights* are universal—that is, 'not contingent on special institutional relations between people'[7]—the 'heightened requirements of equal treatment'[8]—such as a right to democracy, equal citizenship, non-discrimination, equality of opportunity, the amelioration through public policy of unfairness in the distribution of social and economic goods—'are', as Nagel insists, 'contingent that way'[9] and can therefore only be saturated within the special, associative context of the nation state. The stability of any legal system of ordering presupposes the sovereign; and the unique demands which the sovereign makes on the will of its members 'bring with them exceptional obligations, the positive obligations of justice'.[10] So, according to the *discontinuous political conception*,[11] which Nagel advocates, any shift from pure negative constitutionalism to positive constitutionalism seems barred, once we move outside and beyond the state.

But Nagel's specific account of a 'political conception', according to which European populations are not morally obliged to expand their vulnerabilities 'in this way', suggests a paradox, when it comes to the EU. For, on the one hand, the political conception militates in favour of what Europeans call *subsidiarity*: a focus on legitimate diversity of successful and 'living' domestic socio-economic arrangements in the nation state; on responsiveness of law and policy to domestic-local circumstances and preferences, as shaped by domestic public debate; on accountability of decisions to those who benefit from those policy decisions and who must pay for them; and on the viability of sometimes costly redistributive schemes, anchored in a more homogeneous population with a collectively shared 'we-identity' of citizens mutually sharing and bound together by political obligations. And this focus on

---

[5] For an illuminating discussion of Nagel's view, *cf* J Cohen, 'Introduction' in J Cohen, *The Arc of the Moral Universe and Other Essays* (Cambridge, MA, Harvard University Press, 2010) 10–12, and also J Cohen and CF Sabel, '*Extra Rempublicam Nulla Justitia*' in the same volume. Here I am especially interested in the jurisprudential aspects.
[6] Nagel, 'The Problem', n 4 above, 73.
[7] ibid, 76.
[8] ibid.
[9] ibid.
[10] ibid.
[11] ibid, 86.

subsidiarity feeds into, and adds force to, the *democratic–sovereigntist objection to deeper integration*.

But, on the other hand, a political conception of socio-economic justice can also be seen to militate in favour of a muscular social policy and, with regard to the European Court of Justice (ECJ), in favour of a more social jurisprudence at the EU level. That is so, because the evolution of the EU and the question of what competences it should have are of common concern to all individuals, not only as national but as *EU citizens*. The EU's common 'basic structure'—its institutional framework, grounded in the four economic freedoms: the free movement of goods, labour, capital and services—*affects* the living conditions and economic prospects of the citizens of all Member States throughout the EU *individually*. In other words, in the context of the *common market*, it becomes increasingly unrealistic to assume that issues of socio-economic justice can be cabined off and seen as merely arising between citizens of the Member States taken severally.

Here, then is the apparent paradox in full bloom: further (deeper) integration appears to run into the sovereigntist objection (with its adjacent call to 'repatriate' powers and rights); but merely *to do nothing*—by just letting the four freedoms percolate *unfettered* without taking any steps toward social integration and balance—would threaten the moment of shared collective and democratic responsibility associated with legitimacy: the idea that all individuals as *EU citizens* must have a stake and a voice in formulating common policies which shape and transform their individual life prospects.

Yet, as I want to argue, developments in the EU rather suggest the plausibility of a *continuouspolitical conception*—a *discursive continuum* between EU law and the domestic legal systems of the Member States which can be understood along more democratic-experimentalist lines.

To add some flesh on the bare bones of my case for a *continuous political conception*, consider some familiar background. As it is now known, the ECJ initially refused to accept challenges to European Community (EC) measures on grounds of fundamental rights, fearing the impact on the primacy of EC law. The Court was correspondingly seen not as a constitutional court but exclusively as a *Fachgericht*—a specialised court with the final judicial say on the European Internal Market. From this perspective, any interaction, even a tangential contact between Community economic freedoms and national constitutional and social rights, seemed impossible.[12] There was, if you will, a clear and sharp *acoustic separation*[13] between the discourses of the common market (EU integration through law), on the one hand, and of socio-economic justice (associated with the national welfare states), on the other hand.[14]

---

[12] For a representative view, *cf* W Hallstein, 'Europapolitik durch Rechtsprechung' in H Sauermann and EJ Mestmäcker (eds), *Wirtschaftsordnung und Staatsverfassung, Festschrift für Franz Böhm* (Tübingen, Mohr Siebeck, 1975) 211–13.

[13] For the original use of the idea of an acoustic separation in legal studies (somewhat distant from my use here), *cf* M Dan-Cohen, 'Decision Rules and Conduct Rules: On Acoustic Separation in Criminal Law' (1984) 97 *Harvard Law Review* 625.

[14] For a compelling account of the historical background, *cf* G de Búrca, 'The Road Not Taken: The EU as a Global Human Rights Actor' (2011) 105 *American Journal of International Law* 649.

The guiding idea—made explicit by the German ordoliberal tradition of a *Wirtschaftsverfassung*—was that of the EU as an (economic-) liberal transnational order, held together by the principle that Contracting States should not allow the political to contaminate the economic.[15] That tradition saw the role of a new and autonomous European economic law as implementing and protecting a system of open markets and undistorted competition at the supranational level from political interference, while at the same time allowing Member States to retain competence in the area of social regulation compatible with open markets. The lodestar was the '[ordo-] liberal principle ... of the widest possible separation of the two spheres of government and economy ... of Imperium and Dominium'.[16] By observing 'this principle of separation', indeed, by radicalising 'the largest possible depoliticisation of the economic sphere',[17]—it would become possible 'to reduce to a minimum the economic significance of the coexistence of sovereign states with their different legal orders' and systems of administration and separate citizenships. As a consequence, the 'economic process [could be] transferred from the sphere of administration, public law, penal courts, in short, of the "State", to the sphere of the market, of private law, of property, in short of the society'.[18]

But the *acoustic separation* implied unintended consequences. Opposed to ordoliberalism, social democrats began to hold this analysis against the EU and to invert it by addressing what they took to be its spillover costs imposed on non-market spheres of life: they argue that not only can the moment of 'collective responsibility' not be attained at the EU level, but also that collective responsibility at the national level is increasingly being eroded and undermined as EU integration progresses and deepens. As a result, the overall chances for collective fate control by the democratically self-governing people themselves dissipates.

This argument begins with the familiar observation that the political project of European integration was to be realised by an economic programme effectuated through and by the Rule of Law. The pronounced emphasis on 'integration through law' in the early days had, of course, to do with political stagnation at various historical stages of the integration project and could be understood as an audacious but also a prudentially wise choice, insofar as transnational legality helped, as Joseph Weiler pointed out, to prevent free riding and provided stability and continuity to any *acquis* even in periods of political instability and wavering commitment.[19] And yet, according to an influential analysis,[20] the reliance on law also—by way of an unintended consequence—fatefully led, according to that view, to a *double constitutional asymmetry* or bias overall: first, on the substantive level,

---

[15] For theoretical foundations, see F Böhm, 'Privatrechtsgesellschaft und Marktwirtschaft' (1966) 17 *Ordo Jahrbuch für die Ordnung von Wirtschaft und Gesellschaft* 75; W Hallstein, *Europe in the Making* (London, Allen & Unwin, 1972).

[16] W Röpke, *Economic Order and International Law*, Recueil des cours (The Hague, Martinus Nijhoff Publishers, 1954) 207–70, 224.

[17] ibid.

[18] ibid.

[19] Weiler, 'The Political', n 2 above.

[20] F Scharpf, 'On the Double Asymmetry of European Integration. Or: Why the EU Cannot Be a Social Market Economy (2009) *MPIfG Working Papers* 09/12; *cf* also A Supiot, 'Le sommeil dogmatique européen' (2012) 66(1) *Revue française des affaires sociales* 185.

a bias in favour of *economic constitutionalism at the transnational level* to the detriment of *social–political constitutionalism domestically* which remains concerned with socially 'embedded capitalism'[21] and with the externalities of free markets on non-market domains of life: the colonialisation of the lifeworld. Second, and institutionally, an asymmetry between law and politics; a bias in favour of an unencumbered 'supranational'—economic–liberal—*judicial politics* to the detriment of the possibilities and narrowing scope *democratic law and politics 'at home'*—in other words, a concern with an undesirable yet increasing assignment to the ECJ of morally decisive authority in questions concerning society as a whole, which this—legalistically minded, market-focused—Court, as a primarily economic court, is simply ill-equipped to address.

However, this disillusioned analysis also needs to come to terms with the undeniable fact that—perhaps in response to threats expressed by national constitutional courts, perhaps also in response to an ever growing underlying unease with what became to be perceived as a growing democratic deficit of the EU—the ECJ gradually began to shift to a position diametrically opposite to its initial position of acoustic separation and agnosticism. The Court increasingly relied on the European Convention on Human Rights (ECHR) and succeeded in developing its case-law to take full account of the Convention and shared principles derived from the legal systems of the Member States in a hope to provide reassurances to the Member States and their legal communities and the wider public at large.[22]

As I will argue below, these transformations, familiar though they may seem, deserve to be taken seriously and should not be dismissed as the ECJ merely paying lip-service to volatile public moods. On the one hand, EU law, as shaped and developed by the ECJ, opens up to fundamental socio-economic rights considerations and in this process is becoming more hybrid. On the other hand, a closer look at the ECJ's jurisprudence reveals that the ECJ's jurisprudence is not as unilateral or authoritarian as sceptics claim it is. Rather, that jurisprudence opens up a *discursive space* where both—the shared, but always preliminary and contested, EU-wide understandings of fundamental and social principles, on the one hand, and the equally contested domestic conceptions of law, on the other hand—may be mutually justified in the light of one another in an ongoing, interminable and mutually corrective search for *discursive congruence*. In that mutually transformative, discursive process, neither EU law nor domestic law can provide an extra-discursive, neutral

---

[21] JG Ruggie, 'International Regimes, Transactions, and Change: Embedded Liberalism in the Postwar Economic Order' (1982) 36 *International Organization* 379.

[22] For compelling and authoritative accounts, *cf* FG Jacobs, *The Sovereignty of Law: The European Way* (Cambridge, Cambridge University Press, 2007) 50 ff; FG Jacobs, 'The Lisbon Treaty and the Court of Justice' in A Biondi, P Eeckhout and S Ripley, *EU Law After Lisbon* (Oxford, Oxford University Press, 2012); T Tridimas, *The General Principles of EU Law* (Oxford, Oxford University Press, 2006). See also, from a democratic–experimentalist perspective, CF Sabel and O Gerstenberg, 'Constitutionalising an Overlapping Consensus: The ECJ and the Emergence of a Coordinate Constitutional Order' (2010) 16 *European Law Journal* 511; O Gerstenberg, 'Negative/Positive Constitutionalism, "Fair Balance," and the Problem of Justiciability' (2012) 10 *International Journal of Constitutional Law* 904; O Gerstenberg, 'The Justiciability of Socioeconomic Rights, European Solidarity, and the Role of the Court of Justice of the EU' (2014) *Yearbook of European Law* 1–32.

Archimedian standpoint; the metaphor of a simultaneous equation with multiple unknowns seems more appropriate.

III. THE ECJ AS AN EXPERIMENTALIST COURT

According to a compelling account of a democratic experimentalist conception of judicial review,[23] courts act in the first instance as instigators and non-dictatorial overseers of engagement among stakeholders (broadly defined, and public and private, with no hierarchy), in an ongoing process of interpretive clarification of constitutional meaning—a process of subsequent discursive benchmarking. The court serves as arbiter but without having the final word: judicial intervention is *continuum-ising* rather than based on a dichotomic contrast between strong form and weak form review.[24]

At an institutional level, and as a matter of assessing the ECJ's jurisprudence, I will argue that there is only little, or at least inconclusive, evidence for the asymmetry claim. No doubt, all of us can pinpoint numerous *bêtes noirs* among the Court's sprawling case-law.[25] But I believe that a more nuanced account than the one offered by some of the critics of the ECJ's jurisprudence may be given: indeed, the Court has played a benign role by both strengthening and transforming the Rule of Law[26] on countless occasions and is on record for making explicit fundamental legal principles often in surprisingly innovative and unprecedented ways where development was blocked or arrested at the level of *national* law and politics.

In support of this view, consider merely two—at first sight improbable yet momentous—contemporary illustrations.

A. The Right to Healthcare: The Need to Take Individual Circumstances of Pain and Suffering More Fully into Account

In the case of *Yvonne Watts* the ECJ ruled that national health services must refund hospital treatments provided in another Member State if patients waited longer than medically acceptable.[27] But according to critics, this decision epitomises the Court's ill-advised, detrimental role in creating an individual right to jump the

---

[23] *Cf* F Michelman, 'Social–Liberal Constitutionalism, Political–Liberal Thought and the Aims of Judicial Constitutional Review' (MS on file with author), with reference to this author.

[24] For a related set of arguments, *cf* Gerstenberg, 'Negative/Positive', n 22 above, with a comment by Mark Tushnet at www.iconnectblog.com/2012/11/article-review-response-mark-tushnet-and-oliver-gerstenberg-on-rights-adjudication/; and more fully in Gerstenberg, 'The Justiciability', n 22 above.

[25] The notorious *Viking* and *Laval* cases are the usual suspects, which have attracted sometimes vitriolic comment. Case C-438/05 *International Transport Workers' Federation and Finnish Seamen's Union v Viking Line ABP and OÜ Viking Line Eesti* [2007] ECR I-10779; Case C-341/05 *Laval un Partneri Ltd v Svenska Byggnadsarbetareförbundet and Others* [2007] ECR I-11767. But for a different, more nuanced reading of these cases, *cf* Sabel and Gerstenberg, 'Constitutionalising', n 22 above. For a rejoinder to our piece, *cf* A Supiot, 'Le sommeil', n 20 above.

[26] *Cf* Jacobs, *The Sovereignty*, n 22 above.

[27] Case C-372/04 *R, on the application of: Yvonne Watts v Bedford Primary Care Trust and Secretary of State for Health* [2006] ECR I-4325.

queue (or National Health Service (NHS) waiting lists that national services employ to prioritise the spending of limited resources). According to the critics, Ms Watts and others in her position may now, as a consequence of the Court's ruling, seek healthcare in a different Member State, regardless of NHS waiting lists and the well-considered economic spending priorities these lists (and the agencies administering the lists) establish 'at the expense of the health and other social needs of many fellow citizens'.[28]

But this reading of the case is questionable. What the Court did say in *Yvonne Watts* was that a refusal to grant prior authorisation to treatment in another Member State could not be based merely on the existence of waiting lists alone with their predetermined funding priorities,

> without carrying out in the individual case in question an objective medical assessment of the patient's medical condition, the history and probable course of his illness, the degree of pain he is in, or the nature of the disability at the time when the request for authorisation was made or renewed.[29]

And the criteria for this medical assessment must be 'objective, non-discriminatory' and 'known in advance', and based on

> a procedural system which is easily accessible and capable of ensuring that a request for authorisation will be dealt with objectively and impartially within a reasonable time and refusals to grant authorisation must also be capable of being challenged in judicial or quasi-judicial proceedings.[30]

So what the Court here does is

i. to acknowledge the Member States' 'sovereign powers in the field [of health care]';[31] but to require national systems that establish legitimate spending priorities to be run or administered in ways which
ii. fully take individual factors and contextual personal circumstances (such as a patient's degree of pain and suffering, her health prospects, etc) at each stage of the prioritising fully into account; and which
iii. meet the requirements of transparency and procedural fairness;
iv. and also incorporate the Rule of Law requirement of openness to judicial review.

Hence, the Court's decision in *Yvonne Watts* does not amount to creating an atomistic right of the unencumbered self to jump the queue. Rather, Ms Watts—and one may empathise with her—challenged the British system because she felt that system failed to meet those requirements. Indeed, the thoughtful Opinion by Advocate General Geelhoed brings out this point in full, even more clearly than the Court's decision itself. He emphasises the

> inherent tension between, on the one hand, the inevitable existence of waiting lists and their role as an instrument for managing and allocating limited resources and, on the other hand, the interests of patients in receiving adequate and timely treatment.[32]

---

[28] R Bellamy, in correspondence with the author.
[29] Case C-372/04 *Yvonne Watts* [2006] ECR I-4325, para 119.
[30] ibid, para 116.
[31] ibid, para 121.
[32] ibid Opinion of AG Geelhoed, para 86.

But the fault of the national British system lay in its bias towards a target-culture that showed disregard for personal need and necessity:

> [T]he only criterion which at present applies within the NHS context is whether treatment can be provided within NHS targets, and ... these do not take the individual needs of patients sufficiently into account.[33]

So I think the *Yvonne Watts* case is a powerful counterexample to any (constitutional-asymmetry style) analysis that pits the economic against the social, and the European against the domestic. Indeed, it was *the domestic sphere* that was the sphere of purely 'economic' considerations (of a decontextualizing welfare-utilitarian nature, abstracting from personhood); and it is the *European sphere* that opens up a forum for principled moral considerations of personhood, need and circumstance. The European dimension reopens, at the behest of an aggrieved individual, the balancing process that is necessary here and the search for a new compromise via responsible collective decision making. Hence, the *Yvonne Watts* case cannot be seen as evidence for the libertarian–economic atomism the critics bemoan. What the decision throws into doubt is not civic republicanism, but a kind of welfare-utilitarianism which holds individuals at ransom, abstracts from their need and situation, and displays little patience for the requirements of transparency and judicial review. It emphasises their separateness, but not in the libertarian sense, but by giving them democratic voice where there was closure.

B. Adjudicating Consumer Contracts: Attentiveness to an Implicit Human Rights Dimension

The case *Aziz* concerned the question of the possibilities which must be available to a consumer for relying on the unfairness of a term of a loan agreement against the enforcement of the mortgage securing it.[34] Under Spanish law, in the interest of an effective and quick realisation of the mortgage, the grounds on which a debtor may object to those 'simplified' mortgage enforcement proceedings were very limited: those grounds did not include the existence of an unfair term in the mortgage loan agreement, meaning in practice that a debtor must therefore accept the realisation of the mortgage regardless of any unfair term. But according to the principle of effectiveness, the organisation of national procedural law may not impair the assertion of the rights conferred on consumers in Directive 93/13.[35]

Under the contested Spanish procedural law, only in separate declaratory proceedings concerning the validity of the title could the consumer lodge objections to the claim on which enforcement is based and thus allege that one of the terms of a loan agreement was unfair. However, even in those declaratory proceedings the court did not have the possibility of ordering the provisional suspension of

---

[33] ibid, para 90.
[34] Case C-415/11 *Mohamed Aziz v Caixa d'Estalvis de Catalunya, Tarragona i Manresa (Catalunyacaixa)* (ECJ, 14 March 2013). For a more comprehensive discussion, *cf* O Gerstenberg, 'Constitutional Reasoning in Private Law: the Role of the CJEU in Adjudicating Unfair Terms in Consumer Contracts' (2015) *European Law Journal* forthcoming.
[35] Council Directive 93/13/EEC of 5 April 1993 on unfair terms in consumer contracts [1993] OJ L95/29 (Unfair Contract Terms Directive).

enforcement, that is, of the judicial auction of the property. The consumer only has the possibility of influencing the distribution of the proceeds of enforcement or of claiming compensation. As a consequence, as Advocate General Kokott explained in her Opinion, even if the unfairness of a term in the loan agreement on which the mortgage was based were relied on vis-a-vis enforcement against the property, the consumer would not be able, under Spanish law, to prevent the judicial auction and the associated loss of ownership.[36] Once evicted, the consumer cannot recover ownership of his property and 'is limited to subsequent legal protection in the form of damages and … must accept the loss of his home'.[37] While neither the Advocate General nor the Court itself mentioned Article 8 ECHR (possibly in order to avoid troubled waters), the problem here—eviction and loss of a home—clearly has a human rights dimension and concerns the efficacy of Article 8 ECHR in private contractual relations.

The ECJ's First Chamber followed Advocate General Kokott's assessment that such a form of procedure impairs the effectiveness of the protection intended by the Directive 93/13: a mere claim for damages is not conducive to guaranteeing effectively the rights of the consumer conferred by that Directive, because it leaves the consumer defenceless in accepting the realisation of the mortgage and eviction. As the Court observed,

> it would thus be sufficient for sellers or suppliers … to initiate [simplified] mortgage proceedings so as to deprive consumers … of the protection of the Directive, that being so contrary to the Court's case-law, according to which the specific characteristics of court proceedings [under national law] cannot constitute a factor which is liable to affect the legal protection from which consumers must benefit under the provisions of that directive.[38]

The Court ruled that the principle of effectiveness requires that the national court hearing the declaratory proceedings has the possibility of staying the enforcement proceedings provisionally in order to stop enforcement until an assessment of the lawfulness of the contested term has taken place and thus of preventing enforcement creating facts to the detriment of the consumer which would be difficult or even impossible to reverse or rectify. But the Court did not legislate: it did not take the further step of ruling that the consumer must have the possibility to complain that terms are unfair directly in the enforcement proceedings, as a possible consequence of the previous *Banesto* ruling.[39]

Moreover, the Court clarified the concept of 'significant imbalance':[40] a comparative analysis is necessary: national courts must consider what rules of national law would apply in the absence of an agreement between the contracting parties: does the contract place the consumer in a legal situation less favourable than that provided for by the national law in force. In that respect, 'contrary to the requirement of good

---

[36] Case C-415/11 *Mohamed Aziz* (ECJ, 14 March 2013), Opinion of AG Kokott, para 50.
[37] ibid.
[38] ibid, para 62.
[39] Case C-618/10 *Banco Español de Crédito SA (Banesto) v Joaquín Calderón Camino* (ECJ, 14 June 2012).
[40] Case C-415/11 *Mohamed Aziz* (ECJ, 14 March 2013), paras 66 ff.

faith' means that national court must assess whether the seller or supplier, dealing fairly and equitably with the consumer, could reasonably assume that the consumer would have agreed to such a term in individual contract negotiations, also with an eye to the consequences of that term under the national legal system as a whole.[41]

So: an EU-wide understanding of principle gradually crystallises; and yet the Court creates a discursive space for experimentation with domestic private law systems with the aim of achieving congruence with the principle. Moreover, the parties to a bilateral consumer contract must themselves commit to the principles of fairness and reciprocity.

IV. CODA

In my remarks, I have struck a note of caution as regards proposals for a paradigm shift from democracy to a substantive conception of justice. Europeans today are deeply divided not only along the lines of cultural identity but also when it comes to the (applied) meaning of socio-economic justice. The requirement of congruence with a substantive ideal of justice, under those circumstances of constitutional decision making, would lead to blockade and directly feed into the democratic–sovereigntist objection.

But my note of caution is not motivated by agnosticism about socio-economic justice. Rather, I believe that for those who are committed to both—to the EU and to socio-economic justice—the more promising way forward is to concentrate on the task of creating and sustaining common democratic-discursive forums or frameworks within which citizens can carry out discussion about socio-economic justice and, concomitantly, on the question of what service EU law—and the ECJ, in particular—may render in support of this aim of bolstering and sustaining appropriate contexts of encounter and argumentative exchange between the various actors involved, regardless of whether private or public. Such contexts may arise, often as a matter of surprise, in virtually any domain 'directly or indirectly, actually or potentially'[42] affected by the EU, ranging from healthcare to mundane consumer contracts—and many other illustrations could be given. Of course, those forums and frameworks are themselves open to ongoing revision, as experience accumulates. The EU's Rule of Law based transformations suggest that, even in times of deep crisis, the EU can still be a model and test case for re-imagining democratic solidarity beyond the state under conditions of pervasive uncertainty and moral dissensus.

---

[41] ibid.
[42] Case 8/74 *Procureur du Roi v Benoît and Gustave Dassonville* [1974] ECR 837.

6
Justice as Europe's Signifier

SURYAPRATIM ROY[*]

I. INTRODUCTION

EUROPEAN COMMONALITY AND integration have been pursued through institutional rules and their interpretation, and not necessarily through justice. Rather, the agency of justice has been subsumed under such institutional *Diktat*, and does not have a language of its own. Such de-privileging of the agency of justice is also found in scholarly assessments of institutional acts, where categories such as democracy, procedure and welfare infuse meaning into justice. Sites of hermeneutic power such as institutions and scholarly work inevitably describe and explain justice by ascribing certain meanings to it at the cost of others, and it would be trivial to argue that the opportunity for justice to have many meanings should not be foreclosed. Instead, what is contended is that any attempt to understand or mete out institutional justice would necessarily be an exercise in self-legitimation. Thus, what would be preferable is to work towards mechanisms to give justice a voice, rather than define it in institutional terms.

It may seem odd to suggest that justice should have a voice of its own that is not directly attributable to institutions or people, but this is precisely what this chapter advocates. The conceptual basis for the suggestion that justice could have an agency of its own, but that such agency is pre-empted by sites of hermeneutic power is discussed in sections II and III respectively. As will be evident from these sections, this chapter relies primarily on critical social theory concerned with structures that shape normative discourse, and how such discourse in turn creates values and social relations in its own image. It is within this context that I seek to introduce the possibility of allowing a discourse of justice severable from other referents, which in turn would shape normative values and social relations. Section IV identifies the subsuming of justice under discursive categories inimical to the European legal order, namely 'just institutions' and democracy. Finally, given the fact that justice has to operate within the constraints of a legal framework, section V indicates some possibilities of how justice can shape the European institutional complex.

---

[*] I wish to thank the editors for their patience and guidance. I would also like to thank Gerard Delanty for his review and comments.

II. THE SIGNIFYING CAPACITY OF JUSTICE

Justice may mean different things,[1] it may be abused,[2] but it nonetheless seems integral to the human condition. The value of justice may not be dependent on its cognisance by a specific group of persons,[3] and such value is not necessarily attributed to a static point on the space–time continuum. The desire for justice or the pain of injustice could be more sensed than expressed, and may not be adequately captured in normative discourses on social and political life. One objection that could be anticipated is that given such multiplicity of meaning and feeling, justice cannot be separated from other values and perceptions such as fairness and pain, and hence could never have an identifiable language of its own. In fact, the descriptors of justice used here such as 'desire' or 'pain' or 'fairness' have their own sciences, are often fraught with disagreement, and any attempt to talk about them in this space and without relying on a sophisticated epistemology would be frivolous.

The response to this objection draws on Robert Cover's work on violence and language where he suggests that 'prolonged pain does not simply resist language but actively destroys it'.[4] The identification of injustice and the quest for justice could be the way to contest the arbitrary feeling of pain, and has the potential to translate such subjectivity into an identifiable language.[5] The ability of the language of justice to shape and give voice to subjective experience gives justice an agency of its own, which is not an empirical category in itself, but one which allows for articulation and assessment of empirical categories. More importantly, it would allow contestation of institutional decisions including the identification and categorisation of some facets of individual engagement that are considered to fall within the province of law.

The idea that the agency of justice is a discursive category draws on Pierre Bourdieu's idea that individuals operate in a *habitus*[6] which is constructed by the interaction of agency and structure, but where such *habitus* exists independent of—and shapes—individual human agency.[7] Such *habitus* also shapes the *doxa*, or

---

[1] J Waldron, *Law and Disagreement* (Oxford, Oxford University Press, 1999).

[2] As Nader observes: 'In national or transnational contexts of power, the ambiguities embraced by words like justice, injustice or human rights are often there for a purpose—the masking of imperial intent or power disparities that some might call recycled indirect rule'. L Nader, 'The Words We Use: Justice, Human Rights and the Sense of Injustice' in KM Clarke and M Goodale (eds), *Mirrors of Power: Law and Justice in the Post Cold-War Era* (Cambridge, Cambridge University Press, 2009).

[3] B Williams, 'Justice As a Virtue' in B Williams, *Moral Luck: Philosophical Papers 1973–1980* (Cambridge, Cambridge University Press, 1981).

[4] Cover draws on Elaine Scarry's work on the subjectivity of pain. RM Cover, 'Violence and the Word' (1986) 95 *Yale Law Journal* 1601, 1603.

[5] If I may refer to the Batman, his quest for justice arising out of the murder of his parents could be framed as a revenge fantasy, but it acquires moral weight when it is turned into a discourse on justice against oppressors on behalf of the oppressed. Thus, in Cover's terms, just punishment legitimates violence, ibid 1608. Different writers have played with this narrative to suggest that the Batman's butler Alfred secretly disguises himself as villains to keep his master happily cocooned in the moral illusion of his sense of justice (see N Gaiman and A Kubert, *Whatever Happened to the Caped Crusader?* (New York, NY, DC Comics, 2009) or the more popular trend that some of the Batman's villains such as the Joker exist in response to the Batman's oppressive sense of justice.

[6] For an introduction, see C Calhoun, '*Habitus*, Field of Power and Capital: The Question of Historical Specificity' in C Calhoun, *Critical Social Theory* (Oxford, Blackwell, 1995) 132–61.

[7] P Bourdieu and L Wacquant, *An Invitation to Reflexive Sociology* (Chicago, IL, University of Chicago Press, 1992).

the naturalised political language of understanding, debate and contestation.[8] The boundaries of the contestation of power are shaped through permissible ways of contestation; the disadvantaged are mired in hermeneutic injustice as they do not have a language or an epistemology to shape and contest normative structured reality.[9] Instilling a discourse to contest normative structured reality would be the first step.

A discourse to contest structured reality may not assist with the next step of assessing and doing justice. For this, we turn to David Miller who argues that peoples' intuitions and views on justice as well as appreciation of particular contexts are inevitably shaped by social arrangements and human relationships.[10] Thus, rather than trying to understand particular subjective views regarding justice, it would be better for an observer to identify underlying modes of relationships, and he identifies *solidaristic community* (such as family, clubs), *instrumental association* (such as economic relations) and *citizenship* as the basic modes.[11] The aim of a theory of justice is to understand such relationships and provide people with a 'conception of themselves' which does not mistake one relationship for another. Without endorsing Miller's identification of the modes of relationships, it is suggested that both the discourse of justice as well as tools of contestation could benefit from the endeavour to understand arrangements and relationships that shape discourse. However, Miller does not address how such modes interact and are balanced. I argue that institutional *doxa* performs such balancing, and privileges one interpretation over another to suit self-legitimation; what is proposed instead is allowing for a discourse which allows for contestation of such privileging. Notwithstanding its elusive, embedded and perhaps incommensurable nature, justice (and the redress of injustice) appears to be a distinct goal worth pursuing as an end in itself, with social artefacts designed to work towards this end, instead of the other way around.

Thus, justice could be characterised as a floating signifier, which informs organisational and institutional choices, and provides an avenue for contesting the violence contained in such choices.[12] Admittedly, a normative use of the linguistic notion

---

[8] *Doxa* is the manner in which 'every established order tends to produce ... the naturalisation of its own arbitrariness'. P Bourdieu, *Outline of a Theory of Practice* (Cambridge, Cambridge University Press, 1977). Relying on memetics, Balkin characterises the discursive independence of law as 'cultural software' which shapes the way people think and respond. He then proceeds to examine how justice could be separated from ideology in legal frameworks. J Balkin, *Cultural Software: A Theory of Ideology* (New Haven, CT, Yale University Press, 1997).

[9] M Fricker, *Epistemic Injustice: Power and the Ethics of Knowing* (Oxford, Oxford University Press, 2007) 147–75. Judith Butler critiques Bourdieu's conceptualisation of *habitus* and *doxa* as foreclosing the possibility of the 'subversive resignification' of 'authorised' political discourse. J Butler, 'Performativity's Social Magic' in R Shusterman (ed), *Bourdieu: A Critical Reader* (Oxford, Blackwell, 1999) 121–24.

[10] D Miller, *Principles of Social Justice* (Cambridge, MA, Harvard University Press, 1999) 25–26.

[11] ibid. It is important to avoid characterising such modes as properties of nation states, which would privilege the nation state as the appropriate site for achieving justice. Unfortunately, Miller himself has made this argument elsewhere, but there is no basis for viewing the nation state as the appropriate site for facilitating justice, or even fostering a culture of democratic self-determination based on dissent and respect for minorities. See S Benhabib, 'On European Citizenship: Replies to David Miller' (1998) 45 *Dissent* 107.

[12] The notion that contestation as a primary characteristic of justice finds support in Rainer Forst's work: 'I have defined justice as the human capacity to oppose relations of arbitrary rule or domination', R Forst, 'Transnational Justice and Democracy' (2011) *Normative Orders Working Papers* 04/2011, 8. The property of contestation is crucial to the characterisation of justice as a floating signifier; the content of the ambiguous force of justice can be hegemonised by fixed meanings attributed to it by power structures. The conceptualisation of justice put forward in this essay necessitates contesting and struggling with authoritative uses of justice.

of a floating signifier can provoke outrage, as it may convey the property of easy manipulability. However, drawing on the discursive use of a floating signifier as a site of struggle,[13] it is possible to characterise justice as a meaningful signifier that can rupture its ties with a particular signified referent and engage with other referents. I qualify such conceptualisation with the understanding that in an institutional context, decision making precludes the existence of a free-floating signifier. Thus, justice cannot emanate from an autonomous people but is necessarily influenced and shaped by institutional engagement. It is largely for this reason that any attempt to reduce justice to a one-sided discourse—either institutional or democratic–deliberative is difficult to accept. This does not mean that the agency of justice itself needs to be subsumed into the privileged articulation of a particular entity.

However, the agency of justice implicit in its capacity of being a signifier appears to be assumed away in the institutional discourse of the European Union, as well as in the work of some scholars engaged in interpreting and evaluating the functioning of such institutions. The explanation behind this may be historical; the collapsing of justice (and other values, expressions, aspirations) into the maintenance of collective order by way of a self-referential legal system legitimised Europe as a future promised land. But 'the decisional process of the Union'[14] can no longer be considered as Europe's legitimating factor.[15] In this chapter I argue that locating the agency of justice could be considered to be the way forward, instead of lapsing into the attribution of 'primacy to the national communities'.[16] Primacy may be accorded to an institution or community if justice is comparatively enhanced. But first, a discussion on how such assessment may be rendered impossible by foreclosing justice is warranted.

III. FORECLOSING JUSTICE BY INSTITUTIONAL SELF-LEGITIMATION

The European Court of Justice (ECJ) uses the term 'justice' sparingly in its discourse, and on the rare occasion it does, it uses the term as a rhetorical device to support functioning institutional processes. If we take for example its usage in *Köbler*, the Court observed:

> [I]n order to ensure stability of the law and legal relations, as well as the sound administration of justice, it is important that judicial decisions which have become definitive after all rights of appeal have been exhausted or after expiry of the time-limits provided to exercise those rights can no longer be called into question.[17]

Thus, justice is to be administered and it is *eiusdem generis* 'stability of the law and legal relations' as understood in the context of the EU. Again, in *Commission v*

---

[13] See E Laclau, 'Politics and the Limits of Modernity' in A Ross (ed), *Universal Abandon? The Politics of Postmodernism* (Edinburgh, Edinburgh University Press, 1989) 71.
[14] JHH Weiler, 'Europe in Crisis—On "Political Messianism", "Legitimacy" and the "Rule of Law"' [2012] *Singapore Journal of Legal Studies* 248, 267.
[15] ibid, 268.
[16] ibid.
[17] Case C-224/01 *Gerhard Köbler v Republik Österreich* [2003] ECR I-10239, para 38. This usage has been reiterated in Case C-234/04 *Rosmarie Kapferer v Schlank & Schick GmbH* [2006] ECR I-2585, para 20; Case C-2/08 *Amministrazione dell'Economia e delle Finanze and Agenzia delle entrate v Fallimento Olimpiclub Srl* [2009] ECR I-7501, para 22.

Council—where the Commission sought annulment of the Council's move to require Member States to enforce penalties for environmental offences—the Court held that 'the application of the criminal law and the administration of justice'[18] by Member States guaranteed under Articles 135 and 280(4) of the Treaty on the Functioning of the European Union (TFEU)[19] do not pre-empt harmonisation of criminal law for the implementation of environmental policy. In instances where 'administration of justice' is not the reference point for its usage, it is used with regard to procedural issues such as defining the parameters of direct action or 'access to justice'.[20] Deferring justice to other institutional coordinates is borne out in the speech-acts of other EU institutions as well. As Sionaidh Douglas-Scott observes in her contribution to this volume, the EU's 'Area of Freedom, Security and Justice' betrays 'a dominant emphasis on security at the expense of justice and the protection of rights'.[21] It may appear that 'justice' is used as an empty category in these instances, but given that the language of justice is used to legitimise institutional stability and acts such as the administration of security, it clearly acquires significance though its discursive instrumentality. Thus, as far as the EU is concerned, justice appears to be an empty signifier tethered to the self-justifying referent of institutional stability. I refer to this interpretative tactic as a tautological *institutional self-legitimation mechanism*. While the hermeneutic tendency towards institutional self-legitimation is not a novel discovery,[22] I seek to argue that the agency of justice is corrupted as a tool of institutional self-legitimation through justification.

One might argue that just because EU institutions use the term justice in a certain way, it does not mean that they do not *do* justice in other ways, or approach it in an indirect fashion. For example, it could be argued that the interpretative space provided by proportionality and subsidiarity are mechanisms of doing justice. The discourse on justice therefore falls into the scholarly assessment of whether EU institutions do justice, such as in some of the papers compiled in this volume. For instance, Jürgen Neyer's conceptualisation of justice as a right to justification allows justice to be susceptible to institutional meaning, which may preclude any other standards of assessment, including whether the internalised fairness (if at all) is amenable to any mechanism of validation. While Neyer's plea for assessing institutional legitimacy against the yardstick of justice is truly commendable, his conceptualisation provides a way for the institutional self-justification mechanism to be reinforced in scholarly discourse.

Even when scholars critique institutional self-justification, they nonetheless endorse a certain signified referent at the cost of others, which appears to perform an analogous mechanism of hermeneutic self-legitimation. It appears that in order

---

[18] Case C-176/03 *Commission of the European Communities v Council of the European Union* [2005] ECR I-7879.
[19] Consolidated version of the Treaty on the Functioning of the European Union [2012] OJ C326/47 (TFEU).
[20] Case C-50/00 P *Unión de Pequeños Agricultores v Council of the European Union* [2002] ECR I-6677. This boilerplate phrase in ECJ discourse glosses over forms of access *as* justice. P Fitzpatrick, 'Access As Justice' (2005) 23 *Windsor Yearbook of Access to Justice* 3.
[21] S Douglas-Scott, 'Justice, Injustice and the Rule of Law in the EU', in this volume, 51, at 53.
[22] See, eg, J Derrida, 'The Force of Law: The Mystical Foundation of Authority' (1990) 11 *Cardozo Law Review* 919.

to establish the contestability of justice, reliance has been placed on pre-determined theoretical categories such as the 'social', the 'highly competitive market', and even democracy within which the sites, means and even the fact of contestation are captured. Even in Danny Nicol's compelling contribution, this is the descriptive leap— the identification of democracy, characterised as Member State political preferences, to serve as the signified referent. To support the claim that justice is pre-eminently contestable and hence subject to debate, he identifies Member State politics as the signified referent against which such debate should take place, and thereby precludes a thick concept of democracy, or any other referent. While addressing the issue of 'whose justice' appears to be intuitively necessary, inviting and reviewing applications for a suitable definition of a thick concept of democracy appears to be a flawed endeavour, as any chosen model would inevitably determine who[23] or what (if we were to consider the claims on behalf of the biotic community) loses out.

The alternative appears to be to allow justice to be a free-floating signifier, in a Derridean indefinite referral system, where 'there is no transcendental or privileged signified and ... the domain or play of signification henceforth has no limit'.[24] This would, therefore, allow justice to be defined in spatial terms,[25] or in relation to the future (in inter-generational terms which legitimises the spatial reach of EU climate change policy).[26] Unfortunately for the purpose of this volume (and I suspect many others that address institutional or collective decision making), the possibilities of conceptualising justice are limited to their operationalisation by institutions within Europe. And the reconciliation of multiple narratives of justice with the requirement to instil ordered relations would mean the necessity to commit violence upon some concepts, peoples, selves, things. More importantly, it limits justice to a distinct discursive expression, and precludes any other way of appreciating justice. Thus, the process of operationalising justice within institutional constraints would lead to some notion or the other of a justice deficit. The same applies to scholarly assessment, where exacting ontological preferences would find any expression of institutional justice inadequate.

Some analytical relief can be found in Amartya Sen's work, following which justice should not be *measured up to* something 'transcendental', but always *measured against* in a comparative way. In the context of the EU, that would mean that there is a justice deficit only if the EU does not compare favourably against other institutions across spatial boundaries, or possible alternative institutional arrangements. It could also provide an accessible space for a self-defined unit of democracy to contest the meting out of institutional justice over time. This provides opportunities for the identification and resolution of structural institutional injustice such as the systemic

---

[23] For instance, there is no space for the disabled in Rawls' theory of justice. E Anderson, 'Justifying the Capabilities Approach to Justice' in H Brighouse and I Robeyns (eds), *Measuring Justice: Primary Goods and Capabilities* (Cambridge, Cambridge University Press, 2010).

[24] J Derrida, 'Structure, Sign and Play in the Discourse of the Human Sciences' reprinted in P Rice and P Waugh (eds), *Modern Literary Theory: A Reader* (London, Arnold, 1990).

[25] See A Layard, 'Freedom of Expression and Spatial (Imaginations of) Justice' in this volume, 417.

[26] See J Scott, 'The Justice Dimension of the EU's Climate Change Unilateralism' in G de Búrca, D Kochenov and A Williams (eds), *Debating Europe's Justice Deficit: The EU, Swabian Housewives, Rawls and Ryanair* (2013) EUI Working Papers LAW 2013/11.

problem of the financial sector in the EU. Rather than succumbing to the temptation of archaic legal ways of redress such as punishing individual instances of villainy or confining one's readings to where the problem fits into hermeneutic categories such as social rights or the free market, a better referent for justice would be the externalities that are not taken into account by actors operating in the field of finance.[27]

The undertaking of such comparative analysis could be identified as a qualified step towards meaningfully assessing justice in the EU. I say qualified because there is always a referent (or a combination of weighted[28] referents), and Sen's method of identifying referents against which justice is assessed is the Capabilities Approach, which is susceptible to the self-legitimating interpretative trap.[29] In this chapter, I cannot offer a predominant signified referent that can replace procedural coherence or democracy, but only suggest that there are institutional and hermeneutic moderators that lead to such signification. I could, however, complete the image of the floating signifier by filling in a missing piece: endorsing the tethers by which signified referents are attributed to the signifier is the hermeneutic step taken by institutions and scholars in their interpretative capacity. Various strands in social science research concentrate on identifying mediators and moderators to understand factors that influence correlations between variables.[30] Critical theory provides a complementary approach in understanding epistemic privilege, expert methods and ideological preferences which guide the selection of such mediators and moderators. Thus, the interrogation of *power* mediates critical interpretation,[31] which makes its moderation integral to any reflexive discourse.

IV. FORECLOSING JUSTICE THROUGH PRIVILEGED REFERENTS

A. 'Justified Structures of Justification' as Referent

Neyer explains that his conception of justice as a right to justification 'does not praise structures of justification as such' but requires 'fully justified structures of justification'.[32] As to what such justified structures are, he offers: 'inclusive and

---

[27] See M Kumm, 'The Case of Banks and the Financial Transaction Tax in the EU' in G de Búrca, D Kochenov and A Williams (eds), *Debating Europe's Justice Deficit: The EU, Swabian Housewives, Rawls and Ryanair* (2013) *EUI Working Papers* LAW 2013/11. Individual debtor rights and consumer rights are insufficient or perpetuated by the *doxa* of the financial field, which requires the field of finance as such to be considered as a referent. L Coco, 'Debtor's Prison in the Neoliberal State' (2012) 49 *California Western Law Review* 1.

[28] Martijn Boot argues that there are always factors which are inevitably weighted differently in the assessment of justice. M Boot, 'The Aim of a Theory of Justice' (2012) 15 *Ethical Theory and Moral Practice* 7.

[29] Eg the Capabilities Approach does not provide space to assess whether institutional intervention to improve capabilities actually leads to better functioning. See J Wolff and A De-Shalit, *Disadvantage* (Oxford, Oxford University Press, 2007) 37.

[30] For an overview, see AD Wu and BD Zumbo, 'Understanding and Using Mediators and Moderators' (2008) 87 *Social Indicators Research* 367.

[31] Iris Young identifies 'four parameters agents can use for reasoning about their actions and those of others in relation to collective action to redress injustice: *power, privilege, interest* and *collective ability*'. IM Young, *Responsibility for Justice* (Oxford, Oxford University Press, 2011) 144–51.

[32] J Neyer, 'Who Is Afraid of Justice? A Rejoinder to Danny Nicol' (2012) 50 *Journal of Common Market Studies* 523.

efficient procedures for adapting constitutional norms to changing governmental and non-governmental preferences'.[33] He further argues that the promotion of 'second-order values such as transparency, participation, accountability or effectiveness'[34] would lead to greater 'political contestation', which would in turn give effect to the right to justification. By way of 'institutional innovation', he suggests empowering the Conference of Community and European Affairs Committees of Parliaments of the European Union to increase national parliamentary roles in the political process. What is evident in Neyer's conceptualisation is that institutional reform and endorsement of formal principles of administrative or public law is the way to ensure justification, and thereby do justice.

It would be rather simplistic to problematise the purely procedural justice/substantive justice binary, and critique the above plea for reforming political institutions as not being in the service of any outcome. Neyer, infact, explicitly argues against state-centric democratic values ('monopoly of coercion, a shared political culture, a nationwide media')[35] from informing outcomes. Further, at the cost of reading too much into the article, it appears that he does have an outcome in mind—the protection of individual liberty. If all individuals in the EU have access to an institutional framework to contest an imposition of coercion or state violence, then justice would be done. Following this framework, the *fact* that any infringement of liberty needs to be justified by virtue of a proportionality test, or the space provided to 'individual concern' to claim exemption from an EU policy would by themselves imply the operation of justified structures, irrespective of the *interpretative techniques* that accompany the usage of such tools of justification. Take the proportionality principle for example. While the fact of endorsing this principle may reflect a move towards a 'culture of justification', its usage may be in the service of values such as efficiency, and privilege the mathematical exercise of balancing over protecting the incommensurable nature of human dignity.[36] Picking up on this, it is suggested that concentrating on developing just procedures *may result in values being made instrumental to the articulation of such structures*; where all claims to justice would serve the justification of the expressive capacity of such institutions or structures.[37]

To illustrate the limits of restricting justice to justificatory structures and processes, consider the *PI* case,[38] where the issue of sexual assault and rape of a minor by an Italian national permanently residing in Germany was considered by Advocate General Bot to be an indication of insufficient integration into German society, thus meriting deportation from Germany to Italy. As Dimitry Kochenov argues, '[t]he implication of this view is that Germans do not rape their daughters,

---

[33] ibid, 524.
[34] ibid, 527.
[35] ibid.
[36] See S Tsakyrakis, 'Disproportionate Individualism' in this volume, 235.
[37] This prompts the view that if justice is restricted to procedural justice, then outcomes need to be assessed by values other than justice. E Ceva, 'Beyond Legitimacy: Can Proceduralism Say Anything Relevant About Justice?' (2012) 15 *Critical Review of International, Social and Political Philosophy* 183.
[38] Case C-348/09 *PI v Oberbürgermeisterin der Stadt Remscheid* [2012] ECR 1-6355.

but Italians residing in Germany do'.[39] The ECJ did not subscribe to this view, but upheld the deportation on 'imperative grounds of public security', thus interpreting a criminal act in the light of a territoriality signifier. Neyer's framework thankfully would not give space to Advocate General Bot's arguments as a way of doing justice, as it relies on the identification of Member State democratic values. However, the ECJ's collapsing of the wall between a criminal act towards one individual and public security using a free movement paradigm could be considered to fall within a justificatory process, and Mr I's right to justification could be deemed to be exhausted once such reasoning has been institutionally undertaken, even if residence security has been collapsed into public security via an interpretative sleight of hand.

It may appear from the above that the inevitability of interpretation by way of a review process renders 'perfectly just structures' vulnerable to privileged meanings. I would argue that this interpretative space is actually the more contestable component, or the justificatory component of 'justified structures of justification'. Comparing the interpretative space offered by EU courts to, say, the reasoning employed by French administrative courts in deportation cases, it is at least possible to assess the soundness of violence by the former.[40] Institutional decisions which are foreclosed from meaningful ex post-facto assessment because they are the products of an allegedly perfectly transparent, accountable, expert system are yet more problematic, as such values can be operationalised only in institutional terms. The tendency of public law to consider expert decisions as just does not acknowledge that all institutional decisions are ultimately interpretative, and prone to self-justification. Theoretically, this could be because all institutions could be construed to be Frankenstein's monsters (much like those responsible for managing public companies), or a sum of privileged parts. Ironically—as an exploration of the working of the European Commission has demonstrated[41]—limiting justice to the construction of just institutions reinforces statist interests through elite agents who constitute such institutions, rather than moderate such interests. To put it briefly, justification, debate and transparency are clearly important components of institutional structure, but the language and rules of such debate are inevitably institutionally determined. Thus, while Neyer highlights the importance of contestation, my concern is more how *the parameters of contestability cannot make such contestation meaningful*.

Moreover, restricting justice to just processes does not provide a framework for negotiating structural injustice, or instilling a framework for operationalising collective responsibility. In instances where scholars have found shifts in structural justice in the European legal order to be promising, such as the European Court of Human Right's gradual consideration of Holocaust cases,[42] 'just processes' have limited explanatory power. Confining justice to just processes furthers the leeway

---

[39] For a critique of AG Bot's as well as the ECJ's reasoning, see D Kochenov and B Pirker, 'Deporting the Citizens Within the European Union: A Counter-Intuitive Trend' (2013) 19 *Columbia Journal of European Law* 369, 385–86.

[40] M Cohen, 'Reason-Giving in Court Practice: Decision-makers at the Crossroads' (2008) 14 *Columbia Journal of European Law* 77.

[41] L Hooghe, 'Images of Europe: How Commission Officials Conceive Their Institution's Role' (2012) 50 *Journal of Common Market Studies* 87.

[42] See C Lyons, 'Just Fatherlands? The Shoah in the Jurisprudence of Strasbourg' in this volume, 381.

provided to institutions to assume away any structural injustice that may not surface in individual instances of challenging institutional coercion.[43] It does not, for example, address the concern that the periphery of the EU as a whole[44] is unjustly poised, and European law reinforces the specific claims of the centre. Lest it appears that the example of structural justice for Europe's periphery implies a privileging of democracy as the signified referent for justice, we now turn to democracy.

B. Democracy as Referent

Rainer Forst's disagreement with Neyer rests primarily on his view that justice involves contestation, and for that justification needs to be a truly discursive practice. This discursiveness is ensured through democracy:

> [T]his praxis is what we mean by democracy: those who are subject to norms should also be the authority which justifies these very norms—as active subjects of justification and not just in mente or in proxy or in expert discourses.[45]

With regard to the requirement of contestability as a facet of the agency of justice, this view is in conformity with the spirit of this essay. However, while operationalising this view, European institutions as well as scholars are prone to defining 'those who are subject to norms' restrictively, and usually as political collectives operating within the narrative of nation states. Danny Nicol, for instance, argues that justice cannot be separated from democracy, where democracy is conceptualised in terms of the preferences of political parties, and other collectives which characterise the politics of nation states.[46] Any conceptualisation of democracy including notions such as 'those' or 'peoples' is necessarily embroiled in the politics of representation, and categories identified to capture democracy would themselves restrict meaningful contestation. Within the framework of EU law, this is particularly problematic as there is no space for contesting decisions through self-defined collectives, such as class action lawsuits. Even individual concerns are currently voiced through the mouths of Member State courts.[47]

Restricting the tools of discursive contestation is evident in the *Viking*[48] and *Laval*[49] decisions, as well as in Nicol's critique where the plight of workers becomes a story about economic versus social rights, and the need to protect Member States' democratic agency. As Kukovec has argued, such discussion silences the structural

---

[43] K Ehremberg, 'Procedural Justice and Information in Conflict-Resolving Institutions' (2003) 67 *Albany Law Review* 167.
[44] See D Kukovec, 'Taking Change Seriously: The Rhetoric of Justice and the Reproduction of the Status Quo' in this volume, 319.
[45] R Forst, 'Transnational Justice and Democracy' (2011) *Normative Orders Working Papers* 04/2011, 10.
[46] D Nicol, 'Can Justice Dethrone Democracy in the European Union? A Reply to Jürgen Neyer' (2012) 50 *Journal of Common Market Studies* 508.
[47] Weiler, 'Europe in Crisis', n 14 above, 266.
[48] C-438/05 *The International Transport Workers' Federation and The Finnish Seamen's Union* [2007] ECR I-10779.
[49] C-341/05 *Laval un Partneri Ltd v Svenska Byggnadsarbetareförbundet and Others* [2007] ECR I-11767.

centre–periphery problem[50] which the EU faces by equating the condition (or, in Forst's terms, the discursive capacity) of a worker in Finland, Estonia, Sweden, Latvia. While it may be unclear why privileging the concerns of the periphery as a democratic unit should be the preferred method of doing justice in the EU, Kukovec indicates that hermeneutic power may be the reason: 'Because the periphery's social claims, just as free movement claims are structurally weak, progressive politics from the periphery is disabled ... the strong social claims are the existing specific claims of the centre and they run counter to the weak or invisible social claim of the periphery'.[51] Once the under-privileging of the interests of a collective unit of peoples is identified as the problem, rather than defining the unit itself, then it would be possible to do justice for such a signified unit using hermeneutic power as the mediator. This structural violence clearly manifests in several fields of decision making such as the structural financialisation[52] of the Eurozone. The failure of the ruling elite in Greece to manage funds cannot be discounted, but the theory and practice of financialisation in the Eurozone have systematically affected the productive structure of the periphery countries.[53] The category of the periphery as a solidaristic community (to refer to Miller's framework discussed earlier) serves as a more compelling referent than economic relations (or instrumental association) in a justice discourse. Notwithstanding, such a referent may be inappropriate for understanding claims arising out of European citizenship, which may be distorted by ruling elites in periphery countries.

It is primarily because of the politics of defining the contours of democracy and then using this restricted notion to legitimise or contest just decisions that I am sceptical about democracy being the predominant signified referent. Descriptively, although infinite democratic contestation seems appealing, it does not appear to be an unmediated informant of justice in Europe. At its core, if democracy is to reflect human nature, it should incorporate individual and collective tendencies to brutalise, based on the self-justifying moral outrage of violently asserting territoriality and righteous purity. Relying on the ideas of Giambattista Vico, Lief Carter observes:

> No foundational standards exist by which to demonstrate that institutions built on moral principles of justice and human rights are in any way more truthful or accurate than are the institutions built upon religious or ideological fundamentalism or the amoral institutions of competitive play. Only the pragmatic question remains: which institutions in practice seem more likely to reduce the frequency of human brutality?[54]

---

[50] D Kukovec, 'A Critique of the Rhetoric of Common Interest in the European Union Legal Discourse' (13 April 2012) *IGLP Working Papers*, www.harvardiglp.org/new-thinking-new-writing/a-critique-of-rhetoric/.

[51] ibid, 8.

[52] A recent review of the concepts and practices that inform the structural process of financialisation can be found in N van der Zwan, 'Making Sense of Financialization' (2014) 12 *Socio-Economic Review* 99. For an account of how finacialisation moderates the regulatory appreciation of credit risk in the EU, see G Mennillo and S Roy, 'Ratings and Regulation: A Case of an Irreversible Marriage?' (2014) *Harvard Weatherhead Center for International Affairs Working Paper* 04/2014.

[53] VK Fouskas and C Dimoulas, *Greece, Financialisation and the EU: The Political Economy of Debt and Destruction* (Basingstoke, Palgrave Macmillan, 2013).

[54] LH Carter, 'Law and Politics As Play' (2008) 83 *Chicago–Kent Law Review* 1333, 1342.

While characterising justice as a 'moral principle' akin to human rights is problematic, Carter's observation is instructive as relying on the truth of democracy or human expression may require allowing for human brutality. Thus, justice would not necessarily mean giving space to the expressive capacity of peoples or all persons within a people,[55] but on the capacity to assess and contest the privileging of one expression over another.

V. INSTITUTIONAL VIOLENCE AND THE INDIVIDUAL

A. The Market as Europe's Signifier

Following Weiler[56] and Williams,[57] Europe appears to have a justice deficit because in the post-messianic phase, there is no convincing myth or ethos to legitimate the idea of Europe. In the previous section, it was shown that justice could be subsumed into institutional categories, and given that all speech-acts are interpretative in nature, this need not necessarily be the case. It is now opportune to ask—what should be the case? While I hesitate to adopt Weiler's prescription of falling back on national institutions,[58] primarily because it is not clear in which sphere of life national law would be a comparatively more legitimate form of violence, his view that the development of European law has led to 'the placing of the individual at the centre of political attention',[59] and the pros and cons that go with it could indicate the way forward.

In several instances of the European legal order we are faced with situations where the individual is at the centre of attention, but individual voice (either operating individually or through a self-defined collective) is subsumed into other interests, or operates as an agent of adaptive expressions. This happens primarily by tethering individual liberty to the EU discourse of the Internal Market as the primary signifier of the European polity.

The development of case-law and literature on citizenship appear to be attempts to interpretatively free the EU citizen from being defined by the market, and concentrate instead on other referents, such as family unification and the best interests of the child. For this purpose, the ECJ has worked towards broadening the available hermeneutic space by inclusively interpreting the material scope of European law by formulating unwritten rights of citizenship.[60] Using law to contest national and EU rules that abridge the subjective facets of an individual's life could be viewed as a

---

[55] But see G Davies, 'Social Legitimacy and Purposive Power: The End, the Means, and the Consent of the People' in this volume, pp 259.
[56] Weiler, 'Europe in Crisis', n 14 above.
[57] A Williams, *The Ethos of Europe: Values, Law and Justice in the EU* (Cambridge, Cambridge University Press, 2010).
[58] Weiler, 'Europe in Crisis', n 14 above, 268.
[59] ibid, 267.
[60] See Case C-34/09 *Gerardo Ruiz Zambrano v Office national de l'emploi (ONEm)* [2011] ECR I-1177. See D Kochenov and R Plender, 'EU Citizenship: From an Incipient Form to an Incipient Substance?' (2012) 37 *European Law Review* 369.

form of justice superior to another embedded in a situation which does not provide this hermeneutic space. However, the functioning of a citizen seems tethered to the self-realisation of a state-rooted market citizenship through the interpretative uncertainty found in the 'essence of rights' doctrine.[61] This is evident from *McCarthy*,[62] *Dereci*[63] and *Alokpa*[64] where the privileged referents of self-sufficiency and economic participation have pre-empted the operation of other referents, and the lack of interpretative clarity regarding the scope of EU law have reinforced the limited sphere of contesting the state-defined boundaries of who can be accepted as a citizen.

Any qualification of the absolute right to stay anywhere in the EU or the identification of persons as EU subjects by virtue of their ability to participate in an economic activity (as was the case with Mrs McCarthy whose dependence on state benefits was highlighted by Advocate General Kokott[65] and the ECJ judgment, but her status as the full-time carer of her disabled child was conveniently ignored when effectively requiring her to move to another state to be with her husband)[66] imposes on them a responsibility to perform such activities. Prima facie such responsibility to move or perform an economic activity is a violently restrictive notion of liberty.[67] Once such reasoning and selective appreciation of facts are probed a little, it becomes clear that the tether with which the individual is attached to the free market is economic responsibility, and unembedded rational participation (rather than the dignity of a natural person) informs this tether. It may serve us well to keep in mind Iris Young's assessment: 'We lack good conceptual tools for thinking about individual responsibility in relation to structural social processes'.[68]

Further, given that the freedom to choose the 'good life' by moving is not necessarily appreciated by and transformative for all EU citizens,[69] it would be presumptuous to conclude that those who do not move even when this freedom exists do so out of choice, and factors such as lack of information or transparency can hardly be identified as the reason why this is so. Generally speaking, in relation to movement, there is little scope for comparative assessment of the violence committed by collective enterprises that shape education, work and other aspects of life, and

---

[61] 'Market citizenship' does however provide the interpretative space to give leeway to other constitutional principles should the Court choose to do so. N Nic Shiubhne, 'The Resilience of EU Market Citizenship' (2010) 47 *Common Market Law Review* 1597.

[62] Case C-434/09 *Shirley McCarthy v Secretary of State for the Home Department* [2011] ECR I-3375.

[63] Case C-256/11 *Murat Dereci and Others v Bundesministerium für Inneres* [2011] ECR I-1131.

[64] Case C-86/12 *Adzo Domenyo Alokpa and Others v Ministre du Travail, de l'Emploi et de l'Immigration* [2012] (ECJ, 10 October 2013).

[65] Case C-434/09 *McCarthy* [2011] ECR I-3375, Opinion of AG Kokott.

[66] See N Nic Shiubhne, '(Some of) the Kids are Alright: Comment on McCarthy and Dereci' (2012) 49 *Common Market Law Review* 349, 370.

[67] Somek argues that the rhetoric of empowerment of people in the Union cannot lead to emancipation owing to 'subordination to the imperatives of economic performance'. A Somek, 'Europe: From Emancipation to Empowerment' (2013) *LSE Europe in Question Discussion Papers* 60/2013, 9.

[68] Young, *Responsibility for Justice*, n 31 above.

[69] The profiles of those who move indicate the limited transformative potential of free movement on different migrant groups in Member States. N Fligstein, *Euro-Clash: The EU, European Identity and the Future of Europe* (Oxford, Oxford University Press, 2010).

the hermeneutic space offered by happiness and the Capability Approach inspired human development indices can be of little service.[70]

B. The Inverted Monism of Institutional Violence

The above discussion demonstrates that some amount of institutional engagement appears to be necessary even if it is in the pursuit of individual liberty. As such engagement would inevitably entail the making of violent choices to achieve functionality, how do we proceed in conceiving legitimate forms of contestation? To move forward, we could take a step back and turn to Rawls' suggestion of a dualistic notion of justice—one that governs institutional design, and another that governs 'individuals and their actions in particular circumstances'.[71] Liam Murphy has argued that there is no strong argument to support this dualism, given that the normative principles that guide political institutions are derived from those that inform individual choice and conduct.[72] What is happening in the EU could be said to be an inverse of the monism which Murphy advocates—that is, instead of principles of justice arising from people's choices and conduct which can inform institutions, it is justice arising out of institutional operation that are applied to people. The first step is to interpretatively work against this inverted monism, and decluster referents and tethers that inform the characteristics of inversion. This would also indicate whether there is a need for institutional reform. The second step would be to examine whether the sacrificing of the expressive capacity of individuals is warranted in those areas of life where institutional violence is comparatively functional; in areas such as public health, environment and urban planning, decisions in 'public interest' do not compromise dignity, and hence deference to institutional decision-making may be warranted.[73]

To extend the argument for division of labour further, it is suggested that institutional violence may be legitimate when *firstly*, an individual through a deliberative process sacrifices choice-making in certain areas to concentrate instead on things that matter (drawing on Miller's endeavour to clarify misconceptions regarding different modes of engagement,[74] and work towards a meaningful 'reflective equilibrium'[75]); *second*, the paternalism of institutional violence is superior to other forms of collective violence;[76] and *third*, there are avenues for contestation to take into account systemic and unforeseen issues where deliberation may have been of little assistance.

---

[70] John Gardner explains that the reason why Sen's concentration on public action ends at capabilities rather than achieved functionings is because the capabilities approach is restricted to the '"central issue ... of the freedom to choose how to live"'. This concentration on personal autonomy, per Gardner, leads to a 'systematic privileging of one [capability] over the other [achievement]' and leads him to the conclusion that 'people should be free to choose in Sen's sense (and I agree that they should) does not entail, nor even suggest, that we should be less interested in sorting out their plight when they make the wrong choice'. J Gardner, 'Amartya Sen's *The Idea of Justice*' (2011) 6 *Journal of Law, Philosophy and Culture* 241, 245–46.
[71] J Rawls, *A Theory of Justice* (Cambridge, MA, Harvard University Press, 1971) 54–55.
[72] LB Murphy, 'Institutions and the Demands of Justice' (1998) 27 *Philosophy & Public Affairs* 251.
[73] See Stavros Tsakyrakis' contribution to this volume.
[74] Miller, *Principles of Social Justice*, n 10 above.
[75] Rawls, *A Theory of Justice*, n 70 above, 46–53.
[76] As Sunstein and Thaler argue, non-institutional fetters on freedom of choice are inevitable. C Sunstein and R Thaler, 'Libertarian Paternalism Is Not an Oxymoron' (2003) 70 *University of Chicago Law Review* 1159, fn 11.

By way of an illustration, let us consider the issue of climate change. Having the technologies to assess future harm, and the fact that individuals' (or other self-defined collectives') subjective legitimation may not offer a comparatively superior key to functioning, this is an area where the EU could design its legal and political architecture. While expert determination of the science behind climate change may be a legitimate reason for restricting contestation of climate policy,[77] the ways of combating climate change[78] and their effect on different parties is surely a space which should not be foreclosed by deferring to executive action. The utilisation of expert information for privileged gains should certainly be subject to contestation.[79] For example, scholarly assessments of the relationship between consumers and climate change in the EU provide no space for the mechanisms of consumer law to contest greenwashing[80] or similar problems, but rather defer to product regulations which the 'empowered' and informed consumer should be able to discern for herself in the marketplace.[81] This is why in matters where the decisions of the ECJ seem progressive—such as the requirement of EU companies which profit from the EU Emissions Trading Scheme (ETS) to participate in it,[82] or the requirement of foreign airlines to join the EU in combating climate change[83] by constructively thinking about Common But Differentiated Responsibility (CBDR)[84]—there is a mistrust in the self-legitimation of the EU carried out in its restrictive interpretative space, either by keeping the EU ETS free from challenge, or by not explicitly addressing self-interest in energy security in the EU's external climate change policy.[85]

---

[77] In common law jurisdictions, even this has been subject to challenge. See *New Zealand Climate Science Education Trust v National Institute of Water and Atmospheric Research Limited* [2012] NZHC 2297 (7 September 2012); also discussed in the landmark *Massachusetts v Environment Protection Agency* 549 US 497 (2 April 2007).

[78] Due to lack of standing in Europe, a private party cannot really institutionally contest climate policy. Given the litigation space accorded by adversarial legalism in America, various aspects of climate policy have been challenged. See *Association of Irritated Residents v California Air Resources Board* No A132165 (Cal App, 1st Dist, 19 June 2012) for the basis of challenging executive policy regarding a cap-and-trade scheme.

[79] See, eg, the greenwash challenge in Australia. *Australian Competition and Consumer Commission v GM Holden Ltd* [2008] FCA 1428 (18 September 2008).

[80] Greenwashing has been defined differently based on the theories which inform such definitions, but one way of understanding it is the legitimation of commercial activity by providing an environmental gloss. See MF Maniates, 'Individualization: Plant a Tree, Buy a Bike, Save the World?' (2001) 1 *Global Environmental Politics* 3.

[81] Scholarly accounts on the relationship between consumer law and climate change usually focus on climate policy design sans an appreciation of the values that mediate the legal understanding of a consumer, and do not provide guidance as to whether the principles of consumer law offer mechanisms to contest climate-friendly claims made by private parties. See for instance, J de Cendra de Larragán, 'EU Climate Change Law and Consumers' in C Verdure (ed), *Environmental Law and Consumer Protection* (Brussels, Larcier, 2011).

[82] Case T-16/04 *Arcelor v European Parliament and Council of the European Union* [2004] ECR II-211.

[83] Case C-366/10 *Air Transport Association of America and Others v Secretary of State for Energy and Climate Change* [2011] ECR I-13755.

[84] See J Scott, 'The Justice Dimension of the EU's Climate Change Unilateralism' in G de Búrca, D Kochenov and A Williams (eds), *Debating Europe's Justice Deficit: The EU, Swabian Housewives, Rawls and Ryanair* (2013) EUI Working Papers LAW 2013/11, 52–53.

[85] See A Boute, 'The EU's Shaping of an International Law on Energy Efficiency' in F Amtenbrink and D Kochenov (eds), *The European Union's Shaping of the International Legal Order* (Cambridge, Cambridge University Press, 2013).

It is also clear that climate change is not the only referent if we were to consider the pursuit of justice (the EU has conveniently labelled climate change as an environmental issue, which leaves even less room for hermeneutic contestation), but can be declustered into various referents (options considered in formulating executive policy, comparative impacts of policies on different stakeholders, information asymmetry for individuals, precautionary principle, to name a few) and can contribute to developing a more contestable interpretative space. Further, given the role individual and collective action can play in contesting such policies, there is scope for finally reforming access to judicial review in the EU.[86] On the issue of access, there has recently been interest at the European level in encouraging collective redress mechanisms for competition and consumer issues (with consumer welfare tethered to 'drive[ing] competition and innovation';[87] another example of inverted monism). The Commission has been careful to point out such mechanisms are not the same as class action suits.[88] Thus, while articulation of interests of a self-defined collective is not encouraged for any other instance of European law, it is for a signified competition–consumer hybrid. This in effect means that there is no collective redress facilitated in those areas of human engagement where choice making has not been deferred to institutional capability. I do not seek to argue that American litigiousness may necessarily be the way to achieve justice in the European legal order, but only that providing space for greater contestation of institutional decisions may allow claims of justice and injustice to come to the fore, and force an expansion in the hermeneutics of administrative action.

C. Tethering Justice

'The otherness of the other', writes Costas Douzinas, 'means that she is never really present to me; I can approach her only by analogy of the perceptions, intentions and actions available to my own consciousness'.[89] The process of *othering* is most profound where 'the other' is accommodated through tolerance. Slavoj Žižek laments that unlike sixteenth-century Turkey where he finds that no one was forced to live like a Turk,[90] in today's Europe, 'the other is welcomed insofar as its presence is not intrusive, insofar as it is not really the other ... my duty to be tolerant towards the other effectively means that I should respect his intolerance towards my overproximity'.[91] Determining the bounds of proximity is a matter of perspective, and could well be perceived as injustice according to subjective points of view, and it may be argued that the negotiation of tolerance may best not be interfered with.

---

[86] LW Gormley, 'Judicial Review: Advice for the Deaf?' (2005) 29 *Fordham International Law Journal* 655.

[87] European Commission, 'Press Release: Commission recommends Member States to have collective redress mechanisms in place to ensure effective access to justice' (Strasbourg, 11 June 2013). For the tethering of consumer issues to principles of competition, see European Commission, 'Commission Staff Working Paper. Consumer Empowerment in the EU' SEC(2011) 469.

[88] European Commission, 'Press Release', n 86 above.

[89] C Douzinas, 'Violence, Justice, Deconstruction' (2005) 6 *German Law Journal* 171, 177.

[90] S Žižek, 'Against Human Rights' (2005) 34 *New Left Review* 115.

[91] ibid, 120.

The 'other', however, inevitably becomes the central concern of any institutional engagement (or the lack of it). This is not only in resolving conflicts between different peoples, or national policies, but in the way institutions perceive a citizen, a consumer, a migrant or a refugee.

Given the inevitability of 'othering', institutions should not concentrate on determining the truth behind whether injustice has been committed or how justice can be achieved, but prevent a self-referential determination of truth, and use ethical tethers to understand how systemic injustice and individual claims to justice can be dealt with. The agency of justice is captured within the self-justification of power structures operating within the *habitus* of legal relations and in the *doxa* of those who interpret and understand the law. In brief, it is not tolerance but empathy which may be a better guiding principle for appreciating the contours of rights and the scope of EU law.[92] Undoubtedly, empathy would need empirical epistemic import; but as is evident, such empirics would require a critical sensibility to work against the 'deep capture'[93] of elements that inform self-justification. In an article in the *New Yorker*, psychologist Paul Bloom argues that popular support of some acts of charity at the cost of others demonstrates that 'the gut wrench of empathy' can be parochial, advocating instead 'a reasoned, even counter-empathetic analysis of moral obligation'.[94] Indeed, a self-legitimating view of empathy creates an 'appetite for retribution' against people or forms of injustice that one relates to. However, a more nuanced conceptualisation shows that it is precisely to prevent a self-legitimating privileging of forms of suffering or definition of pain that empathy is needed. Institutions cannot ignore systemic violence or a process of 'othering' that a claim to a neutral normative *habitus* perpetuates. To work against such capture, this might require a re-think of appointment practices in EU institutions, developing principles of how to mediate expert knowledge in decision making, and the social arrangements and relationships that inform individual functioning.

VI. CONCLUSION

Europe has famously adopted the cold justice of reason as 'a reaction to the destructive force of politics' eroticism'.[95] The content of such reasons reveals a self-legitimating hermeneutics, which demonstrates the need for interpretative and institutional change to accommodate the agency of justice in the law. While some violence upon different interests is necessary, it is necessary to shape the law to support justice, rather than perpetuate institutional preferences. If institutional discourse (and expert assessment of such discourse) operates to foreclose ways of

---

[92] Transnational human intercourse requires a re-think of 'us' and 'them'. JHH Weiler, 'Thou Shalt Not Oppress a Stranger: On the Judicial Protection of the Human Rights of Non-EC Nationals—A Critique' (1992) 3 *European Journal of International Law* 65.

[93] See JD Hanson and DG Yosifon, 'The Situation: An Introduction to the Situational Character, Critical Realism, Power Economics, and Deep Capture' (2003) 152 *University of Pennsylvania Law Review* 129.

[94] P Bloom, 'The Baby in the Well: The Case Against Empathy' *The New Yorker* (20 May 2013).

[95] U Haltern, 'Pathos and Patina: The Failure and Promise of Constitutionalism in the European Imagination' (2003) 9 *European Law Journal* 14, 19.

assessing and contesting the legitimacy of institutional violence, then there is no way to achieve and comparatively assess whether justice is done. In brief, I do not contend that justice should be dogmatically separate from procedure, democracy or free movement; rather, to say that justice cannot be weighted by any of these components would be inconceivable if the human condition is to have any meaning. But to dogmatically force one of these politically defined components as the sole justifying basis for institutional action would render the reflexivity of justice meaningless. Further, I have not intended to argue that institutional self-justification necessarily leads to undesirable outcomes, which is where comparative analysis becomes useful. Self-interpretation by the ECJ has arguably created a constitutional heritage in Europe,[96] and has broadened the ambit of individual rights. At the same time, the legislative vision enshrined in the Treaty could be said to be an uncritical transplant of the state model, which encourages 'surface activity' at the cost of a functional approach to processes such as comitology.[97] It is perhaps because of the messiness associated with the term justice that more deliberately intelligible categories such as procedure and democracy are used to assess the legitimacy of institutional decisions and are identified as organisational principles. I have tried to demonstrate in this chapter that negotiating this complexity is necessary, as the other categories are not free from tumult, and are prone to precluding other concerns. I have tried to show that such categories are meaningful, but their operationalisation and restrictive definition do not necessarily serve justice. Construing justice as a floating signifier would provide a greater space for representation of interests in any collective endeavour, and leave open the possibility for meaningful contestation of institutional decisions.

---

[96] This is found in Weiler's conceptualisation of the *Sonderweg* for instance. JHH Weiler, 'In Defence of the Status Quo: Europe's Constitutional *Sonderweg*' in JHH Weiler and M Wind (eds), *European Constitutionalism Beyond the State* (Cambridge, Cambridge University Press, 2003).

[97] N Walker, 'After the Constitutional Moment' (2003) *Federal Trust Online Papers* 32/03.

7

'Constitutional Justice' and Judicial Review of EU Legislative Acts

DOROTA LECZYKIEWICZ[*]

I. 'JUSTICE', EU CONSTITUTIONALISM AND JUDICIAL REVIEW

ANALYSING THE LEGAL space created and developed by European Union institutions through the prism of 'justice' faces a range of challenges and difficulties. One of the challenges is providing a convincing account of why the non-state context of the European Union should change nothing about our expectations as to how institutions should behave. Another difficulty is the diversity of traditions and practices of the Member States informing our understanding of 'justice' in the EU. In a diversified and still under-defined conceptual environment of the European legal discourse it is inevitable that we will be faced with a multiplicity of theories of justice. Thirdly, the reasons for employing the concept of justice may not be at all clear. For example, EU scholars may be tempted to revitalise the European discourse by referring to 'justice' in the place of such concepts as subsidiarity and proportionality.[1] In those cases 'justice' changes the discourse only verbally, without adding any new normative content. It follows that the language of 'justice' will bring about a beneficial change only if it is used to perform new tasks, currently not carried out by concepts such as political or social legitimacy.

It is the presumption of this entire volume that 'it *is* appropriate to talk about justice in terms of the EU' (emphasis in original)[2] and for this reason I will not dispute the relevance of justice in the context of the EU. Definitional problems, on the other hand, may be solved by adopting various solutions. One approach is to narrow down the normative reach of the concept of justice, as proposed by Sionaidh Douglas-Scott, and focus on instances of injustice.[3] Another method, applied in this

---

[*] The author would like to thank Professor Ester Herlin-Karnell for her helpful comments. The usual disclaimer applies.

[1] See S Roy, 'Justice As Europe's Signifier: Towards a More Inclusive Hermeneutics of the European Legal Order' in this volume, 79, at 83, 86.

[2] D Kochenov and A Williams, 'Europe's Justice Deficit Introduced' in this volume, 1. On the same point, see also A Williams, 'Promoting Justice After Lisbon: Groundwork for a New Philosophy of EU Law' (2010) 30 *Oxford Journal of Legal Studies* 1.

[3] S Douglas-Scott, 'Justice and Pluralism in the EU' (2012) 65 *Current Legal Problems* 83, 84 and 114. See also S Douglas-Scott, 'Justice, Injustice and the Rule of Law in the EU' in this volume, 51.

chapter, is to identify exactly the context in which 'justice' will be employed and explain how its use enriches the existing discourse. In this chapter I will argue that the concept of justice may be usefully applied to the question of judicial review of EU legislative acts (or more broadly of acts of general application) by the European Court of Justice (ECJ), and that its normative content is not exhausted by the notions of political and social legitimacy. Instead of focusing on the question of the Court's indirect democratic empowerment or public acceptability of judicial outcomes I would like to concentrate on the reasoning practices of the Court in cases involving validity challenges on the ground of violation of EU fundamental rights. I will describe the form of justice with which I will engage as 'constitutional justice'.[4] The adjective 'constitutional' performs a double function here. First, it makes it clear that I am interested in a 'constitutional review' carried out by the ECJ and the General Court, that is, judicial review of legislative acts, as different from administrative review carried out predominantly by the General Court.[5] Secondly, the adjective 'constitutional' is intended also to narrow down the range of grounds of review against which EU legislative acts are assessed. I will focus only on these grounds which have a particularly elevated status. While, formally speaking, all grounds of review operate on the same level fundamental rights constitute an unquestionable constitutional core of the EU.[6]

Mapping out the relationship between EU constitutionalism and judicial review through the notion of justice helps to focus on three distinct ways in which the two can be connected.[7] First, a well-functioning institution of judicial review contributes in a very practical way to the attainment of justice by ensuring that correct values, procedures and principles are observed in the process of law creation and administrative decision making (justice as correctness). Secondly, judicial review contributes to the ethos of justice by engaging institutions of a particular polity in a discourse, forcing them to articulate grounds of their decisions, and by broader participation of citizens in the constitutional process (justice as participation). Thirdly, standards of justice apply to the institution responsible for carrying out the review, a constitutional/administrative court which controls how power is exercised by other institutions (justice as an institutional virtue). 'Justice' in constitutional review may concern both outcomes and the process of review. Process-oriented

---

[4] Cf M Cappelletti, 'Repudiating Montesquieu? The Expansion and Legitimacy of "Constitutional Justice"' (1985–86) 35 *Catholic University Law Review* 1; TRS Allan, *Constitutional Justice: A Liberal Theory of the Rule of Law* (Oxford, Oxford University Press, 2011).

[5] On administrative review in EU law, see P Craig, *EU Administrative Law* (Oxford, Oxford University Press, 2012) 405–45.

[6] Art 2 of the Consolidated version of the Treaty on European Union [2012] OJ C326/13 (TEU) states that 'The Union is founded on the values of respect for human dignity, freedom … and respect for human rights, including the rights of persons belonging to minorities'. Art 6(3) TEU states: 'Fundamental rights, as guaranteed by the European Convention for the Protection of Human Rights and Fundamental Freedoms and as they result from the constitutional traditions common to the Member States, shall constitute general principles of the Union's law'.

[7] On EU constitutionalism, see N Walker, 'European Constitutionalism and European Integration' [1996] *Public Law* 266. According to the thick conception of a constitution, exposed by Raz, a constitution should be 'justiciable'; other acts should be tested for compatibility with a constitution. J Raz, 'On the Authority and Interpretation of Constitutions: Some Preliminaries' in L Alexander (ed), *Constitutionalism: Philosophical Foundations* (Cambridge, Cambridge University Press, 1998) 152.

justice in judicial review entails articulation of reasons and proper engagement with constitutional standards, and is a manifestation of the 'justice-as-justification' conception.[8] Absence of discursive engagement of judicial institutions with constitutional principles, such as the protection of fundamental rights, does not necessarily entail violation of these principles, but it undoubtedly impoverishes the expressive function of EU law.[9] Even when political and social legitimacy are present institutional authentication may be incomplete in the case of justice-as-justification-deficit. A legal system which promotes 'constitutional justice' is a system equipped with concepts and structures ensuring that the review court engages discursively with questions of constitutional validity. In this chapter I will examine whether the EU legal order possesses concepts which act as effective requirements for the reasoning practices of the ECJ. Compliance with these standards is all the more important in a federal system where national courts are ascribed only a very limited function in ensuring constitutionality of EU acts. Moreover they are bound to give EU acts effect, and disapply, in the event of conflict, national standards of fundamental rights protection, prima facie even these of a constitutional status.[10] When we are assessing the success of the pursuit of 'constitutional justice' in the EU, it is thus justified to focus in the first instance on the ECJ.

II. STANDARDS OF CONSTITUTIONAL JUSTICE APPLICABLE TO THE EUROPEAN COURT OF JUSTICE

The jurisdiction and procedures of the ECJ are determined by the EU Treaties[11] and the Statute of the Court, enacted in the form of a Protocol to the Treaties.[12] Article 19(3) of the Treaty on European Union (TEU) ascribes the Court the competence to review acts adopted by Union institutions. Article 263 of the Treaty on the Functioning of the European Union (TFEU) lays down the basic requirements of reviewability and standing and the grounds of review ('lack of competence, infringement of an essential procedural requirement, infringement of the Treaties or of any rule of law relating to their application, or misuse of powers'). It is apparent that grounds of review are laid down by EU treaty law only in a very general manner, and they neither restrict nor direct the Court in the way it should exercise

---

[8] R Forst, *The Right to Justification: Elements of a Constructivist Theory of Justice* (New York, NY, Columbia University Press, 2011).

[9] See CR Sustein, 'On the Expressive Function of Law' (1995) 144 *University of Pennsylvania Law Review* 2021. See also G Davies, 'Social Legitimacy and Purposive Power: The End, the Means, and the Consent of the People' in this volume, 259, who discusses the expressive function of EU law in the context of legislative law making and the Court's review of national rules.

[10] Case 11/70 *Internationale Handelsgesellschaft mbH v Einfuhr- und Vorratsstelle für Getreide und Futtermittel* [1970] ECR 1125; Case C-399/11 *Stefano Melloni v Ministerio Fiscal* (ECJ, 26 February 2013). See D Leczykiewicz, '"Effective Judicial Protection" of Human Rights After Lisbon: Should National Courts be Empowered to Review EU Secondary Law?' (2010) 35 *European Law Review* 326.

[11] Arts 19 and 24 of the Consolidated version of the Treaty on European Union [2012] OJ C326/13 (TEU) and Arts 256, 258, 259, 263–265 and 267–276 of the Consolidated version of the Treaty on the Functioning of the European Union [2012] OJ C326/47 (TFEU).

[12] Protocol No 3 on the Statute of the Court of Justice of the European Union [2010] C 83/210.

its reviewing competence.[13] Until recently, treaty law had also been silent on the content of the Court's justificatory practices. Reasoning of the Court was an unregulated practice.[14] Interpretation of the treaties has been a prerogative of the Court and the Court independently has also been defining rules relating to their application. Therefore, in the context of constitutional review in the EU instead of speaking of regulation to which the Court is subjected, we should speak of 'constraints', external and internal. Some external constraints have come from national judicial traditions giving rise to certain expectations on the part of the Court's addressees.[15] Internal constraints result from concepts which the Court itself developed, such as 'general principles of law', proportionality and 'the Rule of Law'. How do they perform as constraints ensuring that there is no 'justice-as-justification' deficit in EU constitutional review? In my view the single most important issue here is the intensity of the Court's review of legislative acts. Low intensity of judicial review has direct bearing on the apprehensiveness of the Court's justificatory practices. Robust review invites more penetrating examination of constitutional issues and fuller articulation of why and how an EU act complies with EU constitutional norms. So let us take the main constraints created by the ECJ and identify their contribution to the quality of the Court's reasoning in constitutional review cases.

'The Rule of Law', as employed in the case-law of the ECJ,[16] had until recently no impact on the intensity of the Court's review. The use of the concept was generally connected exclusively with procedural issues, such as reviewability of EU acts, standing of non-privileged applicants and jurisdiction of the Court. This cannot be explained simply by the fact that the Court is using a formal, rather than substantive, conception of the Rule of Law.[17] The formal conception too requires

---

[13] Substantively, some regulation of outcomes of review stems from the wording of individual competence-conferring provisions, the principles of subsidiarity and proportionality (Art 5(3) and (4) TEU) and now also the obligation imposed on the Union to respect national identities of the Member States (Art 4(2) TFEU). The process of review remains, however, unregulated, and is predominantly informed by the Court's institutional practice.

[14] The Court's reasoning was obviously subjected to influences and pressures stemming from national legal experiences of individual judges and the constitutional dialogue with Member States' courts. However, these influences and pressures were only indirect and left the Court a lot of flexibility to develop its own style of reasoning. J Bengoextea, L Moral Soriano and N McCormick, 'Integration and Integrity in the Legal Reasoning of the European Court of Justice' in G de Búrca and JHH Weiler (eds), *The European Court of Justice* (Oxford, Oxford University Press, 2001) 43. For more on the Court's reasoning, see H Rasmussen, *On Law and Policy in the European Court of Justice: A Comparative Study in Judicial Policymaking* (Dordrecht, Martinus Nijhoff, 1986); G Conway, *The Limits of Legal Reasoning and the European Court of Justice* (Cambridge, Cambridge University Press, 2012) and G Beck, *The Legal Reasoning of the Court of Justice of the EU* (Oxford, Hart Publishing, 2013). This chapter does not focus, as most contributions on the ECJ, on its law-making activity, also described, somewhat pejoratively, as 'judicial activism'. Instead, the chapter discusses the consequences of independent judicial development of review standards for the justificatory practices of an institution.

[15] This is in line with the fact that in law 'correctness' of legal arguments can be assessed by reference to their acceptability by the relevant audiences. See J Bell, 'On the Acceptability of Legal Arguments' in N MacCormick and PBH Birks (eds), *The Legal Mind. Essays for Tony Honoré* (Oxford, Clarendon Press, 1986).

[16] Case 294/83 *Parti Ecologiste 'Les Verts' v European Parliament* [1986] ECR 1339, para 23: 'It must first be emphasized in this regard that the European Economic Community is a community based on the rule of law, inasmuch as neither its Member States nor its institutions can avoid a review of the question whether the measures adopted by them are in conformity with the basic constitutional charter, the Treaty'.

[17] On the distinction between formal and substantive conceptions of the Rule of Law, see P Craig, 'Formal and Substantive Conceptions of the Rule of Law: An Analytical framework' [1997] *Public Law* 467.

compliance with standards of justification. While the Court readily admits the relationship between the Rule of Law and the institution of judicial review, it does not engage with the question of how intense the review should be in order to substantiate the conclusion that the Union is indeed a community based on the Rule of Law. As a result, the EU law's version of the Rule of Law remains undefined, if not disappointingly empty.[18] It is not until the first *Kadi* judgment of 2008 that we find the ECJ concerned with the 'intensity' of the fundamental rights review in connection with the Rule of Law.[19] The linking concept was the right to effective judicial protection. In the second *Kadi* judgment, delivered five years after the first, the Court confirmed that Article 47 of the EU Charter of Fundamental Rights (CFR), guaranteeing the right to an effective remedy, entails that judicial review of EU acts should be 'effective', which requires the EU courts to ensure that measures affecting persons 'individually' are taken on a sufficiently solid factual basis.[20] In consequence, 'judicial review cannot be restricted to an assessment of the cogency in the abstract of the reasons relied on, but must concern whether those reasons, or, at the very least, one those reasons, deemed sufficient in itself to support that decisions, is substantiated'.[21]

The consequences of the two *Kadi* judgments for the intensity of *constitutional* review in the EU are not however obvious. The Regulation contested by the applicants in the first *Kadi* case was adopted by the Council in pursuance of Articles 60, 301 and 308 of the Treaty establishing the European Community (EC) and included some provisions of general application. Yet, the freezing of funds ordered by its Article 2 applied only to persons and organisations listed by name in an annex to the Regulation, and the measure was annulled only insofar as it concerned the applicants. The measure challenged in the second *Kadi* case was not a legislative act, as this category is very formalistically understood by EU law (acts adopted in a legislative procedure).[22] Neither can it be regarded as an act of general application, given the fact that the Regulation concerned individually only Mr Kadi and the Al Barakaat International Foundation. The *Kadi* saga is a story of administrative review in the EU rather than one of constitutional review.

Another constraint on the Court's reasoning in constitutional review cases stems from the incorporation of fundamental rights as 'general principles' of EU law. In a system which did not have a written catalogue of fundamental rights, the Court

---

[18] S Douglas-Scott, 'Justice and Pluralism in the EU' (2012) 65 *Current Legal Problems* 83; A Williams, *The Ethos of Europe: Values, Law and Justice in the EU* (Cambridge, Cambridge University Press 2010) 80–85.

[19] Joined Cases C-402/05 P and C-415/05 P *Yassin Abdullah Kadi and Al Barakaat International Foundation v Council and Commission* [2008] ECR I-6351. The judgment introduces a concept of 'full review' of EU acts in para 326. Nevertheless, in para 360, the principle of 'full review' is regarded by the Court to be compatible with the doctrine of the 'wide margin of appreciation' enjoyed by the Council. The contested Regulation is annulled because of procedural deficiencies in its adoption.

[20] Joined Cases C-584/10 P, C-593/10 P and C-595/10 P *European Commission v Yassin Abdullah Kadi* (ECJ, 18 July 2013) para 119.

[21] Joined Cases C-584/10 P, C-593/10 P and C-595/10 P *Commission v Kadi* (ECJ, 18 July 2013) para 119.

[22] See Art 289(3) TFEU. Case T-18/10 *Inuit Tapiriit Kanatami and Others v European Parliament and Council of the European Union* [2011] ECR II-5599, para 60, and now confirmed by the Court of Justice in Case C-583/11 P *Inuit Tapiriit Kanatami and Others v European Parliament and Council* (ECJ, 3 October 2013).

102 *Dorota Leczykiewicz*

should be applauded for including within unwritten principles the requirement of fundamental rights protection.[23] However, introducing fundamental rights as 'general principles', instead of incorporating them into Union law the European Convention on Human Rights (ECHR), enabled the Court independently to define the actual level of protection guaranteed to these rights[24] and differentiate the standard between Member States' acts and Union acts (the double standard criticism).[25] Fundamental rights as 'general principles' proved to have a much weaker position against legislative acts than constitutional rights in laws of the Member States.[26] This is visible in particular in the way the Court subjected them to restrictions stemming from the public interest, which the Court controversially identifies with 'goals of the Community'.[27] The Court is making no assessment whether all goals of the EU are sufficiently important to be balanced against fundamental rights. This on its own would be an acceptable practice if stringent review of proportionality ensured that fundamental rights were not unduly restricted in the name of policy goals. Whether the Court has realised this postulate is debatable given the volume of negative comments from legal scholars about the manner in which proportionality review of EU acts is carried out.[28] One of the aspects attracting criticism is the test which the Court uses when it reviews proportionality of EU acts. It maintains that

> [w]ith regard to judicial review of the conditions referred to in the previous paragraph [proportionality], it should be noted that the Community legislature must be allowed a broad discretion in an area such as that in issue in the present case, which involves political,

---

[23] Case 11/70 *Internationale Handelsgesellschaft*, para 4: 'respect for fundamental rights forms an integral part of the general principles of law protected by the Court of Justice. The protection of such rights, whilst inspired by the constitutional traditions common to the Member States, must be ensured within the framework of the structure and objectives of the Community'.

[24] S Douglas-Scott, 'A Tale of Two Courts: Luxemburg, Strasbourg and the Growing European Human Rights *Acquis*' (2006) 43 *Common Market Law Review* 629.

[25] J Coppel and A O'Neill, 'The European Court of Justice: Taking Rights Seriously?' (1992) 12 *Legal Studies* 227; A Arnull, 'The Action for Annulment: A Case of Double Standards?' in D O'Keeffe (ed), *Judicial Review in European Union Law* (The Hague, Kluwer Law International, 2000).

[26] LFM Besselink, 'Entrapped by the Maximum Standard: On Fundamental Rights, Pluralism and Subsidiarity in the European Union' (1998) 35 *Common Market Law Review* 629, 633–36; S Douglas-Scott, *Constitutional Law of the European Union* (Harlow, Pearson/Longman, 2002) 452–54.

[27] Case 4/73 *J Nold, Kohlen- und Baustoffgroßhandlung v Commission of the European Communities* [1974] ECR 491, para 14: 'If rights of ownership are protected by the constitutional laws of all the Member States and if similar guarantees are given in respect of their right freely to choose and practice their trade or profession, *the rights thereby guaranteed, far from constituting unfettered prerogatives, must be viewed in the light of the social function of the property and activities protected thereunder*. For this reason, rights of this nature are protected by law subject always to limitations laid down in accordance with the public interest. Within the Community legal order it likewise seems legitimate that these rights should, if necessary, be subject to certain limits *justified by the overall objectives pursued by the Community, on condition that the substance of these rights is left untouched*' (emphasis added). See also, Case 5/88 *Hubert Wachauf v Bundesamt für Ernährung und Forstwirtschaft* [1989] ECR 2609, para 18; Case C-292/97 *KjellKarlsson and Others* [2000] ECR I-2737, para 45. Also in *Kadi* the Court openly admitted that fundamental rights could be compromised by the security objective. Joined Cases C-402/05 P and C-415/05 P *Kadi and Al Barakaat* [2008] ECR I-6351, paras 342–44 and 363.

[28] G de Búrca, 'The Principle of Proportionality and its Application in EC Law' (1993) 13 *Yearbook of European Law* 105; P Eeckhout, 'The European Court of Justice and the Legislature' (1998) 18 *Yearbook of European Law* 1, 25–27; T Tridimas, 'Proportionality in Community Law: Searching for the Appropriate Standard of Scrutiny' in E Ellis (ed), *The Principle of Proportionality in the Laws of Europe* (Oxford, Hart Publishing, 1999).

economic and social choices on its part, and in which it is called on to undertake complex assessments. Consequently, the legality of a measure adopted in that area can be affected only if the measure is manifestly inappropriate having regard to the objective which the competent institutions are seeking to pursue.[29]

Instructive is the judgment of the Court in the high-profile case of *British American Tobacco*.[30] The case concerned the validity of the Tobacco Products Directive,[31] inter alia, in the light of fundamental rights. The very large size of the new health warnings required by Article 5 of the Directive constituted, in view of the applicants, a serious infringement of their intellectual property rights. The Court's reasoning on the issue of proportionality, which later affects its ruling on the issue of property right's breach, consists of only two paragraphs. The Court simply concludes that the obligations stemming from the Directive for tobacco producers are appropriate measures for attaining a high level of health protection and leave sufficient space for the manufacturers of those products to affix their trademarks.[32] These paragraphs are later referred to by the Court to hold that Article 5 of the Directive, imposing the labelling restrictions, constituted 'a proportionate restriction on the use of the right to property compatible with the protection afforded that right by Community law'.[33] This shows that low-threshold standards not only fail to impose justificatory requirements on the law-making institutions. They also enable timid reasoning of the Court and devalue rights whose observance a constitutional court should ensure.

III. THE CHARTER OF FUNDAMENTAL RIGHTS AS A VEHICLE OF CONSTITUTIONAL JUSTICE

The European Union underwent a comprehensive reform with the Treaty of Lisbon.[34] Is 'justice-as-justification' deficit in the form described in this chapter still a feature of the institution of judicial review of EU legislative acts? Important changes have been made to the Court's jurisdiction, which now encompasses unequivocally acts of the former third pillar (concerning police and criminal matters).[35] Even acts relating to foreign and security policy are subjected to review if, according to Article 275 TFEU, they provide for a 'restrictive measure against a natural or legal person'. Access to the Court by individuals is broadened by the new wording of Article 263 TFEU. Let us now reflect on the changes which the *substantive* standards of judicial review have undergone. Here, the single most important shift is

---

[29] Joined Cases C-453/03, C-11/04, C-12/04 and C-194/04 *R, on the application of ABNA Ltd v Secretary of State for Health and Food Standards Agency* [2005] ECR I-10423, para 69.

[30] Case C-491/01 *R v Secretary of State for Health, ex parte British American Tobacco (Investments) Ltd and Imperial Tobacco Ltd* [2002] ECR I-11453.

[31] Directive 2001/37/EC of the European Parliament and of the Council of 5 June 2001 on the approximation of the laws, regulations and administrative provisions of the Member States concerning the manufacture, presentation and sale of tobacco products [2001] OJ L194/26.

[32] Case C-491/01 *British American Tobacco* [2002] ECR I-11453, paras 131–32.

[33] ibid, para 150.

[34] Treaty of Lisbon amending the Treaty on European Union and the Treaty Establishing the European Community [2007] OJ C306/1.

[35] The Court's jurisdiction as regards pre-existing third pillar acts remained subject to the pre-Lisbon Treaty provisions for a five-year transitional period.

vesting the CFR with the same value as the treaties.[36] This has three implications which show categorically how important it is for a constitutional polity to have a written catalogue of fundamental rights.

The first change concerns the formal recognition of the right to an effective remedy in the CFR and clearly defining its scope. Article 47 CFR, which guarantees this right, covers all 'rights and freedoms guaranteed by the law of the Union'. In particular, it now unequivocally covers fundamental rights protected by the CFR and those enshrined only in 'general principles'.[37] The second change which the CFR brought about concerns the grounds of review of EU acts, more specifically the substantive standard which the Court is now bound to apply. Article 52(1) CFR demands that '[a]ny limitation on the exercise of the rights and freedoms recognised by this Charter must be provided for by law and respect the essence of those rights and freedoms'. Moreover, Article 52(1) prescribes that '[s]ubject to the principle of proportionality, limitations may be made only if they are necessary and genuinely meet objectives of general interest recognised by the Union or the need to protect the rights and freedoms of others'. This provision imposes on the Court three additional justificatory requirements. First, the Court is required to reject all limitations imposed on fundamental rights which are *not* 'provided for by law'.[38] Secondly, the Court is for the first time asked not only to state that in its assessment, the essence of the right has been respected, but also to articulate what is the content of the inviolable essence that was respected by Union institutions, whose preservation enables the Court to conclude that the act is valid. Finally, the provision makes it impossible for the Court to restrict its review of proportionality only to the question of appropriateness of the EU measure for the attainment of its prescribed objective. Further justificatory requirements stem from Article 52(3) and (4) CFR, which require the Court to show with respect to rights guaranteed also by the ECHR that the meaning in which the Court applied these rights is the same as that laid down by the Convention, and that it has interpreted CFR rights resulting from the constitutional traditions of the Member States in harmony with these traditions.

It is early days and it is notoriously difficult to track down evidence of judicial shifts. Cases in which the ECJ reviewed a legislative act after the CFR was made formally binding by the Treaty of Lisbon seem to suggest that the Court is carrying out a fuller review and is justifying its findings about violations of fundamental rights

---

[36] Art 6(3) TEU ascribes the CFR the same legal value as the Treaties.
[37] D Leczykiewicz, '"Effective Judicial Protection" of Human Rights After Lisbon', n 10 above, 333.
[38] This is understood to mean that the limitation has to have a 'legal basis'. Case C-407/08 P *Knauf Gips v European Commission* [2010] ECR I-6375, para 91. This is taken to mean either that the act creating the limitation needs to have a legal character (has to be one of the types of acts generating effects for third parties which the EU is entitled to adopt): Joined Cases C-92/09 and C-93/09 *Volker und Markus Schecke GbR and Hartmut Eifert v Land Hessen* [2010] ECR I-11063, para 66, or more stringently, that the act which creates the limitation 'must have a legal basis', ie, has been correctly adopted under the invoked conference-conferring provision: Case T-187/11 *Mohamed Trabelsi and Others v Council of the European Union* (GCt, 28 May 2013). In a recent opinion, AG Cruz Villalón has argued that the requirement of a fundamental rights restriction to be 'provided for by law' 'must go beyond a purely formal requirement and cover also the lack of precision of the law ("quality of the law")'. Joined Cases C-293/12 and C-594/12 *Digital Rights Ireland v The Minister of Communications, Marine and Natural Resource* (ECJ, 8 April 2014), Opinion of AG Cruz Villalón, para 109.

and the principle of proportionality by using more extensive and more substantive arguments, thereby indirectly defining with greater precision the content of fundamental rights and the inviolable essence.

Sky Österreich[39] is one of the recent cases which particularly stand out. The case concerned the Broadcasting Directive,[40] as amended in 2007, and the question of whether it observed the fundamental freedom to conduct a business of organisations which acquired exclusive rights to broadcast sport events. The Directive required such organisations to allow broadcasters to use, for the purpose of short news reports, short extracts from the matches to which these organisations had exclusive rights at a compensation not exceeding the additional costs in providing access. The Court held that the Directive did not disproportionately infringe their right to conduct a business even though those who possess exclusive rights to broadcast the events could not decide freely with which broadcasters they would enter into an agreement regarding the granting of the right to make short news reports and at what price. The reasoning of the Court clearly shows how Article 52(1) CFR imposes on the Court an appreciable constraint, and requires from it, more successfully that its judicially created equivalent (the general principle of proportionality), the articulation of what 'essence' of the freedom was preserved,[41] and why the solution adopted in the Directive is the least restrictive measure ensuring access of the public to information about sporting events. The judgment explains that the permitted length of footage used and the fact that the holder of rights has to be identified shows that the appropriate balance has been struck between the two competing fundamental rights.[42]

The recent opinion of Advocate General Cruz Villalón in *Digital Rights Ireland* also proves that the CFR will have an impact on the quality of proportionality review of EU legislative acts by demanding a greater emphasis on *sensu stricto* proportionality, that is, the necessity of the solution adopted in the EU measure.[43] Using such a form of review the Advocate General has come to the conclusion that

> Article 6 of Directive 2006/24 [on data retention] is incompatible with Article 7 and Article 52(1) of the Charter is so far as it requires Member States to ensure that the data ... are retained for a period of up to two years

which according to the Advocate General Cruz Villalón went beyond what was necessary to ensure that the data were available for the purpose of the investigation, detection and prosecution of serious crime.[44]

---

[39] Case C-283/11 *Sky Österreich GmbH v Österreichischer Rundfunk* (ECJ, 22 January 2013).
[40] Council Directive 89/552/EEC of 3 October 1989 on the coordination of certain provisions laid down by law, regulation or administrative action in Member States concerning the pursuit of television broadcasting activities [1989] OJ L298/23, amended by Directive 2007/65/EC of the European Parliament and of the Council of 11 December 2007 [2007] OJ L332/27.
[41] Case C-283/11 *Sky Österreich* (ECJ, 22 January 2013), para 49.
[42] ibid, para 63.
[43] Joined Cases C-293/12 and C-594/12 *Digital Rights Ireland* (ECJ, 8 April 2014), Opinion of AG Cruz Villalón, paras 99–152.
[44] Joined Cases C-293/12 and C-594/12 *Digital Rights Ireland* (ECJ, 8 April 2014), Opinion of AG Cruz Villalón, para 152. Directive 2006/24/EC of the European Parliament and of the Council of 15 March 2006 on the retention of data generated or processed in connection with the provision of publicly available electronic communications services or of public communications networks and amending Directive 2002/58/EC [2006] OJ L105/54.

However, the picture is not uniformly favourable. The recent *Melloni* judgment of the ECJ,[45] concerning inter alia the validity of the amended European Arrest Warrant (EAW) Framework Decision,[46] includes only a very short discussion of how the act respects the relevant fundamental rights (the right to an effective remedy, the right to a fair trial and the right of the defence, as protected by Articles 47 and 48(2) CFR). The EAW Framework Decision requires the executing court to recognise criminal judgments of a court of another Member State even where the accused was absent during the trial. What is particularly problematic in the Court's reasoning is a total identification of the CFR standard of protection of the right to a fair trial and the right of the defence with the standard chosen by the EU legislature in the Framework Decision.[47] The Court correctly explains that the content of the EU measure constitutes a compromise between the need to ensure protection of procedural rights of persons subjected to criminal proceedings and the improvement of mutual recognition of judicial decisions between Member States. But the Court fails to notice that where two objectives are in conflict and one of them relates to fundamental rights, Article 52(1) CFR requires the Court to carry out a proportionality review. As a result, no such review is conducted in the judgment.[48]

Furthermore, if we return to the question about the different functions of 'justice' in the context of judicial review, and ask not about the justificatory practices of the ECJ but about the values which such review is promoting, we need to recognise that after the Treaty of Lisbon, fundamental rights review in the EU continues to provide benefits mainly for commercial parties challenging the regulatory reach of EU legislative acts in the intellectual property and now also the social policy field.[49] Of particular interest in this context is the extensive use of Article 16 CFR which guarantees freedom to conduct a business.[50] Asylum seekers, employees and consumers invoke the CFR frequently but in proceedings against Member States. One notable exception is the *Test-Achats* case where it was the EU Directive[51] which was held to be violating a principle of equal treatment between men and women in their access to goods and services.[52] This economic orientation in the use of the CFR in judicial review of EU acts is perhaps compatible with the market-oriented focus of the European Union's own activities, where social protection measures take

---

[45] Case C-399/11 *Melloni* (ECJ, 26 February 2013).
[46] Council Framework Decision 2002/584/JHA of 13 June 2002 on the European arrest warrant and the surrender procedures between Member States [2002] OJ L190/1, as amended by Council Framework Decision 2009/299/JHA of 26 February 2009 [2009] OJ L81/24.
[47] Case C-399/11 *Melloni* (ECJ, 26 February 2013), paras 52–53.
[48] ibid, para 53.
[49] See Case C-70/10 *Scarlet Extended SA v Société belge des auteurs, compositeurs et éditeurs SCRL (SABAM)* [2011] ECR I-11959; and Case C-360/10 *Belgische Vereniging van Auteurs, Componisten en Uitgevers CVBA (SABAM) v Netlog NV* (16 February 2012)on EU intellectual property legislation; and Case C-426/11 *Mark Alemo-Herron v Parkwood Leisure Ltd* (ECJ, 18 July 2013).
[50] See D Leczykiewicz, 'Horizontal Effect of Fundamental Rights: In Search of Social Justice or Private Autonomy in EU Law?' in U Bernitz, X Groussot and F Schulyok (eds), *General Principles of EU Law and European Private Law* (Alphen aan den Rijn, Kluwer Law International, 2013).
[51] Council Directive 2004/113/EC of 13 December 2004 implementing the principle of equal treatment between men and women in the access to and supply of goods and services [2004] OJ L373/37.
[52] Case C-236/09 *Association belge des Consommateurs Test-Achats ASBL and Others v Conseil des ministers* [2011] ECR I-773.

the form of Directives addressed to Member States or of measures not subjected at all to review.[53] But it once again begs the question about the values which Union institutions, including the ECJ, are designed to serve.

IV. JUDICIAL REVIEW—THE QUESTION OF LEGITIMACY OR JUSTICE?

The role of judicial review of acts adopted by Union institutions has been a recurring theme of the Union's legitimacy debate. It has been regarded as relating to both the question of formal and social legitimacy.[54] As Walker observes in this volume,

> the legitimacy of a delegate, or of a fiduciary, or of an efficient or epistemic authority [ie different possible guises of the EU contemplated by Walker], depends on the continuing control of the principal, the clarity of the mandate, or the reducibility of policy competence to knowledge or expertise ... [T]he adequacy of all these justificatory models has been challenged by the expansionary dynamic of the Union. They have become less plausible claims in a supranational polity attenuated from national control, with an ever broader and deeper policy agenda.[55]

What contribution has been made by the ECJ through the institution of constitutional review to legitimacy of the EU? The case-law of the Court has provided numerous and frequent instances of evidence of how imprecise the mandate of the European Union has been, both in terms of its competences and the values it was to promote. The Court has tried to reduce the policy competence of the European Union to politics, on the one hand, and knowledge and expertise, on the other, by classifying more and more issues as involving 'difficult political, social and economic choices'.[56] In this way the Court has not only restricted its own judicial review powers but has also weakened the institution of constitutional review and undermined constitutional justice in the EU. The fact that Union activities concern issues which are often far from uncontested and technocratic entails the necessity for stricter accountability standards. But the political nature of many choices exercised by Union institutions also means that the Court needs to be careful in the way it delineates its jurisdiction. In constitutional theory there is a perennial debate as to whether legislative acts should be reviewable and how to reconcile democracy with the power of unelected judges to invalidate acts adopted by democratically

---

[53] I am referring here to the so-called new governance mechanisms, ie measures falling within the Open Method of Coordination. See G de Búrca, 'The Constitutional Challenge of New Governance in the European Union' (2003) 28 *European Law Review* 814.

[54] For the distinction between 'formal' and 'social legitimacy', or between 'legal validity' and 'legitimacy', see JHH Weiler, 'Epilogue' in A-M Slaughter, A Stone Sweet and JHH Weiler (eds), *The European Court and National Courts. Doctrine and Jurisprudence* (Oxford, Hart Publishing, 1998) 373 and JHH Weiler, *The Constitution of Europe: 'Do the New Clothes Have an Emperor?' and Other Essays on European Integration* (Cambridge, Cambridge University Press, 1999) 77–86.

[55] N Walker, 'Justice in and of the European Union' in this volume, 247, at 251–52.

[56] Case C-233/94 *Federal Republic of Germany v European Parliament and Council of the European Union* [1997] ECR I-2405, para 56; Case C-491/01 *British American Tobacco* [2002] ECR I-11453, para 123; Case C-210/03 R, on the application of: *Swedish Match AB and Swedish Match UK Ltd v Secretary of State for Health* [2004] ECR I-11893, para 48; Joined Cases C-154/04 and C-155/04 R, *on the application of Alliance for Natural Health v Secretary of State for Health* [2005] ECR I-6451, para 52.

elected representatives.[57] Harlow has argued that legal accountability administered by the judiciary is centrally important for the 'constitutional machinery for securing limited government' and is 'the way to provide the element of individual redress and reparation'.[58] According to Majone, judicial review is one of the responses to alleged Europe's democratic deficit because it contributes to substantive legitimacy, making the standards of parliamentary democracy irrelevant.[59] A well-functioning constitutional review contributes to the Union's output legitimacy by promoting effectiveness in the achievement of 'correct' goals.[60] The concept of legitimacy can also be applied more specifically to the ECJ as a benchmark of how a supranational, judicial institution is entitled to exercise its jurisdiction. The chapter argues that the language of legitimacy should be accompanied by that of 'constitutional justice' in order to focus our attention more sharply on the question of institutional authentication of the Court in its constitutional review reasoning. My view is that the shift from legitimacy to justice in the theoretical discussion about the Union's constitutional court will enable us to articulate demanding expectations not only as to outcomes and their social acceptability[61] but also as to the Court's justificatory practices. 'Constitutional justice' will help us think of EU fundamental rights and the principle of proportionality in terms of institutional standards of judicial reasoning.

---

[57] J Waldron, 'The Core of the Case Against Judicial Review' (2006) 115 *Yale Law Journal* 1346; A Kavanagh, 'Constitutional Review, the Courts and Democratic Scepticism' (2009) 62 *Current Legal Problems* 102. For the EU context, see Eeckhout, 'The European Court of Justice', n 28 above, 4.

[58] C Harlow, *Accountability in the European Union* (Oxford, Oxford University Press, 2002) 165.

[59] See also G Majone 'Europe's "Democratic Deficit": The Question of Standards' (1998) 4 *European Law Journal* 5, 22 and 26.

[60] On the role of the Court of Justice in promoting the EU's output legitimacy, see A Menon and S Weatherill, 'Transnational Legitimacy in a Globalising World: How the European Union Rescues Its States' (2008) 31 *Western European Politics* 397.

[61] GA Caldeira and JL Gibson, 'The Legitimacy of the Court of Justice in the European Union: Models of Institutional Support' (1995) 89 *American Political Science Review* 356.

Part Two

8
Politicising Europe's Justice Deficit: Some Preliminaries

MICHAEL A WILKINSON[*]

TODAY OWNERS OF financial capital are working with international organisations and debt-ridden national states to insulate once and for all the economic economy from the moral economy of traditional social obligations and modern citizenship rights—and with greater prospect of success than ever in the four decades since the 1970s. As democratic states are being turned into collection agencies on behalf of a new global haute finance, market justice is about to prevail over social justice, for a long if not an indefinite period of time. In the process those who have placed their confidence as citizens in capitalist democracy must concede precedence to those who have as investors placed their money on it.[1]

I. INTRODUCTION

Europe is awash with deficits. In addition to the various economic deficits engulfing the Eurozone (and elsewhere), the EU has been said to suffer a democratic deficit, a political deficit, and a social deficit, each of which predates the financial and subsequent sovereign debt crises beginning in 2007.[2] None of this is new to the seasoned observer of the EU. Only now, however, is discussion turning to its 'justice deficit'. Not merely pointing to the aggregate of these other deficits, accusation of a justice deficit suggests something more fundamentally rotten at the heart of the project. Justice, after all, is the sovereign virtue.[3]

---

[*] I would like to thank, with more than the usual disclaimer, Floris de Witte, Samuel Tschorne, Alexander Somek and Hans Lindahl.

[1] W Streeck, 'How to Study Contemporary Capitalism' (2012) 53 *European Journal of Sociology* 15.

[2] On the democratic deficit, see S Hix and A Føllesdal, 'Why There Is a Democratic Deficit in the EU: A Response to Majone and Moravscik' (2006) 44 *Journal of Common Market Studies* 533; on the political deficit, see R Dehousse, 'Constitutional Reform in the EC' in J Hayward (ed), *The Crisis of Representation in Europe* (Abingdon, Frank Cass, 1995); on the social deficit, see C Joerges and F Roedl, 'Informal Politics, Formalised Law and the "Social Deficit" of the European Integration: Reflections After the Judgments of the ECJ in *Viking* and *Laval*' (2009) 15 *European Law Journal* 1.

[3] Analysis of Europe's justice deficit could proceed by investigating the treatment of refugees and asylum seekers, allegations of complicity in torture and processes of extraordinary rendition, collusion in wars and occupation of dubious legality, mass surveillance programmes and other threats to civil liberties. None of this will be dealt with here. Justice here will be taken to mean social justice.

Even if it is curious that the measure of this virtue is now expressed in the language of economics, a justice 'deficit'—the very measure of the EU in terms of its justice, or rather, *injustice*—which is where the accusation points, suggests that a threshold has been crossed. After all, dominant strands in the analytical tradition of normative political theory have not infrequently resisted or outright rejected its applicability to domains beyond the nation state—including the nascent EU polity—due to the absence there of the relevant political community.[4] Other commentators continue to *justify* the political, democratic and social deficits beyond the state or to deny them normative significance in the first place.[5]

The purpose here is not to engage directly in debates over the correct theory of the reach and scope of justice claims, over the respective merits of libertarianism and egalitarianism or over the precise limits of the polity within which one may properly speak of justice or injustice. It is rather to consider the way that European integration is altering—whether by exposing, concealing or constraining—the *politics* of justice; in particular, the way integration is destabilising the national frame but not (yet) offering up an alternative platform for subjecting transnational justice claims to democratic contestation.

There is a reason for taking an explanatory rather than a normative approach. Whatever normative theory of social justice we happen to endorse (including its wholesale rejection),[6] the distribution of individual, collective and common goods will in practice, in any really existing society, be determined, at least in part, by political and social struggles for equality. This means not only over the economists' 'scarce resources' but also over public goods such as education and health and non-material goods such as solidarity, recognition and representation.[7] Since in democratic society, ideological superiority will—in theory at least—always be up for grabs, arguments of principle in favour of or against redistribution, recognition and representation will merely be another factor in the fight over and for such goods.

Wolfgang Streeck has recently modelled struggles over distribution on the tension or 'dynamic disequilibrium' between capitalism and democracy, where they are understood not as organised competitions for the accumulation of money or votes but as representing two *principles* or *logics* of resource allocation—market justice and social justice. This enables us to conceptualise a justice deficit as the result of an imbalance in these two logics. And, in Streeck's account, imbalance will tend towards crisis, provoking a reaction of sorts to remedy the imbalance or at least prevent it from becoming critical for the society (section II).[8]

---

[4] See, eg, T Nagel, 'The Problem of Global Justice' (2005) 33 *Philosophy and Public Affairs* 113.

[5] See, eg, J Neyer, 'Justice, Not Democracy: Legitimacy in the European Union (2010) 48 *Journal of Common Market Studies* 903.

[6] On the rejection of patterned theories of justice, see R Nozick, *Anarchy, State, Utopia* (New York, NY, Basic Books, 1974).

[7] Only in part because in practice levels of inequality will depend not only on the basic structure of the state, and its reception to political and social struggles, but also on what has been called the principle of community, the extent to which questions of distributive justice arise for persons in their daily lives. See, eg, G Cohen, 'Back to Socialist Basics' (1994) 207 *New Left Review* 3.

[8] See W Streeck, 'Taking Capitalism Seriously: Towards an Intuitionalist Approach to Contemporary Political Economy' (2011) 9 *Socio-Economic Review* 137; Streeck, 'How to Study Contemporary Capitalism', n 1 above; W Streeck, 'The Crises of Democratic Capitalism' (2011) 71 *New Left Review* 5; W Streeck, 'Markets and Peoples' (2012) 73 *New Left Review* 63.

But in what context is this relationship played out? The contest between market and social justice does not occur in a vacuum. Historically, it is the state that sets the framework for the negotiation and recalibration of the relationship between market and social justice, through institutional and ideological, coercive as well as consensual means (section III).

In recent historical perspective, the political constitution of the post-war state has been conceived as aiming to prevent or forestall crisis by *constraining* the logics of democracy and of capitalism.[9] On this account, the process of European integration is a significant feature of the post-war settlement—designed to prevent majoritarian democratic excesses but without surrendering the state's ability to constrain the logic of capitalism (section IV).[10]

But European integration is now exposing the fragility and dysfunctionality of this settlement. With the apparent boundlessness of markets and extension of market logic, but with democracy struggling to transcend state borders, the structural asymmetry in Europe is now proving *destructive*, not only of the supranational constitution but also of national constitutional settlements. We can conceptualise the EU's 'justice deficit' as representing this imbalance in favour of capitalism and market justice, where, in the absence of a European democratic or social movement, any rebalancing is to come from the executive power of the Member States, or rather from certain among them (section V).

And yet, whatever the prospects of supra- or transnational democracy, Europe's justice deficit is depoliticised with market logic presented in naturalistic terms, making it appear necessary and inevitable, an expression of inescapable pressures to modernise and gain competitiveness. It will be argued that pre-requisite to dealing with the justice deficit is its politicisation. But this may come at a high cost in terms of the stability and unity of the project of integration, and is (therefore) unlikely to come from the top-down, from the political and economic elites who have driven the project since its inception (section VI).

I will suggest in the concluding section (VII), drawing on the recent work of Nancy Fraser, that 'the state'—understood as the framing of relevant boundaries—must itself be politicised, subject to contestation and struggles of recognition and representation. The challenge, it is argued, is to substitute Streeck's dilemma for a trilemma, of market justice, social justice and democratic justice. The purpose of this chapter is not to proffer institutional responses to this trilemma, nor even to specify its social and political conditions; it is to explore some preliminaries for a fuller understanding of the politics of Europe's justice deficit.

II. CONCEPTUALISING A JUSTICE DEFICIT

A justice deficit can be explained functionally as the result of an imbalance between the logic and forces of capitalism on the one hand and those of democracy on

---

[9] I draw here on the work of Jan-Werner Müller, *Contesting Democracy: Political Ideas in Twentieth Century Europe* (New Haven, CT, Yale University Press, 2011).

[10] Chris Bickerton's argument that the post-war logic fundamentally changes in the neoliberal period beginning in the 1970s will also be drawn upon, see CJ Bickerton, *European Integration: From Nation-States to Member States* (Oxford, Oxford University Press, 2012).

the other. A *social* justice deficit would then exist where the former gains an upper hand over the latter. A compelling account of this imbalance—or 'dynamic disequilibrium'—between democracy and capitalism has recently been presented by Wolfgang Streeck.[11] He argues that the relationship between capitalism and democracy will tend towards a critical imbalance as capital tends to dominate, and to such an extent that democracy itself will be threatened, as revealed most dramatically in Europe since the recent financial crises.

In Streeck's account, capitalism and democracy, or 'markets' and 'peoples', represent rival constituencies, with contrasting 'logics of action', which we can label as 'market justice' and 'social justice' respectively.[12] In terms of societal values, these suggest two different principles of resource allocation: one operating according to marginal productivity, and merit on a 'free play of market forces' and the other based on social need, and 'certified by the collective choices of democratic politics'.[13] This reflects a clash in the respective ethical demands of the two major forces in the modern democratic capitalist state, rather than merely a clash of interests between money and votes. If the market imposes a marginal ethics (by advancing the prospect and expectation of rational egoism and competitive accumulation without limits), democratic society promises a maximal ethics (by holding out the prospect of and need for solidarity, collaboration and concern for human well-being).[14]

By rejecting the standard contrast between an amoral market system and moral obligations of solidarity, persons and political communities are in this account instead torn between obligations on either side of the justice balance, obligations that although distinct are not incommensurable. On the one hand, market imperatives present individuals and communities with the duty to adopt and adjust to economic change, to accumulate wealth, to be entrepreneurial in spirit, competitive, and, above all, efficient. On the other hand, democracy calls forth solidarity, the collective obligation to protect weaker individuals from the fallout of capitalist excesses and to prevent or attenuate the 'creative destruction' that is central to liberal progress or 'modernisation'; debate then occurs 'over the moral limits, if any, to the pursuit of economic advantage'[15] where that pursuit and its limits are themselves understood as normative forces.

The paradox is that the market ethos of a capitalist political economy is, for reasons of systemic survival, parasitic upon the moral obligations imposed by social democratic norms.[16] By tempering and correcting capitalist excess, these prevent disequilibrium from turning into outright societal collapse.

There is therefore an interdependence rather than straightforward conflict between the two principles of resource allocation. But this is not a happy or stable

---

[11] See n 8 above.
[12] A Schäfer and W Streeck 'Introduction' in A Schäfer and W Streeck (eds), *Politics in the Age of Austerity* (Cambridge, Polity Press, 2013) 19.
[13] Streeck, 'Crisis of Democratic Capitalism', n 8 above, 7.
[14] Streeck, 'Taking Capitalism Seriously', n 8 above, 137.
[15] Streeck, 'How to Study Contemporary Capitalism', n 1 above, 23.
[16] But, Streeck notes, 'only in a functionalist worldview' is the success of efforts at taming capitalist excesses actually 'guaranteed'. ibid, 156.

relationship. As Streeck concludes, capitalism not only necessitates a continual demand for moral and social support in order for the system to stay afloat, but it is also always undermining that very same support because of its own internal logic. Because of this pathological tendency, capitalism is an inherently 'self-destructive social formation'.[17] Democratic capitalism is then conceivable 'as a political economy in permanent disequilibrium', pushed forward inexorably by continuous innovation on the part of capital and 'pervasive political conflict over the relationship between social and economic justice'. Disequilibrium will periodically lead to crisis, not least because of the inability of capital to think beyond its own short-term interests; even the environmental conditions of our survival are reducible to a mere 'externality'.

With this relationship in view, capitalism is systematically reconfigured, because profits and losses—as well as resultant gulfs in socio-economic equality among persons—are exposed as non-naturalistic, 'the outcome of a struggle between conflicting concepts of and claims to justice' rather than between an irrational moral code and an amoral but rational objective economic law.[18] Rational and public choice philosophy then appear in a new light; rather than purely scientific, positivistic theories that remain above the political fray, they can be seen as performative and ideological, imposing a dominant market logic and narrow view of rationality on neighbouring disciplines and occluding alternative values. Self-interest is the only proper mode of rationality, and, eventually, 'greed is good'. This subordination of discourses of legitimacy to a particular economic rationality is achieved through 'naturalising' the logic of the market. The technocratic dictates of economics then come to speak 'with the pathos of natural law', controlling and even colonising the political debates over justice and inequality.[19] Economics is the method; the aim is the transformation of the soul.[20]

III. HISTORICISING A JUSTICE DEFICIT: THE ROLE OF THE STATE

Although recent political philosophy in the social contract tradition investigates justice primarily as a normative question, seeking for a resolution or reflective equilibrium, Streeck's analysis exposes it as an irresolvable, practical, political problem. This becomes even more apparent when attention is given to the unit within which the question of justice is properly raised, which is frequently but often implicitly, assumed to be a state.[21] And the standard reason given, if one is given at all, is that only within the state does the requisite unity of coercion and community

---

[17] ibid, 25.
[18] ibid, 16.
[19] G Teubner, *Constitutional Fragments* (Oxford, Oxford University Press, 2012) 32–34. For Teubner, the neo-natural law conception of economic rationality is nothing less than 'grotesque' because it substitutes causal explanation for normative legitimacy, bypasses political debate, and overlooks the potential instability of a constitution based on science that has to resolve controversies which cannot be scientifically resolved.
[20] To misquote Margaret Thatcher.
[21] In Rawls's later work, exploring the international basic order, the relevant unit is explicitly a 'people'; see J Rawls, *Law of Peoples* (Cambridge, MA, Harvard University Press, 1999).

exist, generating and sustaining the capacity to provide for basic collective goods.[22] Although in some apparent degree of tension with each other, coercion and community are presented as complementary rather than in competition.

Both are paradigmatic attributes of statehood. First, the capacity to dominate, the monopoly on legitimate violence, which in the Weberian tradition is the defining feature of the modern state and in liberal political theory key to understanding why its authority requires normative justification, is, at least formally, an exclusively sovereign power. To this must be added, second, the sense of being part of a collective endeavour or 'community of fate', necessary for sustaining a functioning public sphere and legitimising any non-trivial redistribution of benefits and burdens. This too is elusive once we move beyond the state's borders.

Only by combining these features in a contiguous manner, when a state not merely coerces but does so 'in our name' or for our collective benefit, are obligations to remedy injustice and duties of redistribution incurred, above the minimum moral duties of humanitarian intervention that might exist outside the state. We ought to be concerned with equality because, and when, we can and do value the reciprocity that it entails. The unity of coercion and community is therefore central to the modern state's capacity to negotiate the tension between capitalism and democracy, market and social justice. Since beyond the state there is no (or at most—as in the case of the EU—only relatively ineffective) political apparatus that unites coercion and community, there can be no egalitarian duties of redistribution.[23]

But from a political perspective, this tension is not resolved in an original position or final determination of where the balance of justice rests; rather, the state provides a more or less stable framework within which the ceaseless competition and interaction of interests and ideas might be negotiated relatively peacefully.[24] In practice, the state manages the tension between capitalism and democracy in order to contain or forestall any crisis that might result from the imbalance in their relationship.

From this perspective coercion and community are also instrumental to the maintenance of stability *in spite of*, and even to legitimise existing and continuing, *inequality*. The idea of a community of fate, binding rulers and ruled, not only facilitates redistribution but also softens, if not eradicates class conflict. It pacifies struggles over justice by appealing to a sense of communal identity, which is not merely left to grow spontaneously or organically, even if it could be nurtured in that way. This is periodically revived as a political project—however insincerely—with communitarian mottos such as that currently in vogue, 'we are all in it together', and ironically by those who only recently urged that 'there is no such thing as society'. From a functional perspective, recall, resources of solidarity are a necessary

---

[22] In Nagel's 'political conception' it is coercion and co-authorship that combine as the relevant characteristics giving rise to obligations of justice within a state, against the cosmopolitan account; Nagel, 'The Problem of Global Justice', n 4 above. Nagel's position is not of course unchallenged: see, eg, A Julius, 'Nagel's Atlas' (2006) 34 *Philosophy and Public Affairs* 176. And there are those in the Rawlsian tradition who have argued for a more cosmopolitan or global basic structure.

[23] We may, however, have moral duties to create such authoritative institutions (and mechanisms of redistribution) in the first place.

[24] I do not claim that the state is merely a neutral arbiter between these forces; it is undoubtedly more complex than that. Beyond some suggestive comments, this will not be the place to go into detail into the history and concept of the state and its role in the balance of justice.

complement to a market economy, to maintain or re-establish order either by rebalancing the justice disequilibrium or encouraging the population to tolerate, accept or at least acquiesce in the inequalities that the market permits, and even depends upon. In the absence of such resources of solidarity, politics will require more coercive mechanisms.

There is, to be sure, nothing new in the perception that the tense and even antagonistic relationship between market and social justice, capitalism and democracy, has a significant political dimension. In an earlier period, Karl Polanyi argued that the destruction caused by the dis-embedding of the market in a liberal capitalist society would lead to a reaction, or 'second movement', of re-embedding through social policies and the re-regulation of markets.[25] It is not only that as a matter of proper sociological understanding, the economy is embedded in society rather than the other way round; it is also that politically, since democracy poses a threat to the logic and interests of capital, the ruling class will attempt to curtail the economic goals of the majority, and by political and even constitutional means if necessary.[26] The perception that capitalism and the individualist ethos of classical liberalism pose a serious threat to the robust 'public' on which democracy itself depends, as John Dewey argued in a different historical and political context, has a similarly vintage pedigree. Dewey of course thought that democracy must permeate all of society, becoming industrial and not merely civil and political; in order to allay the corrupting effects of capitalism and the inequalities it results in, a vibrant public is essential.[27]

And the framing of the justice deficit is political in a second and more basic sense that calls into question any statist assumptions. Although the 'Keynesian–Westphalian' co-evolution of a monopoly of legitimate violence and a community of fate is difficult to envisage beyond the state, it would be an error to think and act as if the state were therefore self-contained or insulated for the purposes of negotiating the tension between capitalism and democracy, market and social justice. Coercion, it must be remembered, can be and frequently is exercised *between* states and even through international institutions that lie over and above states. Both capitalism and democracy are linked to projects of state- and institution-building, both at home and abroad, most obviously in the guise of foreign and imperial adventures, however civilising their missions in the eyes of those who pursued them. Neither coercion nor community, in other words, is autonomous and independent from political action, internally or in external relations.

The framework of assumptions that implied a hermetically sealed national container was of course long ago shattered historically by exposing the links between

---

[25] K Polanyi, *The Great Transformation: The Political and Economic Origins of Our Time* (Boston, MA, Beacon Press, 2001).

[26] 'Inside and outside England, from Macaulay to Mises, from Spencer to Sumner', wrote Karl Polanyi in *The Great Transformation*, first published in 1944, 'there was not a militant liberal who did not express his conviction that popular democracy was a danger to capitalism'. ibid, 234.

[27] See, eg, J Dewey, *The Public and Its Problems* (New York, NY, Henry Holt, 1927). By focusing on the potential of science and experimentation, Dewey arguable neglected the politics necessary to contain capitalism, see MA Wilkinson, 'Dewey's Democracy Without Politics: The Failures of Liberalism and Frustrations of Experimentalism' (2012) 9 *Contemporary Pragmatism* 117.

political freedom, capital accumulation, and imperialism. As Arendt powerfully argues in *The Origins of Totalitarianism*, political emancipation of the bourgeoisie in the late nineteenth century was prompted by their desire for economic expansion, which in turn necessitated expanding the territorial logics of power beyond the nation state.[28] In addition, the assumed role of the bourgeois state and state-sponsored ideology in protecting the security of the individual—determining its openness or closure towards immigration, fixing policies of asylum and assimilation, formulating citizenship tests as well as labour and welfare policies towards foreigners—demonstrates that the internal framework within which democracy and capital 'slug it out' is not fixed in regard to the outside world, but contingent on politics and political action.

Restricting the domain of justice to relations within the state has the effect of legitimising the 'de facto' inequality that exists between states, as if any inequality beyond the state was apolitical, natural, or beyond the domain of human action. Just as it is a mistake, in other words, to see the state only as an enabler of social justice or as an impartial arbitrator of the balance between markets and peoples, it is also a mistake to view it as an arbitrary but necessarily neutralised pivot of the balance of justice.

All of which is to say that the logics of market and social justice do not exist in a vacuum, and so to Streeck's account must be added the political context of their interaction. As a glance at the historical record confirms, to the longevity of the functional disequilibrium must be added its evolution through distinct stages of economic and political development, including, particularly in the second half of the twentieth century in which the project of European integration is born, significant institutional and ideological elements which constrain the logics of capitalism and democracy, and in a way that is not captured by the bare categories of coercion and community.

IV. HISTORICISING A JUSTICE DEFICIT: THE ROLE OF IDEOLOGY

In the post-war period in Western Europe, as classical economic models based on notions of unfettered competition and free markets are replaced with those of late, or 'organised', capitalism based on intervention with market mechanisms, tolerance of oligopoly and the generation and sustenance of large public sectors, government intervention in recalibrating the relationship between democracy and capitalism comes to be taken for granted. This continues to be the case to this day, even if rhetorically and opportunistically dismissed or derided by the cheerleaders of neoliberalism, which does not hesitate to embrace the authoritarian state apparatus if necessary. Whether to ensure the smooth functioning of a market economy, assuage the financial markets, or on more radical accounts, continue the process of accumu-

---

[28] H Arendt, *The Origins of Totalitarianism* (New York, NY, Harcourt, Brace & World, 1968) 123–57. More recently it has also been argued that it is predominantly Western imperialism and intrusion into the Arab world, rather than religious fundamentalism, that is the root cause of the alienation felt by Muslims in Europe today. See P Anderson, 'Portents of Eurabia' *The National* (28 August 2009).

lation through dispossession, ensuring the continuation of the inequalities on which capitalism depends, governmental interference on both sides of the justice balance is ubiquitous.[29]

But not only is the economy increasingly and explicitly entangled with institutions of political democracy and state bureaucracy; struggles over market and social justice also assume more complex political and ideological forms, in part due to the reaction to the series of crises that engulfed Europe and elsewhere in the first half of the twentieth century, in the forms of fascism and Soviet communism. Social, political and economic struggles in the post-war state are tempered by what has been called 'constrained democracy' and 'constrained capitalism', collective commitments—often of a constitutional nature—which encourage or impose limits on the democratic and capitalist logics, in order for society to maintain stability and avoid the extremism that potentially occurs as it relapses—or appears to be in the process of relapsing—into crisis.[30]

First, in Jan-Werner Müller's narrative of post-war democracy in Europe, distrust of popular sovereignty and even parliamentary sovereignty was ubiquitous in the aftermath of the Second World War, with the goal of constraining democratic majorities uppermost in the minds of political and bureaucratic elites, to prevent backsliding into authoritarian extremism.[31] This distrust of politics, and fear of both Right and Left was manifested in concrete national institutions, with liberal constitutionalism and strong constitutional courts in particular developing across the region, most notably in the Federal Republic of Germany, but complemented with supranational institutions in the EU (or European Economic Community as it then was) and the European Convention on Human Rights (ECHR).[32] Not only economically, but also institutionally, this was the hour of the 'European rescue of the nation-state', in Alan Milward's well-known narrative.[33]

But second, there was also, from the beginning of the post-war period until at least the mid-1970s and the dawn of the neoliberal revolution, a Keynesian consensus on the need to protect society from the excesses of capitalism and market justice.[34] As well as laying the foundations for social security and the 'welfare state', this involved a bargain or social contract between capital and labour, a post-war 'class compromise', obtained by a set of mediating institutions, which attempted to organise capitalism in such a way that would unite state and society.[35] This strengthening

---

[29] See further, MA Wilkinson, 'The Spectre of Authoritarian Liberalism: Reflections on the Constitutional Crisis of the European Union' (2013) 14 *German Law Journal* 527.

[30] See further, exploring the history in various national contexts, J-W Müller, *Contesting Democracy: Political Ideas in Twentieth Century Europe* (New Haven, CT, Yale University Press, 2011).

[31] ibid. And on the recent Euro crisis, see J-W Müller, 'Beyond Militant Democracy?' (2012) 73 *New Left Review* 39.

[32] Müller, 'Beyond Militant Democracy', n 31 above, 43–44: 'European integration—this is crucial—was part and parcel of the new "constitutionalist ethos", with its inbuilt distrust of popular sovereignty and the delegation of tasks to agencies that remained under the close supervision of national governments'.

[33] A Milward, *The European Rescue of the Nation-State* (London, Routledge, 1992).

[34] There was, Tony Judt, notes, an 'unusually broad consensus' on this. T Judt, *Ill Fares the Land* (London, Penguin, 2010) 47.

[35] See Bickerton, *European Integration*, n 10 above.

of the bonds between state and society, and between business and labour, was complemented by a commitment to the collective pursuit of broader social goals, including economic development, technical innovation, full employment, regional income distribution and national security.[36] 'Socialism', according to Müller, 'had been implemented from above to constrain capitalism'[37] or as Tony Judt puts it, to save it.[38]

Politically, it was the 'moment of Christian Democracy' and other elite-led and state-sponsored ideologies that pushed for the attainment and entrenchment of stability by curtailing political extremism and avoiding economic imbalances and excessive levels of socio-economic inequality.[39] Constitutional and international commitments, internally, and within the architecture of European legal regimes, increasingly 'take things off the table' for democratic contestation, at least if one wants to play within the rules. And of course the two dimensions of constraint—ideological and institutional—act most effectively in tandem in alleviating the perceived dangers of democratic and capitalist excesses.

The project of European integration was considered a significant means to achieve this, internalising transnational externalities and softening the potential for sovereign violence. Along with the economic benefits thought to accrue from reducing obstacles to trade through the creation of a common market, this was the most convincing rationale for the state's voluntary 'containment' and surrender of 'limited sovereign rights'.[40]

European integration initially was considered a key aspect of the post-war constitutional settlement, a central feature in the narrative of the survival of the democratic sovereign state through constraining its dominant logics. Unlikely to transcend the nation state or represent its evolution into a federal state writ large, because of the difficulty—let alone questionable desirability—of up-scaling the required combination of coercion and community, the EU would instead be an additional bulwark against the dangers of political and economic excesses.

The process was complemented from its early stages by a strong and proactive juridical project to create a transnational rule of law, based on subjective and predominantly economic rights. A glance at the subject matter of the foundational and even revolutionary case of *Costa/ENEL*—often lost in the mist of the supremacy doctrine it gave birth to—is revealing: an Italian law that sought to nationalise

---

[36] ibid, 107.
[37] Müller, *Contesting Democracy*, n 30 above, 131.
[38] Judt, *Ill Fares the Land*, n 34 above, 47.
[39] Müller describes Christian Democracy as 'the most important ideological innovation of the post-war period, and one of the most significant of the European twentieth century as a whole'. Müller, *Contesting Democracy*, n 30 above, 130. The UK does not fit so neatly in this pattern; attaining relative stability and socio-economic equality in the post-war period but without constraining parliamentary supremacy.
[40] For recent accounts of the argument from containment within EU free movement law and citizenship, see F de Witte, 'Sex, Drugs & EU Law: The Recognition of Ethical and Moral Diversity in Europe' (2013) 50 *Common Market Law Review* 1545; and F de Witte, 'Union Citizenship and Constrained Democracy' in AP van der Mei and M de Visser (eds), *Twenty Years Treaty on European Union: Reflections from Maastricht* (Cambridge, Intersentia, 2013).

electricity production and distribution, based on the disputed payment of a 1,925 Italian lire bill.[41]

This ideological and institutional neutering of democratic and market logics was complemented by a 'golden age' of sustained economic growth, which facilitated the (temporary) satisfaction of the demands of both capital and labour, dramatically reducing levels of socio-economic inequality.[42] The precise contribution made by European integration to the peace and prosperity of the 'Trente Glorieuses' is contested. What is not contested is that from the mid-1970s, coinciding with an end to easy economic growth, the 'long downturn', equilibrium between capitalism and democracy has become more difficult to maintain.[43]

The forces of market justice have, in this period of neoliberal ascendancy, come out firmly on top, creating a further critical imbalance in the relation between capitalism and democracy. The current period of crisis demonstrates once again how the state is called on dramatically to intervene, but, in doing so with austerity for the poor and primarily in order to regain international competitiveness under pressures of market justice, is doing so with scant regard for socio-economic equality and considerations of distributive or social justice. What kind of further democratic response, if any, this might lead to, remains to be seen.

In the brief aftermath of the collapse of the Soviet Union, the idea of the co-originality and co-evolution of democracy and capitalism took hold of our collective imagination, a marriage that signified, on some accounts, no less than the end of history itself.[44] Contributing to this eschatological sentiment in Europe was a narrative that paired wider integration with waves of democratisation and market

---

[41] Case 6/64 *Flaminio Costa v ENEL* [1964] ECR 585. The case was spearheaded by two members of the Italian bar actively pursuing the project of creating a European Rule of Law; see, eg, A Vauchez, 'The Transnational Politics of Judicialization. *Van Gend en Loos* and the Making of EU Polity' (2010) 16 *European Law Journal* 1.

[42] According to Bickerton: 'The decades of prosperity were tied to a particular model of both state and society and a specific understanding of the relationship between politics and economics', Bickerton, *European Integration*, n 10 above, 93.

[43] Financially, one solution was thought to be allowing high inflation, which can be seen as 'an expression of anomie in a society which, for structural reasons, cannot agree on common criteria of social justice'; a second then increasing credit: first government debt, then private credit, in both cases 'pulling future resources into present consumption'. If this accumulation of private and public debt foregrounds the most recent financial crisis, one current response in the UK at least is, it appears, more of the same: another debt-fuelled and state-assisted housing bubble. Streeck, 'Crises of Democratic Capitalism', n 8 above, 23. So-called 'privatised Keynesianism', which is advanced as the immediate cause if not the ultimate root of the current economic crisis, is suggested by Streeck as a concession to the democratic pressures exerted by the people. This highlights an ambiguity in Streeck's account. Historically 'privatised Keynesianism' was not, arguably, a response to democratic pressure but to capitalist pressure. For one thing, it occurred most intensely in places where the working class was being weakened—with the neoliberal war on the unions waged by Reagan and Thatcher. Does Streeck's argument imply that without democratic pressures, capitalism would exist in a natural equilibrium? That markets would be self-correcting if left to themselves, unperturbed by democratic pressure? For a different account of the golden age and subsequent 'long downturn' see R Brenner, *The Economics of Global Turbulence* (London, Verso, 2005), emphasising the significance of the global unevenness and competition between national capitalisms.

[44] The reference of course is to F Fukuyama, *The End of History and the Last Man* (New York, NY, Avon Books, 1993). For more nuanced accounts, rejecting both the internal relation and internal tension between capitalism and democracy, see, eg, P Wagner, 'The Crisis of Democratic Capitalism: Reflections on Political and Economic Modernity in Europe' (2011) *LEQS Papers* 44/2011 and before the recent crisis, A Touraine, *What Is Democracy?* (Boulder, CO, Westview Press, 1997).

liberalisation, as first Spain, Portugal and Greece emerge from political dictatorship to join the common market and later the countries of the former Soviet bloc apply for membership of the EU. And the 'Copenhagen criteria' for membership of the EU in the 1990s made the pairing of democracy, the rule of law and human rights with a functioning market economy both formal and explicit conditions.[45]

Any sense of having reached the plateau of liberal democratic constitutionalism was not to last long, however, as, well before the recent financial crisis, the EU began to face a more inward looking constitutional crisis of legitimacy, expressed both in popular rejection of the Constitutional Treaty and in juridical resistance to the constitutional jurisprudence of the European Court of Justice (ECJ).[46] Both global and European narratives of a comfortable reconciliation of democracy and capitalism have now, in any case, been exposed if not completely exploded. Not least the role of the state has increasingly resumed centre stage, even if neoliberalism has proved surprisingly ideologically resilient, as well as economically and politically powerful.[47]

Obituaries for an end of history thesis already deconsecrated by its own author are unnecessary, which is not to say we have definitively moved beyond its paradigms. But however resilient the modern liberal state, the crises and contradictions of democratic capitalism have undoubtedly escaped its confines, becoming Europeanised and globalised, most apparently in the latest economic crises in the Eurozone, which of course were set in motion by events on the other side of the Atlantic.[48] So too the site of struggle between market justice and social justice has now shifted, at least partially, beyond the state, being played out between electorates and financial institutions, governments and international organisations.

V. FRAMING THE EU'S SOCIAL JUSTICE DEFICIT

Through the evolution of political and legal institutions in the EU, both coercive and consensual aspects of political rule would emerge beyond the state, even if only in incipient form. But this gradual outsourcing of political authority and of constitutional checks and balances, rather than protecting the Keynesian–Westphalian 'nation state', now threatens rather to transform it, into a post-Westphalian 'Member State'.[49]

There are many aspects to the erosion of the national political frame and the demise of its social-democratic Keynesian compromise; the precise role that the EU has played in this narrative is far from straightforward. And to be sure, our specific judgement may vary depending on which of the varieties of capitalism from

---

[45] European Council, 'Conclusions of the Presidency' [1993] DOC/93/3.
[46] The strongest resistance in terms of influence has been from the German Constitutional Court. See, eg, D Grimm, 'Defending Sovereign Statehood Against Transforming the Union Into a State (2009) 5 *European Constitutional Law Review* 353.
[47] See C Crouch, *The Strange Non-Death of Neo-Liberalism* (London, Polity Press, 2011).
[48] For an account of this single globalised crisis of financial capitalism see, eg, M Aglietta, 'European Vortex' (2012) 75 *New Left Review* 15.
[49] See Bickerton, *European Integration*, n 10 above, ch 2. I borrow the term Keynsian–Westphalian from Nancy Fraser, 'Reframing Justice in a Globalizing World' (2005) 36 *New Left Review* 69.

amongst the various Member States we take as our exemplar.[50] Even on a single state, the effects of European integration may vary over time, as laws and institutions at national and supranational level themselves evolve.

The purpose of Streeck's account was, however, to suggest that, despite the possibility and actuality of regional variation in terms of the precise political construction of and response to the capitalist economy, there is a singular logic and ethic of capitalism and market justice, which not only can be abstracted from its varieties, but is integral to its institutional and ideational form.

And, however persuasive the varieties of capitalism literature in comparative context, there is a strong current of opinion, in states as varied in their political and constitutional economies as the United Kingdom and Germany,[51] which holds that European integration has been a significant factor in the erosion and even overall demise of the 'Keynesian–Westphalian' compromise due to the structural asymmetries that the EU creates and maintains.[52]

Institutions and practices of social justice, both public and private, at the national level, if not found disproportionate in their effects on trade, may become a burden of comparative disadvantage due to the effects of competition and free movement norms. The juridification of the default rules of free circulation of the factors of production in the EU, combined with the political difficulties of re-regulation or even treaty amendment (in areas where the EU lacks competence), particularly in light of the consensus politics with which it operates, favours and even entrenches a firmly, if not unambiguously, neoliberalising trajectory.[53]

Idiosyncratic features of supranational integration not only combine to prevent cogent political–democratic response to the social dysfunctionality of the market but also deter the creation of possibilities for such response: a central bank unable to buy government debt directly and bound to the single objective of ensuring price stability, the relative lack of labour mobility due to cultural and linguistic heterogeneity, unprecedented wage repression in the largest economic bloc, an eclectic mix of economic development and bureaucracies in different phases of modernisation, and above all the (real or perceived) absence of a supranational community of fate.[54]

The structural asymmetries imposed by Europe's peculiar brand of federalism tips any balance of justice overwhelmingly in favour of market and against social justice, pushing the dynamic disequilibrium of democratic capitalism to tipping point.

---

[50] See, eg, P Hall and D Soskice (eds), *Varieties of Capitalism. The Institutional Foundations of Comparative Advantage* (Oxford, Oxford University Press, 2001).

[51] In the UK context, see D Nicol, *The Constitutional Protection of Capitalism* (Oxford, Hart Publishing, 2010); in the German context see FW Scharpf, 'The Asymmetry of European Integration: Or Why Europe Can't Have a Social Market Economy' (2010) 8 *Socio-Economic Review* 211.

[52] It is Fritz Scharpf, above all, who has conceptualised and described in institutional detail the social and economic imbalances caused by Europe's constitutional asymmetry. See recently, on the role of European law in this process, Scharpf, 'The Asymmetry of European Integration', n 51 above. And for a broader examination of this asymmetry in the terms of constitutional theory, see N Walker, 'The Place of European Law' in JHH Weiler and G de Búrca (eds), *The Worlds of European Constitutionalism* (Cambridge, Cambridge University Press, 2011).

[53] See Scharpf's exhaustive analysis of the asymmetry between market and social rules, law and politics in the EU, 'The Asymmetry of European Integration', n 51 above

[54] See P Anderson, 'After the Event' (2012) 73 *New Left Review* 49.

There are simply insufficient channels of contestation at the supranational level to generate the social and political legitimacy for any Polanyian double movement that might correct these biases and imbalances.

Although there is a powerful and growing body of academic opinion to say that political union must now ultimately ensue, either to deal with the German question or to resolve the Greek problem,[55] the EU emphatically has not itself followed in the footsteps of the statist model or developed a fully fledged transnational social contract. Arenas of distributional conflict are becoming ever more remote from domestic politics, but the imperative to upscale the democratic–political framework for the negotiation and re-negotiation of justice claims has been resisted.[56] The political response to redistributive questions in Europe—to questions of social justice not only within but also between states—has occurred, if at all, *sotto voce*, behind the backs of the electorates.

If taking market logic and market justice beyond the state has been celebrated in Europe in an era of ordo- and then neoliberalism, taking democracy and social justice beyond the state has proven theoretically and practically problematic, to say the least.[57] Democracy, it is only too clear, has not become fully supranationalised in response to the freedom of capital and other factors of production to roam beyond borders. And if the democratic deficit in the EU was already notorious, it has now become critical, with constraints placed on the core of national democratic sovereignty in the European Stability Mechanism (ESM) and the 'Fiscal Compact'.[58]

And yet, on the dominant ordoliberal account, the asymmetry of European integration was entirely justified: the supposed virtues of inter-state competition and the perceived economic benefits of the free circulation of goods, workers and capital better attained without political interference.[59] Founded on 'guarantees of economic freedom', the EU's legitimacy—according to a leading figure in the ordoliberal school—is quite 'independent' of its 'democratic and socio-political future'.[60] From a market liberal perspective, moreover, the absence of a *demos* represented a solution rather than a problem: our reduction to 'mere' individuals, 'consumers' or 'entrepreneurs', is motivated by perfect economic rationality.

An economic constitution celebrates the absence of a *demos* because political redistribution of wealth, whether unjustified or merely irrational, is less likely to be feasible in the absence of community or social solidarity, a 'we-feeling' amongst

---

[55] See, eg, U Beck, *A German Europe* (Cambridge, Polity Press, 2013).
[56] Streeck, 'Crises of Democratic Capitalism', n 8 above, 27.
[57] For an account of the political traits of neoliberalism, see D Harvey, *A Brief History of Neo-Liberalism* (Oxford, Oxford University Press, 2007).
[58] Treaty establishing the European stability mechanism (ESM) (11 July 2011), text available at www.europa.eu/rapid/press-release_DOC-12-3_en.pdf; and the Treaty on Stability, Coordination and Governance in the Economic and Monetary Union ('Fiscal Compact') (2 March 2012) text available at www.european-council.europa.eu/media/639235/st00tscg26_en12.pdf. For analysis, see, eg, M Dawson and F de Witte, 'Constitutional Balance in the EU After the Euro-Crisis' (2013) 76 *Modern Law Review* 817.
[59] The ordoliberal account of the EU is presented by E-J Mestmacker, 'European Touchstones of Dominion and Law' (2007) 58 *Ordo Yearbook of Economic and Social Order* 4. On regulatory competition, see A Sayde, 'One Law, Two Competitions: An Enquiry into the Contradictions of Free Movement Law' (2011) 13 *Cambridge Yearbook of European Legal Studies* 365.
[60] Mestmacker, 'European Touchstones', n 59 above, 7.

the members of a polity.[61] Ordoliberalism, in tune with its neoliberal cousin, 'has more confidence in the economic constitution than in democracy'.[62] This divorce of political authority from control over economic resources leaves market justice to triumph over its rival.

But it is now becoming clear that not only would the EU fail to develop the political capacity to deal with perceived injustice across its borders, it would also impede the existing states from reconciling their own tensions and the writing and re-negotiation of their own social contracts:

> The construction of Europe as an economic and monetary union, without corresponding political and fiscal integration, disabled the protective capacities of Member States without creating broader, European-wide equivalents to take up the slack. Today, the evidence is all around us: Greece is reduced to a protectorate, Spain, Portugal and Ireland are ruled from Brussels, and central bankers set limits to domestic policy even in Germany and France. The upshot is that the project of social protection can no longer be envisioned in the national frame.[63]

Regarding the national level, there is a strong case to say that whatever was left of the Nordic model of welfare capitalism after the neoliberal onslaught of the late 1990s has been further undermined by the rulings of the ECJ in its recent case-law on the free movement of establishment and freedom to provide services.[64] Far from the European rescue of the nation state, the EU now seems to be in the process of contributing to its transformation.

The sense of a serious *imbalance* between capitalism and democracy, caused or exacerbated at least in part by Europe's constitutional asymmetry is becoming increasingly pervasive. Jürgen Habermas, an otherwise avid if not stubborn supporter of the project of integration, now notes that 'political management', 'uncoupled' from the democratic pressures and dynamics 'of a mobilised political public sphere and civil society', is deprived of the motivational strength to resist capitalism, unable 'to contain and redirect' its 'profit-oriented imperatives' into 'socially compatible channels'. As result, governing authorities increasingly 'yield' to the neoliberal pattern of politics:

> A technocracy without democratic roots would not have the motivation to accord sufficient weight to the demands of the electorate for a just distribution of income and property, for status security, public services, and collective goods when these conflicted with the systemic demands for competitiveness and economic growth.[65]

Market discipline had been supposed to perform the function of stabilising economic systems, to compensate for the merely soft, symbolic sanctions against fiscal excess

---

[61] Hayek favoured a form of inter-state federalism to assuage the perceived threat of redistribution. For discussion, see A Somek, 'The Social Question in a Transnational Context' (2011) *LEQS Papers* 39/2011.

[62] J Habermas, *The Crisis of the European Union: A Response* (London, Polity Press, 2012) 129.

[63] N Fraser, 'Triple Movement' (2013) 81 *New Left Review* 126.

[64] For recent analysis, see, eg, E Christodoulidis, 'The European Court of Justice and "Total Market" Thinking' (2013) 14 *German Law Journal* 2006.

[65] J Habermas, 'Democracy, Solidarity and the European Crisis' lecture delivered at Leuven, 26 April 2013. A full transcript is available at www.kuleuven.be/communicatie/evenementen/evenementen/jurgen-habermas/en/democracy-solidarity-and-the-european-crisis.

in the Stability and Growth Pact[66] (violated almost immediately by France and Germany)[67] and for the 'no bail-out' rule enshrined in the Treaty (Article 125 of the Treaty on the Functioning of the European Union (TFEU))[68] that prevented, in theory, transnational sharing of the burdens of any economic crisis, until the ECJ rules otherwise in its *Pringle* decision.[69] But soft measures are now to be substituted for the harder rules contained in the ESM and 'Fiscal Compact'. Although, strictly speaking, these take place outside the EU *acquis*, they threaten the constitutional balance of the European Union, by calling into question the most cherished principles of integration—democracy, Member State equality, the balance of powers, the 'community method', and even respect for the rule of law itself.[70]

If the EU was destined to become a civilised, 'non-imperial Empire',[71] then the financial crisis and responses to it are threatening to tear away this thin veneer of respectability. Disorder, in the present critical conjuncture has spilled over from the economic to the political domain, upsetting not only the 'system integration', but also the 'social integration' of contemporary societies, as the life world becomes increasingly precarious, with austerity programmes, in southern Europe in particular, wrecking lives.

Not only is political democracy in practice suspended in debtor countries, but the economic constitution itself is bypassed, because of the imperatives of the financial markets and the concerns of creditor states.[72] And where that is the case, as, arguably, it already is in countries like Greece, Ireland and Portugal, 'street riots and popular insurrection may be the last remaining mode of political expression for those devoid of market power'.[73] This tampering with an already precarious equilibrium threatens to explode—if not already detonated—into outright revolt in Europe. If there was already a democratic deficit in Europe, there is now a crisis of democracy.

And because of the power—real or imagined—of the troika and even the credit rating agencies themselves, citizens increasingly perceive their governments, 'not as *their* agents, but as those of other states or of international organisations',[74] who utilise the messages sent by the financial markets to control and cajole if not to coerce their populations. The financial markets, we are increasingly informed, will

---

[66] European Council, 'Resolution of the European Council on the Stability and Growth Pacts Amsterdam, 17 June 1997 [1997] OJ C236/1; Council Regulation (EC) No 1466/97 of 7 July 1997 on the strengthening of the surveillance of budgetary positions and the surveillance and coordination of economic policies [1997] OJ L209/1; Council Regulation (EC) No 1467/97 of 7 July 1997 on speeding up and clarifying the implementation of the excessive deficit procedure [1997] OJ L209/6.

[67] A violation side-stepped by the Court of Justice in Case C-27/04 *Commission of the European Communities v Council of the European Union* [2004] ECR I-6649.

[68] Consolidated version of the Treaty on the Functioning of the European Union [2012] OJ C326/47 (TFEU).

[69] Case C-370/12 *Thomas Pringle v Government of Ireland, Ireland and the Attorney General* (ECJ, 27 November 2012). For analysis, see AJ Menéndez, 'The Existential Crisis of the European Union' (2013) 14 *German Law Journal* 453.

[70] See Dawson and de Witte, 'Constitutional Balance', n 58 above.

[71] In the words of José Manuel Barroso, see www.brusselsjournal.com/node/2244.

[72] See C Joerges, 'Europe's Economic Constitution in Crisis and the Emergence of a New Constitutional Constellation' (17 September 2013), www.papers.ssrn.com/sol3/papers.cfm?abstract_id=2179595#.

[73] Streeck, 'Crises of Democratic Capitalism', n 8 above, 28.

[74] ibid, 26.

simply not tolerate certain political outcomes, or more often, political indecision, giving new lease of life to the sentiment that 'time is money'.[75] And international organisations, such as the International Monetary Fund (IMF) and the European Union, are 'immeasurably more insulated from electoral pressure than was the traditional nation-state'.[76] Whereas in the post-war constitutional settlement this insulation (or democratic constraint) was considered one of the EU's supposed strengths—and in the ordoliberal account, a real virtue—it is now increasingly being perceived as a disruptive and dangerous vice.

As a result, extreme nationalist political parties prosper, with promises, however unrealistic, to regain the harnesses of power and smash the mythical power of fate, personified now by faceless bureaucrats and troika representatives. The need to 're-embed' the market economy has been exploited by reactionary movements of right-wing populism rather than transnational movements of pan-European solidarity. The promise of regaining collective autonomy, which only appears institutionally possible at the national level, however illusory in practice, is a far from unattractive platform from which to gain popular electoral support.[77]

In the wake of the financial crisis, we have witnessed the results of capitalism acting 'more like itself', with capital movement and market justice having increasingly strained at the leash of democratic and territorial controls. And in the absence of a European *demos* and democratically legitimate European institutions, it is not markets themselves but strong states that appear to take up the slack, however reluctantly, to ensure the survival of transnational capitalism and the market economy. In this way, the financial crisis has not only revealed the fragility of the constitutional principles of the EU; it has also exposed a horizontal asymmetry between larger and smaller Member States, or economically stronger and economically weaker states, that was previously concealed.

So although strong statehood is lacking at the supranational level, there is at least one contender at the national level, which in conjunction with technocratic governance structures in the EU has been able to call the shots: the Federal Republic of Germany.[78] In the absence of political channels of contestation, dictates and coercive measures prevail. And they appear to emanate from one source in particular. As Perry Anderson puts it,

> in the European simulacrum of federalism, there could be no 'transfer union' along American lines. Once crisis struck, cohesion in the Eurozone could only come, not from social expenditure, but political dictation—the enforcement by Germany, at the head of a bloc of smaller northern states, of draconian austerity programmes, unthinkable for its own citizens, on the southern periphery, no longer able to recover competitivity by devaluation.[79]

---

[75] Accredited of course by Max Weber to Benjamin Franklin.
[76] Streeck, 'Crises of Democratic Capitalism', n 8 above, 26.
[77] This is most evident in Greece with the rise of Golden Dawn. Greece is perhaps unique in also giving rise to a major new left-wing and anti-austerity party, Syriza, which, although maintaining support for the Eurozone was considered a threat by the liberal establishment, particularly in Germany.
[78] See, eg, Beck, *A German Europe*, n 55 above.
[79] Anderson, 'After the Event', n 54 above.

Coercive elements of rule are becoming increasingly prominent and exposed, from the centralised supranational authority and its representatives in the Commission and European Central Bank, to international organisations such as the IMF,[80] as well as among the Member States themselves. Real economic power discrepancies are even becoming translated into political norms, as is the case of the voting weights in the ESM.[81]

European integration not only adds an additional layer of complexity to the relationship between democracy and capitalism; it also makes the core tension more visible. It exposes the justice deficit in broad daylight and the coercion necessary to sustain the background conditions of transnational economic order. Preventing conflict from becoming critical and destructive of the project of the Euro must, we are told, be achieved at all costs.

The post-war narratives of 'constrained democracy' and 'constrained capitalism' therefore appear to be coming to an abrupt end in the current phase of European integration. And, in a conjuncture of exquisite irony, it seems that the constitutional model of the European Union is to be forcefully remade due to the political and economic strength of the one country that integration was supposed above all to contain. Mann's nightmarish vision of a 'German Europe' rather than a 'European Germany' is in danger of becoming a reality.[82]

VI. POLITICISING JUSTICE DEFICITS

There are many attempts to justify the institutional responses to the financial crisis, to suggest, for example, that they are necessary temporarily, in the short term, to ensure the stability of the integration process, or at least its currency, in the long run. There have been attempts to justify the constitutional asymmetries and justice deficits in the EU. Some also deny that European integration creates, contributes to or maintains such deficits at all. But it is becoming increasingly difficult to persuade persons, and indeed entire peoples, that integration merely expands the pie for all, that there are not real transnational redistributive implications of membership in the EU or even that they remain in collective control of their fates. And many influential commentators now argue that Europe will need to engage in huge and explicit redistributive programmes and therefore develop into full political union in order to deal with the social and economic effects of the recent financial crises.[83]

But in the absence of the requisite transnational solidarity to support this democratically, openly and voluntarily, the emergency 'rescue operation' is being conducted in an 'undemocratic, depoliticized, and technocratic mode'.[84] This raises the danger of new forms of authoritarianism emerging, both nationally and transnationally.[85] A recalibration of the 'moral calculus' of integration—of transnational

---

[80] For analysis of the institutionalisation of this 'troika', see Menéndez, 'The Existential Crisis', n 69 above.
[81] See Dawson and de Witte, 'Constitutional Balance', n 58 above.
[82] See Beck, *A German Europe*, n 55 above.
[83] See, eg, C Offe, 'Europe Entrapped: Does the EU Have the Political Capacity to Overcome Its Current Crisis' (2013) 19 *European Law Journal* 595.
[84] ibid.
[85] See Wilkinson, 'The Spectre of Authoritarian Liberalism', n 29 above.

solidarity—will not however to come top-down from elites, but, if at all, from the recognition by the peoples of Europe of the injustice of those suffering from the austerity measures being imposed upon them.[86]

The justice deficit, however, is frequently *depoliticised* by naturalising the ascendency of market justice. There is, for example, a strong tendency to perceive the initial movement of capitalist logic and market justice in quasi-naturalistic terms, as an unstoppable social and evolutionary force, which democratic politics can do nothing more than attempt to tame or civilise in response. This perception of the capitalist economy as natural and autonomous is most explicit and developed in systems theory and can be traced back through to Weber's rationalisation thesis of modernity, and even beyond, to the natural law understanding of the economy that replaces the state with civil society, in the work of thinkers such as Adam Smith and Thomas Paine. Depoliticisation of the public sphere finds support in elite theories of democracy and systems theory, because, in common with the classical doctrines of political economy, they appeal to an evolutionary narrative of social reproduction, whether normatively or merely descriptively.[87]

Common to these varied positions is the viewpoint that the economic is not only autonomous; it is foundational for the polity and for political development.[88] It is a view that even (sympathetic) critics of Weber such as Jürgen Habermas have come to accept.[89] Since the fall of the Berlin wall and the collapse of the Soviet Union, he claims, it has become 'impossible' to break free from the world of capitalism; 'the only remaining option is to civilise and tame the capitalist dynamic from within'.[90] And the transformation of law and politics in the process of European integration, Habermas argues, is bound up with this capitalist dynamics, framed by a 'functionally driven opening' of integration and inclusion followed by a 'socially integrative closure', or re-embedding of the market.[91]

There is a broader point here. Escape from democratic politics signalled by the practice and discourse of ordo- and neoliberalism is not new; its sentiment is as old as philosophy itself. Liberalism's attempt to escape from politics through economics, as Hannah Arendt argued, is not a departure, but a continuation of the philosophical tradition that begins with Plato and ends with Marx.[92] Once a substitute for action is found—which is traditionally the role of the 'absolute', in modern times Sieyès'

---

[86] The term 'moral calculus' is Offe's, see Offe, 'Europe Entrapped', n 83 above.

[87] For Weber rationalisation is an aspect of our loss of freedom in modernity, see, for discussion, eg, K Breen, *Under Weber's Shadow: Modernity, Subjectivity and Politics in Habermas, Arendt and MacIntrye* (Aldershot, Ashgate, 2012). On Smith and Paine, see, eg, M Loughlin, *Foundations of Public Law* (Oxford, Oxford University Press, 2010) 347. Teubner's work is an important exception here, providing a critique of the naturalisation of economic rationality from within systems theory; see Teubner, *Constitutional Fragments*, n 19 above.

[88] Foucault identifies this reversal as central to understanding neo- and ordoliberalism. See M Foucault, *The Birth of Bio-Politics: Lectures at the College de France* (New York, NY, Palgrave MacMillan, 2010).

[89] *Cf* Breen, *Under Weber's Shadow*, n 87 above.

[90] Habermas, *The Crisis of the European Union*, n 62 above, 106.

[91] ibid, 113.

[92] See H Arendt, *Between Past and Future* (London, Penguin, 1968) 17–19. The point is made as strongly in *The Human Condition* (Chicago, IL, University of Chicago Press, 1958) 222: 'Escape from the frailty of human affairs into the solidity of quiet and order', Arendt notes, 'has in fact so much to recommend it that the greater part of political philosophy since Plato could easily be interpreted as various attempts to find theoretical foundations and practical ways for an escape from politics altogether'.

nation or Jefferson's self-evident truths—politics becomes mere administrative execution, analogous to the private economic decisions of the household. The loss of the political comes with the identification of a source of authority 'beyond the sphere of power' and, whether the law of nature or the commands of God, not itself 'man-made'. The source of authority apparently 'beyond the sphere of power' and therefore beyond the sphere of democratic politics is now the market itself and global capital markets in particular, their authority anonymised in the form of barely comprehensible and virtually unaccountable credit rating agencies.

The suggestion of the 'naturalness' of any existing order and the inequalities in which it results is ideologically potent, particularly when it is accompanied by an ethos of competition and an individualism that might be attractive for other moral or cultural reasons.[93] The high water-mark of this reification of the capitalist economic logic is the neoliberal insistence that 'there is no alternative' (TINA), propagated so forcefully by Margaret Thatcher that it was swallowed whole not only by her Conservative but by her 'Third Way' successors, in the UK and elsewhere.[94]

Can the justice deficit be *politicised or re-politicised*? This, it is argued, is a condition for it to be democratised, however democratisation might then be institutionally imagined and implemented. Although this will not of course convince those who deny there is a social justice deficit at all in the EU, it remains, if correct, a contribution to an account of why social (or market) justice deficits are in large measure political artefacts, whether or not they exist in any particular place at any particular time.

The struggle for social justice must be viewed not only in terms of the possibilities of reacting through existing channels to the (actual or perceived) injustice perpetuated by market capitalism but in terms of the creation of markets and of the channels of response to them *in the first place*. We can then consider in particular the way that politics facilitates or hinders a democratic response to that actual or perceived injustice as well as its complicity in the initial movements of market making and inducing the extension of market logic.

Politicisation of the justice deficit points at how capitalist market logic depends upon the state and on political action not only for its maintenance and 'taming', but also for its creation and re-creation. This can occur both through action and inaction. It suggests that the state is at once both problem and solution to the crises of democratic capitalism; both poison and cure.

According to a radical philosophical tradition, the state apparatus is not only responsible for an initial, often violent, movement of original or 'primitive' accumulation that sets up the economic and social conditions for market capitalism (Marx's 'doubly free labourer'), but also constantly or periodically re-constitutes these conditions through 'accumulation by dispossession'.[95] But others—including

---

[93] On the supposed natural quality of the economic order in neoliberalism, see, eg, Foucault, *The Birth of Bio-Politics*, n 88 above. O Parker, *Cosmopolitan Government in Europe* (London, Routledge, 2012). On how neoliberalism splits the left, by co-opting liberal social causes, see Harvey, *A Brief History*, n 57 above.

[94] Thatcher, when asked to name her greatest legacy, famously responds, 'Tony Blair'.

[95] See D Harvey, *The New Imperialism* (Oxford, Oxford University Press, 2003); E Meiksins Wood, *Empire of Capital* (London, Verso, 2003). For an earlier account, see Arendt, *The Origins of Totalitarianism*, n 28 above, 148, drawing on Rosa Luxemburg.

those less radical—have identified political action, coercion and violence, whether through internal corruption, war or in the form of global imperialism ('political capitalism'), as central to at least some types and certain periods of market formation and continuing in aspects of modern capitalism.[96]

Violence, coercion and imperialism, however, are only contingently necessary to alter the balance of forces between democracy and capital. In the most recent era of neoliberalism, to the conceptual dynamic of social and market justice must also be added political and legal changes made to and by the state which tip the balance between democracy and capitalism in favour of capital, such as the hollowing out of state powers, the turn from government to governance, wholesale privatisation programmes, the removal of issues from the democratic agenda and into the regulatory arena of experts and technocrats, and constitutionalisation—and therefore judicialisation—of economic rules, particularly through international institutions.[97] There is a strong affinity between privatisation and regulation on the one hand and technocratic, expert government on the other, and of course in the EU this was captured by Majone's notion of the 'regulatory state', although it is also an aspect of the ideology of 'constrained democracy' that we explored above.[98]

There was, and is, nothing inevitable about the turn to the regulatory state; it is the expression of political choices and planned structures. Placing the political and its most potent manifestation, the modern state, at the root of the political economy of capitalism (whether classical, late or 'post-modern') and the seemingly inexorable spread of market logic, highlights the contingency of the market as an economic and normative form, however powerfully articulated and cultivated institutionally and ideologically. As Joseph Weiler acknowledged with respect to the process of market-building as the centrepiece of European integration:

> A 'single European market' is a concept which still has the power to stir, but it is also a 'single European market'. It is not simply a technocratic programme to remove the remaining obstacles to the free movement of all factors of production. It is at the same time a highly politicised choice of ethos, ideology and political culture: the culture of 'the market' ... premised on the assumption of formal equality of individuals ... Crucially, this not only accentuates the pressure for uniformity, but also manifests a social (and hence ideological) choice which prizes market efficiency and European-wide neutrality of competition above other competing values.[99]

Of course depoliticisation was in some sense a deliberate choice in the designs of the various European communities, which favoured consensual over conflictual evolution, at least the consensus of powerful political and economic elites.[100] The

---

[96] Such as Max Weber himself, with his category of 'political capitalism'. See, eg, R Swedberg, *Max Weber and the Idea of Economic Sociology* (Princeton, NJ, Princeton University Press, 1998) 46–53.

[97] See, eg, S Gill, *Power and Resistance in the New World Order* (New York, NY, Palgrave Macmillan, 2003); D Nicol, *The Constitutional Protection of Capitalism* (Oxford, Hart Publishing, 2010); W Bonefeld, 'Neo-Liberal Europe and the Transformation of Democracy' in P Nousios, H Overbeek and A Tsolakis (eds), *Globalisation and European Integration* (London, Routledge, 2011).

[98] See G Majone, *Regulating Europe* (London, Routledge, 1996).

[99] JHH Weiler, 'The Transformation of Europe' (1991) 100 *Yale Law Journal* 2403, 2477.

[100] For an account, see M Dani, 'Rehabilitating Social Conflicts in European Public Law' (2012) 18 *European Law Journal* 621.

transnational economy would be based on legal guarantees, technical regulations and even 'soft laws' such as the Stability and Growth Pact, rather than centralised political controls subject to democratic contestation. One might say, adopting Weiler's influential narrative, that it was based on this combination of law and technocracy precisely *because* political controls remained with the Member States, reluctant to surrender them, particularly in the early stages of integration.[101]

But once the political nature of transnational market logics is acknowledged, then alternatives to the fundamentals of the current set-up—and not merely tinkering around the edges—might be explored as a genuine possibility. The crisis is, in any case, already exposing the weakness of the rule of law and technology in the face of political response to economic emergency, as developments in the grey zone of the Union method evolve, although it is too early yet to say precisely what this portends.[102]

VII. DEMOCRATISING THE JUSTICE DEFICIT?

The 'Keynesian–Westphalian' negotiation of market and social justice through a combination of 'constrained capitalism' and 'constrained democracy' can no longer be taken for granted, if it has not already been consigned to the history books.[103] We have sketched the role that European integration has played in this negotiation and its transformation, although of course it is a story that touches on all the states of the democratic capitalist world.

The effect of globalisation and Europeanisation has been 'to destabilise' the existing structures of political claims and to change the dynamics of market and social justice.[104] With this destabilisation, even explosion, of the national frame, the assumption no longer holds that the modern territorial state is the exclusive site of justice claims. Neither is it clear that the citizens of such states are exclusively the relevant subjects of debates about justice. As Nancy Fraser argues, not just the 'what' but also the 'who' of justice must now be up for grabs.[105] This is nowhere more evident than in contemporary Europe, where integration now directly raises the question of what, if anything, Germans owe Greeks (or vice versa), either as the result of a 'moral calculus' of integration or for the benefit of their own long-term self-interest.

In addition to the usual first order questions of distribution and recognition within a particular community, second-order questions are increasingly being raised about justice in the EU. Not only the substance of justice, but also the 'frame' is increasingly in dispute, and demands are increasingly being made for a post-Westphalian theory of justice.[106]

---

[101] ibid; Weiler, 'The Transformation of Europe', n 99 above.
[102] See Menéndez, 'The Existential Crisis', n 69 above, for the long view.
[103] Müller himself thinks we have recently turned a corner and that the EU has changed qualitatively, no longer able to lock in states to democratic and social commitments, see Müller, 'Beyond Militant Democracy', n 31 above.
[104] See Fraser, 'Reframing Justice', n 49 above.
[105] ibid.
[106] ibid, 73.

And yet, in recalling the priority of politics we cannot ignore the question of *the political*, or *le politique*, which, fundamentally, defines the parameters of who is to be counted amongst the members of the relevant community, and, in its most infamous formulation, between who is friend and enemy.[107] The point is not merely to highlight the priority of action and contingency over decisionism and necessity, because, as Fraser herself acknowledges, *the political* 'furnishes the stage on which struggles over distribution and recognition are played out'. She continues:

> Establishing criteria of social belonging, and thus determining who counts as a member, the political dimension of justice specifies the reach of those other dimensions: it tells us who is included in, and who excluded from, the circle of those entitled to a just distribution and reciprocal recognition.[108]

The framing of 'the political' determines not only who can make justice claims, by virtue of establishing who is a member of the relevant community, but also how such claims are to be made, judged and acted upon, and of course the precise procedures are significant because they not only exclude certain voices, but also privilege some interests over others in stipulating the rules and conditions of access.

Political justice is therefore concerned chiefly with the idea and the practice of *representation*, where misrepresentation would point to the distinctively political obstacles to equality of representation, in addition to those obstacles to justice presented by maldistribution and misrecognition within a polity.

Misrepresentation can occur at the first ordinary, domestic level of the democratic process, where, for example, the rules and internal constituencies of the electoral system itself are drawn. This is far from straightforward in a compound polity such as the EU, which has to balance the basic principle of the equality of persons with the more complex principle of the equality of states because the constitutional identity of the component parts matters.[109] A balance is sought through the electoral system of the European Parliament, with its system of degressive proportionality, engagement with national parliaments, and in conjunction with forms of indirect representation through the European Commission and Council. Although this balance is difficult in any federal or compound polity it has special resonance in the EU because of the continuing sovereignty claims of the constituent parts, as so forcefully articulated, however disingenuously, by the German Constitutional Court in the Lisbon decision, which insists on maintaining the constitutional power to guarantee its own social state.[110]

Misrepresentation can also occur at a second level, which concerns the basic boundary-setting aspect of 'the political'. Here misrepresentation takes the form of *mis*-framing, where the injustice is not insufficient representation but wrongful exclusion from any kind of political representation. Although the

---

[107] C Schmitt, *The Concept of the Political* (Chicago, IL, University of Chicago Press, 2007). For an account of European constitutionalism which gives priority to the political, but in more dynamic and reflexive terms, see MA Wilkinson, 'Political Constitutionalism and the European Union' (2013) 76 *Modern Law Review* 191.

[108] Fraser, 'Reframing Justice', n 49 above, 75.

[109] See, eg, C Lord and J Pollak, 'Unequal But Democratic? Equality According to Karlsruhe' (2013) 20 *European Journal of Public Policy* 190.

[110] For a critique of the German court's understanding of political equality, see ibid.

process of economic globalisation exposes this mis-framing because it reveals our inter-connectedness in a more comprehensive and immediate manner, it must be remembered, with Arendt, that the Keynesian–Westphalian frame itself mis-framed in significant respects, with political emancipation tied in with legacies of capitalist expansion and imperialism.[111]

If political obstacles to full and fair representation existed within the Keynesian–Westphalian frame of the territorial state, European integration—and economic globalisation more generally—exposes the injustice of the frame itself because those affected by it are marginalised from its political decision-making centres in spite of the legal and political equality they are formally attributed. The enhanced possibility of political gerrymandering comes at the expense of the marginalised and powerless who can only, if at all, channel their claims through relatively ineffective political channels. The allocation of votes in the ESM, weighted by capital contributions, is an example of the normalisation of the conflation of economic and political power, which has potentially dramatic effects on the principle of political representation in the EU.

Europeanisation and globalisation are politicising the normal Westphalian frame of justice by making a dimension of *in*justice more visible. A special kind of meta-injustice is exposed, where some are wrongly excluded from consideration, 'denied the chance to press first-order claims' within a community.[112]

Metapolitical misrepresentation arises when states and transnational elites monopolize the activity of frame-setting, denying voice to those who may be harmed in the process, and blocking creation of democratic arenas where the latter's claims can be vetted and redressed. The effect is to exclude the overwhelming majority of people from participation in the meta-discourses that determine the authoritative division of political space.[113]

In the EU, those who consider their voices silenced by processes beyond their individual and even collective control will take to the streets instead, as we have seen from Athens to Madrid, and from Lisbon to Paris. But, one might ask, in the new light of the redistributive implications of economic and monetary union, why is it that the political code is still predominantly nation versus nation? What explains the absence or weakness of transnational social movements in comparison to the power of transnational capital? Is it a straightforward failure of elites?

To begin to answer this, a third element of social struggle must be explored, working alongside economic and social justice, in order to appreciate the full complexity of the justice deficit: 'emancipation'. Really existing social struggles do not neatly fit the contours of a Polanyian double movement or of Streeck's rebalancing of the relationship between market and social justice. Instead they have exposed problems not only with marketisation and the spread of market logic but also with the socially protective responses to it that, in the name of social justice, have depended on an exclusionary rhetoric of communitarianism, homogeneity and popular consensus.[114] Struggles for emancipation are now cross-cultural, transnational,

---

[111] Arendt, *The Origins of Totalitarianism*, n 28 above.
[112] Fraser, 'Reframing Justice', n 49 above, 77.
[113] ibid, 85.
[114] On the exclusion and sovereign violence of the social contract model see Parker, *Cosmopolitan Government*, n 93 above.

plural and heterogeneous; from feminism to the anti-war movements, Occupy to trade unionism, environmentalism to the *indignados*, the voices of social justice are diverse and dispersed.[115]

A politics of representation must 'aim to democratize the process of frame-setting',[116] to contest the way in which boundaries themselves are drawn. This is no easy task.[117] But what it suggests is that to the tension between the logics of democracy and capitalism must be added the logic of the state, and its external and internal manner of setting the scene for this ceaseless antagonism of interests and values, including the shaping of transnational political spaces such as the EU. Streeck's dilemma of market and social justice must be substituted for a trilemma: of market, social and political justice. Only then might the destabilisation of the national frame signal democracy's graduation rather than its retirement.

---

[115] See the report on subterranean politics, Mary Kaldor, Sabine Selchow, Sean Deel and Tamsin Murray-Leach, 'The Bubbing up of Subterranean Politics in Europe' (2012) available at www.subterrancean politics.eu. In the eyes of the Habermas–Derrida initiative, it was the anti-war movements coordinated on 15 February against the invasion of Iraq that gave birth to a European public sphere. See J Habermas and J Derrida, 'February 15, Or What Binds Europeans Together: A Plea for a Common Foreign Policy, Beginning in the Core of Europe' reprinted in (2003) 10 *Constellations* 291.
[116] Fraser, 'Reframing Justice', n 49 above, 80.
[117] This is an area, however, where democratic experimentalism has presented certain insights about the need to keep open, contingent and provisional the form and content of the democratic community.

9
Whose Justice? Which Europe?

AGUSTÍN JOSÉ MENÉNDEZ

Fruchtbare Fragestellungen werden immer dem staatlichen Leben selbst entnommen.[1]

I. INTRODUCTION

CAN ONE SERIOUSLY claim to be *against* justice? (Is that not tantamount to being, horror of horrors, a partisan of injustice?) Moving from the abstract to the concrete, would anybody in her or his right mind be against nurturing and developing a discourse on justice aimed at shaping the content of European law and the very structure of European institutions and decision-making processes? Can we be against *that* without being the worst kind of conservative possible, the conservative who stands for an impossible status quo?

Against the current and against the odds, and in Tory not Whig spirit, I claim in this chapter that there are good reasons to think twice before enthusiastically endorsing *justice über alles* in general; and, more particularly, that promoting justice to the alpha and the omega on anything European is a bet not devoid of high (political) risks. Better not.

In section II of the chapter, I maintain that the very history of political thought (particularly the history of the uses at which political *philosophy* has been put) should make us very reluctant to engage in justice discourses when divorced or decoupled from democratic politics. Justice has indeed frequently been deployed against democratic politics and against politics *tout court* with a view to pre-empt, deny, and hollow out politics, especially democratic politics. There is the risk that discourses on European justice are used to that effect, and indeed become natural heirs to the now worn out governance and cosmopolitan pluralism fads, so disastrous from a democratic perspective (and from an economic one, too).

At a time when perhaps not only Rome, but also Brussels is burning (and literally, now and again, Athens, Lisbon, Budapest and Madrid *are* in flames), a mere negative note of caution against justice based on the misuses of justice discourses may be found too disappointing by half (and too well known by much more than half). So one cannot and should not avoid asking oneself *what to do Spinelli?* That is the one

---

[1] H Heller, *Staatslehre* (Tübingen, Mohr Siebeck, 1983) 38.

million Euro (or is it Lire, Escudos or Drachmas?) question. It can hardly be avoided when confronted not so much with the problematic but hard to grasp question of what is just in Europe, but with the very concrete injustices galore resulting from the specific policies implemented in the wake of the manifold crises which Europe, and the European Union in particular, has gone through since late 2006. My very modest claim, explored in section III, is that indeed we should engage with political justice, not justice *tout court*, and in particular, that we should focus on the very *unit* of distributive justice in European law and politics.

II. JUSTICE OR DEMOCRATIC POLITICS?

Justice may be the nemesis, not the saviour of democratic politics. There are plenty of precedents of justice discourses playing exactly that role. From Plato's Socrates, political philosophy has been developed, nurtured and shaped by authors who were more than occasionally suspicious of politics and very especially of democratic politics (odd exceptions—perhaps Machiavelli and certainly Spinoza—confirm the rule at the very least until the French Revolution). As the central if not *the* central category in political philosophy, justice has been deployed as a rhetorical device to pre-empt, set aside or hollow out democratic politics. In what follows, I will (1) claim that there are at least three different strategies of depoliticisation through justice claims; (2) define each of the three strategies by reference to the political philosopher (Plato, Hobbes and Godwin) that has been regarded (rightly or wrongly) as champion of each of these strategies, and (3) show how the 'hiding and disguising' use of justice is being mobilised in present discourses on the European crisis.[2]

First, justice can be used to pre-empt politics, and especially, democratic politics, *à la Plato*. A deeply political writer, very much a son of his native Athens and an actor in the period following the defeat of Athens in the Peloponnesian Wars, Plato made justice a full *alternative* to politics. His four key political discourses (*Protagoras, Republic, Statesman* and *Laws*) illustrate this point.[3] Socrates' Plato disbelieves in the power of political education and despises Protagoras for his

---

[2] The choice of these three authors is highly subjective. Other authors could have been picked, but it seems to me that for the present modest purpose of calling the attention of the reader to the dangers of seeking refuge in justice discourses, the subjectivity of the choice may not be that relevant.

[3] See C Castoriadis, *Sur le Politique de Platon* (Paris, Seuil, 1999) (English translation: *On Plato's Statesman* (Stanford, CA, Stanford University Press, 2002). Castoriadis offers an extremely sophisticated analysis of Plato's political thought by considering the 'tension' between the Republic (as the 'ideal' polity model) and the Statesman (and the Laws), where Plato is considering the 'second best' polity. The same intuition about the replacement of politics by justice in Plato's thought was expressed several times by Hannah Arendt. See especially her (unfinished) *Was Ist Politik?* (München, Piper, 1995) (I have read the Spanish translation, *¿Qué es la política?* (Barcelona, Paidós, 1995); there is no English translation yet to my knowledge). Arendt's and Castoriadis' construction is much more refined than the more openly (and partially emotive) R Crossman, *Plato Today* (Oxford, Oxford University Press, 1939) and K Popper, *The Open Society and Its Enemies, Volume 1* (London, Routledge, 1945). It suffices to read the preface that Popper wrote for the second edition to realise the existential involvement of the author in the writing of the book (an engagement for which the book is the better, but Plato's assessment may be a trifle anachronistic).

deeply democratic belief in the transformative power of democratic pedagogics.[4] Both Socrates' Plato in *Republic* and the anonymous Athenian in the *Laws* argue in favour of a static political constitution, one in which everybody fulfils the tasks that have been set for them by *her* nature (that is the original understanding of justice as giving to each what is due to her, later coined by the Romans in the apt and revealing maxim *suum cuique tribuere*).[5] A fundamental anti-egalitarian politics necessarily follows.[6] Rule by the political philosopher (*Republic*) or by the despot who is conveniently disposed to have the philosopher or philosophers whisper in his ear (*Laws*, with the nocturnal council playing a role perhaps not so dissimilar to that of anti-majoritarian institutions in our modern political systems)[7] is indeed a logical consequence of the endorsement of anti-egalitarianism. Plato's justice pre-empts politics because it is prior to politics.

It is not hard to see Platonic streaks in the contemporary debates on the European crises.[8] The very terms in which some institutional actors and even institutions

---

[4] This was perhaps the real dividing issue between Plato and the sophists. Plato was indeed extremely effective in forging the black legend of sophists as venial nihilists. But contemporaries were likely to regard Socrates as yet another sophist. In what remains a widely read general history of Greek philosophy (WKC Guthrie, *A History of Greek Philosophy: Volume III, The Fifth-Century Enlightenment* (Cambridge, Cambridge University Press, 1969), Socrates is characterised as a sophist.

[5] Plato's Republic 433a is the 'locus classicus' for this definition of justice: 'The principle we laid down right at the start, when we first founded our city, as something we must stick to throughout—this, I think, or some form of it, is justice. What we laid down—and often repeated, if you remember—was that each individual should follow, out of the occupations available in the city, the one for which his natural character best fitted him'. Of the many superb recent translations of the Republic, I quote from Plato, *The Republic*, trans T Griffith (Cambridge, Cambridge University Press, 2000) 127. Cicero did then play a key role in fixing the translation of the phrase into philosophical Latin (into the *suum cuique tribuere*). See his *De Officiis*, I.15: 'Everything that is honourable arises from one of four parts: it is involved either with the perception of truth and with ingenuity; or with preserving fellowship among men, with assigning to each his own, and with faithfulness to agreements one has made; or with the greatness and strength of a lofty and unconquered spirit; or with order and limit in everything that is said and done (modesty and restraint are included here)'. I quote from Cicero, *On Duties*, trans EM Atkins (Cambridge, Cambridge University Press, 1991) 7.

[6] Even if, paradoxically, the key cleavages that Plato regarded as relevant were disruptive of some traditional cleavages, including the male chauvinistic one according to which women are naturally subordinated to men. Plato wanted to achieve political stability (and indeed admired the endurance of Egyptian kingdoms) but to get there one would have needed to change radically the way in which society was structured.

[7] On the nocturnal council, see Plato, *Laws*, trans TJ Saunders (Harmondsworth, Penguin, 2004) 461–62 (951d–952c, 960b–969d, especially 951d): 'This Council, which should partly consist of young men and partly of old, must have a strict rule to meet daily from dawn until the sun is well up in the sky The discussion at their meetings must always centre round their own state, the problems of legislation, and any other important point relevant to such topics that they may discover from external sources'.

[8] Plato's philosopher kings were to be selected on the basis of their moral knowledge, not their technical knowledge. But unless one not only shares Plato's belief in the radical inequality of human beings from a normative perspective, but also assumes that Plato's argument was made in full good faith, one may suspect that contemporary 'economic knowledge' (allegedly said to be 'scientific', 'empirically proven') plays a social role similar to Plato's 'moral knowledge'. *Cf* the very peculiar argument of the *Bundesverfassungsgericht* in its 'Maastricht' judgment (BVerfGE 89, 155, 2 BvR 2134/92 and 2159/92 (12 October 1993)), para 96: 'The clear intention of the legislator amending the constitution was therefore to create a basis in constitutional law for the monetary union for which the Maastricht Treaty provides, but at the same time to restrict to this case only the independent powers and rights associated with it which are described here. This modification of the principle of democracy, which is designed to secure the confidence of making payment that is placed in a currency, is justifiable, because it takes account of the special factor, *established in the German system and also scientifically proven*, that an independent central bank is more likely to protect monetary value, and therefore the general economic basis for national budget policy and private planning and disposition, while maintaining economic liberty than are sovereign governmental institutions' (emphasis added).

present the issues at stake and justify different policy alternatives are not only highly charged in moral (if not *moralising*) terms but also smack of Platonism. The analysis of the causes leading to the present crises is dominated by claims concerning the moral failings of the citizenry and the ruling elites of the peripheral states. Southerners (*toutes confondues*) 'lived beyond their means', some national democracies 'failed' due to shortcomings in the political culture of some Member States, the governments of which (and only the governments of which) are highly 'extractive'.[9] These arguments run parallel to those according to which the citizens of core Eurozone states are enjoying the fruits of their sobriety, their institutions managed to maintain discipline rather than falling prey to their democratic instincts to spend, while their elites managed to brave public opinion and take 'very difficult' decisions (unpopular when not verging on bypassing democratic politics) that have now been vindicated.

It would be easy to dismiss such claims as populist mumbo jumbo for electoral consumption were it not for the fact that such claims have percolated into law and policy making. The 'governance' of economic and monetary policy has been reformed so as to get rid of the political *and* discretionary character of fiscal policy. The enactment of what are (alleged) to be strict fiscal rules (stricter medium-term fiscal objectives, with a deficit cap of 1 per cent,[10] a renewed emphasis on the debt ceiling of 60 per cent of the Gross Domestic Product (GDP), coupled with specific deficit and debt reduction trajectories,[11] limits on expenditure growth[12] and automatic correction mechanisms when the trajectory is not followed)[13] comes very close to rule by the philosopher king, albeit with the philosopher replaced by the persons 'in the know' about the 'governance' of the economy (a group that has been

---

[9] Private elites, even banking elites, are less frequently labelled as extractive; instead the more politically correct claim addressed to them is that they 'mispriced risks', which sounds like a venial, not capital sin. But is it?

[10] See Art 2(a), second paragraph of consolidated Council Regulation (EC) No 1466/97 of 7 July 1997 on the strengthening of the surveillance of budgetary positions and the surveillance and coordination of economic policies [1997] OJ L209/1. Further tightened by the Fiscal Compact, 3(1)(a) and (b) to 0.5% GDP, except for countries with debt levels significantly below 60% and clearly 'sustainable' public finances, as in Art 3(1)(d). See the Treaty on Stability, Coordination and Governance in the Economic and Monetary Union ('Fiscal Compact') (2 March 2012), text available at www.european-council.europa.eu/media/639235/st00tscg26_en12.pdf.

[11] For deficit reduction trajectories, Art 5(1), second paragraph of Council Regulation (EC) No 1466/97 of 7 July 1997 on the strengthening of the surveillance of budgetary positions and the surveillance and coordination of economic policies [1997] OJ L209/1; in addition, Art 6(3) establishes a specific limit to the 'deviation' that may occur in the implementation of the budget. For debt reduction trajectories, Art 2(1)(a) of the consolidated text of Regulation (EC) No 1467/97 on speeding up and clarifying the implementation of the excessive deficit procedure [1997] L209/16. For a country such as Italy, with a debt of roughly 120% of its GDP, this implies reducing the debt by 3 GDP points per year. It does not take much imagination to foresee that this will lead to (mis)sale of public assets. And indeed this contributed significantly to the quick rise in the interest rates that Italy had to pay when issuing debt in the early summer of 2011, leading to the 11th chapter in the Eurocrisis.

[12] Art 5(1), third paragraph of consolidated Council Regulation (EC) No 1466/97 of 7 July 1997 on the strengthening of the surveillance of budgetary positions and the surveillance and coordination of economic policies [1997] OJ L209/1.

[13] Art 3(1)(e) Fiscal Compact. For the common principles laid down by the Commission, see European Commission, 'Communication from the Commission on the Common principles on national fiscal correction mechanisms' COM (2012) 342 final.

self-selecting at places such as the Bank of International Settlements for decades).[14] Persons who, should be added, are to be judged not only and perhaps not so much by the *output* their governance produces, but by their moral rectitude (which allows them to take impopular decisions, and persist implementing them even when they seem to fail to produce results). Such norms were introduced first in some core Eurozone countries (Germany being the obvious reference point) thanks to the 'courage' of some leaders, and now should be extended to all Member States also in a 'courageous' way (ie independently of whether a clear majority of the people are against them, and independently of the short-term, mid-term and even long-term social costs).

Furthermore, democratic politics has been largely set aside in countries bailed out both under a formal programme[15] or by the European Central Bank (ECB) under its debt buying programmes.[16] When Papandreou tried to hold a referendum on whether to accept austerity or leave the Eurozone, the Greek Prime Minister was forced to resign. We the people *should* not have the final word on whether to follow

---

[14] A Le Bor, *Tower of Basel* (New York, NY, Public Affairs, 2013). A not-so-angry, albeit less vivid, account is G Toniolo, *Central Bank Cooperation at the Bank for International Settlements* (Cambridge, Cambridge University Press, 2007).

[15] Greece, Ireland, Portugal, Cyprus and Spain. For the first Greek programme, see European Commission, 'The Economic Adjustment Programme for Greece' (2010) *European Economy Occasional Papers* No 61. For the second Greek programme, see European Commission, 'The Second Economic Adjustment Programme for Greece' (2012) *European Economy Occasional Papers* No 94. For the Irish programme, see European Commission, 'The Economic Adjustment Programme for Ireland' (2011) *European Economy Occasional Papers* No 76. For Portugal, see European Commission, 'The Economic Adjustment Programme for Portugal' (2011) *European Economy Occasional Papers* No 79. For Cyprus, see European Commission, 'The Economic Adjustment Programme for Cyprus' (2013) *European Economy Occasional Papers* No 149. For Spain, see European Commission, 'The Financial Sector Adjustment Programme for Spain' (2012) *European Economy Occasional Papers* No 118. The Spanish programme was said to be a 'limited' or 'lite' one, as the loans were 'earmarked' for the 'redress' of the financial sector. Besides the fancy terminology, it is hard to discern much of a difference between a full programme, a programme lite, and no programme under close monitoring on the side of European institutions (especially as this was a result of legislative change and the de facto hegemony of creditor states within the Eurozone). The 'troika' and/or the Commission (and very particularly the Commissioner for Economic and Financial Affairs) have acquired the competences and the proclivities to micro-manage some national economic policies. On the structural roots of the problem and the proclivity to micro-management, see FW Scharpf, 'Monetary Union, Fiscal Crisis and the Disabling of Democratic Accountability' in A Schäfer and W Streeck (eds), *Politics in the Age of Austerity* (Cambridge, Polity Press, 2013). Hungary, Latvia and Romania were subject to what turned out to be experiments in 'economic adjustment programmes' in the immediate aftermath of the crisis. As they were not Eurozone Member States (and all were 'new' Member States), insufficient attention was paid to the phenomenal implications of the formula tested then.

[16] The old securities markets programme and the new, and yet to be activated, outright monetary transactions. On outright monetary transactions, we keep on lacking proper legal regulation. The ECB published a press release on 6 September 2012 concerning the technical features of these transactions. See www.ecb.europa.eu/press/pr/date/2012/html/pr120906_1.en.html. One may be forgiven for speculating whether the lack of a full and proper legal text is not intentional. One could even imagine that the ECB may have considered that the chances of the German Constitutional Court not rendering a judgment rendering legally and/or politically impossible to undertake these transactions may be reduced if the review of German constitutionality has to take place by indirect reference to a press release (doubly indirect, as the German Constitutional Court cannot adjudicate directly on the constitutionality of supranational norms). At the time of going to press, the ruling of the German Constitutional Court was rendered public (available at www.bundesverfassungsgericht.de/en/decisions/rs20140114_2bvr272813en.html). It may well be that the non-publication strategy played a role in avoiding the outright declaration of unconstitutionality of the *Outright Monetary Transactions* (OMT) programme.

austerity policies. *That* was not a question for democratic politics. Indeed, the three main Portuguese parties were forced into the negotiations of the Portuguese programme, taking place *during the electoral* campaign, so as to ensure that whatever the people voted, austerity would be the policy. Similarly, when national democratically elected governments have expressed reservations about austerity policies, pseudo-technocratic governments have replaced them.[17] More insidiously, the six-part and two-part legislative packages,[18] and especially the two regulations on macroeconomic imbalances,[19] have created the institutional means of replacing national democratic politics by the rule of the economic kings in non-majoritarian institutions (the Commission, the ECB and national fiscal boards), institutions that are now formally empowered to micromanage national economies in full disrespect of the division of competences set in the treaties.[20] Internal deflation, as Fritz Scharpf has clearly shown, cannot be implemented through democratic politics.[21]

Secondly, justice can be used as a means of justifying the setting aside of democratic politics in the name of preserving the political community. The ultimate master in this regard is Hobbes. The author of the *Leviathan* was not only the son of fear in an existential sense,[22] but the citizen of a country which had experienced a rapid, radical and destabilising politicisation. It is this context that explains Hobbes' move to turn natural law on its head by defining politics by reference to the moment in which the political order collapses, is on the verge of collapsing or is believed to be about to collapse. Hobbes' state of nature is a thinly veiled reconstruction of

---

[17] Hungary, Romania, Italy and Greece; with the present Letta government in Italy being the utmost example of a *grossekoalition*, perhaps only comparable to the British national government of 1932.

[18] Regulation (EU) No 1173/2011 of the European Parliament and of the Council of 16 November 2011 on the effective enforcement of budgetary surveillance in the euro area [2011] OJ L306/1; Regulation (EU) No 1174/2011 of the European Parliament and of the Council of 16 November 2011 on enforcement measures to correct excessive macroeconomic imbalances in the euro area [2011] OJ L306/8; Regulation (EU) No 1175/2011 of the European Parliament and of the Council of 16 November 2011 amending Council Regulation (EC) No 1466/97 on the strengthening of the surveillance of budgetary positions and the surveillance and coordination of economic policies [2011] OJ L306/12; Regulation (EU) No 1176/2011 of the European Parliament and of the Council of 16 November 2011 on the prevention and correction of macroeconomic imbalances [2011] OJ L306/25; Council Regulation (EU) No 1177/2011 of 8 November 2011 amending Regulation (EC) No 1467/97 on speeding up and clarifying the implementation of the excessive deficit procedure [2011] OJ L306/33; Council Directive 2011/85/EU of 8 November 2011 on requirements for budgetary frameworks of the Member States [2011] OJ L306/41. Regulation (EU) No 472/2013 21 May 2013 on the strengthening of economic and budgetary surveillance of Member States in the euro area experiencing or threatened with serious difficulties with respect to their financial stability [2013] OJ L140/1; Regulation (EU) No 473/2013 of 21 May 2013 on common provisions for monitoring and assessing draft budgetary plans and ensuring the correction of excessive deficit of the Member States in the euro area [2013] OJ L140/11.

[19] Regulation (EU) No 1176/2011 of the European Parliament and of the Council of 16 November 2011 on the prevention and correction of macroeconomic imbalances [2011] OJ L306/25; Regulation (EU) No 1174/2011 of the European Parliament and of the Council of 16 November 2011 on enforcement measures to correct excessive macroeconomic imbalances in the euro area [2011] OJ L306/8.

[20] The formal empowerment is not matched by actual knowledge or political legitimacy, so is bound to either be ineffective or disastrous.

[21] FW Scharpf, *Berlin paper* (on file with the author). *Modus Platonico*, we have created the constitutional framework in which democratic politics is pre-empted so that internal deflation can be. Very Platonic indeed.

[22] According to his very poetic reconstruction of his birth as having been prompted by the fear her mother experienced when the Armada neared the English coast.

the political state in which England found itself in the years immediately preceding and following the Civil War, a state in which the privileges of old are threatened not only and not mostly by the Cromwellian bid to establish a republic, but by the radical democratic project of the New Model Army, not to speak of levellers and diggers; a state in which the defence of the status quo requires transcending if the powerful few are not to see their position threatened, or, what is the same, it is a state of emergency in which an appeal to justice conjures the trick of justifying breaking all the old laws in the very name of order.[23]

Indeed, to the normative potential of a radical democratic discourse written in the grammar of religious dissent but very much constructed with the bits and pieces of the old law (articulated by many, but very cogently by the Levellers),[24] Hobbes opposes a justice discourse that releases the sovereign of any external normative limit in the very name of defending order. The social destabilising potential of a discourse of political and democratic justice which takes seriously the normative underpinning of the law (by standing fast to national democratic constitutions, for example) is conjured up by means of claiming that all normative standards (the natural law of old, the national constitutions of now) subvert and dissolve themselves into chaos and anarchy unless the very definition of such normative standards is in the hands of the sovereign himself. In such a way, Hobbes' justice *cannot but* end up legitimising the law posed by the sovereign, no matter its substantive contents and no matter how disruptive positive law may be regarding the pre-existing law and the pre-existing social costumes.

Strong echoes of the Hobbesian peculiar natural law turn can be found in the political discourses which justify the decisions taken by supranational and national institutions in the name of overcoming the European crises, and in the process, setting aside supranational and national constitutional law (perhaps even the very ideal of the *Rechtsstaat*).[25] The cause of preserving the polity, of conjuring the existential threat to the European Union or this or that Member State, is regarded as the ultimate manifestation of justice, and as such, overriding the arguments that can be made in favour of the respect for 'formal' constitutionality. *Salus populus* as *suprema lex* requires either (1) forcing to the utmost limit the interpretation of the literal tenor of norms (as was the case with the no bail-out clause enshrined in

---

[23] See SS Wolin, *Politics and Vision*, 2nd edn (Princeton, NJ, Princeton University Press, 2004) ch 8; E Meiksinis Wood, *Liberty and Property* (London, Verso, 2011) ch 7; N Bobbio, *Thomas Hobbes and the Natural Law Tradition* (Chicago, IL, Chicago University press, 1993); and the unavoidable, even if very much contested, CB Macpherson, *The Political Theory of Possessive Individualism* (Oxford, Oxford University Press, 1962). The authoritarian potential of Hobbes was explored in depth by Carl Schmitt in the months immediately after his fall from grace as Nazi crown jurist. See C Schmitt, *The Leviathan in Hobbes State Theory* (Chicago, IL, Chicago University Press, 2008) (the book was published in German in 1938).

[24] *Cf* ASP Woodhouse (ed), *Puritanism and Liberty, Being the Army Debates (1647–9) From the Clarke Manuscripts with Supplementary Documents* (Chicago, IL, University of Chicago Press, 1951) and A Sharp (ed), *The English Levellers* (Cambridge, Cambridge University Press, 1998).

[25] A clear distinction must be established here between, on the one hand, the 'official' discourses articulated by public officials and public lawyers with the occasion of the constitutionality review of the different legal norms through which the crisis has been 'governed', and, on the other hand, the discourses put forward in the public sphere, where officials and politicians do occasionally admit that the limits of supranational and national constitutional law have been occasionally infringed.

Article 125 of the Treaty on the Functioning of the European Union (TFEU)),[26] for example by means of imposing an 'internal ranking' of values within the fundamental law, a ranking which indeed may be different in emergency moments than in ordinary times[27] or (2) justifying the claim of the rulers to turn into law anything they call law (with full independence of the extent to which the constitutional standards regarding the formation of the democratic will have been respected or not, as the virtual substitution of parliamentary statutes by the 'soft law' of the Memoranda of Understanding and the 'hard law' of governmental law decrees in peripheral countries shows).[28]

Thirdly, justice is a powerful weapon to hollow out democratic politics when justice is identified with aggregate utility. William Godwin's radical utilitarianism has been a key source of inspiration in this regard (even if rather *malgré* Godwin).[29] In a fundamental passage in his *Enquiry into Political Justice*, Godwin defends the radical impartiality of justice. So impartial are justice claims, that if confronted with the moral dilemma of having to save one, and only one, person from a fire, we should let any relative of ours (including our own kin) burn in the flames and save the Bishop of Cambray (who serves as an exemplar of anybody who is precious to humankind as a whole, who is capable of making much good with his actions).[30] Indeed, we *should* even volunteer to burn ourselves if that renders possible saving the Bishop of Cambray.

Godwin's justice does indeed go further than Hobbes in that this very last limit to any natural obligation, the right of self-preservation, also goes. When Godwin's radical utilitarianism is coupled with a strong sense of pre-political collective identity, it justifies the immolation of each and every individual in the name of saving the collective, a decision which is almost impossible to put forward, even less justify, in a democratic decision-making procedure.

Again, it does not take much to see that some of the key arguments made regarding austerity are modelled on what is taken to be Godwin's template. The massive

---

[26] Consolidated version of the Treaty on the Functioning of the European Union [2012] OJ C326/47 (TFEU).

[27] Indeed, the only semi-plausible argument to be made in favour of the constitutionality of the process of constitutional reform followed in Spain in August 2011, so as to enshrine the golden budgetary rule and the absolute priority of the payment of the creditors of the Public Treasury. And very probably of the Slovenian constitutional reform of 2013, which introduced not only the balanced budget rule, but also ruled out the holding of referenda on the very issues at the core of the reform of 'European economic governance'. Both countries were close to a real fiscal cliff, so that the democratic legitimacy of the decisions is, to say the least, problematic. Given the disastrous consequences of previous experiences with constitution-writing at gunpoint (significantly, Art 231 of the Weimar Constitution through which Germany acknowledged its 'guilt' in the First World War), perhaps a less reckless approach would have been wise.

[28] See C Douzinas, *Philosophy and Resistance in the Crisis* (London, Polity Press, 2013).

[29] Godwin was not only an advocate of a radically impartial conception of justice, but also a radical democrat. See W Godwin, *Enquiry Concerning Political Justice* (Harmondsworth, Penguin, 1976), especially 486–93 (Book V, Chapter XIV). In the latter editions of the *Enquiry*, in which the influence of Mary Wollstonecraft is marked, the tension between radical impartiality and radical democracy is solved in favour of the latter (feelings tame the sharp corners of radical impartiality, it may be said). See also PH Marshall, *William Godwin* (New Haven, CT, Yale University Press, 1984) and M La Torre, 'Anarchismo e liberalismo: Individuo e ragione nel pensiero di William Godwin' (2002) 79 *Rivista Internazionale di Filosofia Del Diritto* 209.

[30] Godwin, *Enquiry*, n 29 above, ch 2.

social, economic and institutional costs of austerity policies are always justified in the name of saving the polity (the European Union, the Member State concerned) and of saving the 'Euro' (a rather vague expression, which is at any rate intended to mean much more than a set of coins and notes).[31] There is ample use of the classical medico–political metaphors (the patient in rude health who requires shock therapy). These are premised on the exchange of concrete and individual sacrifices (which unfortunately mean, in constitutional terms, the 'downgrading' if not 'overriding' of individual fundamental rights or concrete collective goods), which have to be left aside (temporarily, we are told) so as to render effective certain abstract collective goods (fiscal *rigueur*). The radical impartial touch is especially visible when this exchange is defended not on account of long-term economic prosperity, but in the very name of a moral duty which we should follow, also as citizens of a democratic polity, even if that implies hollowing out both the process and the substance of democratic politics. The moral force of the obligation to redeem our past faults (our living beyond our means, as the economist kings remind us) or of preserving and improving our polity (a full-fledged European Union, a 'modernised' Greece, Italy or Spain, capable of competing successfully in international markets, as in contemporary Hobbesian appeals) goes so far as to sacrifice ourselves and our present democratic constitution in a blind utilitarian spirit. It is tempting, indeed, to substitute the Bishop of Cambray for the continued existence of the Euro in Godwin's original sentence. Indeed, the Euro has become anthropomorphised.

In a public discourse characterised by rampant moralisation, there is a serious risk that justice arguments are used *à la* Plato, *à la* Hobbes or *à la* Godwin (*malgré* Godwin) position. As the normative properties of the discourses on 'good governance' or 'cosmopolitan pluralism' have been worn out by the crises, justice discourses stand a good chance of being the last refuge of the powerful few. There is a serious risk that the narratives on European justice end up concealing the ultimate rationales and power objectives which were very frequently hidden behind the governance and cosmopolitan narratives. Justice could provide new, more charming and better cut clothes.

Instead of playing tailors to the powerful, we should focus on political justice, and do so by reference to the positive common constitutional law of the European Union, to the collective of national constitutions that have been enacted through democratic constitution-making processes. In particular, it seems to me that we should stay close to the formula of the Social and Democratic *Rechtsstaat*, which remains, despite the fire and fury of the decisions taken since 2007,[32] the standard of political justice in the European constitutional canon. The regulatory ideal of the Social and Democratic *Rechtsstaat* points to the always complicated but fundamental objective of reconciling the ideals of the *Rechtsstaat*, the democratic state and the social state. The way in which these ideals are reconciled varies from country to

---

[31] A very witty criticism of the ideological function of blank calls to save the Euro in L Canfora, *E l'Europa che ci lo chiede? Falso* (Bari, Laterza, 2013). See also A Bagnai, *Il tramonto dell'euro* (Reggio Emilia, Imprimatur, 2012).

[32] For an overview of the decisions, I refer to Agustín José Menéndez, 'La Mutación Constitucional de la Unión Europea' (2012) 96 *Revista Española de Derecho Constitucional* 41.

country, and from period to period, but there is a concrete and dense elaboration of what this entails in the legislative and adjudicative practice of the Member States. It is on the basis of this much less abstract, much more concrete, legally elaborated standard that we should ascertain the justice of European law and of the European constitution. A justice built on the premise that there is no legitimacy without democratic politics.[33]

III. EUROPEAN CONSTITUTIONAL LAW AS A DEMOCRATIC STRAITJACKET: HOW IT CAME TO BE AND HOW TO START LIBERATING OURSELVES

European integration, and especially European law, contributed to the consolidation and reinforcement of the Social and Democratic *Rechtsstaat* in Europe, both within and outside the European Communities. However, this *positive reinforcing* effect of European integration came to a halt and started to become problematic, when not negative, at some point in the 1970s. Alongside external shocks that revealed looming structural tensions (the two oil crises revealing the contradictions implicit in the post-war economic growth model), the change in the effects of European integration in general and of European law in particular can be traced back to three fundamental developments in the constitutional law of the European Communities.

The first was the shift from the common market to the single market paradigm in the 1970s and 1980s, a shift that realised the potential planted in the treaties by neoliberals and ordoliberals (the German ordoliberals, the Italian Einaudians, the French in the Rueff camp) and was led by some national governments (the British governments led by Callaghan and Thatcher), some national independent players (the *Bundesbank*) and championed by the European Commission and the European Court of Justice.[34]

The second was the asymmetric economic and monetary union decided at Maastricht and implemented in 1999 (largely anticipated by the formal and informal contents of the Exchange Rate Mechanism in the late 1970s). Indeed, the illusion of an unprecedented combination of a unified monetary policy with autonomous national fiscal policies could only be sustained by massive flows of capital which created a dangerous banking union by stealth.

The third has been the series of decisions taken so far in the wake of the recent crises; paradoxically enough, such decisions have radicalised the shift started in the 1970s, and heightened the extent to which the European Union instead of

---

[33] As it seems to me Danny Nicol and Alexander Somek claim, and Jürgen Neyer somehow relativises, in their contributions to this volume, 195ff and 295ff and 211.

[34] The role played by ordoliberals and neoliberals in the drafting of the Rome treaties has been widely discussed, especially on what concerns competititon law (and in general, the 'market' design). See a recent and very nuanced analysis in KK Patel and H Schweitzer (eds), *The Historical Foundations of EU Competition Law* (Oxford, Oxford University Press, 2013). The Labour governments led by James Callaghan (from 1976 to 1979, through the British winter of discontent) broke with the post-war commitment (of both Labour and Conservative) to full employment. See D Sandbrook, *Seasons in the Sun: The Battle for Britain, 1974–1979* (Harmondsworth, Penguin, 2012). The interplay between the Callaghan administration and the International Monetary Fund (IMF), leading to the 1976 British programme, is analysed in a very illuminating way by C Rogers, *The IMF and European Economies: Crisis and Conditionality* (Basingstoke, Palgrave Macmillan, 2012).

contributing to the realisation of the Social and Democratic *Rechtsstaat*, actually undermines it and pre-empts it. Internal deflation, as already stated, is structurally incompatible with the Social and Democratic *Rechtsstaat*.

Dealing with the set of decisions taken in each of these three *transformative constitutional moments* is something that cannot be done without democratic politics. However, democratic politics is not only a matter of *voluntarism*. There are good reasons to conclude that at our present conjuncture, searching for a quick solution to the crises through a pan European democratic constitutional moment could be the quickest way to democratic suicide. The preconditions for a democratic constitutional moment simply are not there. There is a need, however, for democratic tactics. In that regard, it seems to me that a fundamental component of them would be the production of arguments that reveal the problematic character of the cleavages around which European politics is conceived. Despite the deep, rapid and democratically problematic establishment of the single market, political cleavages remain exclusively national in Europe.[35] So much so that it has been relatively easy to make all debates around national lines, avoiding much more relevant socio-economic ones. The bilateral Greek rescue of 2010 was, and perhaps even mainly, a rescue of the creditors of Greece, which happened to be French and German banks to a disproportionate extent.[36] If the Greek state had been capable of increasing its overall debt levels, enjoying for a period historically low interest rates, this was because German and French banks had been so interested in buying Greek debt that the interest rates paid by Greece had become almost the same as those paid by Germany. The rapid growth of the percentage of debt held by non-nationals in all peripheral countries reveals that indeed Greek indebtedness was made possible by Northern creditors.

However, this second dimension of the issue was largely absent from public discussion, certainly from the official discourse of Northern institutional actors. The absence goes a long way to explain that the 'pain' of austerity policies could be inflicted upon the Greek taxpayer, and the Greek taxpayer only. But why should that be so? Indeed, 'contagion' effects may require public actors to avoid rushing decisions that could create uncontrollable dynamics (a good reason to have avoided the talk of default in November 2010 and to have managed the Cypriot crisis very differently indeed).[37] But such 'contagion' effects do not pre-empt either the

---

[35] On the crises being a vehicle of renationalisation, see M Jachtenfuchs and P Genschel, 'Politics Like Any Other. An Institutionalist Account of the Eurocrisis' (on file with the author).

[36] Perhaps the most cogent synthetic rendering of the evidence can be found in Editorial, *Bloomberg* (New York, 24 May 2012), www.bloomberg.com/news/2012-05-23/merkel-should-know-her-country-has-been-bailed-out-too.html. ATTAC Austria has recently calculated that the whole amount lent to Ireland (plus additional taxpayers' money) went into the 'restructuring' of the Irish banks, and thus profited all their creditors. See www.attac.at/presse/attac-presseaussendung/datum/2013/12/27/bailout-ireland.html.

[37] In November 2010, the French and the German Presidents announced their commitment to structural reform of the 'economic governance' of the Eurozone. Simultaneously, they announced that measures would be introduced to ensure that fiscal and financial crisis will be solved through bailing creditors in, and not through public money. This rendered explicit what was implicit from the very start of Monetary Union in 1999, namely, that a state which has renounced the right to monetise its debt and impose compulsory loans on its banks is more likely to go bankrupt than a state that can still print money as a measure of last resort. The announcement by Merkel and Sarkozy pushed up the 'spread' between Eurozone core and periphery states debt.

criminal prosecution of individual reckless bankers, or the legislative reforms which increase the tax burden on financial institutions in the mid- and long run. So the fact remains that the persistence of national cleavages, at a time at which the key cleavages from a socio-economic perspective are rather different ones, does indeed render the underlying problems rather intractable. It forces political decision making into taking useless if not harmful decisions, and makes the necessary and useful decisions impossible. As Claus Offe concludes in his recent book on the Eurocrises, we are entrapped.[38]

My diagnosis is that the trap is very much made of our perception of political cleavages. My prognosis is that a good place to start to change the cleavages is to challenge the unit of distributive justice which prevails in European discourses. European debates remain stuck with the assumption that the proper 'unit' of economic justice is the 'state' or the 'region', not the individual, and that the proper form of economic justice is commutative, not distributive. *For all nationals according to their contributions, not their needs.*

When discussing the two sides of the European budget (revenue and expenses), it is widely assumed that the yardstick of assessment is *national* (at most *regional*) distributive justice, and not *individual* distributive justice. What matters is what Britain, or Italy, or France, have to pay to the European budget, and what each country as a whole receives in total from the EU budget. The expectation is that, overall, there should be a proper relation between what is paid and what is received. Indeed, regional funds were presented as a means of compensating Britain for its being a net contributor, while even cohesion and structural funds, which had clearly redistributive implications, were presented as consideration for accepting deeper economic and monetary union, something that was reflected in the fact that they were not intended or expected to become permanent programmes, contrary to what, for example, the MacDougall report[39] had advocated almost two decades earlier.

This discourse on the unit and character of economic justice has been reinforced, and has shaped, the way in which revenue is collected, and resources spent, in the Union. While the own resources decision in 1970 was aimed at developing the direct taxing powers of the Union,[40] the failure to opt for a clear and transparent formula (like one penny in the pound), and the choice of an obscure and complex equation rendered the Europeanness of Value Added Tax (VAT) invisible. Moreover, in 1984 the decision was taken to increase the EU budget through new national transfers, the weight of which has been increased in successive rounds of budgetary negotiations, diluting the 'ownership' of resources decided in 1970, something fully confirmed by the character of the main expenditure programmes of the EU. Regional, structural and cohesion funds are intentionally distributed nationally and/or regionally, while the Common Agricultural Policy (CAP) also has a clear

---

[38] C Offe, *Europe Entrapped*, London: Polity, 2014. See also 'Europe Entrapped' (2013) 19 *European Law Journal* 595.

[39] European Commission, 'Report of the Study Group on the Role of Public Finance. Volume I: General Report' (April 1977). The text is available at www.ec.europa.eu/economy_finance/emu_history/documentation/chapter8/19770401en73macdougallrepvol1.pdf.

[40] Council Decision of 21 April 1970 on the replacement of financial contributions from Member States by the Communities' own resources [1970] OJ L94/19.

regional and national dimension. Moreover, it has become fully 'natural' to assume that contributing to the EU budget should result in roughly equivalent returns from the EU.[41] The very discourse about 'corruption' in the EU (which is indeed serious, but unfortunately far from peculiar and unique to it, and certainly minuscule when compared with that prevalent in some financial institutions) flirts with the idea that any difference between what is paid and what is received would only feed corruption, even if the Eurocrats would pretend the difference could be used to reduce inequalities across the Union.

The national unit and the commutative logic of European economic justice have two major implications. The first is that they reinforce the view that the relevant 'cleavage' in European politics is nationality. The second is that the proper logic of economic justice is commutative, not distributive. The paradoxical result is that a 'collective' unit of economic justice ends up being extremely 'individualistic' in its implications. 'National' economic justice pre-empts seeing the individual as the proper unit of economic justice, and indeed deactivates discourses about economic justice which consider social divisions along socio-economic lines (in less politically correct days, one is very much tempted to talk of class).

Consider Margaret Thatcher. We know that she wanted her money back, and that she claimed to have got part of it back after Fointainebleau. Thatcher cunningly exploited three basic facts. (1) European revenue remained a matter of state transfers; and (2) European expenditure was absorbed almost entirely by the CAP; so (3) the newly acceded United Kingdom was bound to be presented with a bill much higher than the money being paid from European coffers to Britons. This aggregate 'discrepancy' was turned into a national vindication. It managed to hide in plain sight that the British problem was far more complex than that. What Thatcher wanted to brush aside (and Kaldor or Peter Shore wanted to emphasise) was that the entry into the Communities did not affect equally all Britons. Indeed, how much you benefitted and how much of the aggregate European burden you bore was not determined by your being British, but actually by your socio-economic position, by how your previous income and wealth were affected. Kaldor in particular claimed that entering the common market under the terms and conditions negotiated by Heath was the path of least resistance to implement Heath's *inverse redistribution programme*,[42] a claim that could clearly be extended to Thatcher's more openly neoliberal policy agenda.[43] But the moment one accepts the 'national' unit and the 'commutative' logic at the supranational level, one is indeed laying the ground for the 'commutative' logic trickling down to the national level.[44]

Or consider the True Finns. Their grievances are also based on solid facts. Finland had to face a daunting economic crisis in the late 1980s, a crisis from which it

---

[41] On taxes, I refer to Agustín José Menéndez, 'Taxing Europe' (2004) 10 *Columbia Journal of European Law* 297. On European finance in general, see Agustín José Menéndez, 'The Purse of the Polity' in EO Eriksen (ed), *Making the European Polity* (London, Routledge, 2005).

[42] On Thatcher, see the recently released memo from the Central Policy Review Staff, dated October 1982 ('Long Term Options'), www.discovery.nationalarchives.gov.uk/SearchUI/Details?uri=C13318082.

[43] N Kaldor, 'The Dynamic Effects of the Common Market' in N Kaldor, *Further Essays on Applied Economics* (New York, NY, Holmes & Meier, 1978). On Peter Shore, see P Shore, *Separate ways, Britain and Europe* (London, Duckworth, 2000).

[44] An outcome which was clearly not unwelcomed by the 'dry' faction of the Tory party in the early 1980s (no matter how much resented by the wets).

recovered not without sweat and tears, if not blood.[45] Having learnt the lesson the hard way, the Finnish Parliament was very cautious in the precise way in which institutional structures and substantive policies were shaped before joining Monetary Union in 1999. If Finland had to bootstrap itself, why should Finland be obliged to help the profligate Southerners? And if help comes forward, why should anybody be scandalised if the Parthenon or—as actually happened—a complex and essentially useless[46] financial arrangement is required as collateral *for Finland and only for Finland* providing financial assistance to Greece? This argument, however, fails to consider that not all Finns bore the adjustment burden in the same way in the early 1990s, or that the 'German' and the 'Finnish' (and the latter is fully intertwined with the former) export successes were (in part) rendered possible by the profligate Southerners, who bought many more washing machines and mobile phones than they could have done if not literally showered with cheap credit. More to the point, the 'bail-out' of Greece is a policy alternative to the rescue of German and Finnish financial institutions, the Finnish financial institutions that tried to make a quick Euro through proficient loans to profligate Southerners.[47] Consequently, the ghost of the Parthenon serves the purpose of deleting the subtle differences between the Greek owners of Porsche Cayennes and the Greek unemployed, and between the Finnish banker and the overworked construction worker facing the social dumping from which companies profit at the expense of Finnish and Estonian workers. And in the process, the self-reliant, unencumbered individual is promoted to model citizen also in the national political discourse.

IV. CONCLUSION

In this chapter, I have argued *against* a 'justice turn' in European scholarly (and political) discourses. The history of political philosophy provides many examples of justice being the last refuge of those arguing against democratic politics. Key elements in Plato's, Hobbes' and Godwin's political philosophy provide rather ready-made argumentative strategies with which to cloak escapes from the agora of the polis to the backrooms where the ruling few need not worry about the bewildering herd. There is thus a serious chance that 'justice discourses' come to play a similar role to the inflated 'governance' paradigm of the late 1990s and early 2000s. Instead of escaping into the alleged apolitical objectivity of justice, we should better confront the fundamental tensions underlying the European economic constitution. This is why in the second part of the chapter I have argued that we should consider the clear tension between the unit and kind of economic justice assumed to be proper for the European Union when it comes to the single market (*individual, if not individualistic*) and when it comes to taxing and spending (*national if not regional*). In both cases, justice is confined to commutative, not distributive justice. We should

---

[45] S Honkapohja and E Koskela, 'The Economic Crisis of the 1990s in Finland' (1999) 14 *Economic Policy* 399.
[46] J Cotterill, 'Finland's Still Got a Secret' *FT Alphaville* (12 March 2012).
[47] Although the latter argument works better with regard to Germany; Finnish external private debt is high.

have a serious debate about the discrepancy, and about the hollow character of a solidarity confined to commutative justice. Setting the problem in these terms may well help to avoid both a sacred reverence to the present law of the single market and of economic freedoms in particular (a consequence of the silly taboo of the *acquis communataire*, which is the last refuge of the capital holder) and the development of an authoritarian federalism where the permanent state of emergency not only justifies doing away with democratic politics, but also with the social state. Deciding which distributive justice we Europeans should have is closely intertwined with deciding whose Europe we want to have. The pretence of a European Pareto optimal politics, which was always a fake one, has been shattered for good by the economic crises and by the very ways in which these crises have been governed. It is political freedom, not the equality of servants, that constitutes the essence of any democracy, including European democracy.[48]

---

[48] H Kelsen, *Essence and Value of Democracy* (Lanham, MD, Rowman & Littlefield, 2013. I have read the superb Spanish translation by Juan Luis Requejo: *De la esencia y valor de la democracia* (Oviedo, KRK, 2006).

10

We the People: EU Justice as Politics

DANIEL AUGENSTEIN

I. AUSTERITY

The Member States whose currency is the euro may establish a stability mechanism to be activated if indispensable to safeguard the stability of the euro area as a whole. The granting of any required financial assistance under the mechanism will be made subject to strict conditionality.[1]

WHAT IS REMARKABLE about the 'rescue packages' for Europe's troubled national economies is arguably not the nature or scale of the austerity measures imposed on Member States in economic hardship—drastic as their consequences may be, they very much resemble the World Bank's and International Monetary Fund's (IMF) standard repertoire.[2] Rather, what is remarkable is how the negotiation of the European quid pro quo of money for reform ('strict conditionality') oscillates between the internalisation of economic risks and the externalisation of political accountability.

Viewed from the perspective of the Member States, it is unlikely that, say, the Greek or the German Government could have successfully imposed such austerity measures on their own people on their own political account. While the delegation of political responsibility for unpopular decisions to Brussels is nothing unusual, these days Europe's 'helping hand' provokes unprecedented levels of political protest and resistance amongst Europe's citizenries. Yet it is not the European bureaucracy but national governments that tumble and fall, which sheds light on an often neglected proviso of successful democratic politics: the question is not simply, and no longer, whether a given democratic minority can afford to lose an election in light of the reasonable prospect of becoming the majority next time around; the question is also, and increasingly so, whether a given democratic majority can afford to win an election in light of a reasonable prospect of carrying through its political agenda in the face of significant external constraints. Nota bene, this applies not only to the 'lazy Greeks' but also to the 'domineering Germans'.[3]

Viewed from an EU perspective, the financial predicaments of countries such as Greece, Portugal, Spain, Italy, Ireland and Cyprus are treated as a matter of

---

[1] European Council Decision 2011/199 of 25 March 2011 amending Article 136 of the Treaty on the Functioning of the European Union with regard to a stability mechanism for Member States whose currency is the euro [2011] OJ L91/1.
[2] A Sen, 'Austerity is Undermining Europe's Grand Vision' *The Guardian* (3 July 2012).
[3] ibid.

common political concern that calls for a united European response: together we stand, divided we fall. Accordingly, while European decision makers remain somewhat shielded from national political anxieties, their external interventions into Member State domains are dressed up as 'domestic' reactions to a financial crisis internal to the 'Euro-polity'. At the same time, the European Union appears overburdened by the political responsibility that comes with its attempts at economic reform. While the self-preservation of the polity has been presented as imperative by some (EU integration has become too thick to fail), there are also signs of political disintegration, such as the renewed interest in partitioning Europe's monetary core from its economic and political periphery (multi-speed Europe), repeated calls from certain corners of German politics for Greece to leave the Eurozone (no representation without taxation), and proposals to loosen domestic parliamentary control over Europe's national executives in Brussels (technocracy will solve it).

Appeals to an 'ever closer' Union notwithstanding, the main battles over Europe's financial crisis management are fought outside EU law in state and inter-state ('intergovernmental') fora, which is a poignant reminder of the limitations of a European polity that sought to decouple the legitimacy of a legally constituted transnational market from supranational political and social integration.[4] The German *Bundesverfassungsgericht* (BVerfG), in yet another 'yes but …' decision, gave the green light to Germany's ratification of the European Stability Mechanism (ESM).[5] The more than 37,000 plaintiffs concerned that Europe's new 'bail-out' fund may come with unlimited and irreversible liability risks for their country were told that enhancing their parliament's controlling powers would ensure that German legal authority was still vested in the German people. Yet, in reality, the judicial politics of European legal integration runs at idling speed. According to the BVerfG, while the *Bundestag*'s budgetary powers constitute a central element of democratic *Selbstgestaltung*, intergovernmental decisions do not constitute acts of the German *Staatsgewalt* and are therefore beyond the jurisdictional reach of the Court.[6] The European Court of Justice (ECJ), in turn, held that the EU Treaties and the

> general principle of effective judicial protection do not preclude the conclusion between the Member States whose currency is the euro of an agreement such as the Treaty establishing the European stability mechanism …, or the ratification of that Treaty by those Member States.[7]

In *Pringle*, the plaintiff's goal was to force an Irish national referendum on the ESM Treaty.[8] Part of his strategy was to challenge the legality of Member States' adoption of such a treaty under EU law. In his view, the ESM was designed to ensure price stability and save the Euro, which as part of monetary policy fell within the EU's exclusive competence. Moreover, according to Pringle, the ESM Treaty infringed

---

[4] C Joerges, 'Europa's Wirtschaftsverfassung in der Krise' (2012) 51 *Der Staat* 357.
[5] BVerfGE, 2 BvR 1390/12 (12 September 2012).
[6] ibid, paras 116, 121–23.
[7] Case C-370/12 *Thomas Pringle v Government of Ireland, Ireland and the Attorney General* (ECJ, 27 November 2012), para 186.
[8] Treaty establishing the European stability mechanism (ESM). The text is available at www.europa.eu/rapid/press-release_DOC-12-3_en.pdf.

EU law provisions designed to maintain the Union's financial balance, inter alia the 'no bail-out' clause of Article 125 of the Treaty of the Functioning of the European Union (TFEU).[9] The ECJ disagreed. On the first point, the Court considered that the objective of the ESM was not simply to secure price stability but the stability of the Euro area as a whole which, as a matter of economic policy, fell within Member States' competence.[10] On the second point, the Court retorted that the 'no bail-out' clause only prohibited such financial assistance that would 'diminish the incentive of the recipient Member State to conduct a sound budgetary policy'.[11] Paul Craig has pointed to the tension at the heart of the Court's teleological reduction of Article 125 TFEU; namely, that the very existence of ESM stability support 'diminishes the incentive for budgetary probity by holding out the possibility of assistance in circumstances, or on terms, that the market would not provide'.[12] What is dressed up as common 'economic policy' is really an attempt to regain political control over the European market polity outside the constraints imposed by EU law. As per Advocate General Kokott:

> If a prohibition under European Union law even on indirect assumption of liabilities were recognised, that would hinder the Member States from deploying financial resources in order to attempt to prevent the negative effects of the bankruptcy of another Member State on their own economic and financial situation. Given the mutual interdependence of the Member States' individual economic activities which is encouraged and intended under European Union law, substantial damage could be caused by the bankruptcy of one Member State to other Member States also. That damage might possibly be so extensive that an additional consequence would be to endanger the survival of monetary union[13]

II. PIECEMEAL JUSTICE

The internalisation of economic risks and externalisation of political accountability in Europe's financial crisis management is intimately connected to the double legal segmentation of the 'Euro-polity' into a (supranational) Community method and an (intergovernmental) Union method on the one hand, and, a fully harmonised currency policy and a decentralised economic and fiscal policy on the other hand. The ensuing political division of labour between the Union and the Member States (acting individually and in concert) may suggest a corresponding delimitation of Europe's justice deficit, either along functional (broadly conceived) or national–territorial lines.

---

[9] Art 125(1) of the Consolidated version of the Treaty on the Functioning of the European Union [2012] OJ C326/47 (TFEU) provides that neither the Union nor a Member State shall be liable for or assume the commitments of (other) Member States, without prejudice to mutual financial guarantees to the joint execution of a specific project.

[10] In a somewhat unusual incidence of judicial self-constraint, the Court considered that 'even though the stability of the euro area may have repercussions on the stability of the currency used within that area, an economic policy measure cannot be treated as equivalent to a monetary policy measure for the sole reason that it may have indirect effects on the stability of the euro', Case C-370/12 *Pringle v Ireland* (ECJ, 27 November 2012), para 56.

[11] ibid, para 136.

[12] P Craig, '*Pringle*: Legal Reasoning, Text, Purpose, and Teleology' (2013) 20 *Maastricht Journal of European and Comparative Law* 3, 9.

[13] Case C-370/12 *Pringle v Ireland* (ECJ, 27 November 2012), Opinion of AG Kokott, para 139.

In the former vein, Damian Chalmers has defended the interesting proposition that justice claims in the European Union delimit the legitimate authority of EU law.[14] If justice is what places us in relation to each other, then it needs to be emplaced in political communities. This entails certain limitations for a European Union that does not constitute a state-type form of political organisation but is merely a 'purpose-built organisation' set up to realise certain tasks.[15] According to Chalmers, the EU only has legitimate authority to respond to justice claims generated by conditions of 'mutual dependency' in the realisation of particular tasks and services; and to justice claims salvaging the 'we' from the 'pathologies of the nation-state'.[16] What the EU cannot deliver is justice as substantive equality ('equality of outcome'), which presupposes a relationship between people as *a* people that remains in the exclusive domain of the Member States. Thus, whereas the EU may justly contribute to the realisation of health services, it is not empowered to distribute healthcare across national membership.[17] Richard Bellamy's approach to compartmentalise political justice within and between the Member States is driven by concerns similar to those that underpin Chalmers' 'functional' delimitation of the authority of EU law.[18] Drawing on Rawls and Pettit,[19] Bellamy vests political justice directly in the democratic process that is to 'fairly and publicly adjudicate between our different, partial and fallible, understandings of justice'.[20] A European Union of peoples cannot deliver political justice because it lacks the democratic credentials necessary to qualify for membership in the Rawlsian club of 'well-ordered' societies:

> *Either* one will have a much more minimal view of justice, suitable for regulating separate groups with limited social relations with each other and only bound by their explicit contractual agreements with each other, *or* there will be the danger that the government, including the administration of justice, will be captured by certain sectional groups that will extract rent and oppress the other groups. [Emphasis in original.][21]

It follows that on the one hand, political justice between persons remains confined to the Member States (Rawls' *Political Liberalism*) whereas, on the other hand, the EU is tasked with realising its 'ever closer union among the peoples of Europe' at the

---

[14] D Chalmers, 'Kinship, Markets and Justice in Europe' in G de Búrca, D Kochenov and A Williams (eds), *Debating Europe's Justice Deficit: the EU, Swabian Housewives, Rawls, and Ryanair* (2013) *EUI Working Papers* LAW 2013/11.

[15] ibid, 27.

[16] ibid. Chalmers refers to the latter sphere or 'style' of justice as a 'psychoanalytical condition'. But the problematisation of the 'we' is also a political question in that, as Weiler once put it, the EU creates a 'regime which seeks to tame the national interest with a new discipline'. JHH Weiler, 'To Be a European Citizen: Eros and Civilization' in JHH Weiler, *The Constitution of Europe: 'Do the New Clothes Have an Emperor?' and Other Essays on European Integration* (Cambridge, Cambridge University Press, 1999) 350.

[17] As Chalmers says, 'it is not clear to me why we should be giving health care to, say, our fellow French, not Bangladeshis'. Chalmers, 'Kinship, Markets and Justice', n 14 above, 27.

[18] R Bellamy, 'Political Justice for an Ever Closer Union of People' in G de Búrca, D Kochenov and A Williams (eds), *Debating Europe's Justice Deficit: the EU, Swabian Housewives, Rawls, and Ryanair* (2013) *EUI Working Papers* LAW 2013/11.

[19] Principally J Rawls, *Political Liberalism* (New York, NY, Columbia University Press, 1993); J Rawls, *The Law of Peoples* (New Delhi, Universal Law Publishing, 2008); and P Pettit, 'A Republican Law of Peoples' (2010) 9 *European Journal of Political Theory* 70.

[20] Bellamy, 'Political Justice', n 18 above, 65.

[21] ibid, 65–66.

international level (Rawls' *Law of Peoples*). Bellamy's 'sober conclusion' is that any attempt to address the Euro crisis by way of a political union among at least some of the Member States overburdens the EU and 'will result in a polity that will prove far less capable of sustaining political justice than any of the Member States'.[22]

Chalmers' and Bellamy's proposals to delimit European political justice, while driven by warranted concerns, arguably underestimate what is entailed in having a European Union in common. The EU's 'integration through law' has Europeanised the domestic as it has domesticated the European. Accordingly, attempts to redress Europe's 'justice deficit' along functional or national–territorial lines fail to account for the mutual interdependencies and externalities that come with being (a Member State of) a European Union that has long outgrown its roots in inter-state economic cooperation. The problem with Chalmers' approach is that the impact of EU monetary policy somewhat inevitably 'tramples on' matters of substantive equality reserved to the exclusive political domain of the Member States.[23] At the same time, the separation of purpose as function (of a policy) from purpose as *telos* (of a polity) is difficult to maintain.[24] Pursuing the former without due regard to the latter results in a technocratic discourse based on consequence rather than value, which is arguably one of the root causes of what Chalmers has forcefully denounced as the EU's 'managerialist approach' that privileges market necessities over individual well-being.[25] Relatedly, Bellamy's complaint that 'pressure for the relocation of power at a supranational level is almost entirely elite led', driven by attempts 'to maximise state power through competition, conquest, merger or mutually beneficial bargains'[26] cannot be dismissed out of hand. Yet, his methodological nationalism brushes over the fact that enhancing the EU's own democratic credentials which initiated its transformation from economic policy to constitutional polity was equally an attempt to respond *politically* to the impacts of the expansionist tendencies of European market integration on the Member States. At the same time, a Rawlsian-type political internationalism does little to redress the imbalance between the limited scope of Member States' democratic mandates 'at home' and their wide-ranging powers to govern through EU law 'from abroad'.[27] In sum, given the extent to which having a European Union in common has already pre-empted democratic self-legislation and undermined democratic accountability in the Member States, it is simply too late to tame the European beast with a new functional discipline, or to seek political refuge in the international order of states.

---

[22] ibid, 67.
[23] Chalmers, 'Kinship, Markets and Justice', n 14 above, 28.
[24] See the very instructive B van Roermund, 'The Embryo and Its Rights: Technology and Teleology' (2013) 14 *German Law Journal* 1939.
[25] D Chalmers, 'Political Rights and Political Reason in European Union Law in Times of Stress' in W Sadurski (ed), *Political Rights under Stress in 21st Century Europe* (Oxford, Oxford University Press, 2006) 82.
[26] Bellamy, 'Political Justice', n 18 above, 67.
[27] Recall, eg, Fritz Scharpf's account of the European 'constitutionalisation' of competition law that drove a neoliberal economic policy agenda which was 'beyond even the control of parliamentary supermajorities at the national level', see FW Scharpf, *Governing Europe: Effective or Democratic?* (Oxford, Oxford University Press, 1999) 54.

III. POLITICAL UNITY

The spirits which we have summoned we now cannot banish—the *Sorcerer's Apprentice* awaits his political master.[28] While the further political ramifications of the financial crisis remain uncertain, one thing has become abundantly clear: where the economy drives politics, it becomes increasingly difficult to insulate the EU's common (now: internal) market from its common good. Yet to inquire into the EU's common good—the good that 'we' hold in common—is to posit its political unity.

I have suggested elsewhere that in order to come to terms with the 'touch of stateness' and 'problems of translation' that beset much of the normative analysis of the virtues and pitfalls of the European polity,[29] it may be useful to explore the relationship between two different conceptions of European legal integration: one that centres on the Member States as composing the European Union; and one that centres on the European Union as comprising the Member States.[30] The ensuing multi-perspectival approach guards against reducing the problem of political unity to two well-known statist challenges to the EU's credentials as democratic polity: at a socio-cultural level, the notorious 'no-*demos*' thesis that makes national belonging a condition of democratic self-legislation; and at an institutional level, the evasion of democratic accountability through supranational market integration that disempowers the citizen and undermines the political legitimation of legal coercion. Indeed, viewed from a statist perspective—the Member States composing the European Union—the emerging picture is rather bleak: while the former challenge (no financial solidarity without national identity) has more purchase in the European public debate than one could wish for,[31] addressing the latter challenge (EU institutional reform that approximates the ideal-type of statist representative democracy) may require more than the Union can provide for. The financial crisis gives all reason to be concerned about the future of Europe's national democracies. Yet it is doubtful whether it is possible or even desirable to address these concerns by way of return to the nation state, or by attempting to replicate nation-and-state structures at the European level.

It would be mistaken, however, to collapse the problem of European political unity into the EU's shortcomings *qua* statist representative democracy. Viewed from a supranational perspective—the EU comprising the Member States—the ECJ's early discovery of the principles of supremacy and direct effect not only

---

[28] The reference is to Goethe's *Zauberlehrling*: 'Herr, die Not ist groß! Die ich rief, die Geister, werd' ich nun nicht los'.

[29] On the 'touch of stateness' and the 'problem of translation' see, respectively, J Shaw and A Wiener, 'The Paradox of the European Polity' (1999) *Harvard Jean Monnet Working Papers* No 10/99; N Walker, 'Postnational Constitutionalism and the Problem of Translation' in JHH Weiler and M Wind (eds), *European Constitutionalism Beyond the State* (Cambridge, Cambridge University Press, 2003).

[30] Whereas the former conception ties European legal integration to (inherited) commonalities between the Member States, the latter conception posits the EU as an autonomous legal order in its own right; see D Augenstein, 'Identifying the European Union: Legal Integration and European Communities' in D Augenstein (ed), *'Integration through Law' Revisited: The Making of the European Polity* (Farnham, Ashgate, 2012).

[31] If, with Bellamy, elite-led transfers of power to the supranational level erode political justice from above, new waves of national parochialism in response to the Euro crisis that tie political solidarity to national identity undermine it from below.

challenged the Westphalian linkage of constitutionalism with the state, but also the exclusive unity between the state and its people upon which it rests.[32] At the same time, political unity is not anterior to *any* legal order but revealed in the process of concomitantly positing the polity through law and deriving law from the polity. It is the political representation of a people as a unity (the 'we') that is constitutive of its individuation and legitimised through its reiteration on the part of the real people that come to be represented. Inversely, as Lindahl and van Roermund put it,

> although the legitimacy of legal norms implies that the values protected by law represent the identity of a political community, the identity of the polity is grasped in the values postulated and protected by the legal order.[33]

Accordingly, whatever is deficient about EU political justice is not a problem of political *unity*. By conferring rights on individuals as a matter of European law, the ECJ posits the peoples of Europe as citizens of the European Union. Concurrently, by calling upon this citizenry to cooperate in the functioning of the European Union, the Court derives the authority of EU law from a people of Europe. Rather, what is problematic is the EU's *political* unity; that is, recovering the politics of European market integration from behind the veil of the statist separation between the national-as-political and the European-as-economic. Juxtaposing the BVerfG's *Maastricht* decision with the ECJ's judgment in *Les Verts*,[34] Lindahl and van Roermund have exposed the depoliticising effects of this national/political–EU/economic divide on European polity building:

> By emphasising that a democratic legal order represents the people, the German Federal Constitutional Court purports to rescue the specificity of the political realm vis-à-vis economics. By subordinating legal integration to economic integration, the ECJ seems to reduce politics to economics, and the public to the private sphere.[35]

The old liberal divorce of the economic from the political furnishes the new veneer for aligning conflicting claims to legal authority between EU and Member State polities. This puts the economic cart before the political horse. The European Union's claim to representing the people of Europe—beyond all philosophical quarrels: *to act in our name*—poses the problem of political ownership over the polity. It raises the question of what is being presented to us that we are to endorse as our own. Below the surface of economic expediency, functional spillovers and the like, the inquiry into political justice thus turns on the political justification of the unity of the polity—be it founded on epic tales of common history and destiny or—more mundanely—on the tale of a common market.

---

[32] Case 26/62 NV *Algemene Transport- en Expeditie Onderneming van Gend en Loos v Nederlandse Administratie der Belastingen* [1963] ECR (English Special Edition) 1; Case 6/64 *Flamino Costa v ENEL* [1964] ECR 585.

[33] H Lindahl and B van Roermund, 'Law Without a State? On Representing the Common Market' in Z Bańkowski and D Scott (eds), *The European Union and Its Order: The Legal Theory of European Integration* (Oxford, Blackwell, 2000) 10.

[34] See, respectively, BVerfGE 89, 155 (12 October 1993); and Case 294/83 *Parti écologiste 'Les Verts' v European Parliament* [1986] ECR 1339.

[35] Lindahl and van Roermund, 'Law Without a State', n 33 above, 4. On the dangers of decoupling EU justice from politics see further AJ Menéndez, 'Whose Justice? Which Europe?' in this volume, 137.

IV. FUNDAMENTAL RIGHTS IN THE EUROPEAN MARKET POLITY

Fundamental rights provide a useful avenue for inquiring into the justification of EU political unity. Whether or not one conceives of fundamental rights as co-original with popular sovereignty,[36] they play an important role in the political empowerment of citizens to partake in the definition of the common good. Moreover, this empowering role of fundamental rights in relation to a political community explains why they are 'fundamental' not only for the individual rights holder but also for the self-understanding of the polity as a whole. To borrow from Joseph Weiler, it is the correlation of fundamental rights—concerned with the autonomy and self-determination of the individual—and fundamental boundaries—concerned with the autonomy and self-determination of the community—that epitomises the selfhood of the polity.[37] To dispel the appearance of communitarianism, the relationship between fundamental rights and fundamental boundaries is inherently political: the represented political community empowers the individual against itself as it obliges her in its-own-name. While the correlation of fundamental rights and fundamental boundaries is thus not the expression of a people *qua* existential unity, it cannot be mapped one-to-one onto the supranational European polity, either.[38]

The upshot of Weiler's analysis of the relationship between fundamental rights and fundamental boundaries in the European polity is that the boundedness of fundamental rights in the Member State legal orders prevents the ECJ from adopting a pan-European (maximum/minimum) standard of fundamental rights protection as derived from their national constitutional traditions.[39] EU fundamental rights must safeguard the unity of European law within the Member States while at the same time respecting their diverse national constitutional traditions. As the ECJ held in *Internationale Handelsgesellschaft*,

> recourse to the legal rules or concepts of national law in order to judge the validity of measures adopted by the institutions of the Community would have an adverse effect on the uniformity and efficacy of Community law.[40]

Accordingly, 'the validity of such measures can only be judged in the light of Community law ... [as] an independent source of law'.[41] The Court may interpret

---

[36] J Habermas, 'On the Internal Relation Between the Rule of Law and Democracy' in J Habermas, *The Inclusion of the Other: Studies in Political Theory*, ed CP Cronin and P de Greiff (Cambridge, MA, MIT Press, 2000).

[37] JHH Weiler, 'Fundamental Rights and Fundamental Boundaries: On the Conflict of Standards and Values in the Protection of Human Rights in the European Legal Space' in JHH Weiler, *The Constitution of Europe: 'Do the New Clothes Have an Emperor?' and Other Essays on European Integration* (Cambridge, Cambridge University Press, 1999).

[38] I develop this argument in more detail in D Augenstein, 'Engaging the Fundamentals: On the Autonomous Substance of EU Fundamental Rights Law' (2013) 14 *German Law Journal* 1917.

[39] Weiler, 'Fundamental Rights', n 37 above; on the maximum/minimum standard conundrum see further L Besselink, 'Entrapped by the Maximum Standard: On Fundamental Rights, Pluralism and Subsidiarity in the European Union' (1998) 35 *Common Market Law Review* 929; and M Avbelj, 'European Court of Justice and the Question of Value Choices' (2004) *Jean Monnet Working Papers* (NYU Law School) No 06/04.

[40] Case 11/70 *Internationale Handelsgesellschaft v Einfuhr und Vorratsstelle für Getreide und Futtermittel* [1970] ECR 1125, para 3.

[41] ibid.

EU fundamental rights by 'drawing inspiration from' the national constitutional traditions 'common' to the Member States,[42] and permit derogations from EU law on the basis of national fundamental rights standards provided these standards can be said to be 'shared' among the Member States.[43] Yet such European commonality in the face of national diversity that presents EU fundamental rights as derivative or composite of Europe's national constitutional traditions cannot ground the autonomy of the European Union as a unitary legal and political order.

Inversely, while the proclaimed autonomous interpretation of EU fundamental rights in the light of the European legal order as an 'independent source of law' certainly entails a claim to representing the European Union as political unity, the Court's justification of autonomy does not place fundamental rights at the core of the European polity. As Federico Mancini noted in the early days of EU fundamental rights, while their introduction into the European Community legal order was 'the most striking contribution the Court has made to the development of a constitution of Europe', their protection was 'forced on the Court by the outside, by the German, and, later, the Italian constitutional courts'.[44] At the same time, the recognition of fundamental rights as general principles of Community law not only served to pacify Member States' judiciaries but also shielded the unity of the Common Market against the diversity of Europe's national constitutional human rights traditions. In many ways, the ECJ's early dictum in *Hauer* still holds true today:

> The question of a possible infringement of fundamental rights by a measure of Community institutions can only be judged in the light of Community law itself. The introduction of special criteria for assessment stemming from the legislation or constitutional law of a particular Member State would, by damaging the substantive unity and efficacy of Community law, lead inevitably to the destruction of the unity of the common market and the jeopardizing of the cohesion of the Community.[45]

What renders EU fundamental rights autonomous, and the European Union cohesive, is the unity of the market: the Court bridges the gap between commonality and autonomy with an appeal to uniformity as a functional imperative of economic integration that displays the Internal Market as the fundamental boundary of the European polity. The EU's common market is its common good: the derivative/composite justification of EU fundamental rights with an eye to commonalities between the Member States (composing the European Union) becomes autonomous *only* by virtue of transcending national diversity into the Internal Market that represents the political unity of the European Union (comprising the Member States).

Finally, the ECJ's market-based interpretation of fundamental rights is itself a function of delimiting the 'economic' fundamental boundary of the European polity in relation to the 'political' vested in the Member States. As Philip Alston and Joseph Weiler remarked long before the Charter of Fundamental Rights of the European

---

[42] ibid, para 4.
[43] See, eg, Case C-36/02 *Omega Spielhallen- und Automatenaufstellungs-GmbH v Oberbürgermeisterin der Bundesstadt Bonn* [2004] ECR I-9609.
[44] F Mancini, 'The Making of a Constitution for Europe' (1989) 26 *Common Market Law Review* 595, 611.
[45] Case 44/79 *Liselotte Hauer v Land Rheinland-Pfalz* [1979] ECR 3727, para 14.

Union (CFR) became legally binding, empowering the EU in the field of fundamental rights would run the risk of the 'wholesale destruction of the jurisdictional boundaries between the Community and the Member States'.[46] Because fundamental rights 'directly affect all activities of public authorities and ... also touch upon many areas of social activities of individuals', promoting their protection within EU law may come at the price of further encroaching on domains reserved to the Member States, thus 'trampl[ing] over the equally important democratic and constitutional principles of limited governance and attributed powers'.[47] Accordingly, while post-Lisbon the ECJ appears prepared to take fundamental rights more 'seriously' and to reconsider their relationship with the EU's fundamental market freedoms,[48] the victims of Europe's financial crisis management have thus far not benefited from the Court's new 'human rights friendly' approach.[49] The conclusion of the ESM Treaty did not infringe Pringle's fundamental right to effective judicial protection under Article 47 CFR because 'the Member States are not implementing Union law, within the meaning of Article 51(1) CFR, when they establish a stability mechanism such as the ESM where [the Treaties] do not confer any special competence on the Union to do so'.[50]

V. TO EACH HIS OWN?

> The European Union owes its existence to the efforts of political elites who could count on the passive consent of their more or less indifferent populations as long as the peoples could regard the Union as also being in their economic interests, all things considered. The Union has legitimised itself in the eyes of the citizens primarily through its outcomes and not so much by the fact that it fulfilled the citizens' political will.[51]

As long as the ends of the European integration project that could serve as a vantage point for evaluating its relative successes and failures remain contested,[52] we are constantly thrown back to debates about its means. Yet, when embarking on a journey without destination, the natural instinct is to keep going: perceived failures of the integration process tend to be parried with calls for 'more' and 'better' integration. It is therefore not surprising that the disintegrating effects of

---

[46] P Alston and JHH Weiler, 'An "Ever Closer Union" in Need of a Human Rights Policy: The European Union and Human Rights' in P Alston (ed), *The EU and Human Rights* (Oxford, Oxford University Press, 1999) 23.

[47] ibid.

[48] See, eg, Case C-271/08 *European Commission v Federal Republic of Germany* [2010] ECR I-7087, Opinion of AG Trstenjak; and Case C-515/08 *Criminal proceedings against Vítor Manuel dos Santos Palhota, Mário de Moura Gonçalves, Fernando Luis das Neves Palhota, Termiso Limitada* [2010] ECR I-9133, Opinion of AG Cruz Villalón.

[49] See C Barnard, 'The Charter, the Court—and the Crisis' (2013) 18 *University of Cambridge Legal Studies Research Paper Series* 18/2013.

[50] Case C-370/12 *Pringle v Ireland* (ECJ, 27 November 2012), para 179.

[51] J Habermas, 'Democracy, Solidarity and the European Union' lecture delivered at KU Leuven (26 April 2013). See www.social-europe.eu/2013/05/democracy-solidarity-and-the-european-crisis-2/.

[52] Recall the debate about the *finalité* of European integration triggered by Joschka Fischer's Humboldt speech more than a decade ago: J Fischer, 'From Confederacy to Federation: Thoughts on the Finality of European Integration', speech delivered at the Humboldt University in Berlin (12 May 2000).

the financial crisis have reinvigorated debates about deepening Europe's political integration, in an attempt to rectify the 'birth mistakes' of the Maastricht Treaty.[53] The sheer volume of financial transfers between the Member States seems to leave the Eurozone with a lonely choice: either it abandons its common currency, or it transforms into a veritable European *Bundesstaat*. Under conditions of austerity, Joschka Fischer's political vision of European unification returns as an economic necessity.[54] However, if there is any profound sense in which the financial crisis may trigger a 'moment of transformation' of the European Union,[55] then it is the insight into the fragility of a polity that has put too much of its money on output legitimacy. Beyond the economic mantra of 'smart, sustainable and inclusive growth' lurks a concern with the political implications should the EU fail to deliver. Indeed, it may be that the reasons why the EU has fared worse in the crisis than other major economies despite comparable overall economic performance lie deeper than its often certified lack of effective 'political leadership':[56] the financial crisis goes to the heart of the political identity of the European market polity.

Writing in the mid-1990s, Tony Judt predicted that the belief Europe could continue on its path of integration would prove illusory.[57] The European Community's early success story was based on a lucky historical coincidence of Western European states' economic and prudential self-interest, which was only retrospectively endowed with an ontology of political community:

> [T]he history of the formation of an 'ever-closer union' has followed a consistent pattern: the real or apparent logic of mutual economic advantage not sufficing to account for the complexity of its formal arrangements, there has been invoked a sort of ontological ethic of political community; projected backward, the latter is then adduced to account for the gains made thus far and to justify further unificatory efforts.[58]

That European integration continued no matter what does not necessarily gainsay Judt's thesis—it may simply indicate that the 'real or apparent logic of mutual economic advantage' proved more enduring than he predicted. Only, the problem with Judt's 'after the fact' account of political community is that it conceals how European integration thrives on a process that concomitantly joins and separates the economic and the political. Since the early days of the European Community, economic integration was considered both an end in itself and a means to the end of political integration, as reflected for example in Article 2 of the Treaty establishing the European Economic Community (EEC) of 1958 that envisaged the establishment of a common market to 'promote … closer relations between States

---

[53] See, eg, T Sarazin, 'Geburtsfehler Maastricht' *Frankfurter Allgemeine Zeitung* (17 July 2012).
[54] Fischer, 'From Confederacy to Federation', n 52 above.
[55] European Commission, 'Communication from the Commission of 3 March 2010—Europe 2020: A strategy for smart, sustainable and inclusive growth' COM(2010) 2020 final.
[56] Joschka Fischer has recently taken some time off his new job as oil industry consultant to remind us that 'the real crisis of the EU and the monetary union is not financial but political—or, more precisely, it is a leadership crisis'. The 'price' to be paid for 'the monetary union's survival, and thus that of the European project' is 'more community: a banking union, fiscal union, and political union', see J Fischer, 'The Erosion of Europe' *Project Syndicate* (30 April 2013).
[57] T Judt, *A Grand Illusion? An Essay on Europe*, first published 1996(New York, New York University Press, 2011).
[58] ibid, 23.

belonging to it'.[59] At the same time, economic integration was most successful where it appeared apolitical, that is, where the market was immunised from, and therewith elevated above, political disagreements within and between the Member States. The economic goal of having a common *market* has thus long distracted from the political question of what is entailed in having a market *in common*—as if, as Veitch aptly puts it, 'there was indeed a separate economic realm whose essence could be summed up in the observation that something was economic only insofar as it was not politically supervised, and vice versa'.[60] Somewhat paradoxically, the artificial divorce of the economic from the political has paved the way for European economic *and* political integration, while still persisting in much of today's public debate about the Europe's economic *versus* political constitution. Its real-life implications are most keenly felt in the way Europe's present crisis management oscillates between the internationalisation of economic risks and the externalisation of political accountability.

VI. CONCLUSION

'It's about Europe—it's about you'.[61] As long as EU fundamental rights are reduced to a function of economic integration, and delimited by virtue of the expediencies of financial reform, they will not muster the political strength to break the EU's vicious circle between output legitimacy and economic self-interest. At the same time, if the impacts of the expansionist tendencies of market integration on the Member States propelled the evolution of EU fundamental rights law, fundamental rights may still hold out the promise of a genuine politicisation of the market as the common good of the European polity. Otherwise, the bar for political justice is set very low indeed. Where the 'political' momentum of economic integration becomes its inevitability, we have truly reached the end of politics. The likely response of Europe's citizenry will be further 'counter movements' to the erosion of social justice vianegative integration at the national level,[62] and new waves of political apathy towards the European Union in the late days of European welfare paternalism.[63] This being said, political justice is not a one-way street, and it would be wrong to lay all the blame on Brussels. With an eye to the other crisis of Europe (the unavoidable reference to the Second World War), the great Weimar Republic writer Kurt Tucholsky speculated that a people's political constitution may be less an expression of its true will than an expression of what it is willing to put up with.

---

[59] Treaty Establishing the European Economic Community (Rome, 25 March 1957) 298 UNTS 11.
[60] S Veitch, 'Juridification, Integration, De-Politicisation' in D Augenstein (ed), *'Integration through Law' Revisited: The Making of the European Polity* (Farnham, Ashgate, 2012) 92.
[61] Website of the 'European Year of Citizens 2013', www.europa.eu/citizens-2013/en/home.
[62] See Joerges, 'Europa's Wirtschaftsverfassung', n 4 above, 364, with reference to K Polanyi, *The Great Transformation: The Political and Economic Origins of Our Time* (Boston, MA, Beacon Press, 2001).
[63] Equally provocative and instructive, A Somek, *Individualism. An Essay on the Authority of the European Union* (Oxford, Oxford University Press, 2008).

11

Swabian Housewives, Suffering Southerners: The Contestability of Justice as Exemplified by the Eurozone Crisis

DANNY NICOL

I. INTRODUCTION

THIS CHAPTER FOCUSES on the way in which debate around the EU justice deficit should be conducted, and the role of the scholar therein. Its message is that the content of justice is inherently and inevitably contestable. It therefore counsels against the assumption that academics can concoct general formulae which can somehow satisfy everyone's conception of justice. Rather it argues that we should celebrate *justice as something we argue about*.

Fully accepting the contestability of justice may not come easily for some EU law scholars. The traditions of European Economic Community (EEC) law scholarship since the Community's foundation weigh like a nightmare on the brains of today's academics. In this regard, Joseph Weiler has drawn attention to 'the almost unanimously *non*-critical approach and tradition developed by Community law scholars towards the Court of Justice'.[1] He attributes this non-critical stance to the delight which the European Court of Justice's (ECJ) development of a federal-type legal structure engendered in professors of (traditionally weak) international law, as well as the lack of a strong critical tradition in national law both on the European continent and in the United Kingdom and Ireland, and the absence of a critical symbiosis with sister disciplines, European Community (EC) political science and EC economics, where legal aspects of European integration were often marginalised. Thus generations of EC/EU scholars grew up with the quasi-religious belief that the Treaty of Rome basically met the demands of justice. The role of the EC/EU academic was therefore to defend European integration for all it was worth, since its *just* nature was beyond question. Thankfully this role of academic as defender of the EU faith has been discarded in some respects, and in the wake of the Eurozone crisis it deserves to be wholly swept aside.

---

[1] JHH Weiler, *The Constitution of Europe: 'Do the New Clothes Have an Emperor?' and Other Essays on European Integration* (Cambridge, Cambridge University Press, 1999) 205.

In this regard I draw support from political theorist Chantal Mouffe, who argues that 'End of History' notions of a victory of universal values are misplaced.[2] Mouffe contends that there is always, inevitably, an irreducible character of antagonism within the political scene. Brushing differences under the carpet, she argues, merely leads to disaffection with the political process, and to the growth of other identities around religious, ethnic or nationalist forms of identification. She therefore advocates a healthy democratic process involving a vibrant clash of political positions and an open conflict of interests. We should reach the same conclusion if we frame the debate in terms of the EU justice deficit: justice is a valuable concept precisely *because* it is something we argue about.

In an exchange with Professor Jürgen Neyer in *Journal of Common Market Studies*, he and I clashed over whether the never-ending debate on the EU's 'democratic deficit' could properly be replaced by a debate over its 'justice deficit'.[3] There were various aspects to our disagreement, but in my view the most important by far was that, unlike Neyer, I laid emphasis on *the content of justice being pre-eminently contestable*. One cannot, I argue, entirely replace debate over democracy by debate over justice given the existence of *multiple* and *conflicting* conceptions of justice. Certainly the Treaty on European Union (TEU)[4] and the Treaty on the Functioning of the European Union (TFEU)[5] do not themselves contain an incontestable justice. Neither does the way in which treaty provisions have been interpreted over the years by the ECJ. Indeed, confronted as we are with competing and conflicting conceptions of justice, there is a lack of convincing criteria for distinguishing justice from injustice which can command consensus support. As Jeremy Waldron puts it, there are many of us, and we disagree about justice.[6] I do not believe that scholars can, from their ivory towers, devise a magic formula for justice which can overcome this difficulty. Accordingly we need democracy so that choices over what's just and what's unjust can be constantly made and remade. Therefore the quest for justice cannot be severed from the pursuit of democracy. The inseparability of justice and democracy have been further emphasised by Laura Valentini, who has observed that since in our political world disagreement is pervasive over the very 'truth conditions' of statements about justice, and that accordingly there can be no undisputed criterion for identifying expertise on justice matters, it follows that theories of justice should be centrally concerned with democracy.[7]

---

[2] C Mouffe, *The Return of the Political* (London, Verso, 1993).

[3] J Neyer 'Justice Not Democracy: Legitimacy in the European Union' (2010) 48 *Journal of Common Market Studies* 903; D Nicol, 'Can Justice Dethrone Democracy in the European Union? A Reply to Jürgen Neyer' (2012) 50 *Journal of Common Market Studies* 508; J Neyer, 'Who's Afraid of Justice? A Rejoinder to Danny Nicol' (2012) 50 *Journal of Common Market Studies* 523.

[4] Consolidated version of the Treaty on European Union [2012] OJ C326/13 (TEU).

[5] Consolidated version of the Treaty on the Functioning of the European Union [2012] OJ C326/47 (TFEU).

[6] J Waldron, *Law and Disagreement* (Oxford, Oxford University Press, 1999) 1.

[7] Valentini illustrates differences in these 'truth conditions' by observing that some people believe that just policies are those which maximise *overall* utility, others that they are those which maximise *average* utility, still others might consider laws just if they comply with Kant's or Rawls' tenets, some religious individuals would hold that just laws and policies reflect our status as God's creatures, and so on. See L Valentini, 'Justice, Disagreement and Democracy' (2013) 43 *British Journal of Political Science* 177, 190.

II. CONTESTABLE JUSTICE: PRE-EUROZONE CRISIS EXAMPLES

Professor Neyer's article was written before the Eurozone crisis. The impact of that crisis, I would contend, has served to reinforce my argument about justice's contestability. Self-evidently the Eurozone catastrophe has plunged the EU into a period of unparalleled crisis in which competing claims of justice and injustice have loomed large. Yet in fact EU history has been littered with examples of the contestability of justice long before the disaster with the Euro. In my exchange with Neyer I put forward several examples of the 'justice' of the treaties being in reality highly contestable. I give, for instance, the example of the *Viking–Laval* case-law,[8] which in a separate article I liken to the *Lochner* jurisprudence of the United States.[9] To be sure, there is a case for considering the outcome in *Viking–Laval* to be just. The 'four freedoms' have been part of the EU political package since the EEC's inception, and it can be argued that, had the ECJ decided *Viking–Laval* in a manner favourable to trade unions, this would have been incompatible with the free market in labour costs and thus with the 'Internal Market' which the EU cherishes. It could also be argued that enforcing a free market in wages and conditions helps the economic situation in poorer Member States whose workers can undercut employees in richer Member States, thereby boosting employment in those countries most sorely needing it.

Conversely, there are respectable arguments for considering *Viking* and *Laval* unjust. It is questionable whether the ECJ was merely carrying out the mandate dictated by treaty aims. The EU's objectives clearly purport to combine ideas—the 'social', and the 'highly competitive market'—which are in tension with each other if not downright contradictory, so the ECJ could easily have arrived at the opposite outcome.[10] As for the argument that a free market conception of the Internal Market aids poorer Member States, is it really in the long-term interests of the new Member States to dismantle the welfarism of the older Member States? Would not this likely scupper their own chances for similar development?[11] Indeed, it is controversial whether liberalisation's real beneficiaries are workers in the new Member States or transnational corporations. In treating a highly contestable matter as incontestable the ECJ's stance mirrors the liberal–individualist policies which Eastern European governments have embraced, based on the questionable assumption that what is good for transnational corporations is good for nationals of the poorer Member States.

A further example of the contestability of EU justice is provided by the EU's policy of compelling privatisation. Article 106 TFEU, relating to the application of EU competition law to public undertakings, has been interpreted by the ECJ as

---

[8] Case C-438/05 *International Transport Workers' Federation and Finnish Seamen's Union v Viking Line ABP and OÜ Viking Line Eesti* [2007] ECR I-10779 and Case C-341/05 *Laval un Partneri Ltd v Svenska Byggnadsarbetareförbundet and Others* [2007] ECR I-11767.

[9] D Nicol, 'Europe's *Lochner* Moment' [2011] *Public Law* 307.

[10] Art 3 TEU; L Azoulai, 'The Court of Justice and the Social Market Economy: The Emergence of an Ideal and the Conditions for Its Realization' (2008) 45 *Common Market Law Review* 1335, 1337.

[11] C Joerges and F Rödl, 'Informal Politics, Formalised Law and the Social Deficit of European Integration: Reflections After the Judgments in *Viking* and *Laval*' (2009) 15 *European Law Journal* 1.

removing the ability of Member States to reserve certain activities to their public sectors. This case-law has subsequently been reinforced and broadened by EU liberalisation directives. Whilst the state may still own the previous monopoly firm, it is now required to allow competition with other service providers. Such liberalisation brings in its wake an inevitable degree of privatisation, since it tends to be the private sector which takes advantage of liberalisation rights. Again, the justice implications of this policy are controversial. It might be considered just on the grounds that large public sectors allow Member States to 'selfishly' evade the demands of the single market. More broadly the extension of privatisation can be regarded as just because it is linked to goals of efficiency, competition, innovation and deficit reduction. But this argument is fiercely contested by those who would argue that a policy which fosters privatisation is unjust in shifting wealth from poor to rich, whereas the retention of a large public sector can provide a counterweight to corporations and can soften the impact of market forces on the population.

Thus in picking out the Eurozone crisis as a particularly topical source of the contestability of justice I by no means wish to suggest that other EU treaty policies lack such contestability. Rather, *the very framework of the original common market was highly contestable in justice terms.*[12] If concern for the less advantaged be part of our conception of justice, then as Andrew Williams has pointed out, there is little evidence that the economic freedoms have really assisted Europe's have-nots. Williams observes that to claim the EU as an 'area of freedom' sits uneasily with the extent to which large numbers of, and whole sections of, the population have failed to benefit.[13] Rather than acting as counterbalance to a system that preserves the power of capital and existing inequalities, the EU has offered a veneer of 'goodness' whilst in reality reinforcing that system and placing it on a more secure foundation.[14]

III. EUROZONE CRISIS AND JUSTICE

Let us, then, pursue the example of the Eurozone crisis. Until the crisis erupted, few would have envisaged the single currency as an arguable source of injustice. Perhaps this reflects wilful blindness on the part of a political elite so desperate for European integration that they declined to see the likely effect of eliminating for the less prosperous Member States the right to devalue their currencies. In any event the crisis itself has generated fiercely conflicting arguments over justice.

On one side of the argument we have the view of EU justice put forward by some German conservatives. They have contended that if the economically troubled Member States wish to take advantage of financial help from the richer Member States and remain within the Eurozone, then they must adhere to the agreed strictures of austerity. In justice terms, the poorer Member States lied about their

---

[12] Against this backdrop of contestability it is nonsensical to lavish praise on EU law's 'right to justification' whenever Member States depart from EU norms (Neyer 'Justice Not Democracy', n 3 above), since there can be no certainty that such departures will be unjust.
[13] A Williams, *The Ethos of Europe* (Cambridge, Cambridge University Press, 2010) 224–25.
[14] ibid, 18.

economic circumstances before they joined the single currency, and afterwards embarked on an irresponsible spending spree since the Euro meant cheap money. It would be unjust to inflict on German citizens the need to pay for a 'vacation from reality' on the part of these Member States. Chancellor Merkel explained the position by contrasting the troubled Member States to the Swabian housewife, who characteristically does not spend more than is in the pot. The Swabian ethos is to save first, and then to spend only what has been saved; in the long run, one cannot live beyond one's means.

On the other side of the argument we have a conflicting conception of justice which rejects the Swabian housewife argument and which sees the austerity programme as excessively brutal. Underlying the Swabian housewife argument is the assumption that the poorer Member States are getting their just desserts for having indulged in a feckless spending-spurge. The counterargument needs to be prefaced with the idea, advanced by Neyer himself, that in talking about justice we are focusing on *people*—the ordinary people of Europe, including those of the troubled Member States. If we set aside the frequent linguistic habit of attributing thoughts and deeds to entire nationalities and acknowledge the gulf within states between *people* and *elites*, it might be argued that in establishing the single currency national leaders were embarking on one of the riskiest economic ventures in history—that of uniting 12 different economies in a single currency union—and that the impetus for this reckless project came not from popular groundswell but from national political elites. Insofar as certain Member States may have dissembled regarding their economic situation to gain entry into the Euro, this was perpetrated by political elites not by their publics. It wasn't the ordinary citizen who cooked the books. Yet it is precisely the ordinary citizen who is expected to suffer the consequences. If we take the mass/elite gap seriously it substantially undermines the Swabian housewife argument.

Moreover deeper consideration of the Eurozone crisis reveals a further dimension of justice contestation. The justice argument which has played itself out should be considered side by side with the justice argument which *ought* to be doing so—one which focuses on corporate power. An alternative reading of the Eurozone crisis attributes blame primarily to the financial sector. For example, in the case of Spain, Spanish regional banks, whilst largely unaffected by the United States subprime crisis, essentially replicated the American calamity by creating a subprime crisis of their own. On this reading it is not ordinary Spaniards who are being bailed out but banks. The injustice is that of peoples suffering economic hardship primarily because of the misconduct of banks over which they had no control. If any blame were to be attributed outside the confines of the financial institutions themselves one should blame the political elite for failing to regulate the sector adequately.

These arguments show, once again, that *there are multiple conflicting ideas of what's just and what's unjust.* How is this argument over justice to be resolved if not by democratic means? Herein lies the impossibility of disentangling justice from democracy. The impact of the Eurozone crisis in Cyprus serves to highlight this impossibility. Initially the European Central Bank (ECB), International Monetary Fund (IMF) and President of Cyprus put forward a solution to the Cypriot crisis which they presumably regarded as sufficiently just, and which famously involved imposing a one-off levy on all depositors in Cypriot banks, even on those whose savings would have been fully covered by the 100,000 Euro bank guarantee. Complaints of unfairness to hard-pressed Cypriot savers were warded off with vague talk of the need to counter Russian oligarchs and their money laundering. The Cypriot Parliament, however, rejected the proposal, with not a single vote cast in its favour. National parliamentarians simply did not share the view of justice embodied in the proposal and voted accordingly, the strength of the rejection shocking those who had assumed that a solution of this kind was the obvious, incontestable, way forward. Thus democratic means were used to make a choice over whether the proposal represented justice or injustice, and this serves to emphasise the inseparability of justice concerns and democracy. Thereafter the Cypriot Parliament abdicated its role as justice adjudicator by approving in advance the results of subsequent negotiations. Yet there are compelling arguments to contest the justice of the arrangements which ultimately materialised. Although these arrangements respected the pre-existing bank guarantee, there is a legitimate expectation on the part of bank depositors that they do not expect bank savings to be particularly risky. In other words, there are other (more potentially profitable) things they could do with their money if they are willing to incur risk. In any event, granted there is always the possibility of a bank going bankrupt as part of the normal rough-and-tumble of business activity, depositors do not expect *the state*, in combination with supranational governmental organisations, to engineer the seizure of their savings. As for the 'money laundering Russians' argument, no analysis took place of what proportion of depositors fell within this group, nor was there any consideration of specific, targeted measures which would counter money laundering whilst excluding those savers not participating in criminal activity. The Cypriot scheme is also arbitrary: for example, those who, when the crisis hit, were in the middle of transferring funds from property transactions were hit for no other reason than having their money—possibly just for a single day—in the wrong place at the wrong time. This haphazard quality is difficult to square with the requirements of justice. There is also the lurking suspicion that Cypriot citizens would not have been treated so harshly had Cyprus been a larger and more important country. These arguments may themselves be contested, which merely serves to underline the contestability of justice. The Cypriot Parliament's self-denying ordinance meant that it could not fulfil the normal democratic function of differentiating justice from injustice on behalf of the people it purports to represent.

In my attack on Neyer, I made one subsidiary argument which merits greater attention here. Reflecting on the nature of elections, I observed that political parties offer not only different sets of policies but also different ideas of justice. Thus *arguments about justice are not merely political but party political*. Against this backdrop it would be particularly deluded of scholars to assume that by some philosophical alchemy they can arrive at a single conception of justice which can satisfy everyone. Against this backdrop I am troubled by Andrew Williams' quest to locate 'a suitable and coherent account of substantive justice' for the EU, and I find problematic his insistence that any such plausible account should necessarily 'adapt rather than revolt against' the EU's existing institutional ethos.[15] We should not

---

[15] ibid, 285.

attempt to disguise justice's fiercely controversial nature. Rather we should accept the existence of multiple conceptions of justice many of which lie at different points on the left wing/right wing spectrum. To this end, indeed, we need to reintroduce the words 'left wing' and 'right wing' into our debates concerning competing ideas about justice.

It is worth observing in passing that the same considerations about contestability apply with equal force if we talk in the language of human rights. The orthodox view assumes that human rights are whatever the European Court of Human Rights says they are. But an emerging view rejects the notion of human rights being handed down on tablets of stone from a judicial or any other elite. This view stems from the idea that it is impossible to accept there being only one 'correct' interpretation of the fundamental rights of the human being. As Janet Hiebert observes, a judicial-centric approach to human rights assumes that only judges are capable of resolving social conflicts involving rights in a principled manner; yet many human rights conflicts are amenable to more than a singular, reasonable answer.[16] Marie-Bénédicte Dembour advocates that we should see human rights as a kind of rhetoric, or a system of persuasion, rather than treating them as some glorified mantra which falls so far short, in practice, of what it proclaims.[17] So human rights, like justice, should derive their value from being things about which we disagree and debate.

IV. THE ROLE OF THE SCHOLAR

Against this backdrop of the political, indeed party-political, nature of arguments about justice, scholars should not attempt to devise a more juristic, less polemical and more apolitical conception of justice. I propose a more controversial role in which scholars overcome their aversion to *explicitly* taking sides in the Left–Right spectrum. In this regard we might take a leaf out of the book of thinkers such as Harold Laski and Friedrich A Hayek who assumed a more partisan role. In twentieth-century Britain, academics such as these provided the theories and philosophies for Left and Right respectively. Thus theorists put forward rival views of what is just, as part of a wider debate, with democracy deciding the (temporary) outcome.[18]

Both Laski and Hayek tackled explicitly the question of what would be necessary in order to have a just society. Laski in *The Grammar of Politics* considered from the perspective of justice the range of ways in which property and income could be distributed.[19] He challenged the self-justifications put forward by those rich in terms of property. He argued for a system whereby each person contributes to society according to his powers and is rewarded by society according to his needs. In so

---

[16] J Hiebert, *Charter Conflicts* (Montreal, McGill-Queen's University Press, 2002).
[17] M-B Dembour, *Who Believes in Human Rights?* (Cambridge, Cambridge University Press, 2006).
[18] Danger comes where one view of justice becomes constitutionally entrenched and prevents political communities—elites and electorates—from regularly re-making their choices. I point to the way in which supranational arrangements are overriding democracy in this regard in D Nicol, *The Constitutional Protection of Capitalism* (Oxford, Hart Publishing, 2010).
[19] H Laski, *The Grammar of Politics*, 2nd edn (New Haven, CT, Yale University Press, 1931) ch 5.

doing Laski rejected as a morally inadequate test of worth the idea that remuneration should be fixed by the operation of the market.[20] Likewise he did not support the general communist case for equality of income, though he felt the argument on its behalf was stronger than generally admitted. He has some objections in principle to equality of income (that there seems no justice in an equal reward for unequal effort, and that needs are unequal), but he also believed that 'at least in the early stages of a new social order, habits of differentiation must be given concessions'.[21] Although there was not an atom of logic in the disparities of wealth, 'we cannot as yet travel the whole road to equality'.[22] Laski's approach makes an interesting contrast to the 'normative realism' urged upon us by Jürgen Neyer. Laski recognised the need to trim his sails in deference to the status quo only in terms of the strategic timing whereby justice demands were made. In other words, he believed in making transitional demands. This did not stop him expounding an uncompromisingly radical normative vision for the long term.

Similarly Hayek pulled no punches when expounding his very different views on justice. We should be mindful that for much of his career Hayek was operating in a hostile political environment in which his particular vision of a free enterprise economy was entirely marginalised. Yet Hayek made no concessions to the political reality of the day when advancing his normative vision. He argued robustly that ideas of 'social' justice were inappropriate in the context of the market economy since it involved an impersonal process with no deliberate allocation to particular people. Since under a free enterprise system no human agency was responsible for the material goods in society, there is no individual, nor group of people, against which a sufferer of 'injustice' would have a just complaint. Hayek also contended that belief in 'social justice' was probably the gravest threat to most other values of free civilisation since it would destroy the environment in which personal freedom could flourish. This was because it would be impossible to preserve a market order while imposing upon it some pattern of remuneration based on notions of 'social justice'. If men were to be rewarded in accordance to the supposed merits of their services to society, this presupposed an authority which would not only distribute rewards, but also assign to individuals tasks for the performance of which they would be rewarded. The spontaneous order of the market would be jettisoned in favour of the arbitrary diktat by an organisation.[23]

Plainly Laski and Hayek disagreed starkly about justice. The gulf between them thus confirms the main argument of this chapter, the contestable nature of justice. More interesting still is to consider what the contributions of Laski and Hayek convey about the proper role of the scholar. In this regard it is instructive in particular to dwell on the function of the academic in relation to that of the politician. What did Laski and Hayek add to the political contestations of the periods in which they were writing? I would argue that their value laid in their *distinctive* role vis-à-vis

---

[20] He also argues that in fact the salary for most posts relied on a kind of customary standard of living, not on supply and demand. ibid, 190–91.
[21] ibid, 190.
[22] ibid.
[23] F Hayek, *Law, Legislation and Liberty* (London, Routledge & Kegan Paul, 1982) ch 9.

the politician. Whilst the professional politician may spend some considerable time thinking of the long term, politicians perforce need to focus substantially on the immediate future. By contrast, the academic can devote far more attention to the shape of the society which it is hoped will ultimately be achieved. This was evidently the focus of both Laski's and Hayek's thinking.

However, the more the scholar concentrates his or her attention on the future shape of society *in the long term*, the less it is appropriate to make supposedly 'realistic' concessions to the status quo. This is at variance with the 'normative realism' sought by Jürgen Neyer. Normative realism, he contends, bends normative vision to political pragmatism by drawing a balance between the 'is' and the 'ought'.[24] Neyer argues for sound normative approaches which aspire to political relevance in that their standards are not utopian in the sense of demanding impossible changes.[25] He identifies as a major shortcoming in normative writings that they are politically irrelevant in the sense that they simply do not resonate with reality, with politics as 'the art of the possible'. Yet Neyer himself does not manage to practise what he preaches. At one point in *The Justification of Europe* he proposes an Interparliamentary Constituent Assembly made up of national parliamentarians which would enjoy a monopoly in putting forward treaty reforms. This is rather a radical proposal. Whether national governments and EU institutions would willingly cede the power of initiative in this crucial sphere is questionable, nor more importantly does Neyer seek to weigh up the likelihood of his proposal seeing the light of day. At the end of his monograph, moreover, Neyer explicitly abandons normative realism altogether, in calling for a global document empowering all contracting parties to demand justifications from other contracting parties if they undertake actions which have a constraining effect on their own liberties.[26] A reformed International Court of Justice would have jurisdiction where these reasons were not accepted. Neyer's failure to keep to his own strictures rather undermines his argument for normative realism. On the other hand, Neyer surely has a point when he complains of scholars posing 'impossible' demands. Yet this complaint could be deployed not as a veto on radical demands but rather as an argument for an additional literature on *strategy*, on how we close the normative gap—the gap between the 'is' and the 'ought'—a subject which is seriously under-theorised. It is not a reason to trim our normative sails. To do so would bring the role of the scholar too close to the role of the politician. The more scholars elect to assume a role distinctive from that of politicians, the less they need to kowtow to the existing state of affairs.

V. THE DEPOLITICISATION OF JUSTICE

The converse of Hayek and Laski can be seen where commentators try to depoliticise the search for justice. Justice, I have argued, derives its value from being something

---

[24] J Neyer, *The Justification of Europe: A Political Theory of Supranational Integration* (Oxford, Oxford University Press, 2012) 190–91.
[25] ibid, 20.
[26] ibid, 192.

we argue about. In this regard we should be suspicious of formulae which depoliticise the justice discourse, for instance by seeking to wrench individuals artificially from society. This charge may be levied against John Rawls's famous but much criticised argument for an 'original position'—a hypothetical state of affairs in which any agreements reached are fair. This original position, he contends, must be determined by people collectively debating justice behind a 'veil of ignorance' which prevents them from knowing to which social class they will belong. They must then determine the basis for 'justice as fairness' by reaching consensus according to their own self-interests. Rawls insists that, behind the veil of ignorance, rational persons concerned to advance their interests will choose two principles of justice, as 'everyone's best reply to the corresponding demands of the others' to settle the basic terms of their association:

> *First principle.* Each person is to have an equal right to the most extensive total system of equal basic liberties compatible with a similar system of liberty for all. *Second principle.* Social and economic inequalities are to be arranged so that they are both: (a) to the greatest benefit of the least advantaged, consistent with the just savings principle, and (b) attached to offices and positions open to all under conditions of fair equality of opportunity.[27]

Rawls insists that the first principle be ranked above the second, since if the basic liberties can be exercised, rational persons will not trade a reduction in liberty for an improvement in economic well-being.

Seemingly, therefore, Rawls seeks to assert that the original position offers a single and durable solution to the justice dilemma. Mouffe, however, advances the valid criticism that it is absurd to suppose that 'justice as fairness' could permanently fix social relations. In reality such fixes are precarious because of the permanence of antagonistic forces. Final agreements on justice can never be reached since the public interest is always a matter of debate, and to imagine such a situation is to dream of a society without politics. Mouffe perceives discourse about justice as forming part of unending struggles to fashion different social orders in which specific hegemonies will be established and periods of relative stabilisation only temporarily achieved.[28]

Neyer's version of justice takes the depoliticisation of justice one step further than Rawls. Rawls envisages a procedure leading to substantive justice, whereas for Neyer, justice is a concept limited to procedural matters. He defines justice as the result of a justificatory process. Neyer insists that the right to justification implies that persons or institutions which restrict our freedom are obliged to explain their reasons for so doing to an independent third party equipped with the competence to assess the merits of the arguments.[29] Yet third party adjudication is rarely independent. For instance, the European Court of Justice famously adheres to its teleological approach whereby it prioritises the achievement of the EU's objectives as it defines them. This is not impartiality but partisan politics. Neyer claims to shy away from advocating a substantive idea of justice since more ambitious conceptions of justice seldom find general acceptance in a heterogeneous world.[30] Yet the

---
[27] J Rawls, *A Theory of Justice* (Cambridge, MA, Harvard University Press, 1971).
[28] Mouffe, *The Return*, n 2 above, ch 3.
[29] Neyer, *The Justification of Europe*, n 24 above, 15.
[30] ibid, 18.

procedure he advocates is bound to privilege a certain vision of substantive justice. At various points in his argument Neyer appears to propose better justificatory structures which could avoid any such bias. He argues that the minimal liberal state should enjoy no greater prima facie legitimacy than the activist welfare state: both must justify themselves.[31] He also visualises a European Constituent Assembly which could balance the four freedoms against the social protection of workers, so that European structures of justification would no longer be unduly shielded from critical scrutiny by the requirement of intergovernmental unanimity.[32] Neyer also concedes that structures of justification can in fact promote injustice if established on the basis of an unjustified normative framework.[33] Yet, with a striking lack of coherence, Neyer concludes his monograph by claiming to be cautiously optimistic with regard to the EU status quo at least in the field of EU domestic policy. In fact his praise seems somewhat fulsome. He lauds the EU for promoting the cause of justice by providing effective remedies to horizontal and vertical power asymmetries through its justificatory processes. Yet it is precisely the EU's existing system of justification which has consistently privileged the interests of private enterprise, setting in train the pro-corporation bias which has arguably led to the Eurozone crisis. All in all, Neyer has picked a most unfortunate time to opt out of considering substantive justice and its relationship with the power of private enterprise, something which goes almost unmentioned in his book, for all his talk of power asymmetries.

VI. CONCLUSION

Even in this short contribution, one is struck by the diversity of competing views on justice. It may be associated with economic fairness (Laski), or its applicability to the economic system may be questioned (Hayek). It may be seen as a substantive state of affairs (Laski), or as a procedure leading to a specified substantive outcome (Rawls), or as an entirely procedural matter (Neyer). Against this backdrop, the Eurozone crisis should help us to fully let go of the assumption that the EU treaties represent justice and instead *politicise* the debate on justice by recognising the multiplicity of views on the subject. This approach guarantees the fiercest possible controversy over what's just and what's unjust.

---

[31] ibid, 86.
[32] ibid, 168.
[33] ibid, 151.

12
Is Transnational Citizenship (Still) Enough?

JUSTINE LACROIX

I. INTRODUCTION: TRANSNATIONAL CITIZENSHIP AS A NORMATIVE AND REALISTIC CONCEPT

THIS CHAPTER DISCUSSES how the difficulties encountered by the European Union in recent years—economic and financial difficulties, of course, but above all political threats indicated notably by violations of European principles in some Member States and the growing disaffection with the European project in others—challenge the concept of 'transnational citizenship' as it has been conceptualised by some scholars in the field.

Since its formal introduction in the Treaty of Maastricht[1] in 1991, the topic of European citizenship has given rise to an enormous literature. Considering 'only' the last ten years of the academic debate, Dimitry Kochenov has identified no fewer than nine fundamental disagreements among scholars, divided into three themes: namely, the legal meaning of EU citizenship, EU citizenship's role in the context of the Union's federal structure and EU citizenship's role in the context of people's lives.[2]

I do not intend to delve into these important debates here. My ambition is more limited. I would like to focus on what Kalypso Nicolaïdis and I have previously described as the 'transnational' school of thought, namely a group of scholars who, whatever their disagreements, have in common their view of the EU as a federalism of free states rather than as a federal state. Conceived as a 'third way' between the 'statist' or 'national school'—which considers that democracy can only exist in the nation state—and the 'supranational school', which pleads for a multinational federal state, the transnational school upholds the view that the EU should be conceived as a form of voluntary legal integration of free states based on regular and organised deliberation, and not on their subordination to a higher authority. The

---

[1] Treaty on European Union (Maastricht, 7 February 1992) [1992] OJ C191.
[2] D Kochenov, 'The Essence of EU Citizenship Emerging From the Last Ten Years of Academic Debate: Beyond the Cherry Blossoms and the Moon?' (2013) 62 *International and Comparative Law Quarterly* 97.

mutual recognition of European nations should pave the way for the emergence of a shared civic culture without necessarily heralding the advent of a federal Europe.[3]

The concept of 'transnational citizenship' is built on three pillars: horizontal rights, mutual recognition and Europeanisation of the national spheres.

1. European citizenship is frequently attacked for its alleged lack of meaning. In common usage, to be a citizen of the Union evokes the idea of a direct, vertical link between citizens and the institutions of the European Union. Seen in these terms, European citizenship is something of a disappointment: it grants only the right to elect European deputies seen as distant and unrepresentative, and with it the right to petition the Strasbourg Parliament and to file complaints with the Ombudsman. However, advocates of 'transnational citizenship' have argued that to see European citizenship exclusively through the lens of collective self-government is to miss its essential nature. They posit that citizenship must also be understood as a historical process—open-ended by definition—in which rights are extended to those who do not yet enjoy them.

In this respect, the gains of European citizenship, understood *horizontally*— including the right to freedom of movement and even settlement across the European territorial space, and to (almost) the same privileges as host country residents—are far from meaningless. In a sense one could almost speak of European construction as a 'fourth age of rights', extending the well-known (though historically contestable) trilogy suggested by the sociologist Thomas Humphrey Marshall who distinguished between three stages of citizenship: civil citizenship (affirmation of the principle of equality before the law); political citizenship (recognition of universal suffrage) and social citizenship (implementation of the welfare state).[4] In this scheme, the proposed 'fourth age' would be defined less by the establishment of new rights than by a dramatic expansion of their sphere of influence, far beyond their national roots. Indeed, legally speaking, European citizenship operates principally on a transnational level, since the rights attached to it pertain by and large to relations between a given Member State of the Union and the citizens of a second state. The importance of this type of transnational citizenship is thus that it establishes new relationships of rights between previously unconnected actors, rather than

---

[3] J Lacroix and K Nicolaïdis, 'European Stories: An Introduction' in J Lacroix and K Nicolaïdis (eds), *European Stories. Intellectual Debates about Europe in National Contexts* (Oxford, Oxford University Press, 2010) 14–17. We include in this 'transnational school' authors such as R Bellamy and D Castiglione, 'Between Cosmopolis and Community: Three Models of Rights and Democracy Within the European Union' in D Archibugi, D Held and M Koehler (eds), *Re-imagining Political Community* (Cambridge, Polity Press, 1998); R Bellamy and D Castiglione, 'Legitimising the European Union and Its Regime: The Normative Turn in EU Studies' (2003) 2 *European Journal of Political Theory* 7; F Cheneval, *The Government of the Peoples. On the Idea and Principles of Multilateral Democracy* (Basingstoke, Palgrave, 2001); J-M Ferry, *La question de l'Etat européen* (Paris, Gallimard, 2000); J-M Ferry, *Europe: la voie kantienne. Essai sur l'identité postnationale* (Paris, Cerf, 2005); P Magnette, 'How Can One Be European? Reflections on the Pillars of European Citizenship' (2007) 13 *European Law Journal* 664; JHH Weiler, 'Federalism Without Constitutionalism: Europe's *Sonderweg*' in K Nicolaïdis and R Howse (eds), *The Federal Vision. Legitimacy and Levels of Governance in the United States and the European Union* (Oxford, Oxford University Press, 2001). See also K Nicolaïdis, 'We, the Peoples of Europe' *Foreign Affairs* (New York, November/December 2004); J Lacroix, *L'Europe en procès* (Paris, Cerf, 2004); J Lacroix, 'Does Europe Need Common Values? Habermas vs Habermas' (2009) 8 *European Journal of Political Theory* 141.

[4] TH Marshall, *Citizenship and Social Class* (London, Pluto, 1950).

consecrating new rights as such. As pointed out by Floris de Witte, both the Union and the Member States participate in creating the preconditions for their citizens to have the double benefit of positive welfare entitlements—including healthcare, education or social assistance—and move around wherever the pursuit of their own version of the good life takes them.[5] According to this line of thinking, we are European not by virtue of belonging to a hypothetical European people, but simply because we are treated no differently at home and in the territory of another state.

2. European citizenship thus understood should have a strong transformative influence both on our self-perceptions and our perceptions of others, since the non-discrimination imperative forces us to take into account another's point of view. Consequently, many scholars have suggested reading the evolution of EU citizenship as a process of *mutual recognition* that leads both to a critical assessment of one's own national identity and a transformed perception of other nationalities. Mutual recognition is seen as a horizontal process that establishes a relationship with the other and strengthens self-respect:

> Being a European citizen does not only mean 'feeling European'; more significantly, it means a different way of being a national and having a bond of mutual recognition with nationals of other Member States.[6]

As Joseph Weiler has famously argued, the discipline implied by European law means tempering exclusive and aggressive tendencies to recognise others, with their differences, as partners worthy of respect. Hence the important civilising dimension of the European construct, grounded on the principle of Constitutional Tolerance which Weiler defines as 'an autonomous voluntary act, endlessly renewed on each occasion of subordination to a norm which is the aggregate expression of other wills and other political communities'.[7] In this vision, the EU is dedicated to being a polity composed of a 'persistent plurality of peoples' within which others are recognised as such, rather than being assimilated.[8]

3. This is why the antidote to the dispossession many citizens feel over European matters may best be articulated by re-appropriating European issues in the national arena. Rather than calling for a common identity or a common European public space, we should promote the *Europeanisation of national spheres*. This process assumes that each Member State should incorporate the European dimension into its own national sphere. For many of those who identify with the transnational vein, Europe is more a constitutional polity than an evolving democracy, and the mechanisms that allow citizens to take part in European decision-making processes are a means for the promotion of individual rights rather than the necessary condition for the emergence of a shared civic culture.[9] Though they belong to the

---

[5] F de Witte, *EU Law and the Question of Justice* (PhD thesis, London School of Economics and Political Science, 2012).

[6] Magnette, 'How Can One Be European', n 3 above.

[7] Weiler, 'Federalism Without Constitutionalism', n 3 above, 67.

[8] J-W Müller, 'The Promise of *Demoi*-cracy: Democracy, Diversity and Domination in the European Public Order' in J Neyer and A Wiener (eds), *Political Theory of the European Union* (Oxford, Oxford University Press, 2011) 197.

[9] Lacroix and Nicolaïdis, 'European Stories', n 3 above, 12–17.

same transnational school, some scholars do not content themselves with a vision of Europe that confines democracy to the limits of national spheres. For the latter, the EU is more than a confederation of states since its peoples are also connected through multi-faceted and deep forms of mutual recognition, which Nicolaïdis refers to as a '*demo*icracy' in the making.[10] According to this conception, the EU can be democratically legitimated by a 'plural *pouvoir constituant*' or by 'multiple but connected national politics'.[11] European democracy should be seen not as national or supranational, but as transnational.

It is important to emphasise that the concept of transnational citizenship falls under the definition of 'normative realism', since it is characterised by holding up the link between 'ought' and 'can'.[12] On the one hand, this transnational citizenship is presented as normatively desirable; on the other, it claims to represent an accurate description of the nature of EU citizenship. It is precisely on this last point that the concept starts to fall under a shadow of doubt: this description is fragile, and has been undermined (perhaps irrevocably) by events of the last few years that have made this transnational citizenship, though perhaps still desirable, appear less and less realistic, credible or adequate. This chapter discusses first how the current crisis affecting the European Union has given ammunition to those who claim that there can be no such thing as a 'European citizenship'. In consequence, it raises some worries about the claim that the EU can still be simultaneously conceived as a *demo*icracy on the one hand and promoted as an arena of political and social justice on the other. However, though these doubts should be taken seriously, the chapter concludes that at this moment in time, the implementation of justice in Europe depends on the determined quest to construct a universal field of rights.

II. DEMOICRACY IN CRISIS

The crisis—economic and financial, of course, but perhaps above all the crisis of meaning that afflicts the European construction today—may seem to give comfort to two critiques which come from opposite political directions, yet intersect in several ways.

The first critique depicts Europe as a glaring example of a 'rights utopia' and projects arguments about the fragmentation and narcissism of contemporary society onto the European level. The European construction, it holds, is the ultimate expression of a liberal paradigm whose only aim is to ensure peaceful co-existence between necessarily competing freedoms. In this vision, Europe is built on a common market that allows free exchange of goods and services and on a set of legal regulations that protect this competition and guarantee the right of each monad to live according to his or her own definition of the good life. In this line of thought, European

---

[10] Nicolaïdis, 'We, the Peoples', n 3 above.
[11] K Nicolaïdis, 'European *Demo*icracy and Its Crisis' (2013) 51 *Journal of Common Market Studies* 351, 352.
[12] On normative realism, see J Neyer, 'Europe's Justice Deficit: Justification and Legitimacy in the EU' in J Neyer and A Wiener (eds), *Political Theory of the European Union* (Oxford, Oxford University Press, 2011) 184.

citizenship appears as part of a wider 'culture of narcissism', which Christopher Lasch described as distorting the nature of the public sphere: a form of individualism born of radical fragmentation,[13] in which there is no longer any sense in seeing matters from a collective standpoint. The crisis of meaning that we are witnessing in the European project today—evidenced by Euroscepticism and the momentum of popular resentment at integration—might seem to corroborate the views of thinkers who argued, as long as 20 years ago, that a strong shared identity is the only basis for substantiating aspirations towards both political and social justice.[14]

A second critique depicts European citizenship as a space of unchecked economism and technical professionalisation, features that erode and change the nature of the political sphere. Here, European citizenship is interpreted as the implementation of a neoliberal mechanism. Neoliberalism must be understood in this context not merely as a superlative of hyper- or ultraliberalism: it does not extend existing market freedoms so much as consecrate a completely new political rationale. This is a style of government defined by the economic paradigm infiltrating all other aspects of society: a form of governmentalism which, according to this argument, endangers the very logic of citizenship that makes democracy what it is. In this sense, European citizenship reawakens fears of politics collapsing under the weight of a bureaucratic and market-led tyranny.

Even if one does not agree with all these critiques, it is difficult to deny three developments that reveal some backsliding in the reality of transnational citizenship.

The first is the swing from *recognition to mutual defiance*. Some have expressed a hope that the economic crisis will be a prelude to the gradual Europeanisation of national arenas predicted by the advocates of transnational citizenship. There have indeed been some reasons to think so, since the crisis has witnessed Member States treating the national crises of others—Greece, Italy, Spain—as decidedly domestic issues. But is this really enough to justify Jürgen Habermas' hope that Europe is gradually awakening to a shared destiny? Desirable as this may be, it is hard to deny that as matters stand the Europeanisation of national spheres is marked more by intensifying mutual prejudice (think of the portrayal of German leaders as Nazis or the so-called 'Club Med' countries)[15] than deepening mutual recognition. We can no longer ignore the danger that Europeans, under the pressure of crisis, will cross the fine line between benign indifference and thinly veiled hostility. Also real is the prospect of our common cause gradually disintegrating into a mere collective fear, with each member looking out for its own interests at others' expense. A rampant 'de-Europeanisation' that moves in parallel with flagrant violations of the European principles encapsulated under the banner of Article 2 of the Treaty

---

[13] C Lasch, *The Culture of Narcissism. American Life in an Age of Diminishing Expectations* (New York, Norton, 1991).

[14] For references on this strand of thought see K Nicolaïdis and J Lacroix, 'Order and Justice Beyond the Nation-State: Europe's Competing Paradigms' in R Foot, JL Gaddis and A Hurrell (eds), *Order and Justice in International Relations* (Oxford, Oxford University Press, 2003) and J Lacroix, 'For a European Constitutional Patriotism' (2002) 50 *Political Studies* 944.

[15] J-W Müller, 'The Failure of European Intellectuals?' (2012) *Eurozine*, www.eurozine.com/articles/2012-04-11-muller-en.html.

on European Union (TEU),[16] a development of which Hungary is merely the most striking example.

In addition, one can argue that there has as yet been no 'spill-over effect' from our relationship to the Other European to our relationship with the non-European Other, as was expected. On the contrary, far from conferring a transnational dimension on Europe, the establishment of a 'Europe of police forces' has progressively given the European space all the characteristics of a 'territory' to be defended against a new enemy, both inside and out: refugees and migrant workers.[17]

The second backwards step is that in which *mobility feeds off the progress of the welfare state*. Recent events may appear to affirm the concern expressed by some that according absolute primacy to individual rights could undercut aspirations to social justice. The European construction has extended our rights beyond national boundaries; in this sense, as Floris de Witte emphasises, European free movement law allows 'citizens to find out where the good life lies in twenty-six constellations'.[18] Yet—to take an example that has recently been in the news—some wealthy French citizens currently decide to pursue their own conception of the 'good life' in Belgium since this country is characterised by its low rates of taxation on income from financial and property assets. This is widely perceived as unjust, not only by other French citizens but also by a significant proportion of the Belgian population since income tax on salaried earnings, on the other hand, is very high compared with other European countries.

Thus we see how freedom of movement and the imperative of non-discrimination can in fact undermine the welfare state, in as much as these principles neglect the reciprocal imperative between citizen and state that is the basis for social rights at the national level. Above all, and aside from the special case of tax avoidance, one cannot fail to observe that many of the major population shifts currently witnessed within the European Union arise less from a mutual will to make borders open than from a unilateral and forced movement of young people from the South and the East to the North and the West of Europe—a type of labour drainage that Etienne Balibar has argued has 'quasi-colonial' aspects.[19]

The third regression is that of *citizen apathy towards European construction*—an apathy that may seem to confirm opinions, again expressed by some as long as 20 years ago, that there was no such thing as a European citizen, but only 'users' or consumers devoid of any feeling of loyalty to a particular political community. In the absence of agreement on a model of citizenship to be defended, the figure of the

---

[16] Art 2 of the Consolidated version of the Treaty on European Union [2012] OJ C326/13 (TEU) guarantees the values of respect for 'human dignity, freedom, democracy, equality, the Rule of Law and respect for human rights'. On this topic, see notably KL Scheppele, 'EU Commission vs Hungary: The Case for the Systemic Infringement Action' (2013), www.verfassungsblog.de/en/the-eu-commission-v-hungary-the-case-for-the-systemic-infringement-action/#.UsnO8PvzvF8.

[17] E Balibar, *We the Peoples of Europe? Reflections on Transnational Citizenship* (Princeton, NJ, Princeton University Press, 2004).

[18] F de Witte, 'Integrating National and Transnational Justice Claims' in G de Búrca, D Kochenov and A Williams (eds), *Debating Europe's Justice Deficit: The EU, Swabian Housewives, Rawls and Ryanair* (2013) *EUI Working Papers* LAW 2013/11, 9.

[19] E Balibar, seminar at the Collège de France (27 February 2013), www.college-de-france.fr/site/pierre-rosanvallon.

consumer has instead been reified and in a sense made to represent the 'pioneer' of European construction. This is the source of a motivational crisis that is now forcing the question of the political feasibility of the federation of European states and of a cosmopolitan union. The European political entity relies not on the paradigm of the 'family', but rather that of civil society premised on a form of ethical and political universalism. Several authors have demonstrated that this model is in fact a harbinger of political disaffection and therefore of an increased risk of corruption, over-concentration of power, and even disintegration of political institutions.

III. SOME DOUBTS ABOUT THE 'THIRD WAY'

These threats raise two questions about the future of political and social justice in the EU. First, one may wonder if the proponents of this kind of transnational citizenship[20]—conceived as a 'third way' between the statist or national school and the supranational school—have not over-emphasised respect for national diversity within the European Union. Some observers have rightly commented that the underlying principle of EU institutional reforms is now protection of the rights of states. Not since the failure of the Constitutional Treaty have the European texts so insistently reiterated the emphasis on respect for state prerogatives and national identities. However, those who believe in political justice should admit that diversity is not an end in itself:

> Diversity and pluralism are not values in the same sense as liberty and democracy—everything depends on the answer to the question: 'diversity of what?' It is liberty and democracy that European intellectuals ought to defend.[21]

The end of political justice is the rule of law and liberty. Here, we must follow Jan-Werner Müller's welcome elucidation of mutual recognition, which is all too often trumpeted as the patent mark of the European Union (even while the Union itself is a potent homogenising force) and as an end in itself, while it can in fact lead to a form of bad faith: notably in the presentation of regulatory competition as 'a case of recognizing and respecting national traditions'.[22]

Second, and more importantly for our topic, are political and social justice really attainable in a transnational polity, which is sometimes called a Federation of States and Peoples, a *demoi*cracy or a cosmopolitan union? More precisely, one may ask whether the argument made by Jürgen Habermas in his latest book—in which he advocates a veritable supranational democracy with shared government and the implementation of collective welfare mechanisms, yet claims at the same time to

---

[20] See notably: Nicolaïdis, 'We, the Peoples', n 3 above; Nicolaïdis, 'European *Demoi*cracy', n 11 above; K Nicolaïdis 'The Idea of European *Demoï*cracy' in J Dickson and P Eleftheriadis (eds), *Foundations of European Law* (Oxford, Oxford University Press, 2012); Magnette, 'How Can One Be European', n 3 above. For a long-standing vision of the EU as aspiring to community rather than unity, see JHH Weiler, *The Constitution of Europe: 'Do the New Clothes Have an Emperor?' And Other Essays on European Integration* (Cambridge, Cambridge University Press, 1998).
[21] Müller, 'The Failure', n 15 above.
[22] Müller, 'The Promise', n 8 above, 199.

reject the structure of a federal state—is really defensible.[23] If one agrees that only thoroughgoing fiscal reform (which would involve not only levying European taxes but also implementing provisions for their fair distribution) would remedy the injustices inflicted today in the name of austerity, how then to reconcile this type of interpersonal redistribution on a European scale with an equal and opposite belief; namely, that EU citizenship can only be limited and derivative, and that the political characteristics prized by republicans, such as active commitment, can only be realised at the national level?[24] Put differently, is transnational citizenship still enough or should we move further to build a true supranational citizenship at the European level?

To focus the question further, we may follow Philippe Van Parijs in asking whether today's Europe is in fact

> stuck between two impossibilities. On the one hand the increasing economic impossibility of doing something serious about inequality at the national ... level and on the other hand the persisting political impossibility of doing something serious about inequality at a supranational level.[25]

The suggestions proffered by Van Parijs—a quasi-American strategy founded on personal redistribution at the Union level, along with Union-wide electoral accountability and a shared language (English, of course) to ensure effective communication, coordination and mobilisation among Europeans—may be less attractive, from a purely conceptual point of view, than insisting on the radical novelty of the European polity. They may, however, be the only way to rescue political and social justice in Europe.

But even though this solution may be a necessity, it nonetheless remains improbable. As pointed out by Jürgen Neyer, the EU will, for the foreseeable future, have to live with more than 20 national *demoi* and national democracies. 'From all we observe today, there is neither a demand for, nor a supply of, a European *demos* or a European super-democracy'.[26] It is thus in the name of realism that Richard Bellamy predicts that the likely resolution of the Euro crisis through political union between at least some Member States will result in a polity that will prove far less capable of sustaining political justice than any of the Member States.[27] Yet it might be more accurate to say that it could result in a polity which will prove far less capable of sustaining political justice than any of the Member States *used* to do.

The position that I advocate here is less optimistic than that expressed by Van Parijs and more optimistic than Bellamy's. Less optimistic than Van Parijs in the sense that although I agree with his observation that genuine redistribution at the EU level would doubtless be the only means of reducing the inequalities engendered

---

[23] J Habermas, *The Crisis of the European Union: A Response* (Cambridge, Polity Press, 2012).
[24] R Bellamy, 'Belonging, Rights and Participation Within the EU' (2008) 12 *Citizenship Studies* 597.
[25] P Van Parijs, 'A Quasi-American Strategy for European Egalitarians' (2013) 4 *Green European Journal* 30, 31.
[26] Neyer, 'Europe's Justice Deficit', n 12 above, 172.
[27] R Bellamy, 'Political Justice for an Ever Closer Union of European Peoples' in G de Búrca, D Kochenov and A Williams (eds), *Debating Europe's Justice Deficit: The EU, Swabian Housewives, Rawls and Ryanair* (2013) *EUI Working Papers* LAW 2013/11.

by the common market and common currency, this redistribution appears to be out of political reach for the foreseeable future, since the European budget has already fallen below 1 per cent of the EU's Gross Domestic Product (GDP). In the medium term, it seems unlikely that Europe will be able to take the place of nations as the prime site of social and political integration. There is cause to be more optimistic than Bellamy, however, in the sense that the same observation may also be a spur to conceive of European citizenship as a 'right to have rights' on a larger scale.

IV. A UNIVERSAL FIELD OF RIGHTS?

Put differently, we would do well to take those who criticise European citizenship for being merely legal at their word, and indeed take this aspect as the basis for an alternative answer of our own: that European citizenship is linked to rights more than duties, and to a status more than a shared identity. Rather than endlessly asking how we might encourage political participation and identification to take shape on an extended scale, we must endeavour to build a true community of rights founded on the tenets that Etienne Balibar has called 'equaliberty'.[28] In this regard, it is important to recognise the progress made by a certain number of European treaties and directives in extending the rights of free movement, and consolidating anti-discrimination measures vis-à-vis citizens of non-EU states legally resident within EU borders.

This is an interesting development in view of the fact that several theorists have repeatedly deplored the discrimination or even 'apartheid' that allegedly now divides Europeans from non-Europeans.[29] In the light of the relevant European texts, this is no longer altogether true: if the treaties formally restrict the status of 'European citizen' to Member State nationals, a European directive adopted in 2003 in fact moves towards a (partial) levelling of status between Member State nationals and third-country nationals who are long-term legal residents within EU borders—and thus towards a type of 'residence citizenship'.[30] Although recognition of residence remains within the power of the host country (which therefore holds the key to the 'right to hold rights' at the European level), it is no longer strictly true that holding the nationality of a Member State is a non-negotiable condition for enjoying rights.

If it continued on this track, the EU could take shape as a force progressively breaking down the identity boundaries according to which rights have traditionally been granted. The use of the conditional remains necessary because these tentative steps towards levelling the terrain between the rights of 'Europeans' and those of 'third-country nationals legally resident in the EU' go hand in hand with an ever starker distinction drawn between these and illegal immigrants, whose plight throws into doubt the cosmopolitan ambitions of the European entity. In a short work

---

[28] E Balibar, *La Proposition de l'égaliberté* (Paris, Presses Universitaires de France, 2010).
[29] E Balibar, *Nous, Citoyens d'Europe. Les frontières, l'Etat, le people* (Paris, La Découverte, 2001) 190–91.
[30] Council Directive 2003/109/EC of 25 November 2003 concerning the status of third-country nationals who are long-term residents [2004] OJ L16/44. On this point, J-Y Carlier, *La Condition des personnes dans l'Union européenne* (Brussels, Larcier, 2007).

published in 2013, Mireille Delmas-Mary goes so far as to identify 'dehumanisation' and a strategy of 'open aggression' as the characteristics of a European 'fortress' in which the recourse to criminal or equivalent sanctions (detainment, for instance) is pursued as a hardening of border policy and labour restrictions.[31] Here, I endorse Etienne Tassin's view that far from mere 'collateral damage' from European unification, 'clandestinity may in fact represent the heart of the European conundrum';[32] its importance far surpasses the boundaries of 'a mere question of border policing, which would leave untouched the radically new logic on which political Europe is built'.[33] It is as well to recall that Renaissance humanists and Enlightenment thinkers also dreamt of freedom of movement as a goal, and that Kant based his theory of cosmopolitan rights on the principle of universal hospitality. In this perspective, the political recognition of foreigners, and beyond it a generalised right to free movement, is an important criterion by which to judge the success of public power in honouring its cosmopolitan goals.

This is why it would be better, in harmony with the true nature of the European polity, to revive this movement towards the 'denationalisation of rights', to the benefit of Europeans of course but also of those who do not belong to 'its' nations, to gradually to make Europe an arena for the construction of a 'universal field of rights' premised on a *partial* dissociation of nationality and citizenship. Another possibility to take into account is Pierre Hassner's suggestion of conferring European citizenship upon refugees and stateless persons, those in short who are not citizens of any state. Hassner's view on the place of these individuals whose status is ambiguous or incomplete is that European citizenship, if it must in any case be partial and paradoxical, may as well embrace those qualities by welcoming in those who cannot be citizens elsewhere. This would, Hassner argued, be one way of circumventing the dilemma between the stark abstraction of human rights and national citizenship.[34]

It is worth recalling, indeed, that in an epilogue appended a posteriori to the *Origins of Totalitarianism*, Hannah Arendt forcefully asserted the necessity of this endeavour, and therefore the need to construct what Burke 'with his immense good sense' had deemed impossible: namely, that new discoveries about morality and ideas of liberty might lead towards the recognition of a right to humanity itself:

> The concept of human rights can again be meaningful only if they are redefined as a right to the human condition itself, which depends upon belonging to some human community ... The Rights of Man can be implemented only if they become the prepolitical foundation of a new polity, the prelegal basis of a new legal structure, the, so to speak, prehistorical fundament from which the history of mankind will derive its essential meaning in much the same way western civilisation did from its own fundamental original myths.[35]

---

[31] M Delmas-Marty, *Résister. Responsabiliser. Anticiper* (Paris, Seuil, 2013).
[32] E Tassin, 'L'Union cosmopolitique et la citoyenneté du monde' (2007) 7 *Raison publique* 45, 46.
[33] ibid, 50.
[34] P Hassner, 'Refugees: A Special Case for Cosmopolitan Citizenship?' in D Archibugi, D Held and M Kölher (eds), *Re-imagining Political Community* (Cambridge, Polity Press, 1998).
[35] H Arendt, *The Burden of Our Time*, first published in the US as *The Origins of Totalitarianism* (London, Martin Secker & Warburg, 1951) ch 13.

In other words, though she explicitly rejected the idea of world government, on the basis that this would undermine the plurality of nationalities, cultures and political identities, Arendt might well have endorsed what Jürgen Habermas calls a 'post-conventional' identity based on a relativised sovereignty, a proliferation of checks and balances on power, and a limitation on the power of the nation state achieved through a combination of citizen-led initiatives and international jurisdiction.[36]

As such, it must be made clear that the distinction drawn here between citizenship as 'participation in collective self-government' and citizenship as an 'extension of rights' does not correspond with a distinction between a supposedly 'active' or virtuous citizenship founded on a sense of the public good and a 'passive' or selfish citizenship understood as the mere enjoyment of rights by individuals turned in on their own interests. The fact that European citizenship takes shape more in the logic of human rights, understood as liberties, than in that of citizen rights, understood in terms of participation, does not mean that it has no political dimension. In an article now regarded as seminal, Claude Lefort insisted that human rights, far from concealing the breakdown of social bonds, could also attest to and encourage the formation of new networks of human relationships: they could, in short, bear witness to a new type of legitimacy and a public sphere that both shape individuals and are shaped by them.[37]

In the European context more specifically, two aspects of this 'citizenship of rights' should be emphasised. On the one hand, the fact that rights protect individual interests does not mean that they may not be reclaimed for the purposes of a political project conducted *with* and *for* others: 'in the real world, the striking thing is that these claims (to rights) are generally made in the name of other individuals'.[38] An instance of this type of collective action can be seen today in the mobilisations, led on a European scale by migrants' rights associations, for the extension of the benefits of European citizenship as a whole to legal residents within EU borders or the overturning of 'return' directives issued against third-country state nationals illegally present in Europe. The fact that these types of civic action do not pass through traditional political party channels, and that their claims are for 'rights', by no means excludes them from the political sphere.

That said, however, one must clarify a point that echoes the arguments made by Catherine Colliot-Thélène in her book of 2011, *La Démocratie sans demos*. The book clearly demonstrates that equality of rights has been the main vehicle of 'democratisation of democracies';[39] but the author rather hastily concludes from this that to conceive of democracy we must abandon the ideas of *demos* and sovereignty since 'the pluralisation of the *kratos* makes the *demos* indefinable'.[40] But it is not unlikely that Catherine Colliot-Thélène takes this step only because she relies on

---

[36] J Habermas, *The Postnational Constellation* (Cambridge, Polity Press, 2001) and J Habermas, *Inclusion of the Other: Studies in Political Theory* (Cambridge, Polity Press, 1998).

[37] C Lefort, 'Droits de l'homme et politique' in C Lefort, *L'Invention démocratique* (Paris, Fayard, 1981).

[38] J Waldron, *Nonsense Upon Stilts. Bentham, Burke and Marx on the Rights of Man* (London, Methuen, 1987) 197.

[39] C Colliot-Thélène, *La démocratie sans demos* (Paris, Presses Universitaires de France, 2011) 91.

[40] ibid, 21.

a people conceived as necessarily unitary, and a sovereignty understood as absolute. Now, what is required today is not replacement of the principle of popular sovereignty with an assertion of equal rights but rather, in Pierre Rosanvallon's terms, to 'complicate' democracy by extending its meaning.[41] More specifically, we appear to be witnessing a pluralisation on two fronts.

First of all a pluralisation of *demoi*, in the sense of relevant social communities. Meaningful political sites now vary in character whether we are talking about pension or education reforms, questions of policing and security, family affairs, or currency, fiscal or environmental policy. And despite a frequent assumption to the contrary, the nation state remains the foremost existing embodiment of social community in the contemporary world, let us recall that it is, as things stand, the only site for the redistribution of wealth that exists, or that at least perpetuates itself with more or less stability. If the rule of law has to some extent extended into the European arena, the welfare state has not, and neither is this a hope for the near future.

This warrants a brief parenthesis on the question of sovereignty—a concept which some already appear to regard as obsolete.[42] As Catherine Colliot-Thélène stresses, 'it is inconceivable that sovereignty should be shared'.[43] But if a 'shared' sovereignty is perhaps indeed inconceivable, a *relativised* sovereignty is highly conceivable. In the European framework, state sovereignty is relativised in as much as it is now constrained, both by the choices made by our partners and decisions taken collectively at the supranational level, or by judicial arbitration—whether at the European Court of Justice or at the European Court of Human Rights. This was a state of affairs perfectly captured in the apt subtitle that Paul Magnette gave to his book on the relationship between the state and European construction: *Sovereignty Tamed*.[44] For if it is 'relativised', sovereignty does not disappear altogether. In this sense, European constitutionalism complements internal constitutionalism: internally, the rule of law tempers the majoritarian democratic bias, without however eliminating it—since the sovereign people can change its constitution; externally, European federalism places limits on national democracy, whilst remaining open to the possibility that some such democracies will reject, or even *in extremis* leave the Union. As Kalypso Nicolaïdis underlines in her first principle for a '*Demoi*cratic Ethics',

> Peoples as states must have a de jure right, but also de facto capacity, to choose to enter or exit the Union … Member States must remain master of the Treaties, however difficult accommodations or 'reasonable vetoes' this may imply.[45]

The second form of pluralisation is that of modes of political action linked to a diversification of repertoires for public expression. This is particularly relevant to

---

[41] See notably P Rosanvallon, 'Penser le populisme' *Le Monde* (21 July 2011).
[42] See, eg, G Mairet 'Sur la critique cosmopolitique du droit politique: Europe, souveraineté et démocratie' in G Duprat (ed), *L'Union européenne. Droit, politique et démocratie* (Paris, Presses Universitaires de France, 1996).
[43] C Colliot-Thélène, lecture given at the College de France (13 February 2013), www.college-de-france.fr/site/pierre-rosanvallon/#lm=seminarlq=/site/pierre-rosanvallon/seminar-2012-2013.htm.
[44] P Magnette, *L'Europe, l'Etat et la démocratie. Le souverain apprivoisé* (Brussels, Complexe, 2000).
[45] Nicolaïdis, 'European *Demoi*cracy', n 11 above, 363.

the endeavour of conceiving law in relationship to democracy by recalling that the demands of law and those of democracy

> are connected by a doubly unstable definition. Rights are sought and consolidated. Democracy submerges them and sets the bar higher. This is its untameable essence, which can never be reduced to mere institutional mechanisms.[46]

As Jacques Rancière has demonstrated, it is precisely when one enacts 'the rights that one does not have' that one becomes a political subject.[47]

Yet, here too we must remain cautious. If it is doubtless necessary to leave behind an overly institutional or formal definition of democracy to conceive of cosmopolitan citizenship, it seems a little precipitous simply to substitute 'struggles for rights' for the principle of a self-legislating people. Conceiving of cosmopolitan citizenship means seeking a possible connection between the national and the transnational, between approaches to political commitment termed 'liberal' and those of a more 'republican' bent, between struggles for equal rights and collective self-determination initiatives. Reflecting on democracy in an age of globalisation means bringing out its complexities, to be sure, but not necessarily effecting a complete shift in conceptual register.

V. CONCLUSION

This chapter has not claimed to suggest a solution or 'formula' to resolve the current crisis of the concept of transnational citizenship. It would of course be easy to sideline several of the threats discussed here in view of the fact that *demoi*cracy is a concept intended first and foremost as normative. Easy perhaps, but irresponsible, since as political theorists it is also part of our role to ensure that the concepts we elaborate preserve a link, even if sometimes a distant one, with reality. And from this point of view, we may reasonably fear that the concept of a transnational citizenship based on freedom of movement and mutual recognition may no longer be enough to preserve the gains of the welfare state—or even that these features may destroy what was previously a source of pride for European progressivists. At the same time, there is no simple way out of the paradox since the concept of transnational citizenship remains a crucial one in the wider project of renewing the will to extend a 'right to hold rights' to all those who reside within (or without) European borders. Moreover, those who pursue this latter ambition should keep in mind that citizenship is above all else a *status*. This is important to counter a tendency, prevalent among several theorists of radical democracy, to think about citizenship merely as a form of political action and to deconstruct its definition as a 'status'. The quality of citizenship must first of all not be restricted to mere involvement in political

---

[46] M Chemillier-Gendreau, *De la guerre à la communauté universelle. Entre droit et politique* (Paris, Fayard, 2013) 369.
[47] J Rancière, 'Who Is the Subject of the Rights of Man?' (2004) 103 *The South Atlantic Quarterly* 297. See also EF Isin, 'Two Regimes of Rights' in X Guillaume and J Huysmans (eds), *Citizenship and Security. The Constitution of Political Being* (London, Routledge, 2013) 58.

mobilisation. Many individuals who do not wish to or cannot demonstrate in this way in the public sphere nonetheless enjoy its rights; as the French philosopher Alain put it: 'No one is worthy of rights. This is the very foundation of rights'.[48] We may recall in the same vein that in her text *Nous autres réfugiés* (1943), Hannah Arendt repeatedly emphasised that it is the loss of a legal status in the world that has made pariahs of stateless persons. 'Very few individuals', she wrote, 'have the strength to preserve their own integrity if their social, political and legal status is simply thrown into doubt'.[49]

---

[48] Alain, *Propos sur les pouvoirs*, 29 (5 January 1914) (Paris, Folio, 1985) 93.
[49] H Arendt, 'Nous autres réfugiés' (2013) 144 *Pouvoirs* 5, 12.

Part Three

13
The Evolving Idea of Political Justice in the EU: From Substantive Deficits to the Systemic Contingency of European Society

JIŘÍ PŘIBÁŇ

I. INTRODUCTION

THE PROBLEM OF political justice is a problem of legitimacy. It is, therefore, inseparable from local, national, supranational and global issues of political democracy and functionality. Input legitimacy through democratic values cannot be completely sidelined by output legitimacy through efficiency. The very concept of political justice considers legitimacy a matter of principle and a normative precondition of politics and law.

Although it has proven impossible to replicate at the EU level the systemic complexity and normative preconditions of democratic legitimacy that exists in the politics of Member States, EU judicial and bureaucratic bodies use concepts of justice in their policies and decision making. EU institutions are based on, and actively promote, the values of democracy, equality and respect for human rights that are intrinsic to political justice.

Since the 1950s, administered and expertly driven prosperity, stability, procedural justice and shared political interests and values of Member States have been the added value that legitimated the process of European integration. In the 1990s, democratic mobilisation supplanted the existing processes of technocratic legitimacy. Post-Maastricht, the public was expected to engage in 'ever-closer Union'. When, however, the populations of several Member States rejected the Constitutional Treaty, democratisation proved an obstacle to further integration. In the first decade of the twenty-first century, the split between the EU's calls for democratisation and the crisis of functionality became more acute.

The concept of political justice appears paradoxical because it semantically unifies what needs to be functionally differentiated in modern society; namely, politics and law. Is it, therefore, necessary to contrast political justice with the concept of purely procedural and formalistic legal justice? Is justice a morally substantive concept and ultimate formula of normative legitimation, or an internal formula of functionally differentiated economic, political, legal and administrative systems?

And is this process of functional differentiation specifically related to the EU's post-national and post-sovereign condition, or should one consider it part of the general and evermore globalised social process of systemic differentiation which is merely framed by the Union's institutions and their operations? Any discussion of the EU's deficit of political justice needs to address the functional differentiation of EU politics and law. It especially needs to examine the juridical concept of justice internally developed by the EU's system of positive law and the impact of the Union's democratisation on the Union's self-conceptualisation as a just supranational polity.

In the following text, I therefore start by analysing the concept of political justice as a broad formula for legitimation of both the systems of EU law and politics. Political justice is typical of normative expectations and thus needs to be distinguished from the purely procedural notion of justice in the system of positive law. Discussing political justice in the context of EU law and politics raises questions about the legitimacy of the political authority of EU institutions and the legal normative authorisation of their decisions. I subsequently discuss the concept of political justice as a self-referential concept incorporating expectations of both efficiency and democratic legitimacy, which are evolving at the EU level. The Lisbon Treaty's framework is an example of such coeval enhancements of legitimacy through technocratic efficiency and democratisation. The Treaty's call for the improved efficiency and democracy of EU institutions, however, reveals a structural discrepancy between the EU's politics of supranational governance, which primarily neutralises conflicts by administrative reason and technocratic expertise, and the ever-growing difficulties Member States encounter in attempting to transfer the powers of their democratically legitimate political institutions to the EU.

Theories of EU governance commonly underestimate the importance of democratic decision making and reduce the problem of legitimacy to efficiency. Against this body of theoretical knowledge, I conclude that political justice can neither be left entirely to the neutralising power of administrative reason nor to the expert knowledge of economists, bureaucrats or lawyers; rather, political justice needs to follow the general logic of political modernity and its call for the democratic legitimacy of political authority. The process of democratisation can hardly be discarded as a secondary problem at supranational EU and/or global level. However, this call for democratisation paradoxically weakens administrative legitimacy by technocratic governance of EU experts and makes the EU a significantly more conflict-driven polity replicating a number of problems and conflicts historically associated with the modern state and its political sovereignty. The post-sovereign EU, therefore, cannot avoid the modern politics of democratic sovereignty and, in the absence of a democratically constituted institutional framework, it needs to enhance its democratic legitimacy by strengthening political communication between democratic Member States and supranational EU political institutions.

II. THE LEGAL AND POLITICAL CONCEPT OF JUSTICE: PRELIMINARY THEORETICAL DISTINCTIONS

Hans Kelsen's exclusion of justice from a general theory of law and his identification of justice with relativity, plurality and even a contradiction of moral values and views of law remains a hallmark of modern legal positivism.[1] According to this view, which was profoundly influenced by Max Weber's methodology of a value-free science,[2] justice in the sense of a morality of law is just one manifestation of modern moral relativism and represents nothing but a plurality of public and private opinions.

Legal and sociological positivists perceive morality as a reservoir of merely subjective views and norms that cannot claim objective validity in modern society. Morality is ambivalent because bad action can have good consequences and vice versa. Furthermore, according to positivists, moral arguments are double standards in politics because different political parties use them to attack each other in their struggle for power. The same double standards typical of moral arguments are employed by opposing parties in legal conflicts to enhance the persuasiveness of their legal arguments. All this leads to the conclusion that modern morality is intrinsically polemical and divisive and therefore has lost its integrative function in modern society.[3]

According to legalist views, the concept of substantive justice as an absolute criterion of law's objective authority and general validity loses its persuasiveness in modern society. The purely formalistic and procedural concept of justice as an aspect of the prescriptive form and hierarchical order of positive law appears to be the only alternative to the substantive moral and political concept of justice. According to this positivistic view, the definition of justice thus remains in the realm of positive law and the function and limits of justice are exclusively determined by legal norms. Justice thus becomes an internal matter of the hierarchy of authorisations, efficiency and functionality of legal norms. Instead of moral or political rightness, the concept of legal justice depends on the notion of specifically legal authority. It depends on the functionality of the legal system and cannot be traced to some external substantive principles of just politics and universal morality.

Kelsen's attempt at constructing a pure theory of law is part of the positivistic tradition of modernity typical of the differentiation of social systems, such as economy, politics and law, and the elimination of moral concepts, such as justice, from their internal operations. Weber's distinction of instrumental and value rationality already indicates the impossibility of moral political foundations in modern society.[4] However, the disappearance of ethics as an ultimate ground of political and legal reasoning also indicates the differentiation of political and legal reasoning and decision making. Political power becomes irreducible to the normativity of law and legal norms are equally impossible to explain through the lens of political power and decision making.

Political and legal reasons are mutually exclusive and this exclusivity also means that political and legal concepts of justice are incommensurate. Modern legal and

---

[1] H Kelsen, *The Pure Theory of Law* (Berkeley, CA, University of California Press, 1960) 403.
[2] N Bobbio, 'Hans Kelsen und Max Weber' in M Rehbinder and KP Tieck (eds), *Max Weber als Rechtssoziologe* (Leipzig, Duncker & Humblot, 1987).
[3] For a sociological positivistic view, see N Luhmann, *Paradigm Lost: Die ethische Reflexion der Moral* (Frankfurt, Suhrkamp, 1990) 12.
[4] See, eg, G Oakes, 'Max Weber on Value Rationality and Value Spheres: Critical Remarks' (2003) 3 *Journal of Classical Sociology* 27.

sociological positivism thus criticises the concept of justice as an external and ultimate source of legal validity and reformulates it as an intrinsic value (*Eigenvalue*) of the legal system manifested in its procedures, operations, internal coherence and, most importantly, efficiency as its internal criterion of legitimacy. According to this positivist view, elaborated, for instance, by Niklas Luhmann in his general sociological theory of autopoietic social systems, justice is 'a contingency formula' and 'the concept of substantive justice ... transforms a tautology into a sequence of arguments and makes something that is seen as highly artificial and contingent from the outside appear quite natural and necessary from the inside'.[5]

Early modern theoretical concepts of legal validity are by nature and tradition replaced by the systemic semantics of validity by decisions the content of which is indeterminate, but acceptable through generalised 'dispositions of procedures'.[6] Political values and principles of representative democracy and human rights are turned into internal operations of the constitutional system and, as long as constitutions are considered valid and their principles uncontested, no recourse to the idea of substantive political justice is needed and political values are treated as internal sources of the legal system and formal procedural justice.

According to these positivistic views, political justice is merely an externality of the system of positive law which has no effect on its functionality and potential deficits. Legitimacy is generated through legal procedures and legal validity is secured through decisions made according to these procedures.[7] Political principles and operations internalised by the political system, such as democratic will-formation, majority rule, constitutional separation of power, individual freedom, security and protection against the abuse of power and violence, are internalised by the system of positive law as procedures imposing constraints on arbitrary political decisions by virtue of their systemic operations and not by their principal nature and normative supremacy in a social and political order.

III. POLITICAL JUSTICE AS THE CATEGORICAL IMPERATIVE OF LAW AND THE STATE

This positivist reduction of justice to the internal operations of a legal system reduces the problem of justice to a problem of legal form and the social efficiency of legal rules. If law is a system of objectively valid and enforceable norms and arguments, it does not need any philosophy or political theory of justice. Accordingly, justice is not a condition of the validity of positive law; rather, it is an internal formula stabilising operations and enhancing the efficiency of the modern system of positive law apart from politics and morality.

Hobbes's early modern statement that law's validity is secured by authority and not truth is expanded into a theory of modernity as disenchantment, neutralisation

---

[5] N Luhmann, *Law As a Social System* (Oxford, Oxford University Press, 2004) 445.
[6] N Luhmann, *Ausdifferenzierung des Rechts: Beiträge zur Rechtssoziologie und Rechtstheorie* (Frankfurt, Suhrkamp, 1981) 122–50.
[7] N Luhmann, *Legitimation durch Verfahren* (Frankfurt, Surhkamp, 1969/1983) 28.

or functional and systemic differentiation. Sociological and political theories even speak of 'the disenchantment of the state'[8] and replacement of its representative democratic legitimacy and constitutional settlement by depoliticised forms of governance, expert administration and social steering.[9] According to this view, the state, its organisation and legitimacy do not depend primarily on political principles and values of democracy, responsibility, reciprocity and human rights. The state is considered part of the complex political system of global society which paradoxically acquires new social tasks and increases expectations while losing its central position traditionally associated with political sovereignty. It is no longer the state's authority that makes laws valid but instead the capacity of legal operations to secure steering and governance of global society. In other words, efficiency and output legitimacy completely take over from input legitimation as the normative foundations and principles of politics.

Against these claims, philosophers and theorists of political justice argue that modernity actually radicalises the problem of legitimacy. According to these philosophers and theorists, attempts to reduce political justice to legal or administrative procedures without recourse to normative foundations and principles merely illustrate the scale of this radicalisation.[10] Instead of simply identifying justice with universal normative claims, theorists of political justice often move from looking for a set of normative foundations to legitimate processes of justification[11] as a middle ground between universal validity claims and social acceptance.

In this context, Jürgen Habermas, for instance, states:

> [P]olitical domination must be expressed in the impersonal language of the law in order to satisfy the demand of universality and general validity. Legality is the only technique of government, which can provide modern political domination with legitimacy. Law's legitimacy, however, does not come automatically and the legitimating scheme of the constitutional and democratic rule of law itself must rest on the concepts of the people's sovereignty and basic human rights.[12]

Otfried Höffe argues that postmodernity's farewell to matters of principle is premature. According to Höffe, neither politics nor law can avoid questioning their foundations or the justification of their operations. Höffe relies on Augustine's famous remark—'what are states without justice but rubber-bands enlarged?'[13]—to argue that even legal positivism draws on the qualified notion of authorised power and not just the brute fact of command and enforcement. Höffe maintains that political justice is both a normative and constitutive principle of law and the state.[14]

---

[8] H Willke, *Entzauberung des Staates: Überlegungen zu einer sozietalen Steuerungstheorie* (Königstein, Athenaeum Verlag, 1983).

[9] RAW Rhodes, 'The New Governance: Governing Without Government' (1996) 44 *Political Studies* 652.

[10] M Coakley, 'On the Value of Political Legitimacy' (2011) 10 *Politics, Philosophy and Economics* 345.

[11] R Forst, *The Right to Justification: Elements of a Constructive Theory of Justice* (New York, NY, Columbia University Press, 2012).

[12] J Habermas, *The Theory of Communicative Action II: The Critique of Functionalist Reason* (Cambridge, Polity Press, 1987) 178.

[13] O Höffe, *Political Justice* (Cambridge, Polity Press, 1995) 77.

[14] ibid, 78.

According to him, legal positivism ignores the fact that the Hobbesian perspective of 'validity by virtue of authority'[15] obscures various dimensions of authority, especially its original authorisation by social consent. Even Leviathan's decisions first need to be recognised and consented to by the affected parties.

Furthermore, the original authorisation of power is allegedly accompanied by the power limitation function of both the legal and political system. Legal procedures have both an operative and principled character because their institutionalisation of the original arbitrariness of power involves the principled normative constraints of power.

According to this moral philosophical perspective, the function of political justice, therefore, is both constitutive, in the sense of legitimising authority by consensus, and determinate, in the sense of normatively limiting its exercise. In short, political justice is the organisation of power and its social institutionalisation in the state and other organisations of political unity and community. This is why '[p]olitical justice is the justice of a legal and political system, and as such belongs to the realm of institutional justice'[16] and may even be described as 'the categorical imperative for political and legal orders, or the categorical imperative of law and the state'.[17]

IV. POLITICAL JUSTICE, THE STATE AND THE EU

In modern European history, political justice and its constitutive and limiting functions have traditionally been associated with the state and its constitution. The coercive powers of the state and any other political organisation require legitimacy through these functions of political justice. Political authority's coercion is not merely an execution of brute force. Power manifested in state sovereignty draws on legitimacy through the primary sovereignty of those subjected to it; that is, legal subjects of the democratic state with their basic rights and freedoms. At this moment, Leviathan is replaced by Justitia displaying both the sword, symbolising power, and the scale, symbolising justice, because, as Höffe comments, 'faith in justice without enforcement would be sheer naivety; toleration of political power untutored by justice is the height of cynicism'.[18]

The crucial question, then, is whether principles and values of political justice have lost their legitimising force and whether the state and other local, supranational and global political organisations have become merely organisations of social steering and administration. Have the political form and principles of the sovereign state and democratic government finally been replaced by the neutral efficiency of depoliticised forms of social steering and governance? Is the state and its modern aspirations to political justice, democratic sovereignty, constitutional limitation of power and individual rights just a redundant moralistic strategy unfit to generate legitimacy for the global political system and its supranational and transnational organisations?

[15] ibid, 81.
[16] ibid, 32.
[17] ibid, 41.
[18] ibid, 288.

This set of questions is informed by the conflict between normative and operative concepts of legitimacy; that is to say, between government and governance and between political democracy and social steering. One can subsequently ask if the call for legitimation through social steering and efficient governance is part of the utopian dream of post-conflictual and self-administered society without the coercive power of political institutions.

In context of the EU, one can ask whether the difference between political democratic government and depoliticised technocratic governance is actually replicated in the process of European integration and the structural difference between democratic Member States and supranational EU institutions. The EU's legitimacy through 'the common benefit' is a typical example of legitimacy through efficiency or output, yet the whole post-Maastricht evolution of the Union's economic, political and legal systems is defined by attempts at strengthening democratic legitimacy and reconciling it with the Union's legitimacy driven by expert knowledge and neutralising power of depoliticised governance. The EU has reached a point in its internal development and systemic differentiation at which it must ask whether it needs to constitute legally its 'categorical imperative' of political justice and determine its content. Is the Union, therefore, challenged by the same questions of legitimation like political institutions of the modern state, or does it continue to be a supranational alternative to Member States driven by its internal operations facilitating its legitimacy free of democratic dilemmas, principles and procedures legitimising the modern state politics?

These questions and problems strongly resonate in the evermore complex political and legal reality of the EU and its recent critical developments. For instance, the evolving Eurozone economic crisis is often presented as an apocalyptic moment and as punishment for the cynical politics of EU bureaucrats and promoters of ever-closer Union without democratic consent. The opposite camp of pro-European politicians and federalist campaigners portray the same event as a reason why political and legal integration finally has to catch up with economic integration and warn against more multi-layered and looser forms of European integration in the same apocalyptic tone. As if the Union was facing its ultimate moment of either destruction or salvation!

Stepping aside from these apocalyptic visions and normative urges to deal with social problems in the manner of 'either/or' moralistic solutions and criticisms, it is possible to perceive the current crisis of the EU and all of its deficits as just a moment of increased contingency in the evolution of European society. The apparent EU apocalypse is simply a moment in its societal evolution.

This preliminary remark should not be interpreted as an endorsement of societal functionalism and steering over democratic politics; rather, viewing the EU crisis as an evolutionary moment helps to reconceive of the process of European integration as a contribution to the systemic differentiation and evolution of European society. It also helps to avoid the simplistic and moralistic opposition between the nation state and supranational EU political organisations by highlighting that the EU's political justice deficit actually replicates a number of deficits, dilemmas and paradoxes of legitimacy emerging at the nation state level, which proves that they are general political deficits, dilemmas and paradoxes unlimited by state organisation.

V. FROM THEORETICAL CONTEXTS TO THE LEGAL TEXT: THE LISBON TREATY AND DEMOCRATIC LEGITIMACY

The Lisbon Treaty presents the Union as a system of compound democracy,[19] with the twin representation of citizens and states. Further, it commits the Union to the founding principle of representative democracy, guaranteeing the right for EU citizens to be democratically represented at both EU and Member State levels. The democratic foundations of the Union are further extended by the citizens' right to participate in 'the democratic life of the Union' legislated for in the third section of Article 10 of the Treaty on European Union (TEU).[20] The principle of representative democracy is supplemented by the concept of participatory democracy which is further elaborated by Article 11 of the TEU. Finally, the complexity of the EU's political structures and operations are manifested by closely associating representative democracy with public accountability and multi-party democracy operating at both the Member State and EU level and, therefore, shaping and 'expressing the will of citizens of the Union'.

Specific EU responses to the deficit of representative democracy and political justice are reflected in more general issues of the Union's legitimacy and functioning, accountability, multilevel governance, and commitment to a supranational civic and democratic political culture. The Union's democratic foundation is inseparable from questions of who is represented and how, and which democratic checks and limitations of power apply to the Union. Finally, Member State responses to the level of the Union's democratic legitimacy, especially constitutional court judgments in Member States, need to be addressed to comprehend fully the legal and constitutional complexities and controversies accompanying the Union's political justice deficit.

A. The EU as the Balance Between Efficiency and Democratic Legitimacy

The Preamble to the Treaty on European Union, as amended by the Lisbon Treaty, considers democracy one of universal values specifically related to Europe's cultural heritage. Furthermore, the Preamble perceives democracy as the founding principle of Member States and the basis of the Union's functioning. Article 10 TEU primarily addresses this dual character of democracy as the Member States' founding principle and the Union's internal mode of functioning.

In European studies and EU law literature, it is hardly disputed that the Union is both a transnational community of democratic Member States and a supranational community directly exercising its power over and beyond the EU territory.[21] This form of multilevel governance[22] is an historically and politically unique project

---

[19] S Fabbrini, *Compound Democracies: Why the United States and Europe Are Becoming Similar* (Oxford, Oxford University Press, 2007).

[20] Consolidated version of the Treaty on European Union [2012] OJ C326/13 (TEU).

[21] See, eg, J Richardson (ed), *European Union: Power and Policy Making*, 3rd edn (London, Routledge, 2006); see also W Kaiser and P Sarie (eds), *Transnational European Union: Towards a Common Political Space* (London, Routledge, 2005).

[22] L Hooghe and G Marks, *Multi-Level Governance and European Integration* (Oxford, Rowman & Littlefield, 2001).

which is irreducible to just another kind of international organisation. However, the EU also escapes the logic of democratic nation state-building and state-like popular constitution making. The Union's integration involves economically, politically and legally experimental processes and elements.[23] The incorporation by the Lisbon amendments into the TEU of the principle of representative democracy is then a particular response to the European governance, and is an attempt to find the appropriate legitimation formula for European integration.[24]

The pressures to find a solution to the Union's deficits of democratic legitimacy became increasingly pressing in the post-Maastricht era.[25] Despite imaginative scholarly attempts to present the Union as demanding and deserving models of legitimacy that break with traditional ideas of representative democracy, the appeal of representative democracy survives.[26] An institutional design favouring the executive branch of government needed to be reformed to avoid further alienation and a growing gap between EU governing bodies and those governed by them. The original model of legitimacy of European integration through 'output' became insufficient and needed to be substantially supplemented by legitimacy through 'input' bringing on-board more democratic representation and public accountability of the Union's institutions and their decision making.[27]

The post-national constellation of the EU[28] called for its democratisation to narrow the gap between the Union and its citizens and to deal with the Union's democratic deficit.[29] European political integration based on the limitation of Member State sovereignty[30] resulted in a need to enhance democratic governing and functioning of the post-sovereign Union.[31] As with the failed Constitutional Treaty,[32] the Lisbon reforms sought to strike the right balance between administrative efficiency and democratic legitimacy by strengthening the democratic decision making of the

---

[23] B Laffan, R O'Donnell and M Smith, *Europe's Experimental Union: Rethinking Integration* (London, Routledge, 2000).
[24] A Moravcsik, 'In Defence of the "Democratic Deficit": Reassessing Legitimacy in the European Union' (2002) 40 *Journal of Common Market Studies* 603.
[25] RA Dahl, 'A Democratic Dilemma: System Effectiveness versus Citizen Participation' (1994) 109 *Political Science Quarterly* 23.
[26] AJ Menéndez, 'The European Democratic Challenge: The Forging of a Supranational *Volonté Générale*' (2009) 15 *European Law Journal* 277.
[27] W Wallace and J Smith, 'Democracy or Technocracy? European Integration and the Problem of Popular Consent' in J Hayward (ed), *The Crisis of Representation in Europe* (Oxford, Frank Cass, 1995) 137.
[28] J Habermas, 'The Postnational Constellation and the Future of Democracy' in J Habermas, *The Postnational Constellation: Political Essays* (Cambridge, Polity Press, 2001).
[29] For academic views regarding the EU's democratic deficit, see, eg, Moravcsik, 'In Defence', n 25 above; G Majone, 'Europe's "Democratic Deficit": The Question of Standards' (1998) 4 *European Law Journal* 5; A Follesdal and S Hix, 'Why There is a Democratic Deficit in the EU: A Response to Majone and Moravcsik' (2006) 44 *Journal of Common Market Studies* 533; and finally A Moravcsik, 'The Myth of Europe's Democratic Deficit' (2008) 43 *Intereconomics: Review of European Economic Policy* 331.
[30] For the political and international context of the self-limitation of state sovereignty in the EU, see, eg, J Habermas and J Derrida, 'February 15, or What Binds Europeans Together: A Plea for a Common Foreign Policy, Beginning in the Core of Europe' (2003) 10 *Constellations* 291, 294.
[31] DN Chryssochoou, *Theorizing European Integration*, 2nd edn (London, Routledge, 2009) 136–46; see also N Walker, 'Late Sovereignty in the European Union' in N Walker (ed), *Sovereignty in Transition* (Oxford, Hart Publishing, 2003).
[32] B Crum, 'Tailoring Representative Democracy to the European Union: Does the European Constitution Reduce the Democratic Deficit?' (2005) 11 *European Law Journal* 452.

Union's institutions and increasing the contribution and participation of Member States' democratic institutions in EU decision making.

B. The Principle of Representative Democracy and its Adoption by the European Union

Representative democracy is a form of government in which citizens elect their representatives and grant them political power for a limited period of time.[33] Throughout modern European history, it has been associated with government's respect for and protection of individual liberties (liberal democracy)[34] and parliamentarianism (the legislative body elected in the general election by the people and representing its popular sovereignty).[35] A parliament elected by the people consists of individual members generally organised in political parties or other formations. Parliamentarians are divided into a majority, which supports the executive, or government, and the minority, or opposition, which actively opposes government initiatives but still participates in parliamentary politics and enjoys representation in different parliamentary bodies.

Presently, representative democracy is absent from the EU institutional framework,[36] but representative democracy is the political foundation of the Union. It is a precondition of EU membership, and all Member States are constitutional parliamentary democracies.

Before the end of Cold War and the collapse of the Soviet regimes of 'the people's democracies' in Central and Eastern Europe in 1989 and in the Soviet Union itself in 1991, representative democracy and parliamentarianism had been taken for granted within the Member States of the European Community. The accession of post-dictatorial Greece (1981), Portugal (1986) and Spain (1986) to the European Community confirmed that a constitutional parliamentary democracy was a de facto if not de jure condition of membership. Indeed, before 1993, the Copenhagen criteria were set out for post-communist emerging democracies.[37] Enlargements of EU membership in 2004, 2007 and 2013, however, demonstrate that the political model of representative democracy is now one of the most critical conditions for any state seeking membership. Democracy is a cornerstone of the EU's accession policy and contributes significantly to the belief that the EU is a 'democratic polity' promoting intrinsic democratic values in external relations and global politics.[38]

The EU Treaty lists democracy as one of the foundational values common to all Member States. The quality and standards of democratic politics in Member States is

---

[33] G Sartori, *The Theory of Democracy Revisited: The Contemporary Debate* (Chatham, NJ, Chatham House Publishers, 1987) 21–38.
[34] ibid, 367–98.
[35] K von Beyme, *Parliamentary Democracy: Democratization, Destabilization, Reconsolidation, 1789–1999* (Houndmills, Palgrave Macmillan, 2000).
[36] DN Chryssochoou, *Democracy in the European Union* (London, Tauris, 1998).
[37] W Sadurski, 'Accession's Democracy Dividend: The Impact of the EU Enlargement upon Democracy in the New Member States of Central and Eastern Europe' (2004) 10 *European Law Journal* 371.
[38] R Youngs, *The European Union and the Promotion of Democracy* (Oxford, Oxford University Press, 2001).

consequently an intrinsic part of the EU's multilevel governance.[39] Only recently, in light of growing far right and neo-fascist electoral successes in a number of Member States, did the Amsterdam Treaty establish formal mechanisms for guaranteeing the perpetuation of democratic government in Member States. In 2000, no recourse was made to the Amsterdam Treaty provisions despite the rise of the far-right Freedom Party in Austria. Instead, an 'early warning' amendment to the Treaty provisions, nicknamed 'Lex Austria', was subsequently introduced by the Nice Treaty. The 'Lex Austria' amendment allowed the European Council to make determinations on the existence of 'clear risk' of a serious breach of the foundational democratic values of the EU taking place. The Lisbon Treaty contains similar provisions to ensure adequate protection for constitutional democracy.

C. The Union's Deficit of Representative Democracy and its Constitutional Strengthening at the Member State Level

Despite the increased role of representative democratic legitimacy in European political governance, the Union's democratic deficit has been a growing concern among European and national politicians and the legislative and judicial bodies of Member States have examined its potentially negative effect on domestic democratic politics and legitimacy.

One of the most voiced criticisms of the Union's democratic deficit has traditionally taken the form of constitutional arguments and come from the constitutional courts of Member States. In response to the Maastricht Treaty and the creation of the European Union, the constitutional courts of Member States, and especially those of Germany and Denmark, argued that the process of European integration should not be detrimental to the constitutional principles, authority and standards of democracy enjoyed at the Member State level.[40]

The same concerns caused the constitutional courts of some Member States to review the Lisbon Treaty while it was being ratified. The judgments of these courts, and particularly those of the German and Czech courts, share concerns about the democratic legitimacy of EU institutions, emphasise the principle of Member State sovereignty and insist on the precedence of their democratic nation state constitutions over European law when it is impossible to interpret domestic law in accordance with the EU treaties.[41] The German Constitutional Court has even argued that rights of participation of the German Parliament's chambers in EU matters have not been elaborated to the extent required by the constitutional order of Germany. The Court, therefore, demanded legislative amendments and changes to the German legal system to further strengthen the role of the German Parliament in EU matters.[42]

---

[39] See Arts 2 and 10 TEU.
[40] F Laursen and S Vanhoonacker (eds), *The Ratification of the Maastricht Treaty: Issues, Debates and Future Implications* (Dordrecht, Martinus Nijhoff Publishers, 1994).
[41] See the Judgment No 19/08 Pl ÚS (Constitutional Court of the Czech Republic, 26 November 2008), para 85. For further comments, see J Přibáň, 'From "Which Rule of Law?" to "The Rule of Which Law?": Post-Communist Experiences of European Legal Integration' (2009) 1 *The Hague Journal on the Rule of Law* 337, 357–58.
[42] BVerfG 2 BvE 2/08 (30 June 2009).

D. Legislating for the EU's Participatory and Direct Democracy, Constructing the EU's Civil Society?

The concept of participatory democracy is usually defined against the background of more established notions of representative and direct democracy. Participatory democracy requires extending power and decision making to a broad swathe of the population. Advocates of participatory democracy often criticise representational institutions for limiting democratic participation to voting processes and for insufficient means for voters to control their representatives or hold them accountable.[43] Although all forms of democratic government require public participation, participatory democracy involves an enhanced form of participation that allows those people affected by or interested in political decisions to contribute directly to the decision-making process. This heightened level of engagement is thought to strengthen democracy's general virtues of self-government, self-realisation and self-education through public discussion and civil society.[44]

The EU embraced the concept of participatory democracy to deal with its perceived deficit of democratic representation[45] and to promote alternative forms of democratic legitimacy.[46] The Union's commitment to post-national forms of participatory democracy draws on recent theories concerning political globalisation and post-national democratisation[47] as well as theories of governance that embrace policies of public accountability and the engagement of civil society.[48]

The Lisbon Treaty expands the Union's commitment to increasing political participation by adopting the *citizens' initiative* as a form of direct democracy.[49] The citizens' initiative is an attempt at closing the gap between rhetoric and reality in the Union's commitment to democracy. Until now, direct democracy has played virtually no role in the functioning of the Union. The exercise of direct democracy in EU matters was limited to the national referenda ratifying or rejecting the EU treaties, and these referenda are entirely regulated by the Member States' constitutional systems, not EU law.[50]

Until the adoption of the citizens' initiative under the Lisbon Treaty, Member States practised various forms of direct democracy within their constitutional systems although, apart from the right to petition the European Parliament either individually or collectively,[51] direct democracy had no role in EU politics. Originally

---

[43] C Pateman, 'Participation and Democratic Theory' in RA Dahl, I Shapiro and JA Cheibub (eds), *The Democracy Sourcebook* (Cambridge, MA, The MIT Press, 2003) 41–42.

[44] B He, 'Civil Society and Democracy' in A Carter and G Stokes (eds), *Democratic Theory Today: Challenges for the 21st Century* (Cambridge, Polity Press, 2002) 211–13.

[45] For general comments, see G de Búrca, 'The Quest for Legitimacy in the European Union' (1996) 59 *Modern Law Review* 349.

[46] P Schmitter, 'Democracy in Europe and Europe's Democratization' (2003) 14(4) *Journal of Democracy* 71.

[47] MT Greven and LW Pauly (eds), *Democracy Beyond the State: The European Dilemma and Emerging Global Order* (Oxford, Rowman & Littlefield, 2000).

[48] G Marks et al (eds), *Governance in the European Union* (London, SAGE Publications, 1996).

[49] Art 11(4) TEU.

[50] 'Direct democracy and the European Union ... is that a threat or a promise?' (Editorial comments) (2008) 45 *Common Market Law Review* 929, 930.

[51] Arts 24 and 227 of the Consolidated version of the Treaty on the Functioning of the European Union [2012] OJ C326/47 (TFEU).

introduced by the failed Constitutional Treaty, the citizens' initiative was reformulated and adopted by the Lisbon Treaty to make the Commission more responsive to the collective will of EU citizens.

In legal terms, the citizens' initiative requires the minimum number of one million EU citizens. Furthermore, those citizens must be nationals of a significant number of Member States and the initiative has to relate to matters within the European Commission's powers. Nevertheless, there is a more general goal associated with the citizens' initiative as an element of direct democracy applied at the EU level; namely, the evolution of a transnational European civil society.[52] By voicing and standing for the general interests of EU citizens, a transnational European civil society, which operates beyond the limits of nation states, is expected to act as a counterweight to the lobbying power of interest groups and their specific political goals.[53] Instead of the output-oriented and the interest-aggregation based legitimacy models, the citizens' initiative is part of an input based procedural legitimacy model[54] which is intended to expand democratic deliberation in the post-national EU.

VI. THE LISBON TREATY AND THE JURIDIFICATION OF POLITICAL JUSTICE

The system of European law as updated by the Lisbon Treaty allows for elements of representative, participatory and direct democracy, but it neither facilitates democratic decision making nor does it establish the system of democratic checks and balances which generally characterise the nation state. Instead, it primarily refers to democratic legitimacy as an *external* categorical imperative and precondition of the EU's political and legal systems.

Therefore, neither the political nor the legal systems of the EU have fully operationalised political justice. Although the Lisbon Treaty makes democracy a symbolic foundation, systemic precondition and mode of operation in carefully selected and limited areas of the Union's decision making, the Treaty does not entirely convert general democratic values and principles into specific procedures of decision making. Indeed, the Union's system of positive law is fully operational and its internal concept of formal justice is rich and commonly used by EU lawyers, administrators and judges to enhance the system's efficiency and stability of its operations. However, the Union's political system has not constituted a replica of the constitutional democratic state as a social organisation structurally linking the systems of law and politics. It is impossible to characterise the Union in common terms of territoriality, government, population and (in the case of democratic statehood) popular legitimacy. In the absence of EU democratic government, the complex forms and processes of the Union's political decision making are commonly labelled as a system of European governance.

---

[52] O de Schutter, 'Europe in Search of Its Civil Society' (2002) 8 *European Law Journal* 198.
[53] D Curtin, 'Private Interest Representation or Civil Society Deliberation? A Contemporary Dilemma for European Governance' (2003) 12 *Social & Legal Studies* 55.
[54] C Ruzza and V Della Sala, 'Conclusion: Deliberative Democracy, Input–Output Legitimacy and the Meaning of Civil Society' in C Ruzza and V Della Sala (eds), *Governance and Civil Society in the European Union: Volume 2: Normative Perspectives* (Manchester, Manchester University Press, 2007) 136–37.

Even if democratic state organisation is missing at the EU level, the Union's alternative forms of governing and processes of decision making, nevertheless, are no less powerful. The EU's political system, therefore, circulates power by the self-referential operations of its legal and administrative bodies. The absence of two out of Lincoln's three characteristics of democratic government, namely, government 'of the people' and 'by the people', makes the EU's political system primarily operate 'for the people' or, better, 'for the peoples of the EU'. Nevertheless, this legitimation formula is paradoxically weakened by the process of progressive integration because benefits 'for the people' necessarily become obscured and compromised by political conflicts and even crises emerging and evolving through the system of European politics.

EU politics continues to be informed by tensions between instrumental legitimacy through outcomes and efficiency of EU governance and symbolic legitimacy through democratic values of the EU and its Member States. Efficiency has always been the principle of the EU's political legitimacy while democracy has been its both tacit assumption and desired goal. The Union's efficiency and common benefits were intended to contribute to political stability and democratic accountability at the Member State level. Nevertheless, the evolution of the European polity does not rely exclusively on institutional innovations and technocratic alternatives to the modern democratic state. It becomes ever more challenged by the principles of democratic representation and participation.

VII. LEGITIMACY WITHOUT JUSTICE? ON THE EU'S POLITICISATION AND DEPOLITICISATION

Recent juridification of EU political justice has not established a profoundly democratised or morally and culturally coherent polity with a strong sense of social solidarity and common destiny. The European polity has a fully operational and autonomous legal system, including the principle of formal procedural justice, yet operates without the foundationalist legitimising principle of political justice. The EU has never had a differentiated system of politics operating through processes of democratic will-formation, majority voting, party politics and, above all, popular sovereignty as a general formula ultimately legitimating any decisions of representative bodies.

However, modern politics has never been merely the question of 'By whom am I governed?' It is inseparable from the question of 'How much am I governed?' and the question of 'How well am I governed?' Democratic representation is thus inseparable from limited government and efficient governance. While political justice is hardly just a matter of efficient policy making, no government can claim legitimacy without delivering the expected outputs it has promised and to which the public has consented. The fact that only just politics can be legitimate is as important as the fact that only a functioning and efficient political system can be considered legitimate. General procedures intended to stabilise (check?) arbitrary power facilitate functionality.

The problem of political justice, therefore, is closely linked to the process of transforming political values and principles to general procedures and criteria of decision making. Furthermore, legitimacy through procedure involves a general distinction between politicisation and depoliticisation. This distinction is typical of modern politics, which differentiates between democratic and expert reasoning. Democratic government assumes the expediency, accuracy, correctness and disenchanted politics of social steering while technocratic expert knowledge and governance require democratic consent and institutional framing. Politicisation means democratisation and public deliberation according to public reasoning. Depoliticisation means value-free instrumentality and efficiency facilitated by technocratic reasoning. Politicisation is part of democratic government and depoliticisation is part of expert governance.

European politics, rather than merely constituting new political organisation and forms of deliberation and decision making, thus replicates one of the general operations of the modern political system in which it is the job of politicians to enforce expert knowledge and to translate it to the language of popular sovereignty and will-formation. EU and Member State politicians can keep their decision-making power only if they persuade the public and make technocratic decisions that are democratically legitimate. However, this politicisation of expert knowledge goes hand in hand with the depoliticisation of social conflicts and problems, which turns them into expert problems and technocratic solutions.

Democracy and technocracy are just two different pictures of the same modern political system. In this sense, the Lisbon Treaty has merely recognised the importance of mutual processes of politicisation and depoliticisation when it emphasises both 'democratic accountability' and 'efficiency'. Though reflecting on the typically modern distinction of political reason, this conceptualisation, nevertheless, means a radical departure from the traditional notion of political justice and legitimation in the sense of common normative foundations and value integration. Instead, the Treaty's specific proceduralisation of politics as the process of parallel politicisation and depoliticisation highlights the fragmentation of political justice and the impossibility of controlling expert reason by public reason and vice versa.

Only justice, considered as a contingency formula of both law and politics, accommodates the technocratic reason of expertise and the democratic reason of public deliberation and makes them subject to either legal or political operations. Accordingly, political justice is a paradoxical process of both internal systemic unification and inter-systemic fragmentation.

VIII. POLITICAL JUSTICE AND EUROPEAN POLITY AS OUTCOMES OF FUNCTIONAL DIFFERENTIATION OF EUROPEAN SOCIETY

The Union has transgressed, yet not made completely redundant, one of main structural limitations of modernity—the modern historical *organisation* of societies into nation states. The democratic organisation of Member States challenges the system of EU political governance. In response to this challenge, the Union has undertaken an internal process of democratisation. The political semantics of the nation state, including popular sovereignty, democratic legitimacy, citizenship and constitutional rights, has increasingly permeated post-sovereign EU structures.

Modern state semantics of democratic legitimacy persist. They also change the Union's description and the constitution of the political system operating beyond the nation state and/or international politics. Recent semantic inventions, such as 'constitutionalism without constituent power', 'executive federalism', 'multi-level governance' and 'post-sovereign community', need to be critically reassessed against the persistence and influence of the political semantics of democratic representation, statehood and popular sovereignty. Instead of seeing the Union as statehood in waiting, it rather has to be conceptualised as an organisational framework facilitating the constitution of European society by functional differentiation. Only after this profound theoretical shift has occurred can the notions of a European polity and of political justice be reconceptualised and reformulated as intrinsic parts of European politics. In turn, European politics needs to be considered as one of the many functionally differentiated systems of European society.

Neil Walker has suggested two ways of theorising the concept of polity.[55] One is to insist on the constitutional semantics of a polity constituted by and constituting its shared political destiny and moral solidarity. This prescriptive semantics of polity as society integrated by its constitutional settlement, legitimising moral principles and political organisation contradicts the process of functional differentiation and societal fragmentation. Unlike persons, societies do not have their categorical imperatives and cannot be integrated through moral principles and norms. The concept of polity is not a prescriptive precondition of politics in the sense of a common identity that establishes the political system, its hierarchies and limitations. Polity is not a social or moral foundation of politics.

Walker's other suggestion is to comprehend the concept of polity as a semantic construct produced by internal operations of a functionally differentiated political system. The EU, its organisation, history and development are then persuasive examples of this evolution and the systemic limitation of the meaning of polity beyond state organisation. Tedious debates about the European public, *demos*, moral and political values and shared collective memories and culture only illustrate the impossibility of constructing a European polity as collectively self-constituting, morally integrating and politically organising its destiny. Sceptical voices emphasising the absence of all these prescriptive and imaginative concepts in European politics are as misleading as optimistic calls for Europe as the avant-garde of cosmopolitan democracy and values.

Instead of insisting on these premises, it is possible to reformulate the concept of a European polity in the same manner as the concept of political justice and consider it the semantic self-reflection of European political differentiation. Like any other polity, the European polity is to be treated as the political system's self-legitimation and outcome of the functional differentiation of EU politics and law. Instead of covering the totality of society, it merely refers back to political operations evolving at EU level.

IX. CONCLUDING REMARKS: ON FUNCTIONAL DIFFERENTIATION OF EUROPEAN SOCIETY, POLITICS AND JUSTICE

Recent constitution-making and post-Lisbon Treaty efforts of the EU at enhancing its efficiency and democracy are specific examples of turning political values

---

[55] N Walker, 'The Idea of Constitutional Pluralism' (2002) 65 *Modern Law Review* 317, 347.

and principles of the EU and its Member States into intrinsic procedures through the system of EU law. However, the EU's general commitment to democracy and human rights is not turned into a fully operational system comparable to the constitutional state and the democratic deficit continues to be partly compensated for by the surplus of the functioning system of EU law. The complex process of making the EU both more efficient and democratic has implications for the very notion of European society as a society of functionally differentiated systems of economy, law and politics without ultimate moral and cultural foundations and integration.

The concept of a European polity and its legitimacy through political justice are semantic reflections on a much more general process of evolution of functionally differentiated European society. This society is profoundly supranational and uncontainable by some form of statehood/constitution framing which would make it possible to think of European society as another form of modern national society typical of modern European history.

One cannot imagine European society as a hierarchical unity of principles but only as a network of horizontally differentiated systems governed by their internal rationalities and communication codes. In this sense, the EU's political justice and/or its deficit are intrinsic parts of the political rationality of the EU's political system. Political justice is part of the Union's political problems and not their solution.

The current state of the EU, its policies, public images and self-reflections, are specific examples of a functionally differentiated supranational society politically searching and legally constituting its minimum sense of togetherness and common destiny and looking for the art of common living at an unprecedented scale beyond the 'sacred' bonds of the modern nation state. In the absence of EU democratic statehood and a constitutional polity, technocratic governance paradoxically remains a major force behind the evolution and self-reflection of a European polity and continues to facilitate its legitimacy. A crisis of EU technocratic expertise and governance, such as the Eurozone crisis, subsequently triggers a crisis of the European polity because the European commonality, is not determined by symbolism, but by systemic rationality.

The project of forming an 'ever closer Union' needs, therefore, to be reconceptualised as the 'ever more functionally differentiated Union'. Dealing with the EU's political justice deficit requires analysing and engaging with political processes and operations of the European political system instead of initiating yet another process of law making and legislating for value foundations and legitimation of EU politics. However, this political process hardly can be expected to resolve the Union's recent economic, administrative, legal and other social deficits and crises. It can only contribute to the political semantics and legitimacy of the paradoxical process of European political integration as functional societal differentiation.

14

Justice and the Right to Justification: Conceptual Reflections

JÜRGEN NEYER

I. WHY NOT DEMOCRACY?

MANY OF THE contributions to this book show a growing uneasiness with questioning the EU's democratic credentials.[1] They share the insight that the term 'democracy' should be reserved for describing those political systems which meet the most ambitious normative standards such as political equality, the rule of law and a monopoly of coercion. The EU does not. It is not built on the principle of individual political equality but balances it with state equality. Its rule of law is structurally imperfect due to the fact that its enforcement capabilities are weak and that the application and the interpretation of European law often go hand in hand. The EU's monopoly of coercion, finally, is a topic that is not even on the agenda of the most visionary EUtopianists. The deviations of the EU from minimal criteria of a democracy are all the more serious when considering that they are not some unintended, unfortunate deficits in its organisational structure; rather, they give expression to the well-reasoned conviction that the EU is and shall remain an entity with significant international elements.

Europe is built on its past. It has learned the lessons of international conflict and of the need to accommodate bigger and smaller Member States. Its founding members are proud of their democratic achievements and are fully willing to prolong them into the future. Europe is thus not about overcoming its democratic nation states, but about managing democratic interdependence. Any effort to understand the organisational logic of the EU and to assess its legitimacy that does not take these insights into account will fail. Thus, the EU is not undemocratic by mistake and it is not a democracy in the making. Rather, it is a deliberately different entity that intentionally deviates from some of the constituting principles of democracy. Trying to understand or justify the EU by means of the language of democracy is thus nothing but 'a description of oranges with a botanical language developed for apples'.[2]

---

[1] This article builds on chs 6 and 8 in J Neyer, *The Justification of Europe. A Political Theory of Supranational Integration* (Oxford, Oxford University Press, 2012). I am grateful to comments by Dimitry Kochenov and the participants of the Colloquium on 'Europe's Justice Deficit: Beyond Good Governance? on 22–23 September, 2012 at LSE in London.

[2] JHH Weiler, *The Constitution of Europe: 'Do the New Clothes Have an Emperor?' and Other Essays on European Integration* (Cambridge, Cambridge University Press, 1999) 268.

If the EU, however, cannot become a democracy without forgetting its history and changing its very organisational logic, then it is meaningless to measure it against a democratic standard. The banal result would provide no avenue for reform beyond rejecting the whole enterprise. Applying the democratic standard to the supranational layer of the EU is nothing less than a category mistake. The important question to ask today is not whether the EU is democratic and if its practices differ from the ideal of normative democratic theory. The question to be asked is whether and under which theoretical premises the EU can be justified convincingly. We need to ask whether there is theoretical scope for a realistic normative theory that accepts the EU's most basic structures as a given and that engages in reform measures without, however, becoming mired in a non-reflected affirmation of its practices. An approach is needed that can affirm the EU's structures while criticising its practices at the same time.

II. THE BETTER ALTERNATIVE

A. What is Justice?

Justice is a prime candidate for substituting democracy as the most central analytical term for critically assessing the EU's legitimacy. It is a normative concept with an uncontested validity and it is widely accepted that its applicability does include far less ambitious empirical preconditions than the concept of democracy. Concepts of justice are highly diverse and steeped in tradition. Ever since humanity began reflecting upon the preconditions of ideal society and the corresponding failings of real life, people have sought to define the meaning of justice. Unsurprisingly, notions of justice today carry a broad range of meanings, from a simple reliance on human intuition or 'common sense' to highly abstract and sophisticated theories. Some tend to equate justice with morality or even a general sense of appropriate behaviour. They claim that justice cannot be defined by means of abstract reflection, but that it necessitates an innate sensitivity to what is right and a naturally felt abhorrence of unjust deeds. Others identify it with the selection of those general principles that reasonable people would choose if freed from their materially based interests through the Rawlsian 'veil of ignorance'.[3] Whilst some schools of thought understand justice as a fair distribution of goods according to need, others emphasise the capability of putting resources to good use or the individual contribution to the production of goods.[4] Justice can refer either to a process of distributing goods or to a certain kind of distributional outcome. It can focus on intentions or on achievements. In short, justice is an intrinsically contested concept in terms of scope, conditions and content.

For developing a concept of justice that can be used properly as an analytical category, it is important to cut a path through these issues and to achieve definitional clarity. In this chapter, justice is defined as the outcome of a justificatory

---

[3] J Rawls, *A Theory of Justice* (Oxford, Oxford University Press, 1999).
[4] A Sen, *The Idea of Justice* (Harvard, MA, Harvard University Press, 2009) 12–15.

process in a justified structure of political decision making. This approach to justice takes its inspiration from the claim that human beings have an inalienable right to justification, that is, that we are under no obligation to accept limitations on our freedom except those that can be justified by good reasons. Following Rainer Forst, all individuals have a 'fundamental right to justification', which entails 'no political or social relations of control that cannot be adequately justified to each and every affected individual'.[5] Every use of political power must be justified to all affected individuals, who in turn are expected to accept a well-justified limitation on their liberty. In this understanding of justice, no existing distribution of material goods can claim to represent the just order of things—its mere existence is no evidence of its 'naturalness.'

Nor may any rule-making authority neglect the duty to justify itself by persuasive argument. The right to justification invokes not only a right to defend oneself against illegitimate infringements on individual freedom by political authorities; it also implies a right to demand action. The minimal liberal state enjoys no greater prima facie legitimacy than the activist welfare state. Both are subject to the necessity of justifying themselves, either in their inaction or in their action. The idea of a universal right to justification is rooted in an essentially egalitarian concept of liberty. It presumes the principle that all human beings are born free, protects all citizens equally from unfounded infringements on their liberty and provides a strong defence against arbitrary forms of political authority and control. It implies 'a qualified veto on all norms and practices that cannot be reciprocally and generally justified'.[6] Everyone thus has the right to be protected against an unjustified violation of his or her liberties and to take appropriate action if a violation does occur.

Justice as justification has an intrinsically procedural and discursive character inasmuch as it is the outcome of a well-ordered discourse among political institutions, courts and individuals. Individuals seize their right to justification in conflicts over resource distribution and political influence. Justice as justification is thus a political rather than a philosophical conception of justice that has clear institutional implications. Societies can claim to be just only when they guarantee that all individuals and groups affected by a law are endowed with a fair and full opportunity to participate in law making. The search for justice is a political process in which concerns are articulated, arguments are weighed, objections are considered and justifications are produced. These discourses of justification are necessarily never-ending. Their results are continually called into question because social preferences and attitudes change, technical progress and scientific research bring new knowledge and moral standards shift. Participants in discourses of justification must therefore always be willing to re-examine the validity of old arguments in light of new developments.

The right to justification is not a recipe for transferring conflict into harmony. Its most essential goals are to restrict unjustified infringements on individual liberty and to make the use of political power conditional upon the provision of good

---

[5] R Forst, *Das Recht auf Rechtfertigung. Elemente einer konstruktivistischen Theorie der Gerechtigkeit* (Frankfurt, Suhrkamp, 2007) 10.
[6] ibid, 370.

arguments. It does not overcome asymmetries in power resources but disciplines their use. As a political concept of justice, the right to justification does not attempt to melt different opinions and concerns into a unified idea of what is just and appropriate but rather accepts different opinions as an unavoidable and permanent condition of modernity. Its ambition is to establish a constructive political rivalry among different claims, positions and views and thus to create a procedure through which discord can be channelled into an exchange of mutually acceptable arguments. In practice, such exchanges will often fail to lead to perfect consensus regarding the legitimacy of the action that is being justified. More often than not, deep-seated differences of opinion persist, even after long political discussions have occurred and good arguments have been formulated. Such differences can arise for many reasons including different sources of information, different understandings of the basic underlying problems, antagonistic interests or divergent worldviews. Yet even under these conditions, agreements can be reached that are qualitatively different from the results of mere negotiation processes.

Eriksen has introduced the useful category of 'working agreement' for describing outcomes of this sort, referring to agreements based on 'different, but reasonable and mutually acceptable grounds'.[7] In contrast to agreements based on reciprocated conviction, by which all actors consider the same result to be right and appropriate for the same reasons, the reasons underlying a working agreement can be unreciprocated. One actor might accept a justification out of self-interest, another on moral grounds and yet another for pragmatic reasons. Working agreements are thus a pragmatic compromise around an outcome that we can accept as 'true' or 'right' enough given the constraints of limited time and resources and the incompatibility of worldviews. For this reason, working agreements obtain only temporary validity and may be renegotiated and overturned in the future if important new concerns are put on the table or if actors' interests change. Working agreements implicitly acknowledge the fluidity of preferences and knowledge as well as the imperfection in the conditions under which an agreement was reached. An agreement of this type cannot and does not claim to be able to withstand scientific tests of falsifiability, nor does it even represent 'truth' as popularly understood.

Despite their limited claim to an objective truth, working agreements do not appear out of thin air and cannot be changed on a whim. Individual understandings of shared situations are likely to be accepted only as part of a working agreement—or as legitimate challenges to pre-existing working agreements—if they plausibly reflect the set of values and norms shared by a group of communicating actors.[8] A working agreement thus never appears randomly nor does it merely reproduce any given asymmetry of power resources. It is an outcome of argument, grounded in the group's views and experiences and reflects 'a binding structure of common commitments, one that commands respect for the moment'.[9]

---

[7] EO Eriksen, *The Unfinished Democratization of Europe* (Oxford, Oxford University Press, 2009) 51.
[8] J Habermas, 'Wahrheitstheorien' in H Fahrenbach (ed), *Wirklichkeit und Reflexion. Walter Schulz zum 60. Geburtstag* (Pfullingen, Neske, 1973) 218.
[9] Erikson, *The Unfinished Democratization*, n 7 above, 51–52.

B. What is a Justification?

The concept of justice used here places a strong emphasis on the act of justification through communication. What conditions, then, must speech acts meet in order to be accepted as acts of justification? A justification, according to Rainer Forst, is a morally ambitious speech act that explains the rationale for one's actions or intentions in a manner consistent with the principles of reciprocity and universality. Reciprocity requires that no party involved successfully claims rights or privileges that it denies to others and that the formulation, rationalisation and evaluation of claims are not determined unilaterally. Equally important is the criterion of universality, which requires that the rationale for one's actions be based on arguments that can be accepted by all reasonable individuals affected, irrespective of their policy preferences.[10] Note that in Forst's understanding, justification is essentially a moral category. Justification indicates a type of speech act that demands recognition from others by virtue of its internal structure, that is, because of its universal and reciprocal validity. According to Forst, refusing to acknowledge a perfect justification is an immoral act.

For political scientists infected with some sense of political realism, such a morally loaded category is difficult to apply. Empirical insight tells us that politics and morality are not the closest cousins. After all, recognition of the moral superiority of a speech act seldom motivates powerful actors to abstain from pursuing their individual interests and to accept alternatives that are less beneficial for them. Philosophers of justice might accept as persuasive good moral arguments, provided they are reciprocal and universal, but moral argument rarely forces politicians to change their objectives.

To make the concept of justification compatible with normative realism, it must be divested of some of its moral ballast. For this purpose we can employ a tradition of political theory that can be traced back to John Stuart Mill. Following Mill, one of the most important advantages of free political speech lies in the fact that it helps us distinguish between strong and weak arguments. Controversial exchanges tend to sort out weak arguments and improve the stronger ones.[11] The prime mover of this process is not a shared morality or a process of justice-seeking but an adversarial culture of communication. Mill does not expect participants in justificatory discourses to engage in an altruistic search for objective truth or the common good. Claimants should be encouraged to clash with each other because this forces them to make their respective arguments as persuasive and water-tight as possible. Justification is therefore not necessarily characterised by cooperative consensus-building. In fact, it is more likely to emerge through the interaction of self-interested and rhetorically sophisticated actors. Justifications do not arise naturally through an introspective process of contemplation but rather from within a structure of

---

[10] R Forst, 'Zu einer kritischen Theorie transnationaler Gerechtigkeit' in R Schmücker and U Steinvorth (eds), *Gerechtigkeit und Politik. Philosophische Perspektiven. Deutsche Zeitschrift für Philosophie, Sonderheft 3* (Berlin, Akademie-Verlag, 2002); Forst, *Das Recht auf Rechtfertigung*, n 5 above, 224.
[11] JS Mill, *Considerations on Representative Government* (New York, NY, Prometheus Books, 1991) 42.

interaction. They arise only if agents are compelled to give reasons for adopting certain viewpoints or courses of action.[12] Attempts to disseminate justifications—and to provoke them from others—are most likely to emerge in the context of political contests, as one agent seeks public recognition and attempts to apply pressure on an opponent. Partisanship is thus an important condition of justificatory discourse. It provides incentives to produce intelligible justifications and to engage in efforts at making them as strong and convincing as possible. A proper interpretation of justification thus does not restrict the space for self-interested political action. In fact, it builds on it.

The kind of communication described with the concept of justification employed here is clearly distinct from a 'truth-seeking' mode of communication. Building on Jürgen Habermas's work on the characteristics of truth-seeking, Deitelhoff and Müller,[13] Risse,[14] and others argue that the exchange of claims to valid truth, rightness and the sincerity of competent speakers in communicative situations all belong to a truth-seeking mode of communication. Actors challenge claims to validity inherent in causal or normative statements and seek consensus about their understanding of a situation as well as justifications for the principles and norms guiding their action. This mode of truth-seeking is goal-oriented, just like strategic interaction, but the underlying logic involves seeking argumentative consensus rather than defending one's fixed preferences.[15] Truth-seeking is thus a mode of interaction that is not only based on the assumption that an 'objective reality' actually exists but also implies that the purpose of communicating is to identify what it means. Of course, this is appropriate and useful for the purposes of scientific inquiry. In this form of communication, arguments are brought for and against a particular statement and the only thing that counts is the quality of the argument. The famous 'unforced force of the better argument'[16] compels agreement. In politics, however, the truth-seeking mode of communicative exchange is rare, despite the fact that arguments are often packaged in a claim of universal validity. Indeed, we expect genuine truth-seeking only when topics are of low political salience, when existing interests are weakly structured or when the actors involved in negotiations have no clear political preferences.[17]

The concept of justification employed here assumes that actors are far more self-interested than the concept of truth-seeking allows. Justifications are speech acts that aim at legitimating one's own preferences by providing evidence for their compatibility with the shared goals of the community. Justifications do not require

---

[12] J White and L Ypi, 'On Partisan Political Justification' (2011) 105 *American Political Science Review* 381, 385–86.

[13] N Deitelhoff and H Müller, 'Theoretical Paradise—Empirically Lost? Arguing with Habermas' (2005) 31 *Review of International Studies* 167.

[14] T Risse, '"Let's Argue!": Communicative Action in World Politics' (2000) 54 *International Organization* 1.

[15] T Risse and M Kleine, 'Deliberation in International Negotiations' (2010) 17 *Journal of European Public Policy* 708.

[16] J Habermas, *Vorstudien und Ergänzungen zur Theorie des kommunikativen Handelns* (Frankfurt, Suhrkamp, 2005) 131.

[17] PM Haas, 'Introduction: Epistemic Communities and International Policy Coordination' (1992) 46 *International Organization* 1.

that the individual be predisposed to favour objective truth. They come into play when political action infringes on others' liberties and when this infringement must be explained as being legitimate. They are intended to legitimate an infringement on liberty and to motivate injured parties to accept the infringement willingly, often for the sake of a greater good either for themselves or for the community as a whole. Justifications are therefore highly ambitious speech acts. Their objective is to legitimate the negative effects of one's actions on others by demonstrating their beneficial contribution to a goal that is accepted as being of superior importance. Justifications are typical for political constellations characterised by scarce resources in which material or normative values must be allocated competitively. In such political constellations, the political actor who undertakes or proposes an allocation that is suboptimal from the point of view of other parties brings justifications forward, and they are demanded by those who are disadvantaged or fear disadvantage due to a proposed re-allocation.

C. Substantial and Procedural Preconditions of Justifications

For justifications to be accepted by affected parties as legitimate, a number of demanding substantial and procedural requirements must be met. The substantial requirements include, first of all, that the justification must call upon values and norms shared by both the policy initiator and the addressee of political action:

> Justification depends on certain premises being shared by the agent and the constituency: some degree of common ground, or 'frame resonance' ... is required if justifications are (1) to be recognised and understood as such, and (2) to be received as convincing.[18]

A good justification explains an infringement of freedom in such a way that the disadvantaged party voluntarily accepts it as reasonable and appropriate; at the very least, however, the affected party should not be able to reject it without refuting its own normative convictions (ie committing a 'performative contradiction'). A simple form of justification is, for example, saying that all motorists must drive on the same side of the road to prevent accidents. An affected party cannot challenge the prohibition on any reasonable ground without at the same time rejecting the goal of reducing the overall rate of automobile accidents. Assuming that all motorists prefer fewer accidents to more accidents, a rejection of the rule would amount to a performative contradiction and would be hard to defend publicly. Two other similarly common examples of justifications are the arguments that taxes are necessary for the sake of procuring socially desirable goods, and that punishments for crime are defended by pointing to a hoped-for deterrent effect with a consequent increase in everyone's security. More complex forms of justification are based in controversial moral or ethical problems and link a particular solution to a specific worldview, justifying the resulting new rules as a logical expression of the worldview. Policies on issues such as abortion, religion or other deeply ethical matters require these kinds of complex and philosophically sophisticated justifications to generate acceptance.

---

[18] White and Ypi, 'On Partisan', n 12 above, 389.

Finally, all justifications must present a plausible argument that the policy in question is moderate and entails no more than a necessary minimum of infringement on liberty. We typically reject as arbitrary, unjust and illegitimate any restrictions on our freedom that are not justified in these ways.

Justifications also have a procedural dimension. The degree to which a policy measure is accepted often directly depends on how the concerns of affected parties were addressed. Acceptance-generating justifications are those that sufficiently respond to critical questioning or to objections that the policy sets the wrong goals, makes use of the wrong means or goes too far in restricting liberties. Proper justifications do not end political discourse but open it. Justifications are an integral part of a continuing communicative process. For this reason, actors often modify and update their justifications. They incorporate new viewpoints, adjust their lines of argument and repeatedly re-engage the critical audience. Reason-giving alone is not enough for giving a speech act the credentials of a proper justification. Many argumentative efforts are intended only to legitimate unsuitable, exaggerated or wholly inappropriate infringements of liberty. Thus, the difference between superficial reason-giving and the more meritorious process of justification is that affected parties have a real chance to respond and to see any of their legitimate concerns incorporated into the proposed policy. The latent power of all participants to alter a proposed policy is of crucial importance for turning mere arguing into a proper process of producing justifications. It provides incentives to the policy-proposing party to take the burden of producing good reasons seriously and it gives the affected parties a motivation to engage in a critical discourse.

Justifications, furthermore, are strongly dependent on independent third parties assessing the validity of arguments and distinguishing between proper justifications and mere subjective explanations of individual motivations. In democracies, the public sphere and the media ideally adopt the role of an independent third party. By publicly exchanging policy suggestions and contesting them, the main participants in public policy discourses address themselves to the public at large more often than to each other. A governing party and its opposition both know very well that they are unlikely to convince each other; they do, however, nevertheless engage in political discourse and the exchange of arguments. A most important reason for this ongoing effort is their awareness that they must convince the public of the legitimacy of their policies if they want to stay politically competitive in the long run. Justifications thus have, as opposed to truth-seeking, a triadic rather than a dyadic structure. They are conducted between a policy entrepreneur and a contender, but they also involve an independent third party with the competence to assess the soundness of reasons and to sanction or even prevent policies that lack the buttressing of convincing arguments.

Jon Elster offers a persuasive analysis of the importance of a public sphere for a justificatory discourse.[19] The public sphere, he argues, places three constraints on communication. First, speakers who want to sway a public audience, whether it be a specific audience like a jury or an undefined segment of the general public, have

---

[19] J Elster, 'Deliberation and Constitution Making' in J Elster (ed), *Deliberative Democracy* (Cambridge, Cambridge University Press, 1998).

a strong incentive to put only those preferences on the table that are not too obviously connected to their personal interests. Public audiences find it harder to accept a proposal that is legitimated only by an appeal to the self-interest of its proponent than one that can claim convincingly to be in the common interest. A second constraint follows from the fact that speakers cannot arbitrarily renounce their public positions and arguments. To maintain a modicum of credibility, speakers must keep their arguments consistent and their actions consistent with their arguments. Changing arguments, once they are a matter of public record, often results in a loss of persuasive force if the changes are poorly justified. The freedom of argumentative strategising is thus strictly limited for any speaker who does not wish to be charged with opportunism. A third constraint is that speakers must avoid using a threatening tone in their arguments. The power of the argument must derive solely from qualities inherent to the argument.

The public aspects of the communicative process compel even self-interested and strategic actors to behave *as if* they truly were interested in the public good and *as if* their personal proposal were a step on the path to this goal. Elster speaks here of the 'civilizing force of hypocrisy'.[20] Actors who in truth seek to maximise their own interests or those of their clients, and who care not for the common good, nevertheless often use the mode of justification in political discourse. Only by so doing can they obtain for their position the additional and often necessary boost of public legitimacy. Even if actors are faking their community orientation, they still wind up creating exactly the argumentative mode of communication that is necessary for making good on the right to justification. Simply put, discourses of justification do not require that participants have altruistic attitudes or that they want to promote the common good. They only assume a common normative basis (the substantial precondition) and a receptive and critical public discourse (the procedural precondition) with the power to sanction unconvincing arguments and policies.

Unfortunately, the public context of speech acts is not always conducive to a justificatory discourse. The practice of democracy is often far removed from deliberative ideals. Governments, for example have privileged access to the media and journalists often pay more attention to official government statements and explanations than to the critical remarks of opponents. Furthermore, powerful lobbies can buy media time and create other communicative spaces whilst diffuse interest groups find it very difficult even to stimulate the public interest for a while. The public sphere is not a space free of power relations (a *herrschaftsfreier Raum*) but is subject to a great number of power asymmetries that create unequal access to audiences.

The practice of demanding and giving justifications is not limited to debate in the public sphere. The history of European and national courts in justifying European law is long and well known.[21] It suffices here to underline that the European Court of Justice (ECJ) has for many years applied human rights standards and the principles of subsidiarity and proportionality. All European legal regulations must comply with these standards and principles. It is also true that national constitutional

---

[20] ibid, 111.
[21] K Alter, *Establishing the Supremacy of European Law: The Making of an International Rule of Law in Europe* (Oxford, Oxford University Press, 2003).

courts have in the past served as the most important sites for disciplining political actors and for enforcing the right to justification. They have underlined that all national legal regulations giving effect to European law must be in accordance with national constitutional provisions. The requirement of compatibility with national constitutional law also applies to European treaty law. The German Constitutional Court has won a reputation for scrutinising whether new European treaties are in accordance with the provisions of the German Basic Law and in explicating the conditions that the European treaties must fulfil to withstand legal scrutiny. Lower national courts have also played a major role. The preliminary ruling procedure empowers national private parties to challenge national regulations if they contradict European regulations and if they cannot be justified. The combined effect of both the European and the national layer of judicial scrutiny is to make clear that no legal act, whether European or national, will withstand judicial objection if it cannot be justified for good reasons.

The importance of courts is closely related to the general function of law in fostering justificatory practices. Justificatory working agreements become more likely when discourses are encased in a legal structure. The often-noted phenomenon of the legal formalisation of international politics and the strong role of the law in the process of European integration are important because the law reduces complexity and provides a firm ground for political interaction. Both the formalisation of politics and the strength of law are fundamental for constructive political discourses. Law reduces complexity by either distinguishing between right and wrong or by offering an arbitration procedure that leads to an authoritative assessment. Law also identifies criteria according to which the merits of an argument are assessed and thus distinguishes between relevant and irrelevant facts.

The supportive function of law is one of the main reasons why we are able to get along with each other and why we react in a civilised and respectful manner when confronted with otherness.[22] In modern societies, citizens are all too often overburdened with the challenge of understanding different cultures and of coping with otherness and with seemingly incompatible understandings of right and wrong. Although speaking the same language, people with different cultural backgrounds often talk past one another and fail to understand each other properly. The law is the only medium through which meaningful discourses can be channelled in normatively heterogeneous social contexts and processes of accommodation have a fair chance to take place.

More than in any national state, political relations beyond the state and outside of normatively integrated communities must be characterised by a high degree of constitutional agreement and formal procedure for coping with contending claims to justice, if a right to justification is to be implemented that not only gives lip service to the idea but allows it to obtain practical relevance. The central role of the law in the European integration process is thus of greatest functional importance. It was not only the law's function as a 'mask and shield'[23] which made the Member

---

[22] J Habermas, *Faktizität und Geltung. Beiträge zur Diskurstheorie des Rechtes und des demokratischen Rechtsstaats* (Frankfurt, Suhrkamp, 1992) 57.
[23] AM Burley and W Mattli, 'Europe Before the Court: A Political Theory of Legal Integration' (1993) 47 *International Organization* 41.

States accept the great number of path-breaking decisions of the ECJ in the 1960s and 1970s. German politicians in particular were well aware that international politics without an uncontested rule of law would never be strong enough to tame the anarchy of European post-war society and, later, to manage democratic interdependence. For good reasons, law is the common language and the necessary common standard of rationality for assessing proffered arguments in European politics. It is the only basis on which resilient discursive agreement under conditions of plurality is likely.

D. Limits to the Right to Justification

Justifications are not only a means for safeguarding our legitimate freedoms but also burdens that we can legitimately impose on others.[24] By demanding that others account for their actions and produce reasons in their defence, we oblige others to do something they would otherwise not have done. Justifications therefore have a limiting effect on the freedom of others. It follows from this insight that justifications must be justified, that is, that there must be a limit to the right to justification. The effect that our actions have on the freedom of others determines when and under what circumstances we are obliged to justify them. We do not always and everywhere have a right to demand justifications from someone. We only have the right to demand justifications if and when someone else limits our freedom or attempts to do so. No one needs to justify to a neighbour, for example, what they do inside the four walls of their home. In like manner, France need not justify to Germany or any other Member State of the EU its education, pension or cultural policy as long as these policies have no significant constraining effect on other countries.

It is also clear that only affected persons, and the institutions entrusted with supporting them, have a right to request a justification. Our right to demand justifications is directly linked to limitations of our freedom and ends where those limitations stop. We therefore do not have a right to demand justification of someone only because he or she injured the rights of a third person. Only those injured have the right to demand justification and they also bear the burden of proving that such an infringement occurred. If Sweden, for example, imposes an illegitimate limitation on the import of beef from, say, the United Kingdom, then the United Kingdom, or an affected British legal person, must protest, make the fact of damage plausible and demand a justification. In European politics, the close nexus between suffering damage and having the right to demand a justification is only modified by the right and the duty of the Commission to articulate its concerns whenever it obtains knowledge of illegitimate limitations on liberty in the form of violations of EU law. The Commission acts here according to the will of the Member States as the 'guardian of the Treaties' for the purpose of averting retaliatory measures between the Member States. It thus acts in accordance with the competencies entrusted to it by the Member States.

---

[24] See Neyer, *The Justification of Europe*, n 1 above, 111.

E. Justified Structures of Justification

Supranational structures of justification reduce power asymmetries, create and maintain justification-based discourses and tame the anarchy of international politics.[25] Supranationality creates a space for justificatory discourses and transforms international bargaining into transnational deliberation. This function of the supranational layer of European governance is of crucial importance for assessing the legitimacy of the EU. However, the taming of power asymmetries and the establishment of structures of justification do not lead to greater justice. Structures of justification can further injustice if established on an unjustified normative framework. Legal discourses cement unjust conditions if they merely reproduce norms that reflect the asymmetry of power relationships rather than the outcome of an inclusive and deliberative procedure.

The legitimacy of the EU can therefore only be affirmed to the degree that its structures of justification are established in processes that are fundamentally different to these oft-criticised international practices. EU structures of justification must be the product of justificatory processes, of inclusive and discursive constitutional reflections. In his discussion of fully justified structures of justification, Forst specifies the conditions that the process of justification must meet:

> [P]olitical or social structures or laws have to be based on or [at least] to be compatible with moral norms applicable to them and must be justifiable within appropriate legal and political structures (and practices) of justification.[26]

> Structures of justification must be embedded in a fundamentally just basic political and legal structure ... in which the members have the means to deliberate and decide in common about the social institutions that apply to them and about the interpretation and concrete realization of their rights.[27]

It is important that 'everyone [can] participat[e] effectively in the practice of justification'[28] and that 'dissent should be heard, taken seriously and channelled in such a way that it could lead to a reform of the social structure'.[29] A just structure of justification must provide for the 'possibility of free and equal participation and adherence to proper procedures of deliberation and decision-making'.[30] These are obviously highly demanding conditions. Perfectly justified structures of justification must not contradict prevailing norms of morality, they must be embedded in reflexive procedures for adapting to changing normative preferences and be transparent and open to public participation. Even a perfectly deliberative discourse would be illegitimate if it rested on unfair procedural norms (eg, the exclusion of important stake holders, withholding of information) or unacceptable material norms (eg, the

---

[25] Cf P Allott, 'The European Community Is Not the True European Community' (1991) 100 *Yale Law Journal* 2485.
[26] R Forst, 'The Justification of Human Rights and the Basic Right to Justification: A Reflexive Approach' (2010) 120 *Ethics* 711, 731.
[27] ibid, 736.
[28] ibid, 731.
[29] ibid, 733.
[30] ibid, 734.

violation of basic human rights). In a nutshell, structures of justification are only as good as their normative and procedural context. Thus, only justified structures of justification deserve to be called legitimate.

III. THE EU'S JUSTICE DEFICIT

The EU has already gone a long way towards realising the preconditions of an effective exercise of the right to justification. Its supranational layer of governance is heavily shaped by legal regulations that demand good arguments and provide the incentives for state actors to transform bargaining into legal reasoning. Likewise, the EU's provision that all regulations are subject to legal scrutiny on the part of affected governmental and non-governmental parties has given additional weight to the need to provide sound reasons. The EU has become a political entity that puts more emphasis on the right to justification than any other international body.

It is also clear, however, that the EU's decision-making apparatus is far from perfect and that the EU still has a major justice deficit. Among its many deficiencies, two issues stand out in particular. The first crucial issue is the dominance of national governments in the constitutional process. National governments have the power to shape the discursive framing of the EU's legal discourse by dominating the constitutional process and agenda setting in the European Council. This is an important power resource that works to the detriment of the right to justification. National governments alone can define the distinction between valid and invalid arguments and thereby pre-structure legal discourse. Why is it that social concerns figure so little on the EU's legislative agenda? Why are the four freedoms so prominent in the rulings of the European Court of Justice? The answer is clear: governments have made the relevant decisions and given the constitutional process a clearly liberal orientation.[31] If the EU is to approximate the ideals of a justified discourse in a fully justified political setting then it must strive to overcome this inter-executive bias of the EU and make a huge step toward a profound parliamentarisation of its constitutional process and the European Council.

It is of equal importance that the EU tackles its accountability deficit. Citizens must have choices and be involved in a decision-making process that allows for alternatives to prevailing policies, but many of the most important policies in the EU, such as market-making and monetary policy, are fixed by constitutional provisions and do not allow for any major change. It is equally important that citizens can follow legislative decision making and that they can attribute responsibility for decisions. Transparency is also of crucial importance for the right to justification; however, both transparency and accountability are delicate topics in the European multilevel system of governance.[32] Among the most important characteristics of the EU's institutional structure are the large number of players involved and the complex processes that precede final decisions. In the EU, neither the Commission,

---

[31] FW Scharpf, 'Legitimacy in the Multi-Level European Polity' in P Dobner and M Loughlin (eds), *The Twilight of Constitutionalism?* (Oxford, Oxford University Press, 2010).

[32] M Bovens, D Curtin and P 't Hart (2010), *The Real World of EU Accountability. What Deficit?* (Oxford, Oxford University Press, 2010).

nor the Council, nor the European Parliament can unilaterally pursue their goals without obtaining the approval of the other institutions. It is not just the Member States that have to coordinate their preferences to obtain a qualified majority; the need for coordination also applies to European institutions. The Council cannot act without a proposal on the part of the Commission, and it also needs the Commission to manage implementation. The Commission must formulate its legislative proposals in a way that is likely to pass the scrutiny of both the Council and the Parliament, and it must also secure Member State approval for implementation measures. Furthermore, because the Commission has only limited capacities to enforce European law, it dedicates a great deal of effort to the safeguarding of broad political support for its proposals, consults as many interest groups as possible and prefers to postpone disputed issues rather than to vote on them.

These attributes of European governance mean that decision making and implementation are often informal, opaque and lack clearly traceable lines of responsibility.[33] Control on the part of national parliaments is difficult. The length of the delegation chain combined with the magnitude of administrative discretion makes accountability more of a fiction than a fact. European politics is often conducted among networks of policy experts and technical agencies that are deliberately unaccountable to domestic constituencies to remain credible to their professional communities. Participating non-governmental organisations rarely solve the problem of transparency. They often represent well-organised interests rather than the median voter. Such non-governmental organisations are glad if they succeed in making their concerns heard, even if behind closed doors.

Political outcomes of multilevel policy making are furthermore often the result of a simultaneous process of horizontal compromise between governments and vertical compromise between governments and domestic actors. Under these circumstances, it is often nearly impossible to separate clearly the genuine interests of governments from mere political posturing. Governments can easily argue that a certain negotiation outcome could not be averted, pointing to the extraordinary exigencies of multilevel cooperation. In complex multilevel governance structures like those of the European Union, acts of law can be ratified only if initiated by the European Commission and supported by both a super-majority of Member States and a majority of the members of the European Parliament. In this context, a situation can easily arise in which no one takes responsibility for the result of negotiations. Finger-pointing and buck-passing are inevitable, promoted by an institutional structure that preordains shirking. For similar reasons, in this context the activating dimension of the right to justification, which refers to the right to demand justification for non-action, is weak to non-existent. In front of whose door should political activists shout when no single actor with leadership authority can be identified because every policy outcome is the result of complex negotiations?

In light of these constraints, it seems clear that the right to justification can emerge in complex multilevel systems with multiple veto players only when preceded by a comprehensive right of media access. The level of publicity must be high

---

[33] Y Papadopoulos, 'Accountability and Multi-Level Governance: More Accountability, Less Democracy?' (2010) 33 *West European Politics* 1030, 1034–39.

enough to allow the public to follow and to criticise the legislative process at any time. The intrinsically public and open nature of the legislative process is a time-honoured principle that has been in place ever since authoritarian governance was overcome. It is ignored only in international politics and finds few supporters even in the European Union. The basic rule that legislative assemblies meet publicly so as to allow citizens to monitor the arguments of their representatives critically existed in the Agora of ancient Greece, was practised later in the Roman senate and since then has been a characteristic of all democratic parliaments. Only in international politics is this venerable rule disrespected such that the international legislative process occurs without the buzz of a watchful citizenry. The limited competences of the European Parliament and its ability to raise public awareness occasionally cannot compensate for this defect. The Parliament is still blocked from legislative agenda setting and it is most of the time well below the radar of the public. The need to rethink European parliamentarism and to reflect about new ways and means for reviving it is now urgent.[34] The exclusion of the public's critical eye from the political process is a tradition rooted in the practice of secret diplomacy, a practice that today is normatively and practically superannuated. It is in blatant contradiction to the right of justification, exactly because it makes it impossible to identify the key actors embedded in the interdependent, multilevel governance systems that are characteristic of modern international politics. The establishment of a comprehensive right of media access must therefore be recognised as a necessary precondition for justified structures of justification.

---

[34] *Cf* J Neyer, 'Europe's Sleeping Beauty. European Integration and the Prospects of Parliamentary Democracy' (2014) *Journal of Legislative Studies* (forthcoming).

15

Justice, Democracy and the Right to Justification: Reflections on Jürgen Neyer's Normative Theory of the European Union

RAINER FORST*

I. INTRODUCTION

IN HIS CHALLENGING paper in this volume, drawing on his impressive book *The Justification of Europe*,[1] Jürgen Neyer proposes a new way to conceptualise and assess the legitimacy of the political system of the European Union. Based on a particular interpretation of my idea of a 'right to justification' as the core of a theory of political and social justice,[2] Neyer argues for a shift away from the expectation—which in his eyes is unrealistic as well as undesirable—that the EU be transformed into a transnational democracy. Rather, he suggests using a notion of 'justice as justification' as a standard to both explain and evaluate the EU system from a perspective of what he calls 'normative realism'.

In what follows, I shall make some brief remarks about this intriguing proposal and raise a few questions about it, emphasising the differences between our views. If I were to put it in a nutshell, I would say that whereas I try to bridge the gap between thinking about democracy and thinking about justice, arguing that democracy, if properly understood, is *the* political practice of justice, Neyer is happily using

---

* I wrote this paper during my time as a Senior Emile Noël Fellow at the Jean Monnet Center of New York University's School of Law in autumn 2013. I am grateful for my stay in that excellent research environment made possible by the Center's Director Joseph Weiler, and I thank Gráinne de Búrca for important discussions of the matters discussed here, for kindly nudging me to write this reply and for her comments on an earlier draft. It is in part based on an earlier, short discussion piece of a (different) paper by Jürgen Neyer, published as R Forst, 'Justice and Democracy. Comments on Jürgen Neyer' in R Forst and R Schmalz-Bruns (eds), *Political Legitimacy and Democracy in Transnational Perspective* (RECON Report 13, ARENA Report 2/11, Oslo, University of Oslo, 2011) 37–42. Last, but not least, I want to thank Jürgen Neyer for the many discussions we had over these issues which I enjoyed so much despite, or maybe because of, our persisting disagreements among our many agreements.

[1] J Neyer, *The Justification of Europe. A Political Theory of Supranational Integration* (Oxford, Oxford University Press, 2012).

[2] This idea is fully developed in R Forst, *The Right to Justification. Elements of a Constructivist Theory of Justice* (New York, NY, Columbia University Press, 2012), and in R Forst, *Justification and Critique. Towards a Critical Theory of Politics* (Cambridge, Polity Press, 2013).

this gap to argue that the EU is in part already and in part on its way to being a just supranational polity but not a democracy. Not only does this go against the grain of my conceptual and normative argument (which is the first issue I will address below), it also leads to incoherencies in his approach (the second issue I will address) and finally it conceals from our view what a normatively realistic approach to the EU would require (something I will address only briefly). This last point I add with some trepidation, for, unlike Jürgen Neyer, I am not an EU scholar; nevertheless, I am drawn to a different view from his, given my assessment of the European Union.

II. WHY NOT DEMOCRACY?

Neyer's 'normative realism', which is developed at greater length in his book,[3] is an important approach that attempts a 'rational reconstruction' of the European normative order. But it harbours an ambiguity. Neyer could mean that democracy in the EU is an important goal to desire, yet argue that it is unrealistic and so we should settle for less, that is, some form of justificatory justice within a supranational system of good governance. That would still leave the possibility open that that system could legitimately be developed further into a democratic one—and maybe should be. Or, he could say, which is the stronger thesis, that democracy on the EU level is indeed undesirable and the wrong goal; instead, it should be supplanted by a different 'justice' discourse. I take Neyer to argue for the stronger thesis, when he says that 'the EU is not undemocratic by mistake',[4] but then what are his reasons?

Neyer argues that the EU falls short of three normative standards of democracy: political equality, the rule of law and a monopoly of coercion. But why should we not, following Armin von Bogdandy and Jürgen Habermas,[5] think about the possibilities of developing the EU into a transnational democracy that combines the political equality of all citizens of the Union (represented in a reformed parliament) with the political equality of the states of which they are citizens (represented in another body, parallel to the Council), asking citizens to perform a twofold role as civic norm-makers who balance the interests of the Union and that of states? Furthermore, is the binding character of European law not an expression of the European system being one of the rule of law? Finally, could the enforcement of laws and norms not be realised by a federal system of states, assuming the relevant law-making competences were to be clearly ordered? Neyer's normative realism does not imply, I think, that these questions are conceptually meaningless, so I am not sure why he argues that it is a 'category mistake'[6] to apply democratic standards to the EU. Furthermore, as I will show below, he applies democratic standards to the EU even so.

Essentially, Neyer argues that the EU need not become democratic to function as a proper normative order as long as it is based on the right conception of justice

---

[3] See Neyer, *The Justification of Europe*, n 1 above, ch 2.
[4] J Neyer, 'Justice and the Right to Justification: Conceptual Reflections' in this volume, 211.
[5] A von Bogdandy, 'Grundprinzipien' in A von Bogdandy and J Bast (eds), *Europäisches Verfassunlgsrecht* (Heidelberg, Springer, 2010) 73–120; J Habermas, *The Crisis of the European Union. A Response* (Cambridge, Polity Press, 2013).
[6] Neyer, 'Justice and the Right to Justification' in this volume, 212.

as justification. That conception is adequate for the tasks the EU has and should have. But the success of this argument depends on two things: first, whether such a conception of justice really is an 'alternative' to a democratic framework; second, what kind of legitimation structure a realistic perspective on the EU requires, given its current functions, forms of power and its future tasks. I turn to the first issue in the next section.

III. ALTERNATIVES

Unlike Neyer, I do not think that justice is an 'intrinsically contested concept',[7] for then we would only have partial and to some extent arbitrary definitions of it. I believe that the core concept of political and social justice refers to social relations and institutions that should be free from unjustifiable, arbitrary rule, that is, domination. Thus, justice demands the institutionalisation of what I call a 'basic structure of justification' to make sure that no person is subjected to a normative order that cannot be justified to him or her as a free and equal person, or, in my words, as a justificatory equal.[8] The basis for this notion of political and social justice is what I term the moral *right to justification*, which is another way to express what it means to respect others as 'ends in themselves'.[9] In contexts of morally relevant action, this categorical imperative means that one must act on the basis of norms that can be reciprocally and generally justified to others, and in contexts of political and social justice this means that every normative order which is generally and reciprocally binding must 'earn' such validity through discourses in which those subjected to norms are justificatory equals and can be co-authors of these norms. That is why I consider *democracy* the basic practice of *justice*, since the right to justification as the expression of our autonomy is not just the right to be *provided* with justifications but also the right to be an *agent* of justification: discursively producing, contesting, rejecting and constructing justifications with others. What I call 'fundamental justice' secures the standing of persons within such normative orders by safeguarding basic rights and discursive possibilities, procedurally and substantively. Justification can only take place within a discursive *practice*, yet the criteria of reciprocity and generality at the same time reflexively transcend such practices and allow for their critique. The 'rule-making authority' must not only 'justify itself by persuasive argument', as Neyer says; rather, the rule-making authority must be constituted by those subjected to its norms, and the norms must express the justified judgement of these subjects, arrived at under fair conditions of a basic structure of justification. This is, to make a (very) long story short, my view on justice and justification.

From this, a number of differences between my view and Neyer's follow. He gives the right to justification a libertarian reading by saying that it presumes that 'human beings are born free' and that only restrictions of their freedom or 'liberties' need to be justified—as if there were a 'natural' or 'original' justification for such liberties.

---

[7] ibid, 212.
[8] See especially Forst, *Justification and Critique*, n 2 above, ch 1 ('Two Pictures of Justice').
[9] For the foundational story with respect to Kant, see Forst, *The Right to Justification*, n 2 above, chs 1 and 2.

But this is not how I see things. The right to justification follows from a categorical imperative to respect others as free and equal, but it does not presume that personal liberty is already defined or originally justified as a natural claim. Rather, the moral right to justification equally demands justifications for certain liberties *or* their limits, as it also fundamentally grounds claims to forms of political or social equality or difference. It is thus *prior* to any justification of liberties, not based on them. It is a right to be an author of norms and further rights claims; thus it grounds other rights of a moral or political–legal nature, depending on context.[10] There is no notion of a Fichtean *Urrecht* to natural liberty or non-interference at work here, as Somek, in his critique of Neyer, also appears to think there is (and mistakenly refers to my work for this proposition).[11] The right to justification is a right that discursively grounds further rights to equality, as much as freedom, that is, rights demanded by justice in the first place, as this is the virtue to determine the proper spheres of liberties or claims to equality.

Yet even if the right to justification *were* grounded in some notion of natural freedom, I think it would be the basis for a 'philosophical' conception of justice, and unlike Neyer,[12] I don't think 'philosophical' and 'political' are real alternatives here, as a discourse theory focusing on the relations of justification within a society also is in need of a philosophical grounding. I agree, however, with the following formulation: 'Societies can claim to be just only when they guarantee that all individuals and groups affected by law are endowed with a fair chance and full abilities to participate in law making'.[13] But I wonder why this would not call for a democratic structure of European law making. I will come back to that point.

When it comes to the nature of the justifications to be required in the political sphere, Neyer argues for a watered-down conception of justification, although I agree that we should distinguish contexts of moral and political justification. But as far as I see it, we can only use the dignified term 'justice' for the results of discursive constructions if the social and political conditions of discourse are themselves fundamentally just—which is the point of the idea of fundamental justice. So I am a bit sceptical with respect to Neyer's claim that justice as justification does not 'overcome asymmetries in power resources but disciplines their use'.[14] Here, everything depends on what I call the 'relations of justification' within a society and the

---

[10] See specifically my view on human rights in Forst, *Justification and Critique*, n 2 above, ch 2 ('The Justification of Human Rights and the Basic Right to Justification: A Reflexive Approach', originally in (2010) 120 *Ethics* 711).

[11] A Somek, 'The Preoccupation with Rights and the Embrace of Inclusion: A Critique' in this volume, 302f. Somek speaks about a 'hidden' premise of my conception of the right to justification as an original right 'not to be affected' by others. But that is a premise neither visible nor hidden in my view, as I only argue for a right not to be affected without good reasons given the relevant context of affecting others, which determines the criteria of justification. That is what I say on the pages Somek refers to (Forst, *The Right to Justification*, n 2 above, 213): 'The basic underlying notion ... is of the person with the right to and the capacity for the reciprocal and general justification of morally relevant actions and norms. Whenever human beings act, they are obliged to recognize every morally affected person as someone to whom they owe reasons justifying their actions'. The basic idea here is that of moral respect, not that of already established individual liberties.

[12] Neyer, 'Justice and the Right to Justification' in this volume, 213.
[13] ibid, 213.
[14] ibid, 214.

distribution of the 'discursive power' of persons and groups to construct, contest and co-determine the institutions and laws to which they are subjected. I fear that the reduction of fundamental justice to the rules of a game of 'constructive political rivalry'[15] may not be sufficient to establish the fundamental justice of discursive constructions. We need to distinguish here between the political discourses made possible by fundamental justice and those that are about the essentials of fundamental justice themselves.[16]

Only if we heed the distinction between fundamental and 'normal' political discourse, which Neyer does not sufficiently take into account, can we distinguish different forms of justification. There are purely moral contexts of justification[17] which require moral agents to act on the basis of norms that are reciprocally and generally non-rejectable, as moral norms are not just contingent agreements based on different reasons. When it comes to matters of fundamental justice in contexts of justice (ie contexts of an institutionalised form of social life, or a normative order), justification is not 'pure' in that moral sense, as Neyer says,[18] but it requires shareable (not shared) reasons, as these reasons have to be reciprocally and generally non-rejectable given that the issues here concern the basic standing of persons as legal persons and citizens. Thus, more than a 'working agreement'[19] is required. I do not see how a theory of justice would deserve its name if 'political realism' were to determine that such fundamental norms cannot be more than a mere modus vivendi between the strongest social groups, as Neyer seems to imply.

When it comes to the exchange of arguments in political discourse, then, a moral reason, properly justified, has to trump other considerations. This is what justice demands, whether any form of 'realism' accepts that or not. The 'moral ballast' that the 'normative realist' might want to throw off is, from the perspective of a discourse theory of justice like mine, the moral claim of a minority in danger of being marginalised or overpowered. That is why such persons (or groups) have, if they have a non-rejectable claim to be taken into account, a 'veto right' when it comes to issues of fundamental justice. It would be better if we had a 'realist' theory to inquire into the social and institutional conditions for such a right to be realised.

That does not mean, *pace* Neyer, that I take political justification to be necessarily 'consensus-building'.[20] Political claims will of course be contested. But the point of a theory of justice must be to determine the standards of justification for non-rejectable arguments in a discourse between justificatory equals. Such standards do not answer all questions, but they rule out claims based on privilege and superior power insufficiently justified. Why have a theory of justice that declares the victorious self-interest of winners in an asymmetrical discourse as 'just'?

Does this mean that discourse, as I understand it, is 'truth-seeking' rather than a discourse of persons seeking to win in a political game? No, but it means that when

---

[15] ibid, 214.
[16] Forst, *The Right to Justification*, n 2 above, chs 7 and 8.
[17] For the distinction between different contexts of justification see R Forst, *Contexts of Justice: Political Philosophy beyond Liberalism and Communitarianism* (Berkeley, CA, University of California Press, 2002) ch 5.
[18] Neyer, 'Justice and the Right to Justification' in this volume, 215.
[19] ibid, 214.
[20] ibid, 214.

it comes to the standards of fundamental justice, there is a normative bedrock that must not be determined or violated arbitrarily. To overcome such arbitrariness is the task of justice. That is the normative 'truth' it insists on. So the difference that Neyer emphasises between seeking truth and being self-interested is not a challenge for a discourse theory of justice: the theory simply seeks to identify the normative criteria, procedural and substantive, to identify good justifications, whether they are motivated by self-interest or altruism. For these criteria, the motivations are not important. Motivations are, however, important for the acceptance of basic justice by those subjected, as justice has to be accepted *as justice*, not as a mere compromise.

When Neyer explains his own view of justification, he stresses that justification must proceed from 'values and norms shared by both the policy initiator and the addressee of political action'.[21] That comes close to the requirement of fundamental justice, yet leaves room for such commonality to be arbitrary and to the disadvantage of others if not fixed by the criteria of reciprocity and generality. My view thus avoids the problem that the 'acceptance' on the side of the disadvantaged party may not be truly voluntary and would not deserve to be called 'reasonable'.[22] Need I add here that the theory of justice I defend is a *critical theory*?

Neyer also stresses the need for an additional perspective on reasonable justification striving for objectivity but gives a sociological answer to a philosophical question: In his eyes, the public sphere and the media serve the purpose of an 'independent third party'. I agree that they do play an important role, but I wonder why Neyer thinks that the public is necessary as a third party between 'a policy entrepreneur and a contender', as both entrepreneur, contender and the public form one collective subjected to a normative order, so that there are no strong distinctions between actors and spectators here. Nevertheless, according my view, it is correct to stress the criterion of generality in addition to that of reciprocity.

When it comes to the rationalising force of the law which Neyer emphasises,[23] I think it is necessary to distinguish between processes of law making as legislative processes and those of adjudication and application in legal discourse. Law can have a rationalising as well as an exclusive character (I would add) in both dimensions, but the full force of the right to justification as a right to participate in norm-generating political discourses cannot be sublated in legal practice. The *basic* question of justice is about how norms come about and who is being ruled by them—and thus the question is about the power of setting up these norms in the first place and of changing them, not primarily about the power of using and interpreting them (important as it is). Justice is a constructive and creative human force, not mainly an interpretive one. And where there are norms that bind all subjected equally, justificatory procedures have to be in place in which those subjected to norms can be the authors of these norms.

---

[21] ibid, 217.
[22] ibid, 217.
[23] ibid, 220.

IV. EUROPEAN DEMOCRACY

I wholeheartedly agree with Neyer that supranational structures of justification have to 'reduce power asymmetries' and 'create and maintain justification-based discourses'[24]—and that therefore the legitimacy of the EU structures requires that they are 'the product of justificatory processes, of inclusive and discursive constitutional reflections'.[25] And here he cites my notion of a discursive basic structure of justification ensuring the possibility of free and equal participation. Such participation is the implication of the individual right to justification.

It is a complex question whether the EU realises 'the preconditions of an effective exercise of the right to justification'.[26] Neyer's judgement here (as in his book) is nuanced: the supranational governance structures the EU has established do a good job in transforming 'bargaining into legal reasoning' which is subject to legal scrutiny. I leave aside here any discussion of this or of the many forms in which legal structures and norms carry forward informal power relations, in particular those of an economic kind, and possibly veil them.

What I would like to point out in a brief reflection on the discussion of the 'major justice deficit' of the EU that Neyer presents is that this discussion rests on and reproduces the immanent relation between justice and democracy which a discourse theory of justice establishes and that he wished to avoid in his argument. Neyer names two justice deficits, and they turn out to be deficits of democracy, too. The first one is the dominance of governments in the political process of the EU, and the remedy Neyer suggests is to 'make a huge step towards a profound parliamentarisation'. He does not spell out at this point what exactly this means,[27] but one would probably be on the safe side if one called that a step towards further democratisation.

The second deficit is that of a lack of accountability and transparency of decision making. These processes are criticised as often 'informal, opaque and without clearly traceable lines of responsibility'.[28] This makes, as Neyer argues, '*democratic* accountability more fiction than fact' (emphasis added),[29] which makes it clear that a notion of political justice based on the right to justification calls for democratic forms of responsible decision making. This is precisely the implication Neyer wanted to circumvent. Thus, when stressing the need for public control and media access, Neyer repeatedly affirms the 'intrinsically public and open nature of the democratic legislative process'[30] as a basic principle. Again, I see this as an argument for the application of democratic norms to the EU structure—thus opening up exactly the questions of further democratisation that I alluded to (all too briefly) at the outset. I am not sure whether it is *contre coeur* that Neyer in the end affirms what he denied

---

[24] ibid, 222.
[25] ibid, 222.
[26] ibid, 223.
[27] But see Neyer, *The Justification of Europe*, n 1 above, chs 7–9.
[28] Neyer, 'Justice and the Right to Justification' in this volume, 224.
[29] ibid, 224.
[30] ibid, 225.

in the beginning; in my view, it is the right consequence to flow from an approach based on the right to justification which allows for no *Ersatz* or placebo discourse. Those subjected to a normative order have the right to have a practice of justification established where they can be co-authors of this normative order, and insofar as the EU is such an order, this calls for its democratisation. I do not see a reason why Jürgen Neyer should object, as one cannot claim that only states or national political communities are subjected to the European normative order and not its citizens (and a number of non-citizens) directly.

So we should not divide the European world into domestic democracy and supranational legal justice or intergovernmental forms of governance; rather, we should see justice as tracking down domination where it exists, and what that means depends on 'what is', that is, which forms of domination we find nationally, and transnationally or supranationally beyond states, and internationally between states.[31] There is no conceptual either–or here, since justice is a right-making Goddess wherever she is needed. She always requires that those subjected to norms can become authors of the norms to which they are subject, and that means that participatory practices of justification have to be established. There can be *transnational demoi of subjection* apart from conventionally formed *demoi*, and the EU citizenry clearly is one. This is true more than ever in times of economic crises and their consequences such as imposed financial discipline. Furthermore, this European *demos* is connected with many others beyond its borders, including those it dominates itself. Hence, we should not cling to a reified notion of democracy which prevents people from understanding the powers-that-be. Normative realism, as I would like to redefine the term, starts from a clear understanding of justice and justification as requiring democratic practices, and it calls for these practices where the norms that bind persons or states originate. Today, and in the foreseeable future, decisions taken at the EU level will determine the fate of all European citizens, and if one is concerned about the justice of those decisions, democracy is an essential imperative. Thus, a just political order is a democratic normative order, and we should inquire about ways to think about a just European order along these lines—with and against Jürgen Neyer.

---

[31] On this, see R Forst, 'Transnational Justice and Democracy. Overcoming Three Dogmas of Political Theory' in E Erman and S Näsström (eds), *Political Equality in Transnational Democracy* (New York, NY, Palgrave Macmillan, 2013).

16
Disproportionate Individualism

STAVROS TSAKYRAKIS

I. A TALE OF TWO SOCIETIES

SINCE AT LEAST the publication of Alexis de Tocqueville's famous work *Democracy in America*, common wisdom has it that the United States is an individualistic society par excellence.[1] The judiciary has had more than a fair share in shaping and entrenching this belief, especially during the *Lochner* era (1905–37), when it all but embraced laissez-faire economics,[2] thus giving effect to a strongly individualistic moral philosophy, which praised economic liberty and the right to property. The main tenets of this philosophy can be described as follows: liberty's foundation lies with natural law and consists mainly in the freedom of the individual to acquire property. Accordingly, property rights are elevated to the quintessence of individual freedom. The jurisprudence of American courts has mirrored the priority of property rights. While freedom in other areas, such as freedom of speech, association, and personal life, was systematically curtailed in the *Lochner* era without much resistance from the courts, limitations on property rights were automatically deemed problematic.

We can trace the origin of this philosophy to John Locke. Locke insists that 'the reason that men enter into society is the preservation of their property'.[3] It is true that he also uses the term property in a broad sense, meant to include the life and liberty of individuals. Thus, within 'the general Name, Property', he includes the 'Lives, Liberties and Estates' of persons.[4] Nevertheless, it was around the narrow sense of possession that individualism developed. Whilst Locke's individualism was far from extreme insofar as it acknowledged that the 'perfect freedom' of

---

[1] Tocqueville's description of individuals' mentality in a democracy is that '[t]hey owe nothing to any man; they expect nothing from any man; they acquire the habit of always considering themselves as standing alone, and they are apt to imagine that their whole destiny is in their hands'. Such a democracy 'throws [man] back forever upon himself alone and threatens in the end to confine him entirely within the solitude of his own heart'. A de Tocqueville, *Democracy in America*, vol 2 (New York, NY, Alfred A Knopf, 1945) 99.

[2] Recall Oliver Wendell Holmes's famous phrase: 'The 14th Amendment does not enact Mr Herbert Spencer's Social Statics ... [A] constitution is not intended to embody a particular economic theory, whether of paternalism and the organic relation of the citizens to the State or laissez faire'. *Lochner v New York* 198 US 45 (17 April 1905), 75.

[3] J Locke, *Two Treatises of Government*, ed P Laslett (Cambridge, Cambridge University Press, 1980) para 222. *Cf* paras 85, 94, 124, 134 and 138.

[4] ibid, para 123.

individuals in the state of nature was within the limits of natural law,[5] and although he explicitly allows for the regulation of property,[6] there is no doubt that for him political society has a limited aim; namely, guaranteeing the freedom individuals enjoy in the state of nature.

Contrary to the United States, there has not flourished in Europe an individualistic tradition championing property as the pinnacle of human rights.[7] Notwithstanding the fact that the French Declaration of the Rights of Man deems property to be an 'inviolable and sacred right',[8] the political mainstream never seriously questioned society's right to regulate and restrict private property. Most modern European constitutions enshrine welfare rights (at least for citizens). Restrictions of property have typically been understood to have a distributive task.

However, individualism comes in many different forms. In this chapter I want to argue that recent years have seen the rise in Europe of a type of individualism which, following a conception of freedom that owes more to Thomas Hobbes, ends up being more extreme than Locke's. Needless to say, it goes well beyond the scope of this chapter to map its presence in all fields of social life. So what I propose to do is to indicate its pervasiveness in human rights adjudication. Just like the American courts of the *Lochner* era, human rights courts in contemporary Europe can be seen as the bellwether of an intellectual shift that is under way. Indeed, recent European adjudicative practice carves out a notion of individualism that is at odds with a sound theory of justice.

The touchstone of this peculiarly European brand of adjudicative individualism is the principle of proportionality. Proportionality is not narrowly European. It has become the word of the day in human rights law. It is the prevailing method of human rights adjudication all over the world and has come to shape a whole theory of human rights.[9] That does not make it correct. In fact, proportionality offends our most elementary convictions about human rights. Its failure derives from its individualistic approach to freedom. I start by elaborating this understanding of freedom, which I shall call total freedom, and bringing out its individualistic bias. I argue that total freedom has a striking similarity with the one that Hobbes attributes to human beings in the state of nature. From the state of nature, proportionality lets Hobbes into the city, so to speak. Furthermore, I suggest that due to its individualism, total freedom assumes and reinforces a skewed perception of society and social justice.

---

[5] ibid, para 87.
[6] ibid, para 3: '[P]olitical power then I take to be a right of making laws with penalties of death, and consequently all less penalties, for the regulating and preserving of property'.
[7] The most illustrative example of this is the European Convention of Human Rights (ECHR) itself, which reflects the common constitutional traditions of the signatory (European) states on fundamental rights. Art 1 of Protocol No 1 of the ECHR enounces the principle of peaceful enjoyment of property (para 1), but at the same time it subsumes its use under state control so that it be 'in accordance with the general interest' (para 2). The case-law of the European Court of Human Rights (ECtHR) has always reaffirmed this view (see, inter alia, *Sporrong and Lönnroth v Sweden* App Nos 7151/75 and 7152/75 Series A No 52 (ECtHR (PL), 23 September 1982), para 61).
[8] Declaration of the Rights of Man and of the Citizen, Art 17.
[9] 'By the end of the 1990s, virtually every system of effective constitutional justice in the world, with the partial exception of the United States, had embraced the main tenets of P[roportionality] A[nalysis]'. A Stone and S-J Mathews, 'Proportionality Balancing and Global Constitutionalism' (2008) 47 *Columbia Journal of Transnational Law* 73, 74.

To bring the defects of total freedom into sharper relief, I contrast it to a different conception that draws primarily on the philosophy of Ronald Dworkin. I argue that the latter has significant advantages and should be preferred.

This chapter does not engage in a close examination of how proportionality is used in the case-law.[10] It takes as given that proportionality is the guiding principle of European human rights adjudication. I hope this assumption is not too hard to swallow. To be convinced of its soundness, one needs only take a cursory look at the jurisprudence of the most famous European courts adjudicating human rights such as the European Court of Human Rights, the German Constitutional Court and the UK Supreme Court.[11] Equally, this chapter does not take up the broader project of explaining why individualism has taken hold in Europe, what political and intellectual developments have made it possible. Instead it suggests that individualism has found in proportionality the perfect partner in crime.

II. A PRIMA FACIE RIGHT TO EVERYTHING?

Proportionality is a new label for an old idea. The old idea is balancing. In the 1950s and 1960s, in the context of First Amendment law American judges routinely employed balancing. Absolutists and balancers debated its pros and cons. Absolutists claimed that the First Amendment contained a set of narrowly defined categorical rules. By contrast, for balancing aficionados like Justice Frankfurter, its necessity derived from the fact that human rights are not absolute, so the only way to determine their limits is to balance the value of the right against the value of competing individual and public interests. Frankfurter's approach was criticised for its lack of clarity on a series of issues: what is to be weighed (interests, principles, rights, considerations); how it is weighed (with what metric); who should do the balancing (judges or legislators). Moreover, balancing seemed to leave obscure a more basic issue, which concerns the meaning and import of the relevant constitutional provisions. Even if rights in general are subject to balancing, this does not necessarily mean that our constitutional rights must be balanced. Maybe those who enacted those provisions had already made a balancing judgement about, say, the priority of freedom of speech over other public goals. On the basis of that judgement, they may have intended to entrench certain determinate legal standards that conferred something concrete to the right holder. If that was the judgement that the provisions stood for, should not judges be pre-empted from second-guessing it?

To most of these questions proponents of proportionality rehash old answers. They stress the indeterminacy of human rights norms, which, as Robert Alexy puts it, 'command ... that something must be realised to the highest degree that is actually and legally possible',[12] and come to the conclusion that balancing is inherent in the concept of human rights. This is no different from the claim that, since human

---

[10] For an overview of the use of proportionality in the case law of the ECtHR, see S Tsakyrakis, 'Proportionality: An Assault on Human Rights?' (2009) 7 *International Journal of Constitutional Law* 468.
[11] See, in general, T Hickman, 'Proportionality: Comparative Law Lessons' (2007) 12 *Judicial Review* 31, 32–34.
[12] R Alexy, 'Rights, Legal Reasoning and Rational Discourse' (1992) 5 *Ratio Juris* 143, 145.

rights are not absolute, their content can only be determined through balancing. To the question what shall be placed on the scales, the answer is also much the same: every conceivable individual or public interest. Finally, since proportionality started life as a method of adjudication, it is taken for granted that judges should do the balancing.

The only fresh proposal concerns the specific method of balancing. At this point the concept of proportionality is introduced. Proportionality is a mathematical concept that refers to the relation of two variables to a stable constant. Its use in the context of rights adjudication expresses the idea that some kind of equilibrium is disturbed whenever someone's freedom is restricted in a way that is unsuitable, unnecessary or excessive compared to the benefit that the restriction achieves.

By using the concepts of balance, scale and weight (all concepts coming from the natural sciences) proportionality enjoins us to investigate whether something is adequate, intensive or far-reaching instead of whether it is right or wrong. What are we to make of this shift in focus? Some theorists seem to think that conflicts of values can be reduced to questions of intensity or degree and, more importantly, that intensity and degree can be measured by a common metric (something like a natural force) and that this process will reveal the solution of the conflict. Thus, they argue, proportionality is neutral, objective and rational, and allows us to bypass moral reasoning.[13]

More plausibly, others use the natural science language of balance, scale and weight metaphorically. The value of proportionality, they contend, is that it offers a structure for legal and moral argumentation.[14] But even on the latter view, proportionality is a mistake. That is because its structure is problematic and distorts our reasoning about rights. It is problematic inasmuch as it indiscriminately takes into account any human interest, even those that are worthless or ill-founded. It distorts moral reasoning inasmuch as it requires that we examine to what extent pursuing a competing interest would result in a serious, intermediate or light interference with the right in question. But by placing all interests on the scales and by assigning each of those interests some weight we have already skewed the outcome of the balancing process. Take Dworkin's example of an interest in killing those who criticise me. Are we prepared to assign weight to outrageous interests such as this one in the first place? Once we start going down this road, it makes little difference to assign such interests only a slight weight. The damage will already have been done. So for instance, a small fine for expressing a controversial opinion may start to appear like a minor interference with the right to free speech. Conversely, it may seem to us relevant that the indignation of those who disagree with that opinion is grave. By framing the balance in terms of interests and relative weights we are distracted from proper moral reasoning.[15]

What has gone wrong? At the heart of proportionality's woes is its philosophical starting point, which we can label *Hobbes in the city*. Proponents of proportionality

---

[13] See D Beatty, *The Ultimate Rule of Law* (Oxford, Oxford University Press, 2004).
[14] See M Kumm, 'The Idea of Socratic Contestation and the Right to Justification: The Point of Rights-Based Proportionality Review' (2010) 4 *Law & Ethics of Human Rights* 141.
[15] See Tsakyrakis, 'Proportionality', n 10 above.

introduce within organised society an idea that Hobbes had reserved for the state of nature, namely that 'every man has a right to everything, even to one another's body'.[16] I shall refer to the contemporary variant of this right as the right to total freedom. However, there are two important differences between Hobbes in the state of nature and in the city. First, contemporary proponents of proportionality take the right to total freedom to be only prima facie. Secondly, unlike Hobbes, who did not believe that freedom in the state of nature was of any particular value and was perfectly willing to sacrifice it for the sake of security within a political order, proponents of proportionality maintain that total freedom is of such value that it ought to be optimised along with the freedom of other individuals and other values. It follows from this that any interference with what someone wishes to do is a potential abridgment of her rights or at least the starting point of a human rights inquiry. Activities such as 'falconry',[17] or feeding pigeons on public squares,[18] or spitting on the public sidewalk[19] raise human rights issues just as torture or censorship. From the perspective of this conception, then, there are no specific human rights; rather, individuals have a general right to this kind of total freedom, from which we can derive its more specific emanations after balancing it against competing interests and values to determine in each case whether it will prevail or not. In this sense, it is not far off the mark to say that a prima facie right to everything is equivalent to a prima facie right to nothing in particular. The flipside is that this conception erodes the distinctiveness of human rights as opposed to other human interests.

Is it possible to arrive at a concept of society (let alone a fair society) with Hobbes as our starting point? That is, starting with the notion that society is an aggregate of individuals who by nature have 'a right to everything, even to one another's body' and then trying to figure out how to come together to form a commonwealth. Hobbes' own solution was drastic: a commonwealth is possible only if individuals forfeit not just the right to everything but also all their rights. This was considered his weak point because the absolutism he proposed was not only unattractive, but also incompatible with the principle of individualism he assumed as his starting point. What is the use of having a right if it only serves to licence its forfeiture?

Hobbes' absolutism never became popular. Still, his scheme seems to persist in public discourse, albeit with one basic adjustment. If a peaceful social organisation is possible without forfeiting every right, then such forfeiture is unnecessary. Individuals need only forfeit those rights, the exercise of which is incompatible with peaceful political co-existence, but they may hold on to the rest of them. The scheme becomes clearer if it is recast in terms of freedom. Individuals have an immense amount of freedom; they enjoy total freedom. In a society they are enjoined to sacrifice not their total freedom but just the amount that is necessary to secure the mutual enjoyment of the remaining portion of their freedom under the auspices of

---

[16] T Hobbes, *Leviathan*, ed E Curley (Indianapolis, IN, Hackett Publishing, 1994) 80.

[17] Falconry is the sport of hunting with falcons. Men train the birds to do the hunting. See F Michelman, 'Foxy Freedom?' (2010) 90 *Boston University Law Review* 949, 965. Michelman discusses the activity inspired by a case that was brought before German courts.

[18] BVerfGE 54, 143, 2 BvR 854/79 (23 May 1980).

[19] Spitting on public sidewalks is not an example drawn from an actual case, but a spirited example of Michelman, 'Foxy Freedom?', n 17 above, 952.

a commonwealth. The modified Hobbesian scheme is the basis of what could be called an 'individualistic liberalism'. Its motto is the following: 'the less freedom we give away, the more just a society is'. On this view, the minimal state becomes not merely an efficient social organisation, but something valuable, a realisation of justice.[20]

By adopting the Hobbesian idea that individuals have a prima facie right to total freedom proportionality subscribes to an individualistic liberalism. But this kind of individualism is a methodologically flawed abstraction that makes social justice incomprehensible and, just as was the case with Hobbes, ends up granting no rights to individuals. It is methodologically flawed since it ignores the fact, so well captured by Aristotle, that man is a social being and cannot be conceived outside society. It is society that comes first, not the individual. This means that practices of sharing and accomplishing things with others are prior to the individual pursuing her self-interest. Consequently, we cannot start from the notion of total freedom, since social beings constitutively lack it and society is not the right place to search for it.

Individualistic liberalism is not the only form of liberalism around. I propose we start instead by thinking about how we should regulate the practices of sharing and accomplishing things with others and do so to make them just. Our answers will vary from one social context to the other. We should expect that individual rights will appear further downstream. But, again, the content of those rights will be determined by a notion of fairness in different social contexts. Take intimate relationships. Couples, we often say, are unions that are supposed to strive for the fullest integration towards the achievement of many shared goals. At the same time, though, we insist that persons remain distinct and independent even in intimate relationships. From this we draw more concrete conclusions. We contend, for instance, that one's private correspondence does not belong to the other, or that it is inappropriate for one to spy on the other, even if it is for the purpose of knowing them better.

Political justice follows the same pattern. Theories of justice are theories about our legitimate demands against our fellow citizens. These demands cannot be properly articulated unless we conceive everyone as a separate person whose life is of special importance. Thus, we come to a notion of individuality that derives from and relates to a notion of fair sociability. Basic liberties that grant individuals rights are a cardinal element of a fair society; they are indispensable social arrangements that enable all persons to conduct the plan of life that they deem valuable. The maximisation of liberty is not valuable in itself, but only insofar as it is supported by this notion of fair sociability. We could call such an approach that reconciles the affirmation of individual rights with the primacy of social life liberal sociability. The thrust of liberal sociability, then, is that individual rights are derived from a conception of a just society (one in which everyone has the status of free and equal), rather than from a doctrine that gives methodological priority to the individual and

---

[20] The collapse of communism lent additional support to the idea that what distinguishes a 'minimal' from an 'expansive' state is not efficiency but freedom. Indeed, it was freedom and not welfare that was offered to individuals in exchange for the misery that followed the end of communism.

her total freedom. Under liberal sociability, justice and solidarity find their proper place. We care for justice and solidarity because we are the sort of beings that participate in collective endeavours, which constitutively constrain our liberty and implicate our interests and the interests of others. By contrast, in the individualistic view justice gets a bad name and solidarity is all but eliminated.

There is no space here to make a positive case for this conception of *liberal sociability*, as I call it. My purpose in introducing it is to show that individualistic liberalism is a highly contentious doctrine. In fact, as I argue in the following section, individualistic liberalism propounds a very problematic understanding of human rights.

III. THE LIBERTY OF HUMAN RIGHTS

Does individualistic liberalism with its commitment to total freedom help us grasp the concept of human rights? Take, for example, traffic regulations. Dworkin uses the example of prohibiting driving uptown on Lexington Avenue.[21] Is it helpful to start with a prima facie freedom to drive however someone wishes including uptown and then to examine whether the specific prohibition infringes someone's right? The proponents of proportionality will answer 'yes'. They will balance the loss of freedom of driving uptown with the convenience or order in traffic produced by the existence of the traffic rule, and they will probably find that these values outweigh the loss of freedom. Even so, they will maintain that a loss of freedom has occurred, albeit one that was easily exchangeable for the purpose of optimising freedom overall. Suppose now that new research has indicated that the restriction was misguided, and convenience and order in traffic would be better served by the opposite rule, one prohibiting driving downtown. Are we prepared to say that prohibiting driving uptown was a violation that Human Rights Watch should denounce?

What makes us think that a loss of freedom to drive as we wish, even if it is proven to be grounded on mistaken assumptions, is not particularly grave? Why can we live with it? I guess the answer is that nobody feels offended by the prohibition; nobody feels that the prohibition denies her dignity as a moral agent.[22] On the contrary, someone will feel deeply offended if she is not free to worship the God she wishes or to express her political ideas. The conclusion is that not every curtailment of freedom raises a human rights issue but only the abridgment of certain basic liberties.

Which are these basic liberties? How are we going to distinguish which liberties are basic (or fundamental or preferred) for a society to be just and which are not? Rawls suggests two ways: i) we can use the list of the various bills of rights and declarations of the rights of man;[23] ii) we can 'consider which liberties are essential

---

[21] R Dworkin, *A Matter of Principle* (Cambridge, MA, Harvard University Press, 1985) 189.

[22] 'It is not demeaning for you to accept that a majority of your fellow citizens has the right to fix traffic rules and enforce the rules they fix, provided that the rules they chose are not wicked or desperately foolish'. R Dworkin, *Justice for Hedgehogs* (Cambridge, MA, Harvard University Press, 2011) 367.

[23] 'Throughout the history of democratic thought the focus has been on achieving certain specific liberties and constitutional guarantees, as found for example, in various bills of rights and declarations of the rights of man'. J Rawls, *Political Liberalism* (New York, NY, Columbia University Press, 1993) 292.

social conditions for the adequate development and full exercise of the ... moral personality over a complete life'.[24]

Ronald Dworkin goes one step further in specifying the basic liberties and thus buttressing the contrast between the idea of total freedom and the alternative conception suggested above. He understands total freedom to be the power to act as we wish unimpeded by others or by a political community. He maintains that we do not actually ascribe value to such freedom. We do not think, he says, that there is any moral loss, when the state forbids me to kill my critics. 'If nothing wrong has taken place when I am prevented from killing my critics, then we have no reason for adopting a conception of liberty that describes the event as one in which liberty has been sacrificed'.[25]

The liberty we value is, according to Dworkin, an interpretative concept that is not and should not be co-extensive to total freedom. The liberty we should be committed to is 'the area of [a person's] freedom that a political community cannot take away without injuring him in a special way: compromising his dignity by denying him equal concern or an essential feature of responsibility for his own life'.[26] This is not another formulation of the list of basic liberties. True, insofar as the traditional basic liberties (freedom of speech, freedom of religion, etc) guarantee the 'essential social conditions for the adequate development and full exercise of the ... moral personality over a complete life' (Rawls), these are also included in the Dworkinian formula. Still there are substantial differences.

First, Dworkin's formula seems broader since any interference that denies equal concern and respect qualifies as giving rise to a claim of human right.[27] Second, and more important, it does not allow that 'fundamental or preferred liberties' be determined by collective views. It is not that from the immense amount of freedom we pick some liberties because they seem to us more valuable than others. Doing so would be like imposing on others a certain view about what is a good and valuable way of life. But this would contradict our stated aim, because it would fail to respect everyone's personal responsibility to make the best of their own lives.

But even more fundamentally, Dworkin's formula provides a robust philosophical basis for the kind of liberty we should value. For Dworkin, it is not the role of political society to satisfy our preferences, simply because they are manifestations of our freedom. In fact, political society may and does use its coercive force for all sorts of purposes and restricts freedom in all sorts of ways. There is nothing prima facie problematic about that. What a political society may not do is deny a liberty,

---

[24] ibid, 293. Quite instructively, Rawls felt compelled to utilise the notion of basic liberties in the light of HLA Hart's famous critique of the initial formulation of the liberty principle in *A Theory of Justice*. See HLA Hart, 'Rawls on Liberty and Its Priority'(1973) 40 *University of Chicago Law Review* 551, 553; and J Rawls, 'The Basic Liberties and Their Priority' in J Rawls, *Collected Papers*, ed S Freeman (Cambridge, MA, Harvard University Press, 1999). In important respects, my critique of total freedom echoes Hart's view. The failure he identified in Rawls's original proposal is the one I attribute to the principle of proportionality.

[25] R Dworkin, *Justice in Robes* (Cambridge, MA, Harvard University Press, 2006) 115.

[26] Dworkin, *Justice for Hedgehogs*, n 22 above, 366.

[27] But see Michelman and his Malthus Act hypothetical arguing that sometimes Dworkin's formula could be narrower and not include traditional core liberties. Michelman, 'Foxy Freedom?', n 17 above, 968–70.

Disproportionate Individualism 243

when being denied that liberty would compromise our dignity. In turn, an act is an assault on dignity when it denies someone 'equal respect and concern or an essential feature of responsibility for his own life'.[28] What we really value is dignity. Dignity is the central concept for human rights and all the more specific 'valued liberties' are connected with it. So when, for example, we come to consider that on matters of intimacy we should be free from governmental interference, our view expresses rather the conclusion of an interpretation of the concept of dignity. One of the characteristic ways in which a political society may fail in its duty to act consistently with dignity is when it acts on discriminatory or moralistic grounds. The first type of ground compromises equal standing, whereas the latter vitiates the principle of personal responsibility for one's own life.

These observations help vindicate the view that rights characteristically operate as trump cards.[29] It is not because rights are infinitely more important than the considerations they trump, but because a state that acted on those considerations would thereby assault dignity, and the recognition of the right serves to act as a bulwark against that assault. Consider moralistic and paternalistic laws. These are based on impermissible justifications because they do not respect the ethical responsibility of individuals and thus injure their dignity. So, for example, if the justification for prohibiting bird feeding in the park is that this kind of activity is worthless or a waste of time, this would be an insult to the ethical responsibility of the individuals. The state cannot restrict my choices on the basis that they are not worthy. To do so, would be for the state to make a judgement which the principle of personal responsibility commands that each one of us make for ourselves. But the state can restrict my choices when its reason for doing so does not assume any ethical evaluation. This means that there is no general or prima facie right to feed the birds, to engage in falconry or 'to paint my Georgian house purple'.[30] A state typically prohibits or at any rate regulates those activities on the basis of considerations that do not compromise dignity (such as environmental protection, public health and urban planning). However, the very same activities raise human right issues whenever their justification is based on ethical evaluations. Again, what counts is not freedom as such (the same activity can be restricted without injury) but the protection of ethical responsibility.

Now, someone could say that feeding the birds or falconry is the basic plan of her life; it is not just a preference, like drinking soda instead of orange juice. Does the state show lack of respect for someone's ethical responsibility when, although it abstains from any ethical evaluation, it forbids or makes more difficult on other grounds the pursuit of a central element of my conception of the good life? What is the use of not allowing the state to make ethical judgements about my conception of the good life if it can forbid it altogether for some other reason? This is a question that again shifts our focus from dignity to total freedom. Our claim towards society

---

[28] Dworkin, *Justice for Hedgehogs*, n 22 above, 366.
[29] See R Dworkin, 'Rights As Trumps' in J Waldron (ed), *Theories of Rights* (Oxford, Oxford University Press, 1984) 153.
[30] Painting one's Georgian house purple is Dworkin's example. See Dworkin, *Justice for Hedgehogs*, n 22 above, 346.

is not freedom but respect for our status as moral agents. So, if for example the state acknowledged our freedom to feed the birds, stating that even worthless activities such as this one should be allowed, such an outcome would certainly entail an insult to ethical responsibility, although freedom would be intact.

If we take for granted that every society regulates most of the activities of its members, it would be a disaster to consider every individual preference as an ethical choice that raises a claim of right. We will end up 'moralising' every measure and unavoidably the majority will have to take a stance on every ethical choice. The deliberation would be something as follows: Is your life's plan feeding the birds? Then, it gives you a prima facie right, but so does our life's plan, which is to play football. For us, playing football is more valuable and, since we are many, our choice must have the upper hand. Put differently, if society takes every individual preference as an ethical choice—and thus worthy of protection as a prima facie right—I doubt that the result will be more freedom. Everybody, sometime, will be deeply offended because others will oppose their choices on the basis of their own ethical valuations. The right to nothing in particular will then morph into a right to nothing *tout court*.

It is true that the alternative strategy to forbid regulations that are based on ethical justifications does not guarantee or facilitate any plan of life based on any preference. But the real claim we have from society is not to provide everything we need for the success of our plan, even prima facie. Our claim is not, to use Dworkin's metaphor, to have all possible colours in our palette, but to be able to design our life on the basis of our own value judgements with the colours that are available to all.[31]

IV. HUMAN RIGHTS AND THE COURTS

Now, if we accept that only a few basic liberties are 'essential social conditions' of moral personality in Rawls' sense or are needed to protect against violations of dignity in Dworkin's sense, it is less problematic to subscribe to a constitutional arrangement whereby courts are called to safeguard them from eventual abridgment by entrenching them against the legislative will. In other words, this idea fits well with our traditional ideas of representative democracy and judicial review. By contrast, the concept of total freedom that is implicit in the principle of proportionality renders any interference with a person's total freedom a potential human rights violation or at least the starting point for a human rights inquiry. That definitely seems to reflect the position of the German Constitutional Court, which, as Mattias Kumm notes, 'regards any liberty interest whatsoever as enjoying prima facie protection as a right'.[32] In other words, as Kumm acknowledges, 'the recognition of a general right to liberty and a general right to equality means practically all legislation can

---

[31] ibid, 367.
[32] Kumm, 'The Idea of Socratic Contestation', n 14 above, 151: 'In Germany', Kumm says, 'the right to the "free development of personality" is interpreted as a general right to liberty understood as the right to do or not to do whatever you please. It has been held by the Constitutional Court to include such mundane things as a right to ride horses through public woods, feeding pigeons on public squares, or the right to trade a particular breed of dogs.' (Notes omitted.)

in principle be challenged on human rights grounds, leading to an assessment of its justification in terms of public reason as prescribed by the proportionality tests'.[33]

If in principle every piece of legislation gives rise to a human rights issue, then the judiciary must decide on virtually any question of public policy, from fines for parking violations to the fluctuation of interest rates. Furthermore, in doing so, it is bound to employ a standard that is much more intrusive than mere rational connection. As a result, the boundary between review and appeal is automatically blurred, as is, along with it, the basis of the courts' legitimacy. Legitimacy concerns are intensified when it is supranational courts such as the European Court of Human Rights that are tasked to protect human rights. Having to rely on an expansive understanding of the scope of human rights, they end up becoming the ultimate arbiter of the legality of every piece of national legislation.[34]

Independently of whether such a development would be desirable or not, there is no doubt that it dramatically alters the way we conceive of judicial review, the power of political majorities, the very concept of representative democracy and, ultimately, the role of supranational human rights courts. In reality, this shift would surreptitiously make proportionality not merely the 'ultimate rule of law'[35] but the over-arching method for the moral assessment of any form of human conduct.

V. CONCLUSION

To conclude, I have tried to draw a distinction between two understandings of human rights. On the understanding I favour, limits to 'total freedom' do not necessarily constitute an 'invasion' of valued liberties. Rather, we have to determine which restrictions of freedom count as injuries to the dignity and autonomy of individuals. For a proponent of total freedom, freedom is understood in quantitative terms; the more of it we have, the better. This account, I have argued, is ill-equipped to make distinctions between kinds of invasion of freedom depending on their justification, and on this basis to exclude some justifications as incompatible with the very idea of rights such as freedom of expression, religion and privacy. In fact, insofar as the proportionality test is meant to be neutral and to take at face value a wide range of interests, it lacks the resources to exclude any consideration whatsoever. Thus, it exposes all our rights to a very dangerous vulnerability. More fundamentally, it seems to presuppose a perverse conception of the relationship between the individual and society, one that builds up from a radical individualism.

---

[33] ibid, 164.
[34] This is not to say that judges are eager to take up such an intrusive role or that they actually exercise it. In fact, judges typically devise strategies to limit their interference with political decisions. This applies with even more force at the supranational level. The doctrine of the margin of appreciation is a characteristic example. Often those strategies bear the mark of their origin. They replicate the philosophical confusion and dead ends of the principle of proportionality. If we abandon the principle of proportionality, the usefulness and cogency of such strategies is likely to be greatly diminished. Conversely, when sometimes judges assume an expanded notion of judicial review and proceed to apply proportionality, their judgment seems totally ad hoc and arbitrary. Eg, in *Mamidakis v Greece* App No 35533/04 (ECtHR, 11 January 2007), the amount of a fine, although found by the Greek courts to be proportionate, was held to be excessive by the supranational Court purely on the basis of its amount.
[35] Beatty, *The Ultimate Rule*, n 13 above.

This starting point is deeply misguided. For social beings like us, total freedom is not a value, nor do we want our courts to enforce it. An organised society routinely constrains our freedom; it imposes limits on the ways we can use our shared social, natural and aesthetic environment. Being members of such a society, we should be more concerned that we can live our unavoidably constrained lives in dignity.

Some political ideas have the tendency to recur with slight adjustments in a variety of contexts. Individualism is one of them. Europe prides itself for never succumbing to the extreme individualism that underpinned laissez-faire economic arrangements. It may still be susceptible to individualism though, if it allows the ascendancy of a philosophy the hallmark of which is the prima facie right to everything. If Europe succumbs to individualism it will be exposed to a much graver risk than those associated with a free market: the risk of having the concepts of justice and solidarity seriously undermined.

17
Justice in and of the European Union

NEIL WALKER

I. INTRODUCTION: IN THE NAME OF EUROPEAN JUSTICE

THERE ARE SOME good reasons why we might find justice attractive as an organising concept as we seek to work out what is required for the European Union to achieve and maintain legitimacy before its people(s), and as we endeavour to assess how, where and why it is falling short. These reasons, however, do not offer any guarantees that justice will *in fact* measure up to the task of constructive critique and critical reconstruction. Indeed, some of the factors that might persuade us to invest in the language of justice in the EU context also reflect and reinforce certain shortcomings in the capacity of the 'j'-word to supply a reliable compass of political morality for the world's first post-state polity. In what follows, I will elaborate these points. I will conclude, however, that, while we should be ever alert both to the temptation of overstating the claim of justice as some kind of master discourse in the European context, and to the danger that such a claim merely symptomises rather than resolves the puzzle of supranational legitimacy, there is nevertheless considerable merit in persevering with the project of examining the EU in the name of justice.

The analytical key lies in the potential of the language of justice to impact on the EU legitimacy debate at two levels. It is this double possibility, but also the complexity, even confusion, of the relationship between these two levels, which underscores the promise, but also the pitfalls, of the EU's justice discourse. To understand how this argument proceeds, we must begin with certain peculiarities associated with the concept of justice itself.

II. THE AGILITY OF JUSTICE

Justice is an extremely agile concept. By this I mean more than that it can be shaped and reshaped to mean different things to different people. That certainly is the case. There are many different theories and conceptions of justice, and these are often mutually inconsistent. Justice has no fixed meaning, no settled criteria. It is patently a contentious, and, indeed, a contested concept.[1] Agility, however, suggests something beyond mere flexibility and diversity of theoretical approach towards a

---

[1] See, eg, J Neyer, 'Justice and the Right to Justification: Conceptual Reflections' in this volume, 211, at 212.

common object. It concerns, in addition, the ability of the idea of justice to move nimbly between various sites and to travel smoothly up and down the scale of abstraction; that is to say, its capacity to refer to quite different objects, or focal concerns, and to sound at various quite distinct stages of remove from social and political practice. In particular, justice can refer variously to individuals, or to relations between individuals or among small groups, to particular sectors or segments of common life and common public policy, to certain specific social or political institutions, to the society or the polity as a whole, or, indeed, to the totality of relations across the planet. In a nutshell, justice can be *personal, interpersonal, sectoral, institutional, polity-holistic*, or *global*.

That justice can be understood as a personal trait is a position that goes back as far the classical treatment of Plato and Aristotle. For the Greek philosophers the just individual is a virtuous individual, someone who is guided by a vision of the good. The idea of interpersonal justice, too, has Aristotelian roots. The dyad, or the small group, provides the most immediate context and measure of personal virtue, the setting within which the credentials of the just individual are most directly put to the test. Indeed, it is in the writings of Aristotle that we find the first formulation of the notion of commutative justice—of just action and just consequences considered within the frame of interpersonal transactions. And it is in these same writings that we find the first articulation of the familiar, field-defining distinction, more commonly associated with Aquinas, between commutative justice as the standard appropriate to the micro-context of exchange relations, and distributive justice, which is a standard more appropriate to the macro-context of wider societal relations.

Sectoral justice already assumes just such a macro-context of the just allocation of benefits and burdens across a broader population. The object of analysis here is a particular domain of practice, and of practical consequences. Sectoral justice, then, can refer to a clearly defined social constituency—justice, say, for university students, or for war veterans, or for dementia sufferers. Or, more broadly, it can identify a significant dimension of societal relations and public policy—from environmental justice, or healthcare justice, to something as expansive and open-ended as economic or social justice. An assessment of sectoral justice will often require us to look at the contribution of relevant sectoral institutions, but we are also interested in the justice of a specific category of institutions for reasons apart from a general sectoral audit. These are the public institutions concerned with the provision of civil and criminal justice— police, courts, prisons and the like. For these institutions, justice is such a focal concern that it provides the language of their official (and everyday) description. That is to say, these are nominate institutions of justice—public bodies directly charged with the responsibility of delivering or guaranteeing at a societal level a particular range, type and pattern of just exchanges and outcomes, rather than institutions that exist for other dedicated purposes but whose objectives may also be evaluated in terms of their broader contribution to sectoral justice, or to polity-holistic justice.

Polity-holistic justice, as the label suggests, is concerned with the justice of the political community as a whole. In Rawls's famous formulation, it may only be the 'basic structure'[2] of the relevant polity and society with which such a general theory

---

[2] J Rawls *A Theory of Justice* (Cambridge, MA, Harvard University Press, 1971).

of justice is concerned—the political constitution, the legal system, the economy, the family, and so on. But what distinguishes this perspective from the sectoral or any other approach is that it is concerned with the general responsibility of a political community to promote or secure justice for and amongst its members and associates. Quite how far that responsibility extends—how 'basic' should be the basic structure—is itself controversial between different conceptions of justice, but what all polity-holistic conceptions hold in common is a concern with the overall framework, scope and pattern of the polity's contribution to justice within the relevant community, and so to the justice—or justness of the polity as a whole.

Global justice, finally, extends even further than the polity. It concerns the entire globe, and, to develop a distinction already introduced, it can be conceived of either in holistic terms—with the basic structure of global institutions and arrangements as a whole, or, more commonly, as a series of sectoral projects, from global peace and the global environment to migration policy and access to basic material resources.[3]

The agility of the justice concept makes it particularly well adapted to the situation of the European Union. Granted, one influential recent critique of the European Union holds that its public culture has been progressively concerned too much with the rhetoric of values and too little with the cultivation of individual virtue[4]—including, presumably, the virtue of justice. Yet, however we judge this criticism, in other respects the European Union appears to be a fertile environment for considerations of justice. The four freedoms that lie at the Union's core can all be seen as particular forms of transactional freedom (in respect of the offer and receipt of goods, services and capital, and with regard to labour mobility), and, as such, they are concerned with a certain (if far from uncontroversial) conception of justice in *interpersonal* exchange relations. Less contentiously, the European Union endeavours to make a contribution to various forms of *sectoral* justice—environmental, gender, disability, educational, healthcare, etc—as the upper tier of governance and regulatory capacity within a multilevel continental system. Furthermore, the Area of Freedom, Security and Justice (AFSJ), which has been at the cutting edge of the EU's development beyond social and economic policy for two decades now, provides a clear and prominent example of justice as an *institutional* ideal.[5] And if we consider the EU's external relations, the past 20 years has again[6] witnessed a significant development of that profile, including its key input, for better or worse, within an even more extensive multilevel governance framework into various sectoral dimensions of *global* justice, such as migration, food security and climate change.[7]

---

[3] See, eg, T Nagel, 'The Problem of Global Justice' (2005) 32 *Philosophy and Public Affairs* 113.

[4] See, eg, JHH Weiler, '60 Years Since the First European Community—Reflections on Political Messianism' (2011) 22 *European Journal of International Law* 303.

[5] See, eg, S Douglas-Scott, 'Justice, Injustice and the Rule of Law in the EU' in this volume, 51.

[6] Given early impetus by the 1992 Treaty of Maastricht's development of a Second Pillar of Foreign and Security Policy alongside its Third Pillar of Justice and Home Affairs. On the expansion of the EU's outward-looking global remit more generally, see G de Búrca, 'Europe's *raison d'être*' in D Kochenov and F Amtenbrink (eds), *The European Union's Shaping of the International Legal Order* (Cambridge, Cambridge University Press, 2014).

[7] See, eg, J Scott and L Rajamani, 'EU Climate Change Unilateralism' (2012) 23 *European Journal of International Law* 469.

It is at this point the two-level quality of EU justice discourse comes into focus. To draw upon the terminology of my title, the above analysis demonstrates how all manner of forms and types of justice—interpersonal, sectoral, institutional and global—are relevant to and treated *in* the European Union by its various organs and through its various forms of law and policy. Yet, these examples, for all their dense versatility, do not directly and do not obviously speak to the justice, or justness, *of* the European Union as a whole. For that, we need to return to the final element of justice's flexible remit, namely justice considered in *polity-holistic* terms.

III. THE ELUSIVE LEGITIMACY OF THE EU

It is here, however, that we begin to glimpse some of the potential shortcomings and pitfalls of the EU's discourse on justice. On the one hand, under the various categories considered above, the language of justice is patently capable of making a rich contribution to a full and rounded evaluation of the EU's role in national and transnational affairs. On the other hand, as we shall see, the question of the general polity legitimacy of the EU poses special difficulties, and these are reflected in the treatment of justice, perceived through a polity-holistic lens, as a factor in addressing that question.

The special problems of polity legitimacy are of two types, though they are closely related, and, indeed, shade into one another.[8] In the first place, the very question of whether the EU qualifies as a self-standing polity, such that it makes sense even to think of it as the subject of general legitimacy claims or challenges, is controversial. More specifically, it is not clear that the EU is the kind of entity that meets the necessary minimum external and internal identity criteria—both sufficiently autonomous from other entities and sufficiently integrated in its internal structure and activity profile—that would make appropriate its subjection to the same kind of appraisal of its overall acceptability to it citizens and denizens as other discrete political communities, notably states. Can we even hold that the EU has a general responsibility to promote or secure justice for and amongst its members and associates, and that it should be judged in accordance with its fulfilment or otherwise of that responsibility? And in the second place, to the (inevitably controversial) extent that the EU may be regarded as a self-standing polity, and the previous question can in principle be answered in the affirmative, as there is no supranational genus of which it is a species, the relevant standards by which its legitimacy should be assessed are also deeply uncertain and contentious. If it is at all a distinct polity, it is certainly a highly *distinctive* kind of polity, and so how we go about measuring the legitimacy of its contribution to the world remains a matter of deep disagreement.

How, precisely, does the elusive quality of the EU's general polity legitimacy affect the place of justice—such a familiar discursive theme *in* various of the spheres of action of the EU—at that broader polity-holistic level of debate. To answer this, we need to sketch out a taxonomy of the candidate ways of addressing legitimacy

---

[8] See, eg, N Walker, 'Europe's Constitutional Momentum and the Search for Polity Legitimacy' (2005) 3 *International Journal of Constitutional Law* 211.

within the EU that is sensitive to the deeper contestation over the very idea of polity legitimacy.

IV. FOUR APPROACHES TO POLITY LEGITIMACY

Four broad approaches can be identified, these located along a spectrum of greater or lesser scepticism about the very idea of polity legitimacy in the EU context. On the sceptical side of the divide, we can identify *disaggregated* and *dependent* approaches, while on the polity-affirmative side we can identify *democratic* approaches alongside other approaches to polity legitimacy based upon *collective self-authorisation*. Pursuing a strategy of elimination, let us begin by looking at the two approaches—one from either end of the spectrum—that do *not* directly engage questions of justice. On the sceptical side, there is the dependent approach, while on the affirmative side there is the democratic approach.

The very conditions of emergence of the EU ensured a strong early bias towards dependent forms of legitimacy. Born as an international organisation in the Treaties of Paris[9] and Rome,[10] albeit one with an unusually 'thick' and penetrative policy remit, for its first 30 years the EU tended to be justified in official discourse in terms that reflected the externality of its founding mandate and momentum. Lacking its own conception of popular sovereignty—of independent *pouvoir constituant*—its legitimation strategies were instead linked to various pre-given sources or standards. It was justified primarily in intergovernmental terms, as the delegated 'creature' of its Member States.[11] In turn, legitimation through the indirect authorisation of the Member States encouraged or accommodated other approaches that stressed the modesty, non-contentiousness and containable character of the supranational remit. The EU was treated variously, and often cumulatively, as the recipient and 'trustee' of a clear and clearly delimited legislative or policy mandate,[12] as the disinterestedly efficient or expert 'technocratic'[13] instrument for the realisation of a set of common commitments, or as the indispensable transnational means to pursue a range of shared interests of national states and citizen towards a positive net outcome or 'output'.[14]

However, the legitimacy of a delegate, or of a fiduciary, or of an efficient or epistemic authority, depends on the continuing control of the principal, the clarity of the mandate, or the reducibility of policy competence to special knowledge, experience or expertise alone. And as is well-known, the adequacy of all of these justificatory

---

[9] Treaty Establishing the European Coal and Steel Community (Paris, 18 April 1951) 261 UNTS 140.
[10] Treaty Establishing the European Economic Community (Rome, 25 March 1957) 298 UNTS 3.
[11] See, eg, P Lindseth, *Power and Legitimacy: Reconciling Europe and the Nation State* (Oxford, Oxford University Press, 2010).
[12] See, eg, G Majone, 'Delegation of Powers and the Fiduciary Principle' in G Majone, *Dilemmas of European Integration. The Ambiguities and Pitfalls of Integration by Stealth* (Oxford, Oxford University Press, 2005).
[13] C Lord and P Magnette, '*E Pluribus Unum*? Creative Disagreement about Legitimacy in the EU' (2004) 42 *Journal of Common Market Studies* 183.
[14] As in Fritz Scharpf's 'output legitimacy' in *Governing in Europe: Effective and Democratic?* (Oxford, Oxford University Press, 1999).

models has been challenged by the expansionary dynamic of the Union. They have become less plausible claims in a supranational polity increasingly attenuated from national control, with an ever broader and deeper policy agenda, with multiple veto points that work against any rolling back of community competence, and with a less comfortable 'permissive consensus'[15] amongst key national elites across an ever larger Union.

One response to these developments has been a gradual tendency to view the overall legitimacy of the EU in original rather than derivative terms, and as a matter of resort to internal rather than external criteria. And by that path, with more or less explicit reference to the state as a justificatory template,[16] *democracy* has been treated by many as the natural route to polity self-legitimation. As a relatively autonomous polity with an increasingly capacious and contentious agenda for the allocation of rights, risks and resources, the key to its legitimacy, on this view, lies with the collective self-determination of all those affected by the allocation of rights, risks and resources.

But such an approach has itself long been vulnerable to various objections. One objection questions its basic plausibility, insisting upon the resilience of the so-called democratic deficit. It stresses the record of voter apathy and weak transnational political party organisation even in the face of the progressive empowerment of the European Parliament, indicates the continuing marginalisation of national parliaments despite recent subsidiarity-inspired reforms, emphasises the limited transparency and poor accountability of Council and Commission, and can cite the failure of quasi-populist initiatives such as the (Constitutional) Convention on the Future of Europe to find or nurture a fertile democratic subsoil. On this view, the lack of a European *demos* culturally self-understood as such means that the motivational basis for a genuinely committed and contestatory democracy does not exist or is significantly deficient. A second objection returns to some of the themes of the EU as a dependent polity and questions the appropriateness in general normative terms of a solution which foregrounds democracy. On this view, a key danger of supranational democratic overreach is that Euro-democracy stands in a negative-sum relationship with—and so risks curtailing and chilling—democracy in its culturally more appropriate and more plausible forum of the nation state(s). A third and related objection holds that in its appeal to the unfettered authority of the collective will, the argument from democracy fails in any case to capture the more limited and specialist mandate of the EU as compared to the unlimited political mandate of the state. In terms of its basic architecture and its place in the overall structure of national, continental and global political authority, the EU is simply not a state, and so the kind of argument for a thoroughgoing democratic ethos and audit that attends an entity whose very *raison d'être* is one of collective self-determination should not apply.[17]

---

[15] See, eg, I Down and CJ Wilson, 'From "Permissive Consensus" to "Constraining Dissensus": A Polarizing Union?' (2008) 43 *Acta Politica* 26.

[16] See, eg, F Mancini, 'Europe: The Case for Statehood' (1998) 4 *European Law Journal* 29; E Eriksen, *The Unfinished Democratisation of Europe* (Oxford, Oxford University Press, 2009).

[17] See, eg, A Moravcsik, 'What Can We Learn From the Collapse of the European Constitutional Project?' (2006) 47 *Politische Vierteljahresschrift* 2.

In a nutshell, then, the argument from democracy as a pure alternative to the historically influential dependent approach to polity legitimacy is subject to profound challenge on each of motivational, normative and structural grounds.

It is against this background of an unresolved and deeply unsettled legitimacy discourse that arguments from justice begin to come into their own at both ends of the spectrum. On the one hand, the disaggregated approach to legitimacy focuses on the many particular claims to legitimacy that the EU might make. Whereas the dependent approach to legitimacy *does* address the EU as a singular entity, albeit deploying a thin and derivative model that takes a modest view of the EU's polity status, a disaggregated approach does not concern itself at all with the polity-holistic dimension. That is to say, it does not seek to assess the legitimacy of the EU in accordance with a single test and standard, but instead hones in on particular aspects of its work and applies different criteria to each. What justifies the EU from this perspective is how its various functions and resources contribute to different policy objectives and ethical aspirations in the transnational sphere more generally. The EU, then, on this view, is treated, implicitly or explicitly, as a mere bundle of capacities linked to more or less discrete and diverse objectives, rather than a singular entity whose justification *as such* is a politically salient or even meaningful question.

Though it is by no means the only language that may be adopted in accordance with this methodology, a focus on the many forms of justice pursued *in* the EU, interpersonal, and, in particular sectoral, institutional and global, clearly fits with the disaggregated approach. Justice here provides the double function of supplying an affirmative—and superficially consistent—moral language, but one that lowers the stakes for the EU to a test, or series of tests of consequential benefit. The EU's various institutional and policy platforms are judged for the various things they *do*, rather than the EU as a whole being judged for what it *is*. Indeed, from this perspective, the ontological question of the basic nature and purpose of the EU is entirely missing, and the EU's overall contribution, insofar as it is even a consideration,[18] can only be measured as the sum of its various parts.

In the final analysis, however, the disaggregated approach is vulnerable to some of the same objections as the dependent approach. An approach that unbundles the EU's various functions and capacities may tell us a lot about the justness of these various functions and capacities, but against a backdrop of the EU possessing broad and expanding multi-functional institutional capacity, including significant scope to interfere with the multi-functional capacity of states, this can be no substitute for an approach that looks at it role and contribution in 'joined-up' terms. And so, reverting to the other end of the spectrum, we arrive at a consideration of those approaches, other than a pure democratic approach, which view the

---

[18] I do not mean to imply that those who talk about justice in this way necessarily intend to take a disaggregated approach to polity legitimacy, and in so doing to *dismiss* the significance of more holistic approaches. They may or may not so intend, but the language of differentiated justice can certainly lend support to such a view. On the general trend within EU policy studies towards disaggregating questions of legitimacy and effectiveness, see, eg, M Jachtenfuchs, 'The Governance Approach to European Integration' (2009) 38 *Journal of Common Market Studies* 245.

legitimacy of the EU in original or independent terms. Here, polity legitimacy is a measure of how the EU justifies itself as a matter of self-authorisation, speaking for and to its own collective constituency in light of its own self-standing role and contribution as a polity rather than in terms dictated by external constituencies or standards.

In this final category we find various attempts to discover a register of legitimation for the EU through identifying a bespoke set of values, ideals or aspirations that define European supranationalism on its own special terms and with reference to the common aspirations of the constituent European people(s). One well-known such position goes back to the founding postwar mission of the EU to promote peace and prosperity.[19] But, as the chief sponsor of this approach would be the first to admit,[20] in an age of relative prosperity, however (and, since the financial crisis, increasingly) unevenly distributed, and in which the sounds of war are heard only from beyond the EU's external borders, and in a time where the jurisdiction of the EU stretches well beyond the basics of wealth creation and the avoidance of conflict, something broader and more responsive to the contemporary situation of the European continent is required.

It is unsurprising that a series of renewed efforts to think about the legitimacy of the EU in terms of a morally articulate form of collective self-authorisation have focused on matters of justice. On the one hand, unlike the derivative or disaggregated approaches, the invocation of justice implies an original form of legitimacy.[21] A claim to the justice of a polity or of its institutions is a 'first' or foundational claim. It cannot be 'read off' from some other source, but must instead locate the polity itself as the 'primary agent'[22] or author of its own conception of justice. Yet, on the other hand, as compared to the pure democracy-centred approach, the invocation of justice suggests a basis for legitimacy which can at once be both more specific *and* more universal; more customised to the peculiar needs of the EU since what is 'just' is necessarily tailored to context, as well as more objectively defensible and trans-contextually resonant—the claim of justice being one that also implies adherence to certain general and invariant standards.

Yet justice, if it *is* to be appropriately customised and sufficiently attuned to the situation of the EU as a self-authorising project, cannot be seen as a replacement for European democracy. Rather, it must be seen as a complementary imperative—as something that operates alongside democratic mechanisms or, at least, is tailored in such a way that it exhibits the kind of responsiveness and respect for political equality that we associate with democratic self-rule.

---

[19] See, eg, JHH Weiler, *The Constitution of Europe: 'Do the New Clothes Have an Emperor?' and Other Essays on European Integration* (Cambridge, Cambridge University Press, 1999).

[20] See, eg, Weiler, '60 Years', n 4 above.

[21] See A Williams, *The Ethos of Europe: Values, Law and Justice in the EU* (Cambridge, Cambridge University Press, 2010) ch 8.

[22] O O'Neill, 'Agents of Justice' in A Kuper (ed), *Global Responsibilities* (London, Routledge, 2005), discussed in ibid, 298–99.

It is with this vital but delicate balance that recent attempts to redraw justice as a 'right to justification' are concerned.[23] They combine the democratic spirit of equality of subjective 'right' with the objectivity of 'good reasons' implicit in the notion of a process of justifying political action to all affected. In Rainer Forst's original formulation of the justice–justification nexus, justice refers to 'the human capacity to oppose relations of arbitrary rule or domination'.[24] What he calls 'the principle of general-reciprocal justification' is, he argues, the only means by which justice can be realised. That principle holds that 'every claim to goods, rights or liberties must be justified in a general and reciprocal manner, where one side may not simply project its reasons onto the other but must justify itself discursively'. Such an approach stresses the priority of identifying such contexts or sites of 'general-reciprocal justification' as are associated with deeply recursive relations of power, with the EU clearly providing one such recursive context.

Forst, many of whose ideas have been adapted to the European context by Jürgen Neyer,[25] clearly draws upon a Habermasian tradition of communicative rationality to flesh out a sense of communal justice. What matters, at root, is not the particular institutional form of the 'give and take' of public reason, but the underlying principle of general and reciprocal justification itself. We may avoid, then, the fetishism of certain supposedly paradigmatic institutional forms of 'democracy' whose plausibility and suitability in the EU context may be limited, such as a fully fledged assembly democracy and parliamentary executive, provided that the underlying principle of justification is respected. Equally, we must avoid the fetishism of discourses of expert rationality within specialist epistemic communities, if such rationality is not tested in sufficiently general and reciprocal manner with those it affects.

Yet, in the final analysis, the right to justification operates at too high a level of abstraction to provide, on its own, a compelling answer to the questions of justice in the EU. This, indeed, is evident in the ongoing disagreement between Forst, Neyer and others over the extent to which and ways in which the right to justification can and should incorporate democratic imperatives.[26] If we think back to the motivational, normative and structural problems that attend the problem of supranational democracy, none of these disappears just because democracy is now blended with considerations of justice. Indeed, for Neyer especially, procedures of justification

---

[23] See R Forst, *The Right to Justification: Elements of a Constructivist Theory of Justice* (New York, NY, Columbia University Press, 2007); J Neyer, *The Justification of Europe: A Political Theory of Supranational Integration* (Oxford, Oxford University Press, 2012). See also, the original EU-centred exchange: J Neyer, 'Justice, Not Democracy: Legitimacy in the European Union' (2010) 48 *Journal of Common Market Studies* 903; and (from a critically democratic perspective) Danny Nicol's reply: D Nicol, 'Can Justice Dethrone Democracy in the European Union? A Reply to Jürgen Neyer' (2012) 50 *Journal of Common Market Studies* 508; and the riposte by Jürgen Neyer: J Neyer, 'Who's Afraid of Justice? A Rejoinder to Danny Nicol' (2012) 50 *Journal of Common Market Studies* 523. See also R Forst, 'Justice, Democracy and the Right to Justification: Reflections on Jürgen Neyer's Normative Theory of the European Union' in this volume, 227; J Neyer, 'Justice and the Right to Justification: Conceptual Reflections' in this volume, 211; and D Nicol, 'Swabian Housewives, Suffering Southerners: The Contestability of Justice as Exemplified by the Eurozone Crisis' in this volume, 165.

[24] This and following quotes are taken from his synoptic statement, R Forst, 'Transnational Justice and Democracy' (2011) *Normative Orders Working Papers* No 4/11.

[25] See n 23 above.

[26] ibid.

go a long way in eclipsing more familiar forms of democracy in the EU. In particular, the right to justification cannot fully 'square the circle' of legitimating a polity where we continue to lack common agreement over and commitment to the kind and extent of polity autonomy it should boast or an overlapping common sense of the forms and limits of its legitimate encroachment on national democratic forms.

In some respects, the right to justification may seem to promise progress without having to solve fundamental questions about its democratic pedigree and prospects. In particular, an emphasis on the right to justification is salutary in questioning the privileging of the macro- over the micro-level that we often find in institutional analysis. It tells us that we should oppose, overcome or avoid relations of arbitrary rule or domination wherever they arise, and to do so in all the countless and variously configured sites of decision making in the EU—in Comitology committees and in agencies, in the Open Method of Coordination (OMC) and in national implementation contexts, as much as in the 'high' institutional sites of Commission, Council, Parliament and Court. What matters is the particular context and 'community' of affected persons for any particular policy or decision, and in tracking the countless such communities of the affected, we can deconstruct the singular community of the EU into its many overlapping instances.

Yet this is true only up to a point. As we have already seen, we cannot reduce the legitimacy of a polity to the aggregation of its component capacities and competences, and an appeal to the institutional diversity of the EU only takes us so far. Even in a broadly ramified and weakly centralised polity such as the EU, the macro-level of policy choice retains a steering capacity, and this demands its own 'right to justification' at the macro-scale. The Euro crisis and the move in the Council towards a strong form of 'executive federalism'[27]—discretionary in scope, deeply penetrative in reach, and 'unbalanced'[28] both in its continued emphasis on market freedom over social provision and in the transnational distribution of its burdens—as part of a new cycle of 'integration by fear'[29] in response to that crisis, supplies vividly renewed testimony to this. The EU, more than ever, is palpably more than the sum of its disparate parts, its central institutional settlement requiring its own justification. And certainly Forst himself, at least at the level of general theory, appears to accept this when stating that the conceptual task of constructing and maintaining a 'basic structure of justification' in any particular context is typically given concrete and resilient institutional form in a democratically redeemable 'justified basic structure' which applies recursively across space and time in similar contexts.[30]

V. JUSTIFYING JUSTIFICATION

I began by suggesting that justice possessed certain strengths but also significant limitations as a tool of normative analysis for the European Union. As we have seen,

---

[27] See J Habermas, *The Crisis of the European Union: A Response* (Cambridge, Polity Press, 2012).
[28] See M Dawson and F de Witte, 'Constitutional Balance in the EU After the Euro-Crisis' (2013) 76 *Modern Law Review* 817; see also MA Wilkinson, 'Politicising Europe's Justice Deficit: Some Preliminaries' in this volume, 111.
[29] JHH Weiler, 'Integration Through Fear' (2012) 23 *European Journal of International Law* 1.
[30] Forst, 'Transnational Justice', n 24 above.

justice as a low-tariff, context-specific concept—the justice *in* the European Union of my title—can be a very incisive instrument, provided its disaggregated parts are not understood as fulfilling the function of polity-holistic legitimation. In contrast, justice as just such a high-tariff, polity-holistic ideal—the justice *of* the European Union of my title—tends, by its abstractions and through its contestations, to highlight rather than resolve the more fundamental question of polity legitimation.

Yet, as I have also sought to argue, the kind of democracy-supplementing substantive ideal of collective self-authorisation that the notion of justice—and, in particular, a democratically sensitive conception of justice as an encompassing procedural right to justification—seeks to supply, seems to be the only cogent way of thinking about polity legitimation in the EU. That it cannot easily reconcile democracy with the peculiarities of supranationalism, therefore, is no reason to dispense with justice discourse. Rather, its very capacity to illuminate the heart of the European problem is a good reason to persevere with it.

In so doing, let me conclude by suggesting how we might pursue one more of Forst's insights. Forst's is an ideal theory consciously targeted at non-ideal circumstances. He describes justice as a 'recuperative institution'[31]—with communities of justice throughout history *typically* constituting themselves not in anticipation of new webs of social and political relations but in response to and so '*through*' existing relations of rule or domination'. In other words, the EU, just like many states, was born unfree and 'unjustified'. And, again like many states, its expansion in practice has tended to outpace and evade the constantly adjusting reach of its procedures of justification. It follows that if the continuous attempt to 'recuperate' lost ground is the normal dynamic of an expanding right to justification, there is no need *in theory* to judge the EU as a pathological instance.

There is no reason in principle, therefore, to see the EU as an unprecedented or irremediable case of original (or cultivated) political sin. It may lack the traction of overlapping common sense of its polity potential that aids the development of a strong sense of common political motivation, and it may have to countenance the complex algebra, and sometimes debilitating political gridlock, of facing up to multiple avenues of claims to democratic 'recuperation'—national and supranational—simultaneously. The failure of the first constitutional project a decade ago and the ongoing crisis of common commitment and confidence around the Euro today, certainly provide vivid testimony to this. But the very idea of 'recuperation' as the wellspring of politics—as the basic condition of political action—alerts us to the fact that for as long as Europeans remain deeply implicated in common action—and they have never been *more* mutually implicated—then the need and the impulse to recuperate will remain. And this leaves us with no alternative but to continue to seek to fashion a basic structure of political institutions that satisfies the right to justification of all Europeans.[32]

---

[31] ibid.
[32] For a view which seeks to pursue this through the revival of a constitution-making project, see N Walker, 'The European Union's Unresolved Constitution' in M Rosenfeld and A Sajó (eds), *The Oxford Handbook of Comparative Constitutional Law* (Oxford, Oxford University Press, 2012).

18

Social Legitimacy and Purposive Power: The End, the Means and the Consent of the People

GARETH DAVIES

I. INTRODUCTION

THERE IS A wide acceptance that the EU has a legitimacy problem, at least in the sense that its exercise of power does not enjoy a subjective public acceptance, or perception of legitimacy, appropriate to the scope and extent of that power.[1] Many solutions have been suggested, either involving changes to the structure or working of the EU, or putting forward reasons why the perceptions of the public are misguided and deserve to be rethought. However, this chapter argues that a structural cause of the legitimacy problem has been neglected: the purposive way that EU powers are conferred and defined. This style of conferral has the consequence that it condemns EU law and politics to instrumentality: the pursuit of narrowly defined functional goals, in which other purposes are rendered marginal, at worst illegitimate, or at the very least subordinate to the functional ideals. An important consequence is that politics and democracy cannot take root within the EU, for these imply the possibility of choice between different directions and priorities, and that choice is constitutionally denied.

If political process is not to give the EU legitimacy, then one must look to substance. Laws removed from politics can still win acceptance where they express something which speaks to enough people in a profound enough way that contestation is not needed for legitimacy: that is the saving of constitutions. This is law not just as instrument, but as expression.[2] However, precisely such expressive quality is what EU law lacks. The breadth of vision, the symbolism and the communication

---

[1] Eg R Bellamy and D Castiglione, 'Legitimizing the Euro-Polity and Its Regime: The Normative Turn in EU Studies' (2003) 2 *European Journal of Political Theory* 1; F Scharpf, *Governing in Europe: Effective and Democratic?* (Oxford, Oxford University Press, 1999); G de Búrca, 'The Quest for Legitimacy in the European Union' (1996) 59 *Modern Law Review* 349.
[2] CR Sunstein, 'On the Expressive Function of Law' (1995) 144 *University of Pennsylvania Law Review* 2021; W van der Burg, 'The Expressive and Communicative Functions of Law, Especially with Regard to Moral Issues' (2001) 20 *Law and Philosophy* 31; B Tamanaha, *Law As Means to an End; Threat to the Rule of Law* (Cambridge, Cambridge University Press, 2006).

of values and social norms which can put law above conflict are not achieved when technical rules focus on the pursuit of narrow economic goals.

None of this would matter so much if the EU was but a technical regulator of technical issues, but it is now far bigger than that. Its laws address affectively charged areas of society, such the welfare state, criminal law, immigration and redistribution via the state: areas where passionately held values and beliefs are involved.[3] To exclude both politics and expressivity from the regulation of these fields is to alienate the citizen almost completely.

Nor is the problem confined to EU law. The factor perhaps most threatening to the legitimacy of the EU today is the way that it constrains Member States in its instrumental embrace.[4] The breadth and intensity of EU law is such that states' duties of compliance often deprive them too of the possibility to create non-instrumental, or more-than-instrumental, law, and also make domestic politics increasingly marginal. It still exists, vibrantly so, but the capacity for debate exceeds in many areas the capacity to offer change, inevitably leading to public disaffection. Europeans are being deprived of the chance of responsive expressive government on any level, with a consequent reduction in the legitimacy of law as such.[5]

Is this a problem of justice? This chapter does not offer, nor choose, a theory of justice, and so it must leave that question open. However, the harm that it tries to expose is to the capacity of Europeans collectively to express themselves, determine their environment and their future, and feel recognised and at ease within their systems of government. These are subjective human harms, whose price is in happiness. Because this harm is the product of laws, working according to their own terms, adherents of some formal views of justice might reject its applicability—as Jiří Přibáň's chapter in this volume makes clear.[6] But for others, who share Přibáň's view that 'the problem of political justice is a problem of legitimacy. It is, therefore, inseparable from local, national, supranational and global issues of political democracy and functionality'[7] then the constraining of democracy by EU law will be self-evidently intertwined with the justice of the EU.

Whichever frame is chosen—justice, democracy, legitimacy or happiness—the questions motivating this chapter are concrete ones: how could things be different? What should be done? The inability of the EU in its current form to create law which responds to human beings in their complexity suggests, in answer to these, that either the nature of EU power should be changed, or it should be limited, or its relationship with national law should be rethought. The underlying question is how the functional and the affective can be brought into a better balance in the regulation of the lives of Europeans. Between the rock of political integration and the hard place of fewer EU competences, is there a third way where more can be achieved, but differently, using a different logic of power?

---

[3] The terminology is borrowed from the current 'affective turn' in social science: PT Clough and J Halley (eds), *The Affective Turn: Theorizing the Social* (Durham, NC, Duke University Press, 2007).
[4] Scharpf, *Governing in Europe*, n 1 above; F de Witte, 'Transnational Solidarity and the Mediation of Conflicts of Justice in Europe' (2012) 18 *European Law Journal* 694.
[5] Tamanaha, *Law As Means*, n 2 above.
[6] J Přibáň, 'The Evolving Idea of Political Justice in the EU: From Substantive Deficits to the Systemic Contingency of European Society' in this volume, 193.
[7] ibid.

The chapter is structured as follows: Section II provides a description of how this chapter fits in with the wider debate about legitimacy. Section III explains the expressive role of law in more detail: the ways that law is important in society beyond its immediate goals. Section IV explains more fully why EU law is unable to fulfil this expressive function, how this limits its capacity to win public acceptance, and why its conferred powers exclude politics, democracy, and ultimately legitimacy. Section V then considers how the EU came to this point and the broader logic of power allocation between the Member States and EU. A conclusion considers the future beyond instrumentalism.

II. LEGITIMACY: SUBSTANCE, PROCESS AND EMOTION

The legitimacy under discussion in this chapter is social legitimacy—the subjective acceptance of a government or legal system as legitimate by the public.[8] The scholarly discussion of EU legitimacy is however wider than this.[9] Some research focuses on technical aspects of law or institutions, for example on rules governing accountability, judicial review or transparency. These are all important, but no more than contributory to the social legitimacy of the EU as a whole. Indeed, discussion of these issues in legitimacy terms risks elevating 'best practice' in the eyes of academic experts to the status of constitutive of legitimacy as such, an irony in an EU where expert rule is itself a central controversy.

However, the majority of scholars concerned with public acceptance of the EU see a need for a better representation of interests in EU law, corresponding more closely to the concerns of the public, and more openly debated, and propose various mechanisms for achieving this; broadly speaking they are concerned with using politics to supply legitimacy.[10] Within this frame one may put the scholarship on the democratic deficit, and critical analyses of the working of the European Parliament, the legislative process and political parties at EU level.

Representation of interests and open contestation are also central to much recent legal work. Here the most common criticism of the Court of Justice, and of EU law, is that it is too narrow, and underplays social concerns, whose tension with the economic should not be denied.[11] It is also common to read the suggestion that states should enjoy greater powers of derogation, greater protection for their domestic

---

[8] A Føllesdal, 'Legitimacy Theories of the European Union' (2004) *ARENA Working Papers* WP 04/15.
[9] ibid.
[10] See, eg, n 1 above; VA Schmidt, 'The European Union in Search of Political Identity and Legitimacy: Is More Politics the Answer?' (2010) *EIF Working Papers* No 05/2010; Føllesdal, 'Legitimacy Theories', n 8 above; A Føllesdal and S Hix, 'Why There is a Democratic Deficit in the EU: A Response to Majone and Moravcsik' (2006) 44 *Journal of Common Market Studies* 533; *cf* A Moravcsik, 'In Defence of the "Democratic Deficit": Reassessing Legitimacy in the European Union' (2002) 40 *Journal of Common Market Studies* 603; A Menon and S Weatherill, 'Transnational Legitimacy in a Globalizing World: How the EU Rescues Its States' (2008) 31 *West European Politics* 397.
[11] A Somek, 'Solidarity Decomposed: Being and Time in European Citizenship' (2007) 32 *European Law Review* 787; M Everson and C Joerges, 'Reconfiguring the Politics–Law Relationship in the Integration Project through Conflicts–Law Constitutionalism' (2012) 18 *European Law Journal* 644; de Witte, 'Transnational Solidarity', n 4 above.

institutions and policies.[12] This is echoed in the constitutional pluralism discussion, where the normative suggestion is ever present that national supreme courts offer a desirable balance to the Court of Justice, being the voice of national concerns to its voice of integration.[13] Joerges has offered a variation on this theme, with his conflict-of-law analysis of EU law, which again centres on the need to give more space to non-integration non-EU policies and interests, and to bring the political into the law.[14] All of these perspectives and scholars fit within a broader trend to argue that the conflicts of interest within EU law need to be made more explicit, since only through admitting that interests are opposed is the possibility created for an adequate compromise.[15]

This chapter builds on that scholarship, accepting its themes of re-politicisation and acceptance of conflict. However, it also aims to add something, which it is suggested has been lacking: an explanation of how these ingredients, so necessary to legitimacy, are structurally prevented from blossoming by structural features of the EU. In particular, it is argued that the style of the EU's conferred powers stands in the way of the politics and contestation which legitimacy demands, so that the critiques made in the scholarship above run the risk of missing the point: they call for what is currently constitutionally impossible. Thanks to the EU's structural commitment to defined purposes, meaningful internal contestation is prevented, and this makes an agenda for more politics unrealistic, unless it comes with a readiness to reconsider the very foundations of EU law.

The chapter also builds on the calls above for better and wider representation of interests, but tries to take this challenge beyond procedure to substance: which interests, and why are they not represented now? The chapter suggests that answering this question requires attention to the role of experts in the EU, and the distinctive language and methods that they bring. The EU's commitment to expertise—a corollary of its purposiveness—denies voice to subtle and human concerns, rendering its politics unsatisfying and incomplete. In short, the EU is designed in a way suited to expert negotiation towards concrete goals, not the open contestation about the things that matter to society which legitimacy needs.

These arguments are in many ways a translation of the concerns raised by Koskenniemi about international law.[16] He speaks of fragmentation to capture the way international law has become the domain of purposive technocrats, and he argues that an approach to international law which was originally intended to give

---

[12] Everson and Joerges, 'Reconfiguring', n 11 above; de Witte, 'Transnational Solidarity', n 4 above; M Dawson and F de Witte, 'Constitutional Balance in the EU After the Euro-Crisis' (2013) 76 *Modern Law Review* 817.
[13] For an overview see contributions to J Komárek and M Avbelj (eds), *Constitutional Pluralism in the European Union and Beyond* (Oxford, Hart Publishing, 2012).
[14] C Joerges, 'Conflicts–Law Constitutionalism: Ambitions and Problems' (2012) ZenTra Working Papers in Transnational Studies 10/2012; Everson and Joerges, 'Reconfiguring', n 11 above. Also, de Witte, 'Transnational Solidarity', n 4 above.
[15] D Chalmers, 'The European Redistributive State and a European Law of Struggle' (2012) 18 *European Law Journal* 667; M Dani, 'Rehabilitating Social Conflicts in European Public Law' (2012) 18 *European Law Journal* 621; de Witte, 'Transnational Solidarity', n 4 above; Everson and Joerges, 'Reconfiguring', n 11 above.
[16] M Koskenniemi, 'The Fate of Public International Law: Between Technique and Politics' (2007) 70 *Modern Law Review* 1.

it legitimacy by putting it above politics now has the opposite effect. This politics-denying international law has spread to the point where it threatens to strangle national politics, and as a consequence international law is seen as increasingly problematic itself, with a consequent decrease in its influence and political force.[17]

That argument has not been widely heard within EU law, perhaps because Koskenniemi's primary concern was that international law itself was being weakened by its reliance on experts and narrow goals. Within the EU the role of victim has usually been claimed by the Member States protesting against the indignities they suffer at the hands of rampant EU law. To express concern about the fragility of EU law would until recently have seemed unnecessary. Yet, post-crisis, the debate about what the EU is and should be has become much more fundamental, and to ask whether it is a victim of its own technocratic success and whether it will survive without radical change has become a more plausible and urgent question. The robust legal structure of the EU kept concerns akin to Koskenniemi's at bay for some time, but they may finally have come home.

III. THE EXPRESSIVE ROLE OF LAW

Most laws, and certainly all EU laws, have an immediate and explicit goal to which they are intended to contribute. They are adopted for a reason, a purpose. Their role in achieving that immediate goal may be described as their instrumental role. However, this instrumental role is not all that laws do, and not their only consequence for society. Laws also affect the way people feel about their fellow citizens, and about their government, and about their society generally, and can help create a sense of community and collective identity.[18] They do this partly by being understood not just as tools, but as statements, as expression of values and preferences which individuals hold dear, and which they would like to believe are shared by those around them.[19] A law can be a form of shared credo.

For some laws, such as human rights or non-discrimination rules or core constitutional principles, this expressive role may be both important and evident. These are easily understood as statements about who we are, where we collectively come from, and who we wish to be. However, for more mundane rules, and for economic law, an expressive role will be less immediately apparent and harder to project. Yet even the most functionally oriented or materialist rule of law could be a value bearer, a statement with a deeper understood meaning, if it is seen to be a part of a broader vision of society and of life.[20] The good life has its practical side, and the good society must function, and if the connection is apparent then the merely

---

[17] See similarly E Benvenisti and GW Downs, 'The Empire's New Clothes: Political Economy and the Fragmentation of International Law' (2007) 60 *Stanford Law Review* 595.
[18] See U Haltern, 'Pathos and Patina: The Failure and Promise of Constitutionalism in the European Imagination' (2003) 9 *European Law Journal* 14.
[19] Sunstein, 'On the Expressive', n 2 above; van der Burg, 'The Expressive', n 2 above.
[20] See on this issue in the specifically EU context: F de Witte, 'Sex, Drugs & EU Law: The Recognition of Moral, Ethical and Cultural Diversity in EU Law' (2013) 50 *Common Market Law Review* (forthcoming); JHH Weiler, 'In the Face of Crisis: Input Legitimacy, Output Legitimacy and the Political Messianism of European Integration' (2012) 34 *Journal of European Integration* 825.

functional is elevated to more-than-functional by association. Public commitment to a humble rule may arise where it is perceived in such a context.

Such perceptions could arise from a deep understanding or analysis of the machinery of society and law—a respect for every tiny cog in the machine. However, such an understanding is largely the privilege of the experts of each field. Law may also be seen as carrying deeper statements by virtue of its age: time gives dignity to rules and institutions, and often makes them seem important and precious. Indeed, a connection with the past is one of the very values that laws may express and protect, and which may inspire commitment to them. However, perhaps the most obvious way in which an apparently instrumental rule acquires an expressive role is through politics and debate—where law makers describe it in such terms, and sell it to the public in this way. In a national democracy such as those found in the Member States politicians promote their agendas not only in terms of immediate instrumentality, but in terms of a wider, deeper normative vision which the rules are claimed to support, embody and sustain. This, as well as instrumentality, is the stuff of politics, persuasion of the public, acceptance and ultimately legitimacy.

It may be tempting to dismiss such expressivity as mere sentiment, as a deceptive distraction from law's true effects. However, there are two reasons why expressivity matters. One is that political participation is manifestly influenced by identity, a sense of community and values and not merely by calculations of material or concrete self-interest.[21] Indeed, such calculations are not practically possible for citizens or voters, so broader perceptions of ideology and value-community are a rational part of political choice.[22] The messages that laws send are part of what influences such choice and therefore help determine the instrumental direction that regulation will take. Law's capacity to express facilitates, and may sometimes be a precondition for, its capacity to function.[23]

The second reason is that expression has its own value. While it may be hard to measure, and may not yet have been measured, it is not implausible to suggest that where laws are perceived to respond to the people, to recognise them in their emotional complexity, and reflect their values, then, by making individuals feel both connected and recognised, this adds to the well-being of society.[24] There seems no reason to think that an exclusive legal focus on narrow functional goals, to the exclusion of symbolic or expressive considerations, would necessarily lead to the happiest society.[25] Yet perhaps this is the wrong thought-experiment, since in fact

---

[21] L Hooghe and G Marks, 'Does Identity or Economic Rationality Drive Public Opinion on European Integration?' (2004) 37 *Political Science and Politics* 415; L Hooghe and G Marks, 'Calculation, Community and Cues: Public Opinion on European Integration' (2005) 6 *European Union Politics* 419; D Miller, *On Nationality* (Oxford, Oxford University Press, 1995); *cf* J Habermas, 'Citizenship and National Identity: Some Reflections on the Future of Europe' (1992) 12 *Praxis International* 1.

[22] E Jones, 'Output Legitimacy and the Global Financial Crisis: Perceptions Matter' (2009) 47 *Journal of Common Market Studies* 1085.

[23] Sunstein, 'On the Expressive', n 2 above.

[24] C Taylor, 'The Politics of Recognition' in C Taylor (ed), *Multiculturalism: Examining the Politics of Recognition* (Princeton, NJ, Princeton University Press, 1994).

[25] P Dolan, T Peasgood and M White, 'Do We Really Know What Makes Us Happy? A Review of Economic Literature on Factors Associated with Subjective Well-Being' (2008) 29 *Journal of Economic Psychology* 94.

such a situation is impossible. Expressivity may be perceived whether or not it was intended. Even the most coldly instrumental laws will send a perceived message, but that message will be that considerations beyond function are illegitimate, that all values of importance are embodied in instrumentality, that human and social oddities do not deserve to be recognised.[26] There is an aesthetic even to the denial of aesthetics.[27] However, it is not an aesthetic that will appeal to many, and the expressivity of pure instrumentalism is likely to be one that alienates and angers, rather than bonds or comforts. It says, among other things, that the rule maker has no obligation to respond to the particularities of those he rules.

IV. CONFERRAL, FUNCTIONAL POWERS AND THE EU'S INSTRUMENTAL ORIENTATION

The European Union is a creature of conferred power. Those powers are often conferred in what may be called a purposive way. By this is meant that the powers are defined in terms of the goals to be achieved, such as the protection of the environment, or, most notably, the creation of a single market. The EU then has, subject to certain limits, the power to take the measures necessary to achieve these goals.[28]

The fact that the EU only has the powers conferred to it is conventionally seen as a constitutional safeguard which contributes to the legitimacy of EU action, and of the EU as a whole, by preventing it from growing uncontrolledly and dominating the Member States. Within its sphere it may be supreme, but its sphere, even if large, is limited, goes the logic.

However, to focus on the fact that the EU only has conferred powers, while ignoring the way in which those powers are conferred is to miss the real issue: how exactly EU and national competences interact. The choice to entrust powers to the EU in a distinctive, purposive, way has far-reaching consequences for the way the EU and the Member States function, consequences which threaten the social legitimacy of law in Europe. Not only does it pre-empt choices about the direction of policy, and so exclude politics, but it condemns the EU to a narrowly instrumental way of thinking, that way of thinking is increasingly imposed also on the Member States, and the consequence is that interests peripheral to the goal in

---

[26] U Haltern, 'On Finality' in A von Bogdandy and J Bast (eds), *Principles of European Constitutional Law* (Oxford, Hart Publishing, 2007) 690–91: 'there seemed to be a cold modernist void, a spiritual absence at the heart of the European integration project'.

[27] J Simons, 'Democratic Aesthetics' (2009) 50 *Culture, Theory and Critique* 1.

[28] See Art 114 of the Consolidated version of the Treaty on the Functioning of the European Union [2012] OJ C326/47 (TFEU); A von Bogdandy and J Bast, 'The European Union's Vertical Order of Competences: The Current Law and Proposals for Its Reform' (2002) 39 *Common Market Law Review* 227; I Govaere, 'The Future Direction of the EU Internal Market: On Vested Values and Fashionable Modernism' (2009) 16 *Columbia Journal of European Law* 67; G Davies, 'Subsidiarity: The Wrong Idea, in the Wrong Place, at the Wrong Time' (2006) 43 *Common Market Law Review* 63; S Weatherill, 'The Limits of Legislative Harmonisation Ten Years After *Tobacco Advertising*: How the Court's Case Law Has Become a Drafting Guide' (2011) 12 *German Law Journal* 828, 843; A Somek, *Individualism: An Essay on the Authority of the European Union* (Oxford, Oxford University Press, 2008).

question—although not peripheral to society—are excluded from the law-making process, and ultimately also from adjudication of that law. These interests may be concrete, but they include also the social interest in a law which expresses and binds, and the social interest in law as experiment. Essentially a style of narrow, technical regulation, suitable for certain technical fields, has been extended far beyond these, to socially and humanly complex areas of law where it does not fit. The breadth and power of EU law has come to exceed its legislative imagination.

The following subsections try to show the reality of these problems in four important contexts: the EU legislative process, EU technical regulation, the adjudication of the Court of Justice, and the framing of EU law by the institutions.

A. The Way Law is Made

All EU legislation must have a legal base, an article in one of the treaties which provides authority for the making of that legislation. Such articles are often worded in terms of purposes to be achieved, and grant the EU the power to adopt legislation serving that end.[29] This is true of the most important legal bases in the EU's most impactful policy field, the Internal Market, as well as of the controversial and wide-ranging Article 352 of the Treaty on the Functioning of the European Union (TFEU).[30] The validity of the legislation adopted using these legal bases then turns on whether it genuinely pursues that specific purpose, or not.[31] Other interests may be taken into account—for example, rules aiming at liberalising trade may be drawn up in a way taking account of environmental or social concerns—but the role of such broader concerns is confined to addressing externalities resulting from the pursuit of the primary legislative goal. The peripheral interests may not provide a reason in themselves for the law, however admirable and important they may be.[32] Moreover, these constraints are not merely abstract. The Court has determined that both the claimed purpose of the measure and the claimed need to take account of other interests must be objectively demonstrable, in order to make judicial supervision possible.[33] Each piece of EU legislation must be a tool for a specific and pre-defined purpose.

The contrast is with the law-making process in a national democracy, unconstrained by such principles of legal base. National law is the product of compromise between various standpoints, and may pursue multiple goals simultaneously. There may be no obviously 'correct' way of characterising it: some may consider that it primarily does X, while others think that its importance lies in effect Y. Law usually has complicated effects and can be described in many ways. The EU, however, must

---

[29] Eg Arts 113, 114 and 192 TFEU.
[30] Case C-376/98 *Federal Republic of Germany v European Parliament and Council of the European Union* [2000] ECR I-8419.
[31] Case C-376/98 *Germany v Parliament and Council* [2000] ECR I-8419; Govaere, 'The Future Direction', n 28 above.
[32] Case C-376/98 *Germany v Parliament and Council* [2000] ECR I-8419.
[33] ibid; Case C-405/07 P *Kingdom of the Netherlands v Commission of the European Communities* [2008] ECR I-8301.

keep its eye on a particular purposive ball, to the exclusion of others. Its functions are defined like those of an expert agency, employed just to think about very specific concerns and to achieve them without thinking any more widely than necessary.[34] To suggest that a piece of EU legislation is adopted for reasons other than those referred to in its legal base is to claim that it is invalid, unless those reasons are demonstrably subordinate and dependent ones, mere corollaries of its major goal.

That inevitably informs the way laws are written and proposed. The European Commission, highly aware of the legal framework within which it must work, drafts and presents laws not in terms of wider politics and public preferences, but as expert-approved objectively demonstrable contributions to concrete and specific policy goals.

The legislative process is then condemned to be similarly narrow, since the powers of the European Parliament are equally circumscribed by these competence constraints. The most fundamental political question—which goals the legislator should pursue—is removed from politics. There are no choices here. All that is left to debate is how the pre-defined goals should be achieved, and the extent to which they should be achieved. This is an impoverished political process, which does not, and cannot, represent all the views and interests at stake. Since the purposes of the EU include such contested and controversial matters as ever more open markets,[35] the inability to challenge this reveals the EU legislative process to have little to do with a conventional understanding of representative law making.

This is why politics cannot take root within the EU as currently constituted: because politics implies the possibility for choices between different directions, and that possibility is precisely what the limits to EU powers take away.[36] For a law maker to stand up and propose a law that comes from a wider and deeper normative vision is to invite ridicule or legal challenge.

That is not to say that such visions do not exist. There is certainly political speech within and around the EU that puts forward a full-service vision of Europe, speaking of it not just as an expert regulator of transnational externalities but as an enterprise in which identity, unity, humanity, autonomy and much more are central to its purposes and acts. However, such rhetoric has notably failed to inspire a great public connection with Europe, and one reason may be suggested in the fact that any person speaking in this way is vulnerable to one of two criticisms. Either, if they are close to power, the suspicion arises that they are seeking to avoid limitations on their competence. When they speak of the way the EU should address so many important things, the lawyer at least wants to cry out 'but you can't do that: you have no competence!' If they are outside the inner circle of law makers, then the same rhetoric invites instead the criticism that it is all hot air, empty words: 'what fool paints a picture of something he is prohibited from pursuing?' To the informed viewer, such speech is either dishonest, or utopian.

---

[34] R Dehousse, 'European Institutional Architecture After Amsterdam: Parliamentary System or Regulatory Structure?' (1998) *EUI Working Papers* RSC No 98/11.
[35] See Arts 26 and 114 TFEU; Case C-376/98 *Germany v Parliament and Council* [2000] ECR I-8419.
[36] JS Dryzek, *Discursive Democracy: Politics, Policy, and Political Science* (Cambridge, Cambridge University Press, 1990).

B. Technical Regulation

The focus on immediate purposes is fertile ground for experts, whose role is most apparent where EU law has directly to do with the scientific and the economic. The safety of food, medicine and genetically modified organisms (GMOs) is the domain of specialist scientists, while the regulation of the Internal Market has become an increasingly direct product of applied economics. The former fields are widely criticised for their alleged suppression of value choices, while the latter field is criticised for an alleged implicit acceptance of a particular political bias.[37] However, the suggestion here is that neither criticism quite hits the mark. In neither field is there reason to think that the law is particularly bad when taken on its own terms. If one wants a market without boundaries and food that doesn't make us sick, then, as Majone has in the past suggested, these experts are probably just as good, perhaps better, than any alternative source of regulation would be.[38] It is not that the definitions of 'safe' or 'free trade' are unjustifiable, nor that they are more incompetently pursued than we have a right to expect. Rather, the major problem with these legal fields is that safety and free trade are not the only factors or purposes that ought to be taken into account in making the laws in questions. Food is not just a source of energy, but also a vehicle of culture, emotion and value. A food safety law that determines the kind of food we can buy and sell and eat without taking these things into account is almost inevitably welfare decreasing: it tramples on our profoundly subjective preferences. Yet a food safety law which did set out to create a framework which was a bargain between considerations of risk, tradition, culture, religion and no doubt other factors, would be invalid: it would go beyond the task entrusted to the regulator, unless the non-safety factors were only introduced in a marginal and compensatory way. However, that would almost make things worse; then the subordination of everything to the instrumental EU goal would be painfully apparent, rather than the compromise between diffuse but autonomous passions which we would expect of national law.

The argument is analogous and perhaps more persuasive in the context of the Internal Market. Here experts consider which kinds of rules can make trade between states easier and freer, and they calculate the financial benefits to parties and governments of this facilitation. They may do this imperfectly, but there is no reason to think that they do not meet the professional standards of their field. The real criticism is not of what they do, but of what they are asked to do: to pursue just one purpose. It has become quite apparent over the years that transnational economic freedom has consequences for the shape of the entire economy, and therefore of the state and society. Any measure regulating this field ought to be, again, a compromise between autonomous goals and interests. Instead, one is rendered fixed and non-negotiable, and others are admitted to the discussion only in a minor and subordinate way.

---

[37] M Kritikos, 'Traditional Risk Analysis and Releases of GMOs into the European Union: Space for Non-Scientific Factors' (2009) 44 *European Law Review* 405; C Joerges, 'The Law's Problems with the Governance of the Single European Market' in C Joerges and R Dehousse (eds), *Good Governance in Europe's Integrated Market* (Oxford, Oxford University Press, 2002).

[38] G Majone, 'The Regulatory State and Its Legitimacy Problems' (1999) 22(1) *West European Politics* 1.

The impact of this technocratic style of legislation on relatively concrete and identifiable interests, such as equality, mechanisms of redistribution, individual rights and certain institutions, is one of the major critiques of EU economic law. It is suggested that this is however often over-stated: Member States still have a considerable capacity to counter the 'neoliberal' side-effects of the EU, and to maintain social structures of a different ideological colour. The demise of the welfare state, it may be commented, has been preached now for quite some time.[39] However, there is another critique, which is that a technical orientation towards law leads to over-emphasis on its immediate instrumentality, and under-emphasis on its wider expressive role. National laws and institutions are harmonised away, or destabilised by new EU rules, without full weight being given to their non-instrumental function. In parallel, debate around the new EU laws, being framed by purpose and by expert considerations, will also be unbalanced and narrow, with too much attention to the concrete and quantifiable interests that are easy for experts to address, and not enough attention to the wider role of law. Technocracy has no language and methods for measuring the expressive, so where a technocratic process is central the risk is that narrow instrumentality dominates.[40] Expressiveness, it was noted above, comes when a law is placed in wider context, linked to values and vision. That is more than can reasonably be expected of technical staff.

The tragedy of the EU is then that even if it is in fact doing good work— causing social and economic changes which people would, if presented differently, welcome—it adopts and presents its work from a perspective which is hostile to the life world of most Europeans, denying a place to many of the interests that they care about and values that they hold, failing to embed the worlds of market and science in the worlds of history, culture, identity and autonomy. Almost irrespective of the consequences of EU laws, the purposive narrowness from which they spring is doomed to deny them social legitimacy.

C. Adjudication

It is certainly the case that there is an absence of discussion of the expressive and symbolic value of national law in the case-law of the Court of Justice. Yet while this shows parallels with the legislative process, the dynamic is quite different. In the most impactful case-law it is usually the Treaty itself that is being applied, rather than legislation, so that the question of how and what kind of laws are made is not directly in issue. Rather, it is national law which is being tested for its compatibility with the Treaty, and it is that national law which is the primary object of judicial attention.

In many cases national law fails the test, whereupon it will be set aside, and often repealed or reformed. In order to come to such a conclusion the Court engages in a balancing of interests, and encourages the national judge to do so too. One might expect here that the instrumental, the expressive, the social, the symbolic,

---

[39] Scharpf, *Governing in Europe*, n 1 above.
[40] Dryzek, *Discursive Democracy*, n 36 above.

would all be weighed. Yet while concrete concerns are represented—even if the weight accorded to each may be a continuing subject of controversy—more subtle social consequences of the dismantling of a law or institution are almost entirely unaddressed in the case-law to date.[41]

Indeed, to judge from the cases and opinions of the Advocates General, which show little evidence of Member States arguing that the expressive, or symbolic, or broader social value of a law should be taken into account, one might be tempted to think that Member States are not used to this degree of self-reflection, and certainly not in the context of law suits. A contributing factor may be that the intellectual framework of EU law limits their approach: since they are defending their laws and institutions against the deconstructive effects of EU law they submit to the inclination to meet it on its own terms, and argue in the language of instrumental function. At any rate, law whose role in society is broad and complex is usually presented in narrowly instrumental terms.

However, the intention of national governments should not be central: expressivity does not just arise because law makers set out to express, but when law emerges from a vision, rather than from a narrow set of functional goals. The question is whether such a vision survives EU law, and the case-law raises the suggestion that the stringency of the EU's legal constraints and the strict need to comply with them suppresses precisely such a visionary capacity in the Member States, who are pushed to think in instrumental terms too.

The right balance between expressivity and instrumentalism is an inherently political question, since there is always a certain tension between them: instrumentality demeans the expressive role; the heart is subordinate to the head, the dream to the realistic. EU law stands in the way of Member States achieving this balance, by holding the sword of instrumental adjudication over their heads. It excludes expression not by confrontation, but by silence.

But if EU law is expressively weak, it is nevertheless not entirely without expressive value. The role of individual rights and freedoms in the Treaty has made much of the case-law into a series of very expressive parables about individuals being oppressed by inflexible or closed-minded Member States, and being rescued by the benignly firm hand of EU law.[42] These parables certainly have a strong appeal to the imagination of some, and the extent of their scholarly discussion, and the passion it often contains, evidences their expressive role and the way that they constitute, more than other EU law, a justifying expression of collective values, binding and uniting.

---

[41] See limited and largely dismissive remarks in Case C-148/02 *Carlos Garcia Avello v État belge* [2003] ECR I-11613; Case C-147/03 *Commission of the European Communities v Republic of Austria* [2005] ECR I-5969; Case 186/87 *Ian William Cowan v Trésor public* [1989] ECR 195.

[42] See, eg, Case C-184/99 *Rudy Grzelczyk v Centre public d'aide sociale d'Ottignies-Louvain-la-Neuve* [2001] ECR I-6193; Case C-413/99 *Baumbast and R v Secretary of State for the Home Department* [2002] ECR I-7091; Case C-85/96 *María Martínez Sala v Freistaat Bayern* [1998] ECR I-2691: Case C-200/02 *Kunqian Catherine Zhu and Man Lavette Chen v Secretary of State for the Home Department* [2004] ECR I-9925; Case C-34/09 *Gerardo Ruiz Zambrano v Office national de l'emploi (ONEm)* [2011] ECR I-1177.

However, what is expressed in this law is, sadly, not a vision of the majority, but of the minority.[43] The successful posing of individual freedom to move and live cross-border lives—to escape the bounds of the society into which one is born— even at the cost of institutions and systems, speaks to a small elite, but to much of the population is either an obscure and irrelevant self-indulgent fantasy, or actively threatening to the order upon which they perceive their well-being to depend. The Court takes a symbolic war to the heart of the Member States and the symbolism of these EU rights adds to their force as swords, without the symbolic and expressive importance of national laws being accepted as part of their shield. The only defence arguments which the case-law reveals to carry weight are instrumental ones: finance, immediate health and safety issues, direct institutional stability problems. What this case-law establishes—as clearly as the supremacy of EU law—is the supremacy of EU symbolism, as expressed in vague but legally powerful phrases such as 'the need for a certain degree of solidarity' or the 'fundamental freedoms' and 'destiny' of Europeans as EU citizens.[44] These, expressions quite divorced from text, can nevertheless have legal consequences, whereas the values and meanings carried by national institutions, expressing a more deeply rooted vision of society than the European one, apparently cannot. The Court could be said to have claimed an expressive monopoly.

D. Framing the Law: The Denial of Choice

A final problem of purposive competence is this: It gives us the language of certainty. Instrumental success as a condition for validity entails that law cannot be experimental, or tentative; it must be the correct, and therefore the only, way.[45] This language is both manifestly false by any empirical or rational measure, but also oppressive; in its denial of other perspectives or possibilities—coupled with its dishonesty—it has a dictatorial quality.[46] It alienates, and excludes, and adds to the affective defects of the functioning of the EU.[47] The combination of conferral and expertise provides incentives for parties—Commission, Council and ultimately the Court—to present legislation as inevitable, as compelled, as uncontroversial: to deny that there is a choice.[48] Within the framework of EU law, such an approach is legitimating. However, it marginalises both the citizen and the possibility for politics in the EU.[49]

---

[43] A Somek, 'From Workers to Migrants, from Distributive Justice to Inclusion: Exploring the Changing Social Democratic Imagination' (2012) 18 *European Law Journal* 711.

[44] Case C-184/99 *Grzelczyk* [2001] ECR I-6193; Case C-341/05 *Laval un Partneri Ltd v Svenska Byggnadsarbetareförbundet and Others* [2007] ECR I-11767.

[45] S Frerichs, 'False Promises? A Sociological Critique of the Behavioural Turn in Law and Economics' (2011) 34 *Journal of Consumer Policy* 289.

[46] ibid.

[47] Dani and Chalmers explore how alienation is fed by the exclusion of conflict, in which expertise plays an important role: Dani, 'Rehabilitating', n 15 above; D Chalmers, 'Introduction: The Conflicts of EU Law and the Conflicts in EU Law' (2012) 18 *European Law Journal* 607. Haltern focuses on how alienation results from instrumentalism: Haltern, 'Pathos', n 18 above.

[48] P Magnette, 'European Governance and Civic Participation: Beyond Elitist Citizenship?' (2003) 51 *Political Studies* 139.

[49] ibid.

V. THE POLITICAL CONTEXT OF INSTRUMENTALITY

While the instrumental orientation of EU law limits its capacity to inspire acceptance, let alone affection, this would not be a serious problem if the EU were an organisation of precise, not-too-broad, scope. There is always a role in government for expert agencies, whose legitimacy is derived indirectly from their political context, rather than from their direct connection to the people. A technocratic EU could be a legitimate EU if it were confined to technical fields. However, it has outgrown this coat—if it ever fitted—and reached the point where it regulates areas of significant expressive importance; public services, crime, immigration, as well as having profound structural effects on the organisation of the economy and society more generally. Now, of course, with the economic crisis, a new phase is being entered in which EU rules go to the very heart of the modern state, regulating the capacity and obligations of governments to tax and spend. These rules bite only when governments exceed certain limits, and in that sense work by deterrence as much as by immediate obligation. However, because a violation of the rules is a real possibility for many states, and the consequences are feared, the rules increasingly define the terms of domestic policy thinking in these fields.[50]

This highlights perhaps the greatest problem of EU instrumentality; its effect on Member States. Not only does it lack expressive or affective qualities on its own, but it increasingly denies Member States the choice to respond with sophistication to their electorates.[51] Their capacity to use and adopt law in anything other than a narrowly instrumental way is limited by the constraints of many branches of EU law—free movement, competition, budget rules, safety and social law, to name the most prominent examples. Since Member States must pass stringent EU legal tests in so many fields of law and policy, policy thinking and consequently rhetoric is increasingly confined to 'how do we achieve EU goals?'[52] Affectively important questions such as 'who are we and what do we want?' and 'what laws speak for us?' are excluded to a significant extent. When expressed, they are easily dismissed as peripheral to the goals of trade facilitation, budget control, compliance and implementation, which come from the EU and admit of no compromise. A discussion of national laws as more than decentralised tools of EU policy is often painfully irrelevant. The national legislator now has as its task, perhaps even its primary task, to ensure that the national community complies with the instrumental obligations of Europe. Self-expression and recognition are squeezed out. National politics ceases to be an affectively meaningful debate about society, but becomes a mere adjunct to expertise—at worst an irrelevance, at most a supervisory role.

To a certain extent, this situation arises as a consequence of design and intention. One can plausibly regard the EU in the context of a division of political functions. Member States take care of expression, symbolism and community, while the EU

---

[50] FW Scharpf, 'Monetary Union, Fiscal Crisis, and the Pre-Emption of Democracy' (2011) *MPIfG Discussion Papers* 11/11, 5; K Tuori, 'The European Financial Crisis—Constitutional Aspects and Implications' (2012) *EUI Working Papers* LAW2012/28.
[51] Scharpf, *Governing in Europe*, n 1 above; de Witte, 'Transnational Solidarity', n 4 above.
[52] L Azoulai, 'The "Retained Powers" Formula in the Case Law of the European Court of Justice: EU Law As Total Law?' (2011) 4(2) *European Journal of Legal Studies* 192.

provides expert regulation of transnational issues. It is a division that is not wholly illogical in the light of the nature of many transnational problems, which at the time of the founding of the EU could have been seen as not involving affectively or expressively laden policies. It is also an understandable division of functions given certain features of national politics: it is at least arguable that the symbolic and expressive are over-represented in national politics, and that states struggle, even now, to find space for their 'rational best interests'. In the national context, it may be the instrumental which is often the victim of the expressive. This could arise as a result of capture and far-from-perfect democracy within national political systems: the expressive could function as a useful mask for instrumental inadequacies. Thus the success of Member States at delivering identity, community and expressivity may comfortably sit alongside a relative lack of functional success. While this chapter argues for the importance of the expressive role of law, it does not claim that function therefore does not matter. Rather, the need is to see and use law as something that has many sides and consequences. If Member States have not been good at achieving an optimal balance, the outsourcing of the instrumental part, as part of an implicit deal that could be described as 'save us from ourselves' is understandable. Yet what was not envisaged by all—although perhaps by the European visionaries who always foresaw the ultimate need for political integration—was that the EU would come to impinge upon expressive space—occupying areas of law where expressivity matters—and yet be unable to deliver expressivity, unable to think beyond the instrumental.[53] It is a polity whose power has outgrown its emotional intelligence.

VI. CONCLUSION

Purposive competence has served well for many years to protect the EU from the affective storms of politics and allow it to continue its integrative mission in all weather conditions. Yet in a neatly tragic irony, the technique at the heart of this, the politics-denying blank-faced instrumentalism of the expert, has now defined it as an organisation unable to speak a humanly rich language, lacking the depth or stature to regulate holistically, and only capable of the pursuit of the concrete: insufficiently legitimate to take integration further, or even justify its current state.

Yet the search for a solution places Member States in a conflicted situation. To free the EU from its narrow purpose is necessary if its powers are to meet the standards of intelligence and legitimacy that we expect, but to allow it to pursue broader goals is to give it the power to eat even more sovereignty, and challenge the Member States on the last battlefield where they remain clearly supreme: the fight for the loyalty of the citizen. Precisely because a politically more profound EU would be more legitimate, it would also be more threatening to the Member States.

Is there no third way between giving the EU political depth and breadth—and so effectively creating a widely undesired political union—or rescuing its legitimacy by

---

[53] On self-undermining modernity, however, see U Beck, W Bonss and C Lau, 'The Theory of Reflexive Modernization: Problematic, Hypotheses and Research Programme' (2003) 20 *Theory Culture Society* 1.

reducing its scope and thereby sacrificing policy goals? The most desirable outcome is not more or fewer powers, but a different way of defining and using them, so that the policy goals of the EU relate to those of the Member States without subordinating them.

This question, in various forms, has long occupied EU constitutional lawyers, without success. Neither subsidiarity, nor the role created for national parliaments, nor even the outer limits laid down by national constitutional courts have provided a sense that EU power is adequately defined and contained. EU law has not been able to police itself.

What is needed is a form of EU power in which it takes full account of Member States' interests without taking them over. Social and expressive concerns must be at the heart of EU law making, without the EU having ownership of them. What this suggests is that Member States must be more integrated into the EU, and that EU policy should be designed around Member States as they are, rather than as the EU would like them to be: bring us your institutions, and we will design an open Europe around them.[54] That is a reversal of the current situation, which is: we will give you a free trade area, and you will change to fit it.

The hard practical techniques for achieving this are another project. However, one answer may be less law and more attention to softer ways of achieving policy goals. Seduction often wins more than command, and many laws may bring a price in hostility to the EU which is higher than their immediate instrumental profit. Loyalty to the 'Community method' of legal harmonisation may be betrayal of the Union goals of openness and integration.[55]

At any rate, the current model of an isolated, instrumental EU, dominating the Member States, carries a price that is very high. Not only is the EU condemned to disaffection, but the Member States are reduced to the status of permanent victims. That this is the result of their own collective choice reveals the EU to be a tool for infantilisation. Division of functions between the levels of government has become avoidance of responsibility on both sides rather than constructive cooperation.

Indeed, if there is one fundamental criticism of the way in which power is defined and used it is that it is riddled with dishonesty—it is a process in which Member States help but also harm themselves and then say that they had no choice. The historical roots of this fear of one's own power are well-known. Europe was supposed to be, among other things, a form of self-limitation.[56] However, self-limitation is also limitation of the imagination, and ultimately impairs the ability to create and to act, and, in a final irony, may cause Europe to fail even the most instrumental test of success.

---

[54] C Joerges and M Weimer, 'A Crisis of Executive Managerialism in the EU: No Alternative?' (2012) *Maastricht Faculty of Law Working Papers* 2012/7.
[55] Everson and Joerges, 'Reconfiguring', n 11 above.
[56] Haltern, 'Pathos', n 18 above; J-W Müller, *Contesting Democracy: Political Ideas in Twentieth-Century Europe* (New Haven, CT, Yale University Press, 2011).

Part Four

19

Social Justice in the European Union: The Puzzles of Solidarity, Reciprocity and Choice

JURI VIEHOFF AND KALYPSO NICOLAÏDIS

I. INTRODUCTION

WHAT HAVE WE learned about social justice from the Eurozone crisis? One lesson, we believe, is that there are limits to apprehending social justice between European peoples simply as enlightened mutual advantage, when, in Brian Barry's apt formulation, 'justice is the name we give to the constraints on themselves that rational self-interested people would agree to as the minimum price that has to be paid in order to obtain the cooperation of others'.[1] But if, in fact, social justice in the European context is not reducible to even a sophisticated and indirect pursuit of self-interest then what exactly is it supposed to be? One alternative to think about justice is common and indeed common sense: one starts by asking how much Europeans stand to gain collectively from social cooperation relative to a word where they did not cooperate, and one then suggests principles for fairly distributing the social surplus they have created together, taking into account such things as how much each Member State and its citizens has given up or contributed, or how costly participation in the EU has been. Brian Barry called this common sense view justice as reciprocity. It is a 'hybrid theory of justice' because it combines *justice as mutual advantage* with *justice as impartiality*.[2]

Why do we mention Barry's insights as a starting point for a discussion of social justice in the EU? We think that his discussion, in particular his analysis of justice as reciprocity can help shed light on some of the current positions that prevail in both academic and popular intellectual discussions. In particular, it can help illuminate some of the challenges we face when attempting to construct a theory of social justice for the context of the EU compared to more familiar contexts. More tentatively, we suggest that the EU is (ever so slowly) transforming itself from a social practice whose normative basis can be captured adequately in terms of intuitions about mutual advantage into an institutional arrangement to which more demanding

---

[1] B Barry, *Theories of Justice* (Los Angeles, CA, University of California Press, 1989) 7.
[2] B Barry, *Justice As Impartiality* (Oxford, Oxford University Press, 1995) 46.

principles of socio-economic justice apply. So while remaining, for the time being, a *demoi*cracy—a union of political communities who govern together but not as one—sustaining togetherness and fairness in this union calls for increasingly demanding principles of social justice.[3]

In this chapter, we do not pursue the challenging task of formulating such principles. More modestly, we lay out systematically some of the building blocks that need to be developed and some of the core questions that need to be answered for such an account of social justice in the EU to be persuasive. In order to better understand its particular normative context, we compare and contrast the EU to two domains of political philosophy in which questions of substantive justice have been hotly debated, namely first, the 'standard' case of a closed society for which received theories of socio-economic justice such as John Rawls's *A Theory of Justice* were conceived and, second, more recent debates concerning global justice. Neither our exercise in comparison, nor the topics we single out for future research in the EU context have any claim to exhaust the myriad of differences that exist between, on the one hand, the EU as an institution and any contemporary modern state and, on the other hand, the EU and the global institutional architecture. Our goal is merely to sharpen the focus on those normative differences most relevant to the issues of social justice, that is, those features that will make further investigations of 'EU justice' interestingly different from the more well-trodden paths of domestic and global debates.

But before we venture into the intricacies of different ways of thinking about social justice, we feel the need to briefly comment on the worry that developing an account of justice for the EU might produce the deeply problematic effect of pre-empting and delegitimising its—already weak—process of democratic deliberation.[4] We share the basic liberal commitment that the wielding of coercive political power, including the kind of public power exercised by the EU, can only be rendered legitimate when it operates against the background of political procedures that express the free and equal status of participants. And such procedures must be democratic ones. However, we do not think that a fundamental commitment to this principle of liberal legitimacy stands in the way of developing and refining accounts of social justice for the EU. Quite to the contrary, the task involved in theorising justice is a necessary one that complements democratic legitimacy. Our point here is conceptual rather than substantive: whereas the reflection on adequate principles of legitimacy helps us to recognise the procedures through which political decisions ought to be made—namely democratically—an account of social and distributive justice helps us work out in a systematic fashion to what end political power should be exercised. At the same time, we do not believe that these ends ought to

---

[3] K Nicolaïdis, 'The New Constitution As European "*Demoi*-cracy"?' (2004) 7 *Critical Review of International Social and Political Philosophy* 76; K Nicolaïdis, 'The Idea of European *Demoi*-cracy' in J Dicksonand P Eleftheriadis (eds), *Philosophical Foundations of European Union Law* (Oxford, Oxford University Press, 2012); K Nicolaïdis, 'European *Demoi*cracy and Its Crisis' (2013) 51 *Journal of Common Market Studies* 351.

[4] This is in fact Agustín Menédez's worry, formulated in the opening paragraphs of his contribution to this volume: 'Justice has been deployed as a rhetorical device with the help of which to pre-empt, to set aside or to hollow out democratic politics' (this volume, 137, at 138).

be invoked to bypass the democratic process but rather as a (contested) referent for the transnational democratic debate in Europe. Seen in this light, different accounts of social justice provide indispensable philosophical groundwork precisely for those citizens jointly deliberating about how to democratically create their political order in the common good, whether on a national, supranational or global level.[5]

The structure of this chapter is as follows: First, we explain in more detail what we (and philosophers in the liberal egalitarian tradition of John Rawls and Brian Barry) understand to be the content of domestic principles of social and economic justice, and we suggest why some people may think that this kind of justice only applies within states. This latter point refers to what has often been called the *grounds* of social justice. Subsequently, we focus on three aspects in respect of which the EU interestingly differs from both the contemporary nation state and the global sphere to demonstrate that the EU provides a fertile testing ground for hybrid theories of justice. The first claim we analyse is the position that justice requires solidarity, and that therefore substantive (especially: distributive economic) justice could not be realised amongst EU citizens because solidarity is lacking between them. This issue raises important questions about the sociological prerequisites of substantive social justice, and the EU provides a unique intermediate case between domestic and global conditions in terms of the forms of solidarity that currently exist or plausibly could exist. Second, we look at the claim that social justice in the EU context is different because the goods that ought to be distributed as a matter of reciprocity amongst citizens domestically is very different from those that we find amongst EU citizens. Conceiving of justice as fair reciprocity raises interesting questions about the content of such principles, and again, the EU with its unique features provides an interesting example. Third, we assess the view that the EU could not necessitate substantive requirements of social justice because it is ultimately a voluntary association amongst states. Although we make some substantive arguments about the promise that each of these areas of philosophical analysis bear, the general aim of this chapter is much more exploratory than conclusive: we seek to work out what renders the EU a particularly interesting object to consider questions of social justice, not to 'solve' these questions by advancing a definitive theory.

II. DOMESTIC SOCIAL JUSTICE: CONTENT AND GROUNDS

Let us begin by looking at justice in the 'standard case', the contemporary nation state: liberal theories of social justice take for granted that states realise social justice only when they serve certain functions and bring about certain distributions of justice-relevant goods amongst those subject to their authority.[6] Setting up the issue of social justice in this way raises two important questions: First, in terms of what

---

[5] The argument sketched here is of course Rawls's. See, eg, J Rawls, *Justice As Fairness: A Restatement* (Cambridge, MA, Belknap Press of Harvard University Press, 2001).

[6] We exclude in our discussion here the important issues of rectificatory and criminal justice as well as inter-generational justice. For an illuminating discussion of the application of these kinds of justice to the EU as an institution, see A Williams, 'The Problem(s) of Justice in the European Union' in this volume, 33.

goods must we measure the outcomes that basic institutions bring about? Second, what kinds of distributions should basic institutions bring about? Aside from anarchists who deny that state institutions could ever be just, nearly everybody agrees that as far as the first question is concerned, one necessary feature is that basic institutions provide certain public goods, for example, national defence, policing, the rule of law, healthy environments and other non-rival goods which it is assumed improves all participants' lives. It is an intrinsic feature of these core public goods that when a state provides them, it dispenses them (in some respect) equally to all. But from a liberal–egalitarian perspective, justice also includes the realisation of a just distribution of private (excludable) benefits.[7]

Following John Rawls, we understand the relevant primary social goods to include rights, liberties, opportunities, income and wealth and social bases of self-respect.[8] The enumeration may appear daunting, but we can exclude from redistributive considerations the 'constitutional essentials' among those, for example, the basic liberties understood as those civil and political rights normally guaranteed by a society's legal and political order and focus on 'basic justice', that is, what constitutes a just distribution of resources and opportunities to attain positions of advantage in the economic sphere.[9] What then ought to be guiding principles with respect to the latter, *economic* justice?

A. Benchmark of Equality

What grounds egalitarian shares and fair equality of opportunity as a matter of justice is the conviction that states owe those subject to them particular forms of equal treatment. Rawls argues that states must be understood as fair systems of social cooperation characterised by reciprocity amongst participants and that no person can claim a greater share of the social product than any other without there being a justification for offsetting this benchmark of equality.[10] The argument that Rawls presents is that (a) cooperative practices raise questions of distributive justice concerning what he refers to as common productive surplus, that (b) a state's 'basic structure' is a cooperative practice whose productive surplus comprises nearly all prerequisites for human flourishing, that (c) cooperative practices require equal shares when participants have equal claims to its benefits (subject to considerations of efficiency). Rawls therefore concludes that a state must distribute shares of primary social goods equally amongst participants of social cooperation subject to considerations of efficiency.

---

[7] For some major contributions to the vast 'currency of justice' literature, see M Clayton and A Williams, *The Ideal of Equality* (New York, NY, St Martin's Press, 2000). A defence of primary social goods as the most adequate currency of social justice is presented in J Rawls, *A Theory of Justice* (Cambridge, MA, Belknap Press of Harvard University Press, 1999) and T Pogge, *Realizing Rawls* (Ithaca, NY, Cornell University Press, 1989).

[8] Rawls, *A Theory of Justice*, n 7 above, 79–80.

[9] The distinction is from J Rawls, *Political Liberalism* (New York, NY, Columbia University Press, 1996) 230.

[10] This formulation permits Rawls justification of inequalities in line with the difference principle: where inequalities make the worst off better off it is plausible that nobody could have a reasonable objection to such inequalities.

Interpreting society as a fair system of social cooperation is not necessarily the only way in which we may arrive at a 'benchmark of equality' in determining what counts as a just distribution of the primary social goods of wealth and income. There are alternative grounds for substantive principles of justice that have a benchmark of equality. One thought is simply that equal needs or equal vulnerability to the contingencies of human life (which the basic institutions of society can mitigate to some extent) may be sufficient to ground such an argument, provided that there are no antecedent claims on the good that is to be distributed. One could interpret Rawls as hinting towards this when he mentions the pervasive and comprehensive effect that the basic structure exercises on every person subject to it from the beginning of his or her life.[11] Another argument for equal treatment may derive from further facts about *how* the state relates to those subject to its power, namely by inducing and if necessary forcing people to obey its legal norms. Perhaps there is something specifically problematic about forcing individuals to obey, and the only way to redeem the morally problematic character of such acts is to be found in equal treatment that extends to an equal distribution of primary social goods.[12]

B. Fair Equality of Opportunity

Given such a benchmark, the motivation for a principle of fair equality of opportunity stems from two considerations, one empirical and one normative. The empirical claim is that, given plausible assumptions about human motivation, the complexity of modern societies, and the positive effects of a division of labour on the provision of adequate levels of primary social goods, any institutional system must permit some inequalities in its distribution.[13] Of course, accepting this empirical claim in no way implies accepting the degree of actual material inequality we find in contemporary capitalist societies—but it *does* imply that some incentives are permissible and potentially positively desirable if they can motivate the more talented to be productive in ways that improve the condition of those worse off.[14] The second, normative, assumption is that once an arrangement for social cooperation allows some people to attain more desirable positions in terms of wealth, income and authority, it would be unfair if some would be advantaged in obtaining these positions for reasons unrelated to the task of fulfilling them in ways that serve the common interest.

Equality of opportunity is a widely shared ideal, not confined to conceptions of social justice of the egalitarian brand. But what Rawls called 'fair' equality of opportunity is in fact a very demanding egalitarian ideal, for it requires that 'those

---

[11] Rawls, *A Theory of Justice*, n 7 above, 82; A Abizadeh, 'Cooperation, Pervasive Impact, and Coercion: On the Scope (Not Site) of Distributive Justice' (2007) 35 *Philosophy & Public Affairs* 318.

[12] This is the position defended by Michael Blake and (subject to some further complications) Thomas Nagel. M Blake, 'Distributive Justice, State Coercion, and Autonomy' (2001) 30 *Philosophy & Public Affairs* 257; T Nagel, 'The Problem of Global Justice' (2005) 33 *Philosophy and Public Affairs* 113.

[13] '[A]ny modern society, even a well-ordered one, must rely on some inequalities to be well-designed and effectively organized.' Rawls, *Justice As Fairness*, n 5 above, 55.

[14] Nonetheless, there are powerful arguments stemming from social equality and fraternity that (we think) conclusively speak against permitting inequalities in income and wealth beyond a certain level.

who are at the same level of talent and ability, and have the same willingness to use them, should have the same prospects of success regardless of their initial place in the social system, that is, irrespective of the income class into which they are born'.[15] Defended in these terms, the idea extends beyond the concern that it would be wrong to discriminate between candidates for a position based on features irrelevant for fulfilling the job adequately because equally talented and motivated persons should have equal *prospective* chances of ending up in a desirable position of advantage, independent of contingent facts about such as their social class or family background. Realising fair equality of opportunity thus seems to require basic institutions either to limit well-off persons' abilities to alter others' probabilities of success in economic life, or to significantly extend forms of 'compensation' for those from disadvantaged backgrounds who have not received such additional benefits.

To be sure, the content and ground of social and especially economic justice as laid out by Rawls have been extensively debated. But this is not our object here. Instead, the reasoning we propose is one of differential. Surely, the requirements of justice in the EU can only be equal to or less than those applicable domestically. So the issue for us is to assess one by one the reasons invoked for why these principles might not be applicable to the EU. We do so under three headings, namely, solidarity, reciprocity and choice.

III. IS SOCIAL JUSTICE UNAVAILABLE IN THE EU? SOLIDARITY AS A PREREQUISITE

One objection voiced against the argument that the EU could be subject to forms of socio-economic distribution closer to that which we find within its Member States is that the EU lacks the motivational resources to persuade (citizens in) richer states to comply with demands to redistribute primary social goods to (citizens in) poorer states: there is a lack of *solidarity* amongst EU Member States and citizens that makes talking about substantive justice futile. To adequately evaluate this argument requires addressing at least two distinct questions. On the philosophical level, we must clarify how the concepts of solidarity and justice are connected. Is solidarity merely the empirical prerequisite for institutions that provide substantive social justice? Or is the connection between these values more complex? We begin with a brief conceptual analysis of how we think solidarity is best understood, before tackling the question of how it is related to justice. The further question, which we only touch on peripherally concerns the empirical prerequisites of EU solidarity relations: How deeply engrained are existing solidarities? How likely are they, if at all, to change over time in a more European direction?

A. The Meaning of Solidarity

First, solidarity is a *hybrid* concept, used to describe both an observable *empirical* behaviour amongst people and the normative grounds on which there *ought* to

---

[15] Rawls, *A Theory of Justice*, n 7 above.

be such behaviour. Thus, we could observe both that there is solidarity between members of a group where there ought to be none and that there ought to be solidarity between individuals where there is none at present. Moreover, solidarity is a *social* concept that describes a relation between agents: one is not in solidarity with oneself.[16] However, the fact that solidarity is 'social' still leaves open what it takes to be the proper object or subject of solidarity: can solidarity only exist between actual persons or can it relate to non-human animals or future or past generations. It also begs the question of the kind of relationship that might qualify as such. Some writers—especially those concerned with empirical research—assume that solidarity is necessarily expressed through actual *behaviour* by agents.[17] Other authors think that solidarity does not require particular kinds of behaviour but is better understood as a *disposition* to behave in a specific ways.[18] Second, therefore, solidarity speaks to *motives*. Behaving (or being disposed to behave) in a specific way is not sufficient to be in solidarity. Such behaviour needs to be accompanied by an appropriate kind of *belief*.[19] Acting in ways that benefits somebody else is not sufficient to establish that one is acting *from* solidarity: one might be acting only out of pure self-interest. In all cases, our shared beliefs about the kind of relationship that connects 'us' need to be compatible with the moral reasons that justify acting *from* solidarity: It is fundamental to paradigmatic cases of group solidarity that members of the group believe that they are united by a *just* (morally justified) cause.

B. The Solidarity Compass: Interest, Community, Altruism and Obligation

The intensity of the bonds that exist between members of the myriads of communities of solidarity we recognise around us, as well as the breadth of the issues to which solidarity applies, vary immensely.[20] These two are usually correlated: the broader the set of issues covered by the solidarity relationship, the greater the intensity of the solidarity bonds amongst its participants. But what unique factors account for the intensity of solidarity bonds in solidarity groups, and does solidarity require a threshold level of intensity or range of issues? Here, there is much disagreement in the literature. With an eye to the EU setting, we make a 'pluralist' case about the nature of solidarity bonds, or the motives and contexts that constitute solidarity. In order to do so in a stylised fashion we offer a 'solidarity compass' which locates solidarity at the intersection of two continuums, namely one between (*self*) *interest* and

---

[16] This section draws on K Nicolaïdis and J Viehoff, 'The Choice for Sustainable Solidarity in Post-Crisis Europe' in G Banji, T Fischer, S Hare and S Hoffmann (eds), *Solidarity: For Sale? The Social Dimension of the New European Economic Governance* (Gütersloh, Bertelsmann Stiftung, 2012).

[17] See, eg, the discussion in H Thome, 'Solidarity: Theoretical Perspective for Empirical Research' in K Bayertz (ed), *Solidarity* (Dordrecht, Kluwer Academic Publishers, 1999).

[18] W Rehg, 'Solidarity and the Common Good: An Analytic Framework' (2007) 38 *Journal of Social Philosophy* 7, 8.

[19] J Harvey, 'Moral Solidarity and Empathetic Understanding: The Moral Value and Scope of the Relationship' (2007) 38 *Journal of Social Philosophy* 22, 22.

[20] We use, eg, the term solidarity simultaneously to characterise the close relationship between husband and wife in a marriage, to refer to transnational activist movements focusing on a single political issue or to speak of our feelings about the victims of natural disasters in near and far places.

community, and one between *altruism* and *obligation* (Figure 19.1). We argue that relationships of solidarity usually fall somewhere on these two continuums but not at either extreme.[21] Solidarity therefore describes a relationship that is motivated to some extent by each of these powerful motives, but irreducible to either one of them—this makes it analogous to Brian Barry's definition of reciprocity mentioned earlier.

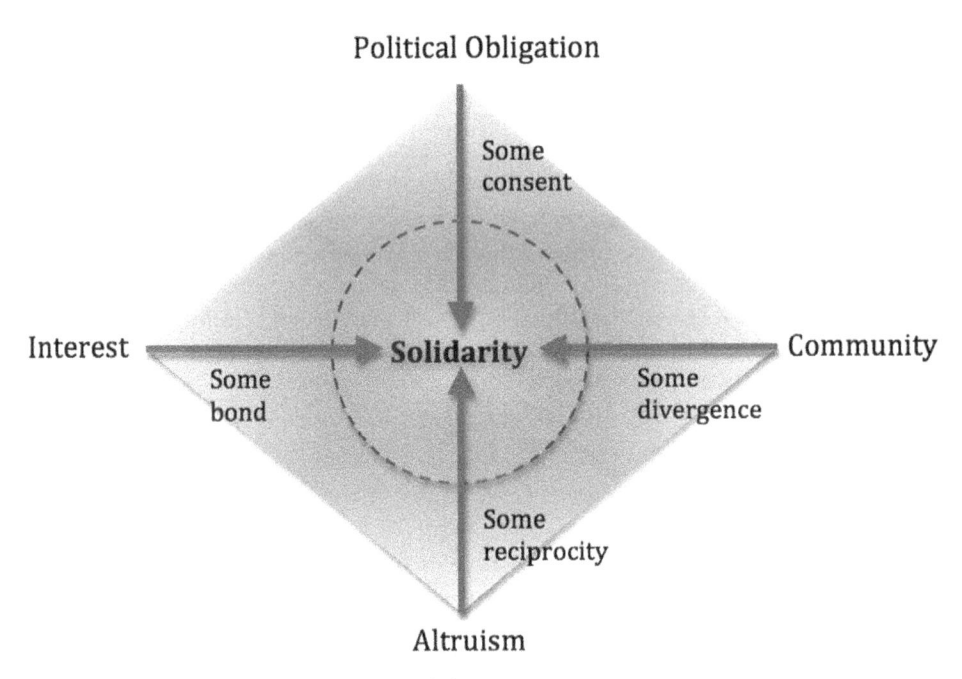

Figure 19.1: The Conceptual Space of Solidarity

(i) Self-Interest versus Community

The most often invoked argument in today's EU debates is that 'solidarity is in Germany's (or France's, etc) interest'. To be sure this is usually qualified as 'enlightened' self-interest or 'long-term' interest, either because it carries expectations of reciprocity or because the positive externalities induced by such solidarity buy a desired outcome (eg sustaining the Eurozone). Abstracting from the EU, we see that for different solidarity groups, there can surely be larger or smaller commonality of such baseline interests, which exist independently from the relationship and which do not internalise others' interests. Commonality simple means that each of person, group or country stands a better chance of realising their independently given interests by participating in the group. If we take the extreme case where individuals

---

[21] By 'display' we here mean that these factors would be mentioned by participants when asked about their reasons to participate in the solidarity group. Our use of 'reasons' throughout is meant to pick out those subjective reasons that agents think they have for participating in a relationship.

cooperate *only* to each realise their independent interest, then few would speak of solidarity at all (but rather of a cooperation or coalition between agents). So mere commonality of interest is not sufficient for solidarity.

This naturally leads to the thought that acting from solidarity requires that one acts in the belief that there also exists some form of loyalty, some kind of pre-existing bond with those one is in solidarity with, which in turn would justify some uncertainty on the nature of the 'return on (the solidarity) investment'. At the opposite end of pure self-interest, therefore, lies what we call the ideal of perfect *community*. Each member identifies with each other member to such an extent that self-interest becomes indistinguishable from common interest: the realisation of each individual's self-interest entails that each other individual's interests are satisfied, that is, they each see the success of their own life as dependent on the success of the group as a whole.[22] We say that solidarity is located somewhere in between the notion of pure self-interest and ideal community, because surely no such comprehensive loyalty is required to invoke the notion of solidarity between members of a group.[23]

What does this tell us about the existence or absence of solidarity in the EU? Member States have come to define their shared interests as ensuring long-term stability in their relationship rather than seeking the highest possible economic benefit for various powerful national constituencies in the short term. This is consistent with saying that there is nothing more than a commonality of interest. But there are also aspects of the EU that seem to transcend the realm of self-interest and to come (at least a little) closer to the ideal of community. Formally, the Treaty of the European Union speaks of an 'ever closer *Union*'. This might not be quite the same as a pledge of full-scale economic solidarity, but the implication is that Member States see themselves as taking part in something that is more than a convenient tool to realise self-interest, namely a relationship of solidarity.

(ii) Altruism versus Political Obligation

Our second continuum is that between altruism and (enforceable) moral obligation. Some think that altruistic behaviour, for example, charity or the simple generosity displayed by the good Samaritan's response to the stranger in need on the side of the road, are also possible instances of solidaristic behaviour. If that were true, then it would show that for some instances of solidarity, there does not seem to be any self-interest or reciprocity involved. But this seems doubtful: While we can imagine being in solidarity with others who cannot reciprocate immediately, we are somewhat wary of the suggestion that solidarity can characterise a relationship without *any* degree of reciprocal link. At the very least, a relationship is more rightfully

---

[22] Feinberg says that the best way to judge different levels of community is by looking at our reactive attitudes: To what extent do I see praise for that person or group as praise *for me*? When that person or group commits a moral wrong, do *I* feel ashamed? J Feinberg, *Harmless Wrongdoing*, vol 4 (Oxford, Oxford University Press, 1990) 234.

[23] We leave open here the question whether it is perhaps even false to speak of 'solidarity' within families, precisely for the reason that they (ought to) realise the perfect ideal of community. The important point is that we can speak of political solidarity where no such strong forms of loyalty exist.

called solidaristic the more people have the ability to influence each other's destiny. But there is also another important aspect that the discussion of altruism brings to the forefront: altruistic acts are in many instances—for example, the case of the good Samaritan—supererogatory, that is, they go beyond what morality strictly requires us to do.[24] By contrast, many things we do in political life we consider non-supererogatory: morality does not make it optional whether we perform them. For example, citizens of states pay taxes, respect the law of the land, serve in times of war.[25] More generally, citizens in a political community plausibly owe obligations of fairness in cooperation to one another such that they mutually uphold each other's rights (see the next section). Not only do most people think that such political obligations are non-optional, but they are also such that most people think they are enforceable.

With this understanding of solidarity in mind, the analogy to the two core debates about domestic social justice and global justice are instructive here: On the one hand, solidarity amongst EU citizens falls short of the kind of solidarity we find amongst co-citizens or co-nationals. It is much less characterised by the kind of sense of obligation or a sense of community. On the other hand, the EU should be seen as much more plausibly as a possible future object for relations of solidarity than the relations amongst everyone on a global scale, amongst whom there is much less by way of community or identifiable interests that can only be realised in the process of cooperation.[26]

Our discussion also points to a second, normative part of the EU solidarity puzzle: Why *should* the existence or absence of solidarity in the EU matter for whether or not egalitarian principles of social justice are to be implemented? After all, the fact that some people fail to see and act on their duties of justice seems an improper basis to conclude that there are no such duties. The best argument here is to be found in the latter Rawls: the relatively weaker developed sense of solidarity amongst citizens of the EU matters once we adopt a certain perspective about what it is that we want a conception of social justice to achieve; it matters if we aim for what Rawls called a *political* conception of justice with a public criterion. Such a conception of justice is not only persuasive to the removed observer but points to the motivational basis of citizens' actions. Once we assume that our conception of social justice requires such a public criterion, we must

> show not merely that it delivers plausible judgments of justice but also that it would perform well in its political role. One must examine how it would be understood, implemented, and followed by actual citizens, what institutional designs they would actually implement under

---

[24] See the discussion in J Seglow and N Scott, *Altruism* (Maidenhead, Open University Press, 2007) 30–31.

[25] See, eg, P Eleftheriadis, 'Citizenship and Obligation' in J Dickson and P Eleftheriadis (eds), *Philosophical Foundations of EU Law* (Oxford, Oxford University Press, 2012). See also G Klosko, *Political Obligations* (Oxford, Oxford University Press, 2005) and JA Simmons, *Moral Principles and Political Obligations* (Princeton, NJ, Princeton University Press, 1979).

[26] Of course, the realisation of common global problems like climate change might also change the disposition of everyone globally to accept that there is a form of community whose interests require joint action. But the sociological basis for this kind of solidarity appears quite weak at present when compared to the EU case.

its guidance, how they would live under such social institutions, and to what extent they would continue freely to endorse this public criterion and any basic structure designed on its basis.[27]

The danger resulting from the lack of solidarity, therefore, is that it could render unachievable the desideratum of being publically acceptable by all participants to social cooperation. Rawls thought that a political conception of justice required a form of social union in which 'human beings have in fact shared final ends and they value their common institutions and activities as goods in themselves'.[28] If EU citizens fail to see themselves as participants in such a social union, then there would be no room for a public political conception of justice.

Is this argument convincing? Rawls himself also provided a powerful response to this line of argument by suggesting that individuals governed by an effective sense of justice will *want* to live on terms characterised by principles of justice with others, if and when they find themselves cooperating in the production of social goods. The upshot from this line of argument for the EU might be the following: rather than being conditional upon the prior existence of certain social bonds and relationships of mutual benefit, justice may *motivate* us to create and sustain such bonds and relationships once certain kinds of (institutional) interaction obtain between us. In other words, solidarity, properly understood, cannot be reduced to an ex-ante emotional attachment but can also be an ex-post effect of reflecting on how we should regulate our actually existing social and political interdependence. The argument is all the more important in the light of our historic knowledge that existing bonds of solidarity—for example, in the case of national citizenship—are more often than not the result of intentional exercises in institutional and social engineering. This of course, was Brian Barry's argument when he concluded (in the context of international justice) that we must complement justice understood as enlightened self-interest with considerations about fairness that do not derive from social bonds or mutual advantage.[29] We do not aim to resolve the difficult question about the sociological prerequisites of just institutions here. But we think that more reflection on the nexus between sociological solidarity and the applicability of substantive principles of justice is required, and that the EU provides a prime example for evaluating some of these questions.

IV. IS SOCIAL JUSTICE FUNDAMENTALLY DIFFERENT IN THE EU? RECIPROCITY AS THE COMMON CORE

The second reason that can be invoked to argue that issues of justice are fundamentally different at the national and EU level has to do with justice as fair reciprocity. At the beginning of this chapter, we discussed the idea defended by Rawls and others that in a society conceived of as a fair scheme of cooperation, those benefiting

---

[27] T Pogge, *John Rawls: His Life and Theory of Justice* (Oxford, Oxford University Press, 2007) 38–39.
[28] Rawls, *A Theory of Justice*, n 7 above, 458.
[29] B Barry, 'Justice As Reciprocity' in B Barry (ed), *Liberty and Justice: Essays in Political Theory 2* (Oxford, Clarendon Press, 1991) 237.

more from cooperation owe those less well off duties of reciprocity in the form of egalitarian shares of primary goods (income and wealth) as well as fair equality of opportunity. If we consider reciprocity a valid ground for social justice domestically, what follows for the institutional arrangement of the EU? In a recent string of publications, Andrea Sangiovanni has provided just such an account of social justice in the EU, which he calls a reciprocity-based internationalist (RBI) conception of EU solidarity.[30] The core proposition is that egalitarian socio-economic requirements 'at all levels of governance can be understood as demands for a fair return in the mutual production of important collective goods'.[31] So whenever individuals or collective agents jointly provide such goods, requirements of socio-economic justice come into play. But because such goods can be provided by different institutional systems or practices to different degrees and in different ways, there is no single set of distributive principles that is triggered by them: where the full set of important collective goods is cooperatively provided, social justice of the kind ideally found at the state level is appropriate (see section II). But where goods are provided to a lesser extent or perhaps in different ways, less demanding and less egalitarian requirements ensue. Given that the kind of distributive principle varies with the institutional form that it is meant to govern, RBI must accomplish the challenging task of deriving such a principle anew for each cooperative context.

To do so, we must ask what kind of collective goods are being provided in each case to determine what kind of socio-economic requirement follows. Sangiovanni identifies three such contexts in the EU case, which he calls *national solidarity* (joint production of collective goods within Member States), *Member State solidarity* (cooperation between EU states), and *transnational solidarity* (cooperation between EU citizens). Unsurprisingly, he finds that (both) principles of solidarity specific to the EU will be less demanding than at the national level.[32] Sangiovanni thinks that the appropriate normative principle applicable to solidarity between Member States is a kind of fair distribution of the surplus that the EU generates paired with an insurance device against those risks of economic disadvantage or harm that states incur as a result of EU membership. Importantly, this principle is subject to the constraint that Member States and their citizens may keep whatever they entered the institutional arrangement with.[33] Thus, social justice amongst EU citizens either directly or through the relationship between their state is not subject to the equality-favouring principles discussed earlier which considers all individual talents to be a 'common asset' that must serve all and especially the worst off.

Approaching EU social justice through the lenses of fair reciprocity is clearly an innovative and potentially very fruitful approach. One core advantage of it is that it pays attention to the *distinctive character* of the EU as a supranational institutional

---

[30] A Sangiovanni, 'Global Justice, Reciprocity, and the State' (2007) 35 *Philosophy & Public Affairs* 3; A Sangiovanni, 'Justice and the Free Movement of Persons: Educational Mobility in the EU and the US' in D Hicks and T Williamson (eds), *Leadership and Global Justice* (London, Palgrave, 2012); A Sangiovanni, 'Solidarity in the European Union' (2013) 33 *Oxford Journal of Legal Studies* 1.
[31] Sangiovanni, 'Solidarity', n 30 above, 6.
[32] ibid, 19.
[33] ibid, 22–23.

arrangement that has taken on important public goods provisions for persons under its authority, and is in this sense very different from the global political landscape whilst obviously still falling short of the full range of goods that states provide to their citizens. Despite this crucial positive point, we want to rehearse here briefly arguments against theories that solely base demands for social justice on fair reciprocity.

To determine obligations for reciprocity, we must ask what counts as having contributed to a particular cooperative scheme and hence who falls under the scope of distributive justice in the first place. A familiar objection, formulated by Brian Barry a long time ago, was that grounding our conception of justice solely on cooperation or reciprocity may have unacceptable moral consequences since it excludes those most vulnerable in contemporary society (children, the severely handicapped, etc) from justice's reach: they would effectively 'fall through the grid', meaning that they would not be owed anything because they have not brought anything to the table.[34] To avoid this charge, Sangiovanni interprets the idea of contribution in a very lax way in the domestic case: it is sufficient to 'make it possible' for others to derive benefits from the state. In short, 'national solidarity says that an individual is integrated into a society when he aids in the reproduction of the state through his participation, contributions, and compliance'.[35] So Sangiovanni avoids Brian Barry's objection to reciprocity theories. But then in turn, one might think that this interpretation creates problems for transnational EU solidarity, or those outside the domestic context. In order for the most vulnerable citizens to be owed egalitarian shares, it must be strictly speaking the case that passive compliance is actually *sufficient*: quite frequently, all that we can say about the contributory effort of the least endowed is that they are not actively undermining the cooperative scheme, for example, that they do not transgress and undermine existing property rules, labour regulation, public order directives and so forth.

But if a person's 'mere passive acceptance', that is, non-interference when she counter-factually could, suffices for that person to be a contributor and owed equal shares, then those outside of a state's borders might also fit the bill. We can make the case that the very viability of states and the societies they protect and beyond this, the benefits that their citizens derive, is based on recognition by state outsiders, starting with territorial integrity and moving on to the recognition of jurisdiction, market standards or intellectual property rights. In the case of Economic and Monetary Union, citizens of some countries have 'made it possible' for citizens of other countries to disproportionally benefit from the scheme by merely passively tolerating the existing set of rules that work in the latter's advantage. So as a matter of theoretical consistency, it seems necessary either to remove from the egalitarian scheme passive compliers on the inside or add them from the outside, thereby questioning the categorical distinction between domestic and EU justice based on the broad notion of reciprocal contribution, making it instead a matter of degree.

---

[34] This was Brian Barry's main objection against (even fair) reciprocity-based theories of justice. Barry, 'Justice As Reciprocity', n 29 above, 235.
[35] Sangiovanni, 'Solidarity', n 30 above, 27.

In short, we believe that fair reciprocity ought to serve as a crucial ground but not the sole ground for obligations of substantive justice in the EU case. In this judgement, we are again indebted to Brian Barry who suggested that we must

> see if there is not some principle of justice complementary to justice as reciprocity that comes into its own when we move outside the special case of justice among contemporaries who are members of the same society. I emphasize that it must be complementary because I believe that justice as reciprocity is here to stay. It is ... a cultural universal, and anyway it makes a lot of sense. Any theory of justice that tried to eliminate justice as reciprocity would be doomed from start. We must therefore seek to show how justice as reciprocity needs to be supplemented, not displaced.[36]

To name just one principle that could supplement justice as reciprocity and might, at least in some cases, take the edge off the latter is the simpler concern that public institutional agents charged with distributing goods amongst persons must at least sometimes do so impartially, where impartiality also includes blindness as to whether or not a person has contributed in *any* meaningful sense to the cooperative surplus.[37]

V. HOW IS SOCIAL JUSTICE DIFFERENT IN THE EU? CONSTRAINED CHOICE AS AN EU MARKER

A third prominent argument in favour of egalitarian socio-economic justice in domestic society starts from the observation that our membership in political society is 'forced', 'coerced' or 'non-voluntary'. The substance of this argument is that the only way to justify or redeem our non-voluntary submission to the authority of the state is to organise the distribution of advantage from social cooperation in an egalitarian way.[38] One upshot of this kind of justification of substantive justice is that because of its non-voluntary character, domestic society and the principles of justice that it requires are categorically and fundamentally different from those private associations and institutions that we—individually and collectively—freely choose to join which do not call for just arrangements.

The implications for distributive justice at the EU level are clear: Membership in the European Union results from state consent. Therefore, at least from the perspective of the state as a collective agent, participation in the social cooperation that the EU gives rise to ought to be voluntary. Does this mean we are in the realm of (voluntary) solidarity not (obligatory) justice? Consider two key aspects of consent starting with *generality*. Every Member State has come to share in the costs and benefits of EU social cooperation by clearly and unequivocally consenting, and so

---

[36] Barry, 'Justice As Reciprocity', n 29 above, 235.

[37] See, eg, the discussion of such arguments in T Scanlon, 'When Does Equality Matter?' (2005), www.politicalscience.stanford.edu/sites/default/files/workshop-materials/pt_scanlon.pdf. This was of course also in certain respect the idea underpinning Barry's conception of 'justice as impartiality'. Barry, *Justice As Impartiality*, n 2 above.

[38] Two prominent recent defenders of such a view, based on the moral wrong of coercion, are Blake, 'Distributive Justice', n 12 above; and Nagel, 'The Problem', n 12 above. For a critique of the argument from non-voluntariness, see A Sangiovanni, 'The Irrelevance of Coercion, Imposition, and Framing to Distributive Justice' (2012) 40 *Philosophy and Public Affairs* 79.

no peripatetic justification concerning tacit consent is required. Moreover, such consent may be withdrawn and each Member State is at least nominally free to exit the institution at any point in time. Indeed, consent is restated for every major revision in the EU's legal and constitutional order since 'Member States are masters of the Treaties'. The second aspect is what we might call the *quality* of consent. We can relatively safely assume that consent to EU membership was in all cases adequately informed and intentional in that it followed after broad democratic deliberation of its costs and benefits. More succinctly: nobody ever signed the Copenhagen Criteria on a whim after a drunken night out. A further aspect of the quality of consent stems from the fact that it was given against a background of meaningful choice: States had and have, perhaps with some important qualifications, acceptable alternatives to EU membership available to them (one only needs to think of Norway or Switzerland). Most people in most states most of the time lack this liberty, either because they would be forced to cooperate should they fail to do so voluntarily, or because, where they have alternative options available to them—usually involving moving out of the country—these options are too costly to count as *acceptable* alternatives.[39] So if it is only the fact of forced or non-voluntary participation in a cooperative scheme that brings demanding requirements of socio-economic justice into play, then, consequently, we should conclude that the EU (being a voluntary association between states) will trigger no such requirements and we do not need a theory of distributive justice for the EU analogous to domestic political society.

How relevant is this apparent difference in terms of voluntariness between the EU and domestic society for questions of socio-economic justice? If we accept the argument from non-voluntariness at the normative level, one question that merits more detailed analysis is to what extent states and the collectives they represent actually do retain meaningful choices regarding distributive options in the actual basic structure of the EU. If EU policies, even while states have consented to them, involve internal distributional consequences which were either not foreseen or at least come to be constrained in ways that might not be foreseen under the initial conditions of choice and consent, then the circumstances of justice also change in the EU. In particular, individual states now start to be expected to uphold obligations stemming from these unchosen dynamics. Under such circumstances, could we not argue that Member States must either engage in egalitarian redistributions or have collective obligations *to restore* the possibility of meaningful choice in individual Member States, from exit from specific cooperative schemes to policy options whose consequences have become clearer? Moreover, we would argue that to the extent that the burden of internalizing such externalities could still be distributed in various ways, such distributions need to be the result of a collective choice on the part of the Member States. But the question remains how such collective choice is most justly delivered.

A different approach to the question of (non-)voluntariness in the context of the EU would be to deny its significance for grounding requirements of *socio-economic*

---

[39] For the general point, see Simmons, *Moral Principles*, n 25 above, ch 2. On the relationship between voluntariness and 'acceptable alternatives', see S Olsaretti, 'Freedom, Force and Choice: Against the Rights-Based Definition of Voluntariness' (1998) 6 *Journal of Political Philosophy* 53.

justice and to insist instead that questions about choice are ultimately questions about legitimacy or *political justice*, that is, the moral justifiability of the exercise of political power. Such questions we ordinarily think ought to be settled by implementing just procedures through which political decisions are reached in the EU. And it is in these procedures that individual national choice should be adequately reflected. In fact, the very idea of the EU as *demoi*cracy relies on the thought that individual peoples freely choose to integrate their institutions, and the specific kind of legitimacy that strikes most as appropriate for the EU is one that proportionally combines elements of majoritarian supranational democratic decision making (which constraints *individual* choice) with the freedom to 'pick and choose' those policy areas in which states want to remain self-determining. Existing EU practices arguably seek to operationalise this idea, but all too clumsily and imperfectly.

Returning to the issue of economic justice that has been the focus of this chapter, the upshot of this view would be that our reasons for endorsing principles of socio-economic justice are analytically distinct from questions of voluntariness, coercion and political legitimacy. Where would this leave us? At the very least, it shows that if we want to construct a multilevel polity that is both just and legitimate, we face difficult questions about how much political choice at the Member State level is compatible with realising social justice at the EU level. The crucial insight that the EU conveys, one might think, is that the realisation of social and economic justice and the realisation of political legitimacy do not always fit nicely together and complement each other, and that we need to think much more about how political institutions (any political institutions!) can be organised in a way that realises both values to the fullest.[40] To bridge the gap as it were, the affect side of transnational solidarity and the kind of social recognition that underpins it matter enormously.

VI. CONCLUSION

Going back to some of Brian Barry's reflections on reciprocity and justice beyond the state, our brief discussion has raised three issues that we consider of particular importance in thinking about the philosophical question of socio-economic justice in the EU. First: how are we to make sense of the claim that we ought not to aspire to a more egalitarian form of socio-economic justice in the EU because of the current lack of solidarity between EU citizens? Second: Even if we overcome the first preliminary objection, should we think that the requirements of social justice are fundamentally different because the EU provides different social goods to its members? Third: How real and how significant is the difference between the EU and domestic society concerning the voluntary nature of each of these associations? If we insist that the EU is distinct because its relevant agents are primarily states, then we must more directly address (a) the empirical accuracy of claims about acceptable alternatives to membership in the EU and in monetary union, and (b) the normative significance of voluntariness and consent for appropriate conceptions of socio-economic justice.

---

[40] A similar conclusion is drawn by Philippe Van Parijs in P Van Parijs, *Just Democracy: The Rawls–Machiavelli Programme* (Colchester, ECPR Press, 2011).

On a final note, we will not spare our readers Brian Barry's own assessment of the European project. Commenting in 2004 on its normative significance and future prospects, Barry doubted whether

> the EU, in its present or any foreseeable future manifestation, will solve more problems than states could have solved by themselves in free co-operation with others. In fact, my contention is that it could do so only as the result of a total institutional transformation that is politically impossible. The worst thing about the EU has been that it banned most of the increasingly sophisticated policy instruments by which individual states had controlled their economies since 1918, but left their replacement to a decision process that was (and is) heavily stacked against equivalent EU-wide intervention ... This automatically inhibited politics from challenging markets successfully.[41]

He concluded by wondering whether 'those of us who accept the objectives of redistribution and a strong welfare state [should] be advocating the abolition of the EU right now?'[42] We disagree with this grim assessment including on the need for total transformation; but we take these clear-headed observations to be a crucial reminder of how complex and how enormous the task of developing appropriate principles of socio-economic justice for the EU is going to be.

---

[41] B Barry, 'What Did We Learn?' in P Van Parijs (ed), *Cultural Diversity Versus Economic Solidarity* (Louvain-la-Neuve, De Boek, 2004) 361–62.
[42] ibid, 366–67.

20

The Preoccupation with Rights and the Embrace of Inclusion: A Critique

ALEXANDER SOMEK

I. THE NEW KID ON THE BLOCK

CURRENT EUROPEAN SCHOLARSHIP does not yet appear to be quite ripe to address the question of justice. Scholars focus on the protection of individual rights and remain largely oblivious to distributions. The question of how the burdens and benefits of social cooperation ought to be allocated does not enter the picture. This prevalent perspective is insufficient. A broader perspective on justice reveals that the European Union is less consistent with justice than with its apolitical counterpart, namely, inclusion. The European Union is an agent of inclusion rather than justice.

* * *

Topics in EU scholarship come and go. Their rise and fall appears to reflect the practical exigencies of the integration process. On some occasions, such topics lend intellectual resonance to political statements. This was to be observed for the ill-fated constitutionalisation debate and also for the changing tides of the quest for a European social model.[1] As one would expect, other themes emerge as an intellectual spill-over effect of institutional experiments, such as the exploration of 'flexibility'[2] or the less short-lived analysis of 'new governance'.[3]

---

[1] The former can be traced to Joschka Fischer's memorable speech at Humboldt University, the latter to statements by Jacques Delors. See the debate at www.centers.law.nyu.edu/jeanmonnet/archive/papers/00/symp.html. On the European social model see more recently, C Hermann and B Mahnkopf, 'The Past and Future of the European Social Model' (2010) *Institute for International Political Economy Berlin Working Papers* No 5, www.ipe-berlin.org/fileadmin/downloads/working_paper/ipe_working_paper_05.pdf.

[2] See the by now classical contribution by S Weatherill, '"If I'd Wanted You to Understand I Would Have Explained It Better": What Is the Purpose of the Provisions on Closer Co-operation Introduced by the Treaty of Amsterdam?' in D O'Keeffe and P Twomey (eds), *Legal Issues of the Amsterdam Treaty* (Oxford, Hart Publishing, 1999).

[3] See, eg, the remarkable anthology, G de Búrca and J Scott (eds), *Law and Governance in the EU and the US* (Oxford, Hart Publishing, 2006).

296 *Alexander Somek*

For quite obvious reasons, the dominant issue of our time is the European sovereign debt crisis. There is a growing debate[4] and an ever-increasing torrent of contributions that attempt to guide the perplexed through the politically disabling world of financial markets, and to pinpoint how the finances of the European Union and the Member States might be stabilised. At the same time, the substance of the measures adopted to sustain the common currency, notably the so-called Fiscal Compact[5] and the amended Stability and Growth Pact,[6] have brought a topic to the surface that is undoubtedly of core relevance to any social institution, namely, the question of justice.[7]

Admittedly, 'justice' has been on the Union's agenda since the conclusion of the Maastricht Treaty.[8] It has been restricted, however, to matters of criminal justice and, by extension, the administration of justice in a transnational context. But this is not the sense in which justice claims its relevance in the context of the current crisis. The peoples of Europe are beginning to wonder whether it is just that high-ranking employees of institutions that have precipitated the crisis continue to enjoy their privileged socio-economic positions while large segments of the population experience hardship and greatly diminished expectations. Moreover, it stands to reason whether the growing supranational constitutionalisation of austerity and

---

[4] For example, there is much discussion about whether the Union ought to have a democratically accountable government. See www.verfassungsblog.de/category/policy/europe/. See also the special issue on the 'Regeneration of Europe' in (2013) 14 *German Law Journal* 441, edited by Moritz Hartmann and Floris de Witte.

[5] The official name of the Fiscal Compact is 'Treaty on Stability, Coordination and Governance in the Economic and Monetary Union'. The text is available at www.european-council.europa.eu/media/639235/st00tscg26_en12.pdf.

[6] The (reformed) Stability and Growth Pact consists of regulations concerning the prevention and correction of excessive deficits and macroeconomic imbalances. See Regulation (EU) 1175/2011 of the European Parliament and of the Council of 16 November 2011 amending Council Regulation (EC) 1466/97 on the strengthening of the surveillance of budgetary positions and the surveillance and coordination of economic policies [2011] OJ L306/12; Regulation (EU) 1173/2011 of the European Parliament and of the Council of 16 November 2011 on the effective enforcement of budgetary surveillance in the euro area [2011] OJ L306/1; Regulation (EU) 1176/2011 of the European Parliament and of the Council of 16 November 2011 on the prevention and correction of macroeconomic imbalances [2011] OJ L306/25; Council Regulation (EU) 1177/2011 of 8 November 2011 amending Regulation (EC) 1467/97 on speeding up and clarifying the implementation of the excessive deficit procedure [2011] OJ L306/33; Regulation (EU) 1174/2011 of the European Parliament and of the Council of 16 November 2011 on enforcement measures to correct excessive macroeconomic imbalances in the euro area [2011] OJ L306/8; Council Directive 2011/85/EU of 8 November 2011 on requirements for budgetary frameworks of the Member States [2011] OJ L306/41; Regulation (EU) 473/2013 of the European Parliament and of the Council of 21 May 2013 on common provisions for monitoring and assessing draft budgetary plans and ensuring the correction of excessive deficit of the Member States in the euro area [2013] OJ L140/11; Regulation (EU) 472/2013 of the European Parliament and of the Council of 21 May 2013 on the strengthening of economic and budgetary surveillance of Member States in the euro area experiencing or threatened with serious difficulties with respect to their financial stability [2013] OJ L140/1. For the legal problems raised, see M Höpner and F Rödl, 'Illegitim und rechtswidrig: Das neue makroökonomische Regime im Euroraum' (2012) 92 *Wirtschaftsdienst* 219; J Bast and F Rödl, 'Jenseits der Koordinierung? Zu den Grenzen der EU-Verträge für eine Europäische Wirtschaftsregierung' (2012) 39 *Europäische Grundrechtezeitschrift* 269; M Dawson and F de Witte, 'Constitutional Balance in the EU after the Euro-Crisis' (2013) 76 *Modern Law Review* 817.

[7] See, eg, H Brunkhorst, 'Kollektiver Bonapartismus? Demokratie in der europäischen Krise' www.eurozine.com/articles/2012-04-17-brunkhorst-de.html.

[8] Treaty on European Union (Maastricht, 7 February 1992) [1992] OJ C191.

retrenchment has created conditions in which Europeans would consider themselves governed by fair institutional arrangements.[9]

In what follows, I would like to point out that current European scholarship seems to be quite ready to address this question. When scholars talk about justice they refer, first and foremost, to the protection of individual rights and remain largely oblivious of how the burdens and benefits of social cooperation ought to be allocated.[10] Justice is believed to be tantamount to respecting and protecting individual rights. The question of how the burdens and benefits of social cooperation ought to be allocated does not enter the picture.

I would like to demonstrate that this perspective is insufficient. I am confident that the examination of two specimens of scholarship will reveal that the pertinent narrow perspective on justice is at best incomplete. *Social* justice must be considered.[11] In the following sections, I sketch briefly the democratic idea of justice and explain why it does not fit the European Union. It will be seen, however, that the Union embraces the apolitical version of equality that goes by the name of 'inclusion'.

II. THE A AND Ω

Williams' study of the ethos of European integration sets out with the bold claim that the European Union has developed an institutional ethos that fails 'to take "justice" seriously as a central defining concern'.[12] He even characterises its current state as 'ethically vacuous'.[13] In his view, this vacuity stems from a functional orientation that merely appeals strategically to values for the entirely self-serving purpose of institutional entrenchment.[14] While Union institutions have often drawn on a variety of values to buttress their claim to legitimacy, the opportunistic[15] deployment of normative rhetoric has left these values in an indeterminate and ambivalent state.[16] At best, both the selection and interpretation of values betray the core interest in market building and preserving a capitalist economic system.[17]

---

[9] For an analysis, see E Chiti, AJ Menéndez and PG Teixeira, 'The European Rescue of the European Union' in E Chiti, AJ Menéndez and PG Teixeira (eds), *The European Rescue of the European Union? The Existential Crisis of the European Political Project* (Oslo, Arena, 2010); see also S Puntscher Riekmann, A Somek and D Wydra, 'Introduction: What is the Purpose of the Union?' in S Puntscher Riekmann, A Somek and D Wydra (eds), *Is There a European Common Good?* (Baden-Baden, Nomos, 2013).

[10] This is true even for the scholar who is most critical of the European Union and aware of larger historical transformations but nonetheless characterises evasions of the duties of solidarity as interferences with human rights. See A Supiot, *The Spirit of Philadelphia: Social Justice vs the Total Market* (London, Verso, 2012) 133.

[11] For a useful contrasting of 'legal' and 'social' justice, see D Miller, *Social Justice* (Oxford, Clarendon Press, 1975) 22.

[12] A Williams, *The Ethos of Europe: Values, Law and Justice in the EU* (Cambridge, Cambridge University Press, 2010) vii.

[13] ibid, 18.

[14] ibid, 273.

[15] Williams' claims are reminiscent of how Niklas Luhmann analysed the opportunistic pursuit of aims by organisations. N Luhmann, *Zweckbegriff und Systemrationalität: Über die Funktion von Zwecken in sozialen Systemen*, 2nd edn (Frankfurt, Suhrkamp, 1977) 47, 203.

[16] See Williams, *The Ethos of Europe*, n 12 above, 264.

[17] ibid, 275–76.

Values do not determine the Union's action; rather, the exigencies of integration account for shifts in their meaning.

Williams believes that the Union's disconnect from justice has been exacerbated by the influence of a legal philosophy that is basically 'a theory of interpretation' rather than an elaboration of values.[18] What he has in mind here is that the jurisprudence of the European Court of Justice (ECJ) presents itself as a teleological interpretation of the treaties and aims to maximise their effect.

Such a diagnosis, if correct, would be quite sobering. The prevalent indeterminacy of value definition and appreciation would even aggravated by the absence of justice 'as a coherent institutional theme'.[19] While the current judicial philosophy is seemingly incorrigible by the ECJ itself,[20] Williams is nonetheless confident that, not least owing to the commendable effects of regional integration,[21] the Union could be moving incrementally[22] towards embracing justice at the heart of its mission. This would suggest that the EU is committed to 'an expanded conception of *human rights*'.[23] Such a conception of human rights should not be overshadowed by the distinction between the internal guarantee of fundamental rights, on the one hand, and the pursuit of an external human rights agenda, on the other; rather, the Union's conception should be of one piece[24] and draw its inspiration from international human rights documents.[25] In this way, the Union could be enlisted to undertake a global human rights agenda that accords priority to the eradication of poverty.[26]

In Williams' view, human rights would also supply the integrating factor regarding other values of the Union, such as democracy, the rule of law or peace. These values should be recast through the lens of human rights.[27] The integrative force as regards the *coherence* of the Union's values would supposedly be inherited from the *socially* integrative force of human rights across borders.[28] As Williams explains:

> [T]he power of the language and practice of human rights rests in their exceptional ability; to draw people together in community; to channel social aspirations; to address fundamental fears; to provide for a means of expressing claims for social change.[29]

A first step in what Williams considers to be the right direction would consist of translating the mandate to 'promote' the Union's values, which is to be found in Article 3(1) of the Treaty on European Union (TEU),[30] into a norm demanding

---

[18] ibid, 18, 252, 274.
[19] ibid, 283.
[20] ibid, 278.
[21] ibid, 286–91.
[22] ibid, 307.
[23] ibid, 20.
[24] ibid, 328.
[25] ibid, 329.
[26] ibid, 335–36.
[27] ibid, 321, 331; 321: 'There is, indeed, good cause to suggest that human rights reflect persistent and convincing social and legal appreciations of how to attain those other values'.
[28] ibid, 321, 325–26, 329.
[29] ibid, 362.
[30] Consolidated version of the Treaty on European Union [2012] OJ C326/13 (TEU).

that fundamental rights be respected, protected and fulfilled.[31] In Williams' opinion, if Article 3(1) TEU were reformulated along these lines it would give rise to affirmative obligations on the part of the Union and Member States to take a proactive approach toward the realisation of human rights. Nonetheless, Williams is also aware that a full-blown turn to justice cannot be brought about by judicial fiat; there must also be legal and institutional reform. On the basis of a new ('full')[32] European Bill of Rights, which would include the emerging international human rights standards,[33] the Union would be transformed into a large-scale human rights organisation the task of which is to oversee and support Member States.[34]

What is most notable about Williams' analysis is that, without anything further, he equates redirecting the European Union toward justice with the adoption of an ambitious commitment to human rights. This reveals that for Williams the realisation of justice is consistent with an ethos that is concerned primarily with individuals, their resources and potentially also their well-being. In fact, this ethos, borrowing Rawlsian parlance, regards individuals as self-authenticating sources of valid claims.[35] In Williams' words this means that individuals have a right to be taken seriously 'as individuals': 'They [human rights] attach to individual demands to be seen as individuals and respected as individuals and to be treated as socially associated with others'.[36]

Remarkably, a similar equation of justice and respect for the individual can be encountered in an *opposite* approach that actually claims that justice already is the normative standard embodied in the European Union. In a recent and controversial article, Jürgen Neyer proposes to swap the currency of the European legitimacy deficit.[37] If a deficit needs to be recognised it is not to be mistaken for a dearth of democracy. In his view, it is profoundly unclear whether it would be even desirable to transform the Union into some transnational democracy. The Union 'is not undemocratic by mistake',[38] not least because the political equality of citizens has not been chosen to be one of its normative principles.[39] Hence, it would be wrong, in Neyer's opinion, to assess the legitimacy of the Union by using democracy as the

---

[31] ibid, 319.
[32] ibid, 331.
[33] ibid, 330.
[34] ibid, 334.
[35] This is how Rawls characterises one essential aspect of freedom. See J Rawls, *Political Liberalism* (New York, NY, Columbia University Press, 1991) 32. For such a characterisation of individuals as 'self-originating' sources of claims, see also T Pinkard, *Hegel's Naturalism: Mind, Nature, and the Final Ends of Life* (Oxford, Oxford University Press, 2011) 136.
[36] Williams, *The Ethos of Europe*, n 12 above, 326.
[37] See J Neyer, 'Justice, Not Democracy: Legitimacy in the European Union' (2010) 48 *Journal of Common Market Studies* 903. In the meantime, Neyer published a book-length exposition of his ideas. See J Neyer, *The Justification of Europe: A Political Theory of Supranational Integration* (Oxford, Oxford University Press, 2012). It is a truly remarkable book. This author has taken the liberty to review it. See A Somek, 'The Darling Dogma of Bourgeois Europeanists' (2014) 20 *European Law Journal* 688–712.
[38] See J Neyer, 'Who's Afraid of Justice? A Rejoinder to Danny Nicol' (2012) 50 *Journal of Common Market Studies* 523, 526. See also J Neyer, 'Justice and the Right to Justification: Conceptual Reflections' in this volume, 211.
[39] Neyer, 'Justice, Not Democracy', n 37 above, 908.

standard.[40] He concludes that it would be more appropriate to rely on the criterion of justice.

What Neyer has in mind, more specifically, is the 'idea of justice as a right to justification'.[41] According to this idea, any person whose freedom has been restricted has a right to demand a justification that amounts to 'good reasons'.[42] Individual freedom must yield only to acts that are sufficiently weighty in order to make such yielding reasonable.

This right to a justification, which Neyer even refers to as a human right,[43] also clearly exhibits an 'individualistic perspective'.[44] Even though the Member States have a right to demand a justification in the context of the Union, their right is derivative of the basic rights of their citizens: '[T]he right to justification is an individual human right and ... governments only act as trustees of their citizen's human rights'. Again, what justice means is articulated with regard to what it takes to take seriously the interests of individuals. It is an open question whether this is a plausible view of justice.

III. THE CATEGORY MISTAKE

Williams' work is remarkably oblivious to the fact that justice is a concept that we encounter in the form of various attempts to flesh out what it means to give each person his or her due. Had Williams been aware of this idea of justice, it would not have escaped his attention that the philosophy of law underpinning the jurisprudence of the ECJ, assuming that there is any,[45] embraces an approach to the distribution of goods and opportunities that strongly supports entrepreneurial freedom, individual initiative and consumer choice.[46] Such a 'philosophy' of law is not necessarily different from the pursuit of justice; rather, it is based on a very specific understanding of it.[47] What is more, it is rather disappointing that Williams, after having indicted the Union for sustaining an institutional ethos that he perceives to be 'chaotic, a patchwork of half-understood and contingent values which are forever in motion, altering

---

[40] Neyer's argument presupposes, of course, that the Union is free to adopt a different standard of legitimacy. It is hard to believe why such a choice would rule out critiquing the Union for not being sufficiently democratic. We would not concede to a dictatorship to retort to the charge of being undemocratic by saying that it does not wish to be a democracy or in the face of the fact that creating a democracy would be 'unrealistic'. For a similar critique of Neyer's idea to limit normative demands to what appears to be 'realistic' under given circumstances (ibid 907), see D Nicol, 'Can Justice Dethrone Democracy in the European Union? A Reply to Jürgen Neyer' (2012) 50 *Journal of Common Market Studies* 1, 6.

[41] Neyer, 'Justice, Not Democracy', n 37 above, 908.
[42] ibid, 908.
[43] ibid, 908, 913.
[44] ibid, 913.
[45] A Somek, 'The Emancipation of Legal Dissonance' in H Koch et al (eds), *Europe: The New Legal Realism* (Copenhagen, DJØF, 2011).
[46] Williams, *The Ethos of Europe*, n 12 above, 272–77.
[47] Arguably, it is wedded to the ideas of justice underlying economic liberalism. See, eg, D Schmidtz, 'Taking Responsibility' in D Schmidtz and RE Goodin, *Social Welfare and Individual Responsibility: For and Against* (Cambridge, Cambridge University Press, 1998). See M Höpner, 'Warum betreibt der Europäische Gerichtshof Rechtsfortbildung? Die Politisierungshypothese' (2010) *MPIfG Working Papers* 10/2.

in form and substance depending on the context of any action',[48] only arrives at the meagre exhortation that in order to pursue justice the Union ought to embrace human rights. It is fairly difficult to see how endorsing human rights might absorb the 'indeterminacy of values'[49] that Williams believes to be the chief deficiency of European law. Any set of human rights is nothing but a motley assembly of potentially colliding limits on action or inaction by governments. No determinate vision of what ought to happen in cases of collision follows from it. Williams's suggestion amounts to replacing the current indeterminacy inherent in the Union's commitment to values with another indeterminacy. It is hence in the very nature of the proposal itself that Williams is therefore incapable of providing 'a complete response' to his call for 'some determinacy of values'.[50]

Not a set of human rights, but what Habermas has called a 'paradigm of law',[51] might give rise to the desired result. Paradigms of law rest on an implicit conception of society and assign various tasks and responsibilities to public institutions and private actors with regard to the enjoyment of rights. Paradigms of this kind, such as the classical legal thought of the Lochner court,[52] can lend coherence to the way in which a set of rights is consistently applied over time. These paradigms cannot be deduced from the rights themselves.

Hence, the desired determinacy cannot flow from human rights per se but only from certain views concerning the social allocation of the responsibility for their enjoyment.[53] These views carry implications for distributive justice. It may not be by accident, therefore, that Williams' exposition more or less consistently ignores the distributive fault lines dividing the Union. It is all the more amazing that a work devoted to justice is oblivious to the rise of social inequality and does not pay heed to the various predicaments that have arisen in the Union in the wake of its last major enlargements. Former Eastern European countries no longer have the opportunity to benefit as much from the structural programmes that benefited Spain and Ireland.[54] The only chance that former Eastern European countries and their businesses realistically have for improvement is to benefit from lower wages and a more business-friendly environment. It is in this context that cases such as *Viking*[55] and *Laval*[56] have signalled intractable conflict.[57]

---

[48] Williams, *The Ethos of Europe*, n 12 above, 250.
[49] ibid, 321.
[50] ibid, 315–16.
[51] See J Habermas, *Faktizität und Geltung: Beiträge zur Diskurstheorie des Rechts und des demokratischen Rechtsstaats* (Frankfurt, Suhrkamp, 1992) 469, 473.
[52] See, eg, M Horwitz, *The Transformation of American Law 1870–1960: The Crisis of Legal Orthodoxy* (Oxford, Oxford University Press 1992) 19–20, 29–31.
[53] On the idea of a social division of responsibility, see Rawls, *Political Liberalism*, n 35 above, 33–34, 185–87.
[54] See G Majone, *Europe as Would-Be World Power: The EU at Fifty* (Cambridge, Cambridge University Press, 2009) 114–15.
[55] Case C-438/05 *International Transport Workers' Federation and Finnish Seamen's Union v Viking Line ABP and OÜ Viking Line Eesti* [2007] ECR I-10779.
[56] Case C-341/05 *Laval un Partneri Ltd v Svenska Byggnadsarbetareförbundet and Others* [2007] ECR I-11767.
[57] See also D Kukovec, 'Taking Change Seriously: The Rhetoric of Justice and the Reproduction of the Status Quo' in this volume, 319.

It follows that equating justice with the protection of rights, while clearly not an implausible manner in which to state the issue, is of little import when it comes to bringing about the desired change of perspective. Giving each person his or her due, if reduced to the protection of rights, is tantamount to saying that the Union's legal system ought to work properly.

What Williams really suggests, albeit in the guise of shifting the orientation of the Union towards justice, is a profound alteration of the *existing* system of rights. Alas, Williams leaves unspecified what this alternative system might look like. This is hardly a way of advocating justice; rather, it is a manner of selling it short.

IV. A RIGHT THAT REALLY ISN'T ONE

It will be seen that Neyer's account is also burdened with the tautology inherent in reducing justice to the protection of rights. What makes Neyer's intervention special, however, is that it tacitly contains its own critique. Before turning to the dialectical virtues of Neyer's text, I would like to dwell, briefly on the rather eccentric idea, which he obviously borrows from Rainer Forst,[58] that there is a human right to a justification.

In Neyer's view, the right to a justification is triggered by restrictions of freedom,[59] which may also originate from omissions.[60] Arguably, in order for freedom to exercise the normative effect of creating a burden of justification one has to assume that interferences with freedom are prima facie wrongful. That interferences give rise to the demand for a justification on the part of the person affected implies that humans have a right to enjoy their freedom without interference from others.[61] Otherwise, there would be no reason for requiring a justification. Thus, the right to be free from being adversely affected by others is the *Urrecht*[62] that precedes the alleged right to a justification. No interfering person would ever come close to the sphere where justice matters if it were not for a right to be free. It would remain inexplicable, in particular, why an interfering person owes the justification to the person whose freedom has been infringed and not, for example, to the public at large.

The question is, then, whether the right to a justification adds something to the right to be free from interference. It would, if it made a difference. It may be possible to triangulate the difference by imagining what the force of the blemished right would be if it were not accompanied by a satellite right to justification.

---

[58] R Forst, *The Right to Justification* (New York, NY, Columbia University Press, 2012). For Forst's reply to Neyer, see R Forst, 'Justice, Democracy and the Right for Justification: Reflections on Jürgen Neyer's Normative Theory of the European Union' in this volume, 227.

[59] Neyer, 'Justice, Not Democracy', n 37 above, 908.

[60] ibid, 909.

[61] This premise is hidden in how Forst introduces the right to justification. According to Forst, any person who is affected by the act of another has a right to demand a justification that respects the principle of reciprocity. Forst, *The Right to Justification*, n 58 above, 213–14. What Forst does not spell out, however, is that such a right is the consequence of the prior right not to be affected by the acts of others. The latter is the *Urrecht* of freedom of which the alleged right to a justification is the consequence.

[62] See JG Fichte, *Grundlage des Naturrechts nach Prinzipien der Wissenschaftslehre* (Hamburg, Meiner, 1979) 111.

Arguably, if it were not for the right to a justification anyone could interfere with the right without having to lay on the table the reasons for doing so. This means, however, that there would be no right to begin with. Conversely it follows that one has a right only if interferences have to be explained with reasons. No right is absolute and not all infringements are tantamount to violations.[63]

From this it follows that the alleged right to a justification is already part and parcel of the right itself. Having a right entails the claim to be offered a reason why the right cannot be enjoyed in this or that situation.[64] The alleged right to a justification is an implication of what it means to have a right. What Neyer (and Forst) have done in creating the 'human right' to a justification is to dissociate the demand for the latter from the right itself. It gives rise to the rather bizarre result that rights without the right to a justification could be interfered with *ad libitum*.

This demonstrates that what Neyer suggests in the name of justice is nothing else, and not more than, the protection of rights. Again, the realisation of justice is reduced to keeping the protection of rights in good order—not a small achievement, admittedly, but a minimalist understanding of justice.

V. AN IMPLIED SELF-CRITIQUE

Intriguingly, Neyer's own article unwittingly contains a critique of its own deflation of the concept of justice. He suggests that respecting the demand for a justification is to accomplish something that is of relevance to justice, namely, disempowering the powerful and supplanting situations in which people merely haggle with the reciprocal use of arguments. Justifications are actually imagined to move things. The obligation of having to resort to arguments is supposed to be an antidote to mere social or economic power. It forces actors who would otherwise easily have their way to present their plans or deeds in the format of reasons. Through the basic norm of reciprocity, according to which no person may reject that which he or she demands from others, clashes among persons with unequal power are transformed into deliberations.[65] Law is the medium through which this transformation takes place. Law introduces structures—and creates exigencies—of justification.[66]

With an eye to the rectification of social or economic power asymmetries through the use of arguments, a *second* understanding of justice comes to the surface. It is more substantive then the tautological right to a justification. The demand for a justification effectively remedies—not generally, but as regards specific conflicts—asymmetries of power, first, in the relationship between Member States and, second, between institutions and those subject to their authority.[67] In this second understanding, justice demands that power present its claims in the vestige of reason.

---

[63] See JJ Thomson, *The Realm of Rights* (Cambridge, MA, Harvard University Press, 1990) 120–22. More precisely, if interferences do not have to avail of a justification the alleged 'right' affected turns out to be a mere 'privilege'.
[64] This proposition would have to be complemented by the proof that no right is absolute. ibid.
[65] Neyer, 'Justice, Not Democracy', n 37 above, 911.
[66] ibid, 910.
[67] ibid, 910–14.

As a result, power loses its grip on social relations. Power becomes translated into reason, which is then in the position to rule.

Never tired of attempting to present supranationalism as the embodiment of reason,[68] Neyer then goes on to remind us that the Union actually does not command any military force and depends, for its effectiveness, on the voluntary implementation by Member States. It depends, in other words, on their loyal support. But whence does this loyalty flow?

In the course of answering this question Neyer tacitly introduces a *third* understanding of justice. The real force of the Union, he contends, originates from the impression on the part of the Member States that the Union actually establishes a fair system of cooperation from which, albeit within limits, even the weaker Member States benefit owing to the existence of structural funds.[69] It is with this remark that Neyer's argument finally arrives at the level of distributive justice.

Neyer presents us with his own view of the dual nature of supranationalism. He envisages national democracies as constrained by transnational justice. However, instead of presenting the walls of transnational justice as self-standing, he explains how the mutual demand for justifications in a context of interdependence is consistent with an improved understanding of democratic self-government. The demand for justification is a means of representing those whose interests are affected by collective choices. Not by accident, Neyer invokes the argument from transnational effects.[70] If cooperating states were not exposed to demands for justification from others 'the external effects of the internal practices of our democracy will impose illegitimate costs on foreigners, or, if foreign democracies do so, on us'.[71] Hence, transnational justice forces any democracy to outgrow its particularity and to represent the interests of outsiders as though they were insiders. Neyer concludes that 'under conditions of interdependence … it is clear that transnational justice and national democracy mutually support and necessitate each other'.[72] Accordingly, the topic of justice finally emerges as distinct from the protection of rights or the realisation of the legal system. He believes that the governments and peoples of Europe loyally support the Union because they perceive the distributions to which it gives rise to be consistent with some normative standard of fairness. Such a view of the matter is consistent with how modern theories of *social* justice invite us to assess normatively the distribution of goods and opportunities in society. What is most often taken to be essential, in this context, is not only the protection of freedoms but also the satisfaction of a certain measure of equality. This, at any rate, has been the thrust of the major theories of justice by John Rawls[73] and Ronald Dworkin.[74]

---

[68] ibid, 919: 'Supranational organizations cannot coerce but only convince'. One imagines seeing this sentence printed on t-shirts in Greece.

[69] ibid, 916.

[70] For a critical discussion, see A Somek, 'The Argument from Transnational Effects' (2010) 16 *European Law Journal* 315–44, 375–95.

[71] Neyer, 'Justice, Not Democracy', n 37 above, 918.

[72] ibid.

[73] See J Rawls, *A Theory of Justice* (Cambridge, MA, Harvard University Press, 1971).

[74] Dworkin's 'theory of justice' is, in fact, a theory of equality. See R Dworkin, *Sovereign Virtue: The Theory and Practice of Equality* (Cambridge, MA, Harvard University Press, 2001).

VI. THE MERIT OF BEING PART OF THE WHOLE

Justice is about giving persons their due. Due is what is lawful.[75] Lawful is what comports with law. What is law in a certain type of society depends on what that society is. A society is, from a distributive perspective, what its members deem to be meritorious. Merit stands for what society believes should be rewarded with goods, influence and, most importantly, political power.[76] In a callicracy, for example, beautiful people have all the money and all the fun. In a timocracy, the members of the military call the shots. Audacious leaders are considered to be not only fit for political office but also worthy of the wealth and prestige that goes along with it. In an oligarchy, wealth is converted into influence. Oligarchs keep politicians on their payroll to exercise power.

What is considered to be meritorious, deserving of the good, accounts for the *deep* constitution of a society. It inaugurates society's ruling force, whose power can pass as acceptable only if it is presented as, and taken to be, an expression of reason.

In an oligarchy the wealthy have the right to rule, for it is assumed that they know how the world works. It does not get any smarter than the smartness of a rich person: Soros, Buffett, Bloomberg—listen when they speak! By contrast, in a timocracy the generals rule, for they know how to enact great deeds and to exercise control. If anyone, they are men of practice. In a callicracy pretty girls and handsome boys enjoy luxury and influence because they know how to charm others. To fall for somebody's beauty is not considered unreasonable in a society of this type.

Any title to rule is based on some claim that the rulers embody the *relevant* aspect of reason. Anyone who has reason has the right to enjoy rewards, for he or she is meritorious. Whoever rules, at any rate, has to be given precedence because of his or her pre-eminence.

At their deepest level, constitutions select merit in presenting one aspect of practical reason as the relevant capacity to persuade and to move others to act. Whatever is an exemplar of reason, thus understood, commands respect.

Democracy is special in that it does not recognise any *special* merit. Nobody can claim to be, by virtue of who he is, an embodiment of reason that is not also equally present in others. If there is merit in democracy it is shared by all those who contribute, to the best of their abilities, to the good of all. Janitor or chief? Who cares? Reason is, therefore, not what originates from the meritorious few but what appeals to the many.

What motivates and moves the many, from a moral point of view, is the absence of distinction. Democracy embraces equality. If a cake has to be divided in an aristocracy the better people (those with greater virtue) are free to take as much as they want first; only later will those of lower distinction have an opportunity to quibble over the rest. In a democracy, by contrast, it is all about equal shares. Nobody matters more than any other.

---

[75] See Aristotle, *Nicomachean Ethics*, trans RC Bartlett and SD Collins (Chicago, IL, University of Chicago Press, 2011) 91 (1129b1).
[76] ibid, 95 (1131a26). The following brief discussion of justice does not at all slavishly follow Aristotle.

VII. RAWLS

Democracies can be persuaded to accept inequalities. It is John Rawls to whom we owe the elementary insight that in systems of cooperation everyone may actually be better off if we do not sustain an egalitarian distribution.[77] Even those who have less than all others might be better off under an unequal distribution if the inequality is conducive to the creation of a greater overall volume of goods. Incentives to earn more will motivate people to exert themselves. Their exertions result in a greater social net product. The net product can be used to make the worst off better off than they would be under conditions of strict equality. Indeed, such a system of incentives may present exertion on the job as a special 'merit', but this reflects the use of common sense to attain the objectives based on the equal freedom of all. The moral praise of hard work, self-sacrifice and success are mere strategies to extract from individuals efforts conducive to a volume of overall output that allows each to have the largest possible share of what is necessary to make individual life potentially good. This is the radicalism underlying Rawls's original idea of the difference principle.

For reasons that cannot be explained here, Rawls would tolerate inequality only as long as it pertains to wealth and social positions, but not for civil and political rights. The latter represent, along with material wealth, an essential component of what he calls 'primary goods', that is, the kind of goods that everyone wants regardless of what he or she wants to do with her life. Everyone wants freedom of conscience. Everyone wants to be in good health. The German philosopher Wolfgang Kersting has expressed the same idea perhaps even more clearly by characterising these goods as follows: they are not everything, but without them everything else would be nothing.[78]

In a democratic society, justice prima facie demands a distribution that satisfies equality. The only inequality that overrides equality is the inequality that promises to give everyone more than they would have under a strictly equal distribution. Justice requires, therefore, social institutions that make it likely that the distribution of wealth and social standing reflects the basic idea of the difference principle.

This explains why the appeal to human rights as criteria of justice is so unsatisfactory. Such an appeal severs the nexus between the idea of justice and the creation of a basic structure of society that allocates rights and responsibilities for the good of all. The importance of this point cannot be overstated. Democratic justice can be meaningfully realised *only* through a common concern for the basic structure of society. For the purposes of distribution, a society that recognises as meritorious only the participation of its members would be unjust if it permitted inequalities regardless of how they are patterned. Whatever is determinative of a pattern counts as part of the basic structure of society.

Evidently, the democratic idea of justice presupposes that human beings have the capacity to control, for better or worse, the institutional arrangements that are

---

[77] See Rawls, *A Theory of Justice*, n 73 above.
[78] See W Kersting, *Recht, Gerechtigkeit und demokratische Tugend* (Frankfurt, Suhrkamp, 1997) 170–212.

relevant to distributions. If human beings did not have this capacity, the democratic idea of justice, and with it the idea of a democratic society, would be spurious.[79] Distributions that adopt participation in society as their ultimate criterion of justice could not be realised if societies did not have the power to control and to correct themselves. It is possible to have a callicracy by bestowing on every possible occasion power and privilege on the beautiful people. It is possible to have an oligarchy on the basis of repeated deference to the moneyed class. It is possible to have an aristocracy by assigning a special place to those who are nobler and finer than others by virtue of their breeding. But it would be impossible to have either an equal distribution, which is arguably not desirable, or a justified unequal distribution without carefully designing, for example, the system of taxation, the various entitlements associated with private property, free movement of labour, corporate law, etc. In other words, the realisation of equality presupposes *comprehensive* political control of other social spheres.[80]

The Rawlsian difference principle does not establish a yardstick that could serve as an exact measure of distributions. What counts, rather, is an ethos that prevails in society.[81] Paradoxically, therefore, the principle should be used rhapsodically to articulate and elucidate moral intuitions. For example, the principle animates an ethos of equality of opportunity that rules out status inequalities of almost 'ontological' proportions as they originate on the grounds of educational distinction. A just society does not support the development of segregated elite institutions, not only because the distinctive qualifications of elites notoriously look greater than they really are, but also for the reason that educational elite status translates into social stratification which benefits the few at the expense of the many. A just society would support highest standards throughout, and different educational facilities for people of different abilities. A just society would end the absurd and appalling privileges that are currently enjoyed by the managerial class. There is no way to justify to ordinary people that their bosses earn a salary that is 300 times larger than their own. A just society is conscious of the fact that nobody is worthier than any other to enjoy the basic good of health. Generally, a society that is animated by the difference principle would sustain efforts to make sure that people live *among* one another as equals and not *past* one another as denizens of entirely different worlds. Any such effort would include the cultural desegregation of neighbourhoods through public housing.

VIII. INCLUSION

Admittedly, this is only a very rough sketch. But it may already suffice to draw a contrast that is highly relevant for the European Union. It is the contrast between justice, on the one hand, and inclusion on the other.

---

[79] This much, I add in passing, needs to be conceded to Hayek. See FA von Hayek, *Law, Legislation, and Liberty. Volume 2: The Mirage of Social Justice* (Chicago, IL, University of Chicago Press, 1978).

[80] See M Walzer, *Spheres of Justice: A Defence of Pluralism and Equality* (Oxford, Blackwell, 1983).

[81] For a fascinating perspective, see GA Cohen, 'Where the Action Is: On the Site of Distributive Justice' (1997) 26 *Philosophy and Public Affairs* 3.

Inclusion represents an application of the equality principle that does not extend to the self-reflexive political concern with the basic structure. Rather, it takes existing distributive structures for granted. What matters is to have those included that have hitherto been excluded. At its core, inclusion treats exclusion as a social ill. It is based on the intuition that the outsiders are prima facie discriminated against by virtue of not being inside. All in! Admitting outsiders is the remedy. More precisely, inclusion is about equal access in any case where someone is confronted with an *arbitrary* barrier. It is recursive in its operation. For example, after foreigners have been admitted to the labour market, any ensuing inequality is relevant if it pre-empts people from participating in society on the ground of some arbitrary factor that creates an insurmountable obstacle of inclusion (eg, race, gender, sexual orientation, age, etc). It is irrelevant, from this perspective, whether a fully inclusive society is marked by large inequalities of wealth. The pattern of distribution does not matter. Inclusion is insensitive to the demands of the difference principle.

With the distinction between justice and inclusion we can return to the European Union. For it is undoubtedly the case that, from a social policy perspective, the European Union is overwhelmingly about inclusion into markets and social protection systems. Its grand social project, the antidiscrimination agenda, aims at the moral purification of markets to provide access for people suffering from social prejudice.

But inclusion represents a deflated form of democratic justice. It retains the emphasis on equality while severing the connection with the basic structure. Hence, it is consistent with inclusion to demand a 40 per cent representation of women on either the governing or supervision board of companies while, at the same time, supporting harsh austerity measures. Inclusion promises equality even to those who are interested in equal opportunities for privilege.[82]

Not surprisingly, the European Union has been largely oblivious of the numerous obstacles that it has put into the path of the realisation of justice. It is a truism that the Union has variously insulated markets against political challenges and intervention. It also lacks most of the competence in the social sphere.[83] Even where formal powers are available they cannot be exercised owing to a problem-solving gap.[84] Where the Union has been successful, such as in the field of antidiscrimination policy, it has shifted the focus from distribution to inclusion.[85] Even worse, the recent developments of Commission proposals and the case-law of the ECJ betray a strong

---

[82] See WB Michaels, *The Trouble with Diversity. How We Learned to Love Identity and Ignore Inequality* (New York, NY, Metropolitan Books, 2006).

[83] See C Barnard, 'Social Policy Revisited in the Light of the Constitutional Debate' in C Barnard (ed), *The Fundamentals of EU Law Revisited: Assessing the Impact of the Constitutional Debate* (Oxford, Oxford University Press, 2007).

[84] See FW Scharpf, 'The Joint Decision Trap: Lessons from German Federalism and European Integration' (1988) 88 *Public Administration* 239; FW Scharpf, 'Democratic Legitimacy under Conditions of Regulatory Competition: Why Europe Differs from the United States' in K Nicolaïdis and R Howse (eds), *The Federal Vision* (Oxford, Oxford University Press, 2001).

[85] Or this is what I have argued. See A Somek, *Engineering Equality: An Essay on European Anti-Discrimination Law* (Oxford, Oxford University Press, 2011).

preference for a liberal social model.[86] This preference makes it difficult to sustain other forms of organising capitalism that are part of the national traditions of the Member States. Finally, monetary union appears to have resulted in the rise of a collective Bonapartism that benefits bankers and harms low earners in the Union.[87]

IX. CONCLUSION

The above analysis gives rise to the following conclusions. First, the notion of justice is given short shrift when it is equated with the protection of rights. This is inconsistent with how we conceive of justice in the context of a democracy. Democracy requires treating others as equals and this excludes treating anything other as meritorious in our readiness to do our bit in a system of social cooperation.

Second, democratic justice is intrinsically related to the possibility of politics. More precisely, it presupposes access to processes with which a society can shape the structures giving rise to patterns of distribution.

Third, if the idea of equality is sustained without extending its power to this structure, it becomes toned down to the demand of inclusion. This is consistent with societies that are static and not concerned with political change. Moreover, it does not pay heed to the distributions that arise as an unplanned result of ubiquitous competition for individual advantage.

That the Union appears to be consistent with inclusion, and not with democratic justice, reveals how deeply it is at odds with democracy.

---

[86] See M Höpner and A Schäfer, 'Eine neue Phase der europäischen Integration: Legitimitätsdefizite europäischer Liberalisierungspolitik' in M Höpner and A Schäfer (eds), *Die politische Ökonomie der europäischen Integration* (Frankfurt, Campus Verlag, 2008).

[87] See for just one example Brunkhorst, 'Kollektiver Bonapartismus?', n 7 above.

21
A Reply to Somek

ANDREW WILLIAMS

I. A GENERAL RESPONSE: A ROMANTIC NOTION

ALEXANDER SOMEK'S CHAPTER in this collection[1] forces me to look again at past work of mine on the EU. This is no bad thing. His comments on my book, *The Ethos of Europe*, or rather on one final section, ask fundamental questions for me: what is the point of scholarship on the history, operation and future of this thing called the European Union?[2] And more threateningly, what is the value of my own contribution? Given our mutual focus on 'justice', this reply is intended less as an effort in antagonism and more a provoked (perhaps provocative) self-reflection.

Reading Somek again makes me think there has been a worrying strand in EU academic studies that is distinctly romantic in nature. A type of melancholia accompanies the critique, which can only see the EU through the lens of the ideal. Anything that the EU does that fails to fulfil not only its own stated purposes but also those desired by more dreamy visionaries is seen as an illustration of its hopelessness. By failing to achieve (variously) world peace, structural equality, the end of poverty within and beyond the borders of Europe, the rescue and fulfilment of democracy, the preservation but dispersal of sovereignty, the saving of the environment, etc, etc, all within some ideal of perpetual prosperity, the EU becomes a heavy disappointment. The approach pervades many accounts, underpins their premises and ultimately predetermines a charge of 'failure'. Whether 'for' or 'against' the EU as an idea or a reality, the project appears doomed.

Of course, such studies do not wear this romantic condition on their sleeves. Ironically, perhaps, critique is wrapped in an appreciation of a realist political tradition. Actors (whether governmental, corporate or individual) are deemed to operate in accordance with a number of vices: self-interest, greed, the maintenance or accumulation of power and wealth. The 'elite', as they are frequently termed (without any proper definition or even appreciation of the comparative quality of such a label), are the target of derision, those who predictably benefit

---

[1] A Somek, 'The Preoccupation with Rights and the Embrace of Inclusion: A Critique' in this volume, 295.
[2] A Williams, *The Ethos of Europe: Values, Law and Justice in the EU* (Cambridge, Cambridge University Press, 2010) referred to throughout this reply as *Ethos*.

disproportionately from the advantages and riches resulting from the EU's activities. The rest just have their burdens either unaddressed or increased.

What is the result of this trend in analysis? The danger for the romantically predisposed is that for all the identification of failure to meet ideal aims, no practical solution is offered. Nothing is capable of satisfying those ideals. Thus when looking to judge whether the EU is 'just' or 'unjust' there can only be one answer.

All this reminds me of Thomas Love Peacock, the little known Victorian satirist. He would have delighted in setting his novels today in the world of European Union critique. His unique ironic style would have been perfect to portray the intellectually rigorous but ultimately cynical nature of much of the enterprise. Peacock would have appreciated the pervading self-reverential earnestness that lacked any obvious practical purpose.

Perhaps for many years this has not been such a terrible affliction, though. For good reasons, scholars of the EU have been kept busy assessing the nature and scope of the Union, examining particular policies, decisions, constitutional proposals, legislative developments and the general impact as well as the history of the project's development. There is always a need to increase understanding and explanation of any phenomenon, any enterprise that affects people's lives, *if* we are to construct programmes of resistance or support. The intellectual underpinning for either is both valid and valuable.

That, at least, has been my self-justification for engaging in the study of the EU, for I would place myself within the cohort of melancholic romantics in case there is any doubt. And this justification has underscored my attempt to examine apparent defects (or deficits) in the EU's justice credentials.[3] What was different about the last chapter of my book, however, was that I sought a plausible way of remedying these defects. I thus placed myself in the camp generally supportive of the Union as a project. By looking to possible reform of the constitutional framework of the EU, of the philosophy underpinning it and its law, I was acknowledging that the enterprise is *capable* and *worthy* of reform. My romantic tendencies have therefore been positive. I am not sure from Somek's contribution whether his romanticism is fundamentally negative.

But before looking a little more closely at this difference, and what I see as a misreading of my work, I wonder whether Somek's identification of the sovereign debt crisis and all that has been done in response as just a 'new topic' for EU scholarship is quite accurate. There is more than a suspicion that recent measures associated with the discourse of 'austerity' (now quickly assuming mythic proportions) have provoked a sense of urgency within the field. There seems to be no longer a place for languid analysis. Critique about justice, distribution, fairness has suddenly assumed a pressing place in EU studies and politics—and perhaps some will say 'about time'. Somek appears to agree insofar as he says there is a 'current crisis' in which the 'peoples of Europe' are beginning to question the justice of a growing gap between

---

[3] See, eg, A Williams, *EU Human Rights Policies: A Study in Irony* (Oxford, Oxford University Press, 2004); A Williams, 'Promoting Justice After Lisbon: Groundwork for a New Philosophy of EU Law' (2010) 30 *Oxford Journal of Legal Studies* 663, and A Williams, 'The EU, Interim Global Justice and the International Legal Order' in D Kochenov and F Amtenbrink (eds), *The European Union's Shaping of the International Legal Order* (Cambridge, Cambridge University Press, 2013).

rich and poor and the fairness of the 'institutional arrangements' which are imposing a 'supranational constitutionalisation of austerity and retrenchment'.[4] In other words, deficiencies of justice are being exposed because of the adversities now being exacerbated or even introduced through and by the EU. Somek is not alone in this view. It is a consistent theme throughout *this* collection.

The question though for me is whether something qualitatively different has happened to challenge the romantics of whichever persuasion. Does austerity represent a new era for the EU or merely shine a powerful torch on what has always been present? Most of the contributions in this book (including my own) tend towards the latter view: austerity is but a heavy straw on the camel's back. All the institutional action and the failures to act within this particular 'crisis' is but confirmation of those structural defects which have long been present. We may see more clearly the 'injustices' of this institution but fundamentally this is a change in emphasis rather than a moment of epiphany. Another crisis in a long history of crises.

My guess is that Somek would agree. There is nothing in his contribution which suggests measures of austerity have qualitatively altered the coordinates of the EU for him. It *remains* unjust because it has always failed to be a vehicle for distribution, a vehicle for justice. Not only that but, as Somek says, it 'has been largely oblivious of the numerous obstacles that it has put into the path of the realisation of justice'.[5] Its challenge to justice has thus been a result of commission as well as omission. The Union is 'deeply' at 'odds with democracy' Somek concludes, emphasising the gravity of the justice deficit in the EU.[6]

On the whole I find it very difficult to disagree. I also think a careful reading of my various (romantic) offerings would reveal a similar position to Somek's.[7] It is true that the 'distributive fault lines' he believes I have ignored were not displayed in statistical detail in my *Ethos* book (though within my exploration of the realisation of values in the EU, those fault lines underpinned every chapter and appeared specifically in my chapter on the value of liberty). But then it has been rare for the romantic scholars of the EU to rely on data (assuming it even exists) that will determine whether the EU has helped entrench or address the great inequalities of wealth distribution within and across its borders. Despite *Eurostat* and its useful data on poverty, there remains little readily available to assess the role and impact of the EU as an institution in its own right. Somek himself provides no such determinative information. His assessment of the unjust is therefore based on assumptions (which I *think* are generally justifiable) that hold the EU as a valid primary *and* secondary agent of justice (and not simply the tool of Member States) and thus an entity to be held responsible. It has emphasised injustice perpetrated by other entities (states or corporations) and contributed its own twist.

The absence, however, of empirical data that can point to the actual impact of the EU in general and over time allows the debate about the benefits/burdens of its existence and operation for individual states or peoples to rest in evidence-free cul

---

[4] Somek, 'The Preoccupation with Rights' in this volume, 295, at 296–97.
[5] ibid, 308.
[6] ibid, 309.
[7] Williams, *EU Human Rights*, n 3 above; Williams, 'Promoting Justice', n 3 above; and Williams, 'The EU', n 3 above.

de sacs (the territory Peacock would also love). Instead, abstract philosophy, often rooted in a different era and a different economy, largely drives the imagination and the judgement about the EU's justness.

This lacuna makes proposing anything other than a simplistic conclusion that the EU is unjust extremely difficult. For, how can solutions be proposed for problems that have not been measured or even, to a large extent, exposed? Undoubtedly, pointing towards obvious inequities in Europe and the lack of success in addressing unequal wealth distribution is a useful and necessary exercise, but it hardly provides a clear sense of what to do about them. Critique then becomes the means and end. That is not what the EU needs, I believe. It is not what the people of Europe need and certainly not those who suffer the effects of austerity measures as an acute condition on top of the ever-present chronic condition of poverty (something which has been evident throughout the EU's history and is not a condition of the banking crisis). I imagine Somek and I would see eye to eye on this.

But if I generally agree with Somek, why would I need to reply?

II. A SPECIFIC RESPONSE

Where Somek takes particular issue with *Ethos* is in my proposal to look towards the promotion of human rights (not fundamental rights) as a means to attain a (more) just EU. He seems to think this is my *solution* and one which glorifies the individual at the expense of distributive justice. He also thinks that I equate 'justice with the protection of rights'. Perhaps I did not make it clear enough but this is not an accurate reading of what was written.

It might, therefore, help for me to clarify what it is I was trying to say, if only to emphasise that my proposal in *Ethos* was to look to a practical attempt to redress injustice rather than continue to stay in romantic limbo. I will do so through identifying three important matters which Somek ignores. He ignores the richness that lies at the heart of a sophisticated appreciation of the rich history of human rights and the need to see them as *both* individual and collective in nature. He ignores the internal/external dimension of distributive justice and indeed the external in the internal dimension. And he ignores the fact that human rights can be a plausible means for demanding a fairer distribution by giving voice to both individuals and communities/sectors in protesting against unfairness and inequality (as well as suffering that results from poverty whether induced in the name of austerity or not).

First, then, to be clear: do I argue that respect for human rights is synonymous with justice? No. A possible important component for achieving justice? Yes. To believe that respect for human rights has no part to play at all in the realisation of justice, distributive or procedural, feels absurd to me. But my argument is that promoting a revised conception of human rights within the EU could be a plausible route towards (a) discussing what kind of justice we should adopt in the EU and (b) how we might assess the continuing development of the EU as a just institution. This is very different from saying that justice = respect for human rights. Indeed, rather than tautological it is antagonistic. By introducing human rights into the constitutional culture of the Union, not only might there be provided a sense of direction but also a sense of challenge, a means by which the EU can be judged and can judge itself.

Similarly, at no point do I claim that justice will be solely or completely fulfilled by looking towards human rights for all answers. Their realisation and respect are necessary but insufficient. Even Rawls might have been persuaded on this up to a point.[8] In addition, I argue that taking the point of human rights (as I define them *not* as Somek assumes I define them) into account wouldcreate a better environment for dealing with injustice. Why? Not because they prioritise the individual at the expense of the collective and not because they equate with how they have manifested themselves in EU legal history as 'fundamental rights'. Rather it is because the discourse and practice of human rights is so much more sophisticated, political and capable of promoting justice than Somek seems to think. Both the collective dimension *and* the individual, both the political and the legal, can be included. One does not have to preclude the others except when applying a highly limited reading of human rights, a reading over which the EU as an institution has presided with its adopted rights language. By unquestioningly assuming that 'human rights' can *only* be about individuals, rather than an essential admixture of individual and community, informing and feeding each other, Somek is guilty of a very narrow reading of the subject.

This is not to say that human rights are flawless or without danger or non-contradictory. Critiques of human rights, of which there are many, have long shown where problems arise, problems which often seem irresolvable. In particular, their co-option by those holding power (economic or political) has been one of the most significant trials for the discourse, not least in the EU. Upendra Baxi, for instance, describes their modern manifestation as 'trade related, market friendly, human rights', suggesting they should therefore be treated with caution.[9]

But Baxi's analysis also provides hope as well as caution. He does not give up on human rights merely because they have become associated with a particular reading of them, a reading which Somek seems to adopt without too much question. Baxi warns that a 'violent epistemic exclusion arises when one focuses merely upon the state/law production of human rights'.[10] He does not discard them because of their abuse or misuse. Instead, he advocates that the future of human rights should lie in 'imparting an authentic voice to human suffering'.[11] Rather than a 'motley' selection of random claims, they have a history set deep in the lives of the oppressed and disadvantaged as well as political and social movements which have sought the very justice (distributive, in particular) that Somek believes is disregarded.

Baxi's view of human rights as a means by which that justice might be re-articulated, is the position I aimed to convey, in part, in my approach to human

---

[8] See, eg, J Rawls, *The Law of Peoples* (Cambridge, MA, Harvard University Press, 2003).
[9] U Baxi, *The Future of Human Rights*, 3rd edn (Oxford, Oxford University Press, 2012).
[10] U Baxi, 'Politics of Reading Human Rights' in S Meckled-Garcia and B Çali (eds), *The Legalization of Human Rights: Multidisciplinary Perspectives on Human Rights and Human Rights Law* (London, Routledge, 2006) 183–84.
[11] U Baxi, 'Voices of Suffering and the Future of Human Rights' (1998) 8 *Transnational Law and Contemporary Problems* 125, 169.

rights in *Ethos*. By imbuing rights with a sense of recognition that they might and could still coalesce voices about and responses to systemic injustice and suffering, might provide a vocabulary upon which collective action is constructed, might give greater strength in advocating for distributive justice, there is hope that a political movement for change could be coordinated. The struggle for equality for the lesbian, gay, bisexual and transgender communities and for the disabled have both benefitted from human rights articulation and are examples which I believe should not be ignored. The task is to translate the advances there to the systemic injustice of wealth inequality.

Perhaps this is naïve. The system may defeat its own rhetoric. That is always a danger. But my approach is patently not one designed to ignore the collective need or systemic injustice in favour of the individual or vice versa. It is subversive *because* it operates within a language accepted by the institution of the EU, but capable of provoking acts and language and politics of resistance. It can aggravate the raw empirical dimension mostly lacking in EU studies by focusing on the lives and experiences of individuals *and* communities.

Somek, however, falls into the trap constructed by those who wish to co-opt the language of human rights for non-altruistic purposes by only seeing human rights as individualistic. Human rights are assumed to be only about individuals as individuals, atomising society so 'we' becomes 'you and I' at best and only 'I' at its most base. They are assumed to be a tool of a liberal elite, whereas the history of human rights has also been relevant in articulating the struggles of disadvantaged communities. By arguing that any 'set of human rights is nothing but a motley assembly of potentially colliding limits on action or inaction by governments' (as Somek puts it) is a powerful but tired critique that accepts the proposition that they have no or only restricted value. This is to undermine and de-value the very people to whom I assume Somek wishes to see justice done. Maybe mine is still a romantic vision of human rights (though I think it is more refined than that). But it is a romance which has provided some (albeit tainted) expression for peoples which *does not* lie wholly contained within and defined by the various international instruments and agencies that Somek seems to see as their only construction. I wonder which discourse Somek might propose that was more 'just' in its ability to speak for those without voice.

Which brings me to my second concern: Somek ignores the 'human' as transcending borders in his critique, something a deeper understanding of human rights takes as given. He ignores the external dimension to the EU in its entirety. He ignores the notion of distributive justice as a global issue. This is strange if the possibility of justice across state frontiers *within* the Union is deemed appropriate. In essence that is only possible if the EU is seen as representing some developing basic structure of society whilst operating concurrently with societies contained by national borders. Somek does not make the case for this. It is another unwritten assumption, which again I am tempted to accept. But if the assumption is plausible then we are in the territory of the cosmopolitan ethic. And if that is accepted, then why should the borders of the EU be the limit? Somek's preference for 'democratic justice' demonstrably fails to address the inequalities sustained by ignoring the 'other' outside a society's borders. My aim on the other hand looks, however imperfectly, to bring the 'other' (wherever he/she/they might reside) within our vision when examining the EU and how justice might be considered a defining value.

Finally, Somek ignores the practical dimension of my preference for valuing human rights. I do not disagree that achieving distributive justice which aims to bring greater resources and opportunities to those who do not have them (or have significantly less than others) is an ideal worthy of pursuit. But the promotion, respect and fulfilment of human rights (in Baxi's and my understanding, *not* as Somek interprets them) is a (not 'the') means by which this might be better realised. By giving voice to communities *and* individuals and their accounts of suffering, the appeal of human rights might better provoke action than the rather opaque call to democratic justice. It is an appeal that *can* do some work towards injustice. That is far better in my view than forever being captured by and limited to a critique of imperfection.

III. A CONTRADICTORY CONCLUSION

It might seem to be contradictory if I conclude my reply as follows: I agree with Somek. I agree with the underlying sentiment. But I think the ethos of a society or institution (putative or actual) is important. And if that is right we should be considering the nature of the ethos that has developed as well as how it might be changed should it appear unsatisfactory. This was the whole point of my book on the subject. What has been the ethos of Europe so far? In my view one has to look at the past as it has accumulated the sediment of values and their expression if we are to fully appreciate what to do in response.

When it comes to choosing that response, we can either say, 'let's jettison the whole project' or look for means by which the project can be altered. Of course the latter option is a perilous one. Who does not appreciate that working from within might lead to co-option? But is the former course any less dangerous? And is it even advocated by those romantic and idealistic critics whose work seems shaped by fundamental antagonism towards the EU as an institution?

There is a political choice here that we all need to make, not just the politicians. It is a choice that critical scholars might be clearer on too.

22

Taking Change Seriously: The Rhetoric of Justice and the Reproduction of the Status Quo

DAMJAN KUKOVEC

I. INTRODUCTION

I WELCOME THE discourse of justice as an opportunity for change in legal thinking. However, my concern is that the rhetoric of justice could also entrench existing legal thinking, which reproduces the current hierarchies in the European Union and the world in general.

When thinking about justice, we usually have in mind the need for *change* of a current and unjust situation. Indeed, justice as a term is constituted by injustice. According to Laclau, 'justice' is an empty term. It is because there is no human situation in which injustice does not exist that 'justice' as a term makes sense.[1] A quest for *change* and *social transformation* should therefore be central to discussions of justice.

We often think about change in terms of refinement and better implementation of legal or economic theories and categories. Justice and change are often conceptualised as more accountability and participation, as resistance to free movement/autonomy considerations and an emphasis on social ones, as resistance to the 'the market', as a general protection of the weaker party, or a better theory or alignment of the entire legal system with general constitutional values and principles. Change is expected to follow from an overtly political discourse that should free us from the shackles of legal language and enable the concerns of the people to be voiced.

The danger of calls for such changes is that, despite the different rhetoric, the repetitive patterns of interpretation, which perpetuate the existing distribution of material and spiritual values, are not addressed. Instead of a resort to one or the other legal category, I will argue that change needs to be thought of in terms of the reversal of unjust hierarchies by legal work.

In section II, I explain the need for legal thinking in terms of hierarchies and address the problem of a particular type of structural hierarchy, the centre–periphery relationship. In section III, I question the possibility of destabilisation of hierarchies

---

[1] E Laclau, *On Populist Reason* (London, Verso, 2005) 96–97.

by the rhetoric of justice. In section IV, I critique the conceptual mode of reasoning in contemporary legal thought and explain how a resort to a particular legal category, the social, and to the idea of the weaker party as a predetermined category, contributes to the reproduction of hierarchies. Section V critiques the promise of change by constitutional rhetoric and specifically by ideas of participation and accountability. In section VI, I give suggestions for legal work which lawyers aspiring to social transformation could undertake.

II. REPRODUCTION OF HIERARCHIES AND THE PERIPHERY

To portray the idea of how lawyers should think about change through law, I first need to outline how I see the legal system. My view of the legal system has a static and a dynamic aspect. Statically, the legal system should be seen as a countless set of compromises, freedoms and prohibitions,[2] or legal entitlements.[3] At the same time, the legal system is also an ever-changing, dynamic structure. The dynamic aspect of the legal system is legal work,[4] that is, the daily work and bricolage[5] we do in our offices, classrooms and courtrooms as judges, scholars, or officials of national authorities or EU institutions.

The static picture of a legal system is thus static only at any one moment in time. The world, legal system and lawyers' interpretations of the legal system are constantly changing. As Heraclitus taught us, no man ever steps in the same river twice, for it's not the same river and he's not the same man. Likewise, every child that is born into a family is, while born into the family of the same name, in fact born into a different family in many respects—with different siblings than the other children, and with parents at different stages of their lives.

Nevertheless, within this ever-changing dynamic, there is constancy. We would always describe the water of a river as wet, and my parents and children will always be my parents and my children. My character, and thus my role as a son and father, will have an invariable dimension in relation to them. Likewise, despite constant dynamism and transformation, there is regularity to legal dynamics, to the way legal dilemmas are debated and to their resolution.

---

[2] D Kukovec, 'A Critique of the Rhetoric of Common Interest in the European Union Legal Discourse' (13 April 2012) *IGLP Working Papers*, www.harvardiglp.org/new-thinking-new-writing/a-critique-of-rhetoric/.

[3] See D Kukovec, 'Taking Change Seriously—The Discourse of Justice and the Reproduction of the Status Quo' (22 September 2012), www.law.harvard.edu/academics/degrees/gradprogram/sjd/sjd-current-students/sjd-candidate-uploads/taking-change-seriously-london-september-2012.pdf; D Kukovec, 'A Critique of the Rhetoric of Common Interest in the EU Legal Discourse' (26 December 2012) (on file with David Kennedy, Duncan Kennedy, Gráinne de Burca and Daniela Caruso). For the notion of Hohfeldian legal entitlements see J Singer, 'The Legal Rights Debate in Analytical Jurisprudence from Bentham to Hohfeld' (1982) *Wisconsin Law Review* 975.

[4] For the inevitability of interpretation and legal work see R Dworkin, *Law's Empire* (Cambridge, MA, Harvard University Press, 1986). Duncan Kennedy defines work as a phenomenological category: D Kennedy, 'A Left Phenomenological Alternative to the Hart/Kelsen Theory of Legal Interpretation' in D Kennedy, *Legal Reasoning, Collected Essays* (Aurora, CO, Davies Group Publishers, 2008).

[5] C Lévi-Strauss, *Savage Mind* (Chicago, IL, University of Chicago Press, 1966).

Lawyers distribute material and spiritual values. It is the legal work and daily decisions of lawyers[6] we need to focus on if we are to take legal change seriously. The task should be to recognise patterns in the dynamic aspect of the legal structure—of the way lawyers, bricoleurs, think and argue, the doctrines and theories we produce and use to construct social reality.

While focusing on justice and change in terms of better emphasis on one or the other legal category or worldview, we tend to forget that the state of injustice concerns the relationships between people in their various functions or between companies, in other words, between various legal subjects. We like to think that we are all created equal, but in the world we live in, people are set in a plethora of different hierarchical situations, some of which are more constant while others are more shifting.[7] While some hierarchies in our lives seem justified, for example, hierarchies based on merit, innovation, or hard work, many are not. Many hierarchies are based on circumstances in which a person is born (such as class, region or family), on education, cultural preferences, seniority or luck and reinforced by the fact that those in a structurally hierarchical position are better positioned to appropriate and exploit the work, merit, innovation and thinking of those who are structurally subordinate.

The existing set of compromises, freedoms, and prohibitions or legal entitlements sets up these hierarchies, and it is the plethora of these constellations that we perceive as 'injustice' that needs to be remedied. Justice, that is, change, should thus be understood as a different set of legal entitlements, structuring different hierarchies, and it is lawyers in our legal work who should rearrange them.

There are countless unjust hierarchies in the world, upheld, ignored or permitted by the legal system. Thinking in terms of centre and periphery brings domination to the fore. My vision of the centre–periphery relationship is a relationship of countless hierarchical relationships with those in a more superior position clustered in a particular space—in social organisations, regions or countries. This clustering further reinforces existing hierarchical relationships. Such a vision of the centre–periphery relationship amplifies the need for thinking in terms of hierarchies, but also distorts conventional pictures of weaker and stronger parties. In terms of countries of the European Union, the centre countries are, for example, Germany or the Netherlands and the countries of the periphery are countries such as Greece or Hungary.[8]

The economic crisis, notably its tragic impact on the European periphery, merely brings to the fore the deeper underlying power relationship between the European centre and periphery. The key question for lawyers is how the legal profession contributes to the reproduction of this relationship.

I have argued that there is regularity in the operation of the legal system that contributes to the reproduction of hierarchies in the Union. The work of European lawyers in antitrust law, state aid law, free movement law, social law, private

---

[6] For a further elaboration see D Kukovec, 'Hierarchies As Law' (2014) 21 *Columbia Journal of European Law* (forthcoming); and D Kukovec, 'Law and the Periphery' (2014) 21 *European Law Journal*.
[7] See n 6 above and D Kukovec, 'Hierarchies As Law' (Harvard Law School, SJD dissertation).
[8] For a detailed definition see Kukovec, 'A Critique', n 2 above; and Kukovec, 'Law and the Periphery', n 6 above.

law, constitutional law and various Internal Market regulations has contributed to the plight of the periphery.[9] The claims of the actors of the periphery are often foreclosed from operating powerfully in the existing consciousness, despite the fact that they often bear the externalities of legal rules. Our legal thinking tends to produce trade surpluses and an upward spiral for the EU's centre and stagnation of the periphery's economies.

While the idea of centre and periphery is far from new,[10] and although economists in the European Union have already used it,[11] the European legal profession and legal scholarship have not addressed the way in which the regular work of lawyers in various legal domains (eg, free movement law, antitrust law or private law) structure the centre–periphery dynamic.

Optimism about enlargement and a belief in the common interest of the Union are just two of the reasons for the absence of centre–periphery analysis in EU legal thinking. It may also be due to the fact that the way of centre–periphery thinking in international legal scholarship, the only legal domain in which this dynamic has so far been used, has been inapposite to European Union law. For example, third-world legal scholarship is based on the rhetoric of orientalism, imperialism or neo-colonialism[12] and could not be applied to the rhetoric of the EU in which all interests are claimed to be taken into consideration and in which inclusion rather than exclusion is the norm.

Indeed, a centre–periphery relationship in the EU cannot be properly understood as structured in a relationship between regions or countries as a whole, that is in terms of the relationship of sovereignty, as highlighted by Third World Approaches to International Law (TWAIL). Thinking in terms of domination of Germany over the Czech Republic, for example, or through concepts such as capitalism,[13] is inapposite to the analysis of legal domination through antitrust law, Internal Market regulation or private law.

The power relationship is a legal relationship between people, groups of people and/or companies at least as much as it is a legal relationship between 'countries' on the level of sovereign powers. The hierarchical structural situation in the EU thus needs to be recognised not only between regions or states, but within classes or categories of people or legal entities. And yet, there is a structure to the positioning of these hierarchies which often overlaps with the spatial position of various actors, such as consumers, companies and workers in the Union, in terms of countries in the Union.

Legal thought and work has ignored the fact that people, workers, consumers and companies in the periphery are in a different situation in the legal and economic

---

[9] D Kukovec, 'Whose Social Europe?—The Laval/Viking Judgments and the Prosperity Gap' (16 April 2010), www.ssrn.com/abstract=1800922; Kukovec, 'A Critique', n 2 above.

[10] See, eg, A Anghie, *Imperialism, Sovereignty and the Making of International Law* (Cambridge, Cambridge University Press, 2005).

[11] M de Cecco, 'Introduction' in M de Cecco (ed), *International Economic Adjustment: Small Countries and the European Monetary System* (Oxford, Blackwell, 1983).

[12] See, eg, Anghie, *Imperialism*, n 10 above; P Chatterjee, *The Black Hole of Empire: History of a Global Practice of Power* (Princeton, NJ, Princeton University Press, 2012).

[13] See, eg, FH Cardoso and E Faletto, *Dependency and Development in Latin America* (Berkeley, CA, University of California Press, 1979). For the critique of the argument of capitalism see Kukovec, 'A Critique', n 2 above; Kukovec, 'Taking Change Seriously', n 3 above; Kukovec, 'A Critique' (on file with Kennedy et al), n 3 above; and Kukovec, 'Hierarchies As Law', n 7 above.

structure than those in the centre. In other words, their structural subordination has not been recognised. In the debate about the *Viking* case[14] the considerations of workers and companies were deemed to be universal despite the fact that companies of the periphery do not relocate to the centre and certainly not in the pursuit of cheaper labour, and workers of the periphery do not protest this relocation. The privilege to protest and block relocation is thus a false social privilege for the workers of the periphery. The autonomy to relocate is a false autonomy for the companies of the periphery.[15]

As structural subordination of various actors of the periphery in the economic and legal structure has not been recognised, the definitions of a weak party in legal vernacular follow a pattern that does not include the weaker parties in terms of the centre–periphery hierarchy. Specifically, the way the notion of vulnerability and weaker party is understood accepts certain weaknesses but not others. For instance, think of the policy of protecting small- and medium-sized enterprises (SMEs). Lawyers often tend to think in terms of the need to protect small companies against big ones, hence a special regime for SMEs in EU law.[16] However, SMEs in the periphery are not in the same structural position as SMEs in the centre.[17] Companies of the periphery, including their small enterprises, have less prestige, less famous brands, a less educated workforce, lower productivity, worse logistics, fewer patents and often less experience with contracts which put them in a subordinate situation in public procurement procedures.[18]

Moreover, it is precisely because such structural subordination is not recognised by law and lawyers that the concerns and injuries of the actors of the periphery are often overlooked in the legal discourse. Despite the fact that they often bear the externalities of legal rules, the claims of the periphery are weak, subordinate and invisible. The legal profession assumes that all actors are in the structural situation of the centre. As a result, harm is understood from the position of the centre. The injuries of the actors in the periphery are structural, repetitive and unrecognised—even by the actors of the periphery themselves.

III. JUSTICE AND SOCIAL TRANSFORMATION

What potential is there for social transformation in aid of the structurally subordinate in the rhetoric of justice? What kind of legal work resulting in what kind of constellation of freedoms and prohibitions is recognised as just change? Enforcement of what kind and whose claims is recognised as 'just'?

My concern is that the claim of justice in legal argument tends to reinforce existing, powerful (conflicting) claims and preferences. The empty notion of justice as a rhetorical move enables particular demands to claim universality. Moreover, 'justice' as a rhetorical move gives particular demands the appearance of unity and coherence.[19]

---

[14] Case C-438/05 *International Transport Workers' Federation and Finnish Seamen's Union v Viking Line ABP and OÜ Viking Line Eesti* [2007] ECR I-10779.
[15] Kukovec, 'Whose Social Europe?', n 10 above; Kukovec, 'A Critique', n 2 above.
[16] See www.ec.europa.eu/small-business/policy-statistics/policy/.
[17] Kukovec, 'A Critique' (on file with Kennedy et al), n 3 above.
[18] Kukovec, 'Whose Social Europe?', n 9 above; Kukovec, 'A Critique', n 2 above.
[19] Laclau, *On Populist Reason*, n 1 above, 96–97.

Particular demands remain closed in their particularism unless there is a radical investment in their becoming universal. The structurally strong claims are deeply imbedded in the legal and political debate. For example, the social argument of workers in the position of the centre are more likely to fill the emptiness of the rhetorical claim of justice. Consequently, existing strong claims are more likely to be recognised as 'just'.

Also, law often provides a forum for the normalisation of exploitation and appropriation. Some arguments in legal discourse are perceived as 'normal', 'reasonable' and conforming to a 'traditional sense of honour' and others as 'political', 'irrational', 'absurd' or 'unreasonable'.[20] In EU legal discourse, arguments that are perceived as reasonable are often those made from the structural position of the centre.[21] By recognising existing strong claims as just, the rhetoric of justice could contribute to their normalisation rather than to their destabilisation. In the EU legal context, the notion of justice may simply further reinforce the existing, visible and strong claims of the centre.

Change for the benefit of some of the hierarchically subordinate is not easily recognised as 'just' transformation. Lawyers arguing for justice may unintentionally promote the existing constellation of hierarchies and existing legal thinking rather than promote legal and social change. In the EU context, this means that social justice, distributive justice, or justice as human rights could again be interpreted from the existing perspective of the centre.

Accordingly, adding the rhetoric of 'justice' to the existing structure of legal thinking, or a realisation of existing theories of justice, has limited transformative potential. Think of a merger case or an odd free movement case—what would the rhetoric of justice add to the debate? Many externalities are hidden from view in our current legal discourse, and they are often not even recognised as 'legal'. They will not be able to enter the legal or the political debate merely with the label of 'justice' added to them. Adding the term justice to current legal thinking risks reproducing existing dilemmas and perceptions ad infinitum. Meanwhile, actual decision making is guided by the same 'reasonable' mindset that would guide decision making without the talk of justice.

IV. SOCIAL EUROPE AND CONCEPTUALISM OF CONTEMPORARY LEGAL THOUGHT

The existing construction of 'social' Europe is an example of structural subordination of various actors of the periphery in which the argument of 'social justice' operates as an affirmation of existing strong claims—the social (as well as autonomy) claims of some of the hierarchically privileged.

Much of the current writing in European legal studies today laments an insufficient emphasis on social considerations in the construction of Europe. Fritz

---

[20] A Somek, 'From Workers to Migrants, From Distributive Justice to Inclusion: Exploring the Changing Social Democratic Imagination' (2012) 18 *European Law Journal* 711.

[21] Kukovec, 'Whose Social Europe?', n 9 above; Kukovec, 'A Critique', n 2 above.

Scharpf, for one, has repeatedly argued that European integration has created a constitutional asymmetry between policies promoting market efficiencies and policies promoting social protection and equality.[22] The perception is that the central provisions of the EU treaties insist upon the vital freedoms for an open and competitive market to operate, but what is missing from this European regime is a vision of distributive justice.[23] As a result, the talk of more social justice calls for a stronger enforcement of social considerations or more human rights as opposed to economic considerations.[24]

The interplay of social and autonomy considerations structures the debate in contemporary legal thought in general, as much as in the European Union. The principle of private autonomy is often opposed, from case to case or across a particular doctrinal domain, by the social principle validating the claims of interdependence. When rights conflict, it is likely to be an autonomy right conflicting with a right to protection against harm. For example, in contract law, the autonomy principle of no liability without fault comes up against the counter principle of 'objective responsibility' (liability based on causation). In economic policy, the efficiency gains from permitting the externalisation of costs confront those of internalisation of costs.[25]

According to Duncan Kennedy, the autonomy claim or autonomy as a doctrine is seen as identifying one as neoliberal or libertarian or free-market conservative. Giving preference to autonomy claims is in contemporary legal thought identified with the right-wing project. The social is now, in the law of the market, almost always a progressive stance, the position of the left.[26]

Indeed, strengthening social, socio-economic human rights or other social or value-laden components of our thinking as opposed to 'neoliberal', economic and 'market' considerations is the guiding line of the progressive legal profession around the world today. It pervades thinking in every domain of law, economic, property, contract and constitutional law.[27] The (anti-)World Trade Organisation (WTO), or the rhetoric challenging the work of international financial institutions, often rests

---

[22] FW Scharpf, 'The European Social Model: Coping with the Challenges of Diversity' (2002) 40 *Journal of Common Market Studies* 645; See also FW Scharpf, 'The Asymmetry of European Integration, or Why the EU Cannot Be a "Social Market Economy"' (2010) 8 *Socio-Economic Review* 211. In private law, a similar argument was made, eg, by H Collins, 'The European Economic Constitution and the Constitutional Dimension of Private Law' (2009) 5 *European Review of Contract Law* 71.

[23] See, eg, Study Group on Social Justice in European Private Law, 'Social Justice in European Contract Law: A Manifesto' (2004) 10 *European Law Journal* 653, 660.

[24] For an outline of such literature see Kukovec, 'Hierarchies As Law', n 7 above.

[25] D Kennedy, 'The Disenchantment of Logic Rationality' (2004) 55 *Hastings Law Journal* 1074.

[26] D Kennedy, 'Three Globalizations of Law and Legal Thought: 1850–2000' in D Trubek and A Santo (eds), *The New Law and Economic Development* (Cambridge, Cambridge University Press, 2006) 64; see D Kennedy, 'From the Will Theory to the Principle of Private Autonomy: Lon Fuller's "Consideration and Form"' (2000) 100 *Columbia Law Review* 94.

[27] Study Group, 'Social Justice', n 23 above, 656; Kennedy, 'Three Globalizations', n 27 above; T Evans, 'Castles in the Air: "Universal" Human Rights in the Global Political Economy' in S McBride and G Teeple (eds), *Relations of Global Power: Neoliberal Order and Disorder* (Toronto, University of Toronto Press, 2011); D Fagundes, 'Property Rhetoric And The Public Domain' (2010) 94 *Minnesota Law Review* 652; GS Alexander, 'The Social-Obligation Norm in American Property Law' (2009) 94 *Cornell Law Review* 745.

on the same assumption.[28] Justice, poverty alleviation, solidarity and advancement of the concerns of the marginalised are channelled to the enforcement of social considerations. This is then often perceived as benefiting all the workers, poor and marginalised. Even South African antitrust courts, which have been branded the most progressive courts in the world, are engaged in the same practice of an ever-stronger enforcement of social claims.[29]

In this picture, for progressive lawyers, the constant enforcement of social, altruist considerations paves a road to progress, it is a 'trajectory toward social justice',[30] while the enforcement of free movement considerations means regression. The position of the right is reversed—the social is seen as regression and free movement as progress. In line with this mode of thinking, the principal legal villain, the source of injustice, for progressive lawyers becomes the claim of private autonomy. In particular, according to the Social Justice Manifesto, as well as many private lawyers,[31] fairness and justice are understood as an acknowledgment and enforcement of social considerations, as the opposite of private autonomy.[32]

The current legal consciousness, which follows thinking in terms of giving preference either to the (universalised existing) social or to the (universalised existing) economic considerations reflects a conceptual understanding of the world. It is a conceptual understanding of the interplay of social and autonomy considerations that does not translate in real life experience, the mode of thinking I have called 'the conceptualism of contemporary legal thought'.[33]

---

[28] See, eg, GC Shaffer, 'The World Trade Organization Under Challenge: Democracy and the Law and Politics of the WTO's Treatment of Trade and Environmental Matters' (2001) 25 *Harvard Environmental Law Review* 1; K Rittich, 'The Future of Law and Development: Second Generation Reforms and the Incorporation of the Social' in DM Trubek and A Santos (eds), *The New Law and Economic Development: A Critical Appraisal* (Cambridge, Cambridge University Press, 2006) 228.

[29] *Minister of Economic Development and Others v Competition Tribunal and Others, South African Commercial, Catering and Allied Workers Union (SACCAWU) v Wal-Mart Stores Inc* 110/CAC/Jul11 and 111/CAC/Jun11 [2012] ZACAC 6 (9 October 2012). For a critique of the reasoning in this case see Kukovec, 'Law and the Periphery', n 7 above.

[30] Rittich, 'The Future of Law and Development', n 28 above, 203.

[31] Study Group, 'Social Justice', n 23 above; Daniela Caruso likewise frames the dilemma in terms of whether and how far to protect weaker parties against abuses of private autonomy, or to what extent to accommodate environmental, cultural and socio-economic concerns in the interstices of private law rules. D Caruso, 'Book Review: Christian Twigg-Flesner (ed), *The Cambridge Companion to European Union Private Law* (2010)' (2010) 24 *European Union Studies Association Review* 27. For the critique of the role of private autonomy see also U Mattei, 'The Nile Perch in European Private Law' in H-W Micklitz (ed), *The Many Concepts of Social Justice in European Private Law* (Cheltenham, Edward Elgar, 2011); Kennedy, 'From the Will Theory', n 26 above; MW Hesselink, 'The Structure of the New European Private Law' (2002) 6(4) *Electronic Journal of Comparative Law*.

[32] Study Group, 'Social Justice', n 23 above, 667: the discussion in private law, as in other fields of law, has focused on achieving a nuanced balance between trade interests and social protection and on the sacrifice of just social causes on the altar of absolute individual freedoms.

[33] For the notion of 'social conceptualism', see K Llewellyn, 'A Realistic Jurisprudence: The Next Step' (1930) 30 *Columbia Law Review* 431; and K Klare, 'The Deradicalization of the Wagner Act and the Origins of Modern Legal Consciousness' (1978) 62 *Minnesota Law Review* 265; and, generally, J Conaghan, RM Fischl and K Klare (eds), *Labour Law in an Era of Globalization: Transformative Practices and Possibilities* (Oxford, Oxford University Press, 2002). For the 'conceptualism of contemporary legal thought', see Kukovec, 'Hierarchies As Law', n 7 above.

Countless sets of analytical mistakes reproduce or are based on this conceptualism: that free movement/autonomy claims are always neoliberal,[34] that the weakest claims will always be the social ones, that justice comes from the realisation of the social claim, that the poor and the marginalised will automatically benefit from them, that there is a clear choice between helping all the poor and helping all the rich, which aligns with either the social or economic claim in contemporary legal thought, to name just a few.

The emphasis on social claims as opposed to autonomy claims or mere resistance to 'neoliberal' solutions can hardly be a recipe for a progressive agenda and change. It might serve a deeply conservative function, entrenching rather than subverting the existing hierarchies in the world and harming the weaker parties rather than advancing their concerns. In particular, emphasis on social justice and values (or generally on leftist politics of benevolent altruism) as the opposite of economic thinking has a limited transformative potential, either in the relations between the centre and periphery, or in the relationships within the centre and within the periphery, because it does not properly address the existing hierarchies within them.

In the context of the relationship between the centre and the periphery, such an approach can harm the latter. First, claims about equity or justice need to be framed as 'social' considerations to be balanced against free movement, despite the fact that what constitutes a social claim or an autonomy claim is a matter of perspective.[35] Second, because the periphery's social claims, just as with its free movement claims, are structurally weak, progressive politics from the periphery is disabled. In the current conceptual understanding of the social and economic considerations in which the universal considerations are those of the centre, the periphery's social and economic claims are systematically foreclosed from operating powerfully. The strong social claims are the existing specific claims of the centre, and they run counter to the weak or even invisible social claims of the periphery.

Indeed, there is a repetitive pattern regarding which social values and whose social values make it into the universalised equation and are then balanced. Often, it is the social and autonomy claim of the structurally privileged that enters into the balancing analysis, the claim of companies and workers of the centre.[36] However, this regularity of the interpretation of 'social' considerations is ignored. Further, the existing legal framework ignores the fact that various actors of the periphery are in a structurally different situation in the legal and economic structure than those in the centre. Consequently, it treats both 'social' and 'free movement' considerations as universal and general to society as a whole, making it difficult to discuss alternative social arrangements—or alternative modes of structuring free movement—that might have different distributional consequences.

Deployment of this dichotomy of (universalised existing) social and (universalised existing) economic considerations results in an endless game of proportionality and balancing between the present strong social and economic considerations,

---

[34] This has been the assumption of the *Laval/Viking* discussion. For one of more recent contributions, see, eg, A Somek, 'From Workers to Migrants', n 20 above, 711, 721.
[35] Kukovec, 'Whose Social Europe?', n 10 above; Kukovec, 'A Critique', n 2 above; Kukovec, 'Hierarchies As Law' (SJD dissertation), n 7 above; Kukovec, 'Hierarchies As Law', n 6 above.
[36] Kukovec, 'Whose Social Europe?', n 9 above; Kukovec, 'A Critique', n 2 above.

with endless reinforcement of existing perceptions of one and the other. Instead of interplay between social and economic considerations, the legal system should be viewed as a set of freedoms and prohibitions, a set of entitlements allocated differently between different actors, thus creating unequal distributions and opportunities. Only through this lens can we stop calling for more social considerations, as if they are general to society as a whole and as if they will improve everyone's lives.

A choice between altruist and individualist policies and ideologies[37] inevitably gives us insufficient guidance for our actions and decisions. We should not ask whether to give a preference to social or economic considerations or individualist or altruist considerations. The question we should ask is *whose* social and *whose* economic considerations in the hierarchical structure we would prefer. Likewise, the question is *what kind* of social and *what kind* of economic considerations we wish to advance.[38] The question we should be asking in our decision making is whose economic growth and whose stagnation do we further through the legal system.

Furthermore, it is erroneous to expect that strengthening the social component of legal thinking would rebalance legal entitlements in favour of 'weaker parties'.[39] When thinking about distribution through law, it is not so straightforward to identify a legal solution favouring the weakest party. The social objectives of the structurally subordinate are not necessarily contained in a specific social claim, but may be hidden in autonomy claims. It all depends on how dilemmas in specific cases are framed. Any particular claim is not inherently a 'social' claim or inherently a claim of 'autonomy'. It is only framed as a social or free movement consideration in particular contingent legal consciousness in which some claims are framed and recognised as social and others as claims of autonomy.[40] Likewise, there is no such thing as an inherent 'market' claim, solution or position as an opposite to a social, non-market claim solution or position. The EU, as well as international financial institutions, are often critiqued for their reliance on the market, but critiqued on the basis of the belief that a general phenomenon, such as the market, in fact exists.[41] The 'market', seen either statically or as a dynamic force of causation, is an illusion.[42] There are only competing constructions of the legal system with competing distributional consequences and competing options of work and decisions of lawyers and other social actors.[43] Thus, we should look to specific legal entitlements and to the specific dynamics of their change and reproduction rather than to legal categories such as the 'market'.[44]

---

[37] D Kennedy, 'Form and Substance in Private Law Adjudication' (1976) 88 *Harvard Law Review* 1685.
[38] Kukovec, 'Whose Social Europe?', n 9 above; Kukovec, 'A Critique', n 2 above.
[39] See, eg, Study Group, 'Social Justice', n 23 above, 659, 660–62, 669.
[40] See Kukovec, 'Whose Social Europe?', n 9 above.
[41] For one such critique see K Rittich 'Global Labour Policy as Social Policy' (2008) 14 *Canadian Labour & Employment Law Journal* 227. For a further critique, see Kukovec, 'Hierarchies As Law', n 6 above; Kukovec, 'Law and the Periphery', n 6 above; and Kukovec, 'Hierarchies As Law' (SJD dissertation), n 7 above.
[42] Kukovec, 'A Critique' (on file with Kennedy et al), n 3 above; Kukovec, 'Hierarchies As Law', n 7 above; Kukovec, 'Hierarchies As Law' (SJD dissertation), n 7 above.
[43] ibid.
[44] ibid.

Honouring social considerations might harm the weakest, not benefit them. For example, when a case is framed as a conflict between companies of the periphery and workers of the centre, where in this picture are the workers employed by those companies of the periphery, whose social objectives are buried in the autonomy claim of the company of the periphery?

Likewise, honouring claims of interdependence, such as a claim of justified reliance upon others, is assumed to benefit the most vulnerable. In reality, it first needs to be determined who in a particular structural situation relied on the statement of another party and who exercised their autonomy. Was the claim of reliance really the claim of the structurally subordinate? Simply because some claims are framed in the language of interdependence is not enough to assume that these claims are those of the weaker party. Would a particular claim of British Petroleum or Nestlé against its worker or distributor be the claim of the weaker party just because in the existing consciousness it would be framed in the language of interdependence and altruism, as reliance? What social objective is hidden in the autonomy claim of the opposite party that is ignored in this conceptual understanding? An inevitable link between the weakest party and the universalised social claim as framed in the existing consciousness is an erroneous conceptual assumption.

Furthermore, there is an idea of the abstract weaker party that is based on the liberal abstraction of the individual and that ignores the complex hierarchical structures in the world.[45] In particular, it is generally assumed in legal consciousness that the identity of the weaker party can be generalised and predetermined. The Social Justice Manifesto, for example, thus postulates an abstraction of a 'weaker party' as the underlying reality of the world and aims to help this presumably pre-existing category. Weaker parties are defined as those with weak bargaining power—consumers, tenants, employees, small businesses, workers.[46] The empty abstraction of the 'weaker party' appears as an eternal entity for the sake of which we need to enforce social considerations or act paternalistically.

However, the identity of the weaker party in any moment in time and in any particular case is subject to interpretation. For example, if a general legal rule claims to favour those least well-off in society, how will the notion of the weakest be interpreted? In terms of the working class in universal terms, as it was in the debate surrounding the *Laval*[47] judgment,[48] or in terms of the working class from the periphery? Likewise, consumers as a class are internally split, based on where in the legal and economic structure they are. In a particular case, a universalised consumer may actually not be the weakest party. A worker of the company going bankrupt as a result of social considerations favouring the consumer might be the weakest party, but he is out of the picture in the pursuit of benevolent social considerations.

Similarly, when we think about benefitting consumers in antitrust law, are we aware that the consumers benefitting from low prices are also workers employed by some companies? The consumers (for instance, of the periphery) who benefit from

---

[45] See, eg, Study Group, 'Social Justice', n 23 above, 661.
[46] ibid.
[47] Case C-341/05 *Laval un Partneri Ltd v Svenska Byggnadsarbetareförbundet and Others* [2007] ECR I-11767.
[48] See, eg, Somek, 'From Workers to Migrants', n 20 above.

antitrust regulation may be employees of the same companies that lose out as a result of antitrust regulation which ensures low prices for these employees as consumers.[49]

Indeed, even when the centre–periphery power relationship has been taken into account, the identity of the 'weaker party' is always subject to interpretation. Moreover, there are repetitive patterns to this interpretation. Consequently, the further danger of the general consciousness of greater emphasis on altruist and social claims is that the indeterminacy of abstract notions, like the notion of the social claim and the claim of the weakest party, is realised in the regular mode of legal interpretation, which consistently interprets some parties as weak and misses many other subordinated interests, thus contributing to the reproduction of the existing distribution of material and spiritual values in our societies and thus to the reproduction of existing hierarchies.

By the naked pursuit of 'social' claims and their automatic linkage to the 'weakest party', the Social Justice Manifesto is a manifesto of transcendental metaphysics divorcing legal reasoning from questions of social fact generally and the fact domination specifically. It deals with the problem of social justice at a purely conceptual level without ever raising the problem of the necessary appreciation of the economic, social and ethical issues which the work of lawyers should engage in the pursuit of justice and advocacy for the most vulnerable. Consequently, such reasoning may well contribute to the reproduction of existing distribution of material and spiritual values in our societies.

V. JUSTICE AS INCLUSION OF THE OTHER AND CONSTITUTIONALISATION

How can there be systemic exclusion in a seemingly exhaustively inclusive society such as the European Union, which has, according to Joseph Weiler, at least in terms of nationality, managed to include 'the other'?[50] Every society is based on exclusion, and therefore it must be a part of a community's self-definition that it constantly negotiates that exclusion and widens its horizons.[51] The European legal order certainly excludes outsiders—migrants, merchants, workers and other actors who physically or legally remain outside of the borders of the Union. Internally, European society appears inclusive. However, every society is equally based on exclusion internally, and it is this dimension that is often missing in constitutionalist and pluralist discourses.

Constitutional discourse often focuses on the synergies of a particular legal order rather than on its externalities.[52] Without doubt, there are numerous benefits and synergies to European integration. However, endless theoretical refinement of the conceptualisation of synergies is not destined to bring about 'justice' or social transformation when the problem of the legal externalities of European integration is not addressed.

---

[49] See Kukovec, 'A Critique' (on file with Kennedy et al), n 3 above.
[50] JHH Weiler, 'Federalism and Constitutionalism: Europe's *Sonderweg*' (2000) 13 *Harvard Jean Monnet Working Papers* No 10/00.
[51] M Koskenniemi, *Gentle Civilizer of Nations* (Cambridge, Cambridge University Press, 2002) 517.
[52] Kukovec, 'A Critique', n 2 above. See also Kukovec, 'Hierarchies As Law', n 7 above; and Kukovec, 'Law and the Periphery', n 7 above.

Legal thinking can cover up life's contradictions, but it can never alleviate them. We only know pain if we know love. We only know a rise if we know a fall. We live neither in heaven nor in hell. There is a downside and cost to *everything* in life. If we ignore this, then externalities, the downsides of legal rules, are hidden from view. Every act of a lawyer, every move of legal work, conscious or unconscious, is built on exclusion, as it creates some externalities. Every act of a lawyer creates a winner and a loser. The question will always be who is excluded and whose justice is being served?

The Social Justice Manifesto, for example, assumes that debating issues in constitutional language promises more justice and inclusion than another legal vocabulary. The assumption is that constitutionalisation will offer a more perfect realisation of a social market ideal.[53] For the sake of social justice, the rules governing markets and contracts need to be aligned and integrated with constitutional principles.[54] The EU treaties and the European Convention on Human Rights (ECHR) have constitutional significance and a hitherto unappreciated importance for the Europeanisation process in private law.

While the language of constitutionalism may bring about a different kind of exclusion than the language of private law does, exclusion is inevitable. How would the hierarchically subordinate interests cease to be excluded in the constitutional rhetoric? More importantly, there is no discussion of how the constitutional language could alter the deep structure of legal work and ideology that regularly excludes some vulnerable interests in society, such as the interests of the European periphery. The Manifesto, like the discussion of constitutionalisation in general, does not grapple with these difficult questions.

The recourse to justice and to documents of constitutional significance may turn out to be a mere addition, decoration and means of justification of the deeply embedded preferences of the legal profession. As such, it cannot serve as a means of deep social transformation, but risks a reproduction of existing legal thinking and of many of the existing hierarchies.

The danger of constitutional and of politicised discourse is a blindness of the systemic exclusion of certain interests from traditional channels of political expression, despite the ubiquitous rhetoric of inclusion and calls for institutional representation and participation.[55] The existing dilemmas and contradictions are merely reproduced in different terms or in a different form.

Furthermore, lack of political accountability is seen as a major source of injustice in governance around the world today.[56] For example, according to Joseph

---

[53] Study Group, 'Social Justice', n 23 above, 670.
[54] ibid, 668.
[55] ibid, 665.
[56] See, eg, N Krisch and B Kingsbury, 'Introduction—Global Governance and Global Administrative Law in the International Legal Order' (2006) 17 *European Journal of International Law* 1; W Wallace and J Smith, 'Democracy or Technocracy? European Integration and the Problem of Popular Consent' in J Hayward (ed), *The Crisis of Representation in Europe* (Oxford, Frank Cass, 1995) 137. On the EU's democratic deficit generally see, eg, A Moravcsik, 'In Defence of the Democratic Deficit: Reassessing Legitimacy in the European Union' (2002) 40 *Journal of Market Studies* 603; G Majone, 'Europe's Democratic Deficit: The Question of Standards' (1998) 4 *European Law Journal* 5; A Moravcsik, 'The Myth of Europe's Democratic Deficit' (2008) 43 *Intereconomics: Review of European Economic Policy* 331. Generally on representation, see, eg, H Pitkin, *The Concept of Representation* (Berkeley, CA, University of California Press, 1967).

Weiler, one of the three most pressing and profound manifestations of the current weakness or crisis in Europe is the lack of political accountability.[57] He argues that even the basic conditions of representative democracy do not operate in Europe. Citizens cannot even elect to replace the government, or, as Weiler put it, to 'throw the scoundrels out'. The form of European governance, indeed governance without government, is such that there is no government to throw out. Weiler asks who has ever paid a real price for failure (rather than misconduct) in European governance?[58]

While the procedural responsiveness of government is an important check on democratic control, the assessment that this is one of the major weaknesses of European governance puts an excessive emphasis on the institutional and procedural mechanism of the Union. The latter is only a small part of the problem of failure and 'injustice' in the European Union.

The central problem of the European Union's legal structure, and of the global society today, is not the occasional excesses of scoundrels. A problem too often ignored in European governance and law generally is that while mechanisms of accountability are able to remove particular people, they are unable to remove the deeply embedded structures of legal thought and preferences of the legal profession that govern irrespective of which specific people are in power, which lawyers deal with a particular issue, and who participates in the government of Europe. Regardless of the lawyer or the politician in power, and regardless of the institution that participates in the construction of Europe, such as the parliament or the executive, some issues are regarded as legal problems and some are not, only some harms are understood as legal harms and legal interpretation will follow some patterns but not others.

The creators of the Euro were not scoundrels; lawyers arguing in the way that reproduces the status quo of material and spiritual values in the Union are also not scoundrels but rather well-meaning people with lofty ideals, as are many people who work on the project of the European Union. However, the fact that people and companies are differently situated in society is too often overlooked. Similarly, the regularity of our own thinking that foregrounds certain considerations and harms but excludes others, is overlooked.

Similarly, calls for a greater participation of poorer regions in the legal process[59] have given insufficient voice to the underprivileged interests in the Union. The idea of participation ignores the deep structures of domination created through law and legal interpretation. Mere institutional participation in the system that does not recognise systemic harm to some of those who participate in the government cannot bring about change. Furthermore, the problem of false consciousness, the fact that people may not always know what is in their best interest, undermines calls

---

[57] JHH Weiler, 'Editorial. 60 Years Since the First European Community: Reflections on Political Messianism' (2011) 22 *European Journal of International Law* 303.
[58] ibid.
[59] F Nicola, 'The False Promise of Decentralization in EU Cohesion Policy' (2011) 20 *Tulane Journal of International and Comparative Law* 65; Daniela Caruso, 'Direct Concern in Regional Policy: The European Court of Justice and the Southern Question' (2011) 17 *European Law Journal* 804.

for representation.[60] The idea of participation as the primary vehicle of democratic decision making assumes that people always know what is best for them and this may anesthetise decision makers. The responsibility of decision makers to act on behalf of the subordinate is blunted or even delegitimised.

Moreover, those in a subordinate position may consent to situations they would prefer to alter and restrain themselves from voicing their concerns, despite the fact that they are fully participating in the system of governance. The conditions of subordination force people to suppress their own interests, discount their own power and consent to situations they would prefer to alter. The barriers of the subordinate are numerous, but subtle. For example, one common barrier to participation is the threat of retaliation—physical, emotional or economic—if an issue is contested[61] by those in a structurally subordinate position.

For example, a small (often peripheral) supplier providing non-branded input for a large branded company or retailer such as Walmart may decide not to contest grossly unfair contractual conditions, because the supplier is concerned about sanction from the structurally superior and more powerful company. The resistance of the supplier is limited, as the articulation of their injury might result in losing the contract with the company that provides them work and income. A supplier might decide that it is wiser to stay a supplier and say nothing about the exploitative relationship that appropriates their labour or innovative work. Institutional participation might do little to prevent or alleviate exploitation.

Finally, can a more robust political discourse of left and right and political contestation bring more justice and undo hidden structural subordination? It is often expected that overtly political language will free us from the shackles of the law, and its hopeless interplay between truth and error, and that the injuries and aspirations of the electorate can be voiced in an overtly political debate. The premise is that once legal language is not an obstacle to popular considerations, when the political deficit has been overcome[62] and when people have an opportunity to voice their concerns and longings, justice can be served.

However, the realisation of ideological abstractions of the left and right is bound to happen in a particular idiomatic fashion. Every political discourse is in the grip of a particular kind of individualism and altruism, of particular understandings of harm and particular models of social and economic considerations. In other words, the realisation of ideological abstractions inevitably occurs within a particular mindset. For example, in the *Laval* and *Viking* discussion, it turned out that the overtly political debate in terms of centre–periphery dynamics is as narrow as legal language, framed from the perspective of the centre.[63]

---

[60] The reaction of the periphery's unions and the legal profession to the judgment of the ECJ in Case C-341/05 *Laval un Partneri* [2007] ECR I-11767 is a case of false consciousness. See Kukovec, 'A Critique', n 2 above; and n 6 above. On false consciousness and paternalism, see D Kennedy, 'Distributive and Paternalist Motives in Contract and Tort Law, With Special Reference to Compulsory Terms and Equal Bargaining Power' (1982) 41 *Maryland Law Review* 563; J Kleing, *Paternalism* (Manchester, Manchester University Press, 1983).
[61] LE White, 'To Learn and Teach: Lessons from *Driefontein* on Lawyering and Power' [1988] *Wisconsin Law Review* 749.
[62] Weiler, 'Editorial', n 57 above.
[63] Kukovec, 'Hierarchies As Law' (SJD dissertation), n 8 above.

A general call for more politics and less law without a critical appraisal of structures that are ingrained in politics and—since the ideology of law is difficult to dissociate from the governing ideology in any particular society—those that are ingrained in law, has a limited range in challenging the existing state of affairs. Without the ability to articulate particular political visions and critiques, power,[64] domination and injustice are reaffirmed.

VI. PROJECTING VISIONS THAT EXPAND THE RANGE OF SOCIAL OPTIONS

Can we unpack the pattern? Can legal work resist the construction of a legal order that does not take the centre–periphery hierarchy or other hierarchies seriously? Can lawyers alter the processes of subordination and possibly reverse existing hierarchies rather than reaffirm and strengthen the injuries that our work generates?

Since injustice is upheld by the dynamism of our work, the striving for justice and for change should be dynamic as well. If change is to be taken seriously, the concerns of the subordinate, as interpreted, need to be brought to the fore and systemically given preference. The lawyer needs to identify the elements, the bricks that structure the patterns of legal work and that prevent us from deciding cases intelligently. The lawyer often needs to destabilise existing interpretations of legal categories and framing of cases, expand the horizon of harms we deem illegitimate and unjust, rethink existing doctrines and theories and construct new ones, reject the conceptualist thinking that pervades legal reasoning, and approach claims of universalisation with scepticism. The lawyer needs to present or decide a case in the best interest of the structurally subordinate according to his vision, intuition and the arguments at hand.

Economic theories, doctrines, theories of justice and other elements of decision making should only be understood as elements of reasoning or justifications for a case, as particular bricks in the hands of a bricoleur, not as sources of ready-made solutions or critiques. Neoliberalism, for instance, has been accused of a variety of evils both in the EU context as well as internationally. However, growth through law or a downward spiral of the periphery is not a result of imminent forces of causation, but a result of a plethora of particular decisions. Economic theories may provide guidance for the construction of a legal system, but a legal system cannot be understood as a reflection of one economic theory or another. Latter claims and critiques thus cannot portray an accurate picture of the structure and construction of the legal system.

Likewise, the goal of reversal of (some) hierarchies is not a realisation of one or another economic theory. No economic theory will give us a formula that we could simply follow or apply in legal interpretation. Economic theories will inform our strategic approaches, but every economic theory, just like every legal theory, will be partial and will lack a determinate force for our decision to reverse a hierarchy in a particular case. Economic theories will only serve as information and provide us with justifications for our decisions and thus support our legal interpretation. They cannot act as substitutes for legal work and for our decisions.[65]

---

[64] Koskenniemi, *Gentle Civilizer*, n 51 above, 517.
[65] Kukovec, 'Hierarchies As Law', n 6 above; and Kukovec, 'Law and the Periphery', n 6 above.

We should think about the centre and periphery relationship as a mode of legal thought, so as to instil in the consciousness of lawyers an awareness of the externalities of our daily work on either the actors of the centre or of the periphery. Domination has been reinforced by the complicity of the dominated. As I have argued, the existing work of EU legal academia and lawyers from the periphery could have been written by any typical Franz or Pierre.[66] The aim of this continuum of legal thought is an expansion of the horizon of acceptable claims, which have been hitherto suppressed or foreclosed.

When there is false consciousness on the side of the structurally subordinate, a decision maker needs to decide against the hierarchically subordinated's understanding of their best interest. Sometimes, particular sensitivity to the concerns of those who are in a subordinate position is important as the structurally subordinate may consent to solutions and situations purely due to their subordinate position. Despite all the declared possibilities of bringing injuries to the fore, such as the principle of democratic participation, the harms to the subordinate remain in the domain of the private. It is the task of lawyers to identify such silenced injuries and design legal strategies to address them.

As the myriad possibilities of exploiting others are too often irresistible to a common person, and the structurally privileged are better positioned to exploit the subordinate than vice versa, the abuse, predation or undue exercise of power by the structurally superior merits special attention by lawyers. Indeed, people in the pursuit of their goals, desires, ambitions and aspirations, or while struggling with their fears and frustrations, do bad things to each other every day. It could be someone you have just sent an e-mail to, a lawyer or CEO of a company whose products you enthusiastically buy, or someone who has just warmly greeted you and your family in the street, or it could be you.

Denial[67] of harm to those who are structurally subordinate and bad faith about injury, exploitation and appropriation of others' work play an extremely important role too. We are often only able to inflict harm on others because we are able to suppress and deny the injury to avoid discomfort we would experience if we faced it. Lawyers should not entertain denial, but face their own and others' discomfort that fuels denial and challenge it.

Finally, the measure of success of the work I am proposing is not necessarily found only in who wins a particular case. Success is also importantly measured by such factors as whether the case identifies a harm and mobilises political (including legal) action behind new social arrangements.[68]

Despite all the effort we put in the dynamic of our legal work to bring about change, with, among others, legal thinking clear of conceptualism, with decisive recognition of various harms to those who are structurally subordinate, or the use of doctrines and theories in a way they appear to favour the periphery, contesting

---

[66] Kukovec, 'A Critique', n 2 above.

[67] D Kennedy, *A Critique of Adjudication* (Cambridge, MA, Harvard University Press, 1998). For a critique of this particular notion of denial see Kukovec, 'Hierarchies As Law', n 6 above and Kukovec, 'Hierarchies As Law' (SJD dissertation), n 7 above.

[68] LE White, 'To Learn and Teach', n 61 above; C Mackinnon, 'Feminism, Marxism, Method, and the State: An Agenda for Theory' (1982) 7 *Signs: Journal of Women in Culture and Society* 515, 536.

denial of decision makers or of hierarchically privileged and contesting false consent of the subordinated, success in the reversal of hierarchies is far from guaranteed. Myriad other elements of legal interpretation could bring us back to the reproduction of the status quo. The haves might keep coming out ahead[69] simply because the community of lawyers recognises some constellations of legal entitlements as 'just' and others as 'unreasonable'. But this should not dissuade us from the struggle for social transformation.

VII. CONCLUSION

Lawyers fundamentally construct social reality, and the burden to reconstruct it importantly lies in their hands. It is lawyers and their daily legal work, choices and decisions that reproduce existing hierarchies or create new ones that we deem to be unjust. And it is precisely on their legal work as a form of constant destabilisation of the existing structure of the legal order that lawyers should focus when seeking justice, and when seeking a different constellation of legal entitlements.

A conscious construction of the legal system cannot have 'the social' or any other legal category as its guiding line. It is not the fate of the social or of autonomy claims or the fate of any other legal category or theory that we should be most concerned with, but the fate of the oppressed and dominated people and the reproduction of unjust hierarchies in our societies, including of those that we have not yet unearthed or that we have not been taking seriously.

The aim of social transformation cannot be a final solution, a perfect social order, theory of justice, ubiquitous affirmations of 'social' considerations nor a stable state of justice, but rather a constant pursuit of 'justice'. The only thing we can be certain of is that once we conclude that we have finished the job, because we have found 'justice' in one form or another—for example, in the right theory or in a state of justice—we know that our sense of justice has been lost.

---

[69] M Galanter, 'Why the "Haves" Come out Ahead: Speculations on the Limits of Legal Change' (1974) 9 *Law & Society Review* 95.

23
Victimhood and Vulnerability as Sources of Justice

ANDRÁS SAJÓ

I. INTRODUCTION

TO UNDO THE justice deficit in Europe the pragmatic issue is how to generate expectations of justice. To meet this challenge one should look at the sources of contemporary justice. The pragmatic issue for legislation and judicial decision making is how (and to what extent) to identify and accommodate the socio-culturally relevant (dominant) expectations of justice. Of course, one should not participate in this venture if one finds the demands of justice morally repugnant.

My present concern is limited to a specific source of contemporary justice that is quite influential in law. I will consider whether and to what extent victimhood and vulnerability are recognised as grounds for restorative and/or (re)distributive justice. Irrespective of the pragmatic issue, the moral issue remains to be confronted: are group victimhood (of past mass human rights violations) and personal or group vulnerability appropriate moral reasons to generate morally compelling justice claims? If so, what are the legal implications of victimhood/vulnerability for legislation and for the courts, and in particular, do they trigger obligations of restorative or redistributive 'state action'? There is a moral intuition of empathy at work here, as people tend to feel sympathy with pain (especially if it is visible), which is characteristic in the case of certain forms of victimisation. In terms of social psychology, the claims of victims can be successful as long as they could mobilise empathy and certain forms of shame. Suffering seems to raise claims of moral virtue, at least intuitively. Nietzsche recognised the relevance of the 'sorrowful history' of a people,[1] although he was concerned about weakness becoming a source of rights claims. A contemporary version of his objection might be that weakness (vulnerability) as a source of (group) rights undermines individual responsibility.

There are, however, important identity-based obstacles to the recognition of the dictates of empathy (like denial of equal status of the victim group or denial of accountability). Vulnerability may also reckon with empathy, which is relying partly on one's own feelings of being open to harm. In both instances, the development of

---

[1] F Nietzsche, *Human, All Too Human: A Book for Free Spirits* (Cambridge, Cambridge University Press, 1996) 174–75 (aphorism 475).

the moral judgement might be hampered by the inability to generalise the potential harm or injury; it is not obvious that members of the majority will conceive of themselves as potential minorities or imagine their already-born children as potentially being born with a disability.

To indicate the impact of victimisation and victimhood on the generation of rights in Europe, I will demonstrate, first, how victimhood became a successful claim for restorative justice after the experiences of the Second World War. I will also consider the socio-psychological conditions that enable or, respectively, hinder the emergence of considerations of justice in regard to victims of mass discrimination and other atrocities. This is followed by a survey of the transposition of victim compensation to various vulnerable groups. Once such transposition has been successful specific restorative and redistributive policies apply. Group vulnerability status remains contested. European social justice reflects these developments in legislation and in jurisprudence: group vulnerability is becoming a source of new legitimacy.

II. GENERATING JUSTICE CLAIMS ON THE BASIS OF 'STATUS'

A. Victimhood

The current European system is based on assumptions generated by the experiences of the Second World War. A genuine concern about victims of past injustice emerged within this frame, but only relatively lately and with a great deal of hesitation, and it is deeply related to *Realpolitik* and affordability. Victimhood became a successful claim for restorative justice in cases of fundamental historical mass human rights violations, at least where genuine or less genuine acceptance of responsibility and related compensation for such past misdeeds occurred.[2]

Concerns about victims of the gravest state-inflicted mass-scale human rights violations satisfy elementary demands of reparative or restorative justice, although a number of social identity and other mechanisms successfully militate against it. Without special compensatory and protective measures, the disadvantageous social position of the victimised will persist. Collective victim status creates special social relations and psychological predispositions on both sides (victim groups and the national collectivity that feels a moral obligation of responsibility). The Canadian Supreme Court concluded that historically created disadvantages, consisting in the deprivation of fundamental human needs, create the likelihood of continued

---

[2] For the resulting special concern (legal sensitivity) for past injustice, see the German Holocaust Denial Case: BVerfGE 90, 241, 1 BvR 23/94 (13 April 1994). 'The historical fact itself, that human beings were singled out according to the criteria of the so-called Nuremberg laws and robbed of their individuality for the purpose of extermination, puts Jews living in the Federal Republic in a special, personal relationship vis-à-vis their fellow citizens; what happened [then] is also present in this relationship today. It is part of their personal self-perception to be understood as part of a group of people who stand out by virtue of their fate and in relation to whom there is a special moral responsibility on the part of all others, and that this is part of their dignity. Respect for this self-perception, for each individual, is one of the guarantees against repetition of this kind of discrimination and forms a basic condition of their lives in the Federal Republic. Whoever seeks to deny these events denies vis-à-vis each individual the personal worth of [Jewish persons]. For the person concerned, this is continuing discrimination against the group to which he belongs and, as part of the group, against him.'

discrimination.[3] Hence, such traditionally discriminated groups are to be provided special protection in order to enable them to participate fully in social life. This statement was made in the context of anti-gay discrimination. The consideration is that of vulnerability (see below).

The recognition of 'victims of history' as a class satisfied certain demands of justice as well as generational and political demands in many countries (eg Germany and South Africa). This was reinforced by empathy felt at injury, which is clearly associated with victimhood. Past suffering as a basis for claims of reparative justice became part of the public discourse, and had good chances of success. Such claims appeal to the consciences of the potential perpetrators and their heirs. Victimhood gained a kind of social respectability, and resulted in a generalised fear to cause harm to potential victims (as a specific though undefined moral class). The reasons for such respectability are not self-evident. Martyrs were venerated from the early days of the persecution of Christians, but it was their unconditional dedication to the religion (ie to a cherished cause) that caused admiration. Modern victimhood is accidental. It is the calamity of the act, in particular the reasons motivating the aggressor, that triggers special concerns for the victim.

The success of victim claims in situations of mass atrocities committed by a majority or by authorities on behalf of majorities or nations is surprising. The presence of past victims and their descendants among the population, or with their ghosts in the minds of the morally sensible members of the community, allows for shaming at the national level. Victim groups may opt for a policy of shaming to shape the public sentiment in their favour. They may rely on exposure of the majority as being beneficiaries of malefactors. But it is relatively easy to resist such complicity by denying causation. There are few of the bodily elements that characterise individual shame, namely the exposition of the body, or of appearing different from the moral person one pretends to be.

Nevertheless, how the judiciary handles past collective injustice against groups of citizens can be of foundational constitutional importance. Injustices that caused suffering and made the oppressed feel shame for their ill-fortune are identified as the foundation of the previous regime. The new constitutional regime emerged to undo that injustice. The grand injustice shamed its victims and the constitution attempts to redeem past suffering by turning victims into beneficiaries. It was understood that the white minority might have moral responsibility for causing humiliation, but to create a new functioning political society, legislators and the South African Constitutional Court preferred reconciliation without giving much preference to victims of apartheid in the name of undoing past injustice.[4]

---

[3] *Egan v Canada (AG)* [1995] 2 SCR 513 (25 May 1995), 518. The South African Constitutional Court followed the Canadian position, see *President of the Republic of South Africa and Another v Hugo* [1997] CCT 11/96 (18 April 1997). The position of the Canadian Supreme Court on the significance of reviewing past discrimination was expressed recently in even stronger form in *Law v Canada (Minister of Employment and Immigration)* [1999] 1 SCR 497 (25 March 1999).

[4] *City Council of Pretoria v Walker* [1998] CCT 8/97 (17 February 1998), paras 1, 43–48. When the Pretoria Municipality charged a consumption-based tariff for electricity and water in former white suburbs and a lower, flat rate in former black townships, the SACC found that the disadvantage to whites was indirect discrimination on the basis of race. The resulting constitutional presumption of unfair discrimination was rebutted because the complainant was a member of a previously advantaged minority group. However, the Court found partly against the policy that was directed against the formerly advantaged group.

Under specific circumstances, where the majority is embedded in shame, there might be reliance upon, and deliberate production of shame for foundational injustice, at least to a limited extent. In Germany the political and intellectual elite successfully imposed shame on the majority for the Holocaust, resulting in specific recognition of victim status.[5] The recognition of inhumanity was consolidated in constitutional law and jurisprudence. The legal measures taken against Holocaust denial and racist speech and the related judicial interpretation illustrate how the foundational constitutional injustice of Nazism was recognised and turned into a source of social shaming. However, the recognition is also dependent on the organised strength of the victim groups: while Jews in Germany, and gradually even those living outside Germany received more and more compensation, the same did not apply to Roma. This was the understanding of the *Bundesgerichtshof*, which denied compensation on grounds of lack of evidence of racial persecution before 1943.[6] This was the approach at least until 1963. In other countries with a different historical responsibility for past wrongdoing there is less recognition of the importance of victimhood, or different types of victims are selected, resulting in little legal compensation for those groups.

Constitutional law that is not animated by empathy towards the victim and by public sentiments of shame (or even guilt) may contribute to the perpetuation of the feelings of injustice, inferiority and insecurity. Where racist speech is construed as protected and therefore the harm to racially targeted group members is judicially non-existent, it is argued that such lack of sensitivity reproduces injustice.[7] The potential victims believe that the state shamefully disregards their fundamental human need of security of life and existence. When authorities tolerate racist attacks this gesture immediately reminds potential victims of the earlier deprivation of their security and suffering.

It must be underlined that certain forms of past injustice are of such a nature that they present special, hard to resist claims on behalf of victims. The injustice of genocide creates moral emotions among bystanders who would expect something similar among those who contributed politically to such developments. One should feel shame and responsibility if one is exposed as a member of a collective, on behalf of which or in the name of which, atrocities were committed. Restorative justice applied to victims would mean that the members of the responsible community deny continuity with the 'evil' characteristics of the community. As to the descendants of perpetrators the 'forms of life' that enabled mass atrocities is what is inherited and this dictates vigilance: responsibility is patrolling our moral borders. 'Our own life is linked to the life context in which Auschwitz was possible ... intrinsically'.[8]

---

[5] Consider Siegfried Lenz's 'Auschwitz bleibt uns anvertraut'. This is the title of the celebrated German writer's speech honouring the German Peace Prize on 9 October 1988. The text is available at www.friedenspreis-des-deutschen-buchhandels.de/sixcms/media.php/1290/1988_lenz.pdf.

[6] J von dem Knesebeck, *The Roma Struggle for Compensation in Post-War Germany* (Hertfordshire, University of Hertfordshire Press, 2011).

[7] Governmental forgiveness might suggest the need to forget. See M Minow, *Between Vengeance and Forgiveness* (Boston, MA, Beacon Press, 1998) 17.

[8] J Habermas, *The New Conservatism: Cultural Criticism and the Historians' Debate* (Cambridge, MA, MIT Press, 1989) 233. According to Müller, 'The suffering of the victims imposed a debt of "intersubjective liability" on successive generations'. J-W Müller, 'On the Origins of Constitutional Patriotism' (2006) 5 *Contemporary Political Theory* 278, 292.

As the Hassidic teacher, Baal Shem Tov stated: 'Remembrance is the secret of redemption'.[9] Recognition of victim status, once institutionalised, will quickly make the potential victims feel more secure and integrated. It improves the moral qualities of society by opening up a learning process. It is only through collective learning that the past can be intellectually processed and neutralised and finally turned into simple history. Accepting the claims of victimhood means taking responsibility for past crimes committed by the state and other social institutions. Such a responsibility dictates that a society must dispose of the falsifications present in its history. When a society ignores this responsibility, it enables falsification of patterns of behaviour that resulted in gross injustice in the past. There will be no moral sentiment guiding us at the reoccurrence of those patterns.

There are, however, formidable cognitive obstacles in the way of forming such feelings. People sustain and even reinforce pre-existing categories and frames, which make them exempt from participating in the chain of past events. Only traumatic collapse of the personal life world and the community that reinforced one's belief and identity gives a chance for breaking cognitive frames. There are a number of coping techniques for dispositional forgiveness, that is, a general tendency to forgive. Strelan indicates that

> individuals may blame an actual situation, for example, the circumstances surrounding a debilitating illness or accident. More likely, however, they may react to the perceived abstract source of the circumstances that led to the situation, by blaming what happened on 'life', or 'an unjust world', or 'fate' ... and also 'the cruel world' that brought about the circumstances which caused the accident.[10]

Self-forgiveness is another important mechanism that applies even where framing of one's act is of no help in denying transgression. Self-forgiveness does not necessarily mean denial of the appropriateness of shame and that harm was caused to others.

> Taking responsibility is a key aspect of self-forgiveness ... in forgiving the self, individuals do not abdicate responsibility for their part in a negative outcome, nor do they transfer blame to circumstances or another.[11]

The recognition of certain group claims of being victims of historical injustice resulted in a competition for entry into the circle of 'certified' victims. Moreover, claims based on victimhood became attractive outside the circle of state-caused injury, for example, in the case of crime victims whose special claims raise important difficulties for due process and the rights of the accused.

---

[9] Quoted in M Bernard-Donals and R Glejzer, *Between Witness and Testimony: The Holocaust and the Limits of Representation* (Albany, SUNY University Press, 2001) 158.

[10] P Strelan, 'Who Forgives Others, Themselves, and Situations? The Roles of Narcissism, Guilt, Self-Esteem, and Agreeableness' (2007) 42 *Personality and Individual Differences* 259, 260. Strelan refers to L Yamhure Thompson et al, 'Dispositional Forgiveness of Self, Others, and Situations' (2005) 73 *Journal of Personality* 313. The contemporary bad reputation of shame (see above) is partly related to the observation that people in depression are less likely to forgive themselves, hence guilt and shame are seen as perpetuating a miserable personal condition that is not conducive to pro-social behaviour. But it does not follow that shame per se causes the depression: the negative effects of shame are related to people with depression.

[11] Strelan, 'Who Forgives Others', n 10 above.

In exchange, victims and potential victims who jumped on the bandwagon accepted their past or residual weakness and current vulnerability. This may well be a strategic claim, as it makes their legal claim stronger. Given the respectability of victim status, many groups choose to argue their claims in similar terms, at the expense of changing their identity into that of a victim instead of claiming historical or other merits (eg, 'victims of the imperialism of other states' instead of 'worthy defenders of the West').

Of course, envy, denial and dire economic realities as well as a more aggressive (often nationalistic) identity limited these restoration claims. The related taboo— namely, that there can be no more state or private action resembling past gross human rights violations, especially against past victims—was often broken. See, for example, the limited compensation granted to victims of communist oppression. The jurisprudence of the European Court of Human Rights (ECtHR) is also criticised for being restrictive in matters of property restitution in Eastern Europe. The treatment of Roma claims in Germany is another example.

It should be added that the recognition of victimhood as rights (entitlements) generating status is resisted in many legal systems, partly because of the specific power relations but also to a considerable extent due to judicial consideration. Victim claims will not work if the injustice can be fended off. Defused injustice does not generate enough shame/guilt for a special recognition of responsibility that is needed for group victim protection. Consider the example of the United States. President Kennedy stated in his 1963 message to Congress on Civil Rights that 'The venerable code of equity law commands "for every wrong, a remedy"'.[12] What made public sentiment more favourable to remedy and the African–American in general was among others shame resulting from exposure of the whites as accomplices of cruelty and oppression.

The US Supreme Court hardly ever endorsed a judicial policy recognising victim status as a means of undoing past injustice. This is consistent with the Supreme Court's general dislike towards empirically non-identifiable standards. Around 1968, at the height of exposure of the injustice of racism, there was a moment when there seemed to be enough public sentiment and legal sensibility for the judicial acknowledgement of past injustice as grounds for enhanced legal protection. Some courts were ready to consider race a 'suspect' category, 'not because [race] is inevitably an impermissible classification, but because it is one which usually, to our national shame, has been drawn for the purpose of maintaining racial inequality'.[13] But this attempt was rejected in the name of policy considerations: shame did not seem to offer clear judicial answers. For the Supreme Court, Rule of Law considerations prevail in the undoing of past injustice. When it came to affirmative action in *Regents of University of California v Bakke*,[14] there was no concern about the collective responsibility that would perhaps justify additional burdens imposed on

---

[12] Doc 124, 88th Cong, 1st Sess 2 (1963). Somewhat later in 1987, Second World War Japanese internees generated enough shame for compensation. See S 1009, 100th Cong, 1st Sess (1987).

[13] *Norwalk Core v Norwalk Redevelopment Agency* 395 F2d 920 (CA2, 7 June 1968), which was referred to in *Gratz v Bollinger* 539 US 244(23 June 2003) (Justice Ginsburg, with whom Justice Souter joined, dissenting).

[14] *Regents of University of California v Bakke* 438 US 265 (28 June 1978).

'innocent' present members of society in favour of victims and their descendants. Even Justice Marshall's passionate language in his partial dissent in *Bakke* that evoked past injustice stopped short of creating a specific duty of restorative justice.[15] But the argument centres on the consequences of discrimination (past and present) on the victim's personality and the needs of a fully integrated society. The victims' group is protected against suspect classification and through affirmative action in view of contemporary dignity (just society) considerations and not because of injustice that turned the group into victims that would trigger restorative justice claims.[16]

Again, in the case of the mentally disabled and gays the recognised history of past discrimination was insufficient for triggering a general constitutional politics of special protection, expressing shame for past injustice. Even those Justices who were sympathetic to a stronger protection of the rights of the mentally disabled by granting them middle level scrutiny would have based this protection on pragmatic considerations, namely the prejudice of the majority, not a moral emotion that *should* develop. 'Most important, lengthy and continuing isolation of the retarded has perpetuated the ignorance, irrational fears, and stereotyping that long have plagued them.'[17] For the majority in *Cleburne*, legislation might have relied on sympathy and pity, but that is not the proper ground for the judicial approach.

In view of the above examples, one can say that the Supreme Court did not accept the general idea that vulnerable groups are subject to political subordination and marginalisation.

B. Vulnerability

Vulnerability is a concern that intends to contribute to the emerging European value system and related generation of the law. Victimhood is translated into vulnerability (members of groups of past mass injustice remain psychologically and materially vulnerable) and this assumption is easily reversed. Vulnerable groups are like vic-

---

[15] ibid. The prevailing consideration in Justice Powell's rejection of any specific consideration of past injustice as a ground for preferential treatment is one of (*otherwise*) sound judicial policy. He refused 'the remedying of the effects of "societal discrimination", an amorphous concept of injury that may be ageless in its reach into the past', and only specific actual instances of present discrimination were held to be redressable. *Bakke* 307, 296–97.

[16] 'The primary purpose of the Civil Rights Act of 1964, however, as the Court recognises, and as I would underscore, is the vindication of human dignity, and not mere economics. The Senate Commerce Committee made this quite clear: "The primary purpose of ... [the Civil Rights Act], then, is to solve this problem, the deprivation of personal dignity that surely accompanies denials of equal access to public establishments. Discrimination is not simply dollars and cents, hamburgers and movies; it is the humiliation, frustration, and embarrassment that a person must surely feel when he is told that he is unacceptable as a member"'. *Heart of Atlanta Motel, Inc v US* 379 US 241(14 December 1964), 291–92 (Justice Goldberg, concurring).

[17] *City of Cleburne Tex v Cleburne Living Center* 473 US 432(23 April 1985) (Justice Marshall, with whom Justice Brennan and Justice Blackmun join, concurring in the judgment in part and dissenting in part). 'Surely one *has to feel sorry* for a person disabled by something he or she can't do anything about, but I'm not aware of any reason to suppose that elected officials are unusually unlikely to share that feeling.' JH Ely, *Democracy and Distrust: A Theory of Judicial Review* (Cambridge, MA, Harvard University Press, 1980) 150, quoted in *Cleburne* 442 (emphasis added).

tims and therefore comparable justice claims may apply. Vulnerable groups (eg, the disabled) and individuals are engaged in a legitimate fight to remove, at least partly, the badge of inferiority and resulting shame. But in terms of language this attempt at liberation, that is easily translated into entitlement claims, had a peculiar consequence. Victim groups started to argue for material improvement and reparation. In this process victim status as such became a legitimate argument for compensation. Hence many other positions of inferiority are perceived as the result of victimisation. Victimhood becomes the key to deny personal responsibility for the individual's fate, disadvantages and sufferings, even where the failure to live up to expectations is due partly to one's own failure. The unpleasant situation is explained as one of victimisation (fault of others). The language of victimhood attempts to impose guilt on those who are blamed for the real or alleged position of the victims.

The partial success of this reversal and its limits are to be understood in the context of the above culture of victimhood. The cultural issue is this: how to generate a situation where a claim is turned into a claim of vulnerability and transformed into (associated with) victimhood that will make claims hard to resist. But once again, there are certain obstacles to such transformation. It is more difficult to prove (impose or self-impose) responsibility for vulnerability than in the case of mass historical injustices amounting to blatant human rights violations, and it is psychologically difficult to mobilise empathy for personal vulnerability, as shame and identity concerns, as well as the need for a belief in personal invulnerability, are often acting against it, especially where empathy-generating suffering is absent.

Nevertheless, the historical or genealogical relationship is obvious. The Roma were historically persecuted and are subject to continued social prejudice and exclusion. This makes them on the one hand vulnerable to harm and on the other hand provides a culturally unchallengeable claim to authorship (agency) in the formation of the situation of vulnerability. Though such factors as national identity-related prejudice and middle-class social angst develop populist arguments about the faults of Roma which would deprive them of the status of a vulnerable group (or 'minority'), the claim that this is a vulnerable class (for purposes of legal classification) fits well into the prevailing European paradigm. Victimhood arguments may apply to other suspect classes (ie groups which receive particular protection), but victimhood arguments are seldom accepted for national or even religious minorities which are political competitors or otherwise pose too powerful a threat. Victimhood is a source of rights generally where the victims remain weak and unthreatening to the political and ideological status quo, showing that extension of special protection is limited by the majority's national culture-oriented bias. While this chapter deals with the use of victimhood and vulnerability in the generation of justice claims, one has to underline the ambiguity of these claims; an ambiguity that may restrict the credibility and scope of related justice claims. Robert Castel refers to those groups that are forced to rely on their traditional identity. Groups, such as migrants, have to refer to particularistic claims:

> The difference from others becomes dangerous only when the rights of humans to be humans are denied, or when human individuals are disparaged for their differences. This is how pertinence to Islam becomes radical Islamism; this leads to the situation where a black

person, only because he is black and despised will complacently assign himself the role of the victim of slaveholders; he will deem appropriate to arrogate compensation for being a victim.[18]

Of course, it is understandable that one intends to turn a history of suffering into a source of power and privilege.[19] Given the moral high ground, victimhood arguments are often irresistible (if well organised) and therefore attractive with problematic consequences for group identity.[20]

Of course, even successful claims for obtaining 'vulnerable group' status (on grounds of past wrongdoing and current resulting vulnerability, perhaps with some showing of actual harm) may have different legal consequences and may not result in the same level of compensation. Roma as a group are denied compensation for past persecution. Instead, at least in human rights law, there is an increasing willingness to create presumptions in their favour in cases involving alleged discrimination.[21] Affirmative action or other special privilege (eg, in regard to Roma culture, or way of life) is not part of European public policies, or, if it exists, it is based on pragmatic social policy grounds rather than a rights-driven approach. In other cases, as in the case of disabled people, there is limited affirmative social action (eg, in the context of mobility), while welfare services (to the extent that they go beyond generally applicable welfare) are not provided as a right, although at least on paper, there seems to be a trend in that direction.[22]

An interesting development is the attempt to extend group vulnerability to socio-economic status. This possibility is recognised as a strategic goal in feminist literature. The socio-economic disadvantage is construed as the result of what Nancy Fraser called misrecognition, where 'institutionalised patterns of cultural value ... constitute some actors as inferior, excluded'.[23] In such a construction of exclusion (which is increasingly detached from socially constructed and/or essentialist characteristics), causation is attributed to social arrangements, even if the actual economic consequences on members of the group are attributable to structural elements of the

---

[18] R Castel, *La discrimination négative*, *La république des idées* (Paris, Seuil, 2007) 99.
[19] See S Steele, *The Content of Our Character: A New Vision of Race in America* (New York, NY, Harper Perennial, 1991) 118.
[20] See in general A Finkielkraut, *Le juif imaginaire* (Paris, Seuil, 1980) 18ff. T Todorov refers to the resulting and unfortunate competition among victims, *Les abus de la mémoire* (Paris, Arléa, 2004) 57. Genocide and Holocaust became trademarks with competing exclusivity claims.
[21] See, eg, *Horváth and Kiss v Hungary* App No 11146/11 (ECtHR, 29 January 2013). The Court refers to 'the positive obligations of the State to undo a history of racial segregation in special schools' (para 127). The Court has further established that, 'as a result of their turbulent history and constant uprooting, the Roma have become a specific type of disadvantaged and vulnerable minority' (para 102).
[22] See, eg, Recommendation Rec(2006)5 of the Committee of Ministers to Member States on the Council of Europe Action Plan to promote the rights and full participation of people with disabilities in society: improving the quality of life of people with disabilities in Europe 2006–2015 (5 April 2006). The Recommendation requires the Member States to 'provide *equal access* to social protection for people with disabilities' (emphasis added). See further B Marin, 'Transforming Disability Welfare Policy. Completing a Paradigm Shift' in C Prinz (ed), *European Disability Pension Policies: 11 Country Trends 1970–2002* (Aldershot, Ashgate, 2003) 23.
[23] N Fraser, 'Rethinking Recognition' (2000) 3 *New Left Review* 116. For additional literature and a review of the European Convention on Human Rights' vulnerability practices, see L Peroni and A Timmer, *Vulnerable Groups: The Promise of an Emerging Concept in European Human Rights Convention Law* (manuscript, 2012). I follow their analysis closely.

given socio-economic system. In more pragmatic terms, old claims for wealth redistribution (in particular in favour of the poor and 'middle' classes, are presented as claims where the fact of the allegedly higher vulnerability serve, often in conjunction with the needs of protection of dignity for the vulnerable group members, as justification for social services that are otherwise not due (eg, in absence of participation in a welfare scheme). The acceptance of this logic is supported by very different concepts of justice and ideologies, ranging from ethics of care to hidden socialist agendas.

The judgment of the European Court of Human Rights in *MSS v Belgium and Greece*,[24] a case concerning an illegally entered asylum seeker, is quite telling. The asylum seeker was considered to be 'a member of a particularly underprivileged and vulnerable population group in need of special protection' comparable to Roma schoolchildren (see, mutatis mutandis,*Oršuš and Others v Croatia*).[25] In *MSS*, the Court found that given the responsibility of the state for the treatment of this applicant, the situation of extreme material poverty of the members of this group amounted to inhuman and degrading treatment. The applicant was wholly dependent on state support, and faced official indifference in a situation of serious deprivation and want incompatible with human dignity.

> Given the particular state of insecurity and vulnerability in which asylum seekers are known to live in Greece, the Court considers that the Greek authorities should not simply have waited for the applicant to take the initiative of turning to the police headquarters to provide for his essential needs.[26]

The definition of vulnerability endorsed by the majority decision in *MSS* contrasted with the Court's established understanding of the term. The notion of a particularly vulnerable group had previously been applied in cases involving gender,[27] race,[28] sexual orientation[29] and mental illness.[30] These groups were historically subjected to prejudice with lasting consequences, which resulted in social exclusion. As argued in the separate judicial opinion in *MSS*, asylum seekers as a group have not historically been subjected to prejudice that had lasting consequences or that resulted in their social exclusion. In fact, they are not socially classified, and consequently treated, as a group. Although some are in fact vulnerable, the Court gave no persuasive reason why asylum-seeker status should constitute a rebuttable presumption in regard to the members of the 'class'. The Court's willingness to find a violation nudged toward an understanding of vulnerability where, dictated by judicial precedent, the state has a general and unconditional positive obligation to provide shelter and other material services to satisfy the needs of an ever-expanding group.[31]

---

[24] *MSS v Belgium and Greece* App No 30696/09 [2011] 53 EHRR 2 (ECtHR (GC), 21 January 2011).
[25] *Oršuš and Others v Croatia* App No 15766/03 (ECtHR, 16 March 2010), para 147.
[26] *MSS v Belgium and Greece* App No 30696/09 [2011] 53 EHRR 2 (ECtHR (GC), 21 January 2011), para 257.
[27] *Abdulaziz, Cabales and Balkandali v United Kingdom* App Nos 9214/80, 9473/81 and 9474/81 Series A No 94 [1985] 7 EHRR 471 (ECtHR (PL), 28 May 1985), para 78.
[28] *DH and Others v Czech Republic* App No 57325/00 [2008] 47 EHRR 59 (ECtHR (GC), 13 November 2007), para 182.
[29] *EB v France* App No 43546/02 (ECtHR(GC), 22 January 2008), para 94.
[30] *Alajos Kiss v Hungary* App No 38832/06 (ECtHR, 20 May 2010), para 42.
[31] *MSS v Belgium and Greece* App No 30696/09 [2011] 53 EHRR 2 (ECtHR (GC), 21 January 2011), Separate opinion of Judge Sajó.

III. CONSEQUENCES OF STATUS CLAIMS ON RESTORATIVE AND REDISTRIBUTIVE POLICIES

The respect for and even cult of victimhood and vulnerability is a welcome development of civilisation vis-á-vis a pseudo-Nietzschean cult of strength and force. However, it remains open to criticisms of paternalism and it may diminish incentives to perform. Moreover, it has generated an unfortunate race for resources where incommensurable sufferings are competing. Such competition diminishes the pressure on taking responsibility where responsibility could be reasonably attributed. It remains to be seen if a vulnerability-dictated social policy is efficient in its distributive consequences or even credible as just. It may result in odd situations, for example, where a parking place is not only reserved for the disabled but is also provided for free, irrespective of the financial means of the disabled car owner. In regard to judicially administered justice, an extended concept of group vulnerability undermines the possibility of ranking: where too many classes qualify, there can be no guidance. Where privileged handling is granted to whole groups (or suspect classes) without clear reasons, the moral grounds of justice (based on responsibility for action) are missing.

The prevailing approaches are subject to criticism, as some problematic groups of victims of past and current discrimination are easily left out from the list (national and religious minorities).

In terms of legislation, a more sensitive understanding of problems of equality has emerged, which tends to take into consideration vulnerability. But this remains primarily within the logic of equality-as-justice, and it cannot solve in itself what kind of equality and non-discrimination (or simply equality as non-discrimination) satisfy justice. The redistributive policies dictated by 'status' are seldom conceived as affirmative action at the level of providing social services or even access to such services. Redistribution may provide vulnerable disadvantaged people with the same benefits that other disadvantaged or ordinary 'qualifying welfare recipients' are entitled to, but there is no consideration for granting the additional amount or service that would undo the special disadvantage of the vulnerable person (or group).[32] The level and even the legitimacy of redistribution based on vulnerability (eg, disability) is contested. Groupthink may have unjust redistributive effects, especially where it precludes means tests. It is remarkable how easily special needs-oriented welfare (eg, disability pensions) is eliminated in the context of austerity, where the disabled and other vulnerable groups seem to suffer more (and are the first target of austerity measures).

IV. CONCLUSION

At least since *Carolene Products*,[33] the protection of vulnerable groups has been the standard purpose of and justification for judicial control over legislation. In

---

[32] This might change in regard to disabled people as the Convention of the Rights of Persons with Disabilities may bring in a new rights paradigm. See P Harpur, 'Embracing the New Disability Rights Paradigm: The Importance of the Convention of the Rights of Persons with Disabilities' (2012) 27 *Disability and Society* 1.
[33] *United States v Carolene Products Co* 304 US 144(25 April 1938).

the American context, this was based on democratic theory: as insular groups were unable to protect themselves in the democratic process against majority bias, the courts have a legitimate basis to intervene (the 'defender' of the weak role, where the showing of certain weaknesses triggers legitimate judicial intervention). Here the justice problem or even deficit lies in the inconsistency of group selection. The protection that is triggered is primarily procedural: it creates presumptions in favour of these groups primarily in the context of discrimination. As the *MSS* case indicates, it is possible to extend the vulnerable group concept to specific welfare entitlements (which may also be reached in many constitutional systems of Europe on grounds of attributing group-specific meaning to dignity). On the other hand, for large categories of recognised vulnerable groups (the disabled in particular), few courts offer special protection against welfare cuts. Currently, the extended welfare granted to asylum seekers on grounds of dignity and vulnerability is contrasted in popular discourse with reduced welfare that applies to all others. Much as they overlap, humanitarian concerns are distinct from human rights—but it remains to be seen the extent to which they will remain so in the eyes of the law.

24

Conceptions of Justice from Below: Distributive Justice as a Means to Address Local Conflicts in European Law and Policy

FERNANDA G NICOLA[*]

I. INTRODUCTION

THE IMPACT OF EU law and policy on social groups has been examined in important scholarly work on European law.[1] Mainstream European legal scholarship, however, seldom makes use of a 'law and society' methodology, committed to an understanding of law, its internal logic and its practice yet influenced by external political and social forces.[2] By means of two different theoretical perspectives, American legal realism and Amartya Sen's idea of comparative justice, this chapter focuses on the impact of European decision making on social groups and local actors embracing different conceptions of justice from below.[3] Lawyers, judges and policy makers in the EU appear more concerned with institutional demands of justice rather its social realisation as revealed by local actors with conflicting visions of justice. The chapter uses distributive justice as a means to reconcile such different visions of the good life.

---

[*] I am indebted to Dimitry Kochenov, Brishen Rogers, Daniela Caruso, Cathy McCauliff, Gianluigi Palombella and Lucia Scaffardi for their comments on this chapter.
[1] See A Vauchez and B de Witte (eds), *Lawyering Europe: European Law As a Transnational Social Field* (Oxford, Hart Publishing, 2013); K Armstrong, *Governing Social Inclusion: Europeanization Through Policy Coordination* (Oxford, Oxford University Press, 2010). See also A Layard, 'Freedom of Expression and Spatial (Imaginations of) Justice' in this volume, 417 (using legal geography as a tool to show how law, space and geography are mutually constituted and reflective).
[2] See DS Clark, 'History of Comparative Law and Society'in DS Clark (ed), *Comparative Law and Society* (Cheltenham, Edward Elgar, 2012). Even though the law and society methodology was prevalent in Europe during the early twentieth century, it remains more prevalent in American legal academia rather than in Europe.
[3] See B Rajagopal, *International Law From Below: Development, Social Movements and Third World Resistance* (Cambridge, Cambridge University Press, 2003).

Even though EU law is not supposed to intervene in domestic disputes arising solely within a Member State without implicating EU norms directly,[4] European judge-made law inevitably redistributes power and resources among private and public actors inside national jurisdictions.[5] The disconnect between the declared duality of EU law and its inexistence due to an overreaching European judge-made law has been central to the work of several authors.[6] In addressing such a disconnect, this chapter takes a distinctive local or municipal perspective. The 'from below' point of departure shows how EU law redistributes power to local actors, groups, and cities with multiple and conflicting conceptions of justice.

Rather than romanticising cities and regions for their communal territorial ties,[7] or praise them as urban innovators to rescue struggling markets,[8] local actors depending on the territorial and jurisdictional context have different preferences that are shaped by and in turn shape EU law. In particular, EU law destabilises traditional and internal distribution of powers by creating unstable multilevel governance alliances with conflicting political goals and different conceptions of justice. This chapter argues that such unstable political local alliances driven by the different conceptions of justice from below rarely surface in European decision making. For instance, in applying general principles of uniformity and proportionality in its interpretation, the the European Court of Justice (ECJ) does not openly address conflicting notions of justice from below that arise in European adjudication.[9] The local and municipal viewpoint often disappears in the ECJ deliberations in which subnational actors have limited standing[10] or their viewpoint is collapsed into the one of their Member States.[11]

---

[4] See M Poiares Maduro, 'The Scope of European Remedies: The Case of Purely Internal Situations and Reverse Discrimination' in C Kilpatrick, T Novitz and P Skidmore (eds), *The Future of Remedies in Europe* (Oxford, Hart Publishing, 2000) and for critical views see N Nic Shuibhne, 'Free Movement of Persons and the Wholly Internal Rule: Time to Move On?' (2002) 39 *Common Market Law Review* 731; and D Kochenov and R Plender, 'EU Citizenship: From an Incipient Form to an Incipient Substance? The Discovery of the Treaty Text' (2012) 37 *European Law Review* 369, 383.

[5] See FG Nicola, 'Invisible Cities in Europe' 35 (2012) *Fordham International Law Journal* 1282.

[6] See P Allott, 'The European Community Is Not the True European Community' (1991) 100 *Yale Law Journal* 2485; G Davies, 'Constitutional Disagreement in Europe and the Search for Pluralism' (2010) *Eric Stein Working Papers* No 1/2010.

[7] See R Thompson Ford, 'Bourgeois Communities: A Review of Gerald Frug's "City Making"' (2003)56 *Stanford Law Review* 231.

[8] See E Glaeser, *Triumph of the City: How Our Greatest Invention Makes Us Richer, Smarter, Greener, Healthier, and Happier* (New York, NY, Penguin, 2011).

[9] See S Tsakyrakis, 'Disproportionate Individualism' in this volume, 235 (explaining how the judges in the US and the EU have mainstreamed proportionality as a given method in adjudication).

[10] See Case C-95/97 *Région Wallonne v Commission of the European Communities* [1997] ECR I-1787; Case C-180/97 *Regione Toscana v Commission of the European Communities* [1997] ECR I-5245; see also Case T-81/97 *Regione Toscana v Commission of the European Communities* [1998] ECR II-2889; Case C-417/04 *Regione Siciliana v Commission of the European Communities* [2006] ECR I-3881; Case C-15/06 *Regione Siciliana v Commission of the European Communities* [2007] ECR I-2591. Several commentators have addressed this problem: D Caruso, 'Direct Concern in Regional Policy: The European Court of Justice and the Southern Question' (2011) 17 *European Law Journal* 804; J Scott, 'Regional Policy: An Evolutionary Perspective' in P Craig and G de Búrca (eds), *The Evolution of EU Law* (Oxford, Oxford University Press, 1999) 625, 636–37 (commenting on the lack of legal standing of individual applicants); S Weatherill, 'The Challenge of the Regional Dimension in the European Union' in S Weatherill and U Bernitz (eds), *The Role of Regions and Sub-National Actors in Europe* (Oxford, Hart Publishing, 2005) 7–8 (in which Stephen Weatherill explains: 'the EC pays for its regional-blindness.... Its formal lack of regard for domestic constitutional arrangements may be combined with activity that in practice severely disturbs those internal patterns').

[11] For a similar analysis in American law see G Frug, 'The City As a Legal Concept' (1980) 93 *Harvard Law Review* 1059. Frug has showed how the invisibility of cities in the American constitutional structure

The first theoretical insight relies on the influence of American legal realism[12] in departing from an understanding of the federal judiciary as a neutral arbiter determining the competences between states and the federal government as two absolute powers within their spheres.[13] Instead of acting as a neutral umpire, the federal judiciary enables the trade-off of powers and resources between various actors at the federal, state and local level according to the Court's political goals.[14] Likewise, in the EU scenario the European judiciary enables unstable multilevel alliances which create trade-offs of power and resources vertically, among various supranational and national actors, but also horizontally, and most importantly among various domestic actors.[15] Local jurisdictions in Europe are not neutral actors, nor 'creatures of the states', but places that acquire or lose power in constant negotiation with each other and with their central governments or the Union.[16] In its application of the principle of proportionality, the ECJ reconciles conflicting moral values arising in its Internal Market jurisprudence between the States and the Union.[17] In the Court's deliberation, however, the ongoing horizontal conflicts and collaborations often disappear or they are subsumed within the classic narrative of mediation of federal versus national tensions.

The second theoretical entry point of this chapter is Amartya Sen's idea of comparative justice.[18] In *The Idea of Justice* Sen both departs from and enriches the dominant theory of distributive justice elaborated by John Rawls.[19] Sen reveals the gap between people's opportunity to obtain primary goods and what people really enjoy because of their preferences. His analysis begins with assessing inequalities instead of creating institutional structures committed to the allocation of primary goods.[20] This consequentialist approach to law overlaps with the 'bad man' theory elaborated by Oliver Wendell Holmes.[21] In departing from abstract legal principles Holmes focuses on the practical consequences of legal norms, which range from paying damages to imprisonment.Sen contributes with his capability approach to enrich Rawls' theory of justice: genuine opportunities that help us value the way

---

influenced the Supreme Court's jurisprudence that reduced cities to either public actors as 'creatures of the State' or as private actors as mere market participants.

[12] See WW Fisher, MJ Horwitz and TA Reed (eds), *American Legal Realism* (Oxford, Oxford University Press, 1995).

[13] See D Kennedy, *The Rise and Fall of Classical Legal Thought* (Washington, DC, Beard Books, 2006).

[14] See R Thompson Ford, 'Law's Territory (A History of Jurisdiction)' (1999) 97 *Michigan Law Review* 843, 921; GE Frug and DJ Barron, *City Bound: How States Stifle Urban Innovation* (Ithaca, NY, Cornell University Press, 2008).

[15] See FG Nicola, 'Another View on European Integration: Distributive Stakes in the Harmonization of European Law' in C Dalton (ed), *Progressive Lawyering, Globalization, and Markets: Rethinking Ideology and Strategy* (Buffalo, NY, William S Hein & Co, 2007).

[16] FG Nicola, '"Creatures of the State": Regulatory Federalism, Local Immunities, and EU Waste Regulation in Comparative Perspective' in S Rose-Ackerman and P Lindseth (eds), *Comparative Administrative Law* (Cheltenham, Edward Elgar, 2010).

[17] See P Kurzer, *Markets and Moral Regulation: Cultural Change in the European Union* (Cambridge, Cambridge University Press, 2001); F de Witte, 'Sex, Drugs & EU Law: The Recognition of Moral and Ethical Diversity in EU Law' (2013) 50 *Common Market Law Review* 1545.

[18] See A Sen, *The Idea of Justice* (Cambridge, MA, Harvard University Press, 2009).

[19] See J Rawls, *A Theory of Justice* (Cambridge, MA, Harvard University Press, 1971).

[20] See A Sen, *Inequality Reexamined* (Cambridge, MA, Harvard University Press, 1995).

[21] See O Wendell Holmes, 'The Path of the Law' (1897) 10 *Harvard Law Review* 457, 460–61.

we live should be the basis for equality.[22] Our individual capabilities should be the barometers for evaluating when opportunities will allow us to achieve desired wellbeing. Equality of suitable opportunities for the person in question will ensure that societal conditions are just for the carpenter and the musician as well as the banker.

Sen assesses the development of a community or a country characterised by territorial and cultural heterogeneity according to the functioning of each locality and its capacity to realise the model of development each particular community values. At times the access to valuable functioning that communities aspire to achieve is constrained by the fact that these communities are located at the periphery rather than the core of the Union.[23] Yet these communities' limited options and aspirations should be compared to assess existing inequalities in our society and different moral conceptions of the good life.

This chapter foregrounds conflicting conceptions of justice from below emerging in European jurisprudence that the Court fails to address through the interpretation of EU proportionality and subsidiarity principles. These conceptions of justice from below shed light on existing ethical differences and unresolved conflicts to achieve the social realisation of actors who are differently situated. Rather than tying local actors and social groups to decisions based on abstract legal principles and institutional demands, the starting point is why injustice arises in particular socio-economic settings. This framing of the justice/injustice question could put European judges or policy makers in the position to anticipate and clarify the unintended effects of their decision making on specific territories and social groups. More importantly, it could provide the opportunity to European judges, lawyers and policy makers to clarify their normative position over conflicts reclaiming different conceptions of justice.

II. DISPLACING THE NEUTRALITY OF THE FEDERAL JUDICIARY AND ITS FEDERALISM DOCTRINES

Pre-realist and formalist ideas of a neutral federal judiciary and its federalism doctrines have played an important role in American and European adjudication. Scholars who have rejected and criticised such doctrines have engaged in judicial debates addressing the social tensions mediated by federalism while mapping the shift from dual to cooperative federalism in the Supreme Court's jurisprudence.[24] Such doctrinal shift in the United States Supreme Court's adjudication reflected the political economic shift from laissez faire to new deal interventionism in the twentieth century. A central figure in American legal realism was the economist and jurist Robert L Hale.[25] His work on private law set aside the pre-realist idea that the free

---

[22] A Sen, 'Development As Capability Expansion' (1989) 19 *Journal of Development Planning* 41, 43.
[23] See D Kukovec, 'Taking Change Seriously—The Discourse of Justice and the Reproduction of the Status Quo' (22 September 2012), www.law.harvard.edu/academics/degrees/gradprogram/sjd/sjd-current-students/sjd-candidate-uploads/taking-change-seriously-london-september-2012.pdf.
[24] See R Schütze, *From Dual to Cooperative Federalism: The Changing Structure of European Law* (Oxford, Oxford University Press, 2009).
[25] See BH Fried, *The Progressive Assault on Laissez Faire: Robert Hale and the First Law and Economics Movement* (Cambridge, MA, Harvard University Press, 2001).

market was a natural condition that led to predictable and efficient outcomes without state intervention. Instead Hale viewed the market as a regulated environment where groups of buyers and sellers constantly acquire or lose their relative bargaining power vis-a-vis other groups and the state.[26] An analogy to the free market idea is the pre-realist notion that the federal judiciary was a neutral umpire meant to police the clashes between independent federal and state absolute spheres of authority.[27]

From a legal realist perspective, federal adjudication rather than interpreting neutral principles created a series of trade-offs among federal, state and local powers.[28] The outcome of federal adjudication was unstable multilevel alliances over specific political and legal outcomes.[29] Therefore for legal realists neither free market policies nor federal legal doctrines offered neutral solutions to the redistribution of resources and power according to a fair criterion of justice.

Some European lawyers have challenged the supposedly neutral and pre-realist interpretation of the ECJ often driven by the need for uniformity in EU law rather than by politically driven motivations. For instance, Gareth Davies has shown how the preliminary reference procedure allows the ECJ to decide a question of 'competence allocation' in a way that undermines its status as a neutral umpire and 'infantilises' national courts.[30] In a similar vein, Daniela Caruso demonstrated that the ECJ has used neutral and technical principles in private law adjudication to achieve the consolidation of 'institutional gains' for European integration.[31] Finally, Tamara K Hervey has called 'imaginative jurisprudence' a progressive approach aiming at rewriting the *Kohll* decision[32] addressing one of the central social rights preserved in the EU legal system, namely the right to healthcare.[33] Rather than using a strictly European framework, the work of all three scholars exemplifies how legal realist lenses have crossed the Atlantic. In particular their work has become part of a global critical discourse in the conceptualisation of legal institutions, private law and socio-economic rights.[34]

---

[26] See generally RL Hale, 'Coercion and Distribution in a Supposedly Non-Coercive State' (1923) 38 *Political Science Quarterly* 470.

[27] This conception of the federal government was predominant during the nineteenth century. See D Kennedy, 'The Globalizations of Law and Legal Thought' in D Trubek and A Santos (eds), *The New Law and Development: A Critical Appraisal* (Cambridge, Cambridge University Press, 2006).

[28] See M Tushnet, 'Following the Rules Laid-Down: A Critique of Interpretivism and Neutral Principles' (1983) 96 *Harvard Law Review* 781, 824.

[29] See generally DJ Barron, 'A Localist Critique of the New Federalism' (2001) 51 *Duke Law Journal* 377.

[30] See G Davies, 'The Division of Powers Between the European Court of Justice and National Courts: A Critical Look at Interpretation and Application in the Preliminary Reference Procedure' in N Nic Shuibne (ed), *Regulating the Internal Market* (Cheltenham, Edward Elgar, 2007).

[31] See D Caruso, 'Private Law and State-Making in the Age of Globalization' (2006) 39 *New York University Journal of International Law and Politics* 1.

[32] Case C-158/96 *Raymond Kohll v Union des caisses de maladie* [1998] ECR I-1931.

[33] See TK Hervery, 'Re-judging Social Rights in the European Union' in G de Búrca, C Kilpatrick and J Scott (eds), *Critical Legal Perspectives on Global Governance: Liber Amicorum David M Trubek* (Oxford, Hart Publishing, 2014) 346, explaining that in rejecting some fundamental premises that shape EU law and policy, such as the creation of a liberal market and that the EU is not a human rights organisation, we can engage in imaginative jurisprudence by 'a literal rewriting of seminal cases through a critical lens'.

[34] See D Kennedy, 'The Globalization of Critical Discourses on Law: Thoughts on David Trubek's Contribution' in G de Búrca, C Kilpatrick and J Scott (eds), *Critical Legal Perspectives on Global Governance: Liber Amicorum David M Trubek* (Oxford, Hart Publishing, 2014).

The relevance of legal realism bears meaning to understand the judicial shifts intrinsic to the interpretation of American federalism. For instance, the Supreme Court developed during the nineteenth century the pre-realist doctrine of dual federalism pursuant to which state and federal power are conceived of as two separate spheres of authority.[35] From the 1930s until the early 1990s, this doctrine was displaced in favour of the principle of plenary powers. This principle conceives of states as autonomous from but nevertheless embedded in federal authority. This shift in doctrinal interpretation of federal powers was coupled by a judiciary initially supporting laissez faire legislation and then shifting to support the New Deal administration committed to social policy.[36] In contrast to dual federalism, American and European scholars committed to social justice have advanced cooperative federalism as a prescriptive theory that enhances federal and state collaboration.[37] The American federal judiciary has used these doctrines at different times to achieve different political economy goals depending on the political shifts on the bench.[38] Legal elites have supported free market liberalism by interpreting the dual sovereignty doctrine, whereas social justice scholars have used cooperative federalism to enhance welfare reforms.

In the 1990s, however, the Rehnquist court began promoting its new federalism doctrine selectively.[39] In doing so, the Supreme Court resuscitated in part the dual sovereignty doctrine even though it appeared to have been abandoned.[40] According to the new federalism doctrine of the Rehnquist court, there exists an overlap between state and federal authority even though they remain separate spheres of power. The development of a new federalism doctrine shows that it is premature to offer its eulogy. Given the predominance of cooperative federalism in the EU and the US, the death of the federalism doctrine is more a normative aspiration than a judicial praxis to interpret federal doctrines. Legal realists have warned against the false expectation that legal doctrines, despite their ideological genealogies, will always lead to desired normative outcomes.[41]

Cooperative localism, albeit different from cooperative federalism, resonates with the federal doctrine of plenary powers developed by the Supreme Court to support

---

[35] See *Parker v Brown* 317 US 341(4 January 1943) (providing an example of dual federalism doctrine in which the states and the federal governments are depicted as two autonomous spheres). While some commentators have criticised the inconsistency of the new federalism and the recurrence of federalist arguments over time, others have promoted alternative and more interactive approaches to federal power. See P Weiser, 'Federal Common Law, Cooperative Federalism and the Enforcement of the Telecom Act' (2001) 76 *New York University Law Review* 1692; RA Schapiro, 'Toward a Theory of Interactive Federalism' (2005) 91 *Iowa Law Review* 243, 246.

[36] See Schütze, *From Dual to Cooperative Federalism*, n 24 above, 123.

[37] ibid 241.

[38] See MJ Horwitz, *The Transformation of American Law, 1780–1860* (Cambridge, MA, Harvard University Press, 1977).

[39] See RH Fallon, 'The "Conservative" Paths of the Rehnquist Court's Federalism Decisions' (2002) 69 *University of Chicago Law Review* 429; DJ Barron, 'A Localist Critique of the New Federalism' (2001) 51 *Duke Law Journal* 377.

[40] EA Young, 'Dual Federalism, Concurrent Jurisdiction, and the Foreign Affairs Exception' (2001) 69 *George Washington Law Review* 139, 142.

[41] See F Cohen, 'Transcendental Nonsense and the Functional Approach' (1935) 35 *Columbia Law Review* 809; and D Kennedy, 'Form and Substance in Private Law Adjudication' (1976) 89 *Harvard Law Review* 1685, 1697.

the legislative supremacy of Congress enacting New Deal legislation.[42] Scholars have used the notion of cooperative localism to highlight the beneficial interaction between federal and local governments in the realm of federal regulatory policies. This cooperation creates pockets of local autonomy often in tension with state-level power.[43] In addition, the cooperation between local and federal authorities at times limits state control on local decision making, which enhances local experimentation.[44] For instance, some federal spending programmes that are directly allocated to counties or municipalities have spurred opposition at the state level against local control of federal funding.[45] The downside of such federal–local cooperation happens when it ends up substituting federal power to state power, thus rendering local government once again creatures of the state rather than experimenting or freely allocating funding according to their needs.[46]

The realist lesson is that advocating for dual federalism, cooperative federalism or localism per se does not produce the normatively desired results of social justice. Legal realism has taught us that legal entitlements, namely the rules of private and public law that undergird institutions, such as markets or federal governments, determine which parties enjoy which sorts of viable legal claims with regard to those institutions.[47] Because all institutions have bundles of rights and entitlements, however, one often risks a categorical error by assuming that the particular bundles will be assigned and distributed in the same way in different jurisdictions and at different time periods.[48] The outcomes of federal doctrines mediating the tensions of political and federal conflicts involving levels of governments need to be evaluated on a case-by-case basis. To take political decisions that will promote distributive justice in the EU, the ECJ will have to set aside its neutral umpire role and openly recognise its counter majoritarian yet democratic role.[49]

---

[42] See, eg, RA Schapiro, 'Judicial Deference and Interpretive Coordinacy in State and Federal Constitutional Law' (2000) 85 *Cornell Law Review* 656, 682 (noting that, after the New Deal, 'the Court desisted from enforcing the non-delegation doctrine, thus allowing Congress broad discretion to allocate legislative power').

[43] See NM Davidson, 'Cooperative Localism: Federal–Local Collaboration in an Era of State Sovereignty' (2007) 93 *Virginia Law Review* 959, 968–74 (explaining new forms of federal–local cooperation in the aftermath of 11 September 2001, post hurricane Katrina and on fiscal federalism).

[44] See S-R Ackerman, 'Cooperative Federalism and Co-optation' (1983) 92 *Yale Law Journal* 1344; J Sarnoff, 'Cooperative Federalism, the Delegation of Federal Power and the Constitution' (1997) 39 *Arizona Law Review* 205; PJ Weiser, 'Towards a Constitutional Architecture for Cooperative Federalism' (2001) 79 *North Carolina Law Review* 663.

[45] See *Lawrence County v Lead-Deadwood School District* 469 US 256 (9 January 1985); see also Davidson, 'Cooperative Localism', n 43 above; J Resnik, 'Foreign As Domestic Affairs: Rethinking Horizontal Federalism and Foreign Affairs Preemption in Light of Translocal Internationalism' (2007) 57 *Emory Law Journal* 31.

[46] See Nicola, 'Creatures of the State', n 16 above.

[47] See RL Hale, 'Bargaining, Duress, and Economic Liberty' (1943) 43 *Columbia Law Review* 603; D Kennedy, 'The Stakes of Law, or Hale and Foucault!' (1991) 15 *Legal Studies Forum* 327.

[48] See WN Hohfeld, 'Fundamental Legal Conceptions As Applied in Judicial Reasoning' (1917) 26 *Yale Law Journal* 710; and JW Singer, 'The Legal Rights Debate in Analytical Jurisprudence from Bentham to Hohfeld' [1982] *Wisconsin Law Review* 975, 993–94 (explaining Hohfeld's fundamental error).

[49] This position has been prominently advocated by JH Ely, *Democracy and Distrust: A Theory of Judicial Review* (Cambridge, MA, Harvard University Press, 1980) in his response to the counter-majoritarian difficulty of undemocratic judicial review articulated by well-known constitutional theorist such as AM Bickel, *The Least Dangerous Branch: The Supreme Court at the Bar of Politics* (New Haven, CT, Yale University Press, 1962).

III. DISTRIBUTIVE JUSTICE IN ADJUDICATION

A mainstream approach to law relies on redistribution of resources and power via tax and transfers, rather than adjudication. According to legal economists, judges should pursue efficiency and set aside distributive goals in adjudication because it is difficult or impossible to redistribute through legal rules, whereas legislatures have the competence to deal with the distribution of resources.[50] Legislative decisions and the government's tax and transfer systems, are likely to be more precise than the decision of a random judge.[51] Even liberal philosophers such as John Rawls who elaborated a rational and normatively grounded theory of distributive justice with 'well-founded justifications' to eliminate arbitrary discrimination was skeptical about relying on judges to apply it. Rawls's difference principle and its 'maximin' distributive criterion aim to redistribute primary social goods to maximise the welfare of the least advantaged.[52] However, Rawls did not view the difference principle as guiding judicial reasoning, instead confining it to the legislative sphere.[53] According to Rawls's difference principle, rational and reasonable beings in the original position would not choose principles mandating total equality among all individuals.[54] Rather, they would choose principles mandating that inequalities must be to the benefit of the worst-off—as, for example, when inequalities 'set up various incentives which succeed in eliciting more productive efforts'.[55] In the global and possibly transitional context, however, scholars have shown the limits of the Rawlsian approach tailored to a national situation.[56]

However, critical scholars have shown that redistribution can be carried out not only through tax and transfer programmes, but also through adjudication.[57] Accepting that members of the judiciary decide on what legislatures deliberate daily might undermine courts' autonomy and legitimacy, especially in civil law countries in which, at least at the declaratory level, judges should be *the mouth of the law*.[58] Even though jurists have long criticised such notions of judicial discretion by showing that civil law courts have wide room to interpret statutory texts,[59] civil law courts' judicial styles still tend to conform to that narrow belief.[60]

---

[50] See L Kaplow and S Shavell, *Fairness Versus Welfare* (Cambridge, MA, Harvard University Press, 2002) 31–35.
[51] See R Cooter and T Ulen, *Law and Economics* (Boston, MA, Pearson, 1999) 4.
[52] See Rawls, *A Theory of Justice*, n 19 above, 62–92.
[53] See B Rogers, 'Justice at Work: Minimum Wage Laws and Social Equality' (2014) 92 *Texas Law Review* 1543.
[54] See Rawls, *A Theory of Justice*, n 19 above, 151.
[55] ibid, 152.
[56] See generally TW Pogge, *World Poverty and Human Rights* (Cambridge, Polity Press, 2002). See J Heath, 'Rawls on Global Distributive Justice: A Defence' (2005) 31 *Canadian Journal of Philosophy* 193.
[57] See D Kennedy, 'Distributive and Paternalist Motives in Contract and Tort Law, With Special Reference to Compulsory Terms and Unequal Bargaining Power' (1982) 41 *Maryland Law Review* 563, 654.
[58] See JH Merryman, *The Civil Law Tradition* (Stanford, CA, Stanford University Press, 1969) 17–18, citing Montesquieu's *De l'Esprit des Loix*.
[59] See B Rudden, 'Courts and Codes in England, France and Soviet Russia' (1949) 10 *Louisiana Law Review* 431; M de S-O-l'E Lasser, 'Judicial (Self-)Portraits: Judicial Discourse in the French Legal System' (1995) 104 *Yale Law Journal* 1325.
[60] See Lasser, 'Judicial (Self-)Portraits, n 59 above.

In the same tradition the judges of the ECJ have been careful not to overstep their boundaries and to exercise prudently their judicial discretion. Even when they make decisions that redistribute power and resources within the Member States, European judges tend not to acknowledge openly the costs and benefits of their decisions. The style of their decisions and the lack of dissenting opinions obscure the distributive consequences at stake in each judgment.[61] Several commentators have criticised the ECJ for its refusal to engage in comparative law by citing or dialoguing with other courts, especially with the European Court of Human Rights, to increase the transparency of its decision-making processes.[62] However, from the interpretation of European private law directives to the application of anti-discrimination principles, European judges redistribute resources and power according to efficiency criteria rather than a principle of distributive justice.[63] Instead of empirical reality, the efficiency claim made by judges to reduce the barriers to trade the single market bears rhetorical power to legitimate new legislative and judicial action on behalf of the EU.[64] European judges attribute the results of their decision-making process to the sophisticated balancing between conflicting interests in light of a proportionality criterion which in their view entails effects on the Union and the Member States but only rarely on local actors, cities, territorial groups and citizens.

There are counterexamples to the judicial style of the ECJ. For instance the Opinion of Advocate General Eleanor *Sharpston* in the *Government of the French Community and Walloon Government v Flemish Community*[65] that was not followed by the Court called on to strike down a reverse discriminatory scheme in Belgium. The Walloon Community in Belgium challenged an insurance scheme adopted by the Flemish Government that was open only to individuals who both lived and worked in the Flanders region of Belgium and not, for example, to those working in Flanders but residing in the Walloon region. The ECJ decided this case by drawing the distinction between two categories of workers: those who have exercised their freedom to move within the EU,[66] and those who have not done so

---

[61] See JL Dunoff and MA Pollack, 'International Judicial Dissent: Causes and Consequences', paper prepared for presentation at the Conference of Europeanists, Washington, DC (14–16 March 2014).

[62] See G de Búrca, 'After the EU Charter of Fundamental Rights: The Court of Justice As a Human Rights Adjudicator?' (2013) 20 *Maastricht Journal of European and Comparative Law* 168; C McCrudden, 'Using Comparative Reasoning in Human Rights Adjudication: The Court of Justice of the European Union and the European Court of Human Rights Compared' (2013) 15 *Cambridge Yearbook of European Legal Studies* 383.

[63] See Case C-183/00 *María Victoria González Sánchez v Medicina Asturiana SA* [2002] ECR I-3901; Case C-438/05 *International Transport Workers' Federation and Finnish Seamen's Union v Viking Line ABP and OÜ Viking Line Eesti* [2007] ECR I-10779; Case C-341/05 *Laval un Partneri Ltd v Svenska Byggnadsarbetareförbundet and Others* [2007] ECR I-11767.

[64] See generally FG Nicola, 'Transatlanticism: Constitutional Asymmetry and Selective Reception of US Law and Economics in the Formation of European Private Law' (2008) 16 *Cardozo Journal of International & Comparative Law* 87.

[65] Case C-212/06 *Government of the French Community and Walloon Government v Flemish Government (Belgian Care Insurance Scheme)* [2008] ECR I-1683.

[66] ibid, paras 37–38. First, those 'Belgian nationals working in the territory of the Dutch-speaking region or in that of the bilingual region of the Brussels-capital but who live in the French or German-speaking region and have never exercised their freedom to move within the European community'. The ECJ held that for these workers 'Community law clearly cannot be applied to such purely internal situations'.

who were prevented from using the insurance scheme.[67] The paradoxical outcome was that EU citizens (non-Belgians) residing in Belgium were better protected than Walloon Belgian citizens who did not move around the Union. Thus, EU law offered more protection than Belgian law. Rather than abandoning the wholly internal situation doctrine, the Court offered a careful analysis of which groups could be protected under EU law because of their ability to move and those that could not.

In her opinion, Advocate General Sharpston suggested a different doctrinal path and rationale that was not followed by the ECJ. While she made the same classification of the ECJ in distinguishing between Belgians who have exercised their right of free movement and other EU citizens versus those Belgians who did not move, Sharpston favoured a broader interpretation of the treaty provisions on European citizenship than the Court. By suggesting the elimination of the purely internal situation in the case, Sharpston advocated extending insurance coverage to all Belgian citizens connected to the Flemish region.[68]

The rationale in Sharpston's opinion was even more significant than her doctrinal interpretation. In her opinion she was suggesting an open evaluation of the distributive effects of the Flemish insurance care scheme for people affected by a prolonged disability. In mentioning that judges should be willing to evaluate the territorial regulatory schemes, she explained that a discriminatory scheme might discriminate per se or it might seek to promote development in underdeveloped territories. In either case, she opined, European judges are well situated to understand the conflict at stake as well as the effects of a domestic regulatory scheme on different local and transnational communities.[69]

In its 2009 decision, the Belgian Constitutional Court had found that 'the Flemish legislation did not infringe the economic and monetary unity of Belgium due to the small amount of money involved and the limited impact of the criticised measures on the free movement of persons in Belgium'.[70]

In their insightful essay, Peter Van Elsuwege and Stanislas Adam show that what should have been a dialogue between the ECJ and the Belgian Constitutional Court through the preliminary ruling became instead a long dispute revealing different conceptions of justice as well as institutional perspectives.[71] For instance, what they call the 'disconguence' between EU and Belgian law arises over the notion of social security, the different conceptions of free movement and the recognition of regional autonomy are based on a mix of problems arising from institutional

---

[67] ibid, para 4. For a second category of workers, 'both nationals of Member States other than the kingdom of Belgium working in the Dutch-speaking region or in the bilingual region of the Brussels-capital who live in another part of the national territory and Belgian nationals in the same situation who have made use of their right to freedom of movement', the ECJ held that EU law precluded the Flemish scheme.
[68] ibid, paras 143–44, Opinion of AG Sharpston.
[69] ibid, para 155, Opinion of AG Sharpston.
[70] See P Van Elsuwege and S Adam, 'The Limits of Constitutional Dialogue for the Prevention of Reverse Discrimination. Constitutional Court of Belgium, Judgment 11/2009 of 21 January 2009'(2009) 5 *European Constitutional Law Review* 327, 330. See also Judgment No 11/2009 (Constitutional Court of Belgium, 21 January 2009), para B.12.3; TAJA Vandamme, '*Prochain Arrêt: La Belgique*! Explaining Recent Preliminary References of the Belgian Constitutional Court' (2008) 4 *European Constitutional Law Review* 127.
[71] Van Elsuwege and Adam, 'The Limits of Constitutional Dialogue', n 70 above, 328.

design as well as divergent visions about which level of government should bear redistributive policies addressing a particular territory or community.[72] The tension in this case arises between subnational redistributive mechanisms that have become politically uncontroversial at the national level but are now put in question by EU law, whether directly or via ECJ decisions.[73] However even if the Court refuses to intervene directly it may rely on the fact that EU law background rules already constrain the actions of Member States.[74]

IV. IN SEARCH OF DISTRIBUTIVE JUSTICE IN COHESION POLICY

The most obvious mechanism to address the uneven distributive impact of Europeanisation was the European Regional Development Fund (ERDF) that was created in the 1970s by the Community. By 1986, European regional or cohesion policies attempted to balance socio-economic inequalities among European regions stressing in the Single European Act an egalitarian commitment to 'harmonious development by reducing the differences existing between the various regions and the backwardness of the least favoured regions'.[75]

In the Lisbon Treaty, EU regional or cohesion policy became explicitly an economic development policy aimed at 'reducing disparities between the levels of development of the various regions and the backwardness of the least favoured regions',[76] which clearly implies addressing disparate levels of wealth, unemployment and capital income across the regions of Europe.[77] In 2009, the Barca report indicated the weaknesses as well as the potential of the current regime that was essential to complement the unification of the Internal Market, the single currency and the erosion of the national welfare state to offer 'equal gains from unification, to have equal access to the opportunities so created as well as equal possibility of coping with risk and threats'.[78] The report attempted to revamp solidarity and distributive justice as constituent of EU cohesion policies well before the current pledges made by Jürgen Habermas and Claus Hoffe to revamp solidarity and democracy in the aftermath of the European financial crisis.[79]

Since the 1970s the EU has encountered numerous challenges in the application of a rational criterion of distributive justice to its cohesion policy. First, the amount

---

[72] ibid, 335–37.

[73] See D Caruso, 'Limitsof the ClassicMethod: PositiveAction in the European Union After the New Equality Directives' (2003) 44 *Harvard International Law Journal* 331.

[74] See Hale, 'Bargaining, Duress, and Economic Liberty', n 47 above; and Kennedy, 'The Stakes of Law', n 47 above.

[75] Arts 130(a), (b), (c), (d) of the Treaty establishing the European Community as amended by the Single European Act [1987] OJ L169; see F Wishlade, 'EU Cohesion Policy: Facts, Figures and Issues' in G Marks and L Hooghe (eds), *Cohesion Policy and European Integration: Building Multi-Level Governance* (Oxford, Clarendon Press, 1996).

[76] Art 174(2) of the Consolidated version of the Treaty on the Functioning of the European Union [2012] OJ C326/47 (TFEU).

[77] See Marks and Hooghe, *Cohesion Policy and European Integration*, n 75 above.

[78] F Barca, *An Agenda for a Reformed Cohesion Policy. A Place-Based Approach to Meeting European Union Challenges and Expectations* (Brussels, Directorate-General for Regional and Urban Policy, 2009) 7.

[79] See J Habermas, 'Democracy, Solidarity and the European Crisis', lecture delivered at KU Leuven (26 April 2013); and C Offe, 'Europe in the Trap', www.eurozine.com/pdf/2013-02-06-offe-en.pdf.

of wealth that ought to be redistributed from wealthy centres to poor peripheries is clearly insufficient to fulfill the promises of a 'regional policy reducing regional economic and social disparities across European states and regions'.[80] At a more substantial level, distributive justice is hard to achieve when Member States are unable to agree that eliminating wealth inequalities among their territories is a foundational commitment for all of society, and not only a benefit for the poor. As a result, many Member States have used cohesion policies as a bargaining tool to obtain resources in return for political compromises. Finally, promoting redistribution on the basis of cooperation among its 28 Member States, with partial surrender of their sovereignty vis-a-vis the Union, will not succeed without such adherence to the requirement of a distributive justice policy. At different times, EU cohesion policies have been used instrumentally by the Member States as a trade-off for political and diplomatic compromises. Often EU cohesion policies were negotiated 'as a side-payment and a redistributive mechanism for budgetary contributions' to compensate states in the context of a new enlargement.[81]

A more dramatic example from 2013 was the freezing by the European Commission of its cohesion and regional funds disbursement to Hungary as a way to put pressure on a Member State that did not respect basic democratic guarantees.[82] While many commentators have reported the 'illiberal' turn in Hungary since 2010 after the constitutional changes led by the conservative Fidesz party,[83] this situation has revealed the lack of mechanisms within the Union to address the infringement of basic democratic and rule of law commitments by the Member States.[84] Due to the absence of such commitments, cohesion policies have become the more readily available political tool used as a short-term and unsatisfactory remedy to force Member States to change their behaviour.[85]

In these examples the notion of territorial cohesion remains a vague concept that is not anchored to a distributive principle of justice. Such vagueness has allowed, for more or less noble reasons, the Member States and the European Commission to use cohesion policies, for want of a better tool, to address European crises in ways that had very little to do with territorial cohesion. Cohesion and regional policies have become a stunning example of how the deliberative forum to express local interests and create more stable multilevel alliances has been taken over by either

---

[80] See M Brunazzo, 'Regional Europe' in M Cini and N Perez-Solorzano Borragan, *European Union Politics* (Oxford, Oxford University Press, 2010).

[81] See Wishlade, 'EU Cohesion Policy', n 75 above.

[82] See K Eddy and J Fontanella-Kahn, 'Brussels Suspends Funding to Hungary over Alleged Irregularities' *Financial Times* (London, 14 August 2013).

[83] See M Bánkuti, G Halmai and KL Scheppele, 'Hungary's Illiberal Turn: Disabling the Constitution' (2012) 23 *Journal of Democracy* 138. For a report on the unstable situation of fundamental rights in Hungary see the Tavares Report: Committee on Civil Liberties, Justice and Home Affairs, 'Report on the situation of fundamental rights: Standards and practices in Hungary (pursuant to the European Parliament resolution of 16 February 2012) (2012/2130(INI))(24 June 2013) A7-0229/2013.

[84] See KL Scheppele, 'What Can the European Commission Do When Member States Violate Basic Principles of the European Union? The Case for Systematic Infringement Actions' (2013), www.ec.europa.eu/justice/events/assises-justice-2013/files/contributions/45.princetonuniversityscheppelesystemicinfringementactionbrusselsversion_en.pdf; C Closa, D Kochenov and JHH Weiler, 'Reinforcing Rule of Law Oversight in the European Union'(2014) *European University Institute Working Papers* RSCAS No 2014/25.

[85] Closa, Kochenov and Weiler, 'Reinforcing Rule of Law Oversight', n 84 above, 19–20.

Member States or EU overriding goals.[86] Despite the prominent debate over the re-nationalisation thesis and its critiques by political scientists,[87] the missing focus has been the lack of a distributive justice commitment in cohesion policies.

V. THE *IDEA OF JUSTICE* AS A COMPARATIVE DEVELOPMENT FRAMEWORK

Amartya Sen's *Idea of Justice* introduces a pragmatic theory of justice that departs from Rawls' foundationalism about institutional structures and their relation to justice. Sen starts from the ground up, thinking about the realisation of justice rather than its definition as an abstract principle.[88] His theory addresses everyday inequalities while also ambitiously providing both a rational and universal theory of justice. Instead of an ideal theory committed to long-term and extensive institutional reforms, *transcendental institutionalism*, Sen engages with an impartial method of reasoning to assess the comparative justice of alternative states of affairs called *realisation-focus comparison* emerging from the Enlightenment tradition.[89] *Transcendental institutionalism* has spurred fundamental work on just institutions with underlying ethical imperatives. In contrast, the *realisation-focus comparison* is concerned with social realisations inspired by comparative approaches to justice.[90] The idea at the heart of the approach that Sen pursues in his work is that competing reasons for justice can co-exist and should be better understood by assessing social inequalities.

Sen's approach resonates with the work of those comparative lawyers engaging with *positive-sociology functionalism* to understand legal change in the context and the territory in which legislation is likely to be implemented, reformed or transplanted.[91] Comparative scholars engaged in legal reform, however, often fail to confront the 'gap' between legal and social practice.[92] Important scholarly work shows how unintended consequences of legal reform and the problem with a one-size-fits-all approach to law ends up undermining, rather than consolidating legal reforms.[93]

---

[86] See Nicola, 'The False Promise of Decentralization in EU Cohesion Policy' (2011) 20 Tulane Journal of International and Comparative Law 65 (showing how cohesion policies and especially their legal implementation have been unsuccessful in tailoring and differentiating their interventions to a particular territory or regions).

[87] See M Pollack, 'Regional Actors in an Intergovernmental Play: The Making and Implementation of EC Structural Policy' in C Rhodes and S Mazey (eds), *The State of the European Union*, Vol 3: Building a European Polity? (Boulder, CO, Lynne Riener, 1995); and for a critique see J Bachtler and C Mendez, 'Who Governs EU Cohesion Policy? Deconstructing the Reforms of the Structural Funds' (2007) 45 *Journal of Common Market Studies* 535.

[88] In a similar way, Neil Walker's 'Justice in and of the European Union' in this volume, 247, at 257, suggests a very incisive instrument of justice *in* the European Union that is 'justice as a low-tariff, context-specific concept'.

[89] See Sen, *The Idea of Justice*, n 18 above, 6 (explaining *transcendental institutionalism*). Sen portrays ideal theories as insufficient to decide political issues because they are designed to apply to a hypothetical world and not real world circumstances.

[90] ibid, 7.

[91] See FG Nicola, 'Family Law Exceptionalism in Comparative Law' (2010) 58 *American Journal of Comparative Law* 777.

[92] See Harvard Law: The Bridge, 'Law and Society', www.cyber.law.harvard.edu/bridge/LawSociety/essay1.htm.

[93] See JL Esquirol, 'The Failed Law of Latin America' (2008) 56 *American Journal of Comparative Law* 75.

In addressing the question of how to promote legal change to spur economic development, David Trubek and Mark Galanter noted that the fact an intense law reform activity had achieved less than they had hoped was, in itself, a significant realisation.[94] In their famous 'self-estrangement' article, Trubek and Galanter show a number of misleading liberal legalist assumptions that heavily constrained the agenda of legal reformers.[95] The gap between the social and legal context was clearly a recipe for failure when attempting to reform a legal regime embedded in socio-economic realities different from those in the United States. Thus, a cautionary note is warranted when applying principles of liberal law reform in rapidly changing societies like the EU.

The liberal legalist assumptions bear a lot of resemblance to the 'economic technology' within EU post-national regimes promoting economic development and growth while heightening the wealth disparities and sovereign debt crisis in some of its poorest regions.[96] Furthermore, the EU remains characterised by profound differences among Member States with diverse levels of economic, political and social stability. Many have recent histories of dictatorships with experiences akin to colonialism not so different from the developing world's experience. Thus the challenge for a European idea of justice is to resist the notion that the EU Member States are territorially homogenous, in full respect of the rule of law and that they are free from poverty, corruption and informal norms.

VI. THREE CHILDREN, A FLUTE AND THE ECJ JURISPRUDENCE

Sen's theory is very much in tune with the notion that justice should be understood according to the types of human lives that people can actually live and the capabilities they have.[97] The famous story that Sen uses to illustrate his theory is the one of three children and a flute. In the story, each child has a competing and compelling reason to claim the flute.[98]

In Sen's example, Anne claims the flute for herself because she is the only one among the three children who can play the flute. Bob also claims the flute because he is the poorest and he does not own any toys. Finally, Carla claims the flute for herself because the existence of the flute is a result of her work and her devotion and commitment to making it. Each child represents a starting point for our conceptions

---

[94] See DM Trubek and M Galanter, 'Scholars in Self-Estrangement: Reflections on the Crisis in Law and Development Studies in the United States' [1974] *Wisconsin Law Review* 1062.

[95] ibid, 1077 stating that '[t]he law and development model assumes that state institutions are the primary locus of social control, while in much of the Third World the grip of tribe, clan, and local community is far stronger than that of the nation-state. The model assumes that rules both reflect the interests of the vast majority of citizens and are normally internalized by them, while in many developing countries rules are imposed on the many by the few and are frequently honored more in the breach than in the observance. The model assumes that courts are central actors in social control, and that they are relatively autonomous from political, tribal, religious, or class interests. Yet in many nations courts are neither very independent nor very important.'

[96] See M Everson, 'The Fault of (European) Law in (Political and Social) Economic Crisis' (2013) 24 *Law & Critique* 107.

[97] See Sen, *The Idea of Justice*, n 18 above, 18.

[98] ibid, 12–15.

of justice in which Anne makes a utilitarian argument, Bob an egalitarian and Carla a libertarian one. Each argument is based on an 'impartial and non-arbitrary reason'.[99] Each one of them needs serious consideration because there is no 'perfectly just social arrangement' that will allow each of them to achieve what he wants and consequently agree with one solution.

This part uses the flute story as an analogy to explore the different conceptions of justice from below emerging in a judicial deliberation of the ECJ. The distributive effects of the Court's decisions, siding with one rather than another conception of justice, are likely to impact unevenly the economic and social development of a specific territory.

The *Rüffert* judgment is an excellent example of conflicting conceptions of justice from below that continues the saga of the *Laval* judgment interpreting the Posted Workers Directive 96/71 that regulates the free movement of workers posted for a limited period of time in another Member State.[100] Even though the Directive was drafted with the aim of protecting workers against social dumping, especially in the construction industry, its interpretation in *Laval* has created an opposite outcome with the influx of former Eastern European workers into Western Europe.[101] The Directive was interpreted by the ECJ to allow only national or collective bargaining agreements that were 'universally applicable', rather than local ones, to apply to posted workers. So labour protections that are not universal, and that do not apply on the entire national territory, were not considered valid by the Court.[102]

In *Rüffert*, the *Bundesland* of Lower Saxony awarded a German contractor who employed a subcontractor established in Poland a public procurement contract to build the Göttingen-Rosdorf prison. The German company signed a contract for an amount of over EUR 8 million that included certain provisions for the protection of workers deployed in public contracting tenders. These provisions required that the contractor and its subcontractors would commit to pay workers the remuneration prescribed by the collective agreement in the place where the obligation was performed. Moreover, these provisions entitled Lower Saxony to impose a penalty or terminate the contract where local labour standards were not respected.[103] When it was found that the contractor had employed a subcontractor who had hired 53 Polish workers at about half of the minimum wage established by the local collective agreement, a penalty notice of approximately EUR 85,000 was issued and the contract terminated.[104]

---

[99] ibid, 13.
[100] See Case C-346/06 *Dirk Rüffert v Land Niedersachsen* [2008] ECR I-1989, interpreting Directive 96/71/EC of the European Parliament and of the Council of 16 December 1996 concerning the posting of workers in the framework of the provision of services ('Posted Workers Directive') [1997] OJ L18/1 and the free movement of services guaranteed in the Treaty under Art 56 TFEU.
[101] See www.eurofound.europa.eu/eiro/1999/09/study/tn9909201s.htm, explaining that '[t]he posted workers Directive, which came into force in December 1999, seeks to prevent free movement of labour within the EU from causing distortions of competition and bringing forms of "social dumping". The basic principle of the Directive is that working conditions and pay in effect in a Member State should be applicable both to workers from that State, and those from other EU countries posted to work there.'
[102] Case C-346/06 *Dirk Rüffert v Land Niedersachsen* [2008] ECR I-1989, paras 21–22.
[103] ibid, paras 6–9.
[104] ibid, para 11.

The question before the ECJ was whether Lower Saxony's higher standards for the protection of workers in public procurement contracts were consistent with the Treaty's free movement of services and the derogations of the Posted Workers Directive.[105] The Courts held, in sharp opposition to the opinion of Advocate General Bot, that Lower Saxony's *Landesvergabegesetz* did not comply with the Posted Workers Directive.[106] The Court rejected a public policy argument made by the German Government arguing that the restriction promoted by the law of Lower Saxony was justified by the 'objective of ensuring protection for independence in the organization of working life by trade unions'.[107] Then it rejected, for lack of evidence, a national welfare argument that the provisions of Lower Saxony aimed at 'ensuring the financial balance of the social security systems [that] … depends on the level of workers' salaries'.[108] These provisions only covered public and not private contracts and the minimum wage protections were geographically limited to the territory of Lower Saxony, rather than being universally applicable to the whole of Germany. Therefore the Court held that the restrictions could not fall under the exception of Directive 96/72.[109] The *Rüffert* court ruled in favour of the free movement of the services of the Polish construction workers posted in Germany at the expense of the local collective agreement on public procurement.[110]

The horizontal dimension of the conflict in *Rüffert* shows Lower Saxony had higher labour standards in public procurement contracts than other *Länder*. The goal of Lower Saxony's legislation was to provide minimum wage protections for employees in public procurement contracts over EUR 10,000. This law served as a model to mobilise other *Länder* as well as the federal government to adopt a nationwide bill imposing higher employment standards throughout Germany.[111] The conflict among the *Länder* on labour standards in public procurement contracts went back to the late 1990s and lasted until 2000. At this point the Conservative party came into power and only six *Länder*out of 16 were able to adopt higher labour standards in public procurement contracts, creating what Florian Rödl called a 'legislative patchwork' in German minimum wage law.[112]

If we apply the story of the three children and a flute to *Rüffert*, the Polish workers represent the libertarian Carla who made the flute. They want to be able to deploy

---

[105] Art 56 TFEU.
[106] Case C-346/06 *Dirk Rüffert v Land Niedersachsen* [2008] ECR I-1989, paras 38–43.
[107] ibid, para 41.
[108] ibid, para 42.
[109] See Art 3(8) Posted Workers Directive; and ibid, para 29.
[110] Case C-346/06 *Dirk Rüffert v Land Niedersachsen* [2008] ECR I-1989; M Franzen and C Richter, 'Case C-346/06, *Rechtsanwalt Dr. Dirk Rüffert, in his capacity as liquidator of Objekt und Bauregie GmbH & Co. KG v Land Niedersachsen*, [2008] ECR I-1989' (2010) 47 *Common Market Law Review* 537.
[111] This case resonates with the living wage initiative launched by several cities in the US. See *New Orleans Campaign for a Living Wage v City of New Orleans* 825 So.2d 1098 (LA, 4 September 2002) (state law pre-empted the local minimum wage); GE Frug, RT Ford and DJ Barron, Local Government Law. *Cases and Materials*, 5th edn (Eagan, MN, West, 2009).
[112] See F Rödl, 'The CJEU's Rüffert-Judgement: A Case for "Undistorted" Wage Competition' (2009) *Harvard European Law Association Working Papers* 2009; F Rödl, 'La Corte di Giustizia CE nel caso Rüffert: per la "non distorsione" della concorrenza in materia salariale' in A Vimercati (ed), *Il conflitto sbilanciato. Libertà economiche e autonomia collettiva tra ordinamento comunitario e ordinamenti nazionali* (Bari, Cacucci, 2009).

their comparatively inexpensive labour at the centre and leave the periphery.[113] The egalitarian Bob is Lower Saxony with welfare legislation protecting the workers' minimum wages. German business, as well as other *Länder* taking advantage of the free movement of services at a cheaper cost, represent the utilitarian Anne.

Once again, each actor in the conflict has a strong justification for obtaining the flute. Each of their justifications is relevant even though, as Damjan Kukovec cautions us, who is the 'weaker party' in this story might change according to the centre–periphery power relationship.[114] While the *Rüffert* judgment reconciles the utilitarian positions of German business and those *Länder* against the minimum wage legislation with the libertarian position of the Polish workers, my point is that the Court does not engage with other distributive implications such as 'dumping', which Bob, the egalitarian, might fear, or the change in power dynamics influencing the negotiation among the *Länder* and the German Government.[115]

VII. CONCLUSION

The focus on conceptions of justice from below is on the plurality of interests at stake, both vertical and horizontal, and their economic development implications when conflicts arise in European law and policy. This chapter reveals the absence of a process and a normative commitment to deploy a criterion of distributive justice to drive cohesion policies and interpret European law. Instead of grasping the complexity of local and horizontal interests at stake that could have entered in the Court's proportionality analysis, or in the articulation of an economic development strategy in cohesion policy, lawyers, judges and policy makers in Europe appear more concerned with institutional demands of justice than its social realisation. In the attempt to shift this perspective, looking at the lens through the conceptions of justice from below sheds light on the imperfect relation between increasing regional disparities and social and economic inequalities on the one hand, and our different capabilities for individual enjoyment on the other.

---

[113] See D Kukovec, 'Taking Change Seriously: The Rhetoric of Justice and the Reproduction of the Status Quo' in this volume, 319.
[114] ibid, 323ff.
[115] See T Walter, 'Germany—The Practical Consequences' in A Bucker and W Warneck (eds), Viking—Laval–Rüffert: *Consequences and Policy Perspectives* (Brussels, European Trade Union Institute, 2010) 50 explaining that '[d]ue to the complicated nature of Germany's federal structure and the associated legal situation regarding public procurement, the *Rüffert* decision has caused major problems ... The two possible consequences are that either German companies are squeezed out of the market or that they are forced to cut their pay levels'.

25

Qu'ils mangent des contrats: *Rethinking Justice in EU Contract Law*

DANIELA CARUSO

I. INTRODUCTION

THE CONCERN FOR justice in the context of EU contract law was central to a scholarly initiative that led, in 2004, to the publication of a Social Justice Manifesto.[1] The Manifesto had the explicit goal of steering the European Commission's harmonisation agenda away from purely neoliberal goals and towards a socially conscious law of private exchange. Contract law would be designed at the EU level so as to become (or remain, depending on the baseline of each Member State) palatable to weaker parties. Today, in the many parts of Europe devastated by rising poverty, dire unemployment rates and collapsing social safety nets, the Manifesto needs to be revised. When mere access to the marketplace is foreclosed by indigence and marginalisation, the promise of contracts that would be sweet towards the vulnerable has the flavour of Marie Antoinette's brioche. This essay revisits the situational premises of the Manifesto, acknowledges its accomplishments, identifies its limits and outlines possibilities for its renewal, both within its original framework and beyond.

The Social Justice Manifesto was a welcome moment of reflection upon the yet undefined trajectory of EU contract law. The concern underlying the Manifesto was that the Commission would spearhead a technocratic, undemocratic and yet definitely ideological project of private law harmonisation—a project geared towards the neoliberal triumph of private autonomy and functionally justified only by the goal of driving down the cost of inter-state transactions. It is important to locate historically both the Manifesto and the project that the Manifesto aimed to oppose. Beginning with the Communication on European Contract Law of July 2001[2] and continuing with the Action Plan of October 2003,[3] the Commission

---

[1] Study Group on Social Justice in European Private Law, 'Social Justice in European Contract Law: A Manifesto' (2004) 10 *European Law Journal* 653, 663–64.
[2] European Commission, 'Communication from the Commission to the Council and the European Parliament on European contract law' COM (2001) 398 final.
[3] European Commission, 'Communication from the Commission of 12 February 2003 to the European Parliament and the Council—A more coherent European contract law—An action plan' COM (2003) 68 final.

seemed poised to launch an ultimately non-sectoral reform of contract law, aimed at bringing 'coherence' among different legal systems and harmonising their guiding rules and principles.[4] The seeming neutrality of such values as coherence and uniformity could not hide the fact that the project was mainly about making life easier for *businesses* operating across borders.[5] The risk was that harmonisation would resuscitate the myth of untrammelled private autonomy and at the same time erode those private law mechanisms, variously devised through the twentieth century by state legislators, courts and agencies, that redressed power imbalances and protected weaker parties. It was therefore important to mobilise the base of private law scholars concerned with questions of distributive justice—or 'social' justice as it was more palatably christened by the Manifesto's authors. The Manifesto highlighted important themes. It noted that private law had an expressive function and needed to reflect the socio-economic complexities of modern societies;[6] that it was a tool for social engineering, and therefore had to be designed with the full consultation of all relevant stakeholders by means of fully democratic processes;[7] and that it had to dovetail with welfare structures that varied a great deal across the different Member States.[8]

In hindsight, the project was of the constructive type. It seemed inspired by the belief that the harmonisation of contract law, if handled properly and guarded from neoliberal hijacking, could be done well and might achieve laudable goals. *L'esprit du temps* nurtured this optimistic streak. The EU was then on the verge of a dramatic expansion, with all the promises of enlargement in full display and none of its (un)intended consequences yet in sight. A supranational constitution, harbinger of political convergence and infused with goals of democracy and solidarity, was then in the making. And in matters of contract a number of legislative measures had already brought a moralising, social tone to the incipient sales law of the EU.[9] The Manifesto signalled a deeper entrenchment of a particular type of contract law scholarship in the constituent bodies of EU contract law, making sure that its values

---

[4] SR Weatherill, 'The Consumer Rights Directive: How and Why a Quest for "Coherence" Has (Largely) Failed' (2012) 49 *Common Market Law Review* 1279.

[5] According to the Commission's Action Plan, in the Common Frame of Reference 'contractual freedom should be the guiding principle; restrictions should only be foreseen where this could be justified with good reasons'.

[6] '[S]ince the market plays an increasingly important role in securing distributive justice for the citizens of Europe, it is vital that its basic regulatory framework—the private law of contract—should embrace a scheme of social justice that secures a widespread acceptance'. Study Group, 'Social Justice', n 1 above, 673.

[7] M Hesselink, 'The Politics of a European Civil Code' (2004) 10 *European Law Journal* 675; D Caruso, 'Private Law and Public Stakes in European Integration: The Case of Property' (2004) 10 *European Law Journal* 751.

[8] T Wilhelmsson, 'Varieties of Welfarism in European Contract Law' (2004) 10 *European Law Journal* 712, 713.

[9] Most notably, Council Directive 85/577/EEC of 20 December 1985 to protect the consumer in respect of contracts negotiated away from business premises (Doorstep Selling Directive) [1985] OJ L372/31; Directive 97/7/EC of the European Parliament and of the Council of 20 May 1997 on the protection of consumers in respect of distance contracts (Distance Selling Directive) [1997] OJ L144/19; Council Directive 93/13/EEC of 5 April 1993 on unfair terms in consumer contracts (Unfair Contract Terms Directive) [1993] OJ L95/29, and Directive 1999/44/EC of the European Parliament and of the Council of 25 May 1999 on certain aspects of the sale of consumer goods and associated guarantees (Consumer Sales Directive) [1999] OJ L171/12.

would not be ignored. And indeed they were not. Procedurally, the drafting of new texts involved the work of scholars affiliated with the Social Justice project.[10] Substantively, the voice of the Manifesto would be heard in subsequent enactments, beginning with Directive 2005/29 concerning unfair commercial practices, which outlawed a number of marketing techniques still permissible in the United States.[11] The 'Recast' Brussels I Regulation, scheduled to enter into force in 2015, reigns in private autonomy in matters of choice of forum when one of the parties is a consumer, an insured party, or an individual employee.[12] The explicit justification for this departure from freedom of contract is the assumed vulnerability of such parties. In the same vein, Commission proposals continue to ban pre-dispute arbitration clauses[13]—a practice that some observers deem fanatically pro-consumer and blind to business needs.[14] More generally, as a matter of course the process of producing new contract law instruments involves balancing autonomy with other values, such as the protection of weaker parties.[15]

In many ways, therefore, social justice scholars can take pride in a job well done and in their well-established presence. There is a sense, however, in which the Manifesto has fallen victim to its own success, as well as to the unfolding of the Euro saga. It is time, therefore, to reassess critically the 2004 Manifesto along two lines—one internal to the project, and one external.

II. INTERNAL CRITIQUE AND SUGGESTIONS FROM WITHIN

A. Perils of Deliberation

The Manifesto, as noted, placed much faith in the possibilities of deliberative processes. Several commentators belaboured the point that EU private law had to be drafted with the full participation of multiple stake holders.[16] This emphasis on

---

[10] The Draft Common Frame of Reference (an opus of 4,795 pages) was prepared by the Study Group on a European Civil Code and the Research Group on EC Private Law (Acquis Group). C von Bar and E Clive (eds), *Principles, Definitions and Model Rules of European Private Law Draft Common Frame of Reference (DCFR)*, Full edn (Munich, Sellier European Law Publishers, 2009).

[11] Directive 2005/29/EC of the European Parliament and of the Council of 11 May 2005 concerning unfair business-to-consumer commercial practices in the Internal Market and amending Council Directive 84/450/EEC, Directives 97/7/EC, 98/27/EC and 2002/65/EC and Regulation (EC) 2006/2004 (Unfair Commercial Practices Directive) [2005] L149/22.

[12] Regulation (EU) 1215/2012 of the European Parliament and of the Council of 12 December 2012 on jurisdiction and the recognition and enforcement of judgments in civil and commercial matters [2012] OJ L351/1.

[13] European Commission, 'Proposal for a Regulation of the European Parliament and of the Council of 21 May 2013 on online dispute resolution for consumer disputes' COM(2011) 794/2; see also European Commission, 'Proposal for a Regulation on a Common European Sales Law' COM (2011) 635 final, Art 84(d). This proposal pays enough attention to consumer protection as to generate the ire of efficiency-minded commentators: R Epstein, 'Harmonization, Heterogeneity and Regulation: CESL, the Lost Opportunity for Constructive Harmonization' (2013) 50 *Common Market Law Review* 207.

[14] MA Aslam, 'B-2-C Pre-Dispute Arbitration Clauses, E-Commerce Trust Construction and Jenga: "Keeping Every Cog and Wheel"' (2013) 7 *Masaryk University Journal of Law and Technology* 1.

[15] N Reich and H-W Micklitz, '*Crónica de una muerte anunciada*: The Commission Proposal for a "Directive on Consumer Rights"' (2009) 46 *Common Market Law Review* 471.

[16] Hesselink, 'The Politics', n 7 above.

process had the side effect of substantive ambivalence. The Manifesto aptly noted that views on social justice were radically different within Europe, and that developing one coherent understanding of contract law in the context of multiple welfare models might prove impossible.[17] Thomas Wilhelmsson was particularly aware of 'internal conflicts within the welfarist perspective':

> What from one point of view may be clearly seen as a welfarist measure, may from some other point of view be regarded as fairly doubtful example. For example ... from the point of view of distributive justice, [precontractual information rules in credit contracts] are problematic, as they tend to improve the position of strong consumers, while offering little help to the more vulnerable ones.[18]

Wilhelmsson then proceeded to assess the contract law *acquis*, as it was in 2004, in light of an articulate taxonomy of welfare models. He found that existing EU instruments—in particular the Unfair Contract Terms Directive—already embraced welfarism, but only in one of its manifestations: the market-rational type, whereby consumer rationality is enhanced by deeper knowledge, wider choice and ability to repent from occasional lapses of wisdom.[19] This meant that alternative forms of welfarism—especially those focused on redistribution and extreme vulnerability—had not yet surfaced in EU contract law, and might never see the light of day.

Over the decade following the publication of the Manifesto, social justice has grown *lato sensu* more visible in the discourse of EU contract law. Yet, its most important feature—its emphasis on the distributive potential of contract rules and principles—has not yet gained the visibility one might expect. The Draft Common Frame of Reference (DCFR),[20] while embracing 'justice' as 'an all pervading principle ... not lightly to be displaced',[21] pays minimal homage to distributive goals[22] and candidly reveals the absence of consensus on what such goals might entail:

> [D]ifferent readers may have different interpretations of, and views on, the extent to which the DCFR suggests the correction of market failures or contains elements of 'social justice' and protection for weaker parties.[23]

---

[17] 'Although the idea of a European model of the social market has gained some currency, at least in contrast to an American model of capitalism, there remains considerable divergences in views about how the details of this model should be articulated and systematised. Indeed, *the existing differences between national systems for providing social welfare and steering market outcomes cast some doubt on the possibility of defining even in abstract terms a convincing interpretation of the European model of the social market*. Thus there is a need to build a consensus around the appropriate principles of a social market.' Study Group, 'Social Justice', n 1 above, 673 (emphasis added).

[18] Wilhelmsson, 'Varieties of Welfarism', n 8 above.

[19] 'If welfarism is understood as signifying mandatory rules protecting the alleged weaker party to the contract ... then practically the whole contract law *acquis* is of this kind [... We] cannot avoid questions such as: welfarist in what respect, from what point of view?' ibid 714.

[20] C von Bar et al (eds), *Principles, Definitions and Model Rules of European Private Law, Draft Common Frame of Reference (DCFR)*, Outline edn (Munich, Sellier European Law Publishers, 2012).

[21] ibid, 84.

[22] 'The promotion of solidarity and social responsibility is not absent from the private law rules in the DCFR.' ibid, 15.

[23] ibid, 10.

Of course such *petites différences* are truly 'irreconcilable visions of humanity and society'[24] and no reconciliation is, to this day, in sight. In some passages, the DCFR drafters seem to doubt the very possibility of defining justice:

> 'Justice is hard to define, impossible to measure and subjective at the edges, but clear cases of injustice are universally recognised and universally abhorred'.[25]

'We know it when we see it' is not much of a yield after a decade of deliberation. With justice so neutralised, the public/private distinction resurfaces, albeit softened by 'however' clauses:[26]

> The promotion of solidarity and social responsibility is generally regarded as primarily *the function of public law* (using, for example, criminal law, tax law and social welfare law) *rather than private law*. However, the promotion of solidarity and social responsibility is not absent from the private law rules in the DCFR.[27]

At an operational level, the DCFR articulates 'justice' as a series of absolutely classical 'qualifications on freedom of contract', such as 'ensuring that like are treated alike'.[28] With a nod to the Manifesto, the DCFR does raise the issue of social vulnerability.[29] The category of 'the vulnerable', however, soon collapses onto the socio-economically neutral notion of 'consumer'[30]—an admittedly dissatisfying proxy for bargaining weakness[31] and definitely not a proxy for low income or marginalisation. Pre-contractual duties to disclose, or post-contractual rights to repent, are only meant to expand and deepen the range of private autonomy. There is nothing truly redistributive here and as always, *diligentibus jura succurrunt*. The truly vulnerable, that is, those incapable of self-care and due diligence, find little solace in such measures.

In hindsight, the Manifesto's main flaw seems to lie in its excessive faith in deliberation and in its ambivalent stance in point of distributive justice. It contained no recipe for identifying weaker parties and embraced no specific redistributive model. Unsurprisingly, given the multitude of interests involved in developing contract law at EU level, the concept of social justice has remained as vague and inconclusive as it was ten years ago.

Going forward, social justice scholars could decide simply to sharpen their focus: insist on the distributive impact of contract law rules and on linkages between markets and welfare;[32] continue to monitor the progress of the Commission towards the adoption of uniform contract law instruments; and make sure that such instruments

---

[24] D Kennedy, 'Form and Substance in Private Law Adjudication' (1976) 89 *Harvard Law Review* 1685.
[25] von Bar et al, *Principles*, n 20 above, 84.
[26] G Bellantuono, 'The Limits of Contract Law in the Regulatory State' (2010) 6 *European Review of Contract Law* 115, 118 ('The DCFR follows the traditional view that gives prominence to the interests of contractual parties and leaves to different branches of law the task of fulfilling other goals, for example ... the distribution of resources to less wealthy classes').
[27] von Bar et al, *Principles*, n 20 above, 15 (emphasis added).
[28] ibid, 84, 88.
[29] 'Many of the qualifications on freedom of contract mentioned above can also be explained as rules designed to protect the vulnerable.' ibid, 88.
[30] 'Within the DCFR the main example of this aspect of justice is the special protection afforded to consumers.' ibid.
[31] 'Whether the notion of the consumer is necessarily the best way of identifying those in need of special protection is a question which has been raised and will no doubt be raised again.' ibid, 89.
[32] H Collins, *Regulating Contracts* (Oxford, Oxford University Press, 1999).

contain enough protection for 'vulnerable' parties. The problem with this course of action is that it might have already delivered all the goods one might ask of it, given its boundaries, its vagueness and its faith in pluralist deliberation. The question is whether more can be done *within* the boundaries of contract law harmonisation. I will outline some possibilities here, before moving on to consider whether the quest for social justice, at this particular historical and political juncture, should rather keep one foot firmly *outside* the realm of contracts.

B. Focusing on Vulnerable Consumers

In February 2013, the European Consumer Consultative Group (ECCG) issued an interesting and detailed 'Opinion on consumers and vulnerability'.[33] The Opinion contains a list of recommendations, seemingly an ideal blueprint for a newly reconfigured social justice manifesto. The ECCG aptly departs from the notion of average consumer and attempts to identify specific markers of weakness, such as illness and disability.[34] It conceives of vulnerability as a trap into which anybody can fall at some point during their lifetime, and recommends therefore a flexible approach to each specific circumstance. In contract law jargon, this is a plea for general clauses and case-by-case adjudication. The Opinion also names specific services which should be universally guaranteed (eg, internet access) and others which should not be handled via autonomous market transactions (eg, home heating). Most notably, the Opinion recommends conducting empirical studies to verify whether existing mechanisms for the protection of weaker parties (eg, disclosure mandates or the ability to switch to alternative service providers) are indeed effective. This emphasis on empirical studies echoes analogous suggestions recently made by prominent contract scholars in the United States, and in particular by Oren Bar-Gill and Omri Ben-Shahar in their commentary to the proposed Common European Sales Law (CESL).[35] The point of such suggestions is that the regulation of private autonomy—through mandatory clauses, black lists or disclosure duties—is only warranted where market failures and systemic harms to consumers have been documented via statistically relevant studies. The ECCG opinion is less worried about unduly constraining private autonomy and instead focuses on identifying new areas of vulnerability, but the bottom line is identical: more data is needed in order to make sure that distributive justice is achieved in consumer transactions.

C. Producing Better Knowledge

To be sure, the Commission has engaged for a while in empirical studies of the EU market. It did produce an impact assessment before issuing the CESL proposal, and the assessment is rife with data. The sort of data that the Commission chose to gather is,

---

[33] European Consumer Consultative Group (ECCG), 'Opinion on consumers and vulnerability' (7 February 2013), www.ec.europa.eu/consumers/empowerment/docs/eccg_opinion_consumers_vulnerability_022013_en.pdf.

[34] The ECCG Opinion cites the work of H-W Micklitz, 'Do Consumers and Businesses Need a New Architecture of Consumer Law?' (2012) *EUI Working Papers* LAW 2012/23, 22.

[35] O Bar-Gill and O Ben-Shahar, 'Regulatory Techniques in Consumer Protection: A Critique of European Consumer Contract Law' (2013) 50 *Common Market Law Review* 109.

however, peculiar. First, a lot of the information that was assembled is qualitative. Firm managers, for instance, were asked to state whether the fragmentation of contract law in the EU was a hindrance to pursuing inter-state marketing strategies. Replies to this question were then given numerical codes depending on whether the hindrance was reportedly severe, non-existent, or something in between. This is how managers' impressions, whether or not supported by hard evidence, were converted into hard numbers and eventually into an accurate-sounding measurement of the loss of business attributable to legal fragmentation.[36]

Second, there was no attempt whatsoever at locating the polled firms or consumers in their socio-economic or even simply national context. Interviewees are de-nationalised and anonymous. The assessment collects data on whether firms deal with customers in one, two or more EU countries, but it does not specify which countries these are, and the vectors of import–export forces within Europe—their directionality or intensity—are nowhere to be seen. Data have no granularity and are systematically aggregate. A nod to firms' relative market power is found only once, in the statement that legal fragmentation is likely to impose higher costs on firms with lower bargaining power in business-to-business (B2B) transactions. This is because leading firms are likely to impose their own choice of law onto their weaker counterparts, placing onto them the burden of acquiring legal knowledge.[37] The implication of this assumption is that the uniformity of sales law would equalise the playing field to the benefit of weaker traders. But with the exception of this casual remark, the entire assessment is controlled by the presumption that strengths and weaknesses are evenly distributed throughout the Union.

In complete contrast to such aggregate data, the pioneering work of Ian Ayres on the impact of race and gender in car-sales dynamics comes to mind as a source of inspiration:[38] identical contract rules can hurt some groups of consumers (or businesses)[39] and benefit others.[40] Interestingly, many other areas of EU policy are supported by highly differentiated, granular and particularised inquiries. The Directorate-General for Regional Policy (DG REGIO), for instance, is a DG where by definition the analysis of socio-economic dynamics is localised and context-specific. But when it comes to establishing the basis for Internal Market legislation, the Commission intentionally blends different realities into statistical averages and takes median values as its legislative basis. This is not the place and time to belabour the resilience of the public–private distinction in EU law, but it is indeed curious that

---

[36] The Commission's use of qualitative interviews has attracted sharp critiques. See J Boyle, 'Two Database Cheers for the EU' *Financial Times* (London, 2 January 2006).

[37] In contrast, in B2C transactions, even large firms can be constrained by the consumer protection regime to which their customers are entitled.

[38] I Ayres and P Siegelman, 'Race and Gender Discrimination in Bargaining for a New Car' (1995) 85 *American Economic Review* 304.

[39] I Ayres, FE Vars and N Zakariya, 'To Insure Prejudice: Racial Disparities in Taxicab Tipping' (2005) 114 *Yale Law Journal* 1613 (documenting customer-side discrimination in tipping cab drivers).

[40] Sellers' ability to pass along the cost of regulation to consumers varies greatly depending on such factors as brand loyalty, which is lower in emerging economies. See, eg, AR Apil, 'Foreign Product Perceptions and Country of Origin Analysis across Black Sea; Studies on Azerbaijan, Bulgaria, Georgia, Russia, and Turkey' (2006) 1 *IBSU International Refereed Multi-disciplinary Scientific Journal* 22, 31 ('In [developing countries such as Romania] consumers typically perceive foreign products, particular those made in higher origin countries, as being of higher quality than domestic products').

when it comes to drafting the law of the market, an enormous pile of economic data showing socio-economic asymmetries can be brushed aside.

While containing several innovative proposals, the ECCG Opinion is completely aligned with the 2004 Manifesto when it conceives of market transactions as governed by uniform laws for all consumers and all businesses throughout Europe; it aims, once again, at producing *Bürgerliches Recht*, with emphasis on an EU-wide, undifferentiated citizen in an undifferentiated market context. There is something eternally appealing about a uniform law for a unified market populated by indistinguishable actors. Its philosophical pedigree is both enlightened (insofar as it enables individual autonomy) and romantic (insofar as it generates communities tied together by a shared set of norms). It is unsurprising that new Member States would want to endorse the project of uniform market rules, thereby signalling their full embrace of the Union's goals and their true belonging. The idea grows all the more appealing when uniformity makes room for vulnerability—again, a horizontal and ubiquitous category—and softens its rules to embrace it. The cold neoclassical assumption by which the two parties to a transaction are formally equal (B=C) is replaced by the warm acknowledgment of unequal bargaining power in consumer transactions (B>C), and the rules are adjusted accordingly.

In the aftermath of the Euro crisis, however, one can detect a few signs of dissatisfaction with even the most vulnerability-friendly versions of uniform laws for the EU market. The bond spreads, brought to the attention of the EU public since the start of the sovereign debt crisis and accompanied by dramatic charts in all media forms, have provided a clear and vivid illustration of the socio-economic cleavages plaguing the Internal Market. One critique, recently phrased by Damjan Kukovec, is that *any* attempt at uniform regulation of the EU market is necessarily blind to the differences between the socio-economic centres and the socio-economic peripheries of the Union.[41] Kukovec questions the overall edifice of EU law as based on a 'rhetoric of common interest' and therefore not equipped even to acknowledge—let alone redress—the pernicious distributive consequences of European integration. Others have addressed directly the issue of private law harmonisation.[42] The uniform regulation of contract law throughout a socio-economically diverse market reproduces, in fact, a fundamental feature of laissez faire—namely, its indifference *by design* to the socio-economic diversity of the market. Ironically, Member States experienced the progressive socialisation and embedding of their private laws in the twentieth century, but the EU is now reviving the nineteenth-century habit of insulating the law of private autonomy from

---

[41] D Kukovec, 'A Critique of the Rhetoric of Common Interest in the European Union Legal Discourse' (13 April 2012) *IGLP Working Papers*, www.harvardiglp.org/new-thinking-new-writing/a-critique-of-rhetoric/.
See also D Kukovec, 'Taking Change Seriously: The Rhetoric of Justice and the Reproduction of the Status Quo' in this volume, 319.

[42] See, eg, F Rödl, 'Private Law, Democracy, Codification. A Critique of the European Law Project' in C Joerges and T Ralli (eds), *European Constitutionalism Without Private Law—Private Law Without Democracy* (RECON Report 14, ARENA Report 3/11, Oslo, University of Oslo, 2011); C Joerges and C Schmid, 'Towards Proceduralization of Private Law in the European Multi-Level System' in A Hartkamp (ed), *Towards a European Civil Code*, 4th edn (Alphen aan den Rijn, Kluwer Law International, 2011) 277; and D Caruso, 'The Baby and the Bath Water: The American Critique of European Contract Law' (2013) 61 *American Journal of Comparative Law* 479.

the larger question of systemic inequality.[43] Can the Social Justice project internalise such critiques and augment its project accordingly?

D. Making Up for Asymmetries

In the abstract, it would be possible to acknowledge the distributive pitfalls of uniform law and to resist any further Europeanisation of contract law. Conscious of the regrettable distributive dynamics of harmonisation, some scholars have considered shifting from uniform rules to a much looser system of coordination among other private law systems within a procedural 'conflicts' model.[44] Others have posited that any problems stemming from legal diversity should be handled through spontaneous processes of self-regulation.[45] Social justice scholars, however, would probably be reluctant to leave the law of the EU market to such local devices, either because of their propensity for centralised market regulation[46] or due to their cosmopolitan, anti-nationalist instincts.[47] But if the reflection on the private laws of the EU market must continue, then a generic focus on horizontal vulnerability is not enough and a closer, more granular understanding of the market—of its many centres and its many peripheries—can no longer be postponed.

The point is *not* to stop working on uniform laws for the market. The prevention of fraud to the consumer, a sensible regulation of access to credit and the outlawing of predatory marketing practices, remain important icons of social justice. The point is to establish an ideological counterpoint to the win–win narrative that has already inspired and justified a number of harmonisation projects—including the adoption of a single currency. The uneven costs and benefits of contract law harmonisation must be tracked and measured. Losers must be identified and helped out of the predicament of false autonomy. Compensatory mechanisms specifically designed to redress the uneven costs of compliance with uniform laws may have to be devised outside the boundaries of contract law (more on this point below).

E. Contracts and Competence Creep

Employment, housing and access to credit are essential aspects of social justice insofar as they are necessary to secure a set of basic entitlements. These fundamental aspects of the human condition had been heavily regulated for over a century

---

[43] Rödl, 'Private Law', n 42 above, 151.
[44] Joerges and Schmid, 'Towards Proceduralization', n 42 above, 295 ('The [Commission's strategy of full harmonization] is at odds with the socio-economic diversity [now deepening] in Europe. In view of this diversity, the imposition of uniform rules on the balancing of market development and consumer demand do not make economic sense. They also risk the destruction of the social fabric of markets and consumption which remains … characterised by national contexts').
[45] F Cafaggi, *Reframing Self-Regulation in European Private Law* (Alphen aan den Rijn, Kluwer Law International, 2006).
[46] The charge of 'statism', moved against the whole project of contract law harmonisation, comes from Epstein, 'Harmonization', n 13 above.
[47] See R Sefton-Green, 'French and English Crypto-Nationalism and European Private Law' (2012) 8 *European Review of Contract Law* 260.

by means of state contract law—a practice that the Treaty of Lisbon, leaving economic and social policy outside the scope of harmonisation, promised to leave untouched. It is now clear that the financial crisis and the measures taken in its aftermath—in particular the conditions attached to 'rescue' measures meant to save insolvent states from bankruptcy—have deeply eroded both private autonomy and the regulatory capacity of the state in such matters.[48] The nature of employment contracts has been radically altered. Post-employment benefits and pensions have been renegotiated with no regard to pre-existing obligations. The Italian *esodati* have been left to wonder about the meaning of sanctity of contracts.[49] Collapsing state and local budgets have caused housing subsidies to shrink, leaving vulnerable tenants to the vagaries of under-regulated landlord–tenant agreements. And in many corners of Europe borrowers have been deprived of financial lifelines. In response to the bursting of the housing bubble, the EU has taken upon itself the role of regulating access to mortgages, again affecting the state's regulation of the housing market in dramatic and unprecedented ways.[50] In sum, the crisis has led to a de facto expansion of EU competences in matters of contract law, and the regulatory capacity of states and local government has shrunk accordingly. 'Social Justice in Contract Law' must now look at much more than consumer protection. Its agenda must embrace contracts that secure housing, employment and access to credit, and it must stay nimble: on one hand, it needs to work alongside the EU legislator when Brussels seems appropriate—or inevitable—as a locus of intervention; on the other hand, it must protect well-functioning local arrangements from supranational interference. In either case, the plot must thicken. The aforementioned contracts affect, much more directly than online shopping, the life of vulnerable subjects and must be placed, at a time of increasing Europeanisation, firmly at the centre of the social justice agenda.

III. THE EXTERNAL CRITIQUE: BEYOND CONTRACT LAW

A. Whither Contracts?

At the time of the Bolkestein proposal, much work was done to keep services of general interest outside of the liberalisation agenda of the Commission.[51] Current versions of that political battle are to be found in the attempt to reconcile the ongoing liberalisation of the energy market with price control and subsidised utility

---

[48] P Tsoukala, 'Euro Zone Crisis Management and the New Social Europe' (2013) 20 *Columbia Journal of European Law* 31; D Chalmers, 'The European Redistributive State and a European Law of Struggle' (2012) 18 *European Law Journal* 666, 667.

[49] P Garibaldi and F Taddei, 'Italy: A Dual Labour Market in Transition. Country Case Study on Labour Market Segmentation' (Geneva, ILO Publications, 2013) *Employment Working Papers* No 144, 24.

[50] European Commission, 'Proposal for a Directive of the European Parliament and of the Council on Credit Agreements relating to residential property credit' COM (2011) 142 final, contains strong limitations on autonomy: credit simply cannot be given if mandatory assessment (conducted by lender) proves negative (Art 14(2) of proposal).

[51] W Kowalsky, 'The Services Directive: The Legislative Process Clears the First Hurdle' (2006) 12 *European Review of Labour and Research* 231.

rates for the poor.[52] The gist of these battles is resisting the privatisation of important relationships and modes of supply. Beginning in the late 1980s, many such battles were lost. Commenting on the White Paper on the Internal Market, Joseph Weiler pointed out that embracing the market was a particular ideological choice that would inform and transform, irreversibly, the ethos of the Community.[53] Marija Bartl's sophisticated analysis of 'market rationality' lucidly portrays the EU's normative lens as heavily controlled by notions of consumerism and efficiency, and notes that the lens has systemically distortive effects.[54] These critiques resonate loudly within contract law discourse. EU law making in contract law is premised on the assumption that contracts are the essence of human exchange across national borders, and that a seamless network of private agreements is a necessary and perhaps even sufficient condition of European unity. This is, again, a particular normative lens that risks framing and distorting the discourse on cross-border exchanges. A Social Justice project that is meant to be a critical voice should not reinforce such distortions and should not let 'contract' alone dictate *the* frame of reference in EU law.

B. Property, Family and Association

The protection of the vulnerable, in the private law tradition of continental Europe, takes place in multiple sites. Entering contracts for goods and services is one way to fulfil basic needs, and the 2004 Manifesto aptly focused on contracts because in this field, thanks to the capacious reach of the Internal Market clause,[55] the EU had conquered much legislative territory. But there is much more in private law than contracts. Current proposals for a European Foundation Statute[56] may be paving the way for EU-wide redistribution of private wealth through the channel of charity.[57] Monitoring such initiatives through the lens of social justice and nurturing their development in the form of secondary legislation should be a feature of a new Manifesto.

Family and property law can also be designed so as to assist individuals in times of weakness, and they have served this function in some Member States more than others.[58] Family and property are areas in which direct harmonisation is largely not allowed by primary EU law, for reasons that range from principled stance to

---

[52] European Commission, 'Communication from the Commission to the European Parliament, the Council, the European Economic and Social Committee and the Committee of the Regions: Making the internal energy market work' COM (2012) 663 final. While the Commission sees subsidised electricity cost as a function of states' social policies and is opposed to price control, the ECCG recommends 'social tariffs': ECCG, 'Opinion', n 33 above, 12.
[53] JHH Weiler, 'The Transformation of Europe' (1991) 100 *Yale Law Journal* 2403, 2477.
[54] M Bartl, 'Market Rationality, Private Law and the Direction of the Union: Resuscitating the Market as the Object of the Political' *European Law Journal* (forthcoming) (manuscript on file).
[55] Now Art 114 of the Consolidated version of the Treaty on the Functioning of the European Union [2012] OJ C326/47 (TFEU).
[56] European Commission, ' Proposal for a Council Regulation on the Statute for a European Foundation (FE)' COM(2012) 35 final.
[57] L Faulhaber, 'Tax Expenditures, Charitable Giving, and the Fiscal Future of the European Union' (2014) *Yale Journal of InternationalLaw* 87; see Committee on Culture and Education, 'Opinion of the Committee on Culture and Education for the Committee on Legal Affairs on the proposal for a Council regulation on the Statute for a European Foundation (FE)' 2012/0022(APP).
[58] P Tsoukala, 'Family Portrait of a Greek Tragedy' *New York Times* (New York, 24 April 2010).

rent-seeking entrenchment.[59] The result of this competence divide is a regrettable hollowing out of EU law scholarship.[60] For instance, the ongoing debate about 'common goods', a desirable mode of ownership for such resources as water or cultural sites,[61] runs on a scholarly track that is entirely parallel to EU discourse.[62] It involves domestic property scholars, comparative law experts and even human rights activists from the Council of Europe, but it has not yet directly engaged EU law circles.[63] When water features in Commission documents, for instance, it is funnelled into EU conceptual buckets.[64] It becomes a *product* that must be *safe* across Europe, must be *priced* correctly, and may open up new *market opportunities*.[65] The strategy of social justice can then only be pursued obliquely, in the form of an exception to market principles in underserved regions. But at the level of EU policy design, social justice cannot partake of the richness of domestic and comparative property debates. It has to deploy contract rhetoric. It has to speak 'marketese'. Going forward, a new Manifesto should explore all the possibilities for social justice that the private law tradition may contain—not just those that happen to dovetail with the current competence divide between Member States and Brussels.

IV. CONCLUSIONS

At the heart of the 2004 Manifesto was the belief that private law had to be linked with larger questions of wealth distribution and with the politics of social justice. It is important, at this stage of European integration, to recall that linkage begins with discourse and that discourse is the level—perhaps the only level—at which legal academia can make a difference. It is time, therefore, to branch out of traditional private law inquiries. At the risk of amateurism, scholars must venture into fields that intersect contract and property but go deeper into the distributive effects of European integration. The Commission's trade deals with third countries, the criteria by which agricultural subsidies are distributed, the cycles of structural funding, the strictures of access to credit and all post-crisis regulatory constraints on markets must be on the radar screen of social justice research. A scholarly project focusing only on the specialty areas of its members would resemble the proverbial drunk searching for his keys under the street light, knowing full well that the keys are somewhere else in the dark.

---

[59] See the timid introduction of legislative competence in matters of family law in 1999 with the Treaty of Amsterdam (1999), now in Art 81 TFEU, or the protection of nationalisation projects guaranteed by the Treaty of Rome in what is now Art 345 TFEU.

[60] The focus on the logic of the market also tends to obscure the redistributive dynamics of different family law regimes. See F Nicola, 'Family Law Exceptionalism in Comparative Law' (2010) 58 *American Journal of Comparative Law* 777.

[61] See, eg, Commissione Rodotà, 'Per la modifica delle norme del codice civile in materia di beni pubblici' (14 June 2007), www.giustizia.it/giustizia/it/mg_1_12_1.wp?contentId=SPS47617.

[62] See S van Erp, A Salomons and B Akkermans (eds), *The Future of European Property Law* (Munich, Sellier European Law Publishers, 2012). This project is still insufficiently concerned with the redistributive dimension of ownership.

[63] Fertile synergies could emerge between mainstream EU property scholarship and new 'common goods' articulations. See A di Robilant, 'Property and Democratic Deliberation: The *Numerus Clausus* Principle and Democratic Experimentalism in Property Law' (2014) 62 *American Journal of Comparative Law* 367.

[64] Bartl, 'Market Rationality', n 54 above.

[65] European Commission, 'A Blueprint to Safeguard Europe's Water Resources' COM(2012) 673 final.

Part Five

26
Just Fatherlands? The Shoah in the Jurisprudence of Strasbourg

CAROLE LYONS[*]

> In the twentieth century, there will be an extraordinary nation. It will be a great nation but its grandeur will not limit its freedom. It will be famous, wealthy, poetic, cordial to the rest of humanity ... it will be called Europe. Europe ... will be called humanity. Humanity, definitive nation ... what a majestic vision![1]

I. INTRODUCTION

THE PRIMARY PREOCCUPATION of this chapter is an examination of how Europe's highest human rights court works through the enduring effects of the 'moral catastrophe' of the Holocaust.[2] The issue of the role of past inhumanity within Europe's present is fundamental and informs (or ought to) the ways in which justice is done and understood in Europe as a whole. This chapter concentrates on one judicial forum, the European Court of Human Rights (ECtHR), and the continuing influence of the Holocaust/Shoah within its jurisprudence. The focus on a particular past in the evolution of European human rights raises general questions as to how history and memory are mediated through the judicial route and, more specifically, how the legacy of Auschwitz has helped to mould the human rights culture which now guides 47 European states, including the 28 EU Member States. The importance of mutual dependency of the EU States has been raised by other contributions to this volume. This chapter suggests that such mutual dependency would be difficult to arrive at in the absence of a parallel mutual confrontation of the past. Mutuality and solidarity, written into, if not consistently respected within, European integration, are rooted in an implicit shared, European responsibility for the shaping of an ethical response to institutionalised racist killing. András Sajó, in his chapter in this collection, discusses the concept of the 'responsible

---

[*] With much gratitude for the generosity of Gráinne de Búrca, Dimitry Kochenov and Andrew Williams.
[1] V Hugo, *'L'avenir' in Paris* (Paris, Introduction to the Paris Guide, 1867) 11 cited in J Derrida, *The Politics of Friendship* (London, Verso, 1997) 264.
[2] J Habermas, 'Democracy, Solidarity and the European Crisis' lecture at KU Leuven (26 April 2013), www.kuleuven.be/communicatie/evenementen/evenementen/jurgen-habermas/en/democracy-solidarity-and-the-european-crisis.

community' in respect of past injustices and how that responsibility equates to 'patrolling our moral borders'.[3] Applied to integration processes in Europe it might be posited that the European (*responsible*) community has Greece (and all the other EU Member States) absorb Germany's past shame,[4] while Germany assists debt recovery in Greece. The constantly alluded to, but nonetheless nebulous, *acquis communitaire* which governs the EU integration compact, is not exactly explicit on such a distribution of debt and disgrace.[5] Turning to European human rights processes specifically, although it might be questioned how much the 'just fatherlands'[6] anticipated while the European Convention on Human Rights (ECHR) was being drafted in 1950 have been achieved, the ECtHR is a forum where an encounter with the past has been taking place, to a greater or lesser extent, for over 50 years. Judge Sajó's chapter asks us to re-examine accepted notions of victimhood which lie at the root of the judicial approach to past collective injustices. This chapter offers a pragmatic complement to that thesis in identifying the stages of Holocaust-specific case-law from Strasbourg and placing an analysis of that Court's approach to the Shoah in the context of a consideration of the extent and nature of a justice deficit in the European legal space.

Digging up the past is all the rage these days. Literally, in the case of King Richard III in a Leicester car park[7] and Federico García Lorca in Andalucia[8] but, more significantly, in the continuing search for those responsible for past injustices such as Hungarian Nazis in an Australian court,[9] Spanish Judge Baltasar Garzón's (ill-fated) pursuit of civil war crimes against humanity in Spain,[10] multiple apologies for past wrongs, slavery, famines,[11] even Wayne Rooney goes to

---

[3] A Sajó, 'Victimhood and Vulnerability As Sources of Justice' in this volume, 337, at 340.

[4] Habermas, 'Democracy, Solidarity and the European Crisis', n 2 above, on the continuing necessity of this 'exchange' for Germany.

[5] The debt element of this 'bargain' has been addressed in the 2011–12 'six pack' and 'two pack' EU economic measures but without concomitant attention to social or historical context. See, generally, B de Witte, H Héritier and AH Trechsel (eds), *The Euro Crisis and the State of European Democracy* (Fiesole, European University Institute, 2013). Read a prosaic definition of the *acquis communautaire* at www.europa.eu/legislation_summaries/glossary/community_acquis_en.htm.

[6] 'I think that from our First Session we can unanimously proclaim that in Europe there will henceforth only be *just* fatherlands.' Pierre-Henri Teitgen, addressing the Consultative Assembly of the Council of Europe, Strasbourg, August 1949, discussing the drafting of the European Convention on Human Rights. He was recalling his father's memory of an inscription on the gates at Buchenwald concentration camp which read 'Just or unjust, the Fatherland'. MW Janis, RS Kay and AW Bradley, *European Human Rights Law: Text and Materials* (Oxford, Oxford University Press, 2008) 14.

[7] The body of the last king of England to die in battle (in 1485) was discovered under a car park in Leicester in 2012: www.le.ac.uk/richardiii/.

[8] 'Spanish judge orders poet García Lorca's grave to be opened' *The Guardian* (16 October 2008), www.theguardian.com/world/2008/oct/16/lorca-grave-spain; and 'Lorca mystery may soon be solved but much of Spain's past remains buried' *The Guardian* (1 December 2014), http://www.theguardian.com/culture/2014/dec/01/-sp-garcia-lorca-mystery-solved-spain-remains-buried.

[9] *Minister for Home Affairs of the Commonwealth v Zentai* [2012]. HCA 28 (15 August 2012).

[10] 'Baltasar Garzón cleared over his Franco-era crimes inquiry' *The Guardian* (27 February 2012), www.theguardian.com/world/2012/feb/27/baltasar-garzon-cleared-franco-crimes.

[11] Such as Prime Minister David Cameron's apology for the killings of civilians in Northern Ireland in 1972 (www.bbc.co.uk/news/10320609) and Prime Minister Tony Blair's apology for the Irish Famine of the 1840s (www.bbc.co.uk/news/uk-northern-ireland-17124401).

Auschwitz.[12] Times change; the culture of commemoration (and confession), now so popular and populist, was sidelined for many years of the twentieth century.[13] Dealing with and genuinely facing up to the past is another matter, long ignored in European legal analysis but now taken more seriously.[14] It is trite to note that any entity which seeks to progress needs to be aware of its history but, nonetheless, this banality does expose a dearth at the core of unity and integration in Europe. The Council of Europe, the EU and their institutions have devoted scant space to the development of a formal recognition of the past which could ethically underpin the highly contested future of European integration. As if from *terra nullius* born, the shiny structures of European unity largely ignored their sombre origins. As András Sajó remarks, 'The current European system is based on assumptions generated by the experiences of World War II … a genuine concern about victims of past injustice emerged within this frame, but only relatively lately and with a great deal of hesitation …'.[15] This lacuna cannot but impact upon the nature and the extent of justice emanating from European institutions.

Andrew Williams, who has written of the 'uncertain soul of Europe',[16] has highlighted the failures of the human rights systems in Strasbourg, heralding a new awareness beyond the conventional appreciation of the ECHR and its Court. These failures are not only at the all too well-known structural, practical level;[17] rather, it is the 'broken dream', 'the disjuncture between the moment of the text, its genesis and the reality of its … application'.[18] The ECHR was drafted in the shadow of the Shoah yet has no regard to institutionalised killing or genocide.[19] He argues that, in ignoring the reality of the Holocaust and absent the recognition of its relationship with the new human rights regime, 'the Convention was a singular failure'.[20] What is at issue is 'the conceptual purpose' of this foundational text; 'the Convention has

---

[12] Wayne Rooney is a footballer who plays for Manchester United and England, 'England players visit Auschwitz and meet Holocaust survivor' *The Guardian* (8 June 2012), www.theguardian.com/football/2012/jun/08/euro-2012-england-players-visit-auschwitz. The issue of footballers' appreciation of the Holocaust and anti-Semitism has arisen also in the case of Nicolas Anelka making an anti-Semitic gesture (the so-called *quenelle*) during a football match in 2013: www.bbc.co.uk/sport/0/football/25870640. This contrasting behaviour was discussed in the UK Parliament during a lengthy debate to mark Holocaust Memorial Day (27 January in the UK and Europe), House of Commons Hansard Debates (23 January 2014), a remarkable debate which included a reading of Primo Levi's poem *Shema*.

[13] The long awaited resolution of the claim of the families of thousands of soldiers murdered by the Union of Soviet Socialist Republics (USSR) in the forest of Katyń in 1940 offers a case study in changing perceptions about justice, memory and responsibility over the second half of the 20th century, *Janowiec and Others v Russia* App Nos 55508/07 and 29520/09 [2014] 58 EHRR 30 (ECtHR (GC), 21 October 2013). See, generally, A Etkind, R Finnin et al, *Remembering Katyń* (Cambridge, Polity Press, 2012).

[14] Eg, the groundbreaking work of, inter alia, Vivian Curran, David Fraser, Christian Joerges and Tom Mertens.

[15] Sajó, 'Victimhood and Vulnerability' in this volume, 337, at 338.

[16] A Williams, *The Ethos of Europe: Values, Law and Justice in the EU* (Cambridge, Cambridge University Press, 2010) 1.

[17] See, generally, S Greer, *The European Convention on Human Rights: Achievements, Problems and Prospects* (Cambridge, Cambridge University Press, 2006).

[18] A Williams, 'Burying, Not Praising the European Convention on Human Rights' in N Walker, J Shaw and S Tierney (eds), *Europe's Constitutional Mosaic* (Oxford, Hart Publishing, 2012) 78; and A Williams, 'The European Convention on Human Rights, the EU and the UK: Confronting a Heresy' (2013) 24 *European Journal of International Law* 1157.

[19] Williams, 'Burying, Not Praising', n 18 above, 79.

[20] ibid.

failed any conception of human rights that includes memorial goals'.[21] What might thus be termed the original sin of the ECHR system is then perpetuated; the entire system of human rights in Strasbourg is corralled by the ECHR, its content, its register, its limitations and the deficits which lie at it source. The Convention text rigidly frames, literally and analytically, the functioning of European human rights so much so that, instead of the now constantly debated institutional and structural reform, it might be apt to wonder if it is not time to cut up the map, *à la* Debord, and discover the text anew.[22] Williams, too, ultimately suggests the need for a 'fundamental re-conceptualisation of the central purpose (or values) of human rights'.[23]

In the mid-1980s, in West Germany, a public debate took place between historians and philosophers engendered by Ernst Nolte's article in the *Frankfurter Allgemeine Zeitung* on 'The Past That Will Not Pass'.[24] Termed the *Historikerstreit*, it provoked lengthy debate about what was seen as Nolte's apologia for the Holocaust and his intimation that a line be drawn under the Nazi past. Since that time, the opposite has arguably been the case; the dramatic political events of 1989, the new Germany and a generalised culture shift towards historical reflection, has resulted in an increased focus on the era of the Second World War. This has been reflected in the ECtHR in leading, recent judgments relating to mass executions in Poland 1940[25] and partisan murders in Latvia in 1944.[26] However, the ECtHR has not always been so preoccupied with events which predated its establishment. The *Stunde Null* mentality, which prevailed in Europe in 1945, passed over inaudibly to the early decades of the functioning of the new European human rights system such that the primordial era of case-law at the ECtHR was affected by a certain degree of historical amnesia.[27] Thus, the judicial forum conceived with a view to ensuring 'the principle of collective responsibility for the maintenance of human rights'[28] did not originally generate a supranational conscience to deal with what had been a, de facto and de jure, supranational infraction. Bates identifies the major motivating force for the ECHR as a collective Western European pact against totalitarianism.[29]

---

[21] ibid, 80.

[22] Guy Debord, in *Psychogeographic Guide of Paris* (Copenhagen, Permild & Rosengreen, 1955) cuts up the map of Paris to facilitate a new perspective on and awareness of the city and take people away from the well-travelled, predictable routes. Following a Debordian line, you might say, further, that the European Convention represents the 'hard' or physical structure of European human rights whereas the Court's case-law is the 'soft', shifting element of Strasbourg justice.

[23] Williams, 'Burying, Not Praising', n 18 above, 93.

[24] See, generally, R Evans, *In Hitler's Shadow: West German Historians and the Attempt to Escape From the Nazi Past* (New York, NY, Alfred A Knopf, 1989).

[25] *Janowiec and Others v Russia* App Nos 55508/07 and 29520/09 (ECtHR, 16 April 2012) and, on appeal, [2014] 58 EHRR 30 (ECtHR (GC), 21 October 2013).

[26] *Kononov v Latvia* App No 36376/04 (ECtHR, 24 July 2008) and, on appeal, (GC) 17 May 2010.

[27] 'We have witnessed periods of historical amnesia before. In the 1950s and 1960s, only a handful of memoirs and studies served to record and recall the Holocaust. The subject was virtually taboo, a consequence of the first and universally affirmed *Stunde Null*'. D Klein, 'The Fate of Holocaust Literature' in S Friedman (ed), *Holocaust Literature* (Westport, CT, Greenwood Press, 1993) xvi.

[28] Council of Europe, *Collected Edition of the 'Travaux Préparatoires' of the European Convention on Human Rights Vol I* (The Hague, Martinus Nijhoff, 1975) 36 cited in Janis, Kay and Bradley, *European Human Rights Law*, n 6 above, 16.

[29] E Bates, *The Evolution of the European Convention on Human Rights* (Oxford, Oxford University Press, 2010) 5, 6. Though this text explores, in depth, the origins and early years of the Convention system, it does not have any index entry under 'Holocaust'.

This focus on creating a bulwark for the denizens of the 'free' West against the perceived threat from the East may account for, though not justify, the relative invisibility of the Holocaust for many decades at the ECtHR.

Generally, Holocaust related jurisprudence oscillates between the infamous (such as Eichmann, Ivan the Terrible), the misconceived or misunderstood (the Nuremberg trial so called had only limited Holocaust related focus)[30] and the largely ignored or unknown (the *Zyklon B* case, a criminal trial in a British military court with no reasoned judgment).[31] Much of this case-law is separated from the contemporary European legal space by distances of time and geography. The European legal order, which can be said, as a whole, to embrace both EU and Council of Europe institutions, has, apparently, been saved many of the challenges of institutionally confronting the collapse into savagery that was the Shoah. Yet, any enquiry into the meaning and limits of justice in Europe would acknowledge that the delivery of justice today needs to take account of lapses in justice in the past. This chapter, therefore, teases out the approach of the Strasbourg institutions towards the Shoah over the decades since their creation. The judgments and decisions looked at here are highlighted not only because of their relevance to an examination of justice in Europe but because of their intrinsic value in themselves in exposing something about the nature of European human rights approaches since 1959. The aim is to cast away the cobwebs from some significant but ignored case-law and to expose the details of some of those whose fate at Strasbourg was shaped by the Holocaust, its reality and its legacy. Dealing with the Shoah is an ongoing process, just as defining the meaning of justice in Europe is a process. In this volume, that latter process is approached largely from the inside, endogenously, from an EU perspective on the EU. This chapter steps back a little from 'Brussels' and examines the nature of European justice from an external perspective based on an assertion that justice has no conceptual borders; the EU and the Council of Europe are a collective experiment in the fashioning of a (just) Europe. As Allot asserts, 'Europe will be made by the Europe that Europe has made. Europe will be made by its own idea of what Europe could be'[32] and that 'Europe' is both Brussels *and* Strasbourg.

The current academic and political preoccupation with the ECtHR has two focal points; reform of the Court system[33] and the accession of the European Union to the ECHR.[34] In other words, the focus is clearly on a modified future. The emphasis in this chapter faces towards the past rather than the future and examines the early decades of human rights adjudication from one specific perspective. The Holocaust constituted an extreme, extensive violation of what would, post facto, be classified as human rights yet Strasbourg proved not to be the locale for collective or

---

[30] See W Schabas, *Unimaginable Atrocities* (Oxford, Oxford University Press, 2012); D Fraser, *Law After Auschwitz* (Durham, NC, Carolina Academic Press, 2005); and KJ Heller, *The Nuremberg Military Tribunals and the Origins of International Criminal Law* (Oxford, Oxford University Press, 2011).

[31] *Case No 9, The Zyklon B Case, The Trial of Bruno Tesch and Two Others* Law Reports of Trials of War Criminals, United Nations War Crimes Commission, Vol 1, London, HMSO (1947).

[32] P Allott, 'The European Community Is Not the True European Community' (1991) 100 *Yale Law Journal* 2485, 2490.

[33] Greer, *The European Convention on Human Rights*, n 17 above.

[34] See P Gragli, *The Accession of the European Union to the European Convention on Human Rights* (Oxford, Hart Publishing, 2013).

high profile claims (which went to Jerusalem or Germany). Instead, the ECtHR records reveal decades of small scale, individual judgments and decisions, more often than not declared inadmissible, and which testify to the absence of any overt consciousness of the specificity of adjudicating Shoah related claims. This approach did, however, gradually begin to alter in the 1990s with Holocaust denial case-law and, more recently, with a heightened awareness of the Holocaust in freedom of expression case-law.

It could be said that the achievement of European human rights justice can be categorised as a type of *fractal* justice, the constantly shifting edges of which can never be fully measured. Nonetheless, some strata are identifiable. The evolution in Shoah related case-law in Strasbourg might be classified as follows:

1950s–80s *Amnesia*—no specific recognition of the uniqueness of the Holocaust despite direct confrontation with victims;

1990s *Negationism*—the emergence of a corpus of case-law on Holocaust denial; freedom of expression (Article 10 ECHR) cases involving Holocaust denial/negation or revision; also post-1989 property related compensation claims;[35]

2010s *Particularity*—case law involving the use of Holocaust related language[36] as well as continuing compensation claims.[37] At the same time a new, overt, insistence that 'the Court is not a forum for the resolution of historical disputes'.[38]

As institutions, the Council of Europe and the ECtHR provide Europe with a unique collective structure for remembrance, which is not replicated elsewhere in Europe. Every European state constantly creates and recreates its own individual history and memory; what Strasbourg offers, under the radar of both general appreciation of the ECtHR as a judicial body and outside the scope of general historical analysis, is a significant source of *European* memory mediated through a judicial lens. The HUDOC database is saturated with beguiling, complex and unexplored narratives, of the victims and the vulnerable of course,[39] but also the victors. The Strasbourg judiciary has over 50 years' experience of exposure to the European past; that time has evidenced ebbs and flows but is always present, even more so today than in 1959. In that respect, it has been, effectively, the first and longest serving transitional court or, perhaps, an involuntary, unintended and unrecognised 'Truth Commission for Europe'. The literature on the ECtHR as a 'manager

---

[35] Such as *Slowik v Poland* App No 30641/96 (ECommHR Decision, 16 April 1998), an unsuccessful attempt to establish ownership of a planned parking lot in Warsaw which had previously been owned by two Jewish people killed in a concentration camp.

[36] Such as *PETA Deutschland v Germany* App No 43481/09 [2012] ECHR 1888 (ECtHR, 8 November 2012) (discussed below).

[37] Such as *Poznanski and Others v Germany* App No 25101/05 (ECtHR, 3 July 2007) (Jewish forced labourers at Auschwitz at the IG Farben factory based there). The applicants asserted that the maximum EUR 7,500 compensation for such slave labour was too low and, generally, that the compensation scheme was established to protect the interest of German industry and not the rights of forced labourers. The application was declared inadmissible.

[38] As stated in *LZ v Slovakia* App No 27753/06 (ECtHR, 27 September 2011) (a Jewish applicant's attempt to stop a village street being named after Jozef Tiso, president of Slovakia during the Second World War), 'the Court is aware of the highly sensitive nature of the issues involved in the present case and its context ... However, it emphasises from the outset that it is not its task to settle possible points of debate among historians' (para 65).

[39] See, further, András Sajó, 'Victimhood and Vulnerability As Sources of Justice' in this volume, 337.

of memory' is sparse as most such work tends towards high profile case-law in Germany (Nuremberg, Frankfurt, etc) or Israel,[40] but the ECtHR has in fact had to process the legacy of the Shoah and the Second World War more frequently than any other single judicial body. This has occurred in spite of the original conceptual failures highlighted above. The *Katyń* judgment[41] is a recent and one of the most high profile of the 'history cases' in Strasbourg. Yet, it is low profile, unremembered decisions which constitute the main body of the ECtHR's claim to a status as an institution 'working through the past'.[42] An examination of widely scattered decisions and judgments from the perspective of the ECtHR encountering Europe's pasts exposes the extent to which 'thick descriptions of everyday life',[43] tragic and non-tragic, are judged and, at one and the same time, the judges themselves judged too, especially from the perspective of the global conceptual purpose they might or could serve in this context.

There are several foundational questions relevant to an attempt to assess the ECtHR as a court of memory/history. First, who is or should be a 'victim' in the Strasbourg system? All Strasbourg applicants are formally classed as 'victims' (under Article 34 ECHR) but this is not inherently a neutral concept (an issue which is further explored in analysis of the National Socialist applications below). There is also the impenetrable question of what people choose to *do* with their memories and their narratives; if you have witnessed *Kristallnacht*, been incarcerated at several extermination/concentration camps and lost all your family at Auschwitz,[44] what can human rights judges offer you? Why would you have faith in a legal system when another such system had so effectively enabled the atrocity? What purpose do human rights courts serve in relation to the uncompensatable? Beyond those questions is a consideration of how memory, mediated through the judicial route, represents and shapes the judges as well as the 'victims'. Furthermore, the governance or management of memory by and in judicial *fora* arguably runs counter to the very nature of memory itself; the very purpose of all judicial decisions is to *close and finalise* the legal issue in hand, to draw a line under the arguments raised, thus institutionalising or forcing a false forgetfulness rather than recognising the validity of a victim's memory and its endurance.

This overview of the work of the ECtHR has a specific interest in examining the Jewish presence in the Strasbourg jurisprudence. Do Jews go to court in Europe?[45] Specifically, to what extent have European Jews benefited from the human rights court which was established as the extermination camps closed? There is widespread dissemination of knowledge about Jewish death within the European arena

---

[40] See, eg, Fraser, *Law After Auschwitz*, n 30 above.
[41] *Janowiec and Others v Russia* App Nos 55508/07 and 29520/09 (ECtHR, 16 April 2012) and, on appeal, [2014] 58 EHRR 30 (ECtHR (GC), 21 October 2013).
[42] T Adorno, 'The Meaning of Working Through the Past' in T Adorno, *Can One Live After Auschwitz? A Philosophical Reader*, ed R Tiedemann (Stanford, CA, Stanford University Press, 2003) 3.
[43] M Stolleis, 'The Spidery Monster: Inga Markovitz's Brilliant History of the GDR's Judiciary' (2007) 8 *German Law Journal* 195.
[44] The facts of *X v Germany* App No 627/59 (ECommHR Decision, 14 December 1961) (Auschwitz survivor), discussed below.
[45] See C Lyons, 'The Persistence of Memory' (2007) 32 *European Law Review* 563 for a similar question posed as regards the European Court of Justice.

(museums, documentation centres, education programmes and the like) but far less awareness of Jewish *life* in Europe, now and then.[46] The victims have become obscured by their killers in the institutional and judicial response to the Shoah. The high profile *Einsatzgruppen* military trials in 1947–48, the Eichmann trial in 1961, the series of extermination camp trials in Germany in the 1970s, the Demjanjuk (wrongly assumed to be Ivan the Terrible) trial in Jerusalem 1986, these have all easily entered the vocabulary and culture of atrocity to the detriment of those millions who were exterminated. Eichmann lives on (thanks to Arendt interalia)[47] but Walter Benjamin's brother, Raphael Lemkin's family, Jerry Springer's grandmothers, and Stephen Fry's great grandparents[48] are all eclipsed and forgotten. There is a superficial parallel in Strasbourg where many of the names of cases/decisions involving Jews are rendered as *X versus* (offering the protection but also the negation of anonymity) but those cases with convicted Nazi applicants from Germany are named and known. In general, it is fair to state that much judicial and academic space devoted to the consideration of the consequences of National Socialism has revolved around its adherents and not its victims; we readily debate the concept of 'banality of evil' in the seminar room but rarely analyse the detail of, for example, the *Einsatzgruppen* trials or of how Treblinka functioned.

The chapter structure adopts the conceit of the concept of *stolpersteine*[49] for an identification of significant markers in the pathway towards the ECtHR's recognition of Shoah specificity within the canon of European human rights. The idea behind the *stolperstein* is to symbolise the return of the lost person to their neighbourhood and community. The focus on Holocaust case-law here suggests that Strasbourg case-law is, too, a means of conveying individual, ignored, Shoah victims back to the European legal community. More generally, ECtHR adjudication is a means of bringing (back) the Holocaust into the realm of European justice. One of the most recent *stolperstein*, from November 2012, is the minority opinion in *PETA*,[50] which forcefully argues for the European wide relevance of the Holocaust and its legacy. Fifty years before, the Strasbourg human rights system and its institutions were relatively oblivious to those few applicants who 'stumbled' before them and making no case for Shoah relevance in the formation of a new human rights system. This chapter outlines the steps on that passage from a dearth of acknowledgement of the relevance of the Holocaust towards a more recent intimation that the uniqueness of the Shoah may necessitate a distinct—and European—interpretation of Convention rights.

---

[46] But see the important, recent series of reports from the EU's Fundamental Rights Agency showing a rise in anti-Semitism across Europe, 'Discrimination and Hate Crime Against Jews in EU Member States: Experiences and Perceptions of Antisemitism' (November 2013), www.fra.europa.eu/en/publication/2013/discrimination-and-hate-crime-against-jews-eu-member-states-experiences-and.

[47] H Arendt, *Eichmann in Jerusalem: A Report on the Banality of Evil* (London, Penguin Books, 2006).

[48] All of whom were killed in various extermination camps.

[49] A project devised and implemented by German artist Gunter Demnig which involves placing small brass plaques—to be 'stumbled' over—in the pavements outside the last known addresses of those killed in the Holocaust. See www.stolpersteine.eu/en/.

[50] *PETA Deutschland v Germany* App No 43481/09 [2012] ECHR 1888 (ECtHR, 8 November 2012), Concurring Opinion of Judges Zupančič and Spielmann.

II. THE LEGEND OF THE JUST MEN

Justice in Strasbourg is primarily the responsibility of the judges of the Court. Now, and in the past, are these judges who can give/write judgments equal to the events they judge,[51] specifically in the context of contentous claims arising from or related to Europe's past? Have victims always been served by 'just men'?[52] Relevant also to a questioning of the who and how of human rights justice in Strasbourg is a recall of the complex juxtaposition of different layers of adjudication in Europe; take, for example, the early 1960s. Seven men in Luxembourg are fashioning, from Dutch tax law and Italian electricity prices, the constitutional foundations of the EU in *Van Gend & Loos*[53] and *Costa/ENEL*;[54] the ECtHR, meantime, in *de Becker*,[55] is adjudicating the claims of a convicted Second World War collaborator; the Commission in Strasbourg is declaring inadmissible the claim of an Auschwitz survivor;[56] in Düsseldorf, criminal judges are dealing with the killing of 900,000 people in one year (the Treblinka trials).[57] In other words, meting out justice, or assessing the quality or extent of that justice, in post-war 'Europe', broadly defined, is not quantifiable on any simplistic level.

There is also the issue of distance from the past, from the events of the specific claim, in Strasbourg case-law dealing with the Holocaust. In the 1960s, during the early phase of Shoah case-law, the judges and members of the European Commission had direct, lived experience of the facts before them. In 2014, the facts will inevitably have become 'history' for the judges (if not always necessarily for the applicants). How might this distance/proximity issue have altered the nature of human rights judging? Barthes reminds us that 'History is hysterical: it is constituted only if we consider it, only if we look at it and in order to look at it, we must be excluded from it. Michelet was able to write virtually nothing about his own time'.[58] The process of dealing with the past, a process which has acquired a (too convenient?) German appellation, *Vergangenheitsbewältigung* is, intrinsically, a delayed process; the past cannot be dealt with as such until it has in fact become the 'past'. This may account for the increased recognition of the Holocaust in the

---

[51] Taussig recalls for us how Nietzsche pleaded 'in vain for historians who can write histories equal to the events they relate', in M Taussig, *Walter Benjamin's Grave* (Chicago, IL, University of Chicago Press, 2006) 7.

[52] This is borrowed from A Schwarz-Bart, *The Last of the Just* (London, Penguin, 1984) 10, where the author refers to 'the Jewish tradition of the *Lamed-waf*. According to this tradition, the world reposes upon thirty six Just Men, the *Lamed-Waf*, indistinguishable from simple mortals; often, they do not recognise themselves. The *Lamed-waf* are the hearts of the world multiplied, into which all our griefs are poured, as into one receptacle'.

[53] Case 26/62 *NV Algemene Transport- en Expeditie Onderneming van Gend & Loos v Nederlandse administratie der belastingen* [1963] ECR (Special English Edition) 1.

[54] Case 6/64 *Costa v ENEL* [1964] ECR (Special English Edition) 585.

[55] *De Becker v Belgium* App 214/56 Series A No 4 (ECtHR, 27 March 1962).

[56] *X v Germany* App No 627/59 (ECommHR Decision, 14 December 1961) (Auschwitz survivor).

[57] See www.holocaustresearchproject.org/trials/treblinkatrial.html.

[58] R Barthes, *Camera Lucida* (London, Vintage, 1993) 65.

last decade or so; the Strasbourg judicial community needed to be 'excluded' (*à la* Barthes) from the Shoah in order to properly confront it.[59]

Adopting an openness to the legacies of the Nazi era does not have to mean a wallowing in guilt or shame but a recognition of the fact that, as Joerges points out, 'this legacy is not merely precious, it is also precarious'.[60] The management of Europe's past(s)[61] is not a duty falling to one or two Member States but is a generalised, European responsibility. One unpredictable outcome of a lengthy reflection on the nature of the legacy is that questions of German accountability have been brought into a European context.[62] This comes to light in *PETA* (discussed below) where the German Government submissions are unusually apologetic in nature.[63]

III. THE COURT OF GRIEF

And so it was for millions who from Luftmensch became Luft.[64]

The legacy of the Holocaust and the Second World War is an enduring (and, paradoxically, increasing) one of loss and grief. How do victims express this grief in Strasbourg?[65] Is it a fallacy that courts are non-emotional, non-sentimental spaces? Even if the text (the Convention) restricts and limits (because of the original sin as discussed above), does this, de facto, curtail the victim's expression of loss? Theodor Adorno suggests that, after Auschwitz, the temporal core is to be found

---

[59] There is perverse example of this in a 2006 judgment of the Austrian Supreme Court referred to in *PETA*; the contested PETA posters with Holocaust victims and animals juxtaposed, which were the subject of litigation in Germany, Austria and Strasbourg, were deemed, in Austria, to aid the process of dealing with the past as they 'had the positive effect of rekindling the memory of the national-socialist genocide. The concentration camp pictures documented the historic truth and recalled unfathomable crimes, which could be seen as a positive contribution to the process of dealing with the past (*Vergangenheitsaufarbeitung*)'. *PETA Deutschland v Germany* App No 43481/09 [2012] ECHR 1888 (ECtHR, 8 November 2012), para 23, referring to Judgment No 6 Ob 321/04f (Austrian Supreme Court of Justice, 12 October 2006).

[60] C Joerges, 'Introduction to the Special Issue: Confronting Memories: European "Bitter Experiences" and the Constitutionalization Process: Constructing Europe in the Shadow of Its Pasts' (2005) 6 *German Law Journal* Special Issue, ed C Joerges and B Blokker 245, 246.

[61] See Christian Joerges on this: '*Was bedeutet: Aufarbeitung der Vergangenheit* is the title of a famous essay by Theodor W Adorno, written in 1959, in which he took issue with what the Germans have coined *Vergangenheitsbewältigung*: How can Germans ever "come to terms" with Auschwitz—*Vergangenheitsbewältigung* is definitely and rightfully resistant against/to translation exercises.' ibid 248.

[62] Exchanges with Christian Joerges, August 2007.

[63] 'The [German] Government considered that they should be granted a wide margin of appreciation allowing a generous definition of the group of affected persons. This applied, in particular, in light of Germany's history, which meant that it was hardly conceivable that a German court would reach a similar conclusion as the Austrian Supreme Court. Given its historical responsibility, it was Germany's duty to ensure that violations of personality rights could be claimed in connection with the Holocaust. The individuals depicted on the photographs were, almost without exception, unable to do this themselves.' *PETA Deutschland v Germany* App No 43481/09 [2012] ECHR 1888 (ECtHR, 8 November 2012), para 36.

[64] Schwarz-Bart, *The Last of the Just*, n 52 above.

[65] Grief: 'This word may be understood in French as: damage, blame, prejudice, injustice or injury but also ... complaint, the call for punishment ... In English ... *grievance* also expresses the subject of the complaint, injustice, conflict, a wrong that must be righted, a violence to be repaired.' J Derrida, *The Politics of Friendship* (London, Verso, 1997) ix.

in the screams of the victims.[66] Who, then, 'screams' (loudest) in Strasbourg, the perpetrator or the victim? From some of the case-law detailed below, one implication is that victims' screams were not very well heard in the early years of European human rights.

Pierre Nora explores the differences between memory and history.[67] It is an analysis which helps us to appreciate the dichotomy between a victim/applicant with memories and the human rights judge who has to respond to the latter. A judicial setting is the embodiment of Nora's memory/history duality and disjunction. *Memory*: origins in primitive/peasant rituals of passing on, in oral tradition; secretive; organic; intimate. *History*: formal; impenetrable; preserve of elites; a reconstitution of what is; besieges and petrifies memory. Nora's perspective would suggest that a (human rights) court can only deal with history but will never be an apt *lieu* for memory reception because it formalises and renders public that which is inherently private.

Hannah Arendt's reflection on the role of the judges at the Eichmann trial resonates in this context also: 'The purpose of a trial is to render justice, and nothing else; even the noblest of ulterior purposes … can only detract from the law's main business: to weigh the charges brought against the accused, to render judgment and to mete out due punishment'.[68] There are arguments which can be made in relation to this statement per se but even more so in the context of human rights adjudication.

Finally, is the function of the (European) human rights chamber limited to doing justice in the case at hand or can a more constitutionally significant role (placing the claim in a larger, historically relevant context) be conceived of for a regional human rights court?[69] This was not the case in the early era of Strasbourg human rights jurisprudence but more recent case-law elevates the Holocaust from an individual compensation claim case level to a higher level as independent factor affecting the interpretation of specific Convention provisions. András Sajó also discusses in his chapter 'how the judiciary handles past collective injustice against groups of citizens can be of foundational constitutional importance'.[70]

At the *Einsatzgruppen* trials in 1947 Judge Musmanno said in his judgment 'these narratives go beyond the frontiers of human cruelty and savagery'.[71] In the decades since then, detailed knowledge about that savagery has become widely available. And, as well as those killing squad military trials in 1947, there have been separate domestic criminal trials in Germany in relation to Auschwitz, Bełżec, Sobibor and Treblinka.[72] Furthermore, the Federal Republic of Germany operated a long-term

---

[66] Adorno, 'The Meaning of Working Through the Past', n 42 above, xviii.
[67] P Nora, 'Between Memory and History: Les Lieux de Mémoire' (1989) 26 *Representations* 7.
[68] Arendt, *Eichmann in Jerusalem*, n 47 above, 253 cited in Schabas, *Unimaginable Atrocities*, n 30 above, 157 where 'History, International Justice and Truth' are discussed at ch 6.
[69] Williams, 'Burying, Not Praising', n 18 above; and S Douglas-Scott, 'Europe's Constitutional Mosaic: Human Rights in the European Legal Space—Utopia, Dystopia, Monotopia or Polytopia?' in N Walker, J Shaw and S Tierney (eds), *Europe's Constitutional Mosaic* (Oxford, Hart Publishing, 2012).
[70] See Sajó, 'Victimhood and Vulnerability As Sources of Justice' in this volume, 337, at 339.
[71] *US v Otto Ohlendorf et al* (Einsatzgruppen) United States Military Tribunals at Nuremberg (1948) Case No 9, TWC Vol IV 1.
[72] See generally Schabas, *Unimaginable Atrocities*, n 30 above; and Fraser, *Law After Auschwitz*, n 30 above.

restitution and compensation scheme for victims of National Socialism.[73] Yet, military tribunals, criminal courts and monetary bureaucracy—it might be asked, is that it? It is notable that the efficiency and smooth running of the institutionalised killing system should be matched with a convenient and minimally disruptive judicial and administrative response. David Fraser's comprehensive examination of post-Shoah adjudication takes in (criminal) courts in France, the US, the UK, Canada and Australia.[74] It does not, tellingly, have a chapter on the European Court of Human Rights. Shoah cases are apparently everywhere save Strasbourg. Judges as far away Canberra[75] 'work through the past', deal with the consequences of an all too *European* period of barbarity yet the human rights judges of Europe have made a less than significant contribution to the judicial appreciation of the Holocaust. Partly this is due to the original sin as discussed, the fundamental failure to include crimes against humanity and a concept of genocide in the ECHR; partly this is due to the inability of the Commission and the Court to determine which types of applicants take the journey to eastern France; partly it is due to the Commission/Court response when a Shoah related case does reach its doors. Could all these factors unintentionally coalescing be said to be an example of Agamben's ethical *aporia* of Auschwitz, of the blindness of law after Auschwitz?[76]

IV. NOMEN EST NUMEN

It is more arduous to honour the memory of the nameless than that of the renowned. Historical construction is devoted to the memory of the nameless.[77]

> When viewing a global picture of case law in Strasbourg, the *punctum* [78] is the case law (or more precisely the lack of it) relating to destruction of European Jewry. This is the detail that 'pricks' when the Strasbourg system is viewed from behind the veil of the Convention text so to speak. One of the decisions which embodies that punctum is the case of *X v Germany*,[79] a European Commission on Human Rights (ECommHR) decision of 1961.[80]

---

[73] Now 'rebranded' as the Remembrance, Responsibility and Future Foundation, www.stiftung-evz.de/eng/home.htm.

[74] Fraser, *Law After Auschwitz*, n 30 above.

[75] *Minister for Home Affairs of the Commonwealth v Zentai* [2012] HCA 28 (15 August 2012).

[76] G Agamben, *Remnants of Auschwitz* (London, Zone Books, 1999), discussed at length in Fraser, *Law After Auschwitz*, n 30 above, ch 3.

[77] Walter Benjamin, Inscription on artwork at Port Bou cemetery, Spain where Benjamin died.

[78] Barthes, *Camera Lucida*, n 58 above, 27 on the concepts of *Studium* (general appreciation (of a photograph)) and *Punctum*: 'The second element will break (or punctuate) the *stadium*, this element which arises from a scene, shoots out if it like an arrow and pierces me. A Latin word exists to designate this wound, this prick. A photograph's *punctum* is that accident which pricks me (but also bruises me, is poignant to me)'; 43: 'The *punctum* is a detail, a partial object'; 45: 'There is another, (less Proustian) expansion of the *punctum*: when, paradoxically, while remaining a detail, it fills the whole picture'; 51: 'What I can name, cannot really prick me. The incapacity to name is a good symptom of disturbance.'

[79] *X v Germany* App No 627/59 (ECommHR Decision, 14 December 1961) (Auschwitz survivor).

[80] The European Commission of Human Rights, which operated from 1954 until 1998 when it was abolished, served as a filtering system for the Court of Human Rights, deciding on the admissibility or otherwise of applications from individuals, who did not have direct access to the Court itself. Many of the early era applications in Holocaust related cases during the *Amnesia* phase failed to pass the admissibility scrutiny of the Commission.

A. *Stolperstein* 1—X (The Auschwitz Survivor)

X survived Auschwitz; his location at this camp can be surmised only from the Commission Admissibility Decision as, like the applicant himself, it is not named and is called camp 'C' only in the Decision.[81] He witnessed his whole family, all his relatives taken to the gas chamber there. He had previously been sent to an unnamed Ghetto and was at several other concentration camps before being liberated by the Russians in 1945. This trauma began on 9 November 1938, *Kristallnacht*,[82] when his father's well-established printing firm was destroyed. After the war, X reopened the family firm in East Germany but relocated the firm to West Germany after his escape from the German Democratic Republic.

X brings this narrative, which encapsulates almost the whole spectrum of Nazi Final Solution measures (pogrom, ghettoisation, extermination) to seek justice at Strasbourg. He may be nameless but he is the living proof, writ judicial, of the history of National Socialism and its legacy. He sees the broken glass of *Kristallnacht*, was moved to a Ghetto then finally, the ultimate last stop, Auschwitz. What differentiates X from millions of others who shared this ordeal, apart from his miraculous survival, is his journey to the ECtHR, bringing this explicit narrative to the heart of the new Europe. X's very witnessing of the smoke of Auschwitz and a human rights judge within 15 years of each other captures the seismic transformations represented by the Strasbourg system. Did even the prospect of *human rights* seem like a parallel universe to somebody who had been deprived of his very *humanity*? At the very least, he provides a form of proof, an undeniable certainty that all this happened, evidence which bypasses the historian, showing the Shoah without mediation, the facts established without method.[83] Not that the Commissioners would not have known this in a general sense as, for them, in 1961, X's story is not 'history' but merely the factual back story of an (ultimately unsuccessful) victim/applicant and is related and recorded as such. The Commission declares X's claim to be inadmissible due to the failure to exhaust domestic remedies in West Germany. However, there is yet another layer of complexity in X's application; his claim is partly based on the fact that in a criminal trial against him in the Federal Republic, the judges were former members of the Nazi party and one of the witnesses for the prosecution was responsible for the arrest and subsequent extermination of his parents in Auschwitz. First, so much for so called de-Nazification. But, how can we appraise a human right forum, which compels an Auschwitz survivor to pursue his claim in a judicial system populated by former persecutors?

---

[81] *Nomem est numen*, to name is to know, but not in the case of this applicant who, previously only a number, is now an anonymous applicant.

[82] '[T]he universally adopted, almost good-natured expression *Kristallnacht*, designating the pogrom of November 1938, attests to this inclination [to use euphemistic circumlocutions in the reminiscences of deportations and mass murder]. A very great number claim not to have known of the events at the time, although Jews disappeared everywhere and although it is hardly believable that those who experienced what happened in the East constantly kept silent.' Adorno, 'The Meaning of Working Through the Past', n 42 above, 4.

[83] See Barthes, *Camera Lucida*, n 58 above, 81, in this vein, discussing photographs of slaves and former slaves.

X is a rare Strasbourg applicant in many respects; very few Jews and no Jewish women or children[84] appear in the early decades of European human rights law. The lack of an appropriate conceptual underpinning of the ECHR is therefore matched by a lack of applicants who might otherwise have exposed the new human rights regime to that which it was largely ignoring. How many European Jews have had the opportunity to formally 'bear witness' to their experiences in a judicial setting, let alone a human rights one? X's multilayered life is of even more interest to legal analysis when his specific complaint is considered: he alleges continuing Nazi bias in the judges he has had to face in post-war West Germany. Sentiment aside, though is difficult not to convey compassion for this persistent victim, this case contains prophetic material which will not reach the academic arena for many decades later. X did not receive justice in Strasbourg, nor presumably in West Germany thereafter given the evidence of continuing anti-Semitism and victimisation. The 1961 Commission was, no doubt, performing a mere administrative task in assessing, formally, the exhaustion of domestic remedies by X. But it seems necessary, at least at this distance, to question how human rights lawyers would have sent an Auschwitz survivor back to West Germany to be judged by former Nazis.

V. THE WRONG KIND OF JUSTICE?

In a book considering the nature of European justice it is worth pondering if justice should serve only the good? Is there an automatic dearth or deficit of justice if the (money) banks are propped up while the queues at the food banks lengthen daily? Is justice to be judged so when it serves only the just? Do the angels get all the (best) tunes in a just system? While this question may be answered in a different way in economic terms, a human rights court delivers justice to those with both clean and dirty hands.[85] Thus it was that Strasbourg institutions have had direct contact with several former National Socialists over the years, such as in the applications and cases of X (1961),[86] *Ilse Koch* (1962),[87] *Heinz Jentzsch* (1970),[88] *Ilse Hess* (1975),[89] and *Anthony Sawoniuk* (2001).[90] Not all of the *stolpersteine*, the markers of remembrance put forward here, are positive; the Strasbourg institutions can be successfully mined for 'the banality of evil' just as much for suffering and injustice.

---

[84] At least 1 million Jewish children and 1.5 million children altogether are estimated to have been murdered taking the 'journey to Pichipoi' (a name invented by Jewish children awaiting deportation in the Drancy prison/holding camp in France).

[85] Recalling the equity maxim that, (s)he who comes to equity must come with clean hands.

[86] *X v Germany* App No 920/60 (ECommHR Decision, 19 December 1961). X, a senior SS officer, was involved in the mass execution of Jews at an unidentified location in the Soviet Union during 1942–43. This Decision was issued five days after the Commission ruled in the *X v Germany* App No 627/59 (ECommHR Decision, 14 December 1961)(Auschwitz survivor).

[87] *Ilse Koch v Germany* App No 1270/61 (ECommHR Decision, 8 March 1962).

[88] *Heinz Jentzsch v Germany* App No 2604/65 (ECommHR Decision, 6 October 1970).

[89] *Ilse Hess v United Kingdom* App No 6231/73 2 DR 72 (ECommHR Decision, 28 May 1975).

[90] *Anthony Sawoniuk v United Kingdom* App No 63716/00 (ECtHR, Admissibility Decision, 29 May 2001).

B. *Stolperstein* 2—X (The SS Officer)

X was a senior SS officer who was involved in the mass extermination of Jews at an unidentified location during 1942–43. He was imprisoned in West Germany after the Second World War but was claiming compensation for being wrongly detained. Here is part of his claim which merits quotation at length:

> In 1961 the District Court of C decided again that the Applicant [X] could not be released as there was a risk that he might flee the country, and it prolonged his detention until 1962. He is claiming damages of 500,000 DM to *compensate him for loss of honour, loss of income, for the distress caused to his family and for the nervous depression from which he suffers as a result of his detention*. He states that he is *merely a scapegoat who exterminated Jews under compulsion* and that the *persons responsible for the atrocities of the third Reich are the Western democracies* and the politicians of the Weimar Republic who, by their stupidity, lack of moral integrity and lack of courage, paved the way for Hitler's assumption of power. [Emphasis added.][91]

Whatever the ultimate result in this case, the very existence of those words in the ECtHR records are a testament to the nature of Holocaust appreciation in the decades after 1945. Furthermore, this mass murderer's words disturb as they draw attention to the role of the Allies in not attempting to prevent the savagery in the first place. X's application for compensation for violation of Article 5 ECHR (delay in trial proceedings) was deemed inadmissible. However, in a manner which was not followed in the X (Auschwitz survivor) application, the Commission here places this SS officer's claim into a wider context, the admissibility being based on the justification of the need for West Germany to have the time to gather evidence for a large trial.[92]

C. *Stolperstein* 3—Heinz Jentzsch (SS Guard)

The *Jentzsch* decision is remarkable in the first instance as the (very lengthy)[93] ECommHR judgment considers war crimes and crimes against humanity (in the context of whether there are special problems of arrest and detention arising in the prosecution of war crimes and crimes against humanity) and it is clearly an application which much exercised the Commission members; there are three individual Opinions (two dissenting).[94]

Heinz Jentzsch was an SS guard at Mauthausen/Gusen concentration camp and was detained pre-trial in Germany from 1961 until 1967. One of the methods of

---

[91] *X v Germany* App No 920/60 (ECommHR Decision, 19 December 1961).
[92] 'Whereas the crimes imputed to the Applicant formed merely a part of the large-scale crimes committed by the SS in the German-controlled territories in Eastern Europe in 1941–45; whereas, consequently, the participation of the Applicant in the mass exterminations at B. in 1942–43 cannot be properly assessed in isolation but must be seen in its full perspective, which can only be obtained by a trial involving all those who participated in the crimes concerned.' *X v Germany* App No 920/60 (ECommHR Decision, 19 December 1961).
[93] Sixty-seven pages with a few hundred pages of appendices; *X v Germany* App No 627/59 (ECommHR Decision, 14 December 1961) (Auschwitz survivor), is only four pages long.
[94] *Heinz Jentzsch v Germany* App No 2604/65 (ECommHR Decision, 6 October 1970).

killing used in Gusen was the so-called 'death bath', forcing ill and/or old prisoners to stand under ice cold showers while being beaten (by Jentzsch and others) to death. He was convicted in 1968 of murdering at least 20 people and sentenced to life imprisonment. He was granted free legal aid to support his application to the ECtHR for compensation for breach of Article 5 (delayed period of detention before trial).

The West German Government argued that in cases of war crimes and crimes against humanity, courts and public prosecutors were in a particularly difficult position which could not be measured by the same standards as ordinary criminal cases.[95] In terms of this chapter's support of Williams' assertion of the lack of original conceptual underpinning of the Convention, it is positive to note that the Commission in *Jentzsch* directly addresses the issue of potential lack of jurisdiction and non-retroactivity. It finds that Article 7(2) ECHR[96] covers war crimes and crimes against humanity. A complication arises because West Germany has entered a reservation as regards Article 7(2) so that it will not be applied except in accordance with the principles of the Article 103(2) of the *Grundgesetz* such that no act can be punished unless it was a punishable offence before it was committed. Thus, 23 years before *Brunner*[97] a 'supranational' judicial entity has a constitutional conundrum arising from National Socialism's long reach. This is resolved in this instance by the Commission's categorisation of Jentzsch's case as based on Article 5(3) and a finding that he *is* entitled to the protection of that provision even though convicted of crimes against humanity. Justice for the dirty handed.

VI. NO SHOAH?

The Strasbourg institutions may have demonstrated a generalised reticence to engage directly with the significance of the Holocaust in the *Amnesia* phase during the 1950s to the 1980s. As we saw above, claims during that period were, largely, individual, compensation type claims. The genres of Shoah case-law, however, segued from the compensation category to freedom of expression cases (Article 10 ECHR) in the 1990s. No longer was the ECtHR faced with individuals with direct, personal experience of a death camp (as a victim or a guard) but instead with writers, journalists and others who claimed that those camps either did not exist or did not operate as death camps. These judgments generated a whole new category of 'hate speech' case-law centered on the denial of the Holocaust. This phase of Shoah jurisprudence, *Negationism*, represents a significant shift in several respects; the focus is no longer on individual Holocaust related claims per se but rather a consideration of the freedom of expression rights of those who contest it. The judgments necessarily move away from a direct confrontation of Holocaust suffering to a generalised, scientific level of appreciation of the Holocaust. Yet, despite the distance in terms of applicants and substance, the ECtHR is, perversely, by this era dealing with the Shoah in a more extensive way than it has done since its establishment. The

---

[95] *Heinz Jentzsch v Germany* App No 2604/65 (ECommHR Decision, 6 October 1970), para 7.
[96] 'This Article shall not prejudice the trial and punishment of any person for any act or omission which, at the time when it was committed, was criminal according to the general principles of law recognized by civilized nations'.
[97] BVerfGE 89, 155, 2 BvR 2134/92 and 2159/92 (12 October 1993).

outcome of a range of cases in this context is the establishment of a precedent that the negation or revision of the Holocaust will engender a specific interpretation of Articles 10 and 17 ECHR.[98] As the Grand Chamber stated in *Lehideux and Isorni*, '[the disputed publication] does not belong to the category of clearly established historical facts—such as the Holocaust—whose negation or revision would be removed from the protection of Article 10 by Article 17'.[99] In essence, after *Lehideux*, it is clearly established that the European human rights system recognises a special level of protection for the facts of the Holocaust. This has been confirmed by the Court in *Witzsch*[100] and *Garaudy*.[101]

VII. 'THE HOLOCAUST ON YOUR PLATE'

We enter a third phase (*Particularity*) of Holocaust jurisprudence with the recent judgments in *Hoffer and Annen*[102] and, especially, *PETA*.[103] Particularity in this context refers to the evolution and maturation of the Strasbourg judicial approach to a point where the unique nature of the Holocaust in Europe's past is recognised above and beyond mere denial scenarios.

D. *Stolperstein 4*—PETA

In 2004, the animal rights organisation, PETA (People for the Ethical Treatment of Animals) planned an advertising campaign in Germany to be called 'The Holocaust on your plate'. This involved posters with death camp photographs on one side opposite images of animals.[104] The intended campaign was challenged by

---

[98] See, interalia, *Marais v France* App No 31159/96 86 DR 184 (ECommHR Decision, 24 June 1996); *Honsik v Austria* App No 25062/94 83 DR 77 (ECommHR Decision, 18 October 1995); *Lehideux and Isorni v France* App No 24662/94 [1998] ECHR 90 [2000] 30 EHRR 665 (ECtHR (GC), 23 September 1998).

[99] *Lehideux and Isorni v France* App No 24662/94 [1998] ECHR 90 [2000] 30 EHRR 665 (ECtHR (GC), 23 September 1998), para 46.

[100] 'Against this background, the Court finds that the public interest in the prevention of crime and disorder due to disparaging statements regarding the Holocaust, and the requirements of protecting the interests of the victims of the nazi regime, outweigh, in a democratic society the applicant's freedom to impart views denying the existence of gas chambers and mass murder therein.' *Witzsch v Germany* App No 41448/98 (ECtHR, Admissibility Decision, 20 April 1999), para 1.

[101] *Garaudy v France* App 65831/01 [2003] ECHR IX (ECtHR, Admissibility Decision, 7 July 2003).

[102] *Hoffer and Annen v Germany* App Nos 397/07 and 2322/07 [2011] ECHR 46 (ECtHR, 13 January 2011).

[103] *PETA Deutschland v Germany* App No 43481/09 [2012] ECHR 1888 (ECtHR, 8 November 2012).

[104] 'The intended campaign, which had been carried out in a similar way in the United States of America, consisted of a number of posters, each of which bore a photograph of concentration camp inmates along with a picture of animals kept in mass stocks, accompanied by a short text. One of the posters showed a photograph of emaciated, naked concentration camp inmates alongside a photograph of starving cattle under the heading "walking skeletons". Other posters showed a photograph of piled up human dead bodies alongside a photograph of a pile of slaughtered pigs under the heading "final humiliation" and of rows of inmates lying on stock beds alongside rows of chicken in laying batteries under the heading "if animals are concerned, everybody becomes a Nazi". Another poster depicting a starving, naked male inmate alongside a starving cattle bore the title "The Holocaust on your plate" and the text "Between 1938 and 1945, 12 million human beings were killed in the Holocaust. As many animals are killed every hour in Europe for the purpose of human consumption". *PETA Deutschland v Germany* App No 43481/09 [2012] ECHR 1888 (ECtHR, 8 November 2012), para 7.

three Holocaust survivors who successfully sought an injunction, though the case spent five years in the German judicial system. PETA then pleaded Article 10 in Strasbourg where, ultimately, no breach was found.

PETA should be given to every first year law student to watch them unravel the labyrinth of human rights versus animal welfare, cultural relativism, historical significance, multilayered adjudication and human rights universality. *PETA* is not an uncomplicated decision; the majority judgment was followed by an, apparently, concurring Opinion from the President of the Court, Judge Spielmann and the Slovenian Judge Zupančič. The latter take issue, in forceful and persuasive terms, with what might be called the *exceptionalism* element of the judgment. That is, German exceptionalism to the extent that the judgment states that the offensive advertising campaign was unacceptable and not permitted by Article 10 but *only* in Germany.[105] This relativisation of freedom of expression is condemned in the minority Opinion, according to which, the debasement of death camp victims by comparing them to hens and pigs should be unacceptable from Azerbaijan to Iceland and not just in Germany. In 1961, the fact of ex-Nazi judges judging an Auschwitz survivor is not a Strasbourg concern but deemed to be a domestic German issue. By 2012, advertising which is offensive to Holocaust victims is very much a matter for Strasbourg adjudication. One important reading of this minority Opinion, if not the judgment, in *PETA*, is the Europeanisation of the legacy of the Holocaust, as brought about by Strasbourg human rights.

VIII. THE ORIGIN IS THE GOAL

Adorno thought it inconceivable that 'life would continue normally' after the Shoah and a sense of shame prevented him writing eloquently about Auschwitz.[106] In 1959, at the same time as the first judgments issued from Strasbourg, he discerned in Germany a rejection of the past that would cheat the murder victims of their right to be remembered, there was 'an empty and cold forgetting':[107] 'Suffering needed to be enabled to speak. Law and philosophy today must be one in which suffering in death camps is present in every one of its sentences'.[108]

How to apply this to the history of jurisprudence at Strasbourg? This chapter began with arguments about the original lack of philosophy and purpose and closes with an acknowledgement that, if 'the origin is the goal',[109] the Strasbourg institutions have gradually, eventually approached that goal/origin. It might still be said

---

[105] 'The Court considers that the facts of this case cannot be detached from the historical and social context in which the expression of opinion takes place. It observes that a reference to the Holocaust must also be seen in the specific context of the German past and respects the Government's stance that they deem themselves under a special obligation towards the Jews living in Germany ... In the light of this, the Court considers that the domestic courts gave relevant and sufficient reasons for granting the civil injunction against the publication of the posters. This is not called into question by the fact that courts in other jurisdictions might address similar issues in a different way'. *PETA Deutschland v Germany* App No 43481/09 [2012] ECHR 1888 (ECtHR, 8 November 2012), para 49.
[106] Adorno, 'The Meaning of Working Through the Past', n 42 above, xi.
[107] ibid, xii.
[108] ibid.
[109] Attributed to Karl Kraus in P Szondi, 'Hope in the Past: On Walter Benjamin' in W Benjamin, *Berlin Childhood Around 1900* (Harvard, Harvard University Press, 2006) 29.

of cases such as X (Auschwitz survivor) above that 'it's as good as if it never happened; the murdered are to be cheated out of the single remaining thing that our powerlessness can offer them: remembrance'.[110] But, taking a route via Holocaust denial, the Strasbourg human rights system has reached a point where the 'origin', the ignored shadow against with the ECHR was drafted, has now acquired a status in the case-law which begins to accord mass extermination and suffering value and recognition in itself.

IX. ENDING

In Europe, there are positions to defend.[111]

It was reported in a Dutch newspaper in February 1942 that potatoes were to be transported to Berlin in heated railway wagons so as to prevent frost damage.[112] The human occupants of German railway wagons at the same time were not so fortunate. In this small insight into a united Europe under German control in 1942, there are echoes of a united Europe of the future. Might it be said that European integration is still overly concerned with potatoes, goods, property, standardisation and health and safety rather than with humanity? And, moreover, that this preoccupation contributes to a hindering of the achievement of justice at the European level?[113]

I suggest at the close of this chapter that, despite the lack of appropriate conceptual underpinning or a founding philosophy in Strasbourg, the current and more recent jurisprudence evidences a human rights system formulating and supplying a kind of justice which now recognises the 'origin' and is beginning to be that which it was not allowed to be in 1950. The Convention *acquis*[114] is enriched and enhanced ultimately rather than devalued by unearthing the 'sins' of the past. In exposing the institutional approaches to Europe's pasts it can be seen that the ECHR is, and needs to be, more than a self-serving collective insurance policy (against totalitarianism).[115] 'The past will have been worked through only when the causes of what happened then have been eliminated. Only because the causes continue to exist does the captivating spell of the past remain to this day unbroken'.[116]

> And praised be Auschwitz. So be it. Maidenek. The Eternal. Treblinka. And praised be Buchenwald. So be it. Mauthausen. The Eternal. Belzec. And praised be Sobibor. So be it. Chelmno. The Eternal. Ponary. And praised be Theresienstadt. So be it. Warsaw. The Eternal. Wilno. And praised be Skarzysko. So be it. Bergen Belsen. The Eternal. Janow. And praised be Dora. So be it. Nuengamme. The Eternal. Pustkow. And praised be ...[117]

---

[110] Adorno, 'The Meaning of Working Through the Past', n 42 above, 5.
[111] Walter Benjamin, justifying his decision not to leave Europe in 1936, discussed by Peter Szondi in his 'Hope in the Past', n 109 above, 33.
[112] *De Courant/Nieuws Van Den Dag* (2 February 1942).
[113] Pope Francis's comments on Europe's failings are in the same vein, 'Pope Francis complains of "haggard" Europe in Strasbourg' BBC News (25 November 2014), http://www.bbc.co.uk/news/world-europe-30180667.
[114] Douglas-Scott, 'Europe's Constitutional Mosaic', n 69 above.
[115] ibid.
[116] Adorno, 'The Meaning of Working Through the Past', n 42 above, 18.
[117] Schwarz-Bart, *The Last of the Just*, n 52 above, 383.

27
An Idea of Ecological Justice in the EU

JANE HOLDER

I. INTRODUCING ECOLOGICAL JUSTICE

THE NATURA 2000 ecological network, established by the Habitats Directive 1992,[1] has a vital and material relationship with the territory of the EU, legally demarcating and categorising land according to the quality and character of its landscape, geology and ecology. Its main device is to connect and protect land for nature conservation purposes, adhering to a trans-frontier pattern of environmental regulation. In this chapter I also present Natura 2000 as having jurisprudential weight by virtue of it providing a testing ground for the reception and strength of *ecological justice* in the EU.[2] This is an emerging category of justice, posing both empirical and ethical questions on a grand scale. Ecological justice is related in some ways to the idea of environmental justice—the just distribution of environmental 'goods' and 'bads', the environmental justice movement having gained considerable strength from the civil rights movement in the US from the late 1960s onwards with a campaign against 'environmental racism'. But, ecological justice adamantly rejects the human-centred foundation of the environmental justice movement, pushing instead for a radical reformulation of justice, with relations between humans and the natural world as its absolute priority. A useful distinction is made by Low and Gleeson who see the struggle for justice as it is shaped by the politics of the environment as including two related aspects: 'the justice of the distribution of environments among peoples' (environmental justice) and 'the justice of the relations between humans and the rest of the natural world' (ecological justice).[3]

The focal point of this chapter is the potentially powerful impact of reordering EU law and governance according to ecological justice principles, beginning with the Habitats Directive, and its construction of the Natura 2000 network, a policy context likely to be most receptive to ecological principles and ideals. The legal

---

[1] Council Directive 92/43/EEC of 21 May 1992 on the conservation of natural habitats and of wild fauna and flora ('Habitats Directive') [1992] OJ L206/7.

[2] Other good testing grounds include Directive 2000/60/EC of the European Parliament and of the Council of 23 October 2000 establishing a framework for Community action in the field of water policy ('Water Framework Directive') [2000] OJ L327/1, and European Commission, 'Proposal for a Directive of the European Parliament and of the Council establishing a framework for maritime spatial planning and integrated coastal management' COM(2013) 133 final.

[3] N Low and B Gleeson, *Justice, Society and Nature: An Exploration of a Political Ecology* (London, Routledge, 1998) 2.

reality, however, is that nature conservation as a policy area in the EU is fraught with tensions existing between developmental and conservatory interests which are barely disguised by the governing principle of sustainable development. The result is the construction of a legal regime which explicitly sanctions the loss and damage of Natura 2000 sites under certain circumstances, helping to negate the ecologically principled approach advanced by the Directive.

In this analysis of ecological justice and its expression in EU law, I highlight the progressive aspects of the Habitats Directive from an ecological point of view, especially the establishment of Natura 2000, before applying ecological justice or 'wild law' thinking as a critique of the Directive's provisions establishing a framework for balancing nature conservation against 'social or economic'[4] interests with frequently harmful effects. My main argument is that taking an ecological justice approach means that judgements about the current sufficiency or deficiency of conditions of justice in the EU cannot be made solely according to the existing and settled set of human-based and legally grounded criteria—procedural fairness, equal or fair distribution of risks and corrective justice via attempts to compensate for the loss of habitats via habitat creation schemes. Instead I put forward a set of ecological criteria (integrity, resilience and coherence) as better able to capture and advance an idea of ecological justice in the EU because they offer more meaningful assessments of the actual ecological state of conservation sites; to further ecological justice, their application could be extended to the protection of sites threatened by 'social or economic interests'.

Significantly for EU law this set of ecological justice criteria challenges the prevalence of individualist and abstract rights-based formulations of justice in favour of an overriding concern with 'viewing the world relationally'[5]—making connections between humans and their environments, through gaining knowledge of the working and inter-relation of ecosystems. The aim is to explore the prospects for ecological law being taken more seriously in the EU, especially when judged against advances, or otherwise, being made in the case of the related categories of spatial justice and environmental justice (which share some concerns but differ in the degree of their acceptance within the EU). In this chapter, extending Fraser's bivalent concept of justice[6] (encompassing distribution and recognition, joined by an idea of parity of participation), I typify each of these categories of justice according to their prevailing concern: spatial distribution of environmental benefits and burdens (*spatial justice*); recognition and place-based participation in decision making (*environmental justice*) and relativist understanding and respecting connections between and within ecosystems (*ecological justice*). I identify important conceptual and practical linkages and knock-on effects between these categories, as well as

---

[4] Art 6(4) Habitats Directive. The preamble lists a broader range of requirements—'economic, social, cultural and regional' to be taken into account in promoting biodiversity as the main aim of the Directive (recital 3).

[5] S Sterling, 'Ecological Intelligence: Viewing the World Relationally' in A Stibbe (ed), *The Handbook of Sustainable Literacy: Skills for a Changing World* (Totnes, Green Books, 2009) 77.

[6] N Fraser, 'Social Justice in the Age of Identity Politics: Redistribution, Recognition, and Participation', The Tanner Lectures on Human Values, delivered at Stanford University (30 April–2 May 1996) available at www.tannerlectures.utah.edu/_documents/a-to-z/f/Fraser98.pdf.

making clear the greater sense of context (the state of the environment) which flows from moving towards an ecological justice approach to decision making and governance structures. At present, though, it is possible to discern only the stirrings of such an approach within EU law, and I give an account of these as indicators of the extent of receptiveness to furthering ecological thinking within EU law.

II. SEEKING ECOLOGICAL JUSTICE IN NATURA 2000

Natura 2000 is the wildly ambitious product of the Habitats Directive (12 years in the making, still not fully implemented,[7] and the subject of enforcement proceedings before the EU courts).[8] Burdened with the epithet of a new millennium, it represents an attempt on the part of the EU to create a 'coherent European ecological network'[9] of areas of land that need special protection because they represent important and threatened habitats, when judged across the whole of the EU's territory. These areas include Special Areas of Conservation, designated under the Habitats Directive, with existing, but often disparate, protected areas, creating the physical means by which species could migrate and flourish. To further give effect to this, the Directive also encourages Member States to provide 'linear and continuous structures', or 'green corridors' such as hedges and rivers, to further help species move between Natura 2000 sites,[10] often across state boundaries. By connecting existing areas in this way, Natura 2000 seeks to counteract the adverse effects on biodiversity of the creation of small 'islands' of habitat which fail to support wildlife in the long term because of the adverse effects of pollutants and developmental strains which tend to surround and impinge upon such isolated areas. Importantly, the Habitats Directive (unlike previous examples of EU nature conservation law)[11] applies to both habitats and a range of species in recognition of their intimate interdependence.

As a result the territory of the EU is shaped by the Habitats Directive in a physical sense. The Directive organises and governs the use and development of land classed as ecologically sensitive (about 15 per cent of the EU—roughly the size of Germany) according to a politically sensitive, multistage and multilevel classification and designation procedure, engaging panels of scientific experts, members of the Commission and, in cases of intransigence, the Council.[12] The EU approaches this organisation of land in a supranational way, though the control it exercises is applied unevenly, with a firm handle on the classification and designation of land,

---

[7] European Commission, 'Composite Report on the Conservation Status of Habitat Types and Species as required under Article 17 of the Habitats Directive' COM(2009) 358 final.

[8] The European Court of Justice (ECJ) has condemned Member States for failing to: implement the relevant provisions (Case C-256/98 *Commission of the European Communities v French Republic* [2000] ECR I-2487); and communicate to the Commission the list of appropriate sites (Special Areas of Conservation (SACs)) in line with the Important Bird Areas (IBAs) and designate or protect a sufficient number of Special Protection Areas (SPAs) (Case C-3/96 *Commission of the European Communities v Kingdom of the Netherlands* [1998] ECR I-3031).

[9] Preamble, recital 6 Habitats Directive.

[10] Art 10 Habitats Directive.

[11] Eg Council Directive 79/409/EEC of 2 April 1979 on the conservation of wild birds ('Wild Birds Directive') [1979] OJ L103/1.

[12] Arts 4 and 5, and Annex III Habitats Directive.

far less so its protection. In conception, if not practice, Natura 2000 is sensitive to the needs of habitats and species and reflects ecological thinking aimed at coherent or holistic protection of nature, in keeping with the idea that such protected habitats and species 'form part of the Community's natural heritage'.[13] But, Natura 2000 is also the product of the extreme influence on the EU's body of environmental law of the principle of sustainable development that economic, social and environmental factors should be taken into account on an equal basis in decision making. A weak form of sustainable development is enshrined in the Habitats Directive's procedures by which the loss or damage of habitats is assessed, negotiated and compensated in order to accommodate social or economic interests,[14] subject to the aim of securing the 'overall coherence' of the network.[15] The strictness of these procedural safeguards is gauged according to a hierarchy of protection, with so-called priority species (wolves, lynx, brown bear, marmot, wolverine, monk seal and others)[16] and habitats (including coastal and inland salt meadows, coastal lagoons, steppes and grasslands, bogs, rocky habitats and caves, and forests)[17] enjoying greater, though notably not absolute, levels of protection.

This legal framework for nature conservation can be judged against a spectrum of human-centred concerns about justice, the mainstay of this volume, with key analytical points being procedural justice, distributional justice and corrective justice (I discuss recognition at a later stage). First, it is notable that procedures for the negotiation of nature in cases of predicted loss or damage of a Natura 2000 site barely conform to recognised international standards of *procedural justice* as set out in the United Nations Economic Commission for Europe (UNECE) Aarhus Convention.[18] Whereas the Convention requires Member States to provide conditions for public participation for a wide array of projects and plans, the Directive grants only restricted opportunities for public involvement in decision making covered by the Directive,[19] and the fulfilment of these opportunities is left entirely to Member States' discretion, creating a participatory 'grey area'.[20]

Second, analysing the Directive's regime for the negation of the loss or damage of Natura 2000 sites according to *distributional justice* calls into question the means by which the Directive seeks to ensure the 'overall coherence' or European-wide coverage of the network in the event of the loss or damage of a Natura 2000 site

---

[13] Preamble, recital 4 Habitats Directive.
[14] Art 6(4) Habitats Directive.
[15] Art 6(4) Habitats Directive.
[16] Annex II Habitats Directive.
[17] Annex I Habitats Directive.
[18] United Nations Economic Commission for Europe (UNECE) Aarhus Convention on Access to Information, Public Participation in Decision-Making and Access to Justice in Environmental Matters (25 June 1998) 38 ILM 515 (1999), 2161 UNTS 447.
[19] Art 6(3) Habitats Directive: '[T]he competent authorities shall agree to the plan or project only after having ascertained that it will not adversely affect the integrity of the site concerned and, if appropriate, after having obtained the opinion of the general public'.
[20] European Parliament, *National Implementation of Council Directive 92/43/EEC* (Brussels, European Parliament, 2009) 35. A comparison can be drawn here with Council Directive 85/337/EEC on the assessment of the effects of certain public and private projects on the environment ('Environmental Impact Assessment Directive') [1985] L175/40; and Directive 96/61/EC of 24 September 1996 concerning integrated pollution prevention and control [1996] OJ L257/6, both of which were amended to comply with the Aarhus Convention.

for 'imperative reasons of overriding public interest', which may include reasons of a social or economic nature.[21] Since the overriding aim of the Habitats Directive is to protect the overall coherence of Natura 2000, achieving this requires judgements to be made about the ecological *significance* of a particular threatened site on an *EU-wide* basis. However in practice, such judgements are necessarily based upon the ecological state of the site at the *local* level.[22] The difficulty is that broader judgements about the extent to which a particular site contributes to the wider network or provides a means by which certain species can migrate throughout the network commonly take place in circumstances of imperfect information about the state of the environment in 'other' parts of Europe.[23] This suggests that decision making by conservation bodies and government is deficient in terms of securing distributional justice, in this context meaning the place and character of development across the EU territory (the subject of spatial justice, discussed below), but also the disproportionate location of environmentally harmful development projects in poor communities (a concern of environmental justice, also discussed below). This difficulty points to a real need to examine empirically the extent to which individual nature conservation areas designated and protected as part of Natura 2000 function genuinely as part of a trans-boundary network, supported by information gathering and disseminating networks operating across state boundaries.[24] In the absence of this, what remains is a picture of decision making about development taking place at the local level, strongly weighted in favour of economic values and expediency, and with the European Commission, offering regulatory oversight by way of issuing opinions on the most sensitive decisions, overwhelmingly supportive of the most ecologically damaging examples.[25] Third, the *compensatory justice* mechanisms in the Directive[26] are characterised by serious fault lines as well as general deficiencies, with the translocation of species and re-creation of habitats rarely working (in fact, often causing more problems than they seek to resolve) and, more fundamentally, acting as a denial of their intrinsic value and worth.

III. MOVING TOWARDS ECOLOGICAL JUSTICE

The previous analysis of the practical working of provisions of the Habitats Directive illustrates the poverty of using human-centred categories of justice in an ecological context such as nature conservation because the reference points—public participation (procedural justice), the spread and distribution of development harmful to the environment (distributive justice) and the artificial creation of habitats or

---

[21] Art 6(4) Habitats Directive.
[22] ibid.
[23] Richard Broadbent, Principal Solicitor at Natural England (personal communication).
[24] Eg via the European Commission-managed Natura 2000 Network Programme, www.natura.org/.
[25] L Krämer, 'The European Commission's Opinions Under Article 6(4) of the Habitats Directive' (2009) 21 *Journal of Environmental Law* 59; and D McGillivray, 'Compensating Biodiversity Loss: The EU Commission's Approach to Compensation Under Art 6(4) of the Habitats Directive' (2012) 24 *Journal of Environmental Law* 17.
[26] Art 6(4): 'If a plan or project must be carried out for imperative reasons of overriding public interest, the Member States shall take all measures to ensure that the overall coherence of Natura 2000 is protected'.

other compensatory measures (compensatory justice) fail to capture the complexity and enormity of what is at stake in decisions likely to bring about collapse and crises in ecosystems. I therefore aim to push further the analysis of deficiencies of justice in this policy context by presenting ecological justice as an entirely new category of justice, far more responsive to ideas about the desirability of maintaining connections between and within ecological systems, and without human reference points at its foundation.

Working through the implications of ecological justice within a discrete policy area such as nature conservation it is clear that this emerging form of justice represents a significant shift in thinking about law and governance. Within EU law, as other legal systems, formulations of justice have primarily been concerned with people, with a sustained focus upon individuals' fair and equal treatment in a range of social and economic contexts: rights of non-discrimination in social life and in the marketplace, rights of access to information and participation in decision making, and rights of redress and compensation. The legal narrative of the European Courts' development of this rights-based jurisprudence describes a move from the recognition of individual social and economic rights as against the state, to a recognition that such rights are capable of being exercised against other individuals (as played out in the long running horizontal effect of directives debate). This was a process of rights creation through 'adversarial legalism' and a strong sense of judicial purpose, if not a full-scale 'rights revolution'.[27] The European Court of Justice (ECJ) demonstrated a remarkable early sensitivity to environmental protection issues,[28] and their strength relative to the four freedoms,[29] and consequently constructed a de facto legal base for policy and legislative activity on the environment.[30] In later cases, the Court strengthened considerably the hand of environmental non-governmental organisations (NGOs),[31] albeit with some notable (and contested) exceptions.[32]

Although recognising environmental protection as an important public interest, overall, the legal development and recognition of rights in the EU has remained faithful to an abstract and individualised version of justice which has been developed in Anglo–American jurisprudence, apart from an appreciation of ecological context. An extreme sense of disconnection with context is the foundation of Rawls' expository and artificial 'original position' device, in which the distribution of natural assets and abilities is veiled, and knowledge about space and time is explicitly excluded from the exercise.[33] Such features make Rawls' 'justice as

---

[27] RD Kelemen, 'The EU Rights Revolution: Adversarial Legalism and European Integration' in T Borzel and R Cichowski (eds), *The State of the European Union. Vol 6: Law, Politics, and Society* (Oxford, Oxford University Press, 2003).

[28] Case 240/83 *Procureur de la République v Association de défense des brûleurs d'huiles usages (ADBHU)* [1985] ECR 531.

[29] Case 302/86 *Commission of the European Communities v Kingdom of Denmark* [1988] ECR 4607.

[30] This legal base was codified by the Single European Act [1986] OJ L169, which inserted an Environment Title into the EEC Treaty.

[31] Case C-44/95 *R v Secretary of State for the Environment, ex parte: Royal Society for the Protection of Birds* [1996] ECR I-3805.

[32] Case T-585/93 *Stichting Greenpeace Council (Greenpeace International) and Others v Commission of the European Communities* [1998] ECR I-1651.

[33] J Rawls, *A Theory of Justice* (Cambridge, MA, Belknap Press of Harvard University Press, 1971).

fairness' rendering of the social contract highly problematic when viewed from an environmental perspective: as a device focused on the optimal structure of society and social institutions' distribution of goods (welfare), it fails to take account of the ecological effects of distribution and use of natural/environmental resources as 'benefits'; the focus is on the redistribution of the benefits or burdens of society, not the reduction of such burdens (such as pollution) with potentially greater impacts upon individual liberty; and, finally, it is a hard task to apply the exercise spatially (issues of global justice are excluded), temporally, and to other species. A less abstract version of justice is developed by Sen who identifies cases of injustice in terms of 'the importance of human lives, experiences ... the freedom to choose our lives'.[34] This 'realisation-focused view of justice' runs counter to Rawls' 'arrangement-focused view of justice',[35] which is drawn up in terms of what would be perfectly just institutions.

Arising from her work examining the lived experience of women, Fraser shifts attention away from distributive justice as the paradigm case for theorising justice to a second type of claim for social justice in the politics of recognition. The goal is 'a difference friendly world, where assimilation to major or dominant cultural norms is no longer the price of equal respect'.[36] Ultimately, however, she develops a bivalent conception of justice, encompassing distribution (political/economic) and recognition (cultural valuation) dimensions, meaning that these categories of justice are not mutually exclusive but are connected by the idea of 'parity of participation'.[37]

This move to a more contextualised and enlarged awareness of justice and the lived experiences of injustice leads to the possibility of *relation* as a third claim of justice. This is as yet less politically recognised and still under-theorised compared to distribution and recognition, but points to ecological relations and connections as forming an ecological base which fundamentally and absolutely affects all other claims and addresses questions about not only what should be distributed, but what are the ecological effects of this? Who matters in distributive decisions—other species, future generations? The prospects for developing such a trivalent concept of justice are here analysed in the legal conditions of the EU, arriving at an idea of ecological justice (*relation*) through analysis of spatial (*distribution*) and environmental justice (*recognition and participative*) categories.

A. Spatial Justice and Territorial Cohesion

It is now possible to identify some broadening of the subject(s) of justice within the EU. Spatial planning provides one example which has gained considerable ground as a policy aim in this respect, especially since its spatial justice element has been repackaged as 'territorial cohesion' (defined initially by the Commission as 'the harmonious and sustainable development of all territories by building on

---

[34] A Sen, *The Idea of Justice* (London, Penguin, 2010) 18.
[35] ibid, 20.
[36] Fraser, 'Social Justice in the Age of Identity Politics', n 6 above, 3.
[37] ibid, 30.

their territorial characteristics and resources',[38] and latterly in terms of the aim that 'people should not be disadvantaged by wherever they happen to live or work in the Union').[39] Territorial cohesion, still containing a spark of spatial justice to the extent that it suggests that there could be solidarity between both people and places, now enjoys a constitutional footing by the new coupling in Article 3 of the Treaty on European Union (TEU),[40] requiring the Union to 'promote economic, social and territorial cohesion' as well as the pursuit of 'solidarity', thus adding an explicit spatial dimension to the EU's existing social, economic, environmental and political agendas. Although, as Antonia Layard argues in this volume, spatial justice is still inadequately examined in the EU context (at least by lawyers).[41]

One interpretation of this progression of territorial cohesion is that it extends the European social model's concern with *social* protection so that it incorporates concerns about *spatial* protection, its aim being 'a just distribution of opportunities of space',[42] with the possibility of it combining ideas of solidarity and identity with visionary or even utopian elements existing outside the market. At some remove from these ideals and goals, however, spatial justice as explained in terms of territorial cohesion has been reshaped and extrapolated by the EU so that its central aim has become the equal opportunity to participate in economic and entrepreneurial activity realised by the provision of 'services of general economic interest'[43] without spatial discrimination, blunting the sharp edge of its redistributive and idealist agendas along the way. The important consequence is that sustainable development and territorial cohesion, as key planks of the EU's spatial policy, are currently dominated by an economic agenda, both in terms of the values expressed and the use of economic methodologies, as illustrated by the adoption of the concepts of 'territorial capital', 'territorial assets' and 'territorial development'.[44] There currently exists only a notional recognition of equality and justice issues in planning and development from an EU perspective, notwithstanding attempts to align territorial cohesion with the European social model.

B. Environmental Justice

I suggested above that the potential exists to develop a serious environmental justice agenda within the EU, in cohort with spatial justice elements. Currently, though, environmental justice is not well shaped as a concern of EU law and

---

[38] European Commission, 'Sixth Progress Report on Economic and Social Cohesion' COM(2009) 295 final.
[39] European Commission, 'Third Report on Economic and Social Cohesion: A New Partnership for Cohesion: Convergence, Competitiveness and Cooperation' COM (2004) 107 final 27.
[40] Consolidated version of the Treaty on European Union [2012] OJ C326/13 (TEU).
[41] See A Layard, 'Freedom of Expression and Spatial (Understandings of) Justice' in this volume, 417.
[42] A Faludi, 'Territorial Cohesion Policy and the European Model of Society' (2007) 15 *European Planning Studies* 567.
[43] Art 16 Draft Constitutional Treaty, '[C]itizens should have access to essential services, basic infrastructures and knowledge by highlighting the significance of services of general economic interest for promoting social and territorial cohesion'.
[44] J Holder, 'Building Spatial Europe: An Environmental Justice Perspective' in J Scott (ed), *Environmental Protection: European Law and Governance* (Oxford, Oxford University Press, 2009).

policy, a product of the lack of a galvanising association with civil rights and race discrimination which gave weight and a sense of urgency to the environmental justice movement in the US. This lack of recognition of environmental justice is, however, out of line with the EU's growing concern with spatial non-discrimination (outlined above), the development of its substantial body of environmental protection legislation over the past 40 years, and the parallel evolution of a well-founded and respected rights jurisprudence—arguably all essential and component parts of environmental justice. The last in particular has tended to be aimed at discrimination of individuals for reasons of race, age or sex, and less so how these identities may inform the treatment of a group as a whole in terms of their exposure to environmental harms and risk. A strongly critical view of the absence of an integrated policy framework within the EU to encourage connections to be made between environmental risk exposure and social status, race or ethnicity has been developed by Schwarte and Adebowale.[45] They compare the existence of well-established procedural requirements for access to environmental justice under EU law (implementing the provisions of the Aarhus Convention) with the absence from the EU agenda of the more politically contentious *distributive* aspects of environmental justice—the fair distribution between communities of environmental 'goods' and 'bads'[46]—and argue for the creative application of the Race Discrimination Directive[47] in such cases. Nevertheless the importance of process remains significant, underlining that environmental justice necessarily seeks to strengthen the connection of communities with a particular *place* through their involvement with decision making affecting their locality, and with opportunities for this shaped by environmental assessment procedures,[48] albeit that such procedures are remarkably weak in relation to nature conservation (as outlined above).

As Schwarte and Adebowale report, in many areas of Europe, but especially in Central and Eastern Europe (CEE), there are widespread environmental inequalities,[49] with a disproportionate number of settlements of Romani people sited near hazardous waste sites, large infrastructure development and former mines.[50] More generally the European Environment Agency reports that the environment-related share of the burden of disease is higher in lower-income countries and that climate change particularly affects vulnerable groups,[51] including children.[52]

---

[45] P Schwarte and M Adebowale, *Environmental Justice and Race Equality in the European Union* (London, Capacity Global, 2007) 4.
[46] ibid.
[47] Council Directive 2000/43/EC of 29 June 2000 implementing the principle of equal treatment between persons irrespective of racial or ethnic origin [2002] OJ L180/22.
[48] M Lee, *EU Environmental Law: Challenges, Change and Decision Making* (Oxford, Hart Publishing, 2005).
[49] Schwarte and Adebowale, *Environmental Justice*, n 45 above, 16.
[50] D Pellow, 'Activist Scholarship for Environmental Justice' in K Korgen, J White and S White, *Sociologists in Action: Social Change and Social Justice* (London, SAGE Publications, 2011) 222.
[51] European Environment Agency, 'Environment and Health' (2006) *EEA Reports* No 10/2005. See also C Varga, I Kiss and I Ember, 'The Lack of Environmental Justice in Central and Eastern Europe' (2002) 11 *Environmental Health Perspectives* 110.
[52] European Environment Agency and WHO Regional Office for Europe, *Children's Health and Environment: A Review of Evidence*, Environmental Issue Report No 29 (Luxemburg, Office for Official Publications of the European Communities, 2002).

410 *Jane Holder*

The vulnerability of certain communities such as the Roma is now being better documented and indicates that the EU's treatment of environmental justice issues, and its responsibility for environmental injustice, is, finally, coming under greater scrutiny,[53] providing a good example of the 'horizontal' nature of the transatlantic journey of the environmental justice movement. Environmental justice is also providing a 'vertical' frame to encompass concerns that do not end at borders but involve relations between countries and global scale issues such as climate change. This presents a significant departure from locally-based assessments of states of justice or injustice—because the impacts of development are now seen on a global scale, although also reverberating within and having impacts on the locality.

In summary, spatial justice and environmental justice are linked by a shared concern with human quality of life and health on a collective rather than individual basis—'a just distribution of opportunities of space',[54] including, increasingly, access to markets, and opportunities to pursue entrepreneurship (spatial justice/territorial cohesion) and the non-discriminatory distribution of environmental 'goods' and 'bads' (environmental justice). These two forms are connected by praxis: spatial justice, as interpreted by the EU as territorial cohesion, is closely associated with a positive approach to hard infrastructure needed to further this (networks of regional airports, business parks, bridges, global ports, high-speed rail and road networks), the development and use of which tends to disproportionately affect poor and ethnic minority communities.[55] Such developments also flatten out environmental diversity and cultural landscapes in favour of a strongly economic rationale of overcoming 'friction' (border controls, 'slow' roads) in the mobility of peoples and goods, creating a European 'monotopia'.[56]

C. Ecological Justice

The above analysis of the state of justice in the EU has focused on the EU's occupation with the economic function of space and, more recently, discriminatory practices in particular places. Both forms of justice take physical conditions of the locality as their context, rather than more abstract notions, but the overriding concern remains human capacity and development. This is highlighted by the Habitats Directive in which the IROPI ('imperative reasons of overriding public interest') formula classifies 'social or economic interests' as potentially capable of 'overriding' ecological concerns about the loss or damage of Natura 2000 sites,[57]

---

[53] K Harper, T Steger and R Filcak, 'Environmental Justice and Roma Communities in Central and Eastern Europe' (2009) 19 *Environmental Policy and Governance* 251.
[54] Faludi, 'Territorial Cohesion Policy and the European Social Model', n 42 above.
[55] O Jensen and T Richardson, *Making European Space: Mobility, Power and Territorial Identity* (London, Routledge, 2004). See a list of such developments drawn from eight case studies of Member States' implementation of the Habitats Directive: N de Sadeleer, C-H Born and M Prieur, *National Implementation of Council Directive 92/43/EEC* (Brussels, European Parliament, 2009) 7–11.
[56] Jensen and Richardson, *Making European Space*, n 55 above, 54.
[57] Art 6(4) Habitats Directive.

a state of affairs which might be compared unfavourably with examples of absolute protection conferred by the (now amended) Wild Birds Directive 1979.[58]

With roots primarily in ecological ethics and philosophy rather than law,[59] ecological justice provides a broad label for a non-anthropocentric paradigm of justice, embracing the idea of nature's own rights, and recognising the intrinsic, rather than functional, value of the natural world. The more theoretical elements of ecological justice have been explored by Baxter[60] and Bosselmann,[61] with key texts being Berry's *The Great Work*[62] and Cullinan's manifesto for Wild Law.[63] Cullinan, an activist lawyer, is highly critical of the current destructive nature of human governance systems, including (especially) law, and recounts the development of a new philosophy, Earth Jurisprudence,[64] based on the idea that humans are only one part of a wider community of beings and that the welfare of each member of that community is dependent on the welfare of the Earth as a whole. From this perspective (aligned with ancient traditions, stories and cosmologies of indigenous peoples), human societies will only be viable and flourish if they regulate themselves as part of the wider 'Earth community' and in a manner consistent with the fundamental laws and principles that govern how the universe functions (the 'Great Jurisprudence'). This conception of the place of humans has profound implications for law, since Wild Law works from the premise that '[t]he Universe is the primary law-giver, not human legal systems'.[65] This means that laws can be assessed for their legitimacy only by reference to a set of higher order, universal, ecological principles. Wild Law UK, a group of lawyers and activists seeking to develop 'Earth-centred governance' in practice, include within this set of principles 'recognition of the intrinsic value of nature as a life support system rather than as a "resource" for the sole benefit of humanity' and 'respecting rights of nature to exist, to habitat and fulfil their role in the community of life, and to restoration from damage'.[66] These principles are drawn from a Draft Declaration of the Rights of Nature,[67] discussed at the UN +20 Rio Conference in 2012, and recognised in the Conference's main output, *The Future We Want*,[68] suggesting at least the arrival of ecological justice on high level law- and policy-making agendas.

---

[58] Art 4 of the Council Directive 79/409/EEC of 2 April 1979 on the conservation of wild birds [1979] OJ L103/1.

[59] See generational analysis by S Emmenegger and A Tschentscher, 'Taking Nature's Rights Seriously: The Long Way to Biocentrism in Environmental Law' (1994) 6 *Georgetown International Environmental Law Review* 545, 552–68.

[60] B Baxter, *A Theory of Ecological Justice* (London, Routledge, 2005).

[61] K Bosselmann, *The Principle of Sustainability* (Aldershot, Ashgate, 2008).

[62] T Berry, *The Great Work: Our Way into the Future* (New York, NY, Bell Tower, 1999).

[63] C Cullinan, *Wild Law: A Manifesto for Earth Justice* (Totnes, Green Books, 2003).

[64] C Cullinan, 'A History of Wild Law' in P Burdon (eds), *Exploring Wild Law. The Philosophy of Earth Jurisprudence* (Adelaide, Wakefield Press, 2012) 13.

[65] ibid.

[66] Wild Law UK, Submission to the HC Environment Audit Committee, Session 2010–12, 20 September 2011.

[67] Global Alliance for Rights of Nature, Draft Declaration of the Rights of Nature (also referred to as the 'People's Sustainability Treaty' and the Declaration of the Rights of Mother Earth. See Global Exchange, *The Rights of Nature: The Case for a Universal Declaration of the Rights of Mother Earth* (San Francisco, CA, Global Exchange, 2011).

[68] United Nations Conference on Sustainable Development, 'The Future We Want', Rio+20 Outcome of the Conference (20–22 June 2012) A /CONF.216/L.1 para 40.

This radically different and ecologically informed view of law and justice is highly theoretical but some of the more practical elements are being worked out and are taking the shape of a 'manifesto' for environmental governance including principles against which legislation may be judged. A partnership between the United Kingdom Environmental Law Association and the Gaia Foundation led to an extensive review of current laws, with the majority judged not to be 'wild',[69] by which is meant that there is little evidence of any consistent intent by legislators to adopt Wild Law principles. The EU's Habitats Directive was scrutinised along these lines, with the conclusion that it offers some opportunity 'for opening up Earth Jurisprudence', but that overall

> this is a 'fire-fighting' measure intended to protect what is left of nature and natural habitats; it is not directed to the protection and enhancement of nature in its own right ... It is certainly helpful that it protects certain aspects of Europe's natural habitats but the underlying attitude is that the human presence is assumed to carry on as always except where it has become so detrimental to nature that the last remnants are threatened. It is suggested that this does not really meet the test of mutual enhancement—it is more a matter of human preservation.[70]

The style and level of protection advanced by the Habitats Directive serves to locate it within 'second generation' environmental thinking[71] (the first generation of environmental law being preoccupied with immediate human self-interest, whether that be for public health reasons, or because of the negative effects of pollution on economic development; the utilitarian rationale of the law was to maximise nature's resources to ensure future exploitation). The second generation (the onset of which is identifiable from the 1970s onwards), was triggered by concerns about 'natural limits' and the 'crisis of survival' and characterised by the enlargement of the immediate interest to encompass the interests of future generations,[72] sentiments now expressed by the intergenerational equity element of sustainable development. As Menkel-Meadow has asked of the state and likely future development of alternative dispute resolution as a discipline of law, how does one know when an evolutionary apogee has been reached?[73] Is environmental law fully developed? If not, what stage has been reached? In the United States, there have been sustained and purposive attempts to categorise these developmental stages of environmental law, focused on debating the respective roles of ecology and law and identifying the need for a greater correspondence between these, for example in work on interdisciplinarity,[74]

---

[69] B Filgueira and I Mason, *Wild Law: Is There Any Evidence of Earth Jurisprudence in Existing Law and Practice?* (London, United Kingdom Environmental Law Association and Gaia Foundation, 2009).
[70] ibid, 9.
[71] Emmenegger and Tschentsher, 'Taking Rights Seriously, n 59 above. A similar analysis is provided by G Winter, 'The Four Phases of Environmental Law' (1989) 1 *Journal of Environmental Law* 38.
[72] This law recognises the intergenerational dimension of the protection of nature (the clearest example of which is the Stockholm Declaration of the United Nations Conference in the Human Environment, UN Doc A/CONF 48/14 (1972) 11 ILM 1416 (1972) 1416, which provides that 'man ... bears a solemn responsibility to protect and improve the environment for present and future generations').
[73] C Menkel-Meadow, 'Is the Adversary System Really Dead?' (2004) 57 *Current Legal Problems* 85.
[74] L Caldwell, *Between Two Worlds: Science, the Environment and Policy Choice* (Cambridge, Cambridge University Press, 1992).

eco-pragmatism,[75] and ecosystem management.[76] A similar analysis informs Chertow and Esty's account of the 'Next Generation Project' which drew together influential ecologists and lawyers to debate the benefits of an ecological approach to regulation, concluding that there is a 'need for a "systems" approach to policy built on rigorous analysis, an interdisciplinary focus and an appreciation that context matters ... fundamentally we seek an ecologism that recognises the inherent interdependence of all life systems'.[77] This work advanced the view that 'most of today's environmental law violates the basic principles of ecology'.[78]

There is a more recent gathering of work building on these generational analyses, but which pushes for a more radical recognition of natural rights and ecological justice through ideas about the Rule of Law for Nature,[79] Nature's Trust,[80] and the development of new forms of ecological governance.[81] Such work envisages ecological law as constituting a distinct third developmental phase characterised by a central concern with ecological relations rather than human development in recognition of the expansiveness of ecological justice and the inter-connections which exist between its subjects.

D. Relation- and Context-Based Ecological Review Principles

It may be possible (though admittedly challenging, both politically and philosophically) to interpret ecological justice as significantly enlarging the concept of justice, by working beyond human rights and responsibilities, and forcing a rethinking of legally accepted notions of participation in legal process, redress and compensation. Such an emerging concept of justice needs careful analysis in terms of the use of ideas of 'nature' and the 'natural' by its adherents, and the severe implications of denying rights an active component—personhood—which is usually connected with democracy and legitimacy. Such a critical agenda extends beyond the remit of this analysis of the centrality within EU law of human-focused and individual rights, which has acted as the driver for defining and furthering the EU as an effective political and legal impact-making project. Nevertheless, working through some of

---

[75] For example, D Farber, 'Building Bridges over Troubled Waters: Eco-Pragmatism and the Environmental Prospect' (2003) 87 *Minnesota Law Review* 851 and D Tarlock, 'Slouching Towards Eden: The Eco-Pragmatic Challenges of Ecosystem Revival' (2003) 87 *Minnesota Law Review* 1173.

[76] R Brooks, R Jones and R Virginia, *Law and Ecology: The Rise of the Ecosystem Regime* (Aldershot, Ashgate, 2007). See also R Keiter, 'Taking Account of the Ecosystem on the Public Domain: Law and Ecology in the Greater Yellowstone Region' (1989) 60 *Colorado Law Review* 923; and D Burnett, 'New Science But Old Laws: The Need to Include Landscape Ecology in the Legal Framework of Biodiversity Protection' (1999) 23 *Environs: Environmental Law and Policy Journal* 47.

[77] M Chertow and D Esty, *Thinking Ecologically: The Next Generation of Environmental Policy* (New Haven, CT, Yale University Press, 1997).

[78] E Elliot, 'Towards Ecological Law and Policy' in M Chertow and D Esty (eds), *Thinking Ecologically: The Next Generation of Environmental Policy* (New Haven, CT, Yale University Press, 1997).

[79] C Voight, *Rule of Law for Nature: New Dimensions and Ideas in Environmental Law* (Cambridge, Cambridge University Press, 2014).

[80] M Wood, *Nature's Trust: Environmental Law for a New Ecological Age* (Cambridge, Cambridge University Press, 2014). This develops an environmental dimension to the public trust doctrine.

[81] O Woolley, *Developing a System of Ecological Governance* (Cambridge, Cambridge University Press, 2014).

the implications of the emergence of ecological justice by examining the working of the EU's Natura 2000 regime in practice, a point can be made that the place, reception and strength of ecological justice can be analysed only partially according to forms of justice such as distributive justice, procedural justice and corrective justice which have provided key evaluative frameworks for *human-centred* judgements about the condition of justice. Although these forms highlight the way certain EU regimes and initiatives such as Natura 2000 work, as I outlined above, a very different set of justice criteria or evaluative frames providing a grounded and material analysis of physical conditions based upon the quality of nature of relations within and between ecosystems is needed before a proper assessment can be made about how ecological justice is 'done' in the EU and other legal systems. Such evaluative frames may be based upon, amongst others, principles of *integrity, resilience and coherence*.

(i) Integrity

This refers to the quality or condition of being whole or complete.[82] An ecological definition identifies ecological integrity as the 'ability of a system to support and maintain a biological community which displays species compositions, diversity and functional organisation analogous to a system which is undisturbed'.[83] In terms of the Habitats Directive,[84] the integrity of a site is defined as 'the coherence of the site's ecological structure and function, across its whole areas, or the habitats, complex of habitats and/or populations of species for which the site is or will be classified'. A site has a high degree of integrity where there is the capacity for self-repair and self-renewal under dynamic conditions and a minimum of external management support is needed.[85] An ecosystem possesses integrity 'when it is wild, and free as much as possible from human intervention'.[86]

(ii) Resilience

Resilience describes the capacity of an ecosystem to maintain its structure, function and identity in the face of perturbation or disturbance, to sustain shocks and disturbances without collapse. For an ecosystem to absorb shocks and disturbances and remain in a functionally similar state requires that there be a threshold between alternatives states that, once exceeded, pushes the system to move from its earlier state towards a fundamentally new configuration. Such lurches in the system's behaviour may occur rapidly. Resilience means the capacity to avoid breaching

---

[82] European Commission, *Managing Natura 2000 Sites: The Provisions of Article 6 of the 'Habitats' Directive 92/43/EEC* (Luxembourg: Office for Official Publications of the European Communities, 2000).

[83] J Karr and D Dudley, 'Ecological Perspective on Water Quality Goals' (1981) 5 *Environmental Management* 55, cited in S Rees et al, 'A Legal and Ecological Perspective of "Site Integrity" to Inform Policy Development and Management of Special Areas of Conservation in Europe' (2013) 72 *Marine Pollution Bulletin* 14, 16.

[84] Under the Habitats Directive, a plan or project may only be granted permission to proceed if it can be 'ascertained that it will not adversely affect the integrity of the site concerned' (Art 6(3)).

[85] Commission, *Managing Natura 2000*, n 82 above, 40.

[86] L Westra, 'Ecosystem Integrity and the "Fish Wars"' (1996) 5 *Journal of Aquatic Ecosystem Health* 275, 278.

thresholds between such alternative states. The more complex and diverse an ecosystem is, the more it is capable of rebuffing and overcoming knocks and shocks and 'bouncing back'.[87]

(iii) Coherence

Coherence refers to the quality of ecological networks to support the favourable conservation status of species (maintaining its population on a long-term basis, the natural range of the species is not being reduced and there is, and will probably continue to be, a sufficiently large habitat to maintain its populations on a long-term basis) (Article 1(i) Habitats Directive)) across the whole of its natural range. Coherence is achieved when the network allows the full dispersal, migration and genetic exchange of individuals between relevant sites in the network and the network is resilient to disturbance or damage caused by natural or anthropocenic factors.[88]

Although embedded in laws,[89] the value of such principles relies upon a body of knowledge and expertise drawn from ecology, biology and environmental studies, operating at the level of individual Natura 2000 sites, but capable of informing and learning from expert information networks spanning different spatial scales and overcoming administrative boundaries. At present such principles are applied mainly for the purpose of designating sites under the Directive, so that certain areas of land form part of the Natura 2000 network, but these may be overridden by the (sadly routine) occurrence of the loss or damage of protected sites for 'economic and social' interests. Elevating these principles so that they guide judgements about loss or damage would come close to achieving absolute protection of nature, subject only to dire emergency.

IV. CONCLUSIONS

Much of this chapter identifies emerging ideas being developed in discussions about the adequacy of and direction of justice within Europe. A critical reading of EU nature conservation law shows ecological justice to amount to more than an expanded version of existing dimensions of justice (as is arguably the case with spatial justice and environmental justice forms). Returning to the 'deficit' theme of this book, ecological justice is considerably impoverished in this context, with much of EU law instead taken up with structuring and legitimising the exploitation of the natural world via trade regimes and development programmes which encapsulate a very narrow and economically grounded conception of development and human progress.[90] More broadly, the burgeoning environmental legal *acquis* is marked by

---

[87] H Leslie and A Kinzig, 'Resilience Science' in K McLeod and H Leslie (eds), *Ecosystem-Based Management for the Oceans* (Washington, DC, Island Press, 2009) 55–56.
[88] R Catchpole, 'Ecological Coherence Definitions in Policy and Practice' (2013) *Scottish Natural Heritage Commissioned Reports* No 552.
[89] Integrity and coherence are both referred to in Art 6(4) Habitats Directive but neither is defined.
[90] D Wood, 'Globalisation and Sustainable Development in the EU' in J Holder and D McGillivray (eds), *Locality and Identity: Social and Environmental Issues in Law and Society* (Aldershot, Ashgate, 1999).

trends of flexibility, managerialism and proceduralisation,[91] which run counter to core ecological needs—the creation and absolute protection of nature conservation sites and networks, supported by networks of experts and communities of practice, and integrated decision-making regimes. This critique applies specifically (and damningly) to the protection regime established by the Habitats Directive which gives significant weight to non-conservatory interests in the name of sustainable development, with severe consequences for ecological conditions even in protected areas.

Against this I have identified some indications of ecological thinking in EU law and policy with growing acceptance of the legal significance of ecological principles such as those which shape the working of the Habitats Directive, such as integrity, resilience and coherence. But clearly such principles have not yet achieved the status of principles of review for administrative action and having impacts upon the determination of rights in a manner similar to those principles expressing human rights values such as non-discrimination, proportionality and fairness. The growing acceptance of the vital importance of the ecological condition of the territory of the EU—within Natura 2000 but vitally also outside such protected areas—sets up the very real possibility of clashes between the principle of sustainable development which, having undergone a process of mainstreaming, sits at the centre of the EU's law and policy-making constitutional and institutional apparatus, and ecological principles which are still likely to be compromised and sidelined because of their currently more marginal position in pockets of policy areas. There may be important signs of receptiveness towards ecological principles in EU legislation, but ideas about how to make manifest ecological justice through the strong application of those principles are currently being developed and debated at some considerable distance from the EU's law- and policy-making bodies.

---

[91] W Howarth, 'Aspirations and Realities Under the Water Framework Directive: Proceduralisation, Participation and Practicalities' (2009) 21 *Journal of Environmental Law* 391; B Lange, 'Searching for the Best Available Techniques—Open and Closed Norms in the Implementation of the EU Directive on Integrated Pollution Prevention and Control' (2006) 2 *International Journal of Law in Context* 67; J Scott, 'Flexibility, "Proceduralization" and Environmental Governance in the EU' in J Scott and G de Búrca (eds), *Constitutional Change in the EU: From Uniformity to Flexibility?* (Oxford, Hart Publishing, 2000).

28

Freedom of Expression and Spatial (Imaginations of) Justice

ANTONIA LAYARD*

Geography is too important to be left to geographers.[1]

I. INTRODUCTION

THE CONTRIBUTION TO this volume made by this chapter is to highlight a specific deficit in EU justice: the lack of a spatial understanding of justice in European legal space(s). The chapter focuses on one broadly accepted incident of justice, freedom of expression. I discuss this through both a concern for justice over space (in particular, access to sites to exercise rights of freedom of expression) as well as for the spatiality of freedom of expression itself. I ask how we frame discussions about justice in both material and discursively spatial terms. While my discussion focuses on decisions reached by the European Court of Human Rights (ECtHR), its norms are applied throughout all EU Member States, so that freedom of expression as framed by the Court can be considered as one incident of 'Europe's Justice'.

This chapter also has the purpose of expanding the reach of legal geography. At times, perhaps paradoxically, legal geography loses legal doctrine. Consequently, the presentation of a case study in this chapter, demonstrates how law and doctrine are infused with spatiality. As this chapter illustrates, by analysing the ECtHR case *Raël v Switzerland*,[2] freedom of expression is spatially produced, using multiple spatial imaginaries in discursive legal decision making. In *Raël*, the prohibition of advertising hoardings in an apparently public space was held not to infringe the applicant organisation's right to freedom of speech, as protected by Article 10 of the European Convention on Human Rights (ECHR). The ECtHR held that there was no unlimited freedom of expression on the public billboards in a municipal square even though far more contentious material could be freely distributed by the

---

* I would like to thank all participants of the seminar upon which this work is based, and also the Durham Human Rights Centre seminar, for their thoughtful and insightful comments which led to many improvements in this paper. I am also very grateful to Dimitry Kochenov for his excellent suggestions.
[1] D Harvey, 'On the History and Present Condition of Geography: An Historical Materialist Manifesto' (1984) 36 *Professional Geographer* 1, 7.
[2] *Mouvement Raëlien Suisse v Switzerland* App No 16354/06 [2012] ECHR 1598 (ECtHR (GC), 13 July 2012).

Raëlian Association through the internet. This finding was considered 'singular, if not paradoxical' by the seven dissenting judges,[3] as well as many commentators. However, as this analysis explains, we can understand this apparent paradox if we use the tools of legal geography.

The starting point for legal geography is that law, space and society are mutually constituted and reflexive, an assumption that is well illustrated in *Raël* and the reason for its selection as a case study. In this application, and doctrinal extension, of legal geographical analysis on the co-production of law, space and society, the analysis draws on the work of Henri Lefebvre and Hannah Arendt. While Lefebvre developed an understanding of the produced nature of social space and the need to understand its physical, mental and lived dimensions, Arendt was concerned to bring a lived perspective to understandings of 'the public' including public space and a *vita activa*. Here, drawing on these insights, I demonstrate how the lived experience differs from the more conventional legal approach taken by the ECtHR in *Raël* (where the Court operated discursively through the legal personality of the Raëlian organisation and their ECHR rights). To put it rather reductively, my key contribution in this chapter is to explain how legal geography works from the site up as well as from the text down. It suggests that the legal decision, the space and the social context in which this dispute took place, are all mutually constitutive. All the judgments are spatially inflected, whether expressly (as in the minority dissents) or in an apparently lack of appreciation of spatiality (as in the majority decision, suggesting instead that this is a dispute about the allocation of municipal billboards).

To investigate the spatiality of the understanding of freedom of expression (one incident of justice) in *Raël*, this chapter considers the work that 'space-talk', or an apparent absence of 'space-talk', does in legal decision making. It draws on two concepts developing in legal geography to explore how spatial understandings might be produced. The first is that of 'splices'—a way of understanding combinations of spatial and legal orderings (public space could be, for example, one such splice). The second is that of 'spatial imaginaries'—exploring how imaginations of the space (whether explicitly articulated or not) take form and do legal work. The analysis suggests that understanding the work splices and legal–spatial imaginaries do might help explain a judgment, such as *Raël*, which in conventional legal terms seems contradictory.

Lastly, this chapter suggests that these observations could contribute to a research agenda in EU law, and to European understandings of justice. The production of EU space—both in terms of jurisdiction but also as a lived, everyday, material reality—depends on social, spatial, political, cultural, ethnic and legal co-production. This much seems obvious. What legal geography can add to discussions on European justice is an investigation into how the interactions between discursive and sociospatial production of the space occur. Identifying geo-legal ordering (splices) and supplementing these with an investigation of underpinning legal–spatial imaginaries,

---

[3] *Mouvement Raëlien Suisse v Switzerland* App No 16354/06 [2012] ECHR 1598 (ECtHR (GC), 13 July 2012), Joint Dissenting Opinion of Judges Tulkens, Sajó, Lazarova Trajkovska, Bianku, Power-Forde, Vučinić and Yudkivska, para 9.

operating on individual sites or within EU jurisdictional space as a whole, can help to uncover implicit or explicit legal–spatial understandings of what 'European space' should be like. These ideas have long been explored in terms of EU teleology and purposive interpretations of the treaties; this adds socio-spatial understandings to these well-established politico-legal discussions. Given the potential productivity for both EU and legal geography scholarship, this extends legal–geographic literatures, which have so far predominantly focused on small-scale urban discussions, to engage in cross-engagement between EU studies and legal geography.

II. RAËL V SWITZERLAND

On 7 March 2001, the Swiss Raëlian Movement sought authorisation from the Neuchâtel police administration to conduct a poster campaign to promote Raëlian ideas. The campaign was to last for two weeks that April and would display posters on billboards located on the public highway. The title of the proposed poster, in large yellow characters on a dark blue background, proclaimed 'The Message from Extraterrestrials' (see Figure 28.1). Lower down, in characters of the same size but in bolder type, was the address of the Raëlian Movement's website, together with a telephone number in France. Right at the bottom of the poster was the phrase 'Science at last replaces religion'. The middle of the poster was taken up by pictures of extraterrestrials' faces, a pyramid, a flying saucer and the Earth. According to its constitution, the aim of Mouvement Raëlien Suisse is to make first contacts, and establish good relations, with extraterrestrials. It also has favourable opinions on cloning and 'geniocracy'.[4]

When the Neuchâtel police administration refused authorisation for the Raëlian's poster campaign in 2001, the Swiss Raëlian Movement began legal proceedings. They alleged that their right to freedom of speech contained in Article 10 ECHR had been infringed (as well as their right to a freedom of thought, conscience and religion in Article 9). The Grand Chamber of the European Court of Human Rights determined the case in 2012. It held by nine votes to eight that Article 10 had not been violated, and so consequently there was no need to examine separately the complaint under Article 9 of the Convention.

In a very brief judgment, the majority of judges sitting as the Grand Chamber rejected the Association's claim that there had been an unjustified restriction on its rights to freedom of expression. Finding that the restriction had taken place, and so would need to be justified under Article 10(2), the key question for the Court was whether these restrictions were 'necessary in a democratic society'. They held that the restrictions could be justified given the margin of appreciation doctrine. They held, first, that it was reasonable to argue (as the Swiss Government had done) that this poster campaign referred 'only incidentally to social or political ideas';[5] and that the advertisement had a certain proselytising function which was consequently,

---

[4] *Mouvement Raëlien Suisse v Switzerland* App No 16354/06 [2012] ECHR 1598 (ECtHR (GC), 13 July 2012), para 12.
[5] ibid, para 62.

Figure 28.1: Swiss Raëlian Movement Poster Campaign

according to the majority, closer to commercial speech than to political speech—thus, the margin of appreciation was broader.[6]

Secondly, the majority held that such a restriction was proportionate to the legitimate aim pursued. They found it illogical to look solely at the poster itself since the poster clearly had the aim of attracting people's attention to the website (the address of that site was given in bold type above the slogan 'The Message from

[6] ibid.

Extraterrestrials'). Instead, they held that it would have been disproportionate to ban both the posters and the website so that, consequently, the more proportionate response was to ban the posters. This would ensure the minimum impairment of the Association's rights even though the posters were, aside from the web address, not considered in any way to be of concern.[7] The Association was, the majority held, able to continue to disseminate its ideas through its website, and through other means at its disposal such as the distribution of leaflets in the street or in letter-boxes. Consequently, this was not a restriction on the Association's ideas, merely on the way in which they were disseminated.[8] Advocate Judge Bratza wrote a concurring opinion voting with the majority 'with some hesitation'.[9]

For the seven dissenting judges who wrote the primary dissent, the decision to prohibit the posters but allow the website to continue with far more controversial material, was 'singular, if not paradoxical'.[10] They rejected the arguments made by the majority that limiting the scope of the restriction to displaying the posters in public places was a way of ensuring the minimum impairment of the applicant Association's rights. Nor were they convinced by the majority's reasoning that that this was a proportionate restriction since the applicant Association was able to continue to disseminate its ideas through its website, the distribution of leaflets in the street or in letter-boxes. They did not agree that this was proportionate given that 'the ban is based on the same criticisms as those levelled at the alternative means'.[11]

Further, making an explicitly spatial point, the minority argued that the majority's decision 'enshrines a particular view of advertising in public space, suggesting that this facility benefits from special status'.[12] The minority, in contrast, believed that 'such status should require increased neutrality on the part of the public authorities, with equal access for all individuals and entities that are not expressly prohibited'.[13] They agreed that precautions necessary to combat the dangers and excesses of sects or associations that seriously contravene democratic values need to be taken. However, they could not understand why a lawful association, with a website that has not been prohibited, should be prevented from promoting its ideas through posters that are not unlawful in themselves. In a separate dissent by three judges, there was more concern about the scope of the doctrine of the margin of appreciation, emphasising the fungible nature of this concept, with the judges stating that it was 'particularly regrettable to see the protection of freedom of expression being diminished in respect of the world view of a minority'.[14] Lastly, in a further separate dissent, Judge Pinto de Alburquerque, agreed with many of the criticisms of the minority as well as lamenting the lack of a 'public forum' in ECHR jurisprudence in which all opinions could be expressed.[15]

---

[7] ibid, para 75.
[8] ibid.
[9] ibid, Concurring Opinion of Judge Bratza, para 1.
[10] ibid, Joint Dissenting Opinion of Judge Tulkens et al, para 9.
[11] ibid, para 9.
[12] ibid, para 11.
[13] ibid.
[14] ibid, Joint Dissenting Opinion of Judges Sajó, Lazarova Trajkovska and Vučinić, para 1.
[15] ibid, Dissenting Opinion of Judge Pinto de Albuquerque, 47.

III. TOWARDS A SPATIAL UNDERSTANDING OF *RAËL*

This, then, was the doctrinal decision that was reached in *Raël*. The ECHR rights of the Association to put up posters on regulated facilities (billboards) were not infringed because this public space was not made available to them. The decision whether to make these billboards available was one to be made by the authorities, in line with their margin of appreciation, and the ban was not disproportionate as other means of dissemination were still available. The space was altered (no posters) through legal (discursive) control. If, however, we also want to understand the spatial framework for freedom of expression, and how justice is spatially produced, we need to understand how legal practice contributes to the construction of spaces (and how spatial understandings contribute to the production of legal principles as here in *Raël*).

Legal geography's emphasis on the production of spaces is underpinned by the work of Henri Lefebvre. His proposition that space is socially produced is now so widely accepted that it 'almost seems an empty formula'.[16] It seems self-evident to modern scholars that '(social) space is a (social) product' and that space is not a neutral background on which society is projected; but that space is 'fundamentally bound up with social reality'.[17] It follows that space 'in itself' can never serve as an epistemological starting position. Space does not exist 'in itself'; it is produced.[18] Legal geographers then take this understanding one step further: (legal) space is a (legal) product. Yet, as the law and society movement has taught us, there can be no law that is not also *in* society—(socio-legal) space then, is a (socio-legal) product. Public spaces such as the billboards or highways in *Raël* are produced; they are not neutral backdrops to the litigation.

This inter-relatedness is the starting point for a legal–spatial investigation of justice, in this case freedom of expression. It reflects the central premise of legal geography: that legality and space are co-constituted, so that 'law is everywhere in space' and 'space is everywhere in law'.[19] Legal and spatial understandings encode sites. We need, say legal geographers, to understand that decisions are not aspatial, occurring solely in the abstract. The influence of Marxist and critical thought is evident in this critique of abstraction even without any references to fetishism or illusion. Soja's formulation of spatial justice makes this heritage particularly clear. He calls for a 'triple dialectic', to acknowledge that 'there are three fundamental or ontological qualities of human existence from which all knowledge follows: the social/societal, the temporal/historical, and the spatial/geographical'.[20] Until now, says Soja, the first two have been privileged.[21] Lefebvre also used a triple dialectic, or a spatial triad emphasizing phenomenological understandings of spaces at a given moment in time: 'spatial practice', 'representations of space', and 'spaces of

---

[16] C Schmid, 'Henri Lefebvre's Theory of the Production of Space: Towards a Three Dimensional Dialectic' in K Goonewardena et al (eds), *Space, Difference, Everyday Life: Reading Henri Lefebvre* (New York, NY, Routledge, 2008) eds.
[17] ibid.
[18] ibid.
[19] I Stramignoni, (2004) 'Francesco's Devilish Venus: Notations on the Matter of Legal Space' (2004) 41 *California Western Law Review* 162, 181.
[20] E Soja, *Seeking Spatial Justice* (Minneapolis, MN, University of Minnesota Press, 2010) 70.
[21] ibid.

representation'. He drew together the dialectics Soja describes by understanding space and time as social products, as socially produced, so that both space and time are 'not only relational but fundamentally historical'.[22]

These inter-relationships resonate with legal geographers who see history and geography, or the historicities and spatialities of the social, fused in the irreducible dynamics of place-as-process.[23] Understanding this inter-relation matters for legal geographers: spatial justice should not be seen as social justice with space as 'add-and-stir', insists Philippopoulos-Mihalopoulos:

> Space is not just another parameter for law, a background against which law takes place, or a process that the law needs to take into consideration. Space is intertwined with normative production in ways that law often fails to acknowledge[24]

Rather than seeking to escape this intertwining then, the task is to identify the modes of analysis that can uncouple time, place and legality. One such tool is to recognise the splicing of legal and spatial orderings together when they occur; another is to uncover the legal–spatial imaginaries, which produce social spaces.

This brings us then to the apparent contradiction at the heart of *Raël*. How could the ECtHR decide that highly contentious material could be disseminated through the internet, while innocuous posters, objectionable only on the basis that they included the website address, were banned from public billboards? This seems almost paradoxical to the dissenting judges;[25] and yet in Lefebvrian thought, this can be understood as more than discourse—it is an example of a lived contradiction (the continuing vitality of this contradiction turns on an understanding of the German word *aufheben* in dialectical reasoning, in contrast to the English *sublate*).[26]

Without engaging too deeply in the theoretical reasoning, then, it is possible to see that there are different geo-legal understandings of the public space here, including the billboards, the internet, the highway and the public forum, and that these can exist concurrently. With power, however, and given the judicial ability of a majority verdict to impose their understanding of the space on others, comes an ability to produce space at any given moment in time. If we accept then that public space is geo-legally-socially produced, the next questions are 'how?' and 'what are the techniques that are being used?' This analysis considers two techniques in turn: splices and legal imaginations.

A. Splices

To understand splices, let us begin with a legal geographic approach of starting with the site, rather than the text. Where is this dispute located? What do we see?

---

[22] ibid, 29.
[23] D Delaney, 'Running with the Land: Legal–Historical Imagination and the Spaces of Modernity' (2001) 27 *Journal of Historical Geography* 493.
[24] A Philippopoulos-Mihalopoulos, 'Spatial Justice: Law and the Geography of Withdrawal' (2010) 6 *International Journal of Law in Context* 201.
[25] *Mouvement Raëlien Suisse v Switzerland* App No 16354/06 [2012] ECHR 1598 (ECtHR (GC), 13 July 2012), Joint Dissenting Opinion of Judge Tulkens et al, para 9.
[26] Schmid, 'Henri Lefebvre's Theory', n 16 above, 32.

One of the distinctive features of legal geography is its emphasis on the ocular.[27] This contrasts with doctrinal legal analysis but is in line with arts and humanities as well as sociological approaches. It considers how different legal discourses see the physical landscape, and how legal provisions and practices are seen from a spatial perspective. The site here is not a neutral empty space upon which law is exercised; it is not a backdrop, but is socio-legally and spatially co-constructed. One way to investigate this co-construction is to identify instances or moments where legally informed decisions and actions take place in 'splices', encodings that combine spatial and legal meanings. Splices are a concept first developed in legal geography by Blomley, who gave the example of a refugee, a splice that implies both a legal status and a spatial dislocation.[28]

Another splice, coupling legal and spatial meanings, is public space. A private home would not feel public, nor would it legally be understood as such. It would be private property, and in many senses a private space (though legal regulations on domestic violence, for example, still apply). Conversely, a shopping centre might feel public to those entering in there, but it can be the private property of its owners who could prohibit any protestors from using this site (as they did in *Appleby v UK*).[29] This would not, in property law terms, be public space. To identify a site as a 'public space' splice, we would have to identify a place that is legally protected as such, which also carries particular spatial and social characteristics. The fact that this legal designation is often missing (as Judge Alburquerque noted in his dissent, there is no equivalent to the North American doctrine of 'public forum' in ECHR jurisprudence),[30] does not nullify the conceptual point—rather it illustrates how vague and poorly understood the 'public space' splice is. Public highways are perhaps the best defined public spaces in this legal sense.

The key point here is that the physical quality of the site alone would not have a bearing on whether or not this was public space (as in *Appleby*). It needs legal meaning (designation) as well. Conversely, public ownership (however defined) is not enough. The European Court of Human Rights at Allée des Droits de l'Homme in Strasbourg, is not privately owned yet it is clearly not a public space open to all, throughout, at all times. And legal categorisation is also not enough. Labelling a hidden corridor as legal public space, would also not *by itself* make the space feel 'public' without clear identification and hospitable access. The use of 'privately owned public spaces' in New York has been highly problematic in practice for this very reason.[31] For a splice both spatial characteristics of a site and legal designation, spatial and legal encodings, are required.

---

[27] I Braverman, 'Hidden in Plain View: Legal Geography From a Visual Perspective' (2011) 7 *Law, Culture and the Humanities* 173.

[28] N Blomley, 'From "What" to "So What?": Law and Geography in Retrospect' in J Holder and C Harrison, *Law and Geography* (Oxford, Oxford University Press, 2003).

[29] *Appleby and Others v the United Kingdom* App No 44306/98 [2003] ECHR 222, [2003] 37 EHRR 783 (ECtHR, 6 May 2003).

[30] *Mouvement Raëlien Suisse v Switzerland* App No 16354/06 [2012] ECHR 1598 (ECtHR (GC), 13 July 2012), Dissenting Opinion of Judge Pinto de Albuquerque, 47ff.

[31] H Grabar, 'A Matchmaker for New York's Privately Owned Public Spaces' *Atlantic Monthly* (23 October 2012).

This combination of both spatial and legal understandings in splices is a key part of the practice of legal geography. As with Arendt's work, the focus on action is central. Scholars are concerned to understand how the spatial and the legal are braided together, moving on from 'the domain of meaning or dematerialised discourse' to focus 'on the pragmatics of world-making' (in Delaney's terminology, the making of the 'nomosphere').[32] Arendt would perhaps have been surprised to hear herself interpreted through legal geography. Yet as Michael Ignatieff paraphrased her views: 'It is citizenship—real actual belonging in political community—not abstract belonging to the human species—which will protect the human rights of all'.[33] Arendt understood very well that citizenship is a lived, geo-legal splice. You must be a citizen of *somewhere* that has been legally defined as sufficient, not a citizen of 'the world' or a community of interest.

Identifying a splice recognises the coming together of legal and spatial practices. As Blomley suggests,

> the world is not given to us, but actively made through orderings which offer powerful 'maps' of the social world, classifying, coding and categorising. In so doing a particular reality is created ... Similarly, space offers a powerful ordering framework. The boundary, which delineates and defines ... is a vital modality of ordering. Space comes with particular and deeply encoded classifications of encoded behaviour.[34]

These spatial and legal orderings are incredibly powerful when they are combined, (literally) making a person a citizen or a refugee or categorizing a site as private property or a public space (however this is defined). Where spaces are encoded with multiple, contested meanings how do we articulate these meanings? One suggestion is that we try to identify the legal–spatial imaginaries that are expressly or impliedly articulated, to understand the work that they are doing in discursively and materially producing the space.

B. Legal–Spatial Imaginaries

Understanding that there are splices, geo-legal codings, does not always explain when the criteria are met. When is a site a public space and when not? What would the practical (social and spatial) consequences of such a designation be and who makes it? One way of exploring these processes is through the identification of 'spatial imaginaries', imaginations of how a place is and should be, in both discursive and material terms. When employed in legal settings, these spatial imaginaries can have significant legal effect, they are then legal–spatial imaginaries.

The concept of 'spatial imaginaries' is often drawn from studies in 'imaginative geographies', which shape our sense of places and people around the world. It was Said in his writing of *Orientalism* in 1978 who suggested most emphatically

---

[32] D Delaney, *The Spatial, the Legal and the Pragmatics of World-Making: Nomospheric Investigations* (London, Routledge, 2010) 23.
[33] M Ignatieff, 'Arendt's Example', Hannah Arendt Prize Ceremony Bremen (28 November 2003) 7.
[34] N Blomley, 'From "What" to "So What?": Law and Geography in Retrospect' in J Holder and C Harrison, *Law and Geography* (Oxford, Oxford University Press, 2003) 29.

that spatial representations do imaginative work; and that these imaginative geographies are the precursors to the seizure and the making, and re-making, of land. He identified imaginative geographies as being mapped out on the basis of a demarcation of familiar space that is 'ours' from one that is 'theirs' (Orientalism is distinct from 'Occidentalism', a space that is not enclosed in this way but acts as a counterweight).[35] Said focused on the work done by cultural practices privileging discourse and language as prime determinants of social reality and production of knowledge.[36] There are important overlaps, though also important differences, with Anderson's argument that nations are produced as imagined communities.[37] Both have contributed significantly to an understanding of the power of imagination in the production of space.

Further, it is clear that these imaginations are not only spatial. Harvey, for example, has built on Wright Mills' seminal work on sociological imagination to stress the ways in which individuals could 'recognize the role of place and space in [their] own biography'.[38] There is an understanding of how social processes, including imagination, create spatial forms. Historical imaginations clearly have powerful effects. Harvey has long argued that imagination and relationality apply to both time and space. Drawing on Leibniz, he argues that 'there is no such thing as space or time outside the processes that define them'[39] and that it if we ask what Tiananmen Square or 'Ground Zero' *mean*, then we have to think in relational terms.

> An event or a thing at a point in space cannot be understood by appeal to what exists only at that point. It depends upon everything else going on around it ... A wide variety of disparate influences swirling over space in the past, present and future concentrate and congeal at a certain point ... to define the nature of that point. Identity, in this argument means something quite different from the sense we have of it in absolute space [fixed, as a grid or frame of reference in which something happens].[40]

Places are historically, spatially and socially situated and historically, spatially and socially imagined.

This focus on imagination is significant in legal geography given its focus on reflexivity: assuming that legal practices produce the space and that each site also affects the use of legal practices. Places, such as the billboards on which the Raëlians are not permitted to exhibit their posters, are not natural or pre-given. As Allen et al write, places are 'constituted out of spatialized social relations—and narratives about them' so that

> there are always multiple ways of seeing a place [places] ... only exist in relation to particular criteria. They are not 'out there' waiting to be discovered; they are our (and others') construction.[41]

---

[35] E Said, *Orientalism* (London, Penguin, 2003) 50.
[36] ibid.
[37] B Anderson, *Imagined Communities* (London, Verso, 2003).
[38] D Harvey, *Social Justice and the City* (Athens, GA, University of Georgia Press, 2009) 24.
[39] D Harvey, 'Space As a Keyword' in N Castree and D Gregory, *David Harvey: A Critical Reader* (Oxford, Wiley Blackwell, 2006) 274.
[40] ibid.
[41] J Allen, D Massey and A Cochrane, *Rethinking the Region* (London, Routledge, 1998) 1–2.

Places in this view are dynamic, not static, relational rather than contained. Yet they are legally produced as well as producing legal practices. The spatial imagination of the site in *Raël* has underpinned a legal authority of the ECtHR, creating a precedent that prioritises decision making by national or local authorities, on what might constitute freedom of expression in each site.

This relationship between imagination and its effect on practice is significant. One of the critiques of *Orientalism*, for example, has been that we are caught in a puzzle that revolves around the relationship between representation and its 'real' object.[42] On the one hand there is

> no relationship between representations and the real (these representations are fabrications), but on the other hand, we are told that these representations work to control and dominate their objects (they are 'made to absorb everything').[43]

This puzzle is partially illuminated in legal geography because there are very evident relationships between the representations and 'the real'. If places are imagined to be one way rather than another, there are powerful legal tools, including mapping and legal ordering, which can restrict any apparent multiplicity. A place can be designated as one person's property or a highway, with such legal determinations having tremendous force. These are more than representations, these decisions have legal effect, albeit effects that are socially and culturally mediated. If the sites in dispute are public spaces, where different groups contest how to use the property and opinions differ, the spatial imagination(s) of one judge or a majority of judges can have powerful effects. Once recognised, this also raises important questions about who possesses the powers of imagination and how these are materially and discursively deployed.

One of the most striking features of *Raël* is that, for a discussion with such significant spatial effects, imposing major restrictions on organisations and associations who wish to display their posters in apparently public spaces, there is so little explicit spatial discussion. The judgment does not, for instance, consider where these billboards are located, on which highway or public square. Nevertheless, this absence of spatial descriptors is also doing work and the legal–spatial imaginaries are still evident.

The majority focus solely on the billboards, these 'regulated and supervised' facilities for the dissemination of information (managed by a private company). They phrase the application as being one of having public space made available to the Association for the dissemination of their ideas. In their view 'individuals do not have an unconditional or unlimited right to the extended use of public space'.[44] The question is whether or not the public space should be made available.[45] They do not talk of 'land' at all and negate the posters' spatial location. The record of the Court has an aspatial quality about it—there are no maps for example illustrating where in Neuchatel the billboards are located, on which street, which square. Conversely, the

---

[42] R Young, *White Mythologies: Writing History and the West* (London, Routledge, 2004).
[43] A Closs Stephens, 'Beyond Imaginative Geographies? Critique, Co-optation, and Imagination in the Aftermath of the War on Terror' (2011) 29 *Environment and Planning D: Society and Space* 254, 261.
[44] *Mouvement Raëlien Suisse v Switzerland* App No 16354/06 [2012] ECHR 1598 (ECtHR (GC), 13 July 2012), para 58.
[45] ibid, para 57.

framing of the dispute by the majority as a bureaucratic question about the allocation of public resources, rather than as a dispute about how freedom of expression might be facilitated in an urban space, is itself a use of a spatial imaginary. It is the lack of 'space-talk' that is doing work here.

This contrasts with the view of the seven dissenting judges who do set out some understanding of what public space should look and feel like; they do not ignore their imaginations. In particular, they are concerned by the notion of allocation, seeing the billboards instead as a public space that 'should require increased neutrality on the part of the public authorities, with equal access for all individuals and entities that are not expressly prohibited'.[46] In a further dissenting judgment by three of the minority, they recognise that '[t]he administration of such public space is, of course, subject to time, place and manner restrictions'[47] and that handing over discretion to the Neuchâtel Police Administration localises these processes. There are norms of neutrality that should govern these spaces, albeit ones that are subject to localised processes.

It is in Judge Pinto de Albuquerque's juxtaposition of the *Women on Waves* case[48] that perhaps best illustrates the legal work done by a spatial imagination. For while the majority distinguish *Raël* from the 'open and public space' of the territorial seas, Pinto de Albuquerque sees a direct comparison: 'The freedom of expression that *Women on Waves* guaranteed in the open maritime space of a State should also be acknowledged in its public space on land. The instant case provided an occasion to affirm that principle explicitly'.[49] Drawing an explicit analogy between open maritime space and public space on land, he is making a material and a discursive comparison suggesting that public space on land *should* be imagined as similar to the open sea with the consequence that this would have for freedom of expression. This was not an extension, however, that the majority of judges felt able to accept.

What then of the internet? To the minority it is 'paradoxical' that the posters are prohibited but the website continues. As they pithily note, '[d]anger, if it exists, does not disappear with borders, wherever they may be'.[50] The majority gives no explanation of why the website should continue, other than suggesting that it 'might [be] disproportionate to ban [it]'.[51] Similarly, Judge Bratza's judgment finds 'nothing contradictory in a decision to refuse permission for public facilities to be used for the purposes of advertising a website, while at the same time taking no steps to close down or restrict access to the website'.[52]

Yet there is here an explanation, which lies in how the internet is legally and spatially imagined and how this contrasts with the billboards. For while it is not clearly articulated, there is a sense in the judgment that the internet is not governable, certainly not by the Neuchâtel Police Administration. The web is not a resource to

---

[46] ibid, Joint Dissenting Opinion of Judge Tulkens et al, para 11.
[47] ibid, Joint Dissenting Opinion of Judges Sajó, Lazarova Trajkovska and Vučinić, para 2.2.
[48] *Women On Waves and Others v Portugal* App No 31276/05 (ECtHR, 3 February 2009).
[49] *Mouvement Raëlien Suisse v Switzerland* App No 16354/06 [2012] ECHR 1598 (ECtHR (GC), 13 July 2012), Dissenting Opinion of Judge Pinto de Albuquerque, 51.
[50] ibid, Joint Dissenting Opinion of Judge Tulkens et al, para 7.
[51] ibid, para 75.
[52] ibid, Concurring Opinion of Judge Bratza, para 5.

be allocated. It is in some sense 'public and open by its very nature', like the sea in *Women on Waves*, according to the majority.[53] And yet the Swiss Government certainly had the powers to ban the website or the Association, there is nothing inherently unmanageable about the internet.

Similarly, there is no explanation of why the distribution of leaflets in the street or in letter-boxes might continue, except for the implication (and it is no more than this given the brevity of the judgment) that neither streets nor letter-boxes are under the management of the authorities. They are certainly governable, though again not through permissions given by the Neuchâtel Police administration as with the billboards. They are not the resource of the local administration. There is another (different) imaginary of public space on the street.

In short then, different legal–spatial imaginations of the billboards, streets and the internet are threaded through *Raël*. They are not shared. In a sense these framings reflect something of Arendt's view on human rights—that they are concerned less with negative liberties than facilitating appearance and flourishing. We need physical public space since: 'deprived of it means to be deprived of reality, which humanly and politically speaking, is the same as appearance'.[54] An Arendtian critique of *Raël* also has a spatial implication, since the Association (and others like them denied the requisite bureaucratic authorisation) can appear or perform only in leaflets or on the internet and not in a lived public space. That is a significant restriction on the *vita activa*.

C. Spatial Imaginations of a European Public Sphere

A spatial understanding of *Raël* asks how public space is understood in legal, social and spatial terms. Yet we are not just concerned with the site itself here, for this too needs to be set into its broader context. Spatial imaginaries are also at work within European legal space, including an imaginary of the public sphere, which may or may not be spatialised, which is pervasive in European thought and finds expression even in the ECtHR. The EU is a physical expression of a political commitment but also to a culture, shared historical narratives, race, ethnicity, religion and social practices. And, increasingly, the EU is also understood explicitly in geo-legal terms, as Azoulai write, as 'a new common space, a space of distribution and common values'.[55]

What then are these common values and how do spatial–legal imaginations engage with them. One such imaginary at work here, particularly in those European countries where there is an understanding of a distinct public sphere, is often framed in terms of a broad acceptance of Habermas' narrative on the evolution of a distinction between the apparatuses of the state and public arenas of citizen discourse and association on the other. He describes the emergence of a 'public sphere', moving some societies (notably England, France and Germany) on from representative

---

[53] ibid, para 58.
[54] H Arendt, *The Human Condition* (Chicago, IL, University of Chicago Press, 1999) 199.
[55] L Azoulai, 'A Comment on the *Ruiz Zambrano* Judgment: A Genuine European Integration' *EUDO Citizenship Observatory* (2011), www.eudo-citizenship.eu/search-results/457-a-comment-on-the-ruiz-zambrano-judgment-a-genuine-european-integration.

publicity. While subsequent analysts have critiqued the idea of an ideal-type, understanding the public sphere 'as involving a field of discursive connections',[56] the ECHR can be understood as providing a framework for consensus building processes instigated through rational deliberation and debate in specified (ideal) conditions.

The influence of this notion of idealised spaces for discussion should not be underestimated. For example, it permeates the minority joint dissent in *Raël*, which identifies the billboards as 'public space that is accessible to all'.[57] In such places, they hold, all speakers have an equal right of use; the government must not exercise censorship and it should apply otherwise permissible restrictions in a way that respects neutrality. 'In democratic Europe' they write,

> in the context of using publicly owned frequencies for the communication of ideas, it is expected (especially where the State controls broadcasting as a monopoly) that the management of the public service will be fair and impartial, allowing pluralism (ie respecting neutrality), precisely because general public access is not possible.[58]

The Habermasian echoes are unmistakable.

This is not surprising. Within a European legal space, in a continent with long histories of both association and repression, we might expect to see a 'European' understanding of how and where freedom of expression, a cornerstone of public dialogue and deliberation, might take place. Neutrality here will inevitably be restricted, for as Neyer writes in this volume, '[t]he public sphere is not a space free of power relations (a *herrschaftsfreier Raum*) but is subject to a great number of power asymmetries that create unequal access to audiences'.[59]

Specifically, for those with a spatial bent, a focus on ideal-types as a normative objective has led to further frustration. Where should this public sphere be grounded in the everyday if citizens are not content to become primarily consumers of goods, services, political administration and spectacle? If the public sphere is still to capture ways and means of mediating between the private interests of everyday life in civil society and the realm of state power, where is this to take place?

A spatial reading of *Raël* contributes to this debate. For by insisting that the billboards are state resources to be allocated, the majority are reducing this space (between the state and the private) significantly. Public space is conceived of here as billboards, rather than the square or the streets that they stand on. By imagining the billboards as the public space under contestation here, it shrinks in both discursive and material terms. In contrast, in his suggestion that 'public space on land' is akin to the 'wide open seas', Judge Pinto de Alburquerque is extending this space (he would legally, discursively, provide for these material spaces).[60]

---

[56] C Calhoun, 'Introduction: Habermas and the Public Sphere' in C Calhoun (ed), *Habermas and the Public Sphere* (Cambridge, MA, MIT Press, 1993) ed.
[57] *Mouvement Raëlien Suisse v Switzerland* App No 16354/06 [2012] ECHR 1598 (ECtHR (GC), 13 July 2012), Joint Dissenting Opinion of Judges Sajó, Lazarova Trajkovska and Vučinić, para 2.1.
[58] ibid.
[59] J Neyer, 'Justice and the Right to Justification: Conceptual Reflections' in this volume, 211, at 219.
[60] *Mouvement Raëlien Suisse v Switzerland* App No 16354/06 [2012] ECHR 1598 (ECtHR (GC), 13 July 2012), Dissenting Opinion of Judge Pinto de Albuquerque, 51.

While in *Structural Transformation*,[61] Habermas identified some of the spaces—the salons, the coffee houses—that facilitated critical–rational public discussions, this is a historical analysis: his discussions of the media and the culture industries are more placeless. As Benhabib has suggested, in this narrative, public space is 'viewed democratically as the creation of procedures whereby those affected by general social norms and collective political decisions can have a say in their formulation, stipulation and adoption'.[62] Such a rather aspatial conception of public space as primarily procedural can also be seen in the majority judgment in *Raël*, which emphasises the margin of appreciation and proportionality.

Consequently for those concerned with spatial justice, it is Arendt who provides a more spatially informed understanding on justice or, to use one of her phrases, 'public happiness'.[63] Rather than arguing for a single grand theory of justice, Arendt reflected on the conditions or requirements for politics, and in particular the joy of participating. For her:

> public freedom consisted in having a share in public business, and that the activities connected with this business by no means constituted a burden but gave those who discharged them in public a feeling of happiness they could acquire nowhere else.[64]

Today, the concern is less a rejection of ideal-types and assertions and identifications of counter-public as the concern that spaces in which the procedures of democracy can physically be exercised (posters displayed, occupation-style protests held) are continually being reduced as particularly urban spaces are managed for aesthetics and commercial gain.

It is this spatial quality of Arendt's work that points up the noted absenceof space in Habermas' parallel investigation of modernity. According to Howell, Arendt 'may not, unlike Habermas'

> have much to say about the way that geographical changes associated with modernization help bring the public sphere into being, but by noting the importance of space to the continuation of the public sphere under conditions of modernity she is able to bring geographical considerations into somewhat sharper focus.[65]

These spatial understandings are in part phenomenological, borne out of a belief that justice is lived, experienced and practised as well as located in text.

Significantly, for those concerned with spatial justice, Arendt's understandings of public freedom or public happiness are more than metaphorical. She praises the *philosophes* of the French Revolution for understanding that public freedom is experienced, lived, noting that they 'under the rule of enlightened absolutism in the eighteenth century'. They understood, said Arendt, that

> freedom for them could only exist in public; it was a tangible, worldly reality, something created by men to be enjoyed by men rather than a gift or capacity, it was the manmade

---

[61] J Habermas, *Structural Transformations of the Public Sphere* (Cambridge, Polity Press, 1992).
[62] S Benhabib, 'Models of Public Space: Hannah Arendt, the Liberal Tradition and Jürgen Habermas' in C Calhoun (ed), *Habermas and the Public Sphere* (Cambridge, MA, MIT Press, 1993) 87.
[63] H Arendt, *On Revolution* (London, Penguin Books, 1990) 110.
[64] ibid.
[65] P Howell, 'Public Space and the Public Sphere: Political Theory and the Historical Geography of Modernity' (1993) 11 *Environment and Planning D: Society and Space* 303, 315.

public space or market-place which antiquity had known as the area where freedom appears and becomes visible to all.[66]

Certainly in philosophy, the spatiality of these questions receive less attention, with Arendt one of the few thinkers who approaches these interactions phenomenologically, thinking explicitly about the space (be it for agonism or association). She was famously reverential of the Greek *Agora* and Roman *Forum*, appearing untroubled by the restrictions on women or slaves from appearing, and perhaps debating public happiness, in this space. Her proposed, and idealised, space for debating 'public happiness' can certainly be critiqued. Nevertheless, Arendt's thinking remains instructive here because she never gave up on the idea that activities aimed at achieving a more just society (however defined) were lived and inescapably spatial.[67] While public space is a splice, a subject of legal and spatial meaning, it is also active and performed, processual and dynamic. To understand legal formulations of public space and where and how freedom of expression is to be permissible, it is important to recognise the many ways in which public spaces are produced.

Yet as lawyers and activists know well, while the idea of a public sphere has become broadly accepted, key disagreements still arise over how it can be operationalised by those outside the central fora of governance or with dissenting views. Where, in other words, is there public space to exercise freedom of expression? Here national authorities have differed. In Germany, for example, the *Bundesverfassungsgericht* has rejected arguments that protestors could be stopped from distributing leaflets in an airport, holding that there is a right to association in those places which are open to the public at large ('wo ein allgemeiner öffentlicher Verkehr eröffnet ist').[68] In England, meanwhile, there is no such understanding of public space. Student occupations in universities and Occupy demonstrators on public highways have been routinely evicted from corporate private or apparently public property (*School of Oriental & African Studies v Persons Unknown*[69] and *Samede v UK*).[70] English courts have relied on *Appleby v UK*, which only suggested that there might be a positive obligation to provide space for freedom of expression in the case of a 'corporate town' where there was no public property[71] (even if this is, as *Raël* demonstrates, and as Occupy protestors found out in London, also highly regulated). As activists know and increasingly lament, while a public sphere is broadly accepted and welcomed, such a public arena of citizen discourse and association is itself legally and spatially constructed. This finding from legal geography is broadly applicable throughout legal practices. Its rather prosaic implication, however, is that freedom of expression must take place somewhere, yet all too often the response is 'not here'.

---

[66] Arendt, *On Revolution*, n 63 above, 133.
[67] Howell, 'Public Space and the Public Sphere', n 65 above; D Mitchell, 'The End of Public Space? People's Park, Definitions of the Public, and Democracy' (1995) 85 *Annals of the Association of American Geographers* 108.
[68] BVerfG 1 BvR 699/06 (22 February 2011).
[69] *School of Oriental and African Studies v Persons Unknown* [2010] 49 EG 78 (EWHC, 25 November 2010).
[70] *City of London v Samede and Others* [2012] EWCA Civ 160 (22 February 2012).
[71] *Appleby and Others v the United Kingdom* App No 44306/98 [2003] ECHR 222, [2003] 37 EHRR 783 (ECtHR, 6 May 2003), para 47.

When we think what spatial form freedom of expression should take, if it is to be a lived activity, part of Arendt's *vita activa*, we can then conjure up different imaginations: public space might be imagined as open (like the seas in *Women on Waves*), as a resource to be allocated (like the billboards, according to the majority), as a resource where neutrality should be emphasised (the jointly dissenting minority) or a public forum, where positive steps should be taken to facilitate free speech (Judge Pinto de Alburquerque). Public space is in many ways an 'ideal-type' and as Habermas has noted, it is 'tempting to idealize the bourgeois public sphere in a manner going way beyond any methodologically legitimate idealization of the sort involved in ideal-typical conceptualization'.[72]

Yet even if we reject these ideal types, these discussions here, of how to spatialise justice, the public sphere or public space are taking place in Europe, which has its own legal–spatial imaginaries. The EU, in particular, may be understood as a legal–spatial imaginary. This raises the question (and a future research agenda): how is EU law spatialised? Can a spatial approach improve our understanding of apparent conflicts both in respect of the apparently paradoxical outcome in *Raël* and in EU law more broadly? For instance, in considering what are 'purely internal' disputes,[73] and what the changing understanding of what 'internal EU space' means (legally, spatially, socially) it is helpful to understand that 'the internal' is itself a splice. It is a geo-positioned area that carries (shifting) spatial and legal meanings.

While EU doctrinal analysis focuses on the two legal orders in the same territory (from the text down), legal geography correlates this from the ground up. It suggests that there are many different splices here: the EU, the internal, the Member State. Each has legal and spatial meaning; spatially they are not quietly co-existing against a neutral geographical backdrop. These EU spaces (and splices) are socially, spatially and legally produced and when, as Azoulai suggests, we are seeing the emergence of 'a new common space' (itself a socio-spatial imaginary with legal implications). These are tectonic shifts in the borders between legal orders,[74] and between splices. And while these 'sites' may be on a different scale, they can be analysed using these spatial, legal geographical, techniques.

IV. CONCLUSION

This chapter has suggested that part of the deficit in our thinking about European justice is spatial. As Soja argues, 'the "spatiality" of justice ... is an integral and formative component of justice itself'.[75] So how do we do this? How do we extract and analyse the spatial understandings in discussions on justice? This analysis has

---

[72] J Habermas, 'Further Reflections on the Public Sphere' in C Calhoun (ed), *Habermas and the Public Sphere* (Cambridge, MA, MIT Press, 1993) 442.

[73] N Nic Shuibhne, 'Free Movement of Persons and the *Wholly Internal* Rule: Time to Move On?' (2002) 39 *Common Market Law Review* 731.

[74] D Kochenov, 'A Real European Citizenship: A New Jurisdiction Test: A Novel Chapter in the Development of the Union in Europe' (2011) 18 *Columbia Journal of European Law* 54.

[75] E Soja, *Seeking Spatial Justice* (Minneapolis, MN, University of Minnesota Press, 2010) 1.

undertaken a legal geographical reading of a case, building on an understanding of splices and legal–spatial imaginations, to think about 'justice in space' to use Pirie's phrase.[76] It has identified two legal–spatial modes of analysis, splices and legal–spatial imaginaries, which are fruitful here. This is only a beginning, there will be many other (better) ways to undertake this task.

Engaging with this project, this analysis has found that the most striking feature in *Raël* is the lack of explicit 'space-talk', the focus on allocation of public resources, reducing the discussion to one of public facilities rather than a vibrant European city centre. This is despite its being a decision with profound spatial effects. It is the ubiquity of this spatial absence that makes Arendt's work so refreshing here, despite its critiques. She resuscitates the idea of a public space, akin to the *polis*,

> permeated by a fiercely agonal spirit, where everybody had constantly to distinguish himself from all the others ... [where the] public realm was reserved for individuality; it was the only place where men could show who they really and inexchangeably were. It was for the sake of this chance, and out of love for a body politic that made it possible to them all, that each was more or less willing to share in the burden of jurisdiction, defense, and administration of public affairs.[77]

This contrasts markedly with the focus on the administration of billboards, contracted out to a private company. Here, there is little space for a *vita activa* Arendt advocated.

It may be of course that we prefer European cities devoid of contentious public debates, that Arendt's ideas of debating public happiness are antiquated or patriarchal. This is not to suggest that the decision in *Raël* is normatively or legally wrong. But by confining the debate solely to doctrinal analysis we are ignoring social–spatial questions, sidelining them by framing the dispute as being about the allocation of billboards. Who and what are our European cities for? Do we have public spaces in which to engage in rational–critical debates in the public sphere? How would a just European city look? Arendt at least propelled her imaginary to the fore, just as the minority in *Raël* did.

The suggestion here is that in debates about justice, it is time to redress the spatial deficit and debate social, spatial and legal imaginaries of how freedom of expression might look, sound and feel. Otherwise, the imaginations of a few judges, hidden in technical, bureaucratic language concerning administrative allocation, will continue to prevail. These (almost non-spatial) imaginations are incredibly powerful, because they have legal force. These imaginations produce (to borrow from Gregory) 'the effects that [they] name'.[78] Addressing the spatial deficit can give us new techniques and practices in which to engage with European justice.

---

[76] GH Pirie, 'On Spatial Justice' (1983) 15 *Environment and Planning A* 465, 469.
[77] Arendt, *On Revolution*, n 63 above, 41.
[78] L Bialasiewicz et al, 'Performing Security: The Imaginative Geographies of Current US Strategy' (2007) 26 *Political Geography* 405.

29
The Just World

DIMITRY KOCHENOV[*]

'You will not certainly die', the serpent said to the woman.[1]

I. INTRODUCTION

THE MAIN CLAIM of this chapter is basic. Justice is not merely manmade: it is also an inherent innate component of being human, some aspects of which can be traced further back into the animal world. The innumerable theories of justice we are dealing with—no matter how seemingly convincing, accepted, or extravagant—not infrequently suffer from one important common flaw, which stands to be corrected. This flaw consists in failing to incorporate a flood of empirical research results dealing with human nature into our justice theorising. When speaking about justice seriously, the link between justice and human nature emerging from evolutionary archeology, biology, psychology, primatology and an array of other disciplines cannot be ignored or interpreted away.

In advancing this straightforward claim, the chapter is not so much concerned with the particular European experience. Yet, a broader view of justice proposed here will definitely help to contextualise other contributions in this edited work. To deliver on the promise of taking human nature seriously, the core of this chapter builds on the presentation of the theoretical and empirical research on justice from a number of non-legal disciplines, tracing the origins of justice to human nature.

The core of the analysis then revolves around two concepts. *The first one* is the Just World—a subconscious implicit belief that the world is fair and that everyone eventually gets what he or she deserves, which is at the core of human psychology. As formulated by Melvin Lerner, the key point about the Just World is that this is one of the key features of human nature, affecting our view of the world whether we want it or not: a built-in justice module.[2] Since having the Just World undermined is a profoundly disturbing experience, humans go to great lengths, subconsciously, to

---

[*] I am overwhelmingly grateful to Gráinne de Búrca, Gareth Davies, Maja Kutlaca, Suryapratim Roy and Andrew Williams for their critical remarks on the first drafts of this chapter.
[1] Genesis 3:4.
[2] See, most recently, MJ Lerner and S Clayton, *Justice and Self-Interest* (Cambridge, Cambridge University Press, 2011).

preserve the feeling: even the most outrageously inequitable situations can receive a subconscious reinterpretation in the vein of the Just World's preservation.[3]

The second concept employed in this chapter is the scope of justice, researched, interalia, by Susan Opotow.[4] In a nutshell, the scope of justice is the field where the Just World functions. All that falls outside the scope of justice is simply ignored, again subconsciously, no matter what: even if the most inequitable and outrageously unfair things happen, the Just World cannot be possibly compromised by anything which is outside the scope of justice. Yet the scope of justice, unlike the Just World itself, is a highly dynamic and malleable concept.

These insights allow us to approach the concept of justice in law in a new light and can have far-reaching effects on the understanding of the key concepts discussed, alongside justice, throughout this volume, including, inter alia, legitimacy, democracy and equality.

Applied to the constitutional context of the EU, the theories this chapter delves into contextualise a number of key theoretical approaches embraced by the authors of the preceding chapters, demonstrating that equating justice with democracy through politicising it in the context of a particular society[5] could amount to playing lip-service to important innate biases of our perception of justice. Viewed in this light, a Member State—or, indeed, any other collectivity or society—cannot be viewed as a 'natural' cradle of justice. Justice has nothing to do with the state and should not necessarily be political. Supranational justice is thus as 'natural' as a state-level justice is. While justice arguments could indeed be used to achieve depoliticisation,[6] the reverse is also possible: politicisation can unquestionably harm justice through exclusion and dehumanisation. Politicised or not, unquestionably we are not dealing with a purely rational realm. In a just society taking natural human biases into account the irrational should also definitely find its reflection in the way how the system of governance operates.[7] Cold reason and pure calculation does not always support human perceptions that the system is just. Moreover, crucially, the difference between procedural and substantive justice[8] seems to disappear entirely, as far as human perceptions are concerned: it is the outcomes that matter.

---

[3] L Montada and MJ Lerner (eds), *Responses to Victimizations and Belief in a Just World* (New York, NY, Plenum, 1998); MJ Lerner and CH Simmons, 'Observer's Reaction to the "Innocent Victim": Compassion or Rejection' (1966) 4 *Journal of Personality and Social Psychology* 204.

[4] S Opotow, 'Is Justice Finite?' in L Montada and MJ Lerner (eds), *Social Justice in Human Relations: Current Societal Concerns About Justice*, vol 3 (New York, NY, Plenum, 1996); S Opotow, 'Moral Exclusion and Injustice: An Introduction' (1990) 46 *Journal of Social Issues* 1.

[5] See, eg, D Nicol, 'Swabian Housewives, Suffering Southerners: The Contestability of Justice as Exemplified by the Eurozone Crisis' in this volume, 165.

[6] In the vein of Agustín José Menéndez's arguments in his 'Whose Justice? Which Europe?' in this volume, 137.

[7] Gareth Davies seems to be absolutely right, in this respect: the worst possible way towards justice lies via the installation and perfection of goal-oriented legal systems and reasoning (just as the one in place in the EU): see G Davies, 'Social Legitimacy and Purposive Power: The End, the Means and the Consent of the People' in this volume, 259, at 262ff.

[8] The presumed existence of this difference seems to be at the core of Jürgen Neyer's reasoning, as his contribution to this collection demonstrates. J Neyer, 'Justice and the Right to Justification: Conceptual Reflections' in this volume, 211.

The possible implications of the theories presented in what follows stretch beyond this handful of issues, however, as it allows us, empowered by the interdisciplinary lens, to have a fresh look at the function and the role of the law in regulating and shaping (just) human societies. These insights can be instrumental for building a just Europe of the future.

II. INTRODUCING KEY ELEMENTS OF THE ARGUMENT

Justice is law's cornerstone: all legal systems make (implicit) justice claims. Who would argue for unjust laws?[9] Law and justice are thus intimately intertwined. Since the time when law and psychology, biology, archeology as well as numerous other disciplines parted ways in the nineteenth century,[10] the landscape of human knowledge has been radically altered by new crucial insights, requiring serious rethinking of some leading postulates underlying legal studies and legal theory, as known today.[11] Concurring with Owen Jones' quite obvious claim, '*any* model of behaviour inconsistent with the foundations of modern behavioural biology is inaccurate and obsolete' (emphasis in the original),[12] it is submitted that taking up-to-date scientific data into account should be the starting point of any meaningful discussion of law as well as of justice, as law's main element.

Building on this premise, in the section that follows this chapter briefly recounts crucial connections between law and the world of science focusing on the rich recent data on justice coming from a number of different disciplines able to enrich our theorising about justice.[13] Crucial in this respect is that recent research makes clear that human intelligence and behaviour is as learnt as it is pre-programmed to cope with the challenges arising in the course of human evolution. As the generally shared understanding in contemporary science has it, there is no firewall between Eros and civilization:[14] biology and thought are intimately connected, both resulting

---

[9] It has been submitted that injustice can be conceptually different from justice—the two are not simply in an antinomian relationship: B Yack, 'Putting Injustice First: An Alternative Approach to Liberal Pluralism' (1999) 66 *Social Research* 1104; J Shklar, *The Faces of Injustice* (New Haven, CT, Yale University Press, 1990) 110. See also S Douglas-Scott, 'Justice, Injustice and the Rule of Law in the EU' in this volume, 51.

[10] OD Jones, 'Law and Biology: Toward an Integrated Model of Human Behaviour' (1997) 8 *Journal of Contemporary Legal Issues* 167, 170.

[11] See, eg, OD Jones and TH Goldsmith, 'Law and Behavioural Biology' (2005) 105 *Columbia Law Review* 405; SM Downes, 'Some Recent Developments in Evolutionary Approaches to the Study of Human Cognition and Behaviour' (2001) 16 *Biology and Philosophy* 575; TH Goldsmith, *The Biological Roots of Human Nature: Forging Links Between Evolution and Behaviour* (Oxford, Oxford University Press, 1991); RD Alexander, 'Biology and Law' (1986) 7 *Ethology and Sociobiology* 167; M Gruter, 'Law in Sociobiological Perspective' (1977) 5 *Florida State University Law Review* 181. See also RL Cohen (ed), *Justice: Views From the Social Sciences* (New York, NY, Plenum, 1986); KR Scherer (ed), *Justice: Interdisciplinary Perspectives* (Cambridge, Cambridge University Press, 1992).

[12] OD Jones, 'On the Nature of Norms: Biology, Morality, and the Disruption of Order' (2000) 98 *Michigan Law Review* 2072.

[13] For some overviews see, eg, LJ Skitka and FJ Crosby, 'Trends in the Social Psychological Study of Justice' (2003) 7 *Personality and Social Psychology Review* 282; W Fikenscher and MT McGuire, 'A Four-Function Theory of Biology and Law' (1994) 25 *Rechtstheorie* 291.

[14] But see, H Marcuse, *Eros and Civilisation: Philosophical Inquiry into Freud* (Boston, MA, Beacon Press, 1955).

from two intertwined lines of evolutionary developments—from biological and socio-cultural evolution.[15] Evolution has direct implications for our (ie 'human') landscape of values and thinking patterns, from arachnophobia to what is due to whom.[16] Knowing these implications is overwhelmingly relevant to law. Adherents of the law and biology movement, among others, made persuasive arguments that denying or ignoring this while approaching law academically can be profoundly disruptive for the discipline.[17]

Moreover, recent research on fairness and what is due to whom in biology, primatology, evolutionary psychology and a number of other disciplines demonstrates that human sensitivity to unfairness and injustice is clearly not unique to our species.[18] What we are dealing with is, in the words of Sarah Brosnan, the 'evolutionary function of justice and fairness'.[19] Justice and fairness are observable in different species including humans and non-human primates.[20] Such recent discoveries can be profoundly informative for the study of justice in humans, with far-reaching implications for the understanding of law and policy.[21] Rather than (mis)representing justice as a uniquely legal–theoretical construct, it is necessary to accept the socio-biological facet inherent in the nature of this concept. The reality of other disciplines should thus necessarily be informing legal scholarship, which is desperately insular, as it stands today.[22]

Living up to the claim that scientific discoveries are relevant to law, in Section IV, the chapter summarises key findings of several relevant disciplines on the nature of justice as a socio-biological, as opposed to a legal–theoretical notion. Justice and fairness can be further developed and explained using the 'Just World' (equally called Justice Motive or Sense of Justice) paradigm, which is the lifetime achievement of Melvin Lerner.[23] The Just World hypothesis presupposes that humans are

---

[15] L Cavalli-Sforza and M Feldman, *Cultural Transmission and Evolution: A Quantitative Approach* (Princeton, NJ, Princeton University Press, 1981).

[16] For an amusing read, see P Westen, 'To Lure the Tarantula From Its Hole: A Response' (1983) 83 *Columbia Law Review* 1186.

[17] See OD Jones, 'Law, Emotions, and Behavioural Biology' (1999) 39 *Jurimetrics* 283. The law and biology movement has been trying to remedy this: DE Elliott, 'Law and Biology: The New Synthesis' (1997) 41 *Saint Louis University Law Journal* 594. Cf Jones, 'Law and Biology', n 10 above, 167.

[18] F de Waal, *Good Natured: The Origins of Right and Wrong in Humans and Other Animals* (Cambridge, MA, Harvard University Press, 1996).

[19] SF Brosnan, 'Justice- and Fairness-Related Behaviours in Nonhuman Primates' (2013) 110 *Proceedings of the National Academy of Sciences* (USA), suppl 2, 10416.

[20] The studies comparing fairness in humans with the studies on non-human primates and other animals are very new and bring about important insights. Sarah Brosnan and Frans de Waal are the leaders of this field. See, eg, SF Brosnan, 'Introduction to "Justice in Animals"' (2012) 25 *Social Justice Research* 109; SF Brosnan and F de Waal, 'Fairness in Animals: Where From Here?' (2012) 25 *Social Justice Research* 336; SF Brosnan, 'Nonhuman Species' Reactions to Inequity and Their Implications for Fairness' (2006) 19 *Social Justice Research* 153.

[21] Eg Brosnan, 'Introduction to "Justice in Animals"', n 20 above.

[22] Among myriads of disciplines generating important knowledge, lawyers have traditionally favoured economics, which, as of itself, is also in need of 'hard-sciences' insights. For an overview of the key problems encountered by comparative lawyers open to other disciplines, see, eg, S Roy, 'Privileging (Some Forms of) Interdisciplinarity and Interpretation: Methods in Comparative Law' (2014) 12 *International Journal of Constitutional Law* 786.

[23] Lerner and Clayton, *Justice and Self-Interest*, n 2 above; MJ Lerner, *The Belief in a Just World: A Fundamental Delusion* (New York, NY, Plenum, 1980); MJ Lerner, 'The Justice Motive: Some Hypotheses As to Its Origins and Forms' (1977) 45 *Journal of Personality* 1; MJ Lerner, 'Justified Self-Interest and Responsibility for Suffering: A Replication and Extension' (1971) 19 *Journal of Human Relations* 388.

naturally endowed with what Lerner calls a 'justice motive'—an 'initial primary automatic reaction',[24] subconscious and natural capacity of construing the world as a just place, where everyone gets what he or she deserves no matter what:

> In essence ... the ... just-world formulation proposed that because of the way *people's minds are structured*, and because they desire to achieve their goals without having terrible things happen to them (whether at the hands of others, the gods, or fate), they try to believe that they live in a just world. [Emphasis added.][25]

Lerner's experimental research established that human beings depend on the sense that the world is just at all stages of their life.[26] This innate sense informs their view of the *self*[27] and also of the surrounding reality to ensure that the sense of justice is uncompromised, thus profoundly altering (or, indeed, shaping) their perceptions of all reality. More and more proofs of this theory are being collected.[28] The implications of Lerner's Just World for the understanding of the law are far-reaching, particularly as far as the understanding of the nature of justice is concerned.

It turns out that justice is not only inherently engrained in nature. It has a somewhat counterintuitive connection with what can be termed 'reality', since the concept of the Just World does not as much help us humans understand the world, as the Just World actually *shapes* what we see, feel and experience. In simple terms, its main function is actually to *bias* human perception of the world, by presenting it as a much more consistent and coherent place than it actually is.[29] In this sense the Just World is particularly relevant for the understanding of the links between justice and different types of human social organisation. A successfully operating Just World ensures that, indeed, our environment is constantly perceived as just no matter what. It has been demonstrated in the literature that deviations from this perception trigger extremely strong emotions and imply the necessity of intervention to ensure that the overall coherence of the world not be compromised. Crucially, Just World research has shown that intervention can take two forms. It can either be an attempt, in fact, to 'restore justice', or, alternatively, it can be a reinterpretation of the whole situation to ensure that the Just World is not compromised. The latter usually results in denigrating innocent victims and multiplying their suffering—a somewhat counterintuitive finding, which is easily explainable logically (the only thing that matters is that the sense of the Just World remains uncompromised) and finds strong experimental support: it is the victim's fault that her situation is so bad.[30]

---

[24] Lerner and Clayton, *Justice and Self-Interest*, n 2 above, 40.

[25] MJ Lerner, 'What Does the Belief in a Just World Protect Us From: The Dread of Death or the Fear of Undeserved Suffering?' (1997) 8 *Psychological Inquiry* 29, 30.

[26] The first steps in the direction of Lerner's discoveries were made in the context of research on children in the 1930s: J Piaget, *The Moral Judgment of the Child* (Glencoe, IL, Free Press, 1932). See also MJ Lerner, 'The Justice Motive: "Equity" and "Parity" Among Children' (1974) 29 *Journal of Personality and Social Psychology* 539.

[27] LJ Skitka, 'Of Different Minds: An Accessible Identity Model of Justice Reasoning' (2003) 7 *Personality and Social Psychology Review* 286.

[28] For overviews, see, eg, C Hafer and L Bègue, 'Experimental Research on Just-World Theory: Problems, Developments, and Future Challenges' (2005) 131 *Psychological Bulletin* 128. See also MJ Lerner and DT Miller, 'Just World Research and the Attribution Process: Looking Back and Ahead' (1978) 85 *Psychological Bulletin* 1030.

[29] Lerner and Clayton, *Justice and Self-Interest*, n 2 above, 191.

[30] Lerner and Simmons, 'Observer's Reaction to the "Innocent Victim"', n 3 above, 204.

As section V demonstrates, justice applies within a certain limited scope: the scope of justice, as humans subconsciously distinguish between the situations which are and are not capable of triggering Just World reactions. Simple physical reality, but also communities perceived as being placed outside such scope, can become victims of reasonable and fairly minded people for no apparent reason, as socio-psychological research shows.[31] While the Just World implies strong subconscious reactions to injustice, these are missing entirely, when an act of injustice happens outside the scope of justice. Susan Opotow, among others, made an important contribution to the study of where the borderline of the scope of justice is to be discovered.[32] The Scope of Justice is crucial for the understanding of the core content of the legal concepts of equality and legitimacy.

Section VI of the chapter deals with the implications for the law of what has been discussed so far, focusing, in particular, on the implications of this analysis for democracy, legitimacy, foundational ideology underlying the legal systems, equality, as well as EU citizenship and the vertical division of powers in the EU's federal structure.[33] It is possible to expect that the claims of equality and justice will only be perceived as genuinely legitimate—not purely legalistic—if they are made within the same scope of justice. This can explain not only genocides and slavery, but also wasteful treatment of natural resources and indifference to the suffering or even extinction of other sentient beings. Lessons to be drawn from the studies of the scope of justice for the effectiveness of legal regulation can be of crucial importance.[34] Approached in a practical vein, while the Just World is built into humans and cannot be either eliminated or seriously altered, the scope of justice seems to be malleable, depending on a particular culture and social strata into which a concrete person is socialised: every new imagined community provides for a new possible way to delimit the scope of justice.[35]

Based on a voluminous body of important non-legal literature, it is suggested that justice is behind our human 'self' and is an extremely complex phenomenon that can definitely be approached empirically. The insights described in what follows are instrumental in potentially nuancing our approach to law in general and the law of the European Union in particular. The Just World and the scope of justice are socio-biological phenomena inherent in human nature across all cultures. While their concrete emanations could be culture-specific, in general they are not based on cultural particularity at all, making far-reaching generalisations on the meaning of justice possible, partly explaining—using the intimate connection between justice

---

[31] S Opotow, 'Predicting Protection: Scope of Justice and the Natural World' (1994) 50 *Journal of Social Issues* 49; Opotow, 'Is Justice Finite?', n 4 above.

[32] Opotow, 'Predicting Protection', n 31 above.

[33] See, for a global overview of this concept, D Kochenov (ed), *EU Citizenship and Federalism: The Role of Rights* (Cambridge, Cambridge University Press, 2015) (forthcoming).

[34] Australian scholar, Julia Davis dealt with the specifics of the legal reasoning in the context of the Just World paradigm: J Davis, 'Judicial Reasoning and the "Just World Delusion": Using the Psychology of Justice to Evaluate Legal Judgments' paper presented at the conference 'Judicial Reasoning: Art or Science?' (National Judicial College of Australia, February 2009), www.papers.ssrn.com/sol3/papers.cfm?abstract_id=2363731.

[35] B Anderson, *Imagined Communities*, 2nd edn (London, Verso, 2006).

and law as a starting point—why every human culture can boast some form of law and an idea of what is and what is not just.

All in all, this chapter then takes its place beside a small number of attempts at a 'cautious stretching of the limits of [lawyers'] naïvity'.[36] It attempts to place the study of justice in a global context of the advances of other disciplines. Such an exercise, although admittedly risky, if not an outright 'barbarism', to follow Marc Tushnet,[37] has potential to inform legal understandings—not merely ornate them, as yet another pure theory would. In other words, barbarism might be a necessity.

III. THE CASE FOR TAKING REALITY INTO ACCOUNT

Recent developments in science have brought about a serious rethinking of the postulated place of humans in the world, as well as the role of both biological *and* cultural evolution in the shaping of human societies.[38] These advances are of direct relevance for the study of law and, especially, for our understanding of justice.

The human mind is an evolved information-processing mechanism, which works on the same principles of physics and bio-chemistry as any other organ of the body: that biology is the necessary basic foundation for all socio-cultural systems is unavoidable. Biology is thus necessarily behind moving our toe, stroking a cat, yawning, or gazing at the sunset. But the biological foundations equally underpin what has also been viewed as innately 'cultural' (as opposed to 'biological'): language and, quite possibly, the basics of human social organisation, including justice, law and, indeed, culture. As explained by Steven Pinker, the essence of language—which is in direct relation to human culture—relies on innate brain modules which belong to the biological essence of 'being human'.[39] This is why your cat, however cultured, cannot converse with you in your language.[40] By analogy, the same could apply to other complex phenomena: certain elaborate taboos, for instance, or deeply held fears, could come directly from the brain—a genetically determined biological organ—representing learnt institutions.[41]

Indeed, scholars demonstrate that the human mind, 'is composed of a large number of functionally specialized information-processing devices: cognitive

---

[36] E Adamson Hoebel, 'Anthropology, Law and Genetic Inheritance' (1982) 5 *Journal of Social and Biological Structures* 335, 337; M Gruter and P Bohannan, 'The Foundations of Law and Morality' (1982) 5 *Journal of Social and Biological Structures* 313; Gruter, 'Law in Sociobiological Perspective', n 11 above; Davis, 'Judicial Reasoning and the "Just World Delusion"', n 34 above.

[37] M Tushnet, 'Interdisciplinary Legal Scholarship: The Case of History-in-Law' (1996) 71 *Chicago–Kent Law Review* 909.

[38] For a compelling overview, see NW Thornhill et al, 'Evolutionary Theory and Human Social Institutions: Psychological Foundations' in P Weingart et al (eds), *Human by Nature: Between Biology and Social Sciences* (Mahwah, NJ, Erlbaum, 1997) (and the literature cited therein). See also WH Durham, 'Advances in Evolutionary Culture Theory' (1990) 19 *Annual Review of Anthropology* 187.

[39] S Pinker, *The Language Instinct* (London, Penguin, 1995). Pinker's example of the forging of grammatically coherent creoles from pidgins by children in one generation is very telling in this respect.

[40] Behemoth of *Master i Margarita* is a notable exception complaining that: 'Kotam pochemu-to govoriat "ty", hotia ni odin kot nikogda ni s kem ne pil Bruderschaft-a' (For some reason, cats are usually addressed familiarly, though no cat has ever drunk *Bruderschaft* with anyone).

[41] Thornhill et al, 'Evolutionary Theory and Human Social Institutions', n 38 above, 204.

adaptations'.[42] According to Nancy W Thornhill and her co-authors looking at such cognitive adaptations of the human brain in their research, 'social "instincts" might allow people to reconstruct [different] features of social life if a catastrophe like enslavement broke the seemingly necessary chains of cultural transmission'.[43] Behaviour—which the law aspires to regulate—is thus also a product of the brain, an organ of our body, which is prone to evolution, resulting in the changes in the behaviours it can generate.

That biological and socio-cultural evolution[44] are correlated and develop hand-in-hand has been convincingly demonstrated by bringing together genetic, archeological and linguistic data: considerable parallelism between genetic and linguistic evolution demonstrated by Cavalli-Sforza and colleagues makes it clear that the strict separation between biology and behaviour would not be a sound starting point in analysing human behavioural evolution.[45] While it is clear that species' success depends on the ability to produce a behavioural response to the morphological and environmental changes, it has become necessary to acknowledge that our behaviour, just like our biology, is also to a large extent fixed by evolution.[46]

Unlike strict responses which numerous animals demonstrate, human response ensuring evolutionary success consisted in the *flexibility* of human behaviour, compared with other animals. To turn to Thornhill et al again,

> if the informational input is changed, the behaviour will often change. So when people with the same cognitive programmes are exposed to different kinds of information, this will cause their cognitive programmes to generate different representations about the world—different knowledge—and this will lead them to behave in different ways. For this reason, one expects to find very few *behaviours* that are universal across cultures, even though all people have basically the same cognitive programmes.[47]

Consequently, speaking of the lack of general human culture as opposed to a large number of particular ones 'is the error of naïve realism', as '"general" and "particular" … are simply different levels at which any system of categorization encounters the same world'.[48]

Social behaviour is thus not a constant natural trait,[49] but it has a constant cognitive adaptation base in our brain. This physiological base pre-programming of our responses to the world and social interactions is crucially important. Some

---

[42] ibid, 213.
[43] ibid, 204.
[44] *Cf* LL Cavalli-Sforza and MW Feldman, *Cultural Transmission and Evolution: A Quantitative Approach* (Princeton, NJ, Princeton University Press, 1981).
[45] LL Cavalli-Sforza et al, 'Reconstruction of Human Evolution: Bringing Together Genetic, Archeological, and Linguistic Data' (1988) 85 *Proceedings of the National Academy of Science* (USA) 6002. See also T Ingold, 'Beyond Biology and Culture. The Meaning of Evolution in a Relational World' (2004) 12 *Social Anthropology* 209; C Bernis, 'The Evolution of Human Biosocial Behaviour' (2000) 15 *Human Evolution* 129.
[46] RG Klein, 'Archeology and the Evolution of Human Behaviour' (2000) 9 *Evolutionary Anthropology* 17.
[47] Thornhill et al, 'Evolutionary Theory and Human Social Institutions', n 38 above, 220.
[48] ibid, 223.
[49] See RD Masters, 'Evolutionary Biology, Political Theory and the State' (1982) 5 *Journal of Social and Biological Structures* 439 (trying to build a model of law and natural sciences interaction based on this insight).

physiological changes, resulting in the apparition of the biological predisposition to flexibility in reacting to the world combined with cooperation,[50] which happened as recently as 50,000–40,000 years ago, are responsible for the explosion of art and culture and, ultimately, for the fact that *homo sapiens* became us,[51] as non-biological, cultural evolution was born:[52] 'she took the fruit thereof and did eat'.[53] In the words of Richard Klein, 'arguably this was the most significant mutation in the human evolutionary series, for it produced an organism that could alter its behaviour radically without any change in its anatomy and that could cumulate and transmit the alterations at a speed that anatomical innovation could never match'.[54]

The cognitive adaptations resulting from biological evolution did not disappear, however: just like chimpanzees, we are not prone to incest and we understand what possession is.[55] Moreover, just like many animals, we know what fairness (justice) is about. Fairness is one of the key tools enabling cooperation and ensuring evolutionary advantage. From this follows, first, that justice/fairness is not merely a theoretical or a philosophical construct. It is also a 'biological problem'.[56] Secondly, given that rules of behaviour became crucial 50,000–40,000 years ago, when cultural evolution, as we know, began, to come with the myriad of flexible options offered by the evolved brain, 'some "concept" of law may [one can speculate] have been *one of the first abstract ideas* formulated by the human mind' (emphasis added).[57]

Make no mistake: of course there is order in some animal societies too. The underlying factors bringing this order about are, in the majority of cases, very different from human societies, however. On the one hand, order can be purely instinctive, if not mechanical, as in the case of bees or termites for instance. On the other, it can also deviate from instincts, being partly shaped also by other factors. Jane Goodall described the latter in her work on chimpanzees as 'order without law'.[58] The most important distinction between purely instinctive behaviour and more complex behavioural patterns, is simple. With pure instincts, the behaviour is fully genetic: it is 'built into the animal from its birth',[59] removing any need whatsoever to impose any rules of behaviour from the outside. If a mistaken bee comes to a wrong hive, it

---

[50] R Boyd and RJ Richardson, *Culture and the Evolutionary Process* (Chicago, IL, University of Chicago Press, 1988).

[51] Klein, 'Archeology and the Evolution of Human Behaviour', n 46 above, 17.

[52] Humans are not the only bearers of culture, if the latter is understood as non-biologically determined evolving behavioural patterns. Some groups of Japanese macaques, for instance, pass the habit of washing sweet potato through generations, Hamadryas and Anubis baboons have different family structures, but females transplanted from one troop to another easily adapt. See, respectively, Gruter, 'Law in Sociobiological Perspective', n 11 above, 191 (fn 32), 195–96. See also memetics literature for a different version of this 'parallel evolution' story: S Blackmore, *The Meme Machine* (Cambridge, Cambridge University Press, 2000); K Destin, *The Selfish Meme* (Cambridge, Cambridge University Press, 2004).

[53] Genesis 3:6.

[54] Klein, 'Archeology and the Evolution of Human Behaviour', n 46 above, 18.

[55] J Goodall, 'Order Without Law' (1982) 5 *Journal of Social and Biological Structures* 353, 357.

[56] Masters, 'Evolutionary Biology', n 49 above, 439, 440 (and the literature cited therein). See also Adamson Hoebel, 'Anthropology, Law and Genetic Inheritance', n 36 above, 335.

[57] M Gruter and P Bohannan, 'The Foundations of Law and Morality' (1982) 5 *Journal of Social and Biological Structures* 313.

[58] Goodall, 'Order Without Law', n 55 above.

[59] ibid. See also RD Alexander, 'Biology and Law' (1986) 7 *Ethology and Sociobiology* 167.

is simply killed without any justice dilemmas or questions asked: malfunctioning in the biological programming not allowing for flexibility is easy to correct.

Justice and fairness thus cannot exist in the groups driven exclusively by instinct: both presuppose an existence of some mental 'golden standard', which directly correlates with the sense of justice,[60] from which some animals would deviate. Otherwise, the concepts of justice and fairness would simply be redundant.

Interestingly, contrary to what social scientists used to presume until very recently, plenty of animals can boast behavioural patterns which are not fully genetically determined, allowing space for flexibility and social learning on top of the instinct. Moreover, recent research demonstrates that the existence of a golden standard is not correlated with linguistic capacity. Not only apes, but also crows and fish seem to have it.[61]

Consequently, also chimps, in one example, unquestionably have law-like concepts, such as possession[62] and incest taboo.[63] Their living together presupposes respect for a number of social rules. This is not a surprise. Every evolutionary biologist would explain that obeying the rules seems to produce an evolutionary advantage.[64] This should also explain why obeying the rules can be pleasurable,[65] eventual deviance notwithstanding; humans clearly derive satisfaction from it, glorifying and elevating their position as the obedient and the meek. Happily reducing oneself to an infinitely tiny part of the societal whole not caring much about the justice or rationale of its actions is thus not only a sign of 'the lack of moral independence',[66] as Michael Walzer had it: it can also be rooted in the ultimate satisfaction of being what we are: human.

All in all, it is clear that contemporary science does not support the idea of a clear separation between the 'body' and the 'mind'—the animal in us and the cultured 'human',[67] which law has traditionally taken for granted. The reason for this is that such dualities used to be accepted as scientifically proven when law emerged as an aspiring scientific discipline: holding itself out as a science[68] and then naturally rediscovering its connection with the social.[69] Even though nobody would honestly

---

[60] F de Waal, 'The Chimpanzee's Sense of Social Regularity and Its Relation to the Human Sense of Justice' (1991) 34 *American Behavioural Scientist* 335.

[61] NJ Raihani, AS Grutter and R Bshary, 'Punishers Benefit From Third-Party Punishment in Fish' (2010) 327 *Science* 171; F de Waal, *Good Natured: The Origins of Right and Wrong in Humans and Other Animals* (Cambridge, MA, Harvard University Press, 1996). See also SF Brosnan and F de Waal, 'Monkeys Reject Unequal Pay' (2003) 425 *Nature* 6955; F de Waal and ML Berger, 'Payment for Labour in Monkeys' (2000) 404 *Nature* 563.

[62] Goodall, 'Order Without Law', n 55 above, 357. Goodall distinguishes three types of possession in chimpanzee society: territory, individual (ie the young), objects 'found, gathered, or made'.

[63] ibid.

[64] For a discussion, see, eg, Gruter, 'Law in Sociobiological Perspective', n 11 above, 193.

[65] ibid.

[66] M Walzer, 'Civility and Civic Virtue in Contemporary America' (1974) 41 *Social Research* 593, 596.

[67] Jones, 'Law and Biology, n 10 above, 167.

[68] Eg C Tomlins, 'Framing the Field of Law's Disciplinary Encounters: A Historical Narrative' (2000) 34 *Law and Society Review* 911.

[69] L Petrażycki, *Vvedenije v izuchenije prava i nravstvennosti* (St Petersburg, 1905); L Petrażycki, *Teorija prava i gosudarstva* (St Petersburg, 1907); E Ehrlich, *Grundlegung der Soziologie des Rechts* (Munich and Leipzig, Duncker & Humblot, 1913) (ones of the first advocates of the necessity to reconnect the study of law with the study of society). See also M Gruter, 'Biologically Based Behavioural Research and the Facts of Law' (1982) 5 *Journal of Social and Biological Structures* 315.

argue for law as existing in a vacuum nowadays' the foundational assumptions behind what law does and whom it regulates, have seemingly remained intact.[70]

Whether lawyers admit this or not, law is most directly rooted in biological and cultural evolution.[71] The trouble is, law and the theories of justice in particular, have never actually come to terms with this reality. Numerous theories of justice and legitimacy view humans as highly abstract and presume that social reality, as hypothesised, can be altered quite radically and effortlessly at the whim of a writer—lawyer or policy maker. This presentation is obviously not true and the absolute majority of the past social experiments failed: Utopias rarely come to life. This brings about an interesting conclusion: studying uniquely morals and norms, in disconnect from a wide array of alternative behaviour-biasing phenomena might be—*en gros*—meaningless.[72]

This is the case even if one does not share the view that 'knowing the law is knowing nothing'[73]—rules can be easily changed, while deeper patterns of human behaviour are studied by other disciplines. Research on the embedded programmes of our mind has been progressing at an impressive pace in the last decades: entirely new avenues of research have been opened.[74] In essence, we often see what we need to see and hear what we need to hear, since 'biological machines are calibrated to the environments in which they evolved, and they embody information about the stably recurring properties of these ancestral worlds',[75] which directly shapes the way how humans see, feel and think. What emerges from these claims, research shows, is that the human brain is not so much attuned to working with content-independent algorithms, as with thick assumptions about the physical world in which humans evolved: it comes 'pre-programmed'. Such pre-programming can be an evolutionary feature manifesting itself first in humans (like the language instinct)[76] or shared with some other animals (like incest avoidance).[77] One of such programmes could be *justice*—or, the Just World.[78]

---

[70] Jones, 'Law and Biology, n 10 above, 170. See also J Tooby and L Cosmides, 'The Psychological Foundations of Culture' in JH Barkow et al (eds), *The Adapted Mind: Evolutionary Psychology and the Generation of Culture* (Oxford, Oxford University Press, 1992) 21; RD Masters, *Beyond Relativism: Science and Human Values* (Hanover, NH, University Press of New England, 1993).

[71] M Gruter, 'The Origins of Legal Behaviour' (1979) 2 *Journal of Social Biological Structures* 43.

[72] For a strong restatement of this, see Jones, 'On the Nature of Norms', n 12 above, 2072. See also L Arnhart, 'The Darwinian Biology of Aristotle's Political Animals' (1994) 38 *American Journal of Political Science* 464.

[73] M Kumm, 'The Idea of Socratic Contestation and the Right to Justification: The Point of Rights-Based Proportionality Review' (2010) 4 *Law and Ethics of Human Rights* 1938.

[74] Thornhill et al, 'Evolutionary Theory and Human Social Institutions', n 38 above, 225 (for a rich overview).

[75] ibid, citing numerous examples based on the research of the assumptions new-born babies have about the world—from language and grammar, to the ability of recognising human faces—which ultimately make learning possible.

[76] Pinker, *The Language Instinct*, n 39 above.

[77] A Maryanski, 'The Elementary Forms of the First Proto-Human Society' (1993) 2 *Advances in Human Ecology* 215. In fact, not only the rape of children, but also infanticide statistics show that the risk of a child suffering at the hands of strangers or adoptive parents is infinitely higher than at the hands of the biological parents: OD Jones, 'Evolutionary Analysis in Law: An Introduction and Application to Child Abuse' (1997) 75 *North Carolina Law Review* 1117.

[78] There is no research engraining the Just World within the context of evolutionary biology, the leading presumption of Just World theorists being that it is essentially a learnt motive. Arguments for implicating biology in the apparition of the sense of justice have been made, however. See, eg, Gruter, 'The Origins of Legal Behaviour', n 71 above.

IV. THE JUST WORLD AND THE LAW

Social cooperation would be impossible without an assumption that others will be fair,[79] which essentially explains why it is unsurprising that Lerner's Just World theory has found numerous experimental confirmations since its first formulation in the sixties.[80] Lerner found that the ingrained sense that the world is a just place makes people intuitively deny reality and forget rational judgement only to save the just world perception. An example of this is the willingness to denigrate the innocent victims of abuse in situations when they cannot be helped, which is described in detail in numerous studies.[81] That they are abused becomes 'their own fault', since otherwise the just nature of the world would be shattered.[82] This is particularly clear from research with religious people, who appear to be more willing to blame the innocent whom they cannot help, as their sense of the Just World is stronger: in the end justice will triumph.[83] There is a general consensus in psychology that 'people may engage in a variety of behaviours that help maintain a sense [of the Just World]'.[84]

Research has demonstrated that the engrained embrace of the Just World is implicit.[85] This is part of our bio-cultural wiring as human beings, rather than a result of rational thinking about justice.[86] Crucially, it cannot be explained through self-interest considerations, as immediate reactions to threats to one's perception of the Just World are often extremely counter-productive, when viewed through the prism of self-interest.[87] Yet, seemingly rational thinking about justice

---

[79] Skitka and Crosby, 'Trends in the Social Psychological Study of Justice', n 13 above, 282.

[80] Lerner and Simmons, 'Observer's Reaction to the "Innocent Victim"', n 3 above, 204. For the most recent restatement, see Lerner and Clayton, *Justice and Self-Interest*, n 2 above.

[81] For an overview, see, Lerner and Clayton, *Justice and Self-Interest*, n 2 above, 36–38, discussing, in particular, the experiments conducted by Hafer and Callan et al. See CL Hafer, 'Investment in Long Term Goals and Commitment to Just Means Drive the Need to Believe in a Just World' (2000) 26 *Personality and Social Psychology Bulletin* 1059; MJ Callan, NW Shead and JM Olson, 'Foregoing the Labour for the Fruits: The Effect of Just World Threat on the Desire for Immediate Monetary Rewards' (2009) 45 *Journal of Experimental Social Psychology* 246.

[82] Lerner and Simmons, 'Observer's Reaction to the "Innocent Victim"', n 3 above, 204.

[83] RM Sorrentino and J Hardy, 'Religiousness and the Derogation of an Innocent Victim' (1974) 42 *Journal of Psychology*, 1974, 372.

[84] Hafer and Bègue, 'Experimental Research on Just-World Theory', n 28 above, 129. See also, eg, J Meindl and MJ Lerner, 'The Heroic Motive in Interpersonal Relations' (1983) 19 *Journal of Experimental Social Psychology* 1; MJ Lerner, 'The Belief in a Just World and the "Heroic Motive": Searching for "Constants" in the Psychology of Religious Ideology' (1991) 1 *International Journal for the Psychology of Religion* 27. Popular erroneous stereotypes also serve the purpose of systemic cognitive distortion of reality to ensure that the sense of justice is not undermined: AC Kay and JT Jost, 'Complementary Justice: Effects of "Poor But Happy" and "Poor But Honest" Stereotype Exemplars on System Justification and Implicit Activation of the Justice Motive' (2003) 85 *Journal of Personality and Social Psychology* 823.

[85] MJ Lerner, 'The Two Forms of Belief in a Just World' in L Montada and MJ Lerner (eds), *Responses to Victimizations and Belief in a Just World* (New York, NY, Plenum, 1998) 247.

[86] This explains the failure of a number of recent experiments to find the justice motive: MJ Lerner, 'The Justice Motive: Where Social Psychologists Found It, How They Lost It, and Why They May Not Find It Again' (2003) 7 *Personality and Social Psychology Review* 388. Lerner introduced a distinction between 'heuristic' and 'systematic' justice in the context of studying the Just World. The first refers to the automatic, intuitive, immediate reactions, while the second is based on having sufficient time to realign thinking with the conventional normatively-appropriate rules (389).

[87] Lerner and Clayton, *Justice and Self-Interest*, n 2 above, 59.

can function—seemingly at least—akin to the Just World by producing ex post facto explanations of unfortunate events, ignoring the lacking factual connections between the perceived fault and de facto unrelated negative consequences. Unlike the Just World, which is an innate reaction, popular flawed rationalising is branded as 'Imminent Justice' in the literature.[88] A clear distinction between norm-enactment (doing what society expects of you) and the Just World (automatic reaction to perceived injustice) is thus crucial.[89]

According to Carolyn Hafer and Laurent Bègue, 'virtually all people, as a result of intrinsic developmental forces in combination with a relatively stable environment, develop a commitment to deserving their outcomes and to organizing their lives around principles of deservingness'.[90] Humans thus live through an implicit 'personal contract' with the Just World—all that there is—and try to shield themselves from any realisations that this contract is broken, or that it, God forbid, appears to be an illusion.[91] It is clear, however, that this state of affairs has to do both with our social interactions, especially in childhood,[92] *and* with, necessarily, the biological organisation of our brain—similar to that of some non-human primates who react fiercely to unfairness.[93] Justice, as is demonstrated by our pursuit of the Just World, is an engrained part of our humanity and is a result of evolution.

Lawyers have long suspected that something akin to Lerner's Just World profoundly affects people's behaviour. German legal theory in particular produced an intriguing literature in this respect, going back to Rudolf von Jhering's famous lecture 'On the Origins of the Sense of Justice'.[94] While an examination of the German debate is interesting,[95] it is crucial to acknowledge that the German legal theory suffered from incurable flaws, as it entirely lacked the crucial empirical component and did not incorporate the advances of other disciplines. The whole exercise started off as an attempt to show that it is *the law* that shapes the sense of justice, not vice versa.[96] From the point of view of everything we have discussed above, this makes no sense at all and cannot be correct.

The very fact that lawyers actively engaged in justice feeling research is telling, however. German scholars were not alone in their endeavour, presenting the law, ultimately, as shaping the essence of what is human—given the role which the notion

---

[88] MJ Callan, JH Ellard and JE Nicol, 'The Belief in a Just World and Immanent Justice Reasoning in Adults' (2006) 32 *Personality and Social Psychology Bulletin* 1646, 1648: 'Immanent justice refers specifically to the causal linking of deeds and subsequent events that are unlikely to be causally connected according to any generally accepted naturalistic analysis'.

[89] Lerner, 'The Justice Motive', n 86 above, 392.

[90] Hafer and Bègue, 'Experimental Research on Just-World Theory', n 28 above, 130. Cf eg Lerner, 'The Justice Motive', n 23 above; Lerner and Clayton, *Justice and Self-Interest*, n 2 above.

[91] Lerner, 'The Justice Motive', n 23 above, 7–8.

[92] Lerner and Clayton, *Justice and Self-Interest*, n 2 above, 20–40.

[93] de Waal and Berger, 'Payment for Labour in Monkeys', n 61 above; Brosnan and de Waal, 'Monkeys Reject Unequal Pay', n 61 above.

[94] R von Jhering, 'Über die Entstehung des Rechtsgefühls', *Österreichische Juristenzeitung* (1877) 7.

[95] For a very informative overview, see, eg, M Rehbinder, 'Questions of the Legal Scholar Concerning the So-Called Sense of Justice' (1982) 5 *Journal of Social and Biological Structures* 341.

[96] ibid, referring to von Jhering's work. Note the similarities with the debate preceding the construction of the German nation and language, as described by Jürgen Habermas: J Habermas, *The Postnational Constellation* (Cambridge, MA, MIT Press, 2001) 1–26.

of justice plays in this process—as well as the core features of a worthy member of a society. This goes back to the idea of a 'good citizen' and the nationalist ideology of a hundred years ago.[97] The culmination of the Soviet legal theory just before the collapse of the state it served, implicitly made allegations which were at least comparable to the German ones: scholars proclaimed the creation of a 'new reality—the Soviet people'.[98] All in all, the German, just as the Soviet *avventure*, demonstrate the connections between legal rules and human experience—in particular the realisation of what is right and what is wrong. These are difficult to deny, so they necessarily beg for explanation.

Lerner's Just World provides precisely such an explanation, which has also now been proven empirically. The explanation it offers works against the disciplinary self-glorifying perspectives German and Soviet lawyers tended to provide and connects the basis of all law—that is, justice—with the socio-biological essence of being human, thus venturing far beyond what any legal–theoretical perspective would ever be able to provide, by taking reality into the picture.

V. THE SCOPE OF JUSTICE AND THE LAW

Justice at the core of our innate Just World perception is equated with a perceived deservedness: what is just is what is deserved.[99] Indeed, this is what our 'compact' with reality is about. This also means that justice does not know a universal standard applicable in all cases and depends on a particular situation as well as on a particular socio-cultural setting. While the substance will then differ from one instance of Just World at work to another, the essence of the Just World as such is universally human. Even though it might manifest itself to a different degree, *all* humans demonstrate it. This is exactly what may best explain the persistent tolerance of the most unquestionable injustice and misery in the world: the human brain, acting through the presumption of the Just World, interprets injustices away either by aggressively assuming that miserable positions are deserved, or by shrinking the Scope of Justice to 'people like us', 'our state' or 'our nation' and the like. The justice of one's world will be defended at all cost precisely due to our vulnerability in the face of realising that the world is not, actually, necessarily just. This vulnerability is what triggers indifference, or even cruel and heartless behaviour.[100] Ensuring that the Just World perception persists is as necessary for a human being as it is overwhelmingly costly. The costs are reduced, however, through being genuinely

---

[97] J Scott, *Seeing Like a State* (New Haven, CT, Yale University Press, 1998).
[98] 'Sovetskij narod' *Bol'shaja Sovetskaja Entziklopedija*, vol 46, 260, reprinted in 2006 (Moscow, Terra).
[99] Lerner, *The Belief in a Just World*, n 23 above, 11: 'A just world in one in which people "get what they deserve"'.
[100] Lerner, 'The Justice Motive', n 23 above, 30. 'As a consequence, any act of help is potentially dangerous and must be avoided' (33), which explains why people prefer (mis)representing their own acts of charity as acts of self-interest: a phenomenon, which is widely documented and also widely used by charity organisations: JG Holmes and DT Miller, 'Committing Altruism Under the Cloak of Self-Interest: The Exchange Fiction' (2002) 38 *Journal of Experimental Social Psychology* 144.

immune to some obvious injustices. Those positions which cannot affect Just World perceptions are characterised as lying outside the scope of justice.

In the words of Lerner, 'the world of victims is located in the hospital, behind bars, "across the tracks," or on the assembly line—or distinguished by a different skin colour or kind of nose'.[101] There appears to be a clear boundary between the cases where justice is and is not relevant. Once again, the scope of justice is not a reflection of a normative position—it is a result of scholars' work on the human reaction to injustice: those in need of help who are outside of our scope of justice will never qualify as victims in our eyes. This boundary is in our mind and the amount of empirical research aiming at understanding the rules behind drawing it is growing.[102] Susan Opotow placed the issue of studying this matter on the agenda of social sciences.[103]

Three key findings on the scope of justice have been described in the literature. First, exclusion from the scope of justice depends on perceived dissimilarity of the target of exclusion (a fish, a Muslim, a homeless person). Secondly, in the situations of high conflict the scope of justice is narrower. Thirdly, exclusion from the scope of justice often depends on the perceived utility of the potential target of exclusion.[104]

Studies of the Holocaust, in particular, seem to confirm the scope of justice idea. Unlike for the perpetrators of Nazi crimes, for the rescuers of the Jews, 'both Jews *and* Nazis [are] "people just like us"'.[105] Research shows that moral choices depend on identity, which correlates with the scope of justice: 'once people create categories ... they feel they must accord equal treatment to all members within that class'.[106] To torture people without undermining one's Just World perception a dehumanising effect has to be created—a clear line drawn between 'us' and 'them'.[107] The scope of justice has implications going beyond human communities, however. One of the main conclusions to derive from the scope of justice scholarship is that the non-human world is usually *par excellence* excluded from the scope of justice, as research demonstrates.[108] The often unbridgeable divide between human and non-human is simply presumed in law—a reality which only rare scholars dare contest.[109]

From Susan Opotow and others' research we know how much the Just World depends on the scope of justice. The scope of justice is a dynamic concept: much more so, than the Just World. The question which arises is what the scope of justice

---

[101] Lerner, 'The Justice Motive', n 23 above, 29.
[102] Eg CL Hafer and JM Olson, 'An Analysis of Empirical Research on the Scope of Justice' (2003) 7 *Personality and Social Psychology Review* 311 (for an overview).
[103] S Opotow, 'Moral Exclusion and Injustice: An Introduction' (1990) 46 *Journal of Social Issues* 1; Opotow, 'Predicting Protection', n 31 above; Opotow, 'Is Justice Finite?', n 4 above.
[104] Opotow, 'Predicting Protection', n 31 above. See also Lerner, 'The Justice Motive', n 23 above, 39.
[105] K Renwick Monroe, 'Morality and a Sense of Self: The Importance of Identity and Categorization of Moral Action' (2001) 45 *American Journal of Political Science* 504.
[106] ibid, 491, also 504 and the references in n 56.
[107] For an overview of the relevant dehumanisation literature see, eg, N Haslam and S Laugham, 'Dehumanization and Infrahumanization' (2014) 65 *Annual Review of Psychology* 399.
[108] S Opotow, 'Predicting Protection: Scope of Justice and the Natural World' (1994) 50 *Journal of Social Issues* 49.
[109] For an example of such contestation see, eg, J Holder, 'An Idea of Ecological Justice in the EU' in this volume, 401.

should be equated to, and whether we should make attempts at shaping its boundaries. While a literature arguing that justice, like democracy, is unfeasible beyond the state is abundant, from Walzer to Nagel,[110] convincing arguments to support this view are largely lacking in history, psychology, biology and even in ethics.[111] Andrew Williams' views on the EU as a potential actor of distributive justice provide an illustration of a more productive approach.[112]

From the point of view of the Just World and the scope of justice scholarship, Walzer, Nagel and a myriad others are trying hard to leave their sense of the Just World uncompromised by obvious injustices. This is done through coming up with arguments that would exclude problem cases from the scope of justice. Arguing dissimilarity—either cultural (Christians versus the Jews), formalistic (those with 'our' passport versus those with 'theirs') or spacial (those from 'here' versus those from 'there') is indeed the *key way*, according to Opotow, to shrink the scope of justice. Plenty justice theorists do precisely that. Human nature itself—the Just World presumption—pushes them to be convinced by their own theorising. Yet, accepting de facto psychologically engrained reasoning, which aims, under overwhelmingly formalistic pretexts, at disempowering the weak from advancing justice claims, is profoundly problematic, once we know humans have such a (seemingly irrational) subconscious inclination to see the world as a Just World and will go to any lengths to remain convinced that this indeed is the case.

VI. BROADER IMPLICATIONS

There is no reason to view the theories described above as deterministic. At most we can aspire to take them into account when building legal–theoretical models of justice or developing the law. They do not teach us the substance of justice or the direction to be taken in articulating it. Given the mechanics of the Just World and of the scope of justice it is clear that the human socio-biological self is not merely about seeking justice, even though we are naturally pre-equipped with the understanding of this concept. It is about presuming that the world is just. The Just World operates—as it should—by preventing us from seeing the whole picture. To ensure that the Just World is not viewed in a deterministic way, critical scrutiny of our natural biases is key to speaking of justice in law 'for real'. A capacity for becoming an actor of justice[113] is thus necessarily related to the question of legal authority:[114] the one which, while taking human cognitive biases fully into account, would provide a broader approach to justice, not constrained or misled by natural human limitations and pre-dispositions.

---

[110] T Nagel, 'The Problem of Global Justice' (2005) 33 *Philosophy and Public Affairs* 113.
[111] Eg J Cohen and C Sabel, '*Extra Rempublicam Nulla Justitia?*' (2006) 34 *Philosophy and Public Affairs* 148. See also V Bader, 'Citizenship and Exclusion: Radical Democracy, Community, and Justice' (1995) 23 *Political Theory* 211.
[112] A Williams, 'The EU, Interim Global Justice and the International Legal Order' in D Kochenov and F Amtenbrink (eds), *The European Union's Shaping of the International Legal Order* (Cambridge, Cambridge University Press, 2013).
[113] ibid.
[114] T Nardin, 'Justice and Authority in the Global Order' (2011) 37 *Review of International Studies* 2059.

A. For Democracy

On the level of reason the only way to sustain the popular position that the scope of justice is not to be extended beyond some highly artificial divides seems to be through equating justice with democracy. The reasons for doing this are fragile, since there are plenty of other ways to determine what is due to whom without democracy. Indeed, while the modern approach to democracy is relatively new, the sense of justice, unquestionably, is 'eternal' for humans as it most probably pre-dates the emergence of the contemporary form of *homo*. Interestingly, what we learn from Lerner is that any social system can be honestly and wholeheartedly embraced by the people as just: it obviously does not matter whether it is a democracy or not.

Needless to say, democracies produce ugly and markedly unjust outcomes cheered by the majorities. We need constitutionalism precisely because we know that this is the case: 'if men were angels no government would be necessary'.[115] At the same time, democracy is such a success precisely because it sends a profoundly misleading, yet welcome signal to 'the minimal human being':[116] no matter who you are and what you think, your voice matters and you are right. John Mueller described the appeal of democracy in the most convincing way.[117] Should such a presentation of reality be correct, there can be no direct correlation between democracy and justice, as the former provides a generally accepted pretext not to broaden the scope of justice of our communities.[118] To be sure, this is not to deny democracy its obvious functional virtues. What we should be cautious about is presenting democracy as a solid pretext to dehumanise groups of individuals by excluding them from the scope of justice.

B. For the Myth of Justice in Law

Any legal system, no matter whether a *demoi*cracy or a plutocracy, is based on a myth of justice and will try selling itself to you based precisely on this myth.[119] The reason why is simple—although Lerner was the first to formulate and test empirically the Just World concept, the essential phenomena it describes could not remain (however counter-intuitive it might seem for some) entirely unnoticed. Consequently, all law, while regulating the human condition, unavoidably draws on the Just World. Margaret Gruter suggested that the fact that the majority of people usually do not question the myth that the law they live under, whatever is the system, is necessarily just, could be a reflection of their biological inner sense of

---

[115] Publius [Madison], Federalist No 51 (6 February 1788).
[116] J Mueller, 'Democracy and Ralph's Pretty Good Grocery' (1992) 36 *American Journal of Political Science* 983.
[117] ibid.
[118] But see, on this connection, the chapters by MA Wilkinson, 'Politicising Europe's Justice Deficit: Some Preliminaries' in this volume, 111; J Přibáň, 'The Evolving Idea of Political Justice in the EU: From Substantive Deficits to the Systemic Contingency of European Society' in this volume, 193 and Nicol, 'Swabian Housewives, Suffering Southerners', n 5 above.
[119] For a somewhat extreme case of arguing for myths, see N Berdiayev, *Tzarstvo duha i tzarstvo Kesaria* (Paris, YMCA-Press, 1949) ch XI.

justice, which overlaps with what the legal system offers.[120] This explanation makes sense, since explaining obedience to the law only through the fear of punishment or peer pressure would be very difficult, especially in a situation where ethically and morally there are no reasons at all to obey the law.[121] Gruter's idea appears to be very much in line with the Just World theory. The only difference is that, when approached from the Just World perspective, it does not matter much what the legal system actually offers in the majority of cases. Indeed, the last thing humans need is to have their sense of the Just World disrupted by seriously doubting the system and disobeying the law. This is why an evolving myth,[122] however obsolete and untrue on the face of it,[123] underlies all the legal systems in the world.[124] Crusades against the myths,[125] while making perfect sense, usually bring about no results in the majority of cases for the same reason. The EU is bound to develop its own vaguely credible myth of justice to go beyond purely rational considerations of economic efficiency and peace.

C. For Legitimacy

While it is clear that humans are predisposed to uphold whatever legal system there is in place, their cognitive efforts to cope with a system that overwhelmingly ignores their preferences can be reduced, thereby diminishing the pressure on the pact with reality which we all embrace, that the world is just. The general problem with legal justice, as identified by Lerner is that 'considerations which are based on other forms of justice—equity, parity, need—may be employed to develop, evaluate, modify the laws, but once the law is established and employed it is the sole determinant of what each person deserves in any given encounter—regardless of their need, investments, inputs, performance etc'.[126] This is not, however, what people innately expect of the law—or the world—as the Just World teaches us. Nodding in the direction of 'need, investments, inputs, performance etc' is thus indispensable for a legal system to be a success. In simple words this amounts to taking the whole picture, especially the extra-legal, fully into account. The connection with the legitimacy of the system is obvious here. One can outline a hypothesis that a legal–political system requiring a more substantial cognitive effort to square what it offers with the Just World would most likely be perceived as less legitimate.

---

[120] Gruter, 'The Origins of Legal Behaviour', n 71 above, 44; Gruter, 'Law in Sociobiological Perspective', n 11 above, 187.

[121] For an overview, see D Kochenov, 'EU Citizenship Without Duties' (2014) 20 *European Law Journal* 482 (and the literature cited therein).

[122] R Barthes, *Mythologies*, trans A Lavers (New York, NY, Farrar, Starus & Giroux, 1972).

[123] Eg D Miller, 'The Ethical Significance of Nationality' (1988) 98 *Ethics* 647.

[124] This is true from 'savage' societies, as they used to be called, to the EU: B Malinowski, *Crime and Custom in Savage Society* (London, Routledge, 1926). See, on the EU story, V Della Sala, 'Political Myth, Mythology and the European Union' (2010) 48 *Journal of Common Market Studies* 1.

[125] See Philip Allott's work in the context of international law, for instance: P Allott, *Eunomia* (Oxford, Oxford University Press, 1990); P Allott, *The Health of Nations: Society and Law Beyond the State* (Cambridge, Cambridge University Press, 2002).

[126] Lerner, 'The Justice Motive', n 23 above, 37.

D. For the Procedural–Substantive Justice Divide

One of the key implications of the Just World theory outlined in the psychological literature is that there is little difference in people's perception between procedural and distributive justice.[127] Experiments show that either you violate 'procedural', or 'distributive' justice principles, it does not matter in the context of the Just World theory. This will only reflect the undeservedness in the eyes of the subject.[128] The distinction between the two thus simply disappears, which certainly puts Jürgen Neyer's claims in an interesting context:[129] whatever the procedure and the discourse, it is the outcomes confirming that the world is just that people aspire to see. Given the innate connection between the Just World and the scope of justice on the one hand and legitimacy on the other, the implication of this is that justice as justification will not necessarily increase the legitimacy of the legal system in the eyes of those whose lives are (negatively) affected by it.

E. For Equality

Another important implication of the theories discussed above concerns the understanding of equality. Equality is in direct correlation with the scope of justice. The Just World theory presupposes that one of the innate ways of dealing with equality problems subconsciously deployed by humans is to shrink the scope of justice. Knowing this, as well as being aware of how flexible the scope of justice is, the task of a law-giver promoting equality is then to counter this natural human tendency. This could be done through the media, education, propaganda, awareness campaigning, etc. To have genuine equality in place, the scope of justice of the majority of the members of a given society has to be enlarged to cover the matters that require equal treatment according to the legislator.

The EU is a great testing ground to see how this functions in practice. The easiest way to check the scope of justice of EU citizens with regards to what the EU stands for is to look at their perceptions of the message behind Article 18 of the Treaty on the Functioning of the European Union (TFEU)[130]—non-discrimination on the basis of nationality. Interesting dynamics emerge from the analysis: inhabitants of the founding Member States, especially in the North of Europe have a radically different attitude vis-à-vis non-discrimination on the basis of nationality, compared

---

[127] Lerner and Clayton, *Justice and Self-Interest*, n 2 above, 98–122 (for an overview).

[128] Eg L Heuer et al, 'The Role of Resource and Relational Concerns for Procedural Justice' (2002) 28 *Personality and Social Psychology Bulletin* 1468; K van den Bos, EA Lind and HAM Wilke, 'The Psychology of Procedural and Distributive Justice Viewed From the Perspective of Fairness Heuristic Theory' in R Cropanzano (ed), *Justice in the Workplace: From Theory to Practice*, vol 2 (Mahwah, NJ, Erlbaum, 2001) 49; K van den Bos, R Vermunt and HAM Wilke, 'Procedural and Distributive Justice: What Is Fair Depends More on What Comes First Than on What Comes Next' (1997) 72 *Journal of Personality and Social Psychology* 95.

[129] See J Neyer, 'Justice and the Right to Justification: Conceptual Reflections' in this volume and the literature cited therein, 211.

[130] Consolidated version of the Treaty on the Functioning of the European Union [2012] OJ C326/47 (TFEU).

with the inhabitants of the newer Member States and the European South. To give an example, while the absolute majority of Swedes do not see any reason to differentiate on the basis of nationality,[131] Poles overwhelmingly hold that possessing Polish nationality makes them somehow special and that other EU citizens, those who are not Poles, should not be compared with them.[132] It is apparent that the confines of the scope of justice differ significantly between the inhabitants of the two countries. Whatever the law says, it is clear that Poles will discriminate, as a result (and will not be disturbed by it) and that Swedes will not. Effectiveness of equality legislation will thus correlate with the scope of justice in the communities where such legislation applies.

F. For the EU's Federal Structure

Continuing with the EU example, even more implications of the Just World theory for the progress of European integration come to light. It has been demonstrated above that the whole rationality of the law should be on the side of the Just World for a legal system to be a success in order to diminish the cognitive efforts invested by its subjects into presenting the whole system as being just to them—no matter how irrational or unkind to them the system is. The EU's problem here is the following: unable to boast a clear and rational division of powers between the national and the supranational legal orders in Europe,[133] which mostly centres around the 'cross-border element' ideology,[134] the EU is structurally built in such a way that numerous equality claims—either under national law, or under EU law—can be formalistically dismissed without citing any substantive reasons or giving any rationally acceptable grounds.[135] This is related to the main ideology behind the EU legal system, which has long been confined to market integration. Having outgrown this ideology, particularly following the introduction of EU citizenship and a gradual extension of EU-level protections to non-economic actors, the EU nevertheless failed to adjust its more or less market-based principles behind the definition of the scope of the law to the new reality.[136] Having gone from the situation where the EU was all about the market,[137] to the situation when the protections of its law (de facto-switching off claims of equality made under national law of the Member States) are

---

[131] J Gerhards, 'Free to Move? The Acceptance of Free Movement of Labour and Non-Discrimination Among Citizens of Europe' (2008) 10 *European Societies* 121. See, esp, 127, fig 1.
[132] ibid.
[133] N Nic Shuibhne, 'Free Movement of Persons and the Wholly Internal Rule: Time to Move on?' (2002) 39 *Common Market Law Review* 731; D Kochenov, 'A Real European Citizenship' (2011) 18 *Columbia Journal of European Law* 55.
[134] For a detailed analysis of its flaws and an exhaustive list of literature, see D Kochenov, 'Citizenship Without Respect' (2010) *Jean Monnet Working Papers* (NYU Law School) No 08/10. See also A Tryfonidou, *Reverse Discrimination in EC Law* (The Hague, Kluwer Law International, 2009).
[135] Kochenov, 'Citizenship Without Respect', n 134 above.
[136] ibid.
[137] N Nic Shuibhne, 'The Resilience of EU Market Citizenship' (2010) 47 *Common Market Law Review* 1597; D Kochenov and R Plender, 'EU Citizenship: From an Incipient Form to an Incipient Substance? The Discovery of the Treaty Text' (2012) 37 *European Law Review* 369.

connected to random acts of birth,[138] highly obscure 'substance of rights'[139] considerations or the nationality of a former wife,[140] the need for justifying the whole system in clear and accessible terms is pressing.[141]

The obvious effects of EU law in operation, when approached from the Just World perspective, can be profoundly troubling and unjust: random citizens are thrown out of the scope of justice for no clear reason: de facto dehumanised.[142] All the problems with such an approach, however acute, are simply interpreted away as non-existent, emphasis being placed instead on the 'market logic' of integration, which is of dubious persuasive value at the current stage of integration.[143] The effects of the EU are thus profoundly unjust and dehumanising not only at the level of its foundations a matter analysed by Andrew Williams in admirable detail[144]—but also at the level of its operation. This is particularly so in the context of the ordinary lives lived by EU citizens. The law that requires a mother of a handicapped child to take a bus to Ireland and return to the UK in order to ensure that her husband is not deported and that the family is not torn apart by the authorities[145] requires a lot of cognitive efforts to square with the Just World and indeed to defend in any context.[146] It is not only frequently incomprehensible; it can also be presented as nonsensical, as the ethical starting point of movement is too problematic to supply a solid starting point for legitimate constitutional analysis. The first fundamental challenge the EU is facing thus concerns reinventing its legitimacy beyond the market logic, to ensure that EU law make basic sense in the eyes of the citizens.

G. For EU Citizenship

The EU can only become fully legitimate, when the majority of EU citizens are included in each others' scope of justice. As has been shown above, currently this

---

[138] Case C-200/02 *Kunqian Catherine Zhu and Man Lavette Chen v Secretary of State for the Home Department* [2004] ECR I-9925; Case C-434/09 *Shirley McCarthy v Secretary of State for the Home Department* [2011] ECR I-3375.

[139] Case C-34/09 *Gerardo Ruiz Zambrano v Office national de l'emploi (ONEm)* [2011] ECR I-1177, para 42. See also M van den Brink, 'The Origins and the Potential Federalising Effects of the Substance of Rights Test' in D Kochenov (ed), *EU Citizenship and Federalism: The Role of Rights* (Cambridge, Cambridge University Press, 2015) (forthcoming).

[140] Case C-403/03 *Egon Schempp v Finanzamt München V* [2005] ECR I-6421.

[141] Kochenov, 'Citizenship Without Respect', n 134 above. For a fascinating discussion of the transnational citizenship scholarship see J Lacroix, 'Is Transnational Citizenship (Still) Enough?' in this volume, 177.

[142] DT Miller, 'Disrespect and the Experience of Injustice' (2001) 52 *Annual Review of Psychology* 527.

[143] For an analysis, see D Kochenov, 'The Citizenship Paradigm' (2013) 15 *Cambridge Yearbook of European Legal Studies* 196.

[144] A Williams, 'Taking Values Seriously: Towards a Philosophy of EU Law' (2009) 29 *Oxford Journal of Legal Studies* 549; A Williams, *The Ethos of Europe* (Cambridge, Cambridge University Press, 2010). But see A Somek, 'The Preoccupation with Rights and the Embrace of Inclusion: A Critique' in this volume, 295. See also Joseph Weiler's brilliant essay 'Bread and Circus: The State of the European Union' (1998) 4 *Columbia Journal of European Law* 223.

[145] An implicit suggestion frequently found in the case-law of the Court of Justice of the European Union (ECJ). Consider *McCarthy* for instance: N Nic Shuibhne, '(Some of) the Kids are all Right' (2012) 49 *Common Market Law Review* 349.

[146] See, for an elaborate criticism, S Iglesias Sánchez, 'A Citizenship Right to Stay? The Right Not to Move in a Union Based on Free Movement' in D Kochenov (ed), *EU Citizenship and Federalism: The Role of Rights* (Cambridge, Cambridge University Press, 2015) (forthcoming).

situation varies greatly from Member State to Member State.[147] In this sense, it is crucial to realise that based on the Just World and the scope of justice, justice and legitimacy are *not* directly connected with each other. On the contrary, the Just World can ensure that people view the most atrocious legal system as legitimate, as long as their vision of the scope of justice extends to embrace the system as well as other individuals covered by the same law. It is thus the scope of justice that is of crucial importance to ensure a legal system's legitimacy. While it would be premature to speculate about the desirable ways to ensure the extension of the scope of justice, its variation vis-a-vis other EU citizens between the Member States demonstrates that it is a dynamic concept and this dynamism should be used by the EU.

It goes without saying that extending the scope of justice to cover all EU citizens will not be an easy task: textbook-friendly political means akin to *Bundesverfassungsgericht*'s *demos*-infused ideologising[148] will not work in the age of post-heroic geopolitics. Indeed, if we approach justice as something inherent in us as human beings, treating it as per se non-generalisable to the different (global) scale would deny our nature as human beings and smacks of racism. The downturn of this reality is also clear. In the words of Slavoj Žižek 'the purely humanitarian, anti-political politics of merely preventing suffering thus amounts to an implicit prohibition on elaborating a positive collective project of socio-political transformation'.[149] Yet, precisely such a positive project could be instrumental in extending the scope of justice. What Žižek outlined is not only true of Europe, of course, but also of the rest of the democratic world.[150] When rights deployed *against* the authority are at the core of any political system in the 'free' world today,[151] politics is reinvented in the vein of washing away the public sphere,[152] *shrinking*, rather than expanding the scope of justice. This is the second fundamental challenge, which the EU will be facing in the years to come, preventing it from making its citizenship fully operational.

VII. CONCLUSION

Working through the Just World combined with the idea of the scope of justice implies going far beyond the simple question of 'what is due to whom', delving into the question of who is human. Throwing a person out of the scope of justice can have a straightforward effect of dehumanisation. The Just World perception, inherent in us, does not only show that justice is not merely another theory, but that it goes much further than any philosophical models, finding a reflection in the

---

[147] Gerhards, 'Free to Move?', n 131 above.
[148] See, for an analysis, JHH Weiler, 'The State *"über alles"*: *Demos, Telos* and the German Maastricht Decision' in O Due, M Lutter and J Schwarze (eds), *Festschrift für Ulrich Everling*, vol 2 (Baden-Baden, Nomos Verlagsgesellschaft, 1995) 1651.
[149] S Žižek, 'Against Human Rights' (2005) 34 *New Left Review* 10.
[150] For this argument in detail, see A Badiou, *Ethics: An Essay on Understanding of Evil* (London, Verso, 2001).
[151] This is not a negative development, but its far-reaching implications should absolutely be taken into account. *Cf* Kochenov, 'EU Citizenship Without Duties', n 121 above.
[152] Žižek, 'Against Human Rights', n 149 above, 3.

deepest corners of our mind. The Just World also demonstrates how dangerous such inclinations in humans can be for law and for freedom. People are profoundly motivated to defend the perception of the world as just: *any* system and *any* law can (and will) be so defended. The Just World can thus bring about injustice: legal authority is necessary to correct this. This also supplies additional arguments for avoiding naturalistic fallacies: it would be a total mistake to present the discoveries from other sciences as a guide for action: they have no relation to 'what ought to be'. The Just World, along with the notion of the scope of justice should be taken into account when constructing legal authority and the legal systems aspiring for justice. The EU, as this volume has been arguing throughout, should definitely be included and will thus have to change a great deal. Ignoring the simple insights from other disciplines, legal thinkers 'risk errors that are harmful, not just intellectually embarrassing'.[153]

---

[153] Jones, 'On the Nature of Norms', n 12 above, 2073.

30

Conclusion

GRÁINNE DE BÚRCA

WE CONCLUDE THIS volume with some reflections, in the light of the contributions of the various chapter authors, on what prompted the book. Why do we seek to stimulate a more active scholarly debate about justice in the European context? What value, if any, is there in framing the critical debate on European integration through the lens of justice?

The book originated in a workshop organised by the three editors, each of whom independently felt that questions of justice had only occasionally been addressed or tackled within scholarly debates on the EU and European integration. Our sense, individually and collectively, was that the normatively oriented literature and debate on Europe had to date been dominated by a range of other discussions on questions such as the democratic deficit, the adequacy of European governance and leadership, the relationship between EU powers and state sovereignty, and the impact of various EU policies. Apart from a growing literature on European human rights and on EU citizenship, analysis of the European Union and its laws and policies from the perspective of justice (other than the narrow meaning officially assigned to that term within the EU's 'area of freedom, security and justice' or AFSJ) seemed largely absent.

This was our sense even before the onset of the Euro crisis, but as the consequences of that crisis unfolded, and as the scale of migrant deaths at and outside Europe's entry points grew, questions of justice appeared to loom ever larger, and the discourse of justice seemed to us to provide an important frame through which the EU and its workings should be evaluated and debated. While the more familiar scholarly focus on the democratic deficit or on the political deficit in Europe had brought many important issues to the fore, an assessment of the EU and its policies in light of our expectations of justice suggested that there was another deficiency to which less attention had generally been given by observers of European integration.

First, a range of EU policies, both external and internal, seem designed to cause or exacerbate what many observers would view as patent injustice. Some obvious examples include—in the external realm—the continued export subsidies for EU products while developing countries struggle to survive and compete economically[1] and, in the internal realm, the policies of austerity which have had perhaps

---

[1] See, eg, Oxfam Briefing Paper 61 (2004): 'Dumping on the World: How EU Sugar Subsidies Hurt Poor Countries'.

their most serious impact on the most vulnerable of Europe's population.[2] Other examples are given by Sionaidh Douglas-Scott in her contribution, and a range of other less heralded injustices are discussed by contributors such as Daniela Caruso who analyses recent initiatives in European private and contract law. Second and more generally, the EU is a powerful political and economic entity which increasingly and pervasively affects the lives of many of those living within as well as outside Europe. Regardless of the sui generis nature of the European Union, this provides ground for asking whether the EU's political and economic system is a just one, and for evaluating the actions of the EU from the perspective of whether or not they promote or hinder justice. And yet, while a lively debate has taken place amongst philosophers about the possibility or otherwise of global justice, and about the meaning and scope of justice in a global context, no developed scholarly debate—as indicated in the contribution of Juri Viehoff and Kalypso Nicolaïdis, who seek to advance exactly that debate in relation to the EU—has yet taken place in the context of European integration. Thirdly, and as pointed out also by Jiří Přibáň, since the EU through its political and legal system—and indeed also the European Convention on Human Rights (ECHR) system—makes claims in the name of justice and purports to dispense justice and to act in the name of justice, it seems important that these claims should be interrogated more closely. Examples of such interrogation can be seen in several of the contributions to this book, including Dorota Leczykiewicz on the quality of judicial and constitutional review by the Court of Justice of the European Union (ECJ), Carole Lyons on how the European Court of Human Rights (ECtHR) has come to deal with questions of historic and intergenerational injustice, Jane Holder on how the EU legal system undermines ecological justice, Antonia Layard on the neglect of questions of spatial justice by the ECHR system, and Fernanda Nicola on how the EU empowers certain local and municipal actors and cities while disempowering others.

It was for these and other reasons—some of which are outlined in the earlier chapters by Andrew Williams and Dimitry Kochenov—that we invited a group of scholars and writers in the fields of law and political theory with an interest in questions of justice in the European context to come and present their ideas at a workshop, and ultimately to write a contribution for the volume. What became evident, however, as the discussion within several chapters of the book illustrate, is that those thinking and writing about the dilemmas of European integration are not all in agreement about the need for a turn to the language of justice in debating the European economic and political project. Some of the reasons for questioning the value of a 'turn to justice' in the scholarship of European integration will be mentioned and addressed briefly here.

Two main and related arguments against the need to bring questions of justice to the centre of the European scholarly debate appear throughout the book. The first, robustly expressed by Danny Nicol, is that justice is an inherently contested political concept and that since it is not possible to reach agreement on a particular conception of justice or any kind of consensus about what the term means, it does not

---

[2] See, eg, Caritas Europe Crisis Monitoring Reports (2013) and (2014), available at www.caritas.eu/the-human-cost-of-austerity-poor-people-paying-for-a-crisis-they-did-not-cause.

provide a useful critical perspective from which to evaluate the EU and its functioning. The second and somewhat related objection, which is voiced in different ways by Agustín Menédez, Oliver Gerstenberg and Jiří Přibáň, is that justice in Europe cannot be considered separately from democracy: the inextricable relationship between the two means that any debate about justice in the European context must be an integral part of the debate about democracy in the EU, and indeed that notions of justice are debated and worked out through democratic procedures. A further argument advanced by Alexander Somek—less an objection to the language of justice being used in the European debate and more a scepticism about the value and authenticity of such a scholarly move—is that the call for such a shift merely reflects a new academic fad, and that European scholars and practitioners are not 'ready' to discuss distributive justice, focusing as they do instead on the protection of individual rights and apolitical notions of social inclusion. A more radical version of this argument is advanced by Damjan Kukovec, who thinks it likely that a shift to the language and discourse of justice in the European context will be mere empty rhetoric, and that claims of justice will only tend to reinforce existing, already powerful preferences.

The editors' intuition that a more developed academic debate about justice in the European context would be valuable does not imply, however, that we consider the crucial debates about democracy in the EU to be in any way irrelevant or misguided. On the contrary, like many of the contributors to the book, we consider that a focus on justice—on what is owed by whom and to whom in the EU context—could complement the robust critical and normative work already being done on how to foster and strengthen democracy in the European integration context.

Similarly, our call for a debate about justice in the European context is neither intended to suggest that the debate about EU human rights policy has been misguided or inadequate on the one hand, nor is it intended to equate the discourse of justice with that of human rights, on the other. Just as the relationship between justice and democracy is the subject of discussion in many of the chapters of this book, so also is the relationship between justice and human rights.

For Andrew Williams, the demands of justice require the European Union to adopt a robust and reformed human rights policy. Alexander Somek challenges this claim by arguing that the appeal to human rights as a criterion of justice is extremely unsatisfactory. An appeal to human rights, he suggests, severs the nexus between the idea of justice and the creation of a basic structure of society that allocates rights and responsibilities for the good of all. Playing around with the existing system of rights protection does not, he argues, get at the basic structure of society or redesign the existing distribution of burdens and benefits. In response to Somek's charge, Andrew Williams replies that to advocate a more thorough and comprehensive EU human rights policy does not necessarily glorify the individual at the expense of distributive justice, nor does it equate justice with the protection of rights. Indeed, just as many other contributors to the book have argued that democracy and justice are closely connected though not one and the same, Williams argues that the articulation and promotion of a satisfactory EU human rights policy could help to clarify what kind of justice is appropriate for the EU to promote, and how the justice of the EU itself, as a political and economic system, might be assessed. Similarly, in Daniel Augenstein's view, the development of a substantial human rights foundation for the EU, far from being apolitical, holds out the prospect of a 'genuine politicisation of the market as the common good of the European polity'.[3]

Yet even if most readers would accept that the promotion of justice and human rights are not alternatives in the EU context but are intertwined in various ways, the challenge laid down by Jürgen Neyer in his contribution to this book and at greater length in his book on *The Justification of Europe*,[4] seems to posit a starker kind of choice between justice and democracy in the EU context, and to present these as alternatives. Neyer argues that it is by design that the EU is not democratic, and that we should seek to appraise and justify the EU's political and economic power by the inappropriate yardstick of democracy, but instead by the yardstick of justice—where justice is understood as 'the outcome of a justificatory process in a justified structure of political decision making'.[5] Neyer's argument that what the EU needs is justice rather than democracy may partly explain the reactions of contributors such as Agustín Menéndez and Oliver Gerstenberg, and indeed also Rainer Forst, from whom Neyer has borrowed the notion of justice as justification. Each of these authors responds to Neyer's proposed separation of justice from democracy by emphasising that the two notions are inextricably intertwined. Indeed for Forst, who firmly rejects the dichotomy drawn by Neyer between democracy and justice, democracy *is* the 'political practice of justice',[6] justice being understood as freedom from arbitrary, unjustified rule or domination.

A cautionary note about seeking to shift debate about the EU to the 'pliable' language of justice is nonetheless also struck by Neil Walker in his chapter. While he does not argue that an appraisal of the EU through the lens of justice is unnecessary, tautological or misguided, he nevertheless cautions—perhaps also in response to Neyer's claim—against any expectation that it can 'solve the legitimacy puzzle' of the EU, and points out that the question of the 'justice of the polity' is a more difficult one than questions of the justice or injustice of particular policies or laws enacted by the EU. There are many possible levels and spheres of justice, and Walker argues that the broader question of the justice of the EU as a political system will remain a difficult one to address—no easier or more tractable than the question of the democratic nature of the EU political system. He warns that the very question whether the EU qualifies as a self-standing polity is controversial, such that we cannot just assume or take for granted the claim that the EU has a general responsibility to promote or secure justice for and amongst its members and associates.

Mike Wilkinson, however, even though he shares with Menéndez, Nicol, Gerstenberg and others the view that justice and democracy are closely connected, takes up the challenge of considering the distinctive questions of justice posed by European Union. Drawing on Wolfgang Streeck's work, he argues that there are very specific features of the EU's transnational system which mean that the tension between capitalism (representing market justice) and democracy (representing social justice) is particularly powerful and takes a very distinctive form. It is distinctive

---

[3] D Augenstein, 'We the People: EU Justice As Politics' in this volume, 153, at 164.
[4] J Neyer, *The Justification of Europe: A Political Theory of Supranational Integration* (Oxford, Oxford University Press, 2012).
[5] J Neyer, 'Justice and the Right to Justification' in this volume, 211, at 213.
[6] R Forst, 'Justice, Democracy and the Right to Justification' in this volume, 227.

not only because the imbalance between capitalism and democracy is so strong in the European Union context but also because this imbalance is both normalised and depoliticised in the EU. In this sense, Wilkinson's analysis supports our contention that there is a need for a more thorough debate about justice in the EU, insofar as the EU presents particular pathologies which are more extreme than those within other political systems. In a related vein, Sionaidh Douglas-Scott argues that the one-sidedness of European integration and the inchoate status of the EU 'presents singular challenges for justice'.[7] Yet despite the temptation to argue that, for reasons of the functional limitation of the EU's scope of authority, questions of justice properly belong to the sphere of domestic political societies, Daniel Augenstein rejects any such attempt to compartmentalise justice and argues that such compartmentalisation fails to recognise and to account for the mutual interdependencies and externalities that come with being a Member State of 'an EU that has long outgrown its roots in inter-state economic cooperation'.[8] In turn, Viehoff and Nicolaïdis in their chapter recognise that the EU is distinct from nation states and that EU society is distinct from domestic societies, and they rise to the profound challenge posed by the 'in between' quality of the EU polity by embarking on the task of trying to articulate which principles of socio-economic justice may be appropriate for the EU.

We strongly support the various attempts made by contributors to this book to begin to grapple with the complex issues posed by asking questions about the justice of EU policies and the justice of the EU polity. While we agree firmly with those who argue that justice and democracy are deeply connected in the European context and that there has long been an active debate about democracy in the EU, we nevertheless consider that there is value in bringing questions of justice in Europe into sharper focus, and in stimulating a more active debate about what can and should be understood as justice in the EU. While it is true that justice is a contested concept and a deeply political one, the fact that there has not been much debate in terms of justice (other than in the superficial AFSJ sense mentioned above) within European studies scholarship suggests to us that it would be valuable to begin a more rigorous debate about what a just European polity and society might look like, and which aspects of European law and policy can be said to enhance or undermine justice. We do not propose the idea of paying closer attention to issues of justice in the European context as a way of seeking a new basis of justification for the European polity to replace that of democracy, nor do we seek to sideline issues of democracy in critiquing or seeking to reform the political and economic system in Europe. Rather our aim is to call for closer attention to questions of fairness and to issues of distribution: or in Somek's terms, to the question of how the burdens and benefits of social cooperation are and should be distributed. It is to prompt further and deeper thinking about how to evaluate as well as to promote the fairness of particular European laws and policies, their impact within and beyond Europe, and the fairness of the European political and economic system and of the polity as a whole. We hope that the chapters in this book may provide an impetus for further research and scholarship in this direction.

---

[7] S Douglas-Scott, 'Justice, Injustice and the Rule of Law in the EU' in this volume, 51.
[8] D Augenstein, 'We the People: EU Justice As Politics' in this volume, 153, at 157.

Index

Aarhus Convention (1998), 46, 404
absolutism, Hobbes', 239–40, 431
accountability (EU), 223–4
adjudication, 269–71
  distributive justice and, 356–9
  redistribution and, 356–7
advertising:
  internet on, 428
  Raël case, 419–21
agency of justice, 79–96
  concept, 80–2
  floating signifiers, as, 81–2, 84
  measurement of, 84–5
altruism, 39
  political obligation and, 285–7
American federalism and legal realism, 354
American legal realism, 351, 352–3
amoral market system, 114
Area of Freedom Security and Justice (AFSJ), 23, 52–3, 249
asymmetries, 128, 375
  double constitutional, 71–2
  power of, 219, 222, 233, 430
austerity, 153–5
  Goodwin's influence, 144–5
  programme, 169
autonomy, 325
  claim, 325, 327
  private, 325
Aziz case, 75–7

'bad man' theory, 351
balancing:
  concept of, 237
  judges, by, 237–8
Barca Report (2009), 359
behavioural patterns, 443–4
Belgium, reverse discriminatory scheme, 357–8
billboards as public spaces, 417–18, 419, 422–3, 426–30, 433–4
biology and law, 437–8
Bürgerliches Recht, 374

capitalism, 115
  depoliticisation and, 129
  financial crisis and, 127
  protecting society from, 119–20
  states and, 117
capitalism and democracy, 115
  constraint and, 120
  co-originality and co-evolution of, 121–2
  disequilibrium (Streek), 112–13, 114
  European integration and, 128
  imbalance of, 125–6
  state control of, 116
  Western Europe, in, 118–19
centre-periphery relationship, 321, 327
  European Union and, 322
  lawyers and, 321–2
  weaker party and, 330
certainty, language of, 271
Charter of Fundamental Rights (2000):
  constitutional justice and, 103–7
  effective remedy, right to under, 104
  European Union Acts, review of, 104
choice:
  constrained as European Union marker, 290–2
  denial of, 271
citizen's initiative, 204–5
citizenship, 8
  definition, 425
  development of, 90–1
  European *see* European citizenship
  rights, of, 187
  stages of, 178
  transnational *see* transnational citizenship
claim of reliance, 329
clandestinity, 186
climate change, 93–4
coherence:
  ecological networks, of, 415
  Social Justice Manifesto, in, 368
coercion:
  community and states, in, 116–17
coercion policy (EU):
  distributive policy and, 359–61
  Lisbon Treaty, in, 359
collective action and European citizenship, 187
collective redress mechanisms, 94
colonialisation, 44–5, 46
Common But Differentiated Responsibility (CBDR), 93
Common European Sales Law (CESL), 372
common market:
  Europe based on, 180–1
  single market becomes, 146
communication and justification, 218–19
community:
  coercion and, 116–17
  rights, of, 185–9
  self-interest and, 283–5
comparative development framework, justice as, 361–2
compensatory justice and Natura 2000 site, 405
competence:
  creep and contracts, 375–6

European Union law scholarship and, 377–8
concept of justice, 303–4
    individuals, for 305
    law and, 303
    Member States and, 304
    social or economic power. 303–4
'conceptualism of contemporary legal thought', 326
conferred power and European Union, 265–7
consent, quality of, 291
constitutional justice:
    Charter of Fundamental Rights, 103–7
    European Union legislative acts and, 97–108
    Standards, ECJ, 99–103
constitutional law and injustice, 340
constitutional pluralism, 262
constitutional systems and justice, 22–5
constraints:
    capitalism and democracy, 120
    internal and external, 100
consumers:
    contracts and loan agreements (Spain) (ECJ case), 75–7
    vulnerable, 372
contestable justice, 167–8
continuous political conception, 70–1
contract law (EU):
    external critique, 376–8
    justice and, 367–78
contracts, competence creep, 375–6
co-operative federalism and localism, 354–5
co-ordination and 'conflicts' model, 375
'Copenhagen Criteria' (EU membership), 122
Court of Justice:
    legislative process and, 269
    national law and, 269–70
crimes against humanity, 393–4, 395–6
    case law, 398
criminal justice, 47–8
    European Union approach to, 47
    negative aspects, 47
    philosophical aspects, 47–8
critical legal justice:
    concept, 59
    human rights and, 60
    rule of law and, 58–60
Cyprus and Eurozone Crisis, 169–70

data collection:
    European Commission, by, 372–5
    qualitative, 373
    race and gender of interviewees, 373–4
decision-making, transparency of, 233–4
deliberative processes in Social Justice Manifesto, 369–72
democracy:
    alternatives to, 229–32
    capitalism see capitalism and democracy
    contours of, 89–90
    crisis, in, 180–3
    democratising the justice deficit, 132–5
    economy and, 119
    European Integration and justice, 9–11
    European Union and, 211–12, 313
    inter-state, 42–3
    justice and, 88, 229, 451
    Member States and, 202–3
    participatory and deficit of democratic representation. 204
    political see political democracy
    polity self-legitimation and, 252–3
    referent, as, 88–90
    sovereignty and, 119
    supranationalisation and, 124
democratic accountability, lack of, 233–4
democratic decision-making, majoritarian supranational, 292
democratic deficit:
    justice deficit, and, 66–77, 166
democratic deliberation, 278–9
democratic justice, 306–7
    inclusion and, 308–9
democratic legitimacy:
    efficiency and, 200–2
    European Union and, 200–2
    Lisbon Treaty and, 200–5
    state semantics of, 207–8
democratic politics:
    financial crises and, 147–8
    justice and, 136–46
    setting aside, 142–4
democratic representation, 206
    deficit of and participatory democracy, 204
demos, 68, 124, 127
    European, 208, 234, 252
    no-*demos*, 158
    sovereignty, 187–8
denial of harm, 335
depoliticisation:
    capitalism and, 129
    European Union, in, 206–7
    technocratic governance and political democratic governance, 199
depoliticising justice deficit, 113, 128–32, 173–5
    principles of justice, 174
    right to justification, 174–5
deservingness, 447, 448
dignity, 243,
    total freedom, to, 243–4
direct democracy, legislation for, 204–5
Directive 93/13, 75–7
discursive contestation, 88–9
disappropriate individualism, 235–46
distribution:
    external and internal, 41
    equality of, 306–7
    goods, of, 112
    law, through, 328
    wealth, of, 39–40
distributional justice and Natura 2000 Site, 404–5
distributive justice, 39–42, 290–1, 301–2
    adjudication and, 356–9

cohesion policy and, 359–61
  domestic states and, 349–65
  'maximin' distributive criterion, 356
  multi-level alliances, 351
  victimhood and vulnerability, 15
division of labour, 92–3
domestic disputes:
  comparative justice and, 351
  European Union law and, 350
double constitutional asymmetry, 71–2
Draft Common Frame of Reference (DCFR), 370–1
Draft Declaration of the Rights of Nature, 411
dynamic disequilibrium, 112–13, 114

Earth Jurisprudence, 411
ecological justice, 17, 410–13
  analysis of, 413–14
  deficiency of justice and, 405–15
  environmental justice and, 401
  evaluation methods, 414–15
  Natura 2000 and, 403–5
  non-anthropocentric paradigm of justice, 411
  sufficiency or deficiency of justice conditions, 402
ecological review principles, relation and context-based, 413–15
economic and monetary union, implementation of, 146
economic constitutionalism, 72
economic law, expressive role of, 263–4
economistic justice, 35
ecosystem, resilience of, 414–15
efficiency and democratic legitimacy as European Union balance, 200–2
Eichmann trial, judges, 391
emancipation, 134–5
Emissions Trading Scheme (ETS), 93
emotion, types of, 65
environmental governance, 412
environmental inequalities, 409–10
environmental justice, 408–10
  aim of, 409
  ecological justice and, 401
  integrated policy framework, absence of, 409
environmental law, development of (US), 412–13
environmental matters (EU), 45–6
equaliberty, 185–9
equality:
  benchmark of, 280–1
  human rights and, 315–16
  inclusion and, 13–14
  Just World and, 543–4
  outcome, of, 156
  rights, of, 187–8
  statehood and, 116
  theoretical views of, 172
equality of opportunity, 281–2
  definition, 281–2
  empirical, 281
  normative, 281

ethical justice, statements of belief 36–7,
Europe:
  common market, based on, 180–1
  justice and, 79–96
  justice in, 137–51
  politicising justice deficit *see* politicising justice deficit
  property rights, in, 236
  social, 324–30
European Arrest Warrant (EAW), 52–3
European Arrest Warrant (EAW) Framework decision case law, 106
European budget, assessment of, 148–9
European Central Bank debt-buying programmes, 141–2
European citizenship:
  extension of rights, 187
  freedom of movement, 178–9
  mutual recognition and, 179
  neoliberalism, 181
  participation in collective self-government, 187
  relationship of rights and, 178–9
  transnational *see* transnational citizenship
European Commission:
  data collection, 372–5
  liberalisation agenda, 376–7
  national budgets, scrutiny of, 54
European constitutional law, 146–50
  common market to single market, 146
  economic and monetary implemented, 146
  Rechtsstaat, implementation of, 146
European Consumer Consultative Group (ECCG), 372
European construction, citizen apathy to, 182–3
European Court of Human Rights:
  establishment of, 383–4
  Holocaust and, 381–99
  Jews and, 387–8
  judges and, 389
  remembrance and, 386–7
European Court of Justice:
  case law *see* European Court of Justice case law
  constitutional justice standards, 99–103
  European Union Acts, review of, 104
  Eurozone crisis and, 165
  experimentalist court, as 73–7
  fundamental rights and, 70
  human rights and, 298
  jurisprudence and concepts of justice, 362–5
  justice and, 82–3
  national budgets, scrutiny of, 54
  redistribution and, 357
  reverse discriminatory scheme ruling, 357–8
  Rule of Law case law, 100–3
European Court of Justice case law:
  fundamental law and, 102–3
  proportionality and, 102–3
  Rule of Law and, 101–3
European crises, Platonic reasoning, 139–41
European democracy and justification, 233–4
European governance, 54, 55, 205–6, 332

European integration, 120–2, 124, 324–5
  case law, 120–1
  democracy and capitalism, 9–11, 128
  justice and, 27
  market justice and, 121
  political, 202
  politicising justice deficit, 112
  process and law, 220–1
  project, 21, 162–4
European law, scholarship and competence, 377–8
European legal realism, 353
European market:
  integration, politics of, 159
  polity and fundmental rights, 160–2
  regulation of, 374–5
European parliament, legislative process, 267
European political justice, 157
European polity:
  building, 159
  differentiation of European society, 207–8
  legitimacy of, 154
European public sphere, spatial imagination of, 429–33
European Regional Development Fund (ERDF), 359
European Stability Mechanism:
  case law, 124, 154–5
  German ratification of, 154–5
European supranationalisation and EU legitimation, 254
European Union (EU):
  accountability 223–4
  assessment of, 311–14
  centre-periphery relationship and, 322
  citizenship and Just World, 455–6
  cohesion of, 161
  competences, 376
  conferred power and, 265–7
  constitutionalism and justice, 97–9
  democracy, 211–12, 313
  democratic legitimacy, deficit of 201
  development and justice, 24–7
  efficiency and democratic legitimacy, 200–2
  experimentalist arrangement, 68–73
  federal structure and Just World, 454–5
  four freedoms, 249
  governance of, 200–1
  human rights and, 298–9, 316–17
  illegitimacy of, 35–6
  injustice *see* injustice
  instrumentality, 259–60, 272–3
  justice *see* European Union and justice
  legal-spatial imaginary, as, 433
  legal structure, 332–3
  legitimacy, 37, 107–8, 222, 250–1
  legitimation, 251, 254
  normative realism and, 228–9
  political justice *see* political justice, in European Union
  political participation, commitment to, 204
  political unity, as, 161
  politicisation and depoliticisation, 206–7, 262
  public acceptance of, 261
  redress, in, 45
  representation of interests, 261–2
  representative democracy, adoption of, 202–3
  romanticism and (Somek), 311–14
  rule of law, 51–66
  social justice *see* social justice (EU)
  social justice deficit, role in *see* social justice deficit (EU)
  sovereigntist objections *see* sovereigntist objections
  states, co-operation between, 26
  substantive justice, 35–8
  symbolism case law, 271
European Union and justice, 23–4, 33–49, 247–57, 297–8
  concept of, 57–8
  development, 24–7
  legitimacy, 212–14
  politics, as 153–64
European Union law:
  authority of and justice claims, 155–7
  domestic disputes, 350
  instrumentality and, 269–60
  justice and, 22–3
  justification of, 219–21
  Member States and, 270
  weakness of, 270
European Union legislative acts:
  Charter of Fundamental Rights, review under, 104
  constitutional justice and, 97–108
  European Court of Justice, review of, 104
  judicial review of, 101
  legislative process, 266–7
  proportionality and, 104
Europeanisation, 134
  national spheres, of 179–80
Eurozone crisis, 53–5, 165–75
  Cyprus and, 169–70
  European Court of Justice and, 165
  German argument for, 168–9
  justice and, 168–70
  pre-crisis case law, 167
  Spain and, 169
exclusion, 330–1
'executive federalism', 256
expressivity:
  economic law, and, 263–4
  European Union law and, 270
  generally, 264–5
  human rights and, 263–4
  instrumentalism and instrumentality, 270
  non-discrimination rules and, 263–4

fairness and justice, 438, 443
federal judiciary, neutral *see* neutral federal judiciary

financial crises:
  democratic politics and, 147–8
  European Integration Project and, 162–3
Finland, economic crisis (late 1980s), 149–50
Fiscal Compact Treaty, Article 7, 55
forgiveness, 341
fractal justice, 386
free circulation and social justice deficit (EU), 122–3
freedom of expression, 428
  'European' understanding, 430
  public space and, 432–3
  spatial justice and, 417–34
  spatiality of, 418
freedom of movement, 41
  European citizenship and, 178–9
freedom of speech, Raël case, 419–21
freedom to choose, citizens', 91–2
fundamental boundaries, fundamental rights and, 7, 160–1
fundamental justice, political discourse and, 231–2
fundamental law, European Court of Justice case law and, 102–3
fundamental rights:
  autonomy and, 161
  broadcasting sport events, 105
  European Court of Justice and, 70
  European Court of Justice interpretation of, 161–2
  European market polity and, 160–2
  fundamental boundaries and, 7, 160–1
  post-Charter of Fundamental Rights case law, 104–7

generality of consent, 290–1
Germany:
  constitutional court's human rights position, 244–5
  European Stability Mechanism, ratification of, 154–5
  European treaties, constitutional court's scrutiny of, 220
  Eurozone crisis and, 168–9
  financial crisis, 127
Godwin, William, on utilitarianism, 144–6
'great jurisprudence', 411
Greek rescue, bilateral (2010), 147
Gross Domestic Product, 54, 140, 185

Habitats Directive (1992), 401, 402, 412
  use and development of land under, 403–4
healthcare, pain and suffering circumstances (ECJ case), 73–5
Heath, Edward, 149
hierarchies, 320–3
Historikerstreit, 384
history and memory, 391
Hobbes and democratic politics, 142–4
Holocaust, 17
  case law, 390–2, 397–8
  denial of, 396–7, 398–9

European Court of Human Rights and, 381–99
identity, 449
jurisprudence, 385, 397–8
legacy, 390–1
human behaviour and human mind, 441–2
human nature and justice, 435–57
human rights, 69
  citizenship and, 186–7
  concept of, 314–15
  courts and, 244–5
  critical legal justice and, 60
  critique of, 315
  equality and, 315–16
  European Court of Justice and, 298
  European Union and, 298–9, 316–17
  expressive role of, 263–4
  Germany's constitutional courts and, 244–5
  Holocaust denial, 398–9
  individual rights and individualism, 299–300, 316
  justice and 314–17
  liberty of, 241–4
  practice of, 315
  socio-economic, 325–6

identity and Holocaust, 449
ideology and justice deficit, 118–22
illegitimacy and European Union, 35–6
imaginations, 426–7
  see also legal-spatial imaginaries
'imperative reasons of overriding public interest' (IROPI) formula, 410
inclusion, 307–9
  definition, 308
  democratic justice and, 308–9
  equality and, 13–14
  justice and, 308, 330–4
  rights of, 295–309
individual liberty, 86, 90
individualism:
  adjudicative and proportionality, 236–7
  disproportionate, 235–46
  human rights, 316
individuals:
  European Union, in, 39
  institutional violence and, 90–5
injustice (EU), 36, 52–7, 61–5
  collective, 339
  constitutional law and, 340
  emotion and, 65
  examples of, 3
  foundational and shame, 340
  internal market and, 14
  justice and, 63, 80
  market freedoms and, 56
  Member States and 56–7
  restorative justice and, 340
  social justice issues, 55–6
  theoretical views of, 172
institutional self-justification, 83–4
institutional self-legitimation and justice, 82–5

institutional violence, 92
  individuals and, 90–5
  inverted monism and 92–4
instrumentalism and instrumentality:
  European Union and *see* European Union, instrumentality
  expressivity and, 270
  Member States and, 260
integration:
  European *see* European integration
  justice and, 21, 28
'integration through law', 71, 157
integrity, ecological, 414
inter-generational justice, 43–6
internal market:
  Europe's signifier as, 90–2
  individuals and, 90
  injustice and, 14
  regulation of, 268
international law, 262–3
internet, 428–9
inverted monism, 94
  institutional violence and, 92–4

Jews and European Court of Human Rights, 387–8
judges:
  Eichmann Trial, at, 391
  European Court of Human Rights and, 389
judicial review:
  European Union acts and, 101
  justice and, 97–9
  legitimacy and, 107–8
  standards, changes to, 103–4
Just Word hypothesis, 438–9
  concept of, 435–6
  equality and, 453–4
  European Union citizenship and, 455–6
  European Union federal structure, 454–5
  German legal theory, 447–8
  interventions under, 439
  justice and, 439, 449–50, 451–2
  law and, 446–8
  legitimacy and, 452
  procedural-substantive justice divide and, 453
  research on, 446–7
  Soviet legal theory, 448
justice:
  agility of, 247–50
  benchmark of equality and, 281
  comparative development framework, 361–2
  concept of, 3, 212–13
  constitutional systems and, 22–5
  contestable, 167–8
  contract law (EU), 367–78
  deficiencies of ecological justice, 405–75
  democracy and, 227–34
  democratic *see* democratic justice
  dualistic notion of, 92
  egalitarian, 362–3
  Europe, in, 137–51

  European Court of Justice and, 362–5
  European integration and, 9–11, 27
  European Union, in *see* European Union and justice
  Eurozone crisis and, 168–70
  fairness and, 438, 443
  foreclosing through referents, 85–90
  fractal, 386
  global, 249
  human nature, 435–57
  human rights and, 314–17
  impartiality as, 277–8
  inclusion and, 308, 330–4
  institutional aspects, 249
  integration and, 21, 28
  Just World hypothesis and, 439
  justification and, 213
  law myth and Just World, in, 451–2
  legal-spatial investigation, 422
  legitimacy and, 5, 11, 22
  libertarian, 362–3
  Member State sovereignty and, 3–5
  mutual advantage, as, 277–8
  national and supranational aspects, 15–16
  paradigm of and ecological justice, 411
  party political aspects, 7–8, 170–1
  philosophy of law, 300–1
  politics, pre-empting, 138–42
  polity-holistic, 248–9
  'recuperative institution' as, 257
  relation, 407
  restorative, 338
  rhetorical, 28–9
  right to justification, 255–6
  scope of *see* scope of justice
  sectoral, 248, 249
  social change and, 334
  state and, 35
  status quo and, 319–36
  sufficiency or deficiency of ecological justice and, 402
  types of, 21–2
  utilitarian, 144–6, 362–3
justice claims, 132–3
  depoliticisation strategy, 138
  European Union and, 155–7
  impartiality and, 144
justice deficit:
  concluding remarks, 459–63
  definition, 113–14
  democratic deficit and, 66–77, 166
  depoliticisation of, 113
  'major justice deficit', 233
  types of, 233–4
  undoing, 337–48
justice-as-justification-deficit, 99
justification, 215–17
  communication and, 218–19
  definition, 215
  depoliticisation of justice, 174–5
  European democracy and, 233–4

Index   471

European Union justice deficit and, 233–5
European Union law of, 219–21
forms of, 217
justice and, 213
justified structures of, 222–3
legitimacy (EU) and, 222
multi-level policy making and, 224–5
normative realism and, 215–16
political discourse and, 230–1
pre-conditions of, 217–21
procedural dimension, 218
public sphere and, 218–19
right to, 213–14, 221, 229–30, 302–3
third party and, 218, 232
transparency and, 223
truth-seeking and 216–17
'justificatory structures of justification', 85–8

law:
  biology and, 437–8
  concept of justice and, 303
  European integration process and, 220–1
  functions of, 220
  Just World hypothesis and, 446–8
  philosophy of and justice, 330–1
  roots of, 445
  science and, 437–41
  scope of justice and, 448–50
  society and, 264
lawyers:
  centre-periphery relationship and, 321–2
  legal change and, 321
legal geography, 418
  spatial and legal aspects, 425
legal language, use of, 333
legal positivism, 194–5, 197–8
legal realism:
  American, 351, 352–3
  European, 353
legal-spatial imaginaries, 425–9
  European Union as, 433
legal system and hierarchies, 320–3
legal thinking:
  justice and, 324
  Social Europe and, 324–30
legitimacy:
  collective authorisation approach, 254
  democracy-centred approach, 254
  dependent approach, 253–4
  disaggregated approach, 253–4
  economic rationality and, 115
  European Union and, 37, 250–1
  Just World and, 452
  justice and, 5, 11, 22
  justificatory model of, 251–2
  operative, 9
  political justice and, 8–9
  politicisation and, 6
  polity *see* polity legitimacy
  procedure, through, 204
legitimation applied in European Union, 251

liberal sociability, 240–1
liberalisation agenda and European Commission, 376–7
liberalism, 129–30, 240
liberty:
  basic (Dworkin formula), 242–3
  basic, society for, 241–2
  human rights of, 241–4
  individual, 86, 90
Lisbon Treaty (2007):
  democratic legitimacy and, 200–5
  details of, 200
  political justice, juridification of, 205–6

margin of appreciation doctrine, 419, 422
market:
  amoral market system, 114
  injustice and, 56
  social justice and, 117
  transactions, ECCG opinion, 374
  uniform laws for, 375
mass atrocities and victim claims, 339
Member States:
  concept of justice, 304
  democracy and, 202–3
  European Union instrumentality and, 272–3
  European Union law and, 270
  injustice and, 56–7
  instrumentality and, 260
  representative democracy and, 203
  sovereignty and justice, 3–5
memory:
  European Court of Human Rights and, 387
  history and, 391
misrepresentation, 133–4
modernity, 196–7
monism, inverted, 92–4
mortgage loan agreement (Spain), ECJ case, 75–7
multi-level alliances, distributive function, 351
multi-level policy making and justification, 224–5
mutual dependency conditions, 156
mutual recognition, 183

National Health Service (UK):
  Yvonne Watts case, 73–5
national law:
  Court of Justice and, 269–70
  legislative process, 266–7
national socialist case law, 394–6
Natura 2000:
  definition, 401
  distributive justice and, 404–5
  ecological justice and, 403–5
  procedures under, 404
  sites, 410
natural law (Hobbes):
  applications of, 143–4
  definition, 143
nature conservation, legal framework, 404
negationism, 396
neoliberalism and European citizenship, 181

Index

neutral federal judiciary and federalism doctrines, 352–5
no-*demos* thesis, 158
non-discrimination rules, 263–4
non-voluntariness, 291
normalisation, 324
normative realism:
  European Union and, 228–9
  justification and, 215–16
  theoretical views of, 173

Open Method of Coordination (OMC), 256
ordoliberalism, 71, 124–5
'original position' device, development and recognition of rights, 406–7
othering, 94–5

paradigm of law, 301
'parity of participation', 407
participatory democracy:
  and democratic representation, 204
  legislation for, 204–5
party politics and justice, 170–1
'past that will not pass', 384
PI case (ECJ), 86–7
place-as-process, 423
Plato:
  European Crises and, 139–41
  justice pre-empting politics, 138–9
political accountability, lack of, 331–2
political action and public expression, 188–9
political and social justice and transnational polity, 183–4
political conception, discontinuous, 69–70
political democratic government and depoliticised technocratic governance, 199
political democracy:
  debtor countries, in, 126–7
  practice of justice, 227–34
political discourse:
  fundamental, 231–2
  justification and, 230–1
  normal, 231
political justice, 42–3, 292
  definition, 133
  differentiation of European Society, 207–8
  European Union, in, 193–208
  Hayek on, 171–3
  Laski on, 171–3
  legitimacy and, 8–9
  Lisbon Treaty (2007) and, 205–6
  Natura 2000 sites, 404
  Neyer, on, 172–3
  operation of legal system and, 196–8
  Rechtsstaat formula and, 145–6
  state and, 198–9
  veto right and, 231
political participation, EU commitment to, 204
political unity, 158–9
  European unity and, 161
politicisation, 6, 206–7

politicising justice deficit, 111–35
  European integration and, 112
  state and, 117
politics:
  European Union justice as, 153–64
  justice pre-empting, 138–42
polity:
  concept of, 208
  legitimacy, approaches to, 251–6
  self-legitimation and democracy, 252–3
presumed justice, 27–8
prevention (criminal justice), 47
'principle of general reciprocal justification', 255
Pringle case, 154–5
privatisation, 167–8
procedural justice *see* political justice
property rights:
  Europe, in, 236
  United States of America, in, 235–6
proportionality:
  adjudicative individualism, 236–7
  concept of, 238
  European Court of Justice case law and, 102–3
  European Union acts and, 104
  principle, 86
  sensu stricto, case law 105
  social and economic considerations, 327–8
  total freedom and, 238–9
  value of, 238
prosecution (criminal justice), 47
public expression and political action, 188–9
public freedom, 431–2
public happiness, 431, 432
public space, 423, 424, 428
  billboards are, 417–18, 419, 422–3, 426–30, 433–4
  definition, 431
  freedom of expression and, 432–3

Raël case, 417–18, 419–21
  European Court of Human Rights judgment, 423
  space-talk and, 434
  spatial understanding of, 422–33
reality and law, 441–5
Rechtsstaat formula, 145–7
reciprocity, 277
  social justice and, 287–90
  theory, 289
recognition to mutual defiance, 181–2
redistribution:
  adjudication and, 356–7
  European Court of Justice and, 357
redistributive justice, 64
reflexibility and imaginations, 426
relativism, 64–5
remembrance and European Court of Human Rights, 386–7
representation of interests (EU), 43, 261–2
representative democracy:
  definition, 202
  development of, 202

Index 473

European Union deficit of, 203
European Union's adoption of, 202–3
Member States and, 203
rescue packages, 153–4
'residence citizenship', 185–6
resilience of ecosystem, 414–15
'responsible community', 381–2
restoration claims, limiting factors, 342
restorative and redistributive policies and status claims, 347
reverse discriminatory scheme (Belgium), 357–8
right to justification:
  decision-making and, 256
  depoliticisation of justice, 174–5
  justice and, 255–6
right to stay, 91–2
rights:
  creation and adversarial legalism, 406
  denationalisation of, 186
  extension of and European citizenship, 187
  inclusion of see inclusion of rights
  'original position' device, 406–7
  rights-based jurisprudence, 406
role of law, expressive, 263–5
Romani people, 409–10
Rüffert judgment, 363–5
rule of law:
  concept, 59
  critical legal justice and, 58–60
  European Court of Justice case law, 100–3
  European Union, in, 51–66
  lack of, examples, 60
  visual images of, 61–3

science and law, 437–41
scope of justice, 436, 440
  democracy and, 451
  Just World and, 449–50
  key findings, 449
  law and, 448–50
'second generation' environmental thinking, 412
self-interest, 39, 93, 115, 283–5
shame and foundational injustice, 340
Shoah:
  case law, 389–90
  denial of, 396–7
  European Court of Human Rights and, 381–99
single European market, 131
single market and common market, 146
'Six-Pack', 54, 55
small and medium-sized enterprises (SME), protection of, 323
social and economic rights against individuals, 406
social behaviour, 442–3
social claims, 327
social co-operation, Rawl's arguments, 280
social Europe, 324–30
social justice (EU), 12–13, 130, 277–93
  constrained choice as an European Union marker, 290–2

  development of, 326
  domestic, 279–82
  injustice in, 55–6
  market and, 117
  reciprocity and, 287–90
  setting up, 279–80
  solidarity and, 282–7
  theoretical views of, 172
social justice deficit:
  European Union's role, 122–8
  free circulation, 122–3
  political union and, 124
'social justice in contract law', 376
Social Justice Manifesto, 331, 367–9
  aim, 367
  background to, 367–8
  coherence and, 368
  consequences of, 370–1
  critique of, 369–76
  deliberative processes in, 369–72
  evaluation of, 368–9
  harmonisation in, 368
  themes, 368
  weak point, 371
social legitimacy:
  definition, 261
  power and, 259–74
social protection and spatial protection, 408
socio-economic justice, 291–2
  political conceptions, 70
socio-political constitutionalism, 72
solidarity:
  conceptual space, 284
  definition, 282–3
  lack of, 286–7
  Member State's, 288
  moral obligations, 114
  national, 288
  reciprocity-based internationalist (RBI), 288
  self-interest and, 283–5
  social justice and, 282–7
  solidarity compass, 283–7
  transnational, 288
sovereign debt crisis, 312–13
sovereigntist objections, 68–70
  defensive, negative and positive fundamental rights and, 69
  human rights and, 69
sovereignty, 188
  democracy and, 119
  Member States and justice, 3–5
space, social, 422
space-talk, 427–8
  Raël case and, 434
Spain and Eurozone crisis, 169
spatial imaginaries, 425–6
spatial imagination:
  European public sphere of, 429–33
  example of, 428
spatial justice, 422–3
  definition, 408

freedom of expression, 417–34
  territorial cohesion, 407–8
spatial protection and social protection, 408
Special Areas of Conservation, Member States' obligations, 403
splices, 423–5
state:
  contract law, 375–6
  justice and, 35
  political justice and, 198–9
  politicisation of justice deficit, 130–1
  regulatory, 131
statehood:
  attributes of, 116
  equality and, 116
  justice deficit and, 115–18
states:
  capitalism and, 117
  coercion and, 117
  nineteenth century development, 117–18
status claims and restorative and redistributive policies, 347
status quo and justice, 319–36
Strasbourg human rights system and Holocaust denial, 398–9
structural injustice, 87–8
structural subordination, 322–3
  social transformation, 323–4
subnational redistributive mechanisms, 358–9
subsidiarity, 69–70
substantive justice, 34, 195
  European Union and 35–8
  themes, 38–48
supranationalism, 304
  integration, 123

technical regulation, 268–9
  impact of, 269
  internal market and, 268
territorial cohesion, 360–1
  spatial justice and, 407–8
Thatcher, Margaret, 149
theory of justice, 63–4, 231
  modes of relationships, 81
third party and justification, 232
third way, 183–5
Third World Approaches to International Law (TWAIL), 322
total freedom, 242
  dignity from, 243–4
  proportionality and, 238–9

transnational citizenship, 177–90
  concept of, 177–80
  European construction, 182–3
  pillars of, 178–80
  recognition to mutual defiance, 181–2
  supranational citizenship, 184–5
  welfare state and mobility, 182
transnational polity and political and social justice, 183–4
transparency, 224
  justification and, 223
Treaty on European Union (TEU):
  Articles 2 & 3, 24, 54–5
truth-seeking and justification, 216–17

United States:
  environmental law, development of, 412–13
  property rights, 235–6
utilitarianism and justice, 144–6

victim claims and mass atrocities, 339
victim status:
  collective, 338–9
  recognition of, 341
victimhood, 338–43
  European Court of Human Rights and, 382
  rights, recognised as, 342–3
  vulnerability and, 15, 343–5
victims, 449
  definition, 387
  nameless, 392–4
  victim status *see* victim status
  'victims of history', 339
Vienna Action Plan, 53
vulnerability, 343–6, 448–9
  definition, 346
  socio-economic status, 345–6
  victimhood, becomes, 343–4
vulnerable consumers and family and property law, 377–8
vulnerable groups:
  status claims and, 345
  victimhood and, 344–5

weaker parties, 329
  centre-periphery power relationship, 330
welfare state and transnational citizenship, 182
'well-ordered' societies, 156
Wild Law and Wild Law UK, 411
Wirtschaftverfassung, 71
working agreements, 214